COST ACCOUNTING
Third Edition

**Accounting Data
for Management's Decisions**

Nicholas Dopuch
University of Chicago

Jacob G. Birnberg
University of Pittsburgh

Joel S. Demski
Stanford University

HARCOURT BRACE JOVANOVICH, INC.

New York   San Diego   Chicago   San Francisco   Atlanta
London   Sydney   Toronto

Printed in the United States of America

Library of Congress Catalog Card Number: 81-82170

ISBN: 0-15-514201-1

Preface

In writing this third edition of *Cost Accounting*, we have tried again to present the essential issues of cost accounting thoroughly yet concisely enough for use in an introductory course. We have included sufficient material to keep students gainfully occupied for a full semester. However, by omitting subsets of materials, the instructor can easily adapt the book to a quarter system. Indeed, we have covered 90 percent of the material in a single quarter at our respective schools (for example, by omitting the materials in Chapters 11, 13, and 15).

The book is intended to be conceptual in nature. We try to present cost accounting issues against a backdrop of the demands that users internal to the firm make on the accounting system. The central theme, then, is not how to do cost accounting, or the presentation of a list of techniques, or even a set of recipes to follow in particular circumstances. Rather, the orientation is one of emphasizing the continual choices that the accounting system designers must face.

The text is designed to minimize prerequisites. We do not assume prior exposure to financial accounting. Indeed, the only use made of the double entry system is in Chapters 11 and 12, where we explicitly deal with cost assessment issues in financial reporting. The ways in which various cost accounting transactions are entered in the financial accounts are illustrated at appropriate points throughout the text. The four basic control accounts used in a firm's cost accounting system—raw materials, work-in-process, finished goods, and overhead costs control—are illustrated in numerous exhibits, along with other accounts that are essentially just embellishments on this fundamental system.

Similarly, models from such fields as economics, finance, and management science have had a significant impact on traditional approaches to managerial decision making and, therefore, cost accounting. This is reflected in two ways in this text. First, we use the concept of a formal model to ask the question of which cost accounting techniques are appropriate. Break-even analysis, constrained profit maximization, capital budgeting, and inventory control are all used as illustrative settings. In each case we refrain from presenting lists of formal models and instead concentrate on the most simple illustrative formulation. This has the advantage of not placing undue demands on the students and of allowing direct focus on the conceptual issues at hand.

Second, we make extensive use of the notion of information, and of expected returns if we improve information, in a decision theory setting. Most of this is done with an assumption of risk neutrality, simply to ease the student's burden. At times, however, the notion of risk aversion is critical to understanding a cost accounting issue. If the student has no prior exposure to decision theory, the instructor may wish to move somewhat slowly through the material in Chapter 1.

As noted, the text is conceptual by design. This presumes an inclination to ask questions about the nature of cost accounting as opposed to its procedures per se. Comparative advantage dictates, we feel, pursuit of a conceptual approach in the classroom.

In line with this conceptual approach, we have altered the chapter sequence from that employed in earlier editions. We begin by emphasizing the information production nature of the cost accounting function. Chapters 2 and 3 cover essential ideas of cost classification and cost estimation. Equipped with this background, we then consider demands for cost accounting information in analysis and evaluation. The analysis exploration, Chapter 4, is in the short-run setting of cost–volume–profit analysis. Here the emphasis is on the demands such decision problems place on the cost accounting system and the economic view of how they ought to be resolved. Other decision settings of capital budgeting and inventory control are postponed until the end of the text (Chapters 14, 15, and 16).

Chapter 5 introduces cost accounting demands associated with control problems. We begin with a discussion of performance evaluation in Chapter 5, then introduce standards and budgets in Chapter 6, and follow with variance analysis procedures in Chapter 7. Chapter 8 treats the important question of assessing the significance of deviations from the standard or the budget.

This completes the core material in the text. Cost allocation is examined in Chapter 9, from the perspective of decomposing a complex choice problem. Viewed in this manner, we are able to rationalize cost allocation practices and more fully understand their enigmatic nature. Chapter 10 extends the introduction of complexity by examining decentralization and the demands it places on the cost accounting function.

Chapters 11, 12, and 13 deal with financial reporting. Here we begin with a general survey in Chapter 11, and then provide an in-depth treatment, in Chapter 12, of product cost assessment for financial reporting purposes. The master budget—the accountant's model of financial events for planning purposes—is the subject of Chapter 13.

Finally, as already noted, the last three chapters contain explorations of decisions that are designed to repeat the conceptual content of Chapter 4, but in a variety of contexts.

The text is intended to be somewhat robust in terms of alternative sequencing. Chapters 14, 15, and 16 may be pursued at any point beyond Chapter 4. Similarly, the financial reporting materials in Chapters 11, 12, and 13 may be pursued after Chapter 3.

Each chapter presents a list of suggested references, usually drawn from a diverse set of authors and writings. A new advanced text, Robert Kaplan's *Advanced Management Accounting* (to be published by Prentice-Hall in 1982) covers most of the same topics, but with the added depth of treatment that we typically associate with an advanced course.

The conceptual and decision-making focus of this text make it rigorous. The Third Edition has several features designed to assist the student in comprehending the text and in working the problems. Review Problems have been added to each chapter. There are typically three to six of these problems in the chapter. They take material incrementally or cover major areas within a chapter. By doing these problems as the chapter is read, the student will be better prepared to work the end-of-chapter problems. Solutions to the Review Problems can be found at the back of the text. We continue to label each problem indicating the area or topic to be covered. This should help students in working the problems and instructors in assigning the problems. As in past editions, we have taken time in setting up problems to raise thought-provoking questions, to remind the student of the real issues that underlie seemingly mechanical computations, and to point out the many facets of a seemingly simple decision. We have done more of this in the Third Edition with the hope that it will assist students and help them to gain greater insight into using information in managerial decisions. Finally, more difficult problems—sometimes anticipating later coverage, sometimes more integrative, sometimes requiring an extension of techniques introduced in a chapter—are included in the problem sets and indicated with an asterisk.

Many problems have been revised and a number of new problems have been added. We feel that the problem sets are robust and challenging and are one of the important features of this text. We have tried mightily to eliminate errors in problems and solutions. We welcome your calling our attention to any errors you may find.

We are indebted to numerous people for their help in the many stages of preparation of this book. William Beaver, Stanford University, Richard Lindhe, Northeastern University, John Kennelly, University of Illinois at Chicago Circle, and William Voss, Ohio University, all contributed valuable resources in the production of earlier editions. Steve Dowling, Harcourt Brace

Jovanovich, and Rick Antle, University of Chicago, performed in a similar capacity in the production of this edition.

We are also indebted to the AICPA and the IMA for their permission to use numerous problems that appeared on previous professional examinations.

Finally, we again acknowledge a special (and large) debt to our respective families. They have been patient and encouraging, to say the least.

Nicholas Dopuch
Jacob G. Birnberg
Joel S. Demski

Contents

vii

The Cost Accounting Function

In its broadest sense *cost accounting* is concerned with the production of cost (and revenue) data for various purposes. These purposes, in turn, range from historical product cost determination for taxation or external financial reporting purposes, through historical product, segment, and manager evaluation within the firm, to cost and revenue predictions in support of various decisions.

Our study of cost accounting will emphasize managerial considerations, an orientation that manifests itself in two important ways. First, we will focus on the production of data that are useful to individuals within, or internal to, the organization. Indeed, in pursuing this topic we assume the student is familiar, at the introductory level, with financial accounting, its procedures, and its primary concern with the production and presentation of data to individuals and groups external to the firm. In this text, therefore, we shall not be concerned with financial statements, reports to government agencies, and so on. Rather, we shall focus on management's use of accounting data.

Second, our managerial focus will *not* emphasize various accounting techniques per se. Rather, we will emphasize the continuing question of which accounting technique is appropriate in which circumstance. More precisely, we shall deal with the ways in which the accountant can determine what data are useful for management's decision making and how to classify and transmit these data.

Accounting Information Within a Firm

The purpose of this initial chapter is to introduce our topic and motivate its study. To begin, we define a *firm* as any organization concerned with the production of any type of commodity. The firm may be a proprietorship, partnership, corporation, government agency, church, or any other form of organization. Similarly, the commodity produced may be a manufactured consumer durable, such as an automobile; a private-sector service, such as a stock brokerage advisory report; a public-sector service, such as public health services; and so forth. For the sake of specificity in our discussions, we will usually focus on the upper levels of management in a manufacturing firm. Selected end-of-chapter problems, in turn, are designed to focus attention on the utilization of accounting information in other types of firms.

Information is a broad, generic term used to describe data that are useful. The essence of management is decision making; we therefore emphasize accounting data that are useful in managerial decision making. Precisely how the data are used is a situation-specific question, but in broad terms we think of the data as being used to improve the quality of management's decisions. Hence, we view cost accounting as a factor of production in the sense that it is used in the production of quality decisions.

Within any firm, we encounter a number of users of information, who face a number of different types of decision problems. For pedagogical reasons, however, we classify the decision problems under the two broad managerial functions of *planning* and *control*. Every manager makes planning decisions— which resources should be acquired, how they should be used, what products should be sold, and so forth. These decisions must then be implemented, usually by subordinates to whom are delegated various responsibilities. This assignment of responsibilities for the implementation of decisions is the first phase of control. The second phase of control involves comparing results achieved with those anticipated when decisions were made about resource utilization. Essentially, then, control consists of decision implementation coupled with a feedback process comparing actual to anticipated results, with corrective action taken where necessary.

Of course, this feedback process subtly merges into another round of planning decisions. And the planning versus control distinction becomes further blurred when we recognize that subordinates, such as divisional managers, also engage in planning. Nevertheless, it remains a useful structure for exploring the role of cost accounting.

Further note that the scope of the planning and control functions within a firm will depend on the responsibility delegated to particular managers. For example, a foreman may be responsible for meeting a production quota set for his department. He has available a given set of machinery and equipment and a given labor force, so his responsibility is restricted to the efficient assignment of workers to machines to meet his output quota. To meet this responsibility, he must rely on his knowledge of the relative skills of the workers, their wage rates, and the capacity of his machinery and equipment. When he compares the actual output in a given time period with the hours and wages required to achieve that output, he is able to evaluate both the individual workers and his particular work assignments.

In contrast, a supervisor in charge of several departments is less concerned about specific work assignments in any one department. Rather, he concentrates on the total performance of each department and how the departments must be coordinated to achieve the output for which he is responsible. In addition, he may initiate proposals to acquire more personnel or new machinery and equipment or to authorize repairs and maintenance of existing equipment.

As we move up the organizational structure, the responsibility assigned to managers increases. At the top level, responsibility will include deciding which resources should be acquired and when, how these resource acquisitions should be financed, how the firm's activities should be organized, which outputs should be produced, and so on.

In each of these settings we encounter a potential use for information. The foreman may be interested in technical characteristics of his equipment, the supervisor in the cost of alternative production schedules, and the manager in the profitability of a new product. Their interest does not, though, imply that all such information should be produced and made available to the various individuals. Producing and using information consumes resources. By implication, the choice of what information to produce (and for whom) is one of the firm's resource allocation problems. We term this the firm's *information problem*.

Decision Problems and Information

Quite naturally, our study of cost accounting is a study of the firm's information problem. Unfortunately (or fortunately), we cannot approach this subject by simply laying out a "cookbook" of well-engineered recipes for each and every situation. The conceivable array of possible and interesting situations is far too broad and complex. Besides, our philosophical orientation is one of viewing accounting as a factor of production; in studying the economics of production, we do not encounter files of recipes. Instead, a choice-oriented view, with different circumstances and different prices combining to determine the appropriate factor mix and output schedule, is what we encounter. This is the view we offer in our study of cost accounting.

Pedagogy, however, convinces us to approach this study in stages. Initially, we examine terminology, models of cost behavior, and cost estimation. This is followed by extensive work on short-run planning decisions and control decisions. The relationship to financial reporting is then explored. Finally, additional planning decisions and their respective information problems are explored.

In more specific terms, Chapters 2 and 3 deal with cost classification and methods of cost estimation. Accounting data typically reflect revenue and cost implications of various resource allocations. Cost is, however, a subtle concept. Indeed, numerous concepts are in use largely because (we suspect) what is a useful expression of cost varies with the decision situation at hand.

Hence, we begin our study with a careful examination of these concepts in Chapter 2. In turn, actually implementing one of these concepts—and actually producing the cost datum in a particular circumstance—is itself a nontrivial yet vital exercise that cuts across all decision situations. For this reason we immediately pursue, in Chapter 3, the question of cost estimation.

Equipped with terminology and estimation concerns, we then examine a series of short-run planning decisions and their associated information problem. This is the topic of Chapter 4 (cost–volume–profit decisions). Additional exploration of the important theme of linking the firm's accounting system to its planning process is presented in Chapters 14 and 15 (investment decisions) and Chapter 16 (inventory decisions). This allows for additional reflection on our basic theme as well as for consideration of important planning considerations beyond the short-run horizon of the typical cost–volume–profit setting.

Another important theme, however, is the planning–control relationship. For this reason we immediately follow Chapter 4 with an exploration of the control process and the accounting considerations therein. In particular, we recognize that economic activity is conducted under conditions of uncertainty. This uncertainty extends from the point at which the nature of the decision is first formulated, to the alternatives to consider, to the estimates of the benefits and costs that would result from following the different alternatives. Because of this uncertainty, management may design a control system to help ensure the implementation of its chosen alternatives and to see that a desirable balance of benefits and costs is realized. (There is a tendency to insist upon a statement of maximizing benefits less costs, or some such expression. However, it is well to realize that deep problems are associated with such a description of choice behavior, and we will therefore confine our use of the terminology "costs and benefits" to a general euphemism for whatever the goals of management happen to be.)

A common idea in any such control system is the notion of *performance evaluation*. Its basic nature and relationship to the information problem associated with planning decisions is explored in Chapter 5. In turn, performance evaluation often relies on budgets for the various segments in a firm. (A budget typically reflects standards for resource consumption, given a particular level of output achieved.) The use of budgets in this manner is broadly outlined in Chapter 6. Techniques for comparing actual with budgeted (or standard) results are developed in Chapter 7. And the significance of the resulting "variances" between actual and budgeted results, in terms of possible control responses and future planning adjustments, is analyzed in Chapter 8.

Planning and control considerations are, however, far more subtle than merely making, implementing, and monitoring choices. In a large organization, the decision activity is parceled out among a number of managers—partly for training purposes, partly because of diseconomies of scale in decision analysis, and partly because of communication costs. At this point, then, we also encounter an information problem associated with coordinating these various managers. One version of the problem arises when the activities of one manager impose a cost or benefit on another (as when a service center supplies other departments). Here we encounter the dilemma of cost allocation (Chapter 9). Another version arises when the firm formally organizes itself into divisions, and we encounter the question of designing divisional reporting systems that are consistent with the divisionalized and probably decentralized structure of the firm (Chapter 10).

Finally, it is also important to recognize that cost accounting for managerial purposes is not completely divorced from external financial reporting concerns. Economies of scale often result in one reporting system fulfilling multiple purposes. In addition, some financial reporting topics are traditionally reserved, for whatever reason, to the study of cost accounting. Hence, we also offer a brief look at cost accounting issues that arise in external financial reporting. Chapter 11 provides a general survey and Chapter 12 looks at product costing in more depth. Moreover, many of these issues reemerge in a managerial setting when the basic accounting model is used for planning purposes. Hence, our study of the relationship between financial and managerial reporting concludes, in Chapter 13, with an examination of financial planning models.

Selection of the Accounting System

Our central theme in the text, then, is examination of a series of decision problems and their associated information problems. Before proceeding, the student should be aware that each such information problem can be approached and analyzed in a systematic manner. While the theory that supports such analysis is beyond the scope of an introductory text, its basic nature and philosophy are readily outlined. And in this sense, our text should be viewed as a series of systematic analyses of information problems.

Quite simply, we always view the accounting system as a factor of production. One accounting system is viewed as better than another if it produces higher quality decisions. Of course, what decisions each will produce (as well as distinguishing their quality) is a nontrivial task, and we must also be careful to balance decision improvement and cost. But the idea is straightforward. Consider the following simple example.

Suppose the proprietor of a manufacturing firm must decide whether to accept a special order from a customer. He has two alternatives: accept or reject the order. He anticipates that rejection will cause no ill feelings; thus he calculates the net increase in his profits as precisely zero if he rejects the order. If he accepts the order, he will receive $550,000. The cost of making the special item is not known with certainty, but he estimates that it will cost either $400,000 (good news) or $600,000 (bad news), depending on how

EXHIBIT 1-1 _____

Analysis of the Special Order

	EVENT	
Choices	Low Production Cost	High Production Cost
Accept:		
Profit outcome	$150,000	−$50,000
Reject:		
Profit outcome	$0	$0

much time is needed for its manufacture. Hence, acceptance will result either in a net gain of $150,000 or a net loss of $50,000, while rejection will produce neither gain nor loss. These data are summarized in Exhibit 1-1.

The proprietor regards the two production cost events as being equally likely. That is, if he accepts the order, he expects to incur a gain of $150,000 with a probability of .50 or a loss of $50,000 with a probability of .50. The expected value of profit if the order is accepted is therefore .50($150,000) + .50(−$50,000) = $50,000, and that from rejection is, of course, $0. If the proprietor's objective is to maximize his expected gain, he will accept the offer.[1]

Is it possible to improve the quality of this choice? Looking at Exhibit 1-1, the answer is surely negative if the low production cost results. But the high production cost is another story. Suppose it were possible to learn, in advance of accepting or rejecting the offer, what the production cost actually will be. If the low cost results, the offer will be accepted and the profit will be $150,000. If instead the high cost results, the offer will be rejected and the profit will be $0. The events are equally likely, and the expected profit is .50($150,000) + .50($0) = $75,000.

Note that in this case the proprietor defers his choice (whether to accept or reject) until all uncertainty is removed. We refer to this advance revelation of the production cost as *perfect information*. Once the information is received, the proprietor knows exactly what will happen for each choice. The information is perfect.

Indeed, the proprietor would pay up to $25,000 for such information, since his best prospect without the information carries an expected profit

_____

[1] Note that a more thorough analysis would not focus on the expected value of profit. For example, the firm will make $150,000 or lose $50,000 here. Is this gamble necessarily better than no gain or loss for certain? Similarly, how much would we have to pay you to flip a fair coin, winner pays loser a million dollars? Aversion to risk is introduced by using a particular utility function and evaluating decisions by the expected value of the utility that may result. Presuming risk neutrality and evaluating decisions by the expected value of their resulting profit is, however, sufficient for our limited purposes.

of $50,000, while with the information the expected profit is $75,000. We term this $25,000 difference the *expected value of perfect information*.

Of course, most information is not perfect. Nevertheless, we would never pay more for any information than the expected value of perfect information. $25,000 is the maximal improvement in our proprietor's decision. To pay more than this amount for *any* improvement would be illogical.

To illustrate the analysis of imperfect information, suppose now that (before deciding whether to accept or reject this order) the proprietor has the option of analyzing a set of special orders already in production. Such analysis will provide information on what his production costs might be. He estimates that the cost of setting up the necessary accounting records and analyzing whatever data are reported will be $10,000. Thus, under any of the possible outcomes, he now incurs an additional cost of $10,000. This will change the outcome to a net loss of $10,000 if he rejects the new order and either a net gain of $140,000 or a net loss of $60,000 if he accepts it.

One of three possible conclusions will be drawn from an analysis of the results. In general, the production cost will be significantly below budget, significantly above budget, or fairly close to budget. If the current production cost is below budget, the proprietor estimates that it will also be below budget on the new order, with a probability of .90. Similarly, if the current production cost is above budget, he estimates that it will also be high on the new order, with a probability of .90. If, however, current cost is quite close to budget, he will retain his original 50–50 opinion concerning the cost of producing the new order. These probability assessments and profit outcomes are summarized in Exhibit 1-2.

—————————————————————————————————— **EXHIBIT 1-2**

**Accounting Information for Analysis
of the Special Order**

	EVENT	
	Low Production Cost	High Production Cost
Conditional probability of the event, given accounting report indicating:		
Low recent production cost (probability = .25)	.90	.10
Normal recent production cost (probability = .50)	.50	.50
High recent production cost (probability = .25)	.10	.90
Accept: Profit outcome	$140,000	−$60,000
Reject: Profit outcome	−$10,000	−$10,000

If the proprietor invests in the accounting system and subsequently receives data indicating that the current production cost is significantly less than anticipated, he then regards the $140,000 gain as occurring with probability .90 and the $60,000 loss as occurring with probability .10. The expected value is .90($140,000) + .10(−$60,000) = $120,000 and the order will be accepted. Alternatively, if the cost data indicate a high recent production cost, the expected value of accepting the order is .10($140,000) + .90(−$60,000) = −$40,000 and the offer will be rejected, with a net loss of $10,000. Similarly, if the recent cost experience is normal, the offer will be accepted, with an expected profit of .50($140,000) + .50(−$60,000) = $40,000.

We see, then, that the action to be taken by the proprietor depends on which datum he receives from the accounting system. Were this not the case—that is, were his action choice completely invariant to the accounting data—the accounting system would be useless. But usefulness alone does not imply desirability. *Accounting information may be too expensive.* To consider this issue, we must also know how likely the various report outcomes are. Let us say that past experience leads the proprietor to believe that the probability of a below-budget or an above-budget report is .25 each and the probability of a near-budget, or normal, report is .50. At this point, then, the proprietor has two alternatives. He can accept the order out of hand, with an expected profit of $50,000, or he can invest $10,000 in the accounting system and accept or reject the order depending on the specific report he receives. The expected profit associated with the decision to invest in information is the sum of the expected profits for the three possible reports, weighted by their respective probabilities:

$$.25(\$120,000) + .50(\$40,000) + .25(-\$10,000) = \$47,500 < \$50,000$$
$$\text{accept} \qquad\qquad \text{accept} \qquad\qquad \text{reject}$$

Thus the proprietor will not install the accounting system. (You should verify, however, that decreasing the cost of the accounting system by a sufficient amount will reverse this conclusion.)

If you are familiar with decision "tree" representations, Figure 1-1 will offer an alternative but equivalent view of these examples. In any event, two points should be noted. First, the proprietor uses the accounting system to revise his beliefs. He did not know whether it would cost him $400,000 or $600,000 to produce the special item, and he initially regarded each event as equally likely. However, his opinions could be changed by additional information. Indeed, this is the characteristic of information: It can alter the recipient's opinions or beliefs. However, it is useful only if it alters the recipient's opinions enough to change his or her decision.

Second, the proprietor evaluates the question of whether to install the accounting system by focusing on consequences—in this case, profit outcomes. His method of analysis is to ask what decisions would follow receipt of

(1) **No information**

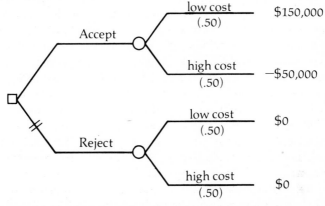

Expected profit = .50 ($150,000) + .50 (−$50,000) = $50,000

(2) **Perfect information**

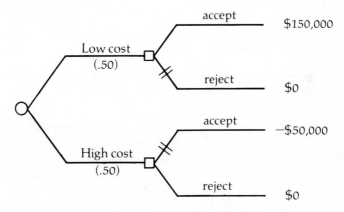

Expected profit = .50 ($150,000) + .50 ($0) = $75,000

FIGURE 1-1 cont.

(3) **Imperfect information** (with $10,000 cost)

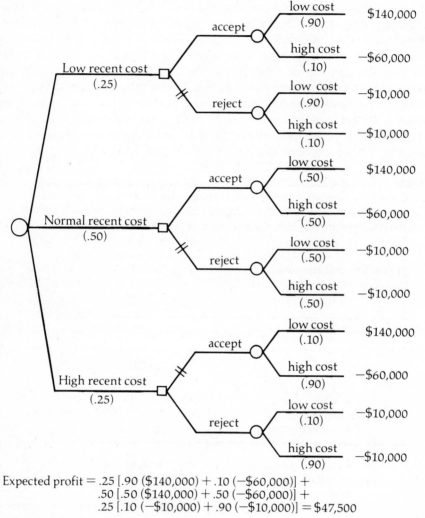

Expected profit = .25 [.90 ($140,000) + .10 (−$60,000)] +
.50 [.50 ($140,000) + .50 (−$60,000)] +
.25 [.10 (−$10,000) + .90 (−$10,000)] = $47,500

*Chance nodes are designated by ◯ and choice nodes by ☐, with respective probabilities in parentheses. Inferior choices are broken with a II designator.

each possible set of data and what consequences (profit) would follow these decisions.

In this manner, then, we are able to conceive of the use of accounting data and evaluate accounting alternatives in terms of the quality of the decisions they produce. It is this idea that provides the basis for selecting among accounting alternatives. Of course, detailing the outcomes, probabilities, risk preferences, and so on is difficult if not impossible as we allow the complexity of our decision situations to increase. Indeed, complexity dictates that while such analysis may be an aspired goal, we are forced to balance cost and quality and engage in simplified analysis. For example, when considering alternative methods of predicting overhead, we will rely, in Chapter 3, on heuristic, goodness-of-fit criteria rather than formal analysis of the quality of the resulting decisions. But our central theme should be apparent: The firm's information problem is a resource allocation problem.

REVIEW PROBLEM

Consider a manager who is attempting to decide whether to implement a new production technique. Implementation will cost, he estimates, $50,000. But the savings are uncertain: They will be either $80,000 or $10,000, implying net gains of $80,000 − $50,000 = $30,000 and $10,000 − $50,000 = −$40,000 (see Exhibit 1-3). The manager also assesses a .60 probability that the savings will be $80,000 (and thus a .40 probability that they will be $10,000).

EXHIBIT 1-3

Cost Savings Outcomes

	EVENT	
	High Savings	**Low Savings**
Implement	$30,000	−$40,000
Do not implement	$0	$0

Required (a) Calculate the expected net gain for each of the alternatives.
(b) Calculate and interpret the expected value of perfect information.

Conclusion

In this chapter we have outlined the purpose and structure of this book. In the process of operating a firm, a manager must choose between conflicting alternatives without complete knowledge of the effects of each course of action. Thus, proper acquisition and use of available information is a requisite for good management.

It is the accountant's task to supply at least some of this information. In this book we shall discuss how the accountant chooses and transmits information and how the manager can use the information. We shall emphasize the fact that the accountant is continually choosing among alternative accounting methods; that is, he, too, is a manager. By implication, then, a major goal of this book is to acquaint the student with this choice-oriented point of view as well as with the various accounting alternatives that might be used in different situations.

Supplementary Readings

American Accounting Association, Committee on Managerial Accounting Reports, 1970, 1971–72.

Anthony, R.N., *Planning and Control Systems: A Framework for Analysis*. Harvard University Graduate School of Business, 1965.

Anton, Hector, "Some Aspects of Measurement and Accounting," *J. Accounting Research*, Spring 1964.

Demski, J.S., *Information Analysis*. Reading, Mass.: Addison-Wesley, 1980.

Demski, J.S., and G.A. Feltham, *Cost Determination: A Conceptual Approach*. Ames, Iowa: Iowa State Press, 1976.

Kassouf, S., *Normative Decision Making*. Englewood Cliffs, N.J.: Prentice-Hall, 1970.

Luce, R., and H. Raiffa, *Games and Decisions*. New York: Wiley, 1957.

Marschak, J., and R. Radner, *Economic Theory of Teams*. New Haven, Conn.: Yale University Press, 1972.

McFarland, Walter, *Concepts for Management Accounting*. New York: National Association of Accountants, 1966.

Questions and Problems

1. It is often popular to talk about managerial accounting and financial reporting as if these were two separate disciplines. To what extent do you consider them similar? Different?

2. What do we mean by the term *useful data?* Can data be useless? Can information be useless?

3. Discuss at least two ways the accountant could ascertain what data might be useful to a department head. What are the strengths and weaknesses of each?

4. What is the primary purpose of the organized institution called a business firm?

5. Does the accounting system determine the form of the institution's organization or does the organization determine the nature of the accounting system?

6. One of the major changes taking place in business organizations is the increased use of computers. How might this alter the nature of the accountant's task?

7. More firms are using operations research techniques, such as inventory tech-

niques and mathematical programming. How does this alter the accountant's task?

8. Many accountants talk of developing a "total information system for the firm." How does this compare to the accounting system?

9. **Expected Value of Perfect Information**
Ralph must select one of three investments: *One* is a real estate venture that will produce $2,000,000 if the economy is "healthy," but nothing if it is "ill"; *two* is vintage sports car speculation that will produce $400,000 if the economy is "healthy" or $800,000 if it is "ill"; and *three* is a loan to his trustworthy banker that will produce $600,000, regardless of the economy's health. We summarize the options and possible outcomes below:

EVENT

	"Healthy" Economy	"Ill" Economy
One	$2,000,000	$ 0
Two	400,000	800,000
Three	600,000	600,000

The probability of a healthy economy is .70 and the probability of an ill economy is .30.

(a) What is the expected cash flow for each of Ralph's options?
(b) Assuming Ralph evaluates options in terms of their expected cash flow, what option should be selected?
(c) What is the expected value of perfect information?

10. **Evaluation of Information**
Refer to Ralph's options in Problem 9 and suppose he can purchase a report that purports to predict the economy's future health. If good times are predicted, the probability of a healthy economy is .75 (and the probability of an ill economy is therefore .25). But if bad times are predicted, the probability of a healthy economy is .50 (and the probability of an ill economy is therefore .50). Consistency requires that the probability of a good times prediction is .80 and the probability of a bad times prediction is .20. The report will cost $1,000.

(a) What should Ralph do if he acquires the report and it predicts good times?
(b) What should Ralph do if he acquires the report and it predicts bad times?
(c) Should Ralph acquire the report?
(d) What is the maximum price Ralph should pay for the report?

*11. **Effect of Risk Aversion** [2]
Suppose Ralph is risk averse and evaluates decisions in terms of the expected value of the utility of their cash flow. His utility for cash flow is $\sqrt{1 + (\text{cash flow}/1,000)}$.

---

[2] Problems denoted with an asterisk (*) are intended for students who have more than the typical level of analytic skill. They expand on subjects covered in the respective chapters.

(a) Suppose Ralph is offered a fair coin bet on $1,000. If the coin is "heads" he wins $1,000, while if it is "tails" he must pay $1,000. Verify that Ralph would have to be paid $250 to accept such a gamble.

(b) Refer to Ralph's options in Problem 10 and verify that with this utility function he not only finds the report useful but would gladly pay $1,000 to receive it.

(c) Explain the difference between the results in (b) above and those in Problem 10.

*12. **Information Evaluation and Probability Revision**

Ralph is now constructing a special product for an individual customer. The only catch is whether the constructed product is of acceptable quality. If it is acceptable he will net (revenue less cost) $400, but if it is unacceptable legal reprisals, unfavorable publicity, and so on, will reduce his net gain to −$250. (The two events are equally likely.) At an incremental cost of $400 Ralph may, however, inspect the product and completely repair it if the quality is, indeed, unacceptable. In other words, Ralph has a choice of inspecting (which guarantees neither gain nor loss) or not inspecting (which offers a potential gain of $400 or a potential loss of −$250).

Ralph also faces an accounting issue. He has an additional option of acquiring—at a cost of $5—a cost control report that will shed some light on the quality issue. To keep things as simple as possible, we view this cost report as telling Ralph one of two things: costs on a similar job are either "high" (HC) or "low" (LC). This information, in turn, may tell Ralph something about the quality of the product in question. In particular, if the quality is indeed unacceptable, the probability of either measure is .50. If the quality is acceptable, however, the probability of a low cost (LC) is .80. Should Ralph pay for such a cost report? Put another way, which accounting treatment or method is "best" in this situation: none or the special study? (Hint: Use Bayesian revision to determine that the probability of acceptable quality given a "low" cost message is 40/65, and so on.)

Cost Classifications

Cost accounting has developed in response to a rather pervasive desire on the part of managements to control the consumption of scarce resources used in the production and distribution of goods and services. Generally, there are alternative mixes of resources that may be employed to produce and distribute a given level of output, and management's objective is to choose those mixes that minimize the costs of obtaining various output levels. This holds for both profit-seeking and nonprofit organizations, since neither type has an unlimited supply of "free" resources available to it.

The optimal production mix, however, usually must be determined under conditions of uncertainty regarding the actual prices that must be paid to acquire them and the output levels that will be achieved for various mixes, as well as the ability and willingness of subordinates to achieve planned output levels from the particular mix of productive factors made available to them. Over time, we have learned that *feedback* information on actual results relative to planned results provides a useful basis for improving future decisions on input mixes and for increasing the probability that subordinates will carry out their responsibilities. For example, forecasts of future prices and input/output relationships may be improved by an analysis of past forecast errors on these variables, say, by suggesting which forecasting methods provide more accurate forecasts. The ability and willingness of subordinates to achieve planned output levels for the mixes they have available may be increased by linking penalties and rewards to the extent to which they actually do so.

The use of cost data for feedback purposes has led to the development of numerous cost classifications that are designed to focus on various aspects of the planning and control phases of management. To illustrate these classifications, we will work with a simple firm consisting of three departments: production, distribution, and administration. Assume that costs are aggregated into three categories of input services: materials, labor, and a catchall called overhead (utilities, rents, depreciation, supervision, and so on). During the prior period, the firm produced 10,000 units of output and incurred the following costs:

	Production	Distribution	Administration
Materials	$15,000	$ 5,000	$ —
Labor	18,000	20,000	25,000
Overhead	12,000	10,000	15,000
Total	$45,000	$35,000	$40,000

Each unit of output sells for $15.00. Suppose that 8,000 units were sold, leaving 2,000 finished units in inventory. No beginning inventory was present.

Note that considerable cost classification has already taken place here. A direct cost is one that can be unambiguously identified with some product. In a manufacturing setting, we typically classify the manufacturing cost into direct material, direct labor, and overhead. Direct material consists of the cost of all materials that can be unambiguously and economically identified with the manufactured products. Subassemblies would be classified as direct material, while minor items such as small hardware presumably would not. Direct labor consists of the cost of all labor service that can be unambiguously and economically identified with the products. Machine operators would be costed as direct labor, while inspectors typically would not. All other manufacturing cost elements are classified as overhead; examples are rent, depreciation, and any labor and materials not classified as direct costs.

You should further notice, as we proceed through the illustration, how each cost item may be reclassified under various headings, depending on the purpose of the analysis. For example, our first illustration deals with cost classifications as either product or period costs. This distinction is useful in preparing financial statements such as income statements and balance sheets. As a second illustration, consider cost classifications based on the behavior of cost items as some activity variable changes (for example, output levels or direct labor hours worked). Some cost items (strictly variable costs) will vary strictly with changes in the activity variable, whereas other cost items (strictly fixed costs) will remain at a fixed amount irrespective of changes in the activity variable. Still other cost items (mixed costs) will reflect behavior patterns between these two extremes. Additional illustrations deal with basic cost classifications useful in controlling and planning operations (controllable versus noncontrollable costs, sunk costs, opportunity costs, and incremental costs).

As a sort of preview, consider the cost item, direct labor. This is considered a product cost since amounts incurred are charged to the inventory account, "work in process," then traced through "finished goods" inventory, and then to "cost of goods sold" as finished goods are sold during a particular accounting period. Direct labor is also a strictly variable cost, or so treated, since we would expect to incur no costs at an output level of zero, but increasing costs as the output level increases. Therefore, direct labor is classified as a controllable cost for those responsible for assigning direct labor to production. In addition, it is an incremental cost within a decision evaluation of whether to increase output levels over some previously established amount. Direct materials costs could be classified in a similar manner—that is, as a product cost, a strictly variable cost, a controllable cost, or an incremental cost of expanding output levels. But the same does not hold true for all overhead items, as the illustrations will show.

Product Versus Period Costs

Traditionally, an evaluation of the efficiency of firms centered on the relationship between the costs incurred in producing units of output and their selling prices. In order to enable managers and others to make interfirm comparisons of this relationship, accountants developed rules for assigning costs to production departments and then apportioning these costs between units sold and those remaining in inventory. Cost assignment is typically based on a full-costing principle in which *all* manufacturing costs, whether fixed or variable with respect to output levels, are assigned to physical units of output, thereby producing an average full-cost per unit. As units are sold, they are removed from the inventory account and charged to cost of sales on the basis of their computed full-cost per unit. From financial accounting, we know that as input prices change over time, different full-costs per unit will enter the inventory account, creating a problem as to which per-unit costs are to remain in inventory and which should be assigned to output units. The accountant solves these problems by computing averages of the per-unit costs or by adopting various flow assumptions, such as the assumption that the first units in (and their per-unit costs) are the first out (FIFO) or the last units in are the first out (LIFO). For the moment we will avoid this inventory accounting problem by assuming that all 10,000 units entered inventory at the same full-cost (price) per unit.

Given that total production costs were $45,000, the average cost per unit for 10,000 units produced this period was $4.50. Since 8,000 units were sold, we assume the accountant would allocate 8,000 $\times$ $4.50 = $36,000 to cost of sales for the period and 2,000 $\times$ $4.50 = $9,000 to the ending inventory valuation for finished goods.

Under financial accounting rules, all distribution costs and administration costs incurred during an accounting period are charged to sales as "period" costs. The main reason is simply that it is difficult, if not impractical, to determine the relationship between the incurrence of these costs and the production (and sale) of individual units of output. Hence, we have the distinction between *product* and *period* costs.

An illustrative income statement based on these rules would appear as follows (ignoring some detailed accounting calculations):

Sales (8,000 × $15.00)		$120,000
Cost of goods sold (8,000 × $4.50)		36,000
Gross profit on sales		$ 84,000
Less period costs:		
Distribution (selling)	$35,000	
Administration	40,000	75,000
Net operating income		$ 9,000

Many cost accounting issues arise in determining production costs, particularly in allocating these costs to units of output for inventory and costs of sales computations. One issue is whether to allocate all categories of production costs to units produced or merely to allocate a subset of these—for example, only those costs that vary with output levels (variable costs). The issue is known as the absorption (full-cost) versus direct (variable) costing issue. Another issue concerns the allocation of common or joint costs that are incurred in the production of two or more different types of outputs (products or product lines). The allocation of overhead costs to different "products" is illustrated in Problem 23 at the end of this chapter. A special type of common cost is a manufacturing cost jointly incurred with no discernible basis for ascertaining how its level varies with changes in the output levels of the individual products or product lines. These costs are called *joint costs;* methods of and reasons for allocating them will be discussed in later chapters. These and other allocation issues cannot be ignored or treated lightly, since firms' accountants require that all manufacturing costs be allocated to units of outputs for the preparation of traditional income statements and balance sheets. Moreover, various regulations, such as those of the SEC, the IRS, and the CASB[1] are pertinent here.

The gross classification of costs as production, distribution, and administration is not particularly useful for management's internal decisions. We turn now to classifications designed to facilitate management's internal planning and control decisions.

REVIEW PROBLEM 1
Statements Supporting the Cost-of-Goods-Sold Calculation _____

We assume the student has some background in the double-entry system of accounting. (The basic procedures for cost accounting are briefly summarized in Appendix B to Chapter 11.) The typical system uses three control accounts for each production department: raw materials control, work-in-process control, and finished goods control. The basic transactions for

---

[1] Securities Exchange Commission, Internal Revenue Service, and Cost Accounting Standards Board, respectively.

the raw materials account are like any other inventory account: Beginning inventory value *plus* purchases *less* ending inventory value *equals* the cost of materials used in production.

The work-in-process account is a little more involved. This account receives the costs of materials used in production, labor costs incurred in production during the current period, and overhead costs assigned to current-period production. The latter are usually assigned on the basis of some direct input, such as direct labor. For example, overhead might be assigned on the basis of $3 per direct labor hour used in production. If 20,000 hours were used in production, the overhead costs assigned or allocated to production would amount to $60,000. This method of allocation is used primarily because overhead costs are incurred (recorded) at discrete points in time, whereas output is continually being produced. Again, to illustrate, vacation time is incurred primarily in the summer months. If units produced in the winter months are to receive a charge for vacation costs that will be incurred in the following summer months, some system of overhead allocation must be employed. The rationale for spreading such overhead costs is simply that vacation time is an additional employment cost of each worker who devotes his time to all units of production.

The accounting equation for work-in-process is, therefore, beginning inventory of costs carried over from a prior period (for units not completed in the prior period) *plus* costs incurred in the current period (to complete old units and work on new units) *less* costs assigned to current units not yet completed *equals* the cost of goods manufactured in the current period.

This total for the cost of goods manufactured is transferred to the finished goods control account. Beginning inventory of costs for finished goods *plus* cost of goods manufactured *less* ending inventory of finished goods *equals* the cost of goods sold for the period.

Assume the following:

Beginning inventory of raw materials	$10,000
Purchases of raw materials	50,000
Ending inventory of raw materials	12,000
Beginning inventory of work-in-process	30,000
Direct labor costs incurred (10,000 hours)	50,000
Overhead costs allocated to production	45,000
Ending inventory of work-in-process	23,000
Beginning inventory of finished goods	20,000
Ending inventory of finished goods	30,000

Required   (a)   Determine the cost of direct materials for the current production period.

(b)   Calculate the cost of goods manufactured for the current period (costs to finished goods).

(c)   Calculate the cost of goods sold for the period.

(d)   Calculate the overhead rate per labor hour.

Present these calculations in detail in the order required so that a(nother) novice could follow them and be able to explain their meaning.

Fundamental Cost–Volume Relationships _____

One of the more fundamental classifications of costs for planning and control purposes is based on whether the costs tend to be fixed or variable in relation to changes in some measure of activity. We denote this activity measure by x and the total cost function by

$$TC = f(x)$$

If TC is a constant amount, regardless of x, we say the cost is a strictly fixed cost. If TC varies with x and is zero when $x = 0$, we say the cost is strictly variable. This is, of course, a rather gross simplification, since very few, if any, cost items are strictly fixed or strictly variable.

More important, however, is to recognize that practical considerations demand that a simplified cost function be employed. Linear approximations are by far the most common. Here, we approximate the cost function with

$$TC \approx a + bx$$

where the intercept is a and the slope is b. Within this linear setting, we identify three cost behavior patterns: (1) strictly variable, in which case the cost would be expressed as $TC = bx$, with b representing the average change in cost per unit change in x, (2) strictly fixed, wherein $TC = a$, a constant, and (3) semivariable which is a combination of the first two, so that $TC = a + bx$.

A slight variation on this theme allows us to identify a fourth major category, semifixed, or the "step cost" phenomenon. Here $b = 0$, but the a intercept depends on x in a discontinuous manner. That is, the cost would be at a level of a_1 for activity levels from zero to x_1; a_2 for activity levels between x_1 and x_2; a_3 for activity levels between x_3 and x_4; and so on. In some cases, the steps might be equal jumps, in which case $a_2 = 2a_1$; $a_3 = 3a_1$; and so forth.

The four cost models are illustrated in Figure 2-1(a)–(d). In every case, the vertical axis measures the total cost and the horizontal axis indicates the level of x, the activity variable.

Strictly Variable Costs

As implied in part (a) of Figure 2-1, a strictly variable cost is equal to zero at $x = 0$, then increases in a linear model at the average rate of b per unit change in x. Of course, a strictly variable cost need not increase at a constant rate (a linear function); in fact, it may be necessary to recognize that cost functions are nonlinear, having, say, a squared term (x^2) or perhaps even a cubed term as well (x^3). The latter, which appears in Figure 2-2, reflects

FIGURE 2-1

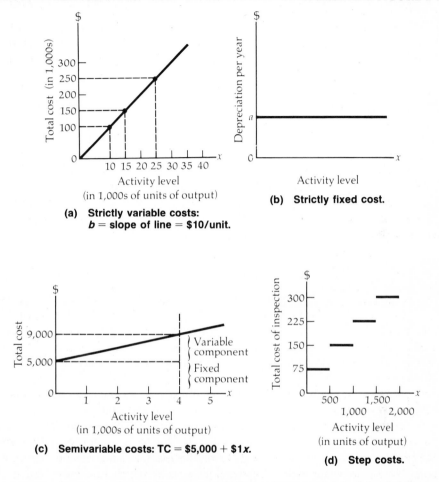

(a) **Strictly variable costs:**
   b = slope of line = $10/unit.

(b) **Strictly fixed cost.**

(c) **Semivariable costs: TC = $5,000 + $1x.**

(d) **Step costs.**

different degrees of efficiency in using an input factor at various levels of activity. (How would a learning situation appear?) Note that the slope of the cost line is steeper at the upper end of the activity scale, with the more efficient interval in the mid-range.

The typical assumption leading to a linear estimate of a cost item is that firms tend to operate in the efficient interval, so that a linear estimate, shown as the dashed line in Figure 2-2, is an adequate representation of the behavior of total costs in that operating interval. Some would argue that few costs are strictly variable, since some level of cost incurrence would be observed at an output level of $x = 0$ because of various operating constraints. For example, many firms commit themselves to holding a given level of skilled workers even if output levels drop below the points at which these workers

FIGURE 2-2 _____

Linear estimates of a nonlinear function.

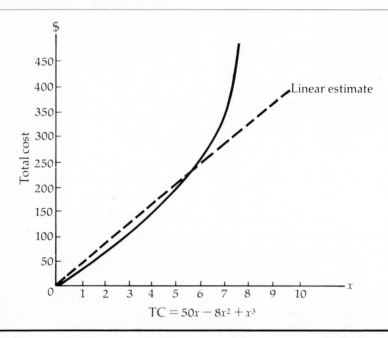

$$TC = 50x - 8x^2 + x^3$$

are actually being utilized in the production process. Under such an assumption, the cost item might appear as in Figure 2-3, where the fixed portion of the cost (the solid horizontal line) represents the firm's commitment to hold a certain number of workers who can handle output levels up to the point where the cost starts to increase. At that point, additional workers are hired, and the cost increases at an average rate of the labor cost per unit. Note, however, that we can achieve the same estimate of total cost beyond the critical output point by drawing a straight line from the origin to the critical point and beyond.

Costs typically classified as strictly variable are direct materials and direct labor in production departments, supplies in distribution and administration departments (given some appropriate activity variable, such as orders filled, or invoices or letters processed), commissions and other payments based on units sold or dollars of revenue, and labor costs in nonproduction departments that can be linked directly with some activity variable (again, orders filled, letters typed, invoices or cases processed, and so forth). In terms of our previous illustration, we will assume that the labor and materials costs in production are strictly variable, as are the materials costs in distribution. The other cost items will be classified under one of the other three types discussed next.

_____FIGURE 2-3

**Labor costs, assuming a fixed level of costs up to x_1, and an
increase in costs, at an average of $10x, beyond x_1.**

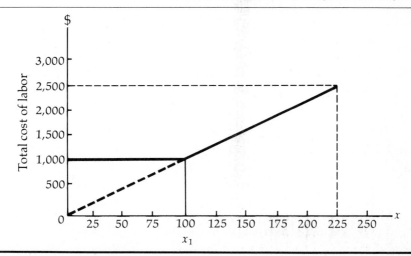

Strictly Fixed Costs

As shown in part (b) of Figure 2-1, a strictly fixed cost remains constant
for the entire output range. Some items that might fit this characterization
are time-depreciation on plants and buildings, administrative salaries, and
higher-level supervisory salaries. Regarding the first, we assume that no matter
what the output level, the depreciation of plants and buildings will be at a
constant amount per time period (say, a year). The same assumption applies
to the salaries of higher-level personnel, such as presidents, vice-presidents,
plant supervisors, and the like. Of course, in practice other cost items are
classified as strictly fixed, even though they more closely fit the pattern of
the step cost [part (d) of Figure 2-1]. For example, depreciation on machines
and equipment is usually graphed as a strictly fixed cost item, when in fact
we would expect total depreciation on all of these items to increase in steps
as output levels are expanded and additional amounts of these assets are
acquired. The same holds for insurance and taxes on personal property (equipment, machines, and inventories) held by the firm. These items will increase
with additional holdings of personal property, yet they are usually graphed
as strictly fixed costs. The reason is simple: We assume that firms have made
decisions regarding what levels of these particular assets are to be acquired,
and it is the fixed costs associated with these decisions that is being graphed.

This brings to mind an important assumption underlying cost classification. It is generally assumed that firms have made preliminary decisions regard-

ing their probable range of operations and the proper balance between fixed and variable input factors, so that cost classifications of strictly variable and strictly fixed costs actually reflect these preliminary decisions. This probable range of operations is usually defined as the *relevant range* for cost analyses.

For the purposes of our illustration, we will assume that all of the costs in the administration department and the overhead cost item for distribution may be classified as strictly fixed. That leaves us, then, with only the task of classifying the overhead item in production and the labor costs in distribution, which we will classify as semivariable or mixed cost items.

Semivariable and Step Costs

A semivariable cost is one that has a fixed component, a, but then increases with activity at the constant rate of b per unit change in x [see part (c), Figure 2-1]. Many overhead items in production are typically classified as semivariable costs—for example, utilities, maintenance, and indirect labor. Certain licensing arrangements may also result in semivariable costs; an example would be a fixed payment per month plus a certain percentage of sales. Note also that when we aggregate individual cost items into single functions for departments, plants, firms, or other operating units, the total cost function will behave as a semivariable cost, with a fixed component equal to the sum of all fixed items and a variable rate equal to the sum of the individual variable rates.

Further note that the interpretation of such a linear cost model is a somewhat delicate issue. We have already stressed the approximate nature of the linear cost model, coupled with the confinement of the activity measure to some relevant range. The fixed component, then, should be interpreted as the *intercept* and the variable component as the *slope* of the linear approximation in the relevant range. We do not know what the cost will be at $x = 0$, unless zero activity is in the relevant range. The issue will be stressed in the next chapter, where we examine methods for determining the cost model.

Step (or semifixed) costs are much more pervasive than we might imagine since, under the appropriate definition of the unit of activity, practically every cost item can be characterized as a step cost. For example, suppose a unit of output requires one pound of materials priced at $10 per pound. If we graphed the change in materials cost per unit change in x, we could show the total cost function as a series of steps, with each change equal to $10. The same holds for direct labor, which might call for 2 hours of labor per unit with a labor rate of $7.50 per hour. Each unit of output then results in a cost of $15 so that the total labor cost changes in steps equal to $15 per step. The insignificance of the steps, given a large number of output units produced, is what leads us to ignore them and, instead, to graph materials, labor, and other step costs as a continuous function. This is illustrated in Figure 2-4.

But this simplification is not justified when the steps are significant (occurring at several discrete points, with each change being nontrivial in amount). Here, we must either assume some output level and then estimate the cost as a fixed cost appropriate for that output level, or graph the discontinuous function explicitly. The two treatments are illustrated in Figures 2-5 and 2-6 for two different cost items (inspection and indirect labor). The choice of treatment is guided by practical considerations. Our guess is that the first treatment is the more prevalent one in practice, simply because it results in a continuous cost function that can be used in estimating future costs for planning and controlling operations.

Referring back to our illustration, we will assume that the overhead costs in production are of the semivariable type, with a fixed component of $10,000 and a variable portion of $2,000. In practice, such breakdowns would be based on an analysis of individual overhead cost items and on experience with their typical behavior with respect to output changes. We will also assume that labor payments in distribution result in fixed costs of $5,000 and variable costs of $15,000.

We can now summarize the breakdown of costs for our firm and calculate its total (linear) cost function.

	Variable Costs	**Fixed Costs**
Production		
Materials	$15,000	$ —
Labor	18,000	—
Overhead	2,000	10,000
Total	$35,000	$10,000
Distribution		
Supplies	$ 5,000	$ —
Labor	15,000	5,000
Overhead	—	10,000
Total	$20,000	$15,000
Administration		
Labor (salaries)	—	$25,000
Overhead	—	15,000
Total	$ —	$40,000
Grand total	$55,000	$65,000

First, we will summarize these figures into three cost functions, one for each department. Since production produced 10,000 units of output, its cost function would be $TC_p = \$10,000 + (\$35,000/10,000)x_p$, or $TC_p = \$10,000 + \$3.50x_p$. Recall that the firm sold only 8,000 units, so the cost function for the distribution department would be $TC_d = \$15,000 + (\$20,000/8,000)x_s$, where x_s represents units *sold*, or $TC_d = \$15,000 + \$2.50x_s$. Finally, the administration department has a fixed component of $40,000, with no variable costs, regardless of the number of units produced or sold.

FIGURE 2-4

The step cost of direct labor treated as a variable cost.

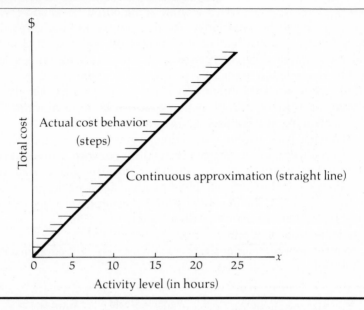

FIGURE 2-5

The step cost of inspection treated as a fixed cost. The expected cost is $225 for the output level between 1,000 and 1,500 units.

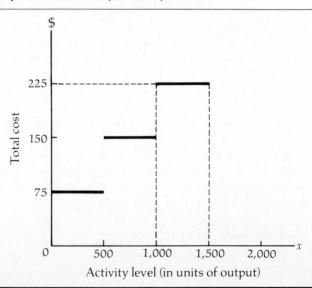

_____FIGURE 2-6

An indirect labor cost treated as a semifixed cost.

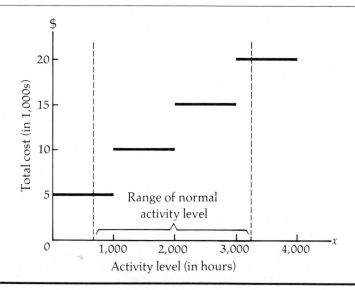

To combine these into a single cost function for the firm, we let x represent units produced *and* sold, on the assumption that inventory changes will be zero for whatever decisions are based upon this aggregate cost function. For example, for a decision of whether to expand output, we would assume that whatever the level of additional units produced, they will all be sold during the time period of their production. Similarly, if we were attempting to determine the firm's expected break-even point for a typical operating period, we would assume that the number of units needed to break even would be produced and sold during the same time period. The expansion calculation will be illustrated later; the break-even point for our firm would be determined as follows. The number of units needed to break even occurs at an output that produces a zero profit, or the output point where total revenues equal total costs. Our firm's total cost function for units produced *and* sold is TC = ($10,000 + $15,000 + $40,000) + ($3.50 + $2.50)$x$ = $65,000 + 6x$. Given a selling price of $15 per unit, the firm would break even when 15x$ = $65,000 + 6x$, with x as the unknown. By appropriate manipulation, we solve for x_{be} = 7,222.22, or 7,222 rounded off. How firms might use this simple calculation, as well as other variations, will be discussed in Chapter 4.

REVIEW PROBLEMS 2 and 3
Cost Behavior Patterns _____

The following problems review the basics of cost classifications (2) and some complicating factors that lead to rather hybrid cost behavior patterns (3). These hybrid patterns are typically suppressed in practice. They may be significant enough in some situations, however, to warrant dealing with them explicitly.

2. Classify each of the following as being *usually* fixed (F), variable (V), semifixed (SF), or semivariable (SV).

   (a) factory electrical power
   (b) factory manager's salary
   (c) advertising
   (d) depreciation on machinery
   (e) factory rental
   (f) maintenance of machinery
   (g) direct labor
   (h) supplies and other indirect materials
   (i) supervisory personnel
   (j) royalty payment that guarantees a minimum amount
   (k) overtime premiums
   (l) property taxes and insurance

3. In the following graphs, assume total cost is measured on the vertical axis, while activity levels are measured along the horizontal axis. Indicate which graph depicts each cost–volume relationship described. If you do not find a graph that is appropriate, draw your own.

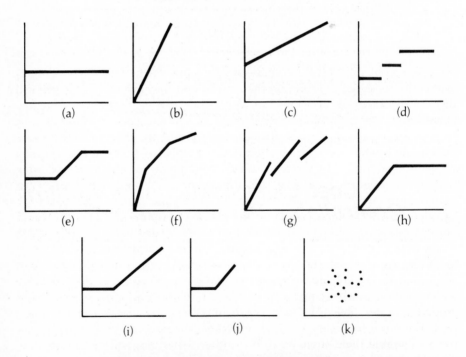

(a)   (b)   (c)   (d)

(e)   (f)   (g)   (h)

(i)   (j)   (k)

(1) Salespeople are paid solely on commission.
(2) Salespeople are paid solely on commission. As their volume increases, however, the rate decreases: for example, 30% on the first $10,000, 25% on the next $10,000, and 20% on any sales beyond $20,000.

(3) The lease requires rental payment of 1% of net sales. Minimum rent is $1,000 per month.

(4) Electric rates are as follows:

First 5,000 kilowatt-hours	$.07 per kilowatt-hours
Next 10,000 kilowatt-hours	.09 per kilowatt-hours
Above 15,000 kilowatt-hours	.10 per kilowatt-hours

Minimum billing per period is $100.

(5) A supplier agrees to furnish widgets at the following prices:

$1.00 per pound for any order of 1,000 pounds or less
$.80 per pound for any order from 1,001 to 2,000 pounds
$.70 per pound for any order of 2,001 pounds or more

(6) The plant is leased for $12,000 per year.

(7) The licensing agreement for a patent requires payment of a royalty of $.10 per unit, with a maximum annual payment of $100,000.

(8) The cost of the company's accident insurance plan is based on the hours actually worked by the employees. Company policy requires a stable work force adequate in size to meet expected volume in the short run without overtime.

(9) A machine is leased at a rental of $10 per hour.

(10) The contract signed with Universal Maintenance provides service for the firm's machinery. The contract sets a fee of $10 per hour. However, the company agrees to guarantee Universal at least $100 per month in billings, and Universal "insures" the company against any monthly bills in excess of $700.

Cost Classifications for Control: Controllable Versus Noncontrollable Costs

Most cost control systems rely on budgets for *costs allowed* to achieve a given output level. Individuals in charge of costing units (such as departments) are expected to incur actual costs consistent with their allowed costs once the actual output level is known. This is of significant concern to these heads, since their compensation (wages, bonuses, and promotion) is often based on the degree to which they can keep their actual costs below or equal to their allowable costs. Of course, many events may occur during a particular operating period that are beyond the immediate control of the heads of costing units, but that nevertheless affect the levels of their incurred costs. Recognition of this problem has given rise to the notion that costs incurred within a particular costing unit should be classified as either controllable (by its head) or noncontrollable. Presumably, the individual in charge of the costing unit would then be evaluated in terms of the controllable costs. This notion is somewhat simplistic, however. It will be dealt with in Chapter 5; for the moment, we will concentrate on the classification itself.

Many noncontrollable costs reflect decisions made outside the costing unit. For example, most decisions regarding the machinery and equipment available to costing units are made by those responsible for determining the firm's capital needs. The fixed costs associated with these assets, therefore, are outside the immediate control of the heads of these costing units. Actual costs incurred in one department and transferred to another costing unit are also outside the direct control of the receiving unit's head, and this is one reason such costs are transferred at some "standard" cost rather than at the actual cost.

It is not always clear which costs are controllable by a responsibility unit head and which are noncontrollable. Typically, costs that are fixed for an operating period are classified as noncontrollable, particularly if their levels reflect capacity acquisition decisions made in prior periods. Apart from this simple rule, the issue of which costs are controllable and which are noncontrollable may have to be resolved through interactions between responsibility unit heads and their immediate supervisors, given some actual operating setting. Applying the simple rule to our illustrative firm, labor and material costs would be classified as controllable costs, as would the variable portions of the overhead cost items. The fixed costs would be classified as noncontrollable by the respective unit heads.

The fact that fixed costs tend to be noncontrollable within current operating periods has provided a major impetus for the so-called "zero-based" budgeting systems, which became popular in the late 1970s. Fixed costs that represent capacity decisions of the past, including the decisions to hold a given level of skilled workers whether in production, distribution, or administration, can be reduced only by reviewing the original decisions to acquire these capacities and reducing or eliminating those capacities no longer needed. Zero-based budgeting deals primarily with the reviewing procedures that lead to reassessments of these prior capacity decisions.

Under the more typical procedures of budgeting, costing units are controlled by what are known as "flexible budgets." These are nothing more than a series of budgets for costs allowed to achieve various output levels. In order to use a flexible budgeting system, we need only separate our cost items between variable and fixed, which we have already done for our firm. Thus, the flexible budget for production for any output level of x achieved during a particular operating period could be stated as $BTC_p = \$10,000 + \$3.50x_{act}$, where x_{act} represents actual output. This budgeted cost would then be compared to the actual costs incurred within the production department. If more detail is required, the flexible budget could be constructed on an item-by-item basis: labor costs allowed $= \$1.80x_{act}$, materials costs allowed $= \$1.50x_{act}$, and overhead costs allowed $= \$10,000 + \$.20x_{act}$.

A similar type of budget could be constructed for the other two departments, except that sales would be the activity variable for the distribution department to budget its variable costs, and the administration budget would simply be a fixed budget for each operating period.

REVIEW PROBLEM 4
Controllable Versus Noncontrollable Costs

At the beginning of an operating period, suppose a particular responsibility unit receives a budget that lists the output expected from this unit, along with the costs allowed to achieve this budgeted output. The output might be physical units of production, hours of services to be performed (for example, maintenance), or specific jobs budgeted (such as audits of an accounting firm or layouts for an advertising firm). In other words, assume we are dealing with a budget that can be developed for any responsibility unit for which a specific output can be defined and measured. The cost items included in the budget are of the typical classes: labor; materials or supplies; and various overhead costs, such as depreciation, insurance and taxes, indirect or supervisory labor, and rents. The responsibility unit has various equipment and machinery consistent with the technology needed to produce its output, as well as a labor force consisting of personnel of various skills.

The budgeted or allowable costs are based upon *past* observations of the relationship between incurred costs and various output levels, with adjustments to take into account changes in operating conditions between present and past operating periods. The personnel within the unit are assigned to various tasks on the basis of the skills required for the tasks and their availability. Overhead costs that vary with output are linked to the amount of labor time consumed during the period (which obviously fluctuates with the level of output actually achieved).

Required   (a)   Given the above description of this unit's operating conditions, discuss whether it is reasonable to label labor costs as controllable; that is, discuss the types of decisions affecting labor costs that are under the control of the unit head.

         (b)   Repeat (a) for direct materials (if any).

         (c)   What overhead items are likely to fluctuate with labor usage? Would they be controllable?

         (d)   What fixed overhead items might be incurred in this department? Would they be controllable?

Cost Classifications
Related to Planning Decisions

Additional cost classifications have been developed to facilitate an evaluation of various alternative actions in the area of managerial planning, particularly those alternatives related to the allocation of existing capacities to outputs.

Incremental Costs

Incremental costs may be defined as the change in total costs that will occur as the result of moving from one plan of action to another. The typical reference point is the present plan of action, so the incremental costs would be the change in costs resulting from a substitution of another plan of action for the present one. The present plan of action might consist of the current method of production and the alternative could be a change in the level of machinery or equipment, in the level or mix of skilled personnel, or in the grade (and price) of raw materials. Or, alternatively, the present plan might be a given level of output of product A, under existing technology, and the alternative would be a change in the level of output of A, a substitution of output B for A (with a change in technology as well), or various combinations of the two. A decision rule for the latter type of alternative evaluations would be to expand (or change) output levels (or mixes) if the incremental revenues resulting from the change exceed the incremental costs associated with it. A rule for the first set of alternative evaluations would be to change the method of production if the incremental costs of the specified future levels of production under the alternative plan are negative. Of course, this type of decision rule assumes a known cost and revenue structure or risk-neutral behavior.

We will show only one type of decision problem using our illustrative firm. Recall that the firm produced 10,000 units of output and sold 8,000 of these. Suppose the distribution department informs top management that sales could be increased to 10,000 units per period if the firm increased its advertising expenditures by $5,000 per operating period to cover special campaigns. Assuming the firm can meet this additional production output without changing its inventory requirements, we can evaluate this alternative by estimating the incremental revenues from producing and selling 2,000 units per period and comparing these against the incremental costs associated with this new output level.

Incremental revenues	$2,000 \times \$15.00 =$		$30,000
Incremental production costs			
Materials	$2,000 \times \$\ 1.50 =$	$3,000	
Labor	$2,000 \times\ \ \ 1.80 =$	3,600	
Overhead	$2,000 \times\ \ \ \ .20 =$	400	
Incremental distribution costs			
Supplies and labor	$2,000 \times\ \ \ 2.50 =$	5,000	
Advertising		5,000	17,000
Incremental profit			$13,000

Note that we used our initial classification of costs as fixed and variable to estimate the change in costs as output is expanded and that we assumed costs classified as fixed will remain unchanged as the firm expands its sales and production by 2,000 units. This assumption may be unrealistic, since some costs classified as strictly fixed might have been step costs, which could increase if output and sales are expanded by a significant amount. The point to keep in mind, then, is that the incremental costs of an alternative action will exceed the sum of the changes in variable costs to the extent that costs originally classified as fixed also change with the alternative action.

Sunk Costs

Sunk costs are costs associated with prior decisions that should have no bearing on current decisions. This classification of costs is probably more useful for its effect on decision attitudes than on any calculation of costs to be used in making decisions. To illustrate, suppose a firm holds an asset with a recorded (book) value of $10,000. The $10,000 is the remaining amount of the original cost of the asset to be depreciated over future periods if the asset is held and used in the future. The asset could be sold today for $5,000. The firm is interested in evaluating whether to sell the old asset and acquire a new and more efficient one or to continue to operate with the old asset. Most individuals do not like to recognize a loss on a sale, which is what would occur if the firm sold the old asset. That is, the present book value of $10,000 for the old asset is not the relevant cost to consider in deciding whether to replace the old asset. The relevant figure is the present market price of the old asset, which is $5,000. The $10,000 is a sunk cost and should be considered in the decision only if the sale of the old asset affects present or future taxes.

Of course, practically all decisions by firms have an effect on their taxes, which means their managers cannot ignore the book values of assets in making their decisions. But we often hear such comments as, "I cannot sell that item for $5 per unit, because it cost me $10 per unit to acquire (or manufacture)." In a competitive market, buyers are not interested in what a seller had to pay to acquire what he has up for sale. His costs are sunk costs.

Individuals often reflect a similar tendency to let sunk costs affect their decisions. Consider an individual who invests in an advanced degree in some field or discipline, then finds that he cannot market his talents when he receives his degree. It is quite natural for such an individual to be reluctant to "throw away" this investment and to seek alternative employment (even though the investment has a low or nonexistent current market value). The cost of his educational investment is a true sunk cost in this case, since there are no tax effects should he decide to abandon his original degree ("sell" his asset) and seek something else.

Actually, the sunk cost notion arises in a specification of so-called relevant costs. When faced with a particular decision, the profit-maximizing manager is interested in the impact on profits. Suppose some cost element remains the same across all of the alternatives under consideration. If so, it is *irrelevant* to the profit-maximizing decision at hand. Otherwise the cost element is relevant. Sunk costs are irrelevant (ignoring taxation questions). They are not affected by the decision at hand; indeed, they typically have already been incurred.

The relevant cost focus has considerable appeal, because it stresses the consideration of cost elements that are affected by the decision at hand. This is easy enough to rationalize in a setting of certainty, such as one of profit maximization, where revenues and costs are known. But uncertainty and risk aversion cloud the issue because of portfolio considerations. Thus, the relevant cost notion does not have universal appeal.

Opportunity Costs

The opportunity cost of adopting a particular course of action is defined as the net benefits foregone by not adopting a next best alternative course of action. Opportunity costs are usually associated with the utilization of capacities, both physical and human. To illustrate, our exemplary firm holds a productive capacity which we will assume will continue to be used to produce and sell 10,000 units of output. Suppose the next best alternative is to rent the facilities to some other firm or to produce an entirely different product. The opportunity cost of using its capacity for present output is the net benefit given up by not using the capacity in the best of the other alternatives. If the next best alternative were the rental arrangement, the opportunity cost would be rent foregone; if it were producing a different product, we would compare the net cash benefits of producing the other product to what we are now obtaining. The analysis of opportunity costs is important, because many styles of analysis rest on opportunity cost assessments, yet typical accounting systems report what was and not what could have been.

The situations described in the discussion on sunk costs also involve opportunity costs. That is, the opportunity cost of holding an asset, rather than selling it, is the market price foregone by not doing so. Individuals incur opportunity costs whenever they allocate their time and effort to one activity rather than to the next best alternative activity. (Wouldn't you rather be playing golf or running than reading this?) For example, top management may be willing to pay the extra premium for their subordinates to fly supersonic transports, because the opportunity costs of having these executives spend twice as much time in the air in regular aircraft exceeds the extra premium costs of the supersonic transports. This is especially true after the tax benefits of the write-off of the ticket costs are considered.

REVIEW PROBLEM 5
Different Cost Classifications for Different Purposes _____

If we now think back over the material of this chapter, we can recall how the same cost item could be classified along several different dimensions. The various dimensions were illustrated using a simple firm with only three departments and three basic cost items. The principles are the same for large, complicated firms, although the actual task of classifying their costs may be mind-boggling at times. Rather than summarizing the ways in which our illustrative firm's costs may be classified, we are providing this review problem, which illustrates the various classifications of costs discussed in the chapter.

For the relevant cost data in items (1)–(13), indicate which of the following is the best classification.

(a)	sunk cost	(f)	semifixed (step) cost
(b)	incremental cost	(g)	controllable cost
(c)	variable cost	(h)	noncontrollable cost
(d)	fixed cost	(i)	opportunity cost
(e)	semivariable cost	(j)	common cost

(Each item is independent except as indicated.)

(1) Jones, Inc., is thinking about selling an old punch press. The press has a book value of $10,000. In evaluating the decision to sell the press, the $10,000 is a(n) _____ .

(2) As an alternative to the old press, Jones, Inc., can rent a new one. It will cost $1,500 a year. In analyzing its cost behavior, the rental is a(n) _____ .

(3) To run the firm's presses, there are two alternative courses of action. One is to pay the operators a base salary plus a small amount per unit produced. This makes the total cost of the operators a(n) _____ .

(4) As an alternative, the firm can pay the press operators a flat salary. It would then use one machine when volume is low, two when it expands, and three during peak periods. This means that the total operator cost would now be a(n) _____ .

(5) The punch press mentioned in (1) could be sold for $4,000. If the firm considers retaining and using it, the $4,000 is a(n) _____ .

(6) If the firm wishes to use the punch press any longer, it must be repaired. For the decision to retain and use the press, the repair cost is a(n) _____ .

(7) The punch press cost has been allocated to the department on an hourly basis, even though the machine will likely be obsolete before it physically deteriorates. This cost will appear to be a(n) _____ with respect to changes in volume.

(8) The punch press is charged to the head of each department at a rate of $1,500 a year. In evaluating the department head, the charge is a(n) _____ .

(9) If you own 100 shares of a corporation's stock, their current market value is a measure of the _____ cost of holding these shares.

(10) A salesman considers each customer carefully. It is his policy to draw on his expense account only for potentially large customers. Management is willing to let each salesman allocate his entertain-

ment as he sees fit. In measuring the salesman's efficiency, the entertainment expenditure is a(n) _____ .

(11) A different salesman is told that it is company policy to entertain
every customer whose volume is over $50,000 and never entertain
a customer whose volume is less than $10,000. His entertainment
cost for the group whose volume is over $50,000 is a(n) _____ .

(12) The data are the same as in (11). In evaluating the salesmen, the
amount expended on customers whose volume is under $50,000 is
a(n) _____ .

(13) The data are the same as in (11). In evaluating the sales manager
who set the guidelines on entertaining, the amount expended on
customers whose volume is over $50,000 is a(n) _____ .

Conclusion

The various cost classifications discussed in this chapter may seem somewhat
vague at this point, since we could not discuss the details regarding the uses
of each classification or many of the problems encountered in developing
these classifications. Hopefully, the ambiguity will disappear in subsequent
chapters, where these classifications appear in the context of specific planning
and control decisions. The problem of classifying costs and other data for
management uses is a dynamic one, with each new decision calling for a
different perspective regarding the appropriate figures to report.

In the next chapter, we consider methods (models) used to estimate
the cost functions for decision units within the firm or for the firm as a
whole. As we have already noted, estimates of cost functions in terms of
their fixed and variable portions are fundamental to planning and control
decisions.

Supplementary Readings

Articles

Anthony, R.N., "Cost Concepts for Control," *Accounting Rev.*, April 1957.

Bedford, N.M., "The Nature of Business Costs: General Concepts," *Accounting Rev.*,
Jan. 1957.

The 1955 Committee on Cost Concepts Underlying Reports for Management Purposes,
"Tentative Statements of Costs Underlying Reports for Management Purposes,"
Accounting Rev., April 1956.

Books

Davidson, S. and R.L. Weil, eds., *Handbook of Cost Accounting*. New York: McGraw-
Hill, 1978, Ch. 2.

Demski, J.S. and G.A. Feltham, *Cost Determination: A Conceptual Approach*. Ames, Iowa: Iowa State Univ. Press, 1976, Ch. 4.

The Uses and Classification of Costs, *Research Series No. 7;* reprinted in *N.A.A. Bull.* (May 1946, now published as *Management Accounting*).

Questions and Problems

1. What is the distinction among variable, incremental, and relevant costs?
2. What is meant by product costs?
3. What is meant by period costs?
4. Administrative costs are generally fixed costs. Are these controllable or noncontrollable?
5. Why is the concept of a relevant range so useful to accountants in analyzing cost behavior patterns?
6. Which of the following costs are likely to be controllable by the head of a production department?

    (a) quantity of raw materials used
    (b) electricity for machinery
    (c) charge for floor space
    (d) machinery depreciation
    (e) unit price paid for materials

    (f) insurance on machinery
    (g) direct labor
    (h) idle time
    (i) scrap costs

7. Give an example of a situation where a particular variable cost is not an incremental cost in a given decision.
8. Give an example of a decision where a fixed cost may become an incremental cost.
9. Contrast a sunk cost with other types of nonincremental costs.
10. Are fixed costs also sunk costs?
11. Indicate some potential problems that may arise if semifixed costs (step costs) are treated as semivariable (continuous) or strictly fixed.

12. **Cost Volume**
    Using the graphs shown in Review Problem 3, indicate which graph depicts each type of cost behavior described in the following statements. If you do not find one that is appropriate, draw your own.

    (1) The newly negotiated labor contract freezes the labor force at its present level. This is sufficiently large that overtime is unlikely.
    (2) The company's advertising budget is based upon what management feels is necessary to meet its competition.
    (3) There is currently a shortage of skilled laborers. Under no circumstances will any be let go, because they may be difficult to rehire when needed later.
    (4) The company pays its share of the social security tax.
    (5) Supplies are purchased subject to quantity discounts: that is, $.10 per unit

EXHIBIT 2-1 _____

Cost Account	Amount
Cleanup crews	$ 1,000
Department supervisor	5,000
Depreciation on machines	10,000
Direct materials	30,000
Machine operators	10,000
Electricity	500
Lubricants	650
Inspectors (quality control)	2,000
Rent on building	1,000
	$60,150

Beginning inventory: 1,000 units (½ completed), $6,000
Units started in production: 11,000
Ending inventory: 2,000 units (⅔ completed), $14,000

in lots of 10,000 or less, a 2 percent discount on the next 10,000, and a 5 percent discount on any units over 20,000.

(6) Supervisors are hired as they are needed as production expands.
(7) The club where the officers entertain clients requires annual dues as well as a charge for those services used by the members.

13. *Production Cost Classifications*
From the data in Exhibit 2-1 for Department X of Widgets, Inc., (a) prepare a cost of goods manufactured schedule for June 1978, (b) indicate which costs are likely to be fixed and which variable, and (c) determine how many completed units were sent to finished goods.

14. *Controllable Costs*
Using the data in Problem 13, classify the various items according to whether they are controllable or noncontrollable by the supervisor of the manufacturing department.

15. *Cost Classification*
Annee Company provides you with the cost items, as indicated in Exhibit 2-2, for two different volumes of production. Classify these data into

(a) product costs and period costs,
(b) costs controllable and noncontrollable by the department head,
(c) variable, fixed, or semivariable costs (a strictly variable cost would have a constant per-unit cost; a semivariable cost would have a decreasing per-unit cost).[2]

16. *Cost Controllability*
The data in Exhibit 2-3 are from the operations of a particular cost center in a plant with one machine and its operator. Indicate which of the costs listed are

_____
[2] That is, if $TC = bx$, then $TC/x = b$, which is a constant, but if $TC = a + bx$, then $TC/x = (a/x) + b$, which decreases with larger values of x.

_____EXHIBIT 2-2

Account Title	40,000 Units	50,000 Units
Administrative costs	$ 1,000	$ 1,000
Advertising	1,500	1,700
Depreciation on machines	4,000	4,000
Heat, light, and power	1,200	1,350
Insurance on plant	25	50
Lathe operators	10,000	12,500
Machine repairs	600	625
Paint, lacquer, and varnish	1,000	1,250
Raw materials	80,000	100,000
Rental of plant	5,000	5,000
Sales, salaries, and commissions	8,000	9,000
	$112,325	$136,475

controllable by the machine operator. Of those remaining, which are controllable by his immediate supervisor? Which are controllable by the plant superintendent?

17. *Incremental Cost Analysis*
The XYZ Company is considering a special order for 100,000 widgets at a price below the going market price. Because of the size of the order, the company wishes to analyze its costs. Exhibit 2-4 shows the most recent production cost statement.
Production during the period was 500,000 widgets.

(a) Which costs are likely to be incremental costs?
(b) Which costs, if any, represent sunk costs?
(c) What factors would you consider in assessing the opportunity cost of producing the 100,000 widgets?

18. *Determination of Responsibility for Cost Control*
The entire operations of a regional office of Branches, Inc., had up to now been under the regional sales manager. He had supervised both the production and

_____EXHIBIT 2-3

Account Title	Amount
Raw materials	$1,000
Electricity for running the machine	100
Depreciation on the machine	700
Rental for floor space	200
Preventive maintenance on the machine	300
Operating supplies	35
Factory-wide general and administrative costs	20
	$2,355

EXHIBIT 2-4

XYZ Company
Production Cost Statement
March 1982

Materials		$100,000
Direct labor		80,000
Prime cost		$180,000
Supplies and indirect materials	$10,000	
Supervisory personnel	25,000	
Depreciation on equipment	15,000	
Taxes	1,000	
Factory rental	4,000	$ 55,000
Total costs		$235,000

sales forces. It has now been decided at the home office to provide him with two new assistants. One will be in charge of the salespeople, and the other will supervise production. The current regional manager will coordinate production and sales, negotiate such major items as leases and advertising, and call on potentially large institutional customers.

(a) From the accounts found on the performance report of a previous period, shown in Exhibit 2-5, indicate which costs are now controllable by the assistant in charge of production and which are controllable by the assistant in charge of sales.

(b) If any of the previously controllable costs are not controllable by either assistant, indicate why this is true.

EXHIBIT 2-5

Branches, Inc., Region A
Cost Report Form 6A
May 1982

Controllable costs
  Raw materials
  Direct labor
  Indirect variable costs
  Rental of auto fleet (negotiated annually in late December)
  Entertainment for institutional clients
  Entertainment for other clients
  Region A variable office overhead
  Advertising
Noncontrollable costs
  Fixed production overhead
  Rent of plant and office
  Sales commission (per company-wide plan)

19. **Opportunity Cost Measurement**

The Annee Company has received an order for a product it does not usually produce. It has available the machines and operators needed to fill the order. Some discussion has arisen over the extent and amount of the incremental costs. The available information is summarized below.

Exium. The order requires 1,000 units of this material. While Annee never uses Exium in its regular operations, records indicate that it acquired 10,000 units of it as part of a recent special purchase. The cost records show 4,000 units being carried at $4.00 per unit. According to the purchasing department, it would cost $8.00 per unit to replace it. However, the best offer they had when they tried to sell it earlier was $3.50 per unit.

Whyite. Two thousand units are required. This material is used regularly, and Annee has a large inventory of it. The average cost per unit of the current inventory is $2.50. The market price is now $3.00. Purchasing estimates that if it uses the Whyite in this order, it will reorder one month sooner than usual. At that time, the seasonal decline will have dropped the price of Whyite to $2.75. This is above the expected seasonal low of $2.20.

Zeebium. Only 500 units are needed. This material is carried in large quantities in Annee's inventory. The average cost is $.10 per unit. Because of the heavy usage and poor storage characteristics, it must be purchased weekly. The current price is $.12 per unit.

Scrapite. About 1,000 units are needed. This is a by-product of one of Annee's other processes. It is sometimes salable at prices of up to $1.00 per unit. However, it typically must be hauled away by a local scavenger at a cost of $1.00 per case. Each case contains 25 units.

Labor. All of Annee's employees are guaranteed pay for a 40-hour work week even when work is unavailable. At present, the hours actually worked average about 35. The production manager indicates that the order will require 10 hours of his time at $12.00 per hour and about 70 hours of worker time at $5.00 per hour plus 10 hours at time-and-a-half in order to meet the deadline.

(a) What is the relevant cost of each of the raw materials?
(b) What is the relevant labor cost figure?

20. **Incremental Cost Versus Product Unit Cost**

In the light of the discussion in this chapter, review this decision: "We took the order because the $5.00 they offered per unit was more than our *per-unit* cost of production. I have shown these in the report that follows. We always gain when we sell a unit for more than it cost us to produce it. It is as simple as that."

COST OF PRODUCTION

	Regular Production (25,000 Units)	New Level of Production (30,000 Units)
Variable costs	$ 25,000	$ 40,000
Fixed costs	75,000	85,100
Total costs	$100,000	$125,100
Cost per unit	$4.00	$4.17

(a) Why do you agree or disagree with the analysis?

(b) If you disagree, how would you alter the analysis?

(c) Suppose a decision unit's cost function is TC = $50,000 + $5x, where x represents units of output. What is the average total cost per unit at x = $10,000, $20,000, and $30,000?

21. **Some Issues in Budgeting and Allocating Overhead**

Assume a production department reported incurred overhead costs as follows for the month of April 1982:

Variable	$20,000
Fixed	$37,800

Production was 10,000 units and required 20,000 direct labor hours. Using these relationships and other data, the following budgeted data were provided to the production department head regarding his department's activities for May 1982:

Budgeted production	12,000 units
Budgeted labor	25,200 hours (slightly more, on average, than last month)
Budgeted overhead	$63,000 ($37,800 plus $1 per direct labor hour)

Actual results for the month:

Production		11,000 units
Direct labor		24,200 hours
Actual overhead		
Variable	$24,200	
Fixed	37,800	$62,000

(a) Using the relationship between budgeted production and budgeted labor hours, how many hours of labor should have been used to achieve 11,000 units of output? If there is a difference between your figure and actual hours, does the difference represent a favorable or unfavorable deviation?

(b) Assume the production department head is held responsible for variable overhead. What should she have spent this month for such items? Was there a favorable or unfavorable deviation? (Note, you have to decide whether to use actual direct labor hours as the activity base or the standard hours she should have used.)

(c) At the beginning of the month, the cost accountant determined that each output unit to be produced during the month should be charged at a rate of $2.50 per direct labor hour worked on a unit in order to absorb total overhead costs. Show how he obtained this overhead rate.

(d) Assume he did use this rate to allocate overhead to production. What would be the total overhead costs allocated to this month's production based on (1) actual direct labor hours and (2) standard direct labor hours allowed for 11,000 output units?

(e) Your answer to (d) should not have been $62,000 in either case. The difference represents an "underapplication" of overhead costs (incurred exceeded applied). Does the underapplied overhead reflect an error in the variable rate, the fixed rate, or both?

(f) Because of the problem reflected in (d) and (e), some accountants advocate treating fixed overhead costs as period costs and only allocating variable overhead costs to units of output. What is your opinion?

22. **A Preview of Process Costing**

Suppose a production department is controlled by a "flexible budget." Recall that at the end of an operating period a department's budget is adjusted to reflect *costs allowed for actual output* achieved.

Assume the total variable costs allowed per unit of output achieved is $10.00 per unit. The department in question is part of a processing firm that has incomplete units carried over from a prior period (beginning inventory) and incomplete units carried over to the subsequent period (ending inventory). The respective amounts and their estimated degree of completion are:

Beginning inventory	5,000 units	½ complete
Ending inventory	6,000 units	⅔ complete

A total of 10,000 new units were started in production during the month, and 9,000 completed units were sent to finished goods.

Note the relationships: Beginning inventory *plus* units started *equal* units to account for. The latter is split between units completed (9,000) and ending inventory (6,000), ignoring any possible spoilage or waste.

(a) How many of the 10,000 units started were also completed in the same time period?

(b) How many of the 9,000 completed units came from the beginning inventory?

(c) Assume these units are homogeneous in all respects (they are exactly alike in terms of production requirements). What was the level of output achieved by this department during the current period? (*Hint:* The correct answer requires explicit consideration of the stages of completion of both inventories, resulting in what are known as equivalent units of output.)

(d) Assume the correct answer to (c) is 10,000 equivalent units of output (not the correct answer). Actual variable costs were $105,000. What were the allowable variable costs for this level of output achieved, and what was the sign of any deviation between actual and allowable costs?

(e) Note from (d) how the accountant determines the standard or allowable costs for output in a process-type of firm. This is based on a standard cost per equivalent unit of output achieved. Suppose we wish to determine the actual cost per equivalent unit of output. What is this per-unit cost?

23. **Job-Order Costing**

In Problem 22, we introduced a basic calculation to process costing (that is, equivalent units of output). Here we illustrate some basic procedures for firms that account for their production on a job-by-job basis.

Suppose a job-order firm starts production in this period with no work-in-process (that is, beginning inventory is zero). It receives orders for three special jobs: 101, 102, and 103. During this period, costs were incurred as follows:

	Direct Materials	**Direct Labor**
Job 101	500 lb @ $5/lb = $2,500	1,000 hr @ $12/hr = $12,000
102	300 lb @ $2/lb = 600	750 hr @ $11/hr = 8,250
103	200 lb @ $5/lb = 1,000	500 hr @ $10/hr = 5,000
Totals	1,000 lb = $4,100	2,250 hr = $25,250

These data are taken from requisitions of materials for specific jobs and from time tickets prepared by workers indicating the time (and rates) applicable to each job. Total overhead incurred was $11,250. Job 101 was "finished," but jobs 102 and 103 require additional work in subsequent periods.

Suppose the firm's accountant wishes to cost out each job. The "direct costs," labor and materials, can be traced to each job based on the data above. However, the "indirect costs," overhead, will have to be *allocated* to each job based on one or the other of the direct inputs (labor or materials). Typically, labor hours are used as the basis for allocating overhead costs, but they need not be. If overhead costs are assumed to vary more with material usage, then pounds of raw materials would be the overhead basis; the same would hold for overhead costs that vary with direct labor dollars, another possible basis.

(a) Using direct labor hours as the basis for allocating overhead, determine the assignment of overhead costs to each job. Complete the job costing by assigning direct materials and direct labor costs to each job.

(b) Determine the total cost of goods manufactured for this job-order firm (beginning inventory of jobs *plus* current costs *minus* ending inventory of jobs).

(c) Assume job 101 resulted in revenues of $30,000. What was the gross profit (revenue *minus* cost of completing the job)?

(d) Suppose we had used pounds of material for the allocation of overhead. What would be the gross profit on job 101 under this method of overhead allocation?

(e) Assume a sales engineer receives a commission on jobs based on the gross profit achieved on each. Which method of overhead allocation would (s)he prefer, (a) or (d)?

(f) Discuss the propriety of using accounting figures, such as gross profit, as a basis for compensation plans. Is there a "true" allocation formula?

*24. **Relevant Costing**

Ralph currently owns a firm which he estimates will yield the following net cash returns, depending on the future state of the economy. For our purposes, Ralph predicts one of three states will occur, with equal probability of occurrence:

	Boom	**Stagnate**	**Bust**
Net cash returns	$50,000	$10,000	$3,000

Ralph paid $10,000 to acquire this firm, but he still has $5,000 that he could invest. He is currently undecided between a risky investment and a safe investment, with the net cash returns again dependent upon the future state of the economy. The net cash returns for the two investments are:

	Boom	**Stagnate**	**Bust**
Net cash returns (safe)	$ 6,000	$6,000	$6,000
Net cash returns (risky)	15,000	5,000	0

(a) Assume Ralph is risk-neutral (that is, he maximizes expected values). Which alternative should he choose?

(b) Assume instead that Ralph is risk-averse and that he tries to maximize the expected value of the *square root* of net cash returns as of the end of the period. Which alternative should he now choose?

(c) How does the prior decision to acquire the firm for $10,000 enter into your analysis for (a) and (b), if at all? What does this tell you about the notion of relevant cost?

*25. **Approximate Cost Functions**

Ralph has the following nonlinear cost curve, where x denotes units of output:

$$TC(x) = (\tfrac{1}{3})x^3 - 8x^2 + 65x + 260$$

(a) Plot $TC(x)$ for $0 < x < 10$.

(b) Determine Ralph's fixed and marginal costs.

(c) Consider the neighborhood $4 < x < 8$. Determine Ralph's cost at $x = 4$ and $x = 8$, and then construct a linear approximation to $TC(x)$ by drawing a line between these two points. (Specifically, the *slope* will be $[TC(8) - TC(4)] / [8 - 4]$.)

    (1) Plot this approximation on your graph of $TC(x)$ for $0 < x < 10$.

    (2) Using this "local linear approximation," determine Ralph's fixed and variable costs.

    (3) Can you think of another method of approximating $TC(x)$?

Cost Estimation

In Chapter 2, we discussed some classification schemes for segregating cost data that are useful in various decision situations. In this chapter, we focus on the methods used by the accountant to develop estimates of costs for planning and controlling operations.[1] Recall that a cost item may be classified initially as variable, fixed, semivariable, or semifixed when associated with some activity measure x. If we exclude semifixed cost items by treating them as special cases and also assume linear cost functions, we can define any cost item by the equation $TC = a + bx$, where the measure of activity x is, for example, output, direct labor hours, or pounds of materials. For strictly variable cost items, $a = 0$; similarly, for strictly fixed items, $b = 0$. Semivariable cost items have nonzero values for a and b. This is a crude definition of a cost item, since it literally implies that for any particular level of activity—say, $x = 100,000$—the estimate of cost is a constant ($TC_{100,000} = a + 100,000b$).

A better definition of a cost item would allow for some randomness in the definition by the insertion of an error term, e, which may be interpreted as a measure of the error in the estimating equation. (We will, however, retain the linearity assumption.) That is, the observed cost will be $TC_i = a + bx_i + e_i$, and the estimated cost is $\hat{TC}_i = a + bx_i$, where i represents a particular pairing of a cost to an activity level. The difference between observed and estimated costs, e_i, has an expected value of zero, since we assume positive deviations will equal negative deviations over a sample of estimates. Thus, the expected cost is

$$E(TC_i) = E(a + bx_i) + E(e_i) = E(a + bx_i) + 0 = \hat{TC}_i$$

---

[1] We ignore problems in deriving revenue estimates for different levels of activity. Estimates of revenues involve questions about advertising, promotion, and price elasticities (that is, the effect of price changes on total revenues). We assume that estimates of these effects can be supplied by the marketing department.

In the remaining sections, we discuss some methods for estimating $E(a + bx)$, dropping the i subscript for convenience. With one of the methods, regression analysis, the assumptions about the distribution of the error term, e_i, become important in assessing the statistical properties of the estimated equation(s).

The first sections of this chapter are devoted to a description of various methods that can be used to obtain estimates of the two parameters of our cost equation. Later, we will discuss some problems in evaluating alternative estimating equations. Different estimates of the same cost item may be obtained, because we use different estimating methods or different samples of data (including different measures of activity) to obtain values for the parameters.

Methods used to obtain cost estimates are divided into two broad categories: engineering estimates and estimates based on an analysis of past cost data. Briefly, the engineering method relies on a specification of the physical relationship between the inputs to some productive process and the observed output from the process. In contrast, the analysis of past cost data does not rely on explicit statements of the relationship between physical inputs and a level of activity. Rather, relationships are inferred from an observed association between different levels of costs and different levels of activity.

In general, the more pervasive problems of cost estimation occur in the use of past data. Therefore, the major portion of this chapter is devoted to the various methods of using past data. However, we will first discuss some aspects of the engineering method.

The Engineering Method

The engineering method received its name primarily because the physical relationships between inputs and outputs in manufacturing can often be derived from the engineering specifications of manufactured outputs. However, the method is not restricted to manufacturing; the familiar time-and-motion studies that are applied to well-structured administrative and selling activities, such as typing and order filling, involve essentially the same type of analysis.

Every productive process is designed to yield a certain amount of physical output, given a particular mix of materials, labor, and capital equipment. Once the relationships between the prime factors of production and output are established, the total cost of labor and materials can be estimated by assigning prices and wage rates to the physical input requirements. The cost derived in this manner is nevertheless an estimate because of the uncertainty in the production process, such as uncertainty in the specified allowances for waste in materials usage and for different levels of labor efficiencies.

Suppose we are considering the operations of a single department that uses raw materials, labor, and a certain type of machine to finish a product.

The raw materials needed are specified by engineering to be 1.5 pounds of material A per unit of output, where A represents a certain type and quality of material. On the basis of an engineering study (such as a time-and-motion study), it is determined that each worker takes an average of 2 hours to finish a unit of output on his machine. The total prime cost (TPC), or direct material plus direct labor cost, of producing one unit of output will be

$$TPC = 1.5(\text{Cost of material A}) + 2(\text{Wage rate of labor})$$

Of course, the total cost of producing a unit of output must also include some cost of operating the machine, but many of these costs are difficult to associate directly with individual units of output. Moreover, there are also other costs incurred in the department in the production of various levels of output that do not appear in the cost equation. These include the costs of supervision, of utilities, of cleaning up, and of maintaining the machine, to name just a few. It may be possible to associate these costs with the department, in which case they are direct costs of the department, but it is virtually impossible to associate them with specific units of output. Therefore, an accurate estimate of the *total* cost of output cannot be obtained with the engineering method, because of the secondary relationships between some inputs and the output of the department.

It is not surprising, then, that the engineering method is generally used only to derive estimates of the relationships between major items of materials and direct labor and some output variable. The resulting estimates are fairly accurate, because these relationships can be directly inferred, observed, and measured. In addition, they can be adjusted to reflect what the relationships should be under assumed conditions of efficiency. But estimated equations for other cost items usually must be obtained from an analysis of past cost data or from pure subjective assessment.

Another drawback of the engineering method is that it tends to be expensive in actual practice. Different mixes of materials may be used to produce the same type of output, and an estimate of the material cost of output must be adjusted to reflect the actual mix of materials to be used. Similarly, an estimate of direct labor used in production will be affected by the degree of skills assumed to be possessed by the people who will work on the output. These skills must be specified in the cost estimate. Finally, a measure of the time required to produce a unit of output may necessitate a detailed and costly analysis of the physical movements required in each task. As a general rule, we would expect the engineering method to be used when the costs of materials and labor represent significant portions of the total cost of output and the relationships between material and labor inputs and outputs remain stationary over time. If the latter condition holds, the estimating equations for these costs can be used in future periods without extensive adjustments.

Analysis of Historical Cost Data

The analysis of past cost data yields estimates of future costs based on the actual cost relationships of previous periods. The degree to which these analyses are appropriate depends on the extent to which cost relationships in the future will correspond to those in the past. For example, if a firm in a stable economy is considering only a superficial style change in a product, such as an expanded variety of colors, historical cost relationships should be reliable. If the change being considered is extensive enough to bring about changes in the underlying cost structure, however, the unadjusted historical cost data are inappropriate.

The graph of the cost function could have a variety of shapes, depending on the relationships between costs and the identified activity variables. As in the previous chapter, however, we will assume that we are dealing with simple linear relationships of the form $TC = a + bx$, where a is the level of all fixed costs, x is an index of the level of activity, and b is the (variable cost or) average of the marginal rates of change in total cost with respect to changes in x. Although this is the standard practice and terminology, it is important to keep in mind that $TC = a + bx$ is an approximation. In literal terms, then, a is the *intercept* and b is the *slope* of the approximate linear model of cost behavior.

Preliminary Steps in the Analysis of Cost Data

Regardless of the specific techniques that are used to analyze past cost data, certain preparatory steps are useful in increasing the reliability of the results. These steps are especially important if we wish to employ more rigorous techniques of analysis.

(1) Examine the data to determine whether the accounting policies produce any significant bias.

(2) Examine the data to determine if the observations seem to be drawn from a "stationary process." In other words, check them for "homogeneity" in the relationship between cost and the activity variable(s).

(3) Ascertain that the appropriate activity variables are selected. (In our illustration we will usually use some index of output. However, this is done only for convenience.)

(4) Plot the data to show either the relationship between costs and activity variables or the deviations of actual costs from forecasted costs.

Examination of Data. The importance of the first step should be clear. In processing cost data, the accountant classifies and reclassifies the data to reflect direct and indirect responsibility for the incurrence of costs. These cost classifications may create a potential source of distortion in the cost–volume relationship being observed. That is, the cost function developed and the related estimate of b, the per-unit variable cost, may reflect altered and not actual relationships. In order to guard against this and other potential hazards, the following guidelines should be observed:[2]

(1) *The cost data and activity data should be of the same period.* It is possible that some of the costs of a given period, say a week, are not entered into the records of a department until the following week. Thus, the output of period 2 might be matched against the costs of period 1, the output of period 3 matched against the costs of period 2, and the output of period n matched against the costs of period $n - 1$. If the level of activities is at all volatile, this misallocation between time periods will have a disruptive effect on the estimation of variable cost. In addition, some firms may classify purchases of supplies and other minor items of inventory as an immediate cost or expense at the time of purchase. If purchases are irregular or made in periods of low activity, the relationship between the amount of purchases and the activity measure will be spurious. In such a case, the *requisitions* of these items (orders to move the items from storage to production) should be used to measure the relationship between costs and activity levels.

(2) *The data should be properly classified by costing unit.* This consideration relates primarily to attempts to develop cost functions for costing units or individual departments. Improper cost classifications by costing units may lead to inaccurate statements of the relationships between costs and outputs of these units. Although these effects may be balanced out in the firm-wide cost function, the decisions within particular departments may be adversely affected.

(3) *The extent to which costs of the costing unit are the result of accounting allocations should be determined.* If a substantial portion of the fixed costs of a firm is allocated to different costing units according to output, the variable cost coefficient in the cost equation will be overstated. Thus, the accountant's allocation process may result in making fixed costs of the firm appear to be variable costs of the different departments. As an example, assume that straight-line depreciation is allocated on a per-unit basis to product A.

---

[2] This list is not exhaustive but merely illustrative. These requirements, as well as a more detailed discussion of the problems involved in statistical cost analysis, can be found in J. Johnston, *Statistical Cost Analysis.* New York: McGraw-Hill, 1972, Ch. 3. Also see G. Benston, "Multiple Regression Analyses of Cost Behavior," *Accounting Rev.,* Oct. 1966. A particularly interesting application is reported by R. Kaplan, "Management Accounting in Hospitals: A Case Study," in Livingstone and Gunn, eds., *Accounting for Social Goals.* New York: Harper and Row, 1974.

$$\text{Depreciation} = \$1,000$$
$$\text{Output of product A} = 1,000 \text{ units}$$

Therefore, depreciation per unit = $\$1,000/1,000$ units = $1 per unit of product. If all other variable costs for product A have been estimated to be $5 per unit, the estimate of the total variable cost from a naive analysis of past data will be $6 per unit. But suppose in another period only 800 units were produced. The allocation would be $\$1,000/800 = \$1.25$ per unit, for a total variable cost of $6.25 per unit. Thus, the allocation of fixed costs can lead to fluctuations in unit costs that bear no relationship to changes in total costs as output varies as well as to overstatement of the slope approximation.

(4)   *The time period under consideration should be long enough to permit collection of meaningful data, but short enough to reflect different rates of activity.* For example, if cost data were collected hourly, significant differences could occur that were related to the time of day. Workers may be more efficient at midmorning and less efficient just after lunch and prior to the end of the day. Therefore, the hourly observations would include the effect of time of day on cost. On the other hand, too long a time period may result in an artificial smoothing (an unwarranted averaging) of production and costs. If activity varies weekly, monthly data could artificially smooth production data by including both high and low weeks. In that case, the exact relationships between costs and activities at these high and low readings would not be observed.

Observation of Data for Homogeneity.   Data must be checked to ensure that the cost changes reflect only changes in the activity variable. If changes have occurred from period to period in technology, skills of the labor force, or the price level of the inputs, the cost measurement will be an amalgam of the change in output *and* changes in the environment. Thus, the cost data will not be homogeneous from observation to observation. Nonhomogeneous observations often result from technological differences in costing units producing identical outputs. In order to work with a large number of observations covering a wide range of outputs, it may be necessary to work with the cost data of many similar departments. If the nature of the operations of the departments varies, the behavior of costs will reflect this diversity.

Selection of Activity Variable(s).   This step is analogous to the model-building stage in any research project. While the cost relationship will usually be simple, involving only a few variables, it must be hypothesized before the analysis can be carried any further. Generally, we should choose an activity measure on the basis of a reasonable belief that some relationship exists between the variable and the cost being estimated. The variable used in the estimation should be the one that exerts the major effect on the cost observed. Among the most widely employed variables are direct labor hours, machine hours, and the number of units produced.

Plotting. The final step, plotting a scatter diagram, is actually the first step to be performed in the estimation of the cost–volume relationship. Cost observations are plotted against the activity scale to see how the variables interact. Extreme observations, or *outliers,* are readily apparent from such a plotting. These observations can later be investigated to find out if they are nonhomogeneous or simply instances of extreme behavior that occur even in a well-ordered situation (a "stationary process").

Quite often, an examination of a scatter diagram will indicate the validity of the hypothesized relationship between the cost and the activity variable chosen. Also, by "eyeballing" the scatter, the accountant often can determine whether any relationship exists between the variables and, if so, whether it is more reasonable to fit a linear rather than a curvilinear cost function to the data.

Methods Used to Derive Cost Equations from Past Data

Once the data have been processed, several alternative methods may be used in their analysis. The methods vary in their difficulty and cost and in their potential usefulness in more complicated situations. Three of the methods discussed here—account classification, the high–low method, and visual curve-fitting—generally provide only rough estimates of cost–volume behavior. The fourth, statistical curve-fitting, is a more formal approach and often more useful in analyzing complex cost relationships. All, however, are techniques for *curve-fitting.* We have already developed a linear model that relates cost to some activity index or independent variable. (It is common practice to refer to x as an independent variable; we think of the cost as being caused by the activity summarized in the independent variable.) We also have some observations of total cost and their associated values of the independent variable. The question is how to use these observations to determine the slope and intercept of the posited cost model.

Note that when the observations cluster around an imaginary line, as in Figure 3-1, the estimated relationship between cost and the independent variable can be determined by an informal fit of the line to the data. In such cases, the results from the four methods of estimation will not differ markedly, since the pattern of cost behavior is so clear. Hence, even a crude method should yield a reasonable approximation. In contrast, an array such

FIGURE 3-1

Cost observations reflecting a linear relationship between cost and output.

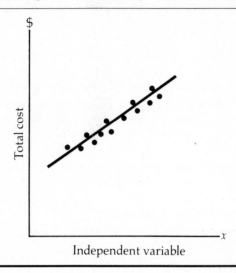

as that shown in Figure 3-2 reflects a less clear cost relationship, and more than one line can be drawn through the data. A more formal criterion for choosing the line may be appropriate here. A simple model of cost behavior, such as the linear model we have hypothesized, often will not explain a significant proportion of the variation in cost. The linear cost function can explain the observed trend upward with increasing values of x, but it cannot explain the wide variation in cost for virtually identical levels of activity. A more elaborate (multivariate) estimation procedure may be required before most of the variation can be explained.

Before illustrating how we may derive estimates of the coefficients a and b from past relationships, let us review some basic algebra regarding linear lines. Suppose we have two observations on a linear cost line, $TC_1 = a + bx_1$ and $TC_2 = a + bx_2$. It is then an easy task to solve for the unknowns, a and b. This can be accomplished by subtracting one equation from the other. The a term cancels and the result, depending on whether we subtract TC_1 from TC_2 or TC_2 from TC_1, will be:

$$b^* = \frac{TC_1 - TC_2}{x_1 - x_2} = \frac{TC_2 - TC_1}{x_2 - x_1}$$ [3-1]

In words, the slope of a linear line is equal to the change in the vertical axis divided by the change in the horizontal axis. This is shown in the following graph:

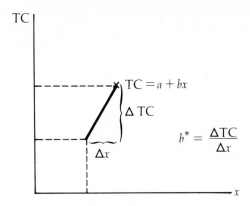

To obtain an estimate of the a term in the cost equation, merely take either *point on the line*—that is, TC_1 or TC_2—and solve. Hence:

$$a^* = TC_1 - b^* x_1 = TC_2 - b^* x_2 \qquad [3\text{-}2]$$

These simple calculations are used in estimating the a and b cost parameters for the following three cost estimation methods: account classification, the high–low method, and visual curve-fitting. For regression estimates of

_____FIGURE 3-2

Linear cost functions with different estimates of the cost equation TC = *a* +*bx*.

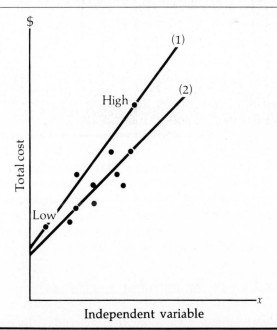

costs, we rely on more formal properties to fit a line to the data, which in turn lead to different methods of solving for a and b in the cost equation.

Account Classification

Perhaps the simplest formal procedure uses only a *single* observation of cost and activity level, say $\widehat{TC}$ and $\hat{x}$. This gives us one equation with two unknowns; we must therefore introduce additional information. The account classification method accomplishes this by classifying $\widehat{TC}$ into fixed and variable categories: $\widehat{TC} = FC + VC$. In effect, we separately estimate $FC = a^*$ and assume $TC = FC$ when $x = 0$. Going back to Equations [3-1] and [3-2] we then use

$$TC_1 = FC \quad \text{with} \quad x_1 = 0$$

and

$$TC_2 = \widehat{TC} \quad \text{with} \quad x_2 = \hat{x}$$

Hence:

$$b^* = \frac{TC_2 - TC_1}{x_2 - x_1} = \frac{\widehat{TC} - FC}{\hat{x}} = \frac{VC}{\hat{x}}$$

and

$$a^* = FC$$

In less abstract terms, examine the data in Exhibit 3-1. The estimate of the cost equation would be

$$TC = \$20,000 + \frac{\$112,000}{4,000} x$$

$$= \$20,000 + \$28x$$

The account classification method of cost estimation has the advantage of being fast and therefore inexpensive. It can be revised regularly to account for changes in cost structures or cost classifications. However, the technique has obvious weaknesses that limit its applications:

(1) It relies heavily on the initial decision to classify an account as fixed or variable.
(2) It relies on a single observation to determine the cost equation.

_____ EXHIBIT 3-1

Control, Inc.
Total Costs for Department A

Account	Amount	Variable	Fixed
Raw materials	$ 50,000	$ 50,000	
Direct labor	60,000	60,000	
Indirect labor	10,000		$10,000
Depreciation	5,000		5,000
Repairs and maintenance	2,000	2,000	
Administrative overhead	500		500
Various overhead items	4,500		4,500
	$132,000	$112,000	$20,000

Volume: 4,000 units			
Fixed costs			$20,000
Variable cost per unit		$28.00	

(3) It fails to recognize that some classifications of costs have both fixed and variable portions.

The importance of the initial division of the accounts between fixed and variable costs is readily apparent in the final cost estimates. A great deal of judgment enters into this step. If the distinction is not clear-cut, two accountants could disagree on the proper classification. The significance of differences in estimates depends on whether decisions would be affected. For example, if the indirect labor in Exhibit 3-1 is in fact variable, the variable cost per unit will increase by $2.50 ($b = \$30.50$) and fixed costs will decrease to $10,000. This might be insignificant for such purposes as broad price guidelines, but significant in the decision to accept or reject a specific order.

Closely related to the problem of whether an account balance is fixed or variable is the question of whether a particular transaction should be charged to one account or another. If the choice is between two accounts in the same category, both being either variable or fixed costs, the problem has no implications for the average variable cost estimate of cost behavior or for total fixed costs. However, if the accounts in question are in different categories, the result will be an over- or underestimation of the variable cost per unit (the b coefficient) and a corresponding under- or overestimation of the total fixed costs.

Similarly, the accountant's decisions to allocate a cost to one costing unit or another can alter the estimates of the various costing units' cost functions. It is difficult to determine accurately the effect of the activity levels of several production departments on a service department's costs. A misallocation of a service department's costs among the production departments could produce errors in the classification of the total costs of these production departments.

The classification of semivariable costs poses another problem. Many practitioners of the cost classification approach to cost analysis place semivariable costs in the variable category and then use rules of thumb to estimate the fixed portion of the total variable costs arrived at in this manner. For example, one may assume that 10 percent of the total costs that have been labeled strictly variable at output level x_0 are in fact fixed.[3] The reasonableness of such an approach to the semivariable cost dilemma depends on how well we can segregate the fixed portion from the variable costs.

Finally, the accounting method ignores the possibility of variations in the cost relationships from one observation to another. Generally, the latest observation is used to determine the cost equation, and there is no adjustment for any variability in the relationship among different activity levels or different time periods.

Thus, the account classification method should be used only when a crude approximation of cost behavior is sufficient for making decisions. Since cost estimates based on account classifications involve highly subjective judgments, the estimates may lack the precision desired for decisions that involve substantial sums or that are sensitive to cost estimation errors. This method seems especially inappropriate for determining cost standards to be used in measuring efficiency of performance.

The High–Low Method[4]

A natural alternative to account classification is to use *two* observations. This is termed the *high–low method,* so called because it usually relies on two extreme activity levels—the highest and the lowest—to reflect the change in cost that results from changes in activity.

Consider the following examples. Costs are $TC_1 = \$32,000$ at $x_1 = 1,000$ units of output and $TC_2 = \$41,000$ at $x_2 = 2,000$ units of output. Directly applying Equations [3-1] and [3-2], we determine the slope and intercept of our presumed linear cost model:

$$b^* = \frac{\$41,000 - \$32,000}{2,000 - 1,000} = \frac{\$9,000}{1,000} = \$9 \text{ per unit}$$

and

$$a^* = \$32,000 - \$9(1,000) = \$41,000 - \$9(2,000) = \$23,000$$

---

[3] For an example of this procedure, see *Explanation of the Development of Motor Carrier Costs.* Washington, D.C.: Interstate Commerce Commission (ICC) Cost Finding Section, 1959.

[4] For a detailed discussion of this technique (as well as of the previous approach), see "Separating and Using Costs as Fixed and Variable," *N.A.A. Accounting Practice Report No. 10,* reprinted in *N.A.A. Bull.,* June 1960.

FIGURE 3-3

Estimate of the cost equation TC $= a + bx$.

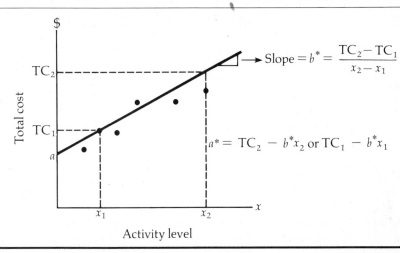

Activity level

Though having the virtue of relying on two observations, this procedure ignores any information contained in any of the other observations. In addition, there is some question about the appropriateness of using extreme values for reference points in calculating the slope and intercept of the cost function.[5] Since these two extreme volumes reflect only the overall variation, the resulting cost equation does not take into account the presence of any unusual situations. In fact, when the extreme points are not typical, the function calculated will actually reflect an abnormal rather than a normal cost relation. For example, the line fitted to the high and low points in Figure 3-2 tends to overstate the variable cost per unit. While the high–low method provides a quick estimate of the cost function, we reiterate our earlier caution that the data must be examined to determine how well the line represents the actual cost relation.

Visual Curve-Fitting

Now suppose we have $n > 2$ observations of cost and activity. One way to use all of these observations in the fitting of our linear model is to plot the data and *visually* draw the TC line. We then select two points on this line and determine the slope and intercept. The calculations are illustrated in Figure 3-3.

The major criticism of the visual curve-fitting method is that it lacks

---

[5] An alternative is to take, say, the second highest and the second lowest costs and their associated activity levels. Taking the highest and lowest costs seems to be the more common method, however.

objectivity. Each accountant using the same cost data to estimate the cost equation may choose a different line to describe the relationship between cost and activity. A discussion of the relative aesthetics of two or more different functions, each fitted visually to the same data, is not likely to resolve the problem of which line is more appropriate.

Some criteria for choosing the "best" line must be selected. For example, one criterion might be to choose the line that is closest to the most observations [line (2) in Figure 3-2]. Another criterion might be to choose the line that minimizes the sum of the absolute deviations from the line or one that minimizes the squared deviations about the line. The latter is the criterion used in a statistical estimate of costs.

REVIEW PROBLEM 1
The High–Low Method Versus Account Classification _____

Assume you have production cost data available for three levels of output: 10,000 units, 15,000 units, and 20,000 units. The items at the 20,000 output level have been classified by your assistant as being variable or fixed.

	OUTPUT LEVELS			CLASSIFICATION
	x_1 (10,000)	x_2 (15,000)	x_3 (20,000)	(at x_3)
Materials	$ 20,000	$ 30,000	$ 40,000	Variable
Labor	30,000	45,000	60,000	Variable
Overhead				
Indirect supplies	10,000	15,000	20,000	Variable
Indirect labor	18,000	22,000	26,000	Variable
Utilities	6,000	7,500	9,000	Fixed
Supervision	10,000	10,000	10,000	Fixed
Depreciation	12,000	12,000	12,000	Fixed
	$106,000	$141,500	$177,000	

The company anticipates an output level in the next period between 18,000 and 22,000 units.

(a) Using the data and the assistant's classification for 20,000 units, determine a cost function of the form $TC = a + bx$ by the account classification method.

Show your solution: $a =$ _____ $b =$ _____

(b) Using the appropriate data, determine the cost function by the high–low method

Show your solution: $a =$ _____ $b =$ _____

(c) Your two estimates should differ because of the "forced" classification of items into fixed and variable categories under the account classification method. Which item(s) in the listing of data has (have) both a fixed and a variable component? Indicate the fixed and variable portions of each "mixed" item.

	Fixed Portion	Variable Rate
Item _____	$a =$	$b =$
Item _____	$a =$	$b =$
Item _____	$a =$	$b =$

Statistical Curve-Fitting

The use of statistical regression to measure cost relationships provides a more rigorous framework for deriving cost estimates than the three methods just discussed. A line is chosen to relate cost observations and activity levels such that the sum of the squared deviations of the observations around the line is minimized. This gives us a criterion that establishes a well-understood and widely used basis on which to analyze the observations. Moreover, the method provides techniques for extending our analysis to nonlinear functions and for incorporating more than one activity variable to explain the cost behavior observed. It permits us to calculate a measure of the "goodness of fit" of cost observations to activity levels; the correlation coefficient measures the extent to which changes in the activity variable(s) account for changes in the cost observations. Finally, with the use of important specification as-sumptions, it allows us to make statements about possible errors by construct-ing, for example, statistical "confidence limits" for the slope (or variable cost) estimate.

In Figure 3-4 a linear "least squares" trend line has been fitted to the data shown in Exhibit 3-2 on page 63. The calculations are shown in Exhibit 3-3. To understand this construction, remember that we want to fit a linear model to the given cost and output observations. We denote each cost observa-tion by TC_i and its associated output by x_i. Our model is

$$\hat{TC}_i = a + bx_i$$

and we want to determine a and b parameters so that $\hat{TC}_i$ is as "close as possible" to TC_i for $i = 1, 2, \ldots 6$. "Close as possible" is *defined* to be a squared error criterion: $(TC_i - \hat{TC}_i)^2$. It is instructive to plot or at least examine $TC_i - \hat{TC}_i$ in Figure 3-4. We determine a and b so as to minimize the total of these squared errors:

$$E^2 = \min_{a,b} \sum_{i=1}^{n} (TC_i - \hat{TC}_i)^2 = \min_{a,b} \sum_{i=1}^{n} (TC_i - a - bx_i)^2 \qquad [3\text{-}3]$$

Note that E^2 is zero if the model perfectly matches all of the observations; otherwise, it is always positive.

FIGURE 3-4 _____

Estimate of the cost equation using the least squares technique (the data are from Exhibit 3-2).

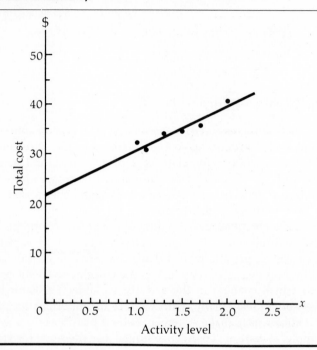

In a technical sense, now, the problem in [3-3] is a simple programing problem. Differentiating with respect to a and b and setting these derivatives equal to zero provides the so-called "normal" equations in Exhibit 3-3.[6] Of course, ready-to-use computer and hand calculator packages are typically employed to circumvent the drudgery of personally performing the calculations.

In any event, this procedure provides us with $a^* = \$21.91$, $b^* = \$9.02$, and $E^2 = 4.81$. This is the minimum value of E^2; for this reason, a^* and b^* are called *least squares* estimators. From this we obtain a measure of the goodness of fit of this line to the given observations. We let $\overline{TC}$ be the mean of the observed costs $\left(\dfrac{1}{n} \sum\limits_{i=1}^{n} TC_i \right)$. If we set $b = 0$, we would estimate $\hat{TC}_i$ as the mean cost, $\overline{TC}$. This provides an error measure of $\bar{E}^2 = \sum\limits_{i=1}^{n} (TC_i - \overline{TC})^2$. You should think of this as our cost estimate irrespective of the independent variable at hand. We now use this to define the *coefficient of determination* as

_____

[6] The good student will convince himself/herself that second order conditions are satisfied and that we do indeed identify the minimizing values of a and b with this procedure.

_____ **EXHIBIT 3-2**

Costs Observed
in the Output Range
of 1.0 to 2.0 Units

Pairing (i)	Units Produced (x_i)	Total Cost (y_i)
1	1.0	$32
2	1.5	35
3	1.7	36
4	1.3	34
5	2.0	41
6	1.1	31

$$r^2 = \frac{\sum_{i=1}^{n}(TC_i - \overline{TC})^2 - \sum_{i=1}^{n}(TC_i - a^* - b^*x_i)^2}{\sum_{i=1}^{n}(TC_i - \overline{TC})^2}$$

$$= \frac{\overline{E}^2 - E^2}{\overline{E}^2}$$

The *best* possible case exists when $TC_i = \hat{TC}_i$ for all observations, or $E^2 = 0$. Here, $r^2 = 1$. The *worst* possible case exists when $b^* = 0$ (which implies

_____ **EXHIBIT 3-3**

Pairing (i)	Units Produced (x_i)	Total Cost (y_i)	x_i^2	x_iy_i	y_i^2
1	1.0	$ 32	1.00	32.0	1,024
2	1.5	35	2.25	52.5	1,225
3	1.7	36	2.89	61.2	1,296
4	1.3	34	1.69	44.2	1,156
5	2.0	41	4.00	82.0	1,681
6	1.1	31	1.21	34.1	961
	8.6	$209	13.04	306.0	7,343

$$\Sigma y = na + b\Sigma x \quad \text{or} \quad 209 = 6a + 8.6b \qquad [1]^a$$
$$\Sigma xy = a\Sigma x + b\Sigma x^2 \quad \text{or} \quad 306 = 8.6a + 13.04b \qquad [2]^a$$
$$a^* = \$21.91$$
$$b^* = \$ 9.02 \text{ per unit}$$
$$r = \frac{n\Sigma xy - (\Sigma x)(\Sigma y)}{\sqrt{n\Sigma x^2 - (\Sigma x)^2}\sqrt{n\Sigma y^2 - (\Sigma y)^2}}$$

$$= \frac{6(306) - (8.6)(209)}{\sqrt{6(13.04) - (8.6)^2}\sqrt{6(7,343) - (209)^2}} \qquad [3]^a$$

$$= \frac{38.6}{40.2} = 0.96$$

[a] The summations are over $i = 1, 2, \ldots 6$. Subscripts are suppressed in these equations but are understood to be $i = 1, 2, \ldots 6$.

TC_i is *totally* unrelated to the independent variable, as evidenced by the observations). Here, $E^2 = \bar{E}^2$ and $r^2 = 0$. Another way to view this is to envision r^2 as the percentage variation in TC_i that is explained by the $\hat{TC}_i = a + bx_i$ model. In our example, $r^2 = .92$, $\bar{E}^2 = 62.83$, and $E^2 = 4.81$:

$$\frac{62.83 - 4.81}{62.83} = .92$$

Thus, 92 percent of the variation in TC_i (about its arithmetic average or mean) is explained by the linear cost model identified in Exhibit 3-3.[7]

Another way to express this goodness of fit measure is with the *correlation coefficient,* which is the square root of the coefficient of determination. Its sign is the sign of b^*. Thus, the best possible case would be perfect correlation of $r = \pm 1$. We obtain $r = +1$ if all the observations lie on $TC_i = a^* + b^* x_i$ and the line extends upward to the right ($b^* > 0$); we obtain $r = -1$ if there is a perfect fit and the line extends downward to the right ($b^* < 0$). The worst case is zero correlation. In our example, we have $r = +\sqrt{.92} = .96$.[8]

The previous discussion illustrates two of the advantages of using statistical curve-fitting to obtain a cost estimate. (1) We can calculate a measure of the goodness of fit (r^2) that gives some indication of how reliable the estimate may be in the future. A high r^2 might lead us to expect smaller forecast errors than would lower measures of r^2. (2) The method permits us to derive a cost estimate that is based on an objective criterion: Minimize the sum of the squared deviations around our estimating line. This leads to a unique estimating equation for a given sample of observations.

Additional Assumptions.   There are other advantages as well. If we can make certain assumptions about the distribution of the TC_i for repeated samples at a given x_i, then confidence limits can be set for our estimates of a, b, and the expected cost, $\hat{TC}_i$. More specifically, $\hat{TC}_i = a + bx_i$ can be viewed as an estimate of the true relationship between TC_i and x_i, $TC_i = \alpha + \beta x_i$, where α and β are the true parameters of the equation. Suppose we set a fixed value for x, denoted by x_0, and take repeated samples of TC_0. We would

---

[7] Those who have had statistics will recall that a sample estimate of the variance around the mean of some variable, in our case $\overline{TC}$, is the sum of the squared deviations of each observation from the mean divided by $n - 1$, where n is the number of observations. This, in turn, allows us to interpret r^2 in terms of the percentage of variance that is explained by the model.

[8] This is a so-called *unadjusted* r^2. You will often be confronted by an *adjusted* r^2, which is adjusted for degrees of freedom. In particular:

$$r_{adj}^2 = \frac{1-k}{n-k} + \frac{n-1}{n-k} r^2$$

where n is the sample size and $k - 1$ is the number of independent variables. The point is that adding new variables cannot decrease r^2. We adjust r^2 in such cases to "account for" the additional variables.

not expect the value of TC_0 to be the same for all samples taken. Our equation $\hat{TC}_0 = a + bx_0$ is really the estimate of the mean or expected value of TC_0, given the activity measure x_0. Thus, regression analysis is simply another form of sampling, and certain assumptions must be made about the population distribution of the TC_i for different x_i before statistical inferences can be made.

In more precise terms, then, suppose we *assume* the true cost model is

$$TC_i = \alpha + \beta x_i + e_i$$

That is, the true model is linear. The α and β values are unknown but constant, and e_i is a random error term. Each e_i, in turn, is *independently* drawn from a normal distribution with a mean of zero and a variance of σ^2. We thus assume that the expected cost at the independent variable level x_i is $\alpha + \beta x_i$ and that the unexplained cost associated with the expectation is drawn from a normal distribution with a variance independent of x_i. These additional assumptions allow us to use classical statistics techniques to obtain estimates of α, β, and σ^2, as well as measures of the possible errors in these estimates. We solve for a^* and b^* in exactly the same way as before (minimizing E^2), but the interpretation of these estimators is now quite different. For example, b^* is an unbiased estimator of β (though we do not require a normality assumption for this conclusion), *and* we have a measure of the potential error in the b^* estimate. In particular, the b^* sampling distribution is known in this case (it is the Student t distribution). This allows us to make error statements, construct confidence limits, and so on.

We will not go into this subject in any detail, because of the presumed statistical training. It is important, however, that you be aware of the richness of statistical theory at this point. Equally important is that you be aware of the assumptions that are employed to produce these additional insights.

Returning to the example in Exhibits 3-2 and 3-3, a typical computer-based analysis presents the results in the following type of format:

$$\hat{TC} = \$21.91 + \$9.02x$$
$$(1.91) \quad (1.30) \qquad r^2 = .92$$

The numbers in parentheses below each coefficient are the standard errors. The coefficient divided by its standard error is what is used to provide the measure of error in the estimator. A high ratio is a sign of low error and vice versa. But this extremely casual interpretation follows from the additional assumptions.[9]

---

[9] The reader is referred to a statistical text, such as J. Johnston, *Econometric Methods*, 2nd ed. New York: McGraw-Hill, 1972, Ch. 1. To whet your appetite, the standard error of the regression estimate is $s_e = \sqrt{E^2/(n-2)}$ (where, again, n is the number of data points). In turn, the standard error of the b^* estimate is $s_b = s_e/\sqrt{\Sigma(x-\bar{x})^2}$ (where $\bar{x}$ is the sample mean of x_1, $x_2, \ldots x_n$). Granting all of our noted assumptions, b^*/s_b is characterized by a Student t distribution with $n-2$ degrees of freedom. This is why "significance" is attached to the ratio of b^* to s_b.

In our opinion, the proper interpretation of such a display is twofold. First, $a^* = \$21.91$ and $b^* = \$9.02$ are the a and b values that minimize the E^2 criterion given the sample observations. Second, *if* we admit additional assumptions, statistically based interpretations are available. It is important to be aware of the additional assumptions in moving from the first to the second interpretation. For example, it would often be contended that 9.02/ 1.30 = 6.94 is overwhelming evidence of a variable cost of about \$9 per unit of x (indeed, any ratio beyond ± 2 is typically regarded as satisfactory). Technically, however, this statement follows from a classical hypothesis test and is based on important and stringent assumptions.

A final advantage of statistical regression is that it allows us to choose estimates of cost–activity relationships, even though they may not be linear. For example, suppose we have a relationship $y = ax^b$, which implies that y increases exponentially for increasing values of x. Taking logarithms of both sides of this equation, we have $\log y = \log a + b(\log x)$, which is in the same linear form as our previous equations. The normal equations for solving for a and b will be the same as before except that $\log y$ and $\log x$ will be used instead of the observed values. This particular relationship has some significance for cost estimation, because it describes the general effect of learning on the average time used in production. The equation is discussed further in a later section.

Limitations of Statistical Methods.   As should be obvious from our cautious approach, the use of statistical methods is not without some difficulties and limitations. First, there is the basic problem of obtaining a sufficient number of observations to support the distribution assumptions and to reduce the standard error. The variance of the error term, σ^2, is not known and must be estimated by the square of the standard error:

$$s^2 = \Sigma (TC_i - \widehat{TC}_i)^2 \frac{1}{n-2}$$

where n is the number of observations. The error measures and confidence intervals for α, β, and TC_i depend on this measure, and these will be quite large if the standard error of the estimating equation is large. Note that the error is reduced as n increases.

Similarly, the confidence intervals and error measures are dependent on the range of the observed values of the independent variable x. They will be relatively wide again if the range is limited. But this is not at all uncommon in firms and departments, since the activity levels tend to be clustered from one time period to the next.

The number of observations can be increased by using additional time periods for which cost observations are available. Unfortunately, this raises some practical problems. First, increasing the number of time periods in the analysis runs the risk that the process from which the cost observations are taken is not stationary over time. Changes in technology and in the prices of input factors will produce nonrandom disturbances if the error terms tend to be some function of time. In addition, the accounting systems of firms and departments do not usually provide for an accumulation of cost data in sufficiently disaggregated form over many time periods. Instead, cost data of individual costing units are usually aggregated in order to prepare performance reports for entire functions, and the original observations often cannot be recalled. Storing disaggregated data would result in added costs that, in combination with the first factor, may not be justified. Recall from Chapter 1 that the costs and benefits must be weighed to make an "optimal" information system choice.

We can also raise some questions about the validity of using the least squares criterion as a basis for cost estimation. The least squares estimate minimizes the sum of the squares of the deviations of actual cost observations from their estimates. By its very construction, it imputes a disproportionate weight to the influence of larger deviations compared to smaller ones. It also implies that under- and overestimates have the same penalties for errors. Whether this is true will depend on how the estimate will be used. And a manager may wish to use an estimate that has alternative properties. For example, if the penalty for errors is a constant, independent of the size and direction of error, then we would use the mode (the most likely value) of a population as a forecasting base, because we would wish to be correct as often as possible. This would be analogous to using the mode of the cost distribution for a given value of the activity measure, if one existed. If, instead, the penalty for errors is proportional to the size of error, but independent of its direction, then we would wish to minimize the sum of absolute deviations between actual and estimated values. This could be accomplished by selecting the median of a population. Indeed, there are algorithms (solution techniques) for determining a regression line that does minimize the sum of the absolute deviations.[10]

Apart from these concerns of data availability and appropriateness of the least squares criterion, we should also remember that we are discussing the estimation of a cost function from a collection of past data. Whether we adopt a highly subjective approach, such as account classification, or embrace a sophisticated statistical approach, the fact remains that we are producing the estimate by processing past data.

Problems in Using Past Data for Cost Estimates

There are inherent difficulties in trying to derive cost estimates from an analysis of past relationships between a cost item and some activity variable. Some of these difficulties may be present whether we use statistical regression,

---

[10] For an illustration of one algorithm, see W.F. Sharpe, "Mean–Absolute–Deviation Characteristic Lines for Securities and Portfolios," *Management Science*, Oct. 1971.

the high–low method, or visual curve-fitting, although they are more likely to be encountered with the first method. The statistical method generally requires more observations, and it may be difficult to find sufficient data.

Historical Relevance. First, there is the problem, mentioned previously, of using past relationships between cost items and activity variables as a basis for predicting future relationships. In many instances, past relationships can be adjusted for known changes in the process, such as inflation or significant changes in the labor and material content of an output. Many changes are subtle, however, and creep into the analysis unnoticed. As a result, biased estimates of the parameters are obtained without the exact nature of the bias being known.

The account classification method does not suffer from this problem, because it relies on only one observation. We have not performed any empirical studies of the problem, but we suspect that firms rely on this method because of an intuitive belief that the process being sampled is not stable over time.

A related problem in cost estimation is the extrapolation of the equation to cover ranges of activities not observed. A cost equation is generally valid only within the range of the actual values of x used to estimate the parameter values. For example, the values of a and b shown in Figure 3-4 imply a level of fixed costs of \$21.91 when $x = 0$. In fact, the equation gives no information about the costs at activity levels outside the range of observations. Any extrapolation beyond the range of observed values is a matter of judgment. For example, the crosses in Figure 3-5 might be the observations if x were less than x_1 or greater than x_2. The dots represent the actual observations in the range x_1 to x_2. Using the dots only, our equation might be $TC = a + bx$, or line (2). If we also included the crosses at activity levels below x_1, we could come up with line (1), or $TC' = a' + b'x$. If we used all the crosses and the dots, our line might be closer to line (3), which tends to fall between lines (1) and (2).

The pattern of actual and assumed observations in Figure 3-5 suggests a nonlinear cost function that has a steeper slope in the lower and higher ranges of activity than in the middle range (see Figure 3-6). This type of function is generally believed to be more typical for firms, because it is often assumed that their productive activities are less efficient at the low and high ends of their capacities. Whether this is true is an empirical question we do not consider here. The important point is that fitting straight lines to nonlinear functions results in extreme shifts of the cost equation, depending on which set of observations is used to arrive at the estimate. (Indeed, it is possible to have $a^* < 0$ in such circumstances.)

Cross-Sectional Data. The exact shape of the cost function of a firm or department may be unimportant for cost estimation if the derived equations

————————————————————————————————FIGURE 3-5

Cost estimates using actual and assumed observations over different intervals: (1) from 0 to x_2, (2) from x_1 to x_2, and (3) all observations.

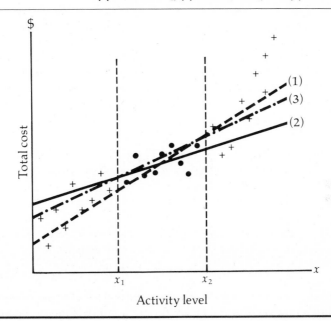

Activity level

are to be used to generate estimates only within the range of activity levels used in the analysis. The range may, in fact, encompass many of the normal operating decisions of management if the operations of firms and departments do cluster within restricted ranges of activity levels. Some decisions, however, may require an analysis of the cost relationships outside the observed range of operations of a single department or of the firm itself. Some insight into the cost behavior pattern outside this range may be gained from the use of data across several similar departments or similar firms. The latter may not be feasible in practice,[11] so we concentrate on the use of cross-sectional data from similar departments.

Very often a firm is composed of nearly homogeneous departments (divisions), each consisting of several individual costing units that are engaged in essentially the same type of activity and differ only in their scale of operations. If these departments are truly homogeneous, then the observations from each may be treated as samples from the same underlying process. This will provide a pooled data base that reflects a wider range of activity levels

———————

[11] Benston used cross-sectional analysis to draw inferences about the shape of cost curves for individual banks; see G. Benston, "Economies of Scale and Marginal Costs in Banking Operations," *National Banking Rev.*, 1965.

FIGURE 3-6 ───

**The curvilinear relationship between cost and activity
(the data are the same as in Figure 3-5).**

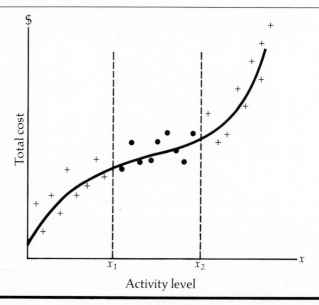

Activity level

than would be observed from any single costing unit. One problem discussed earlier, concerning time series data, is thereby circumvented, since the number of available observations during a single time span is increased.

Of course, the use of cross-sectional analysis assumes that there are costing units within a firm whose operations are sufficiently homogeneous that observations from them may be pooled. The nature of the homogeneity assumption can be illustrated by referring to the data shown in Exhibit 3-4. This exhibit shows a single observation of the relationship between cost and output from each of 10 departments. The sampling assumption that would justify a pooling of these observations is that if output could be varied in any one of these departments from 15,000 to 35,000 units (Departments 1 and 6), the observed cost would vary from approximately $180,000 to $320,000 along a trend line fitting the other cost observations to their respective outputs. This implies that the technology employed in each department is essentially the same or that it can be adjusted quickly and without significant cost to wide changes in activity levels.

Apart from this, there is another problem associated with cross-sectional data that limits its applicability, particularly with the statistical method. Recall that statistical regression analysis (as opposed to curve-fitting) assumes that the cost observed for a given value of x has a distribution with an expected value $a^* + b^*x$ and a variance around this expected value. The tests for

EXHIBIT 3-4

Cost Observations over a Range
of 15,000 to 35,000 Units of Output

Dept. No.	Units Produced	Labor Costs
1	15,000	$180,000
2	20,000	210,000
3	18,000	190,000
4	27,000	270,000
5	19,000	200,000
6	35,000	320,000
7	30,000	290,000
8	25,000	255,000
9	23,000	240,000
10	32,000	308,000

significance and the calculation of confidence intervals rest on the further assumption that the variance of the cost around its expected value is constant, regardless of the value of x. This is referred to as the *assumption of the homogeneity of variances.*

Referring back to Exhibit 3-4, the assumption is that the distribution of unexplained costs is identical at 15,000 units and at 35,000 units. In practice, it is conceivable that the costs could reflect a much higher variance around $320,000 than around $180,000.[12] Generally, a plotting of the relationship between the cost item and activity levels will indicate whether the assumption is being violated. There are also formal tests of the homogeneity of variances assumption, but they are usually used when relationships cannot be plotted— for example, when several independent variables are used in a single equation.

Causality and Association.   It is essential to distinguish between causality and mere association in cost estimation. Ideally, an activity variable should be used in an estimating equation only if it can be argued that changes in this variable are causally related to observed changes in the cost. For example, we can argue that output is the primary explanatory variable for changes in direct labor and direct materials costs. However, overhead costs are more directly dependent upon other inputs than upon output. Supplies are usually consumed as a function of raw materials inputs; indirect labor costs usually vary with the amount of direct labor hours worked; repairs and maintenance are influenced by machine time; and so on. It is true that these overhead costs would also vary with output, but this is primarily because their (intermediate) causes are associated with output.

Statistical texts cite numerous instances where high correlations are ob-

---

[12] This is discussed more fully in R. Jensen, "Multiple Regression Models for Cost Control— Assumptions and Limitations," *Accounting Review,* April 1969.

served but no causal relationship exists.[13] The danger is that the correlations result, because the dependent and independent variables are themselves correlated with still another unexamined variable whose influence can destroy or reduce the observed correlation in future analyses. For example, indirect labor may increase with direct labor, but the latter may be inefficient and output may not increase correspondingly. Using output in the estimating equation in this case could result in large errors because of direct labor's influence on the amount of indirect labor cost incurred.

Distribution Assumptions.   Another set of problems in the use of past data to obtain cost estimates is the importance of the statistical assumptions. Recall that a constant-coefficients linear model and an independent, normally distributed error term provide a basis for assessing the reliability of the estimates. In turn, violation of these assumptions, as we have warned, calls such reliability assessments into question. One should, of course, never expect to encounter such a perfectly specified setting. So the real question is how to test the assumptions and what to do when the tests are negative. Again, however, our goal is to ensure your awareness of important and subtle matters that are best addressed in a statistics text.

Violations of the error term assumptions—normally distributed with an expected value of zero, a constant variance, and no serial (auto-) correlation—can often be revealed by analyzing the printout pattern(s) of the error term. There are also formal tests to determine violations of the normality, constant variance, and autocorrelation assumptions. Examples are the Bartlett test for the variance assumption[14] and the Durbin–Watson test for (a first-order version of) the autocorrelation assumption (see Problem 28).

Heteroscedasticity.   Heteroscedasticity refers to a *violation* of the assumption of a constant variance in the error term. If the error term does not have a constant variance, the statistical tests used to construct confidence limits around individual coefficients (the *a* and the *b*), and around the cost estimate, are not valid.

Heteroscedasticity usually arises because of scale problems. Increased levels of costs will be observed with increased levels of the activity variable. We would expect the variability of these levels to increase as well. Heteroscedasticity may also be observed if we attempt to fit a linear equation to a nonlinear cost curve. The observed values will deviate further from their estimates as we take readings at the lower and higher ranges of output (see Figure 3-5).

---

[13] One of the criticisms originally voiced against the early studies associating heart attacks and smoking was that the studies merely confirmed the fact that many smokers are highly emotional people who are prone to heart attacks, an intermediate variable that was ignored.

[14] See M.S. Bartlett, "The Use of Transformation," *Biometrics* 111, 1947.

FIGURE 3-7

A linear line fitted to a nonlinear function. Negative estimation errors predominate below x_1; positive errors predominate above x_2.

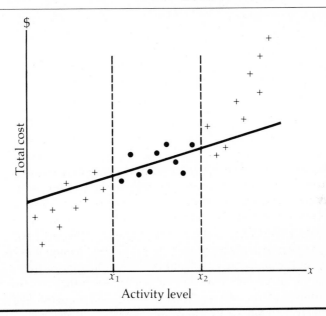

The scale problem may be alleviated simply by scaling the observations (that is, by dividing by a scale factor). Transformations of the data may also alleviate the problem of a nonconstant variance. (One typical transformation is to regress logs of the dependent variable against logs of the independent variables.) Another possible transformation is to regress square roots of the data.

Autocorrelation. Autocorrelation refers to a lack of serial independence in the error term. That is, the expected value of the correlation of e_i to e_j, $i \neq j$, is nonzero. This characteristic may arise when we attempt, again, to fit a linear estimate to a nonlinear cost curve. To illustrate, we have fitted a single linear line to the data from Figure 3-6 as shown in Figure 3-7. Note that the observations in the lower range of output tend to fall below the estimate, whereas in the higher range they fall above the estimate. The negative error terms in the lower range and the positive error terms in the higher range will produce serial (auto-) correlation in the residuals.

Another source of autocorrelation is "cost stickiness." A firm may expand its output during several periods with normal increases in the inputs needed to achieve higher levels of outputs. Then, when output levels have to be reduced, these higher levels of inputs tend to persist, thus resulting in higher costs than previously for a particular output value. One reason these costs

EXHIBIT 3-5————————————————————————————————

Cost Observations Reflecting Increased Costs as Output Declines to the Previous Level

Period	Volume (units)	Cost
1	1,000	$11,000
2	1,500	14,500
3	2,000	16,500
4	2,500	18,000
5	2,000	17,000
6	1,500	15,500

persist at higher levels is that firms simply do not wish to cut back on their pools of skilled labor during temporary reductions in output.

The figures in Exhibit 3-5 illustrate cost stickiness. We have two readings for output levels 1,500 and 2,000 and one each for 1,000 and 2,500. While the two different costs observed for output levels 1,500 and 2,000 could have resulted from random fluctuations, repetitions of this sequence of observations would raise doubts about this explanation. A simple plot of the cost observations against output levels may not reveal the presence of cost stickiness. When the timing of the observations is included, however, the ratchetlike nature of the cost behavior becomes apparent (see Figure 3-8). Note that if we had fitted a line to more or less split the data, as we would if we regressed cost against output, the error term would be negative for periods 1, 2, and 3, but positive for 5 and 6.

FIGURE 3-8————————————————————————————————

Observations in (a) ignore time sequence, but in (b) time sequence is considered.

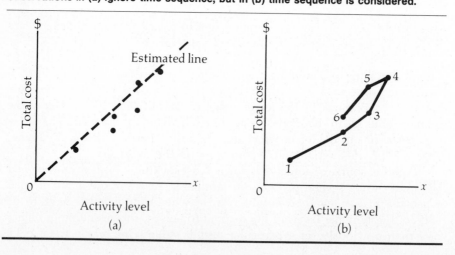

Autocorrelation leads to underestimates of the standard errors of the regression estimates. These, in turn, render the confidence tests inappropriate. The problem may be alleviated by transforming the data to remove nonlinearity; by using index numbers to account for price and technology changes; by inserting dummy variables to handle cost stickiness, seasonality, and the like; or by regressing first differences of costs against first differences of the activity variable(s). That is, regress $TC_t - TC_{t-1}$ against $x_t - x_{t-1}$ for all t.

Model Selection. A final, and far from trivial, difficulty here is selection of the estimating model itself. Up to this point we have presumed the use of a linear model defined on a particular independent variable. We could, however, envision numerous alternatives, consisting of linear and nonlinear relationships, alternative independent variables, and combinations of independent variables. Estimation of a learning curve is an important example of a nonlinear relationship, and multiple regression provides an example of combinations of independent variables. Both topics are treated subsequently. Here, we concentrate on alternative independent variables in a linear model.

Assuming that a linear model is appropriate, suppose we want to estimate an overhead cost, but are not clear on whether the independent variable should be machine hours or direct labor hours. Ideally, we would use our understanding of the situation's economics to select one of the variables. But suppose either one is acceptable on such grounds. Then we would seek insight from the data themselves. We might construct the least squares model for each and rely on a goodness of fit comparison, to determine which variable has a lower standard error, higher coefficient of determination, or seemingly more reliable slope estimate (in terms of intuition and statistical significance, where the relevant assumptions have been checked). Alternatively, we might consider a *hold-out* approach and estimate the model with only some of the data, then check its accuracy on data that were not used in the estimation process.

Remember, however, that any such process is highly subjective. The ultimate issue concerns the use to be made of the cost estimation. Here, we return to the theme of Chapter 1. Suppose the use of model 1 will lead to decision A and the use of model 2 will lead to decision B. The fundamental question is choice between decisions A and B, not between models 1 and 2.

For example, suppose an estimate of a cost item is used to determine whether to accept or reject a contract. If the cost item is overestimated, the decision maker would reject an order when in fact the order should have been accepted. His loss is measured by the amount of profit he forgoes on the rejected order. If the amount of profit is small, the disutility of the incorrect decision may be insignificant. Now consider the effect of an underestimate of the cost item. In this case, the decision error is to accept an order when in fact the order should be rejected. The opportunity loss would be measured by the difference between expected and actual profit, with the latter being smaller. Here again, the disutility of this loss in profits could be insignificant.

But suppose the estimation error is large. In the case of overestimation, the decision maker would find himself rejecting profitable orders quite frequently, and eventually his competitors could force him out of business. The same result could occur in the case of underestimation, since the decision maker might be paying out more money than he receives, or at least realizing smaller profits than some of his competitors.

A common assumption is that the loss function associated with different estimation errors is quadratic rather than linear. Under this condition, we would expect that the decision maker would be willing to pay disproportionately more to avoid large estimation errors. Moreover, the situation might be such that he would also be willing to pay more to avoid underestimation errors than he would to avoid overestimation errors even of the same magnitude. This could be justified if bankruptcy is approached faster with the former than with the latter.[15]

A formal analysis of the effects of estimation errors is difficult to implement in practice. A particular cost estimate may be used in many different kinds of decisions, and some of these may be made by a decision maker who himself is uncertain about the kind of decision model he uses. There are many so-called unstructured decision situations (such as advertising and research) that are not susceptible to modeling. As a result, the decision process of the decision maker cannot be expressed in precise mathematical form. In addition, the accountant may not be able to develop a probability distribution for different estimates of the cost items, in which case the expected opportunity costs of relying on any particular estimate cannot be calculated. Therefore, the evaluation of cost estimates may have to be based on less demanding approaches to the problem.

As one possibility, the accountant might evaluate different estimates on the basis of some general criterion. For example, he or she might assume a particular form of utility function and choose an estimating method that promises to minimize losses consistent with that utility function. Recall that the least squares method is consistent with a quadratic loss function. Alternatively, the criterion to minimize the sum of the absolute differences between actual and estimated costs is consistent with a linear cost function. Still other criteria could be used, but we will not elaborate on these.[16]

The choice between estimating methods may also depend on other cost considerations. For example, regression models make more demands on the accounting system in terms of the amounts of disaggregated data that need to be stored from previous periods than, say, the accounting method. The latter can be implemented with only the most recent observation available.

---

[15] This is not an unusual situation, since many personal lawsuits require that the plaintiff demonstrate the incurrence of actual rather than potential losses.

[16] For additional insights into the problem, see R. Barefield, "Comments on a Measure of Forecasting Performance," *J. Accounting Research,* Autumn 1969, and J. Demski and G.A. Feltham, "Forecast Evaluation," *Accounting Rev.,* July 1972.

In general, we would expect regression models to outperform other estimation methods that rely on past data, but this would not be true if the sampling assumptions were violated. If a process that generates a cost observation is subject to extreme changes in technology or input prices, then a reliance on past observations would not be reasonable. In such cases, an extrapolation of the cost from the most recent single observation might be the best method possible.

The choice of estimation method should depend on the expected benefits and the expected costs of obtaining each estimate. Whether this analysis is conducted informally or formally must be left up to the individual estimator, because the issues to resolve are complex and often controversial.[17]

The basic point, in other words, is that we often analyze past data to derive cost estimates. This is a well-practiced procedure and has the benefit of classical statistics to guide its application. But in conceptual terms it must be remembered that (because of complexity) we typically treat these as "estimating problems" when, in reality, we are dealing with decision problems. Do not lose track of the basic principle that the ultimate criterion is the estimate's utility in practice.

REVIEW PROBLEMS 2 AND 3 ─────────────────────────────────

2. **Alternative Activity Bases and Estimators**
   (a) *Relevant Activity Basis.* Because the sealing department of the Ajax Company works on several of the firm's products in one period, there is some question of the relevant basis for cost estimation. Each of four different department supervisors suggested a different basis for cost–volume analysis. The departmental overhead costs and the four possible indices of activity are shown in Exhibit 3-6. From the data given, attempt to resolve the conflict by finding what appears to be the best single index of volume. (*Hint:* Use graph analysis.)
   (b) *Comparing the Results of Two Methods.* Fit a straight line to the data using direct labor hours (DLH) as the index of volume. Calculate it by

   (1) the high–low method
   (2) least squares

   Let $x =$ DLH and $y =$ cost; $\Sigma x^2 = 151,658,500$; and $\Sigma xy = 641,476,000$. Compare the results of the two methods.
   (c) (1) Calculate the least squares estimate of the cost equation assuming that machine hours is the proper index of volume. Here $\Sigma x^2 = 26,255,350$ and $\Sigma xy = 265,994,000$.
       (2) Plot the cost equation on a graph of the data; comment

─────────────

[17] This issue is not unique to accounting. The variables to consider in assessing forecasts are treated in a more general context in statistical texts. For example, see R.G. Brown, *Smoothing, Forecasting and Prediction of Discrete Time Series.* Englewood Cliffs, N.J.: Prentice-Hall, 1963, sec. V. Also see H. Theil, *Economic Forecasts and Policy.* Amsterdam: North-Holland, 1965, sec. II.

EXHIBIT 3-6

Overhead Cost per Quarter	Units Produced	Direct Labor Hours	Machine Hours	Weights of Units Produced
$12,500	1,000	4,090	750	15,000
18,000	1,075	3,700	1,725	23,000
16,000	1,130	3,750	875	21,800
19,200	1,060	5,350	2,050	20,050
11,800	1,050	1,600	1,660	12,000
14,900	1,080	3,100	1,720	17,000
17,600	1,010	3,320	1,950	16,000
13,800	1,080	2,490	1,550	19,300
15,400	1,020	2,980	1,100	13,900
14,200	1,050	2,500	1,240	21,400
13,000	1,010	4,100	960	13,250
16,500	1,060	4,150	1,470	14,100

on the results.

(d) What additional considerations might be important in your selection of an estimating model here?

3. **Alternative Estimates and the Opportunity Costs of Forecast Errors**
Assume you have two production cost estimates as follows ($x =$ units of output):

(1) High–low $\quad$ $TC_1 = \$25,000 + \$7.50x$
(2) Regression $\quad$ $TC_2 = \$30,000 + \$7.00x$

Management is highly confident it can sell at least 18,000 units of output next period at a price of $12.00/unit. The estimated selling and administrative costs are:

Variable $\quad$ $1.50/unit
Fixed $\quad$ $14,000

(a) What is the expected profit given the *production cost* estimate of $TC_1 = \$25,000 + \$7.50x$?
(b) Management is worried that the second estimate, $TC_2 = \$30,000 + \$7.00x$, may be a more accurate estimate of what production costs will be next period. If this were the true estimate, management would push to sell at least 20,000 units by increasing fixed selling and administrative expenses from $14,000 to $22,150. What is the expected profit, given these data: Total variable costs = $7.00 + $1.50 = $8.50 and total fixed costs = $30,000 + $22,150.
(c) Suppose management accepts the second estimate and produces 20,000 units with the added costs. However, only 18,000 units

are sold, and actual production costs are found to be TC = $25,000 + $7.50x$. The 2,000 units in inventory result in added storage costs of $0.50 per unit. What is the opportunity loss of not knowing in advance that actual sales would be only 18,000 and that actual costs would be consistent with TC_1? Show calculations. (*Hint:* Use the optimal decision for 18,000 units produced and sold as a base against which to compare the actual results of the decision taken.)

(d) The calculation in (c) provides the basis for a measure of the "value of perfect information." It can be expressed generally as the "optimal value of the objective function given actual realization of parameter values less the actual value of the objective function given actual decisions." In effect, we do not come away completely empty-handed when we make forecast errors, but we do not come away with a full hand, either. Discuss this measure as a practical basis for evaluating alternative estimates.

The discussion to this point stresses the conceptual issues and illustrates simple or elementary approaches to formalized cost estimation. We reiterate the importance of combining accounting with statistical expertise when considerable data are available and high-quality estimates are essential. The two remaining sections, Multiple Regression and Learning Curves and Cost Behavior, explore additional technical issues and are, therefore, probably more accessible to advanced students.

Multiple Regression

Thus far, we have assumed that changes in cost are a function of a single independent variable and a random factor. In many cases, this may be a reasonable assumption. Consider a repairman working on a particular type of machine. His task for each job is the same: to disassemble the equipment, clean it, and lubricate certain parts. The job is identical for each machine, but the repairman does not work at a constant speed. His time on 10 identical jobs might range from 2 hours and 50 minutes to 3 hours and 5 minutes. One cause of this variation might be that the worker is less efficient some days than others. Another source might be disturbances in the environment— for example, the foreman passes by and chats. Whatever the cause, these differences are small and are usually difficult to isolate, so they are included in the random factor.

However, one particular cause of variation from job to job can be predicted. This is the variation due to differences in the type or age of machine worked on. Different machines will have different maintenance requirements. For example, used machines may take longer on a job than new ones. Typewriters may take less time to overhaul than desk calculators. These variations can be taken into account explicitly through the use of multiple regression techniques that estimate simultaneously the relationships between costs and several causal variables. The following example, taken from an early application, indicates how such a problem might be approached in measuring the time necessary to perform a given task.[18]

Workers in the repair department clean and lubricate various types of small office equipment. Typically, these items are typewriters, desk calculators, and adding machines. It is believed that the time involved is not the same for each type of machine. Thus, simple linear regression relating hours and total units completed would be inappropriate. One of the assumptions is that the desk calculators require greater amounts of time, and it is felt that they should be treated separately to verify this. Essentially, management wishes to estimate the repair time required for each class of machine. The functional equation may be expressed as

$$H_i = a + b_1 T_i + b_2 A_i + b_3 C_i + e_i$$

where H_i = total hours worked during period i
$\quad a$ = overhead of indirect time
$\quad b_1$ = estimate of the time required to overhaul a typewriter
$\quad T_i$ = number of typewriters overhauled during period i
$\quad b_2$ = estimate of the time required to overhaul an adding machine
$\quad A_i$ = number of adding machines overhauled during period i
$\quad b_3$ = estimate of the time required to overhaul a desk calculator
$\quad C_i$ = number of desk calculators overhauled during period i
$\quad e_i$ = random error term for period i

During the past eight weeks the work performed was as shown in Exhibit 3-7.

Multiple regression techniques are used to estimate the a and b_i values;[19] the results are

$$a = 8 \text{ hours}$$
$$b_1 = 1.456 \text{ hours}$$
$$b_2 = 2.047 \text{ hours}$$
$$b_3 = 4.016 \text{ hours}$$

---

[18] This example is taken from Paul R. McClenon, "Cost Finding Through Multiple Correlation Analysis," *Accounting Rev.*, July 1963.

[19] See any standard statistics text for the formulas. The details for this problem can be found in McClenon, "Cost Finding." A typical display would be:

$$\hat{H_i} = 7.878 + 1.456 T_i + 2.047 A_i + 4.016 C_i$$
$$\quad (1.416) \quad (.098) \quad (.055) \quad (.076)$$

with $R^2 = .999^+$ (adjusted $= .999$). Recall that standard errors are displayed in parentheses below their respective coefficients.

_____EXHIBIT 3-7

Machine Repair Time Over the Eight-week Period

Week	Typewriters	Adding Machines	Calculators	Hours
1	5	7	8	64
2	7	9	6	64
3	9	5	5	53
4	9	7	4	54
5	8	8	3	51
6	9	10	3	57
7	9	10	2	53
8	9	10	1	49
	65	66	32	445

In the context of this example, we interpret the results as implying that, on the average, almost an hour and a half is required to recondition a typewriter, a little more than two hours is needed to repair an adding machine, and four hours are required to overhaul each desk calculator. In each week, almost eight hours are spent in miscellaneous overhead tasks.

To determine the *direct* costs of performing any one of these tasks, we have to multiply each term by the direct labor rate. Assuming that wages are equal for all workers, total labor costs during period i, C_{Li}, are

$$C_{Li} = (a + b_1 T_i + b_2 A_i + b_3 C_i) W_i$$

where W_i is the wage rate during period i.

The reliability of this estimate can be measured. That is, if the assumptions of least squares are met, we can construct confidence limits for C_{Li} and the individual coefficients of the equation. The exact procedures are too involved for discussion here. Computer programs exist that provide the required calculations, and these may be relied upon once the distribution assumptions are found to be reasonable.

Multicollinearity

The assumptions required to move from curve-fitting to statistical analysis are the same here as in the single independent variable case, with one addition. This is multicollinearity. It occurs when the multiple independent variables, x_j, are highly correlated. To illustrate, suppose we wish to estimate total overhead costs as a function of two independent variables: direct labor hours and machine hours. The data on the three variables are shown in Exhibit 3-8. A careful reader would observe that the values assigned to x_2 are approximately 120 percent of the values assigned to x_1 (some random error was purposely inserted).

EXHIBIT 3-8 _____

Multicollinearity in x_j

Total Overhead Costs	Direct Labor Hours (x_1)	Machine Hours (x_2)
$11,000	1,000	1,200
14,500	1,500	1,850
17,000	2,000	2,400
18,500	2,800	3,350
18,000	2,500	3,000
18,500	2,900	3,500
19,000	3,500	4,300
19,500	4,000	4,800

If we regressed x_2 against x_1, we would obtain a very high r^2 (almost 1.0). Suppose we set x_2 exactly equal to $1.2x_1$, then try to run a multiple regression of total overhead costs as a function of x_1 and x_2. The normal equations to solve for a, b_1, and b_2 would be:

$$\Sigma \, \text{TOH} = na + b_1 \Sigma \, x_1 + b_2 \Sigma \, x_2 \qquad [3\text{-}4]$$

$$\Sigma \, \text{TOH} \, x_1 = a \Sigma \, x_1 + b_1 \Sigma \, x_1{}^2 + b_2 \Sigma \, x_1 x_2 \qquad [3\text{-}5]$$

$$\Sigma \, \text{TOH} \, x_2 = a \Sigma \, x_2 + b_1 \Sigma \, x_1 x_2 + b_2 \Sigma \, x_2{}^2 \qquad [3\text{-}6]$$

Rewriting x_2 as $1.2x_1$:

$$\Sigma \, \text{TOH}' = na + b_1 \Sigma \, x_1 + b_2 \Sigma \, 1.2x_1 \qquad [3\text{-}7]$$

$$\Sigma \, \text{TOH}' \, x_1 = a \Sigma \, x_1 + b_1 \Sigma \, x_1{}^2 + b_2 \Sigma \, x_1 \, 1.2x_1 \qquad [3\text{-}8]$$

$$\Sigma \, \text{TOH}' \, 1.2x = a \Sigma \, 1.2x_1 + b_1 \Sigma \, x_1 1.2x_1 + b_2 \Sigma \, (1.2x_1)^2 \qquad [3\text{-}9]$$

Note that Equation [3-9] is simply 1.2 times Equation [3-8]. Hence, we do not have three linearly independent equations, which means we cannot solve for three unknowns: Only two of them can be determined.[20]

Of course, we rarely encounter perfect multicollinearity. But it may be present to a degree sufficient to render estimates of the *individual* coefficients for the x_j unreliable. Indeed, we may observe in our example that total overhead costs $= a + b_1 x_1 + b_2 x_2$ with $b_2 < 0$, implying that TOH can be decreased while we hold x_1 constant and *increase* x_2. If x_2 is some measure of input use, we would not expect increased levels of x_2 to lead to lower levels of overhead costs (see Problem 27, for example).

---

[20] Those who have had matrix algebra will recognize that the determinant of the 3×3 matrix implied by Equations [3-7], [3-8], and [3-9] would be zero.

The presence of multicollinearity is not as serious a problem if we are only interested in estimating total overhead costs as a function of both independent variables. That is, the estimates of total overhead costs as both variables change will still be reliable (providing the other assumptions are met). The effect of multicollinearity is to increase the error measure associated with the collinear variables and thus reduce our confidence in making statements of how total overhead costs may vary in response to marginal changes in these variables.

Of course, we can always eliminate multicollinearity by simply discarding one or the other of the correlated independent variables. But this may reduce the overall predictability of our cost equation. One compromise approach is to first regress, say, x_2 on x_1, obtaining an estimate of the relationship between x_2 and x_1. Then we take the error term from this equation, which captures the unexpected changes in x_2 *not explained by* x_1, and insert this error term in the overhead cost equation. Thus, $\widehat{\text{TOH}} = a + b_1 x_1 + b_2 (e_{1,2})$.

Finally, to have some appreciation for these remarks, return to the original example in Exhibit 3-6. It turns out that T_i and C_i are highly collinear (with a correlation of $-.821$). Suppose we drop C_i and reestimate the model. This provides:

$$\hat{H}_i = 7.910 - .313 T_i + 2.329 A_i$$

How do we interpret the negative coefficient? One possible answer is that C_i is an important independent variable that has been excluded from the model *and* is correlated with one that is included. In this case, b_1 will capture the effects of both T_i *and* C_i; eliminating C_i therefore biases our estimate of b_1. Conversely, using all of the variables provides us with unbiased estimates (assuming requisite assumptions), but with error measures inflated by the collinearity.

Dummy Variables

Thus far, we have assumed that any independent variable that is to be used in an estimating equation can be measured in a natural manner (such as units of output). However, there are many instances where a cost relationship may not be described in such a refined way. For example, we may believe that the time of the year, week, or day can influence the level of a particular cost item, but apart from this no more specific statement can be made. Time may be treated as a dummy variable that has only two values assigned to it: a 1 when its influence is to be included in the estimating equation and a 0 otherwise. To illustrate, suppose our estimating equation is $\widehat{\text{TC}} = a + b_1 x_1 + b_2 x_2$, where x_2 is a dummy variable representing the winter season. We may choose to assign a zero value to x_2 unless the observations of TC occur in the winter, in which case x_2 receives a value of 1. Note that this dummy variable merely shifts the intercept of our estimating equation by the amount of its coefficient, b_2, whenever $x_2 = 1$.

Dummy variables provide a useful technique for including the influence of unusual factors, but it would be preferable if a more refined relationship could be defined between the cost item and these factors.

REVIEW PROBLEM 4
Multiple Regression and the Use of Dummy Variables _____

The following is designed to illustrate the nature of multiple regression solutions by way of adding a dummy variable to the analysis. (This problem was first suggested to us by W.W. Cooper.)

The president of your company approaches you as his chief statistician and expresses his concern about difficulties being experienced in estimating the costs of producing an important item. He asks you to prepare an analysis that will provide some improvement over present methods of estimating these costs for budgetary projections and other purposes. He supplies you with data from the controller's records over the past six periods as a basis for your analysis (see Exhibit 3-9).

(a) Determine the relationship between output and cost, ignoring the timing of the observations.
(b) Repeat (a), but add a dummy variable x_2 to the cost equation:

$$TC = a + b_1x_1 + b_2x_2$$

where x_2 is assigned a value of 0 if the change in output from the previous year is positive and a value of 1 if the change is negative. The normal equations are

EXHIBIT 3-9 _____

Total Cost and Production
for the Past Six Periods

	ITEM X	ITEM Y
	Units Produced (000)	Total Cost ($000)
Period		
1	1.0	11.0
2	1.5	14.5
3	2.0	16.5
4	2.5	18.0
5	2.0	17.0
6	1.5	15.5
$n = 6$	10.5	92.5

$$\Sigma \, TC = na + b_1 \, \Sigma \, x_1 + b_2 \, \Sigma \, x_2$$
$$\Sigma \, TC \, x_1 = a \, \Sigma \, x_1 + b_1 \, \Sigma \, x_1{}^2 + b_2 \, \Sigma \, x_1 x_2$$
$$\Sigma \, TC \, x_2 = a \, \Sigma \, x_2 + b_1 \, \Sigma \, x_1 x_2 + b_2 \, \Sigma \, x_2{}^2$$

(c)   How might you detect the presence of cost stickiness?

Learning Curves and Cost Behavior

It is observed that in many situations an organization improves its levels of performance on a given job as its members repeat the necessary tasks of the job. This has given impetus to the development of "learning curves," which illustrate the amount of improvement that can be expected as the cumulative amount of work performed increases.[21]

The learning curve phenomenon is relevant for business decisions when the reduction in production time per unit leads to a reduction in the unit cost.[22] Later units can be produced at a lower cost per unit than earlier ones. Thus, an estimate of total or incremental costs of production should be adjusted for savings arising from learning.

Learning effects may be expressed by the simple equation

$$y = ax^{-l}$$

where y = average number of labor (or machine) hours per unit
   a = number of labor (or machine) hours for the first unit
   x = cumulative number of units produced
   l is a measure of the "learning" improvement

If we graphed y against x, we would observe an exponentially decreasing function as x is increased (Figure 3-9). This can be converted to a linear function by plotting log y against log x:

$$\log y = \log a + (-l) \log x$$

The linear transformation is shown in Figure 3-10.

An 80 percent learning curve has been found to be typical in the airframe and other industries. That is, in these industries, every time output is doubled, average hours per unit are 80 percent of the previous figure. For example,

---

[21] For a summary of the history of learning curves and a discussion of their potential usefulness, see Frank J. Andress, "The Learning Curve as a Production Tool," *Harvard Bus. Rev.,* Jan.–Feb. 1954; W.B. Hirschmann, "Profits from the Learning Curve," *Harvard Bus. Rev.,* Jan.– Feb. 1964; and W.J. Abernathy and K. Wayne, "Limits of the Learning Curve," *Harvard Bus. Rev.,* Sept.–Oct. 1974.

[22] The argument in this section assumes that the labor force has no slack time for which it must be paid. It is also assumed that an hourly, not a piece, wage rate prevails.

FIGURE 3-9

Cumulative average labor time.

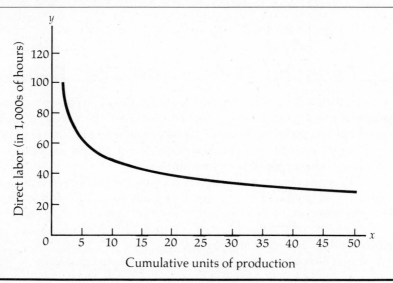

FIGURE 3-10

Cumulative average labor time plotted on a log-log scale.

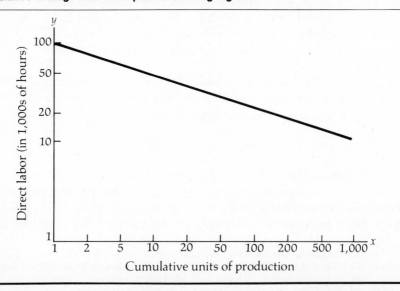

Figures 3-9 and 3-10 reprinted by permission of the *Harvard Business Review.* From "The Learning Curve as a Production Tool" by Frank J. Andress (Jan.–Feb. 1954). Copyright © 1954 by the President and Fellows of Harvard College; all rights reserved.

_____EXHIBIT 3-10

Calculations for a Theoretical Learning Curve:
Learning Rate = 80 Percent

	QUANTITY (IN UNITS)		TIME (IN HOURS)	
Lot No.	Per Lot	Cumulative	Total	Average Time per Unit
1	15	15	600	40.0
2	15	30	960	32.0 (40.0 × 0.8)
4	15	60	1,536	25.6 (32.0 × 0.8)
8	15	120	2,460	20.5 (25.6 × 0.8)
16	15	240	3,936	16.4 (20.5 × 0.8)

if 600 hours are required for 15 units, or an average of 40 hours per unit, the average for 30 units would be 0.8 × 40, or 32 hours; for 60 units, the average would be 25.6 hours; and so on. The calculations are illustrated in Exhibit 3-10.

The average time for any output may also be computed using the equation $y = ax^{-l}$. As it turns out, $l = .3219$ for a learning improvement of 80 percent. In this example, we do not know a for the first unit, but only for the first batch of 15 units. Suppose we let $x =$ the number of cumulative lots of 15 units each. For lot 8 (120 units), $y = 40(8)^{-.3219}$ and

$$\log y = \log 40 + (-.3219)(\log 8)$$
$$= 1.6021 + (-.3219)(.9031)$$
$$= 1.3114$$

or

$$y = 20.5 \text{ (approximately)}$$

which is the figure shown in Exhibit 3-10 for 120 cumulative units.

Estimated values for a and l in the learning curve equation can be determined from simple regression analysis after converting average hours per unit, y, and cumulative output, x, into logarithms and inserting these values into the normal equations.

REVIEW PROBLEM 5
Learning Curves and Expected Costs _____

The MEC Company has just completed the assembly of 150 units of a new system. The company is now considering a new order for 50 additional units. Management has noted that the number of direct labor hours required for each unit seems to be declining. For the first 50 units produced, the average hours per unit were 580. After producing another 100 units, the average hours per unit over the total of 150 units dropped to 398. These two observations imply a learning curve function of the form $y = ax^{-l}$.

(a) Using these two points on the curve, derive the values for a and l, so that the average hours for 200 units can be determined. (*Hint:* $\log 580 = \log a - l \log 50$ and $\log 398 = \log a - l \log 150$.)

(b) Using your values from (a), calculate the total hours required to assemble 200 units in total.

(c) Suppose labor rates average $10 per hour. What will be the incremental labor cost if the new order is accepted?

Conclusion

We have outlined some of the better-known methods that are used to develop estimates of cost equations. These estimation techniques range in difficulty from the simple (for example, the high–low method) to the extremely difficult (that is, multiple regression); the latter may require the combined talents of an accountant and a statistician.

As we indicated earlier, the engineering method represents the most direct approach to an estimate of future costs. It is expensive to implement, however, and can be used only for the direct labor and materials categories. If the estimate is reliable over time, it can be used in many different decisions and the expense will be justified. Indeed, this is the assumption when engineering estimates are used to set standards for the control of labor and materials (see Chapter 6). The control function demands reliable estimates of what a cost should be.

Less reliable estimates are suitable for many special types of decisions. For example, the high–low estimate often proves sufficient for the typical break-even or cost–volume–profit analysis (to be discussed in Chapter 4).

Statistical techniques are generally justified when the estimates are to be used in recurring decisions. The expense involved in gathering and analyzing the data for multiple regression is not usually justified if the estimate of the cost equation is to be used for only a single decision. Hence, these techniques are more suitable for use in developing cost data for such decision models as linear programing (Chapter 4), capital budgeting (Chapter 14), and inventory (Chapter 16). The implementation of these models requires repeated estimates of various costs. Since statistical methods yield reasonable measures of costs, these methods are also suitable for the development of standards for controlling costs, especially overhead costs.

It is important to remember, though, that we are actually dealing with cost and value-of-information questions at this point. Whether an estimate should be further refined is a question of whether the additional information is worthwhile. And choice between two estimation procedures is akin to choice between information systems. This will be discussed further in Chapter 4, when we begin to embed our study of cost accounting in a specific choice context.

Supplementary Readings

Articles

Benston, G., "Multiple Regression Analysis of Cost Behavior," *Accounting Rev.*, Oct. 1966.

Gynther, R.S., "Improving Separation of Fixed and Variable Expenses," *N.A.A. Bull.*, June 1963.

Hirschmann, W.B., "Profits from the Learning Curve," *Harvard Bus. Rev.*, Jan.–Feb. 1964.

Jensen, R., "Multiple Regression Models for Cost Control: Assumptions and Limitations," *Accounting Rev.*, April 1967.

Kaplan, R., "Management Accounting in Hospitals: A Case Study," in Livingstone and Gunn, eds., *Accounting for Social Goals*. New York: Harper and Row, 1974.

Le Brone, H., "The Learning Curve: A Case Study," *Management Accounting*, Feb. 1978.

McClenon, P.R., "Cost Finding Through Multiple Correlation Analysis," *Accounting Rev.*, July 1963.

"Separating and Using Costs as Fixed and Variable," *N.A.A. Accounting Practice Report No. 10*, reprinted in *N.A.A. Bull.*, June 1960.

Books

Davidson, S. and R.L. Weil, eds., *Handbook of Cost Accounting*. New York: McGraw-Hill, 1978, Ch. 2.

Dean, J., *Statistical Cost Estimation*. Bloomington, Indiana: Indiana University Press, 1976.

Demski, J.S. and G.A. Feltham, *Cost Determination: A Conceptual Approach*. Ames, Iowa: Iowa State Univ. Press, 1976, Ch. 4.

Johnston, J., *Econometric Methods*, 2nd ed. New York: McGraw-Hill, 1972, Chs. 1, 2, and 8.

_____, *Statistical Cost Analysis*. New York: McGraw-Hill, 1972, Chs. 3 and 4.

Kelejian, H.H. and W.E. Oates, *Introduction to Econometrics*. New York: Harper and Row, 1981, esp. Chs. 2–4.

Questions and Problems

1. Comment on the following statement: "Since we live in a changing world, past cost data are of little or no value to managers in planning their future course of action."

2. The manager of Department A asked for a "rough estimate" of our variable cost at our normal range of volume. The accountant used the high and low figures within the normal range in making his estimate. He submitted this estimate with the note, "If you need more precise data, let me know" to the department head. Do you approve or disapprove of this procedure? Why?

3. In the fall of 1980 the Nihton Motor Car Manufacturing Company made a detailed statistical study of its cost behavior. It was interested in determining its variable cost. In August 1981 the firm made plans for the 1982 model year, which runs from fall 1981 through summer 1982. The managers were about to use the 1980 data when it was suggested that some changes might have occurred in the interim. Assuming that each set of the changes listed below reflects the *only* changes that occurred, discuss the appropriateness of using 1980 data for estimating the 1981–82 model year's variable costs. (Each part is independent of all other parts.)

   (a) The outer trim is being relocated, a new grill has been added, and the dashboard has been restyled.

   (b) The trunk and rear fender line have been altered to give it a curved instead of a flat look. Carpeting, formerly an option, has replaced the rubber floor mat on all models. New outside trim has replaced last year's.

   (c) While no changes have been made in the mechanical systems, the body is being entirely restyled to fit the new sporty image.

   (d) Nihton is adding a longer luxury sedan to the top of its line.

4. In measuring total food costs per meal, exclusive of any preparation costs, a study found the total cost to include a fixed component, that is, $TC = a + bm$, where m is the number of meals. Is a positive intercept reasonable here?

5. A recent study of Department A's costs found that the least squares fitted to the data exhibited a negative fixed cost. The department head has rejected the entire study. What is one likely cause of a negative intercept?

6. (a) Could the high–low method yield a negative fixed cost?

   (b) Could it yield a fixed component to total cost where none in fact exists?

7. Could the analysis of accounts, that is, the accounting method, result in a negative fixed cost?

8. What is the underlying principle or assumption of the engineering approach to cost estimation, and where is it likely to be used?

9. If a firm followed the engineering approach for making its cost estimates, how, if at all, would the accountant assist in the process?

10. Economists speak of *curvilinear* cost functions, while accountants usually speak of *linear* cost functions. How can this be reconciled?

11. What are the economic interpretations of the b coefficients from a multiple regression equation of cost estimates?

12. How would you make up a set of data that are completely consistent with the assumptions of statistical regression analysis?

13. (a) The regression program fits a line such that the sum of the squared errors, that is, $\Sigma (TC_{act} - TC_{est})^2$, is a minimum. What type of loss function relating losses to errors is implied by this criterion? Show as follows:

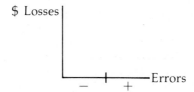

(b) Another possibility would be to fit a line such that the sum of the absolute deviation, $\Sigma|TC_{act} - TC_{est}|$, is minimized. What type of loss function is implied by this criterion?

14. Regarding the use of multiple regression analysis in the control of branch costs, Robert Jensen makes the following comment:[23] "Unfortunately, heteroscedasticity is more likely to exist among operating costs of branch operations than is homoscedasticity. *Therefore, the untested assumption of homoscedasticity in multiple regression application in cost control is untenable.*" [Italics in the original.] Define the condition of homoscedasticity. What are some of the operating conditions that vary from branch to branch that might lead to heteroscedasticity?

15. One of the assumptions of regression analysis that is not discussed in the chapter is that the disturbance terms are independent of (uncorrelated with) the explanatory variables. For example, large deviations between actual and estimated costs are not associated with large or small values of the output variables. Benston[24] gives an illustration of how this condition[25] might arise in cost analysis. Suppose a relationship between total overhead costs and output is being estimated. Included in overhead costs are charges for maintenance and repairs, which usually arise during idle or slack periods and are therefore negatively correlated with output. Discuss the consequences of such a condition.

16. ***Application of the Analysis of Accounts Method***
The head of the grinding department of Phoenix, Inc., has divided his overhead costs into those he considers fixed and those he feels are variable. The accounting

---

[23] Jensen, "Multiple Regression Model," p. 269.
[24] Benston, "Multiple Regression Analysis," p. 668.
[25] Actually, this condition reflects the fact that unspecified factors are correlated with the explanatory variables.

department requested this division, so that it could estimate the grinding department's cost equation. His separation is as follows:

Fixed Costs		Variable Costs	
Depreciation of machines	$1,000	Electricity	$1,555
Supervision	900	Machine supplies	425
Rent, taxes, etc.	400	Cleanup crew	1,380
Standby repairmen	700	Grinding wheels	630
	$3,000		$3,990

The costs are for the month of July 1981, when the department worked 1,900 machine hours.

(a) From these data, calculate the overhead cost function using the analysis of accounts (accounting method).
(b) What is your evaluation of this approach to cost estimation?

17. *Analysis of Accounts*
The seasoning department of Modern Antiques performs an artificial aging process on all its products. After being cut out and sanded, the unassembled parts are sent to this department on carts. They are then placed on a conveyor belt that carries them through a chemical shower. After the shower they are placed in trays and soaked in a water and chemical mixture for 24 hours. The final phase of the process requires their removal to the electric kiln for drying. The parts are then transferred to the assembly department.

The seasoning department has a work force of seven: six workers and the foreman. The latter is responsible not only for supervising the workers but also for setting the controls on the various machines. The workers move the

EXHIBIT 3-11———————————————————————

**Modern Antiques
Seasoning Department
Cost Report
June 1981**

Chemicals used by machines	$13,000
Depreciation on machines	500
Electricity	3,000
Floor space charge	450
Heating costs (exclusive of kiln)	380
Labor	3,000
Supervisor's salary	1,000
Supplies—machines	200
Supplies—workers' gloves, etc.	160
Total costs	$21,690

Total machine hours worked: 400

parts from machine to machine and handle the cleanup and very simple maintenance functions.

The department works as little as 50 percent of the time during the off season and some overtime during the peak season. Typically, it is working on parts about 80 percent of the time. The remaining time is spent keeping the equipment in good repair, since none of the crew is let go during the off-peak months.

The listing of departmental costs in Exhibit 3-11 deliberately omits any fixed and variable cost dichotomy. From these data, calculate the fixed costs and variable costs per machine hour using the analysis of accounts technique.

18. *Cost–Volume Data Analysis*

The Special Novelty Button Company prints political, advertising, and carnival buttons. They have limited data available and want you to use it as best you can to analyze their cost–volume behavior. It is agreed in advance that costs initially will be considered a function of sales dollars.

(a) Analyze the data to determine the firm's cost function.
(b) What alternative bases might be used instead of sales dollars? Why?

Period		Sales	Cost
Jan.–June	1974	$37,000	$33,600
July–Dec.	1974	65,000	33,000
Jan.–June	1975	32,000	29,600
July–Dec.	1975	31,000	28,800
Jan.–June	1976	35,000	32,000
July–Dec.	1976	45,000	25,000
Jan.–June	1977	29,000	27,200
July–Dec.	1977	39,000	35,200
Jan.–June	1978	42,000	37,600
July–Dec.	1978	60,000	31,000
Jan.–June	1979	36,000	32,800
July–Dec.	1979	40,000	36,000
Jan.–June	1980	37,000	33,600
July–Dec.	1980	48,000	26,200

19. *Basis of Activity*

The grinding department of Ajax, Inc., has just received a report on its cost behavior from one of the firm's management trainees. After several unsuccessful attempts, he fitted a least squares trend line to the department costs that had a very high r value. In this instance, it is a phenomenal $r = .98$. His formula is $25,000 + $10.50I$, where I is the number of indirect labor hours worked.

The department manager is quite concerned, since he had expected a cost formula related to machine hours, direct labor hours, or units of production. The indirect labor costs are primarily for cleanup crews and quality control personnel.

The manager has brought the report to you for your reaction. Prepare a report for him.

(a) Indicate whether this equation should be used to predict the costs for each period of next year. Either provide support for the department head's skeptical reaction or try to allay his fears.

(b) The department head has offered to supply you with any other information you might wish. The report contains only the equation and an explanation of how to use it. What other data might you request and why?

20. **Determination of Cost Behavior**

The quarterly financial data below were taken from the records of the Peerless Division of Quality Products, Inc. You have been asked to determine a linear cost equation for the overhead costs that can be used by the managers during the coming year to guide their activities and assist in decision making. Although they normally would require a more formal, statistical approach, they will accept other methodologies if you can justify their use.

	Quarter	Output	Overhead Costs
Year 1	1	9,000	$390,000
	2	11,000	410,000
	3	12,000	420,000
	4	10,000	410,000
Year 2	1	10,500	$410,000
	2	11,800	431,000
	3	14,000	434,000
	4	12,500	430,000
Year 3	1	13,000	$435,000
	2	15,000	440,000
	3	16,500	470,000
	4	14,500	450,000

21. **Graphic Analysis of Data**

Quality Products is also concerned with total cost behavior at its Peerless Division. It has made the following data available to you. Plot the data, then discuss how you might proceed to estimate the total cost equation. What additional data might you desire? What questions would you raise with management?

	Quarter	Output	Total Cost
Year 1	1	9,000	$ 775,000
	2	11,000	860,000
	3	12,000	924,000
	4	10,000	820,000
Year 2	1	10,500	$ 820,000
	2	11,800	945,000
	3	14,000	1,180,000
	4	12,500	1,020,000
Year 3	1	13,000	$1,100,000
	2	15,000	1,225,000
	3	16,500	1,320,000
	4	14,500	1,185,000

22. **Application of High–Low Method**

Period	Manufacturing Overhead	Units Produced
1st quarter, 1980	$1,000,000	14,500
2nd quarter, 1980	925,000	13,050
3rd quarter, 1980	800,000	12,000
4th quarter, 1980	750,000	11,500
1st quarter, 1981	900,000	12,900
2nd quarter, 1981	685,000	10,000
3rd quarter, 1981	840,000	11,800
4th quarter, 1981	970,000	14,200

Given the data above:
(a) Calculate the fixed and variable costs using the high–low method.
(b) If the data for the second quarter of 1981 had been $730,000 and 10,000 units, how would this change your estimates? Compare the two sets of estimates by plotting actual against predicted costs.

23. **Application of High–Low Method**
Everglo, Inc., is interested in estimating the cost of its new deluxe foam polishing cloths. The engineering and purchasing departments, as well as the accounting department, have been consulted. Together they have developed estimates for the cost of the foam rubber cloth and the chemicals needed to treat the cloth. The only remaining component of cost to be determined is the cost of impregnating the foam sheet with the chemicals. This, according to the engineering department, can be done on the existing equipment. It is anticipated that sufficient idle time will be available on the machines. The relevant data are as follows:

Month	Impregnating Department Costs	Square Feet of Material Treated
June 1980	$1,800	182,000
July 1980	1,200	125,000
Aug. 1980	1,600	167,000
Sept. 1980	1,760	150,000
Oct. 1980	1,000	100,000
Nov. 1980	2,050	187,000
Dec. 1980	1,520	175,000
Jan. 1981	1,040	116,000
Feb. 1981	1,400	160,000
March 1981	2,400	200,000
April 1981	1,280	148,000
May 1981	1,160	137,500

(a) Using the high–low technique, calculate the cost of impregnating each cloth. Assume that each cloth requires one square foot of material and that there is no waste in cutting the material into cloths.
(b) Evaluate the usefulness of the high–low method in this situation.

24. **Analysis of Regression Results**
Ralph's Sauna, Ltd., is a manufacturer of custom electronic instruments and analog computer components. All "jobs" are manufactured to customer specification; the firm is, in fact, a classic example of the job shop. The firm has become

interested in its cost-function and is in the process of attempting to estimate its manufacturing overhead costs. A single manufacturing department was focused on, and the following data were obtained (for the most recent 16 months):

Total Departmental Overhead	Total Direct Labor Hours	Material Units	Orders Processed
$25,835	878	970	88
27,451	1,088	934	100
28,611	1,281	667	108
32,361	1,340	1,243	110
28,967	1,090	964	90
24,817	1,067	903	67
29,795	1,188	876	88
26,135	928	820	28
31,361	1,319	984	19
26,006	790	933	90
27,812	934	966	93
28,612	871	940	87
22,992	781	518	81
31,836	1,236	1,017	236
26,252	902	881	92
26,977	1,140	751	140

A computer program has been used to analyze these data. The results are:

Dependent Variable	Independent Variable	Coefficient	Standard Error	t-Value	Adjusted r^2
1	2	8.50	1.93	4.4	
	3	6.95	2.21	3.2	
	4	6.59	7.19	.9	
	Intercept	12,052	2,286	5.3	
Std. error of estimate		1,281			.76
1	2	8.88	1.87	4.7	
	3	7.06	2.19	3.2	
	Intercept	12,190	2,267	5.4	
Std. error of estimate		1,273			.76
1	2	10.98	2.27	4.8	
	Intercept	16,310	2,421	6.7	
Std. error of estimate		1,646			.60
1	3	10.68	3.26	3.27	
	Intercept	18,277	2.98	6.14	
Std. error of estimate		2,027			.39

A correlation matrix shows:

	Overhead	Labor	Material	Orders
Overhead	1.0000			
Labor	.7913	1.0000		
Material	.6580	.3489	1.0000	
Orders	.3253	.2420	.1324	1.000

Required (a) (1) Develop, (2) present, and (3) defend what you think is the most "reasonable" estimate of the recently experienced manufacturing overhead cost function.

(b) Interpret the coefficients and independent variable(s) in your answer to (a).

(c) Do you think your answer to (a) would also provide a "useful" prediction of the manufacturing overhead that might be experienced next month?

(d) For what purposes do you think management might use your answer to (a)?

25. ***Analysis of Regression Results***

Ralph's Division (RD) is, for your convenience, a two-product, two-department firm. The two departments are code-named I and II, and the two products are designated A and B. Ralph's first problem is to determine a satisfactory production schedule; in thinking about this problem, he decides to analyze the firm's overhead structure. The accountant tells him that manufacturing overhead averages "about $9 per direct labor hour." The accountant also supplies Ralph with the following data for the 10 most recent quarters.

RD OVERHEAD AND VOLUME DATA

Period	DL Hours in Dept. I	Overhead in Dept. I	DL Hours in Dept. II	Overhead in Dept. II	Total DL Hours	Total Overhead
1	984	$12,600	1,841	$13,200	2,825	$25,800
2	967	11,500	2,143	17,000	3,110	28,500
3	710	9,200	1,980	15,500	2,690	24,700
4	1,040	11,900	1,610	11,200	2,650	23,100
5	1,015	11,650	1,485	10,600	2,500	23,250
6	940	11,200	2,160	17,300	3,100	28,500
7	950	11,000	1,600	11,100	2,550	22,100
8	640	8,400	2,100	16,900	2,740	25,300
9	680	8,600	1,940	15,400	2,620	24,000
10	1,018	11,980	1,567	11,200	2,585	23,180

A computer program has been used to analyze these data. The results are:

Dependent Variable	Independent Variable	Coefficient	Standard Error	t-Value	Adjusted r^2
6	1	8.51	1.40	6.1	
	3	10.09	.83	12.1	
	Intercept	−1,357	2,471	−.6	
	Std. error of estimate	538			.94
2	1	9.47	.85	11.1	
	Intercept	2,337	777	3.0	
	Std. error of estimate	392			.93
4	3	10.59	.49	21.6	
	Intercept	−5,579	915	−6.1	
	Std. error of estimate	382			.98

Dependent Variable	Independent Variable	Coefficient	Standard Error	t-Value	Adjusted r^2
6	5	10.03	.87	11.5	
	Intercept	−2,617	2,404	−1.1	
Std. error of estimate		565			.94

A correlation matrix shows:

Variable	1	2	3	4	5	6
1	1.00	0	0	0	0	0
2	.97	1.00	0	0	0	0
3	−.56	−.47	1.00	0	0	0
4	−.61	−.54	.99	1.00	0	0
5	.05	.13	.80	.76	1.00	0
6	−.06	.03	.85	.82	.97	1.00

Required (a) After surveying these results, Ralph picks the model relating total manufacturing overhead to total direct labor hours. State (indicating the intercept and slope values and the independent variable) the model Ralph is proposing to use and give a brief interpretation of the coefficients.

(b) Ralph calls an accounting friend to show him the model. Regardless of your answer to (a), suppose Ralph submits a model that has a negative intercept. The friend inquires about the negative intercept, and Ralph is subsequently embarrassed when he is informed by technical personnel that actual manufacturing cost for any quarter with zero production will be approximately $4,000. How do you reconcile (or compare) the $4,000 datum with the negative regression intercept?

(c) Suppose Ralph now obtains relevant data and runs a regression that relates the cost of direct material in A to units of product A. The results are

$$(\widehat{DM\ Cost})_A = -407.8 + 3.14A$$
$$(98.2)\quad(1.01)\qquad r^2 = .83$$

Provide Ralph with a brief interpretation of the negative intercept.

26. **Statistical Issues in Cost Estimation**
(a) The data below reflect a specific violation of an assumption of regression, using the equation:

$$TC_{est} = a + b_1x_1 + b_2x_2$$

x_1	x_2	Costs
10	13	5,000
20	25	10,500
30	40	14,800
40	52	21,000
50	65	24,750
60	75	30,100
70	90	36,000
80	105	41,650

(1) What is the violation?

(2) What is the main effect of this violation in terms of the estimation equation and its coefficients?

(3) Would you expect this violation to occur often in cost estimation using a model with two or more independent variables? Explain.

(b) **Cost Stickiness**

How would cost stickiness show up in a typical plot of the residuals? Explain, indicating one method for handling this problem.

(c) **Learning Curve**

How would a learning curve be revealed in a typical plot of the residuals? Explain.

(d) **Correct Form of the Model**

Assume you have run a regression and obtained the following estimate for total costs as a function of x (this is an estimate and not based on an actual regression):

$$\widehat{TC}_{reg} = -136 + 100x$$

The actual cost observations used to obtain this estimate were as follows:

Output, x	TC_{act}
3	337
4	354
5	375
6	406
7	453
8	522
9	619
10	750
11	920
12	1,138
13	1,407

Using the high–low method of cost estimation, you would obtain the following estimate:

$$\hat{TC}_{HL} = 16 + 107x$$

(1) Plot the residuals from the regression equation and indicate what statistical violation would be observed.

(2) What is the likely source of the violation? (This is especially obvious if we worked with the high–low estimates.)

(3) What adjustment would you make either to the model or to the data (or both) to alleviate this problem?

27. **Multicollinearity**

The data in Exhibit 3-12 have been given to you for analysis. They relate to the average costs observed for two different output measures for the past operating periods.

EXHIBIT 3-12

Output Measures		Total Overhead Costs					
x_1	x_2	C	$x_1 C$	$x_2 C$	$x_1 x_2$	x_1^2	x_2^2
1.0	1.5	1,500	1,500	2,250	1.5	1.0	2.25
2.0	3.1	1,900	3,800	5,890	6.2	4.0	9.61
3.0	4.5	2,200	6,600	9,900	13.5	9.0	20.25
4.0	6.2	2,500	10,000	15,500	24.8	16.0	38.44
5.0	7.7	2,800	14,000	21,560	38.5	25.0	59.29
6.0	9.0	3,500	21,000	31,500	54.0	36.0	81.00
21.0	32.0	14,400	56,900	86,600	138.5	91.0	210.84

There are three possible equations you could use to predict future overhead costs:

$$C = a + b_1 x_1 \qquad [3\text{-}10]$$
$$C = a + b_2 x_2 \qquad [3\text{-}11]$$
$$C = a + b_1 x_1 + b_2 x_2 \qquad [3\text{-}12]$$

(a) Calculate the parameter values for each equation.

(b) Discuss the criteria that might be used to choose among these three estimates.

(c) What are some potential problems in using Equation [3-11]? Are any of these evident in the data?

28. **Application of Statistical Regression**

The following is based on an actual study by R. Kaplan[26] in which he estimated nursing hours of various types. These hours were required at various nursing stations and were based on data from a large hospital in the Pittsburgh area. Initially, Kaplan used the following model:

$$y_{tj} = a_{0k} + a_{1k} x_{tjk} + e_{tjk}$$

[26] Kaplan, "Management Accounting in Hospitals."

where x_{tjk} = nursing hours of type k worked in month t at station j
    $k = 1$; registered nurses
    $k = 2$; licensed practical nurses
    $k = 3$; aides and orderlies
    $k = 4$; *total* nursing hours
    y_{tj} = patient days during month t at station j
      $t = 1$ represents July 1969; $t = 24$ represents June 1971
      $j = 1, \ldots 20$

The results were summarized as follows for $k = 1$:

r^2	$<.05$	$.05-.15$	$.20-.30$	$>.30$
Number	14	2	2	2

Durbin–Watson	$0-.5$	$.5-1.0$	$1.0-1.5$
Number	8	7	5

(a) Evaluate these results in terms of the statistics reported. The critical values for Durbin–Watson are 1.16 (positive autocorrelation) and 2.67 (for negative autocorrelation) at a 95 percent confidence level.

(b) Kaplan examined the residuals (e_{tjk}) and noted a pattern of mostly negative for $t = 1, \ldots 12$ and mostly positive for $t = 13, \ldots 24$. That is, the *regression* estimates *over*estimated y_{tj1} during the first year and *under*estimated y_{tj1} during the second.

   (1) What are some possible reasons for this?

   (2) In the absence of any specific information, what could be done to alleviate this problem? (The use of a dummy variable is one.)

(c) Kaplan inserted a dummy variable J_{tj} which took on the value of 0 for $t = 1, \ldots 12$ and 1 for $t = 13, \ldots 24$. The results were:

r^2	$0-.2$	$.2-.4$	$.4-.6$	$.6-.8$	$.8-1.0$
Number	2	5	5	7	1

Durbin–Watson	$.6-1.0$	$1.0-1.25$	$1.25-1.5$	$1.5-1.75$	$1.75-2.0$
Number	6	3	6	2	3

Compare these results to the previous ones, assuming the critical values for Durbin–Watson are 1.08 and 2.57.

(d) Kaplan used patient days as the activity variable. Indicate some problems in using this single activity variable for all stations, for all t, and for all k.

(e) In examining the results in (c), Kaplan noted some unusual jumps during the months of April and May. These were the months during which there is an upsurge in student nurse hirings. How would you adjust for this effect?

29. **Learning curves**

The average number of minutes required to assemble trivets is predictable based upon an 80 percent learning curve. That is, whenever cumulative production doubles, cumulative average time per unit becomes 80 percent of what it was at the previous doubling point. The trivets are produced in lots of 300 units, and 60 minutes of labor are required to assemble the first lot.

Using the concept of the learning curve and the letters listed below, select the best answer for each of questions (1) through (5).

Let TT = total time
MT = marginal time for the xth lot
M = marginal time for the first lot
x = lots produced
b = exponent expressing the improvement;
b has the range $0 \leq b < 1$

(1) A normal graph (that is, not a log or log-log graph) of average minutes per lot of production, where cumulative lots are represented by the x axis and average minutes per lot are represented by the y axis, would produce a

   a. linear function sloping downward to the right.
   b. linear function sloping upward to the right.
   c. curvilinear function sloping upward to the right at an increasing rate.
   d. curvilinear function sloping downward to the right at a decreasing rate.

(2) A log-log graph of average minutes per lot of production, where cumulative lots are represented by the x axis and average minutes per lot are represented by the y axis, would produce a

   a. linear function sloping downward to the right.
   b. linear function sloping upward to the right.
   c. curvilinear function sloping upward to the right at a decreasing rate.
   d. curvilinear function sloping downward to the right at a decreasing rate.

(3) The average number of minutes required per lot to complete four lots is approximately

   a. 60.0.
   b. 48.5.
   c. 38.4.
   d. 30.7.

(4) Average time to produce x lots of trivets could be expressed as

    a. Mx^{b+1}
    b. Mx^{-b}
    c. MT^{b+1}
    d. Mx^{b-1}

(5) Assuming that $b = -0.322$, the average number of minutes required to produce x lots of trivets could be expressed as

    a. $40.08x^{0.678}$
    b. $40.08x$
    c. $60x^{-0.322}$
    d. $60x^{1.322}$

[AICPA adapted]

30. **The Smyth Corporation: Learning Curves** [27]
The Smyth Corporation has just completed the assembly of the 50th unit of a complex new guidance system for missiles. The company has been invited to bid on a new order of 100 additional units. Management has observed that the cost of assembly seems to be declining with each unit completed. After completing 10 units, the average cost per unit was $953, and after completing another 40 units, the average cost per unit over the cumulative total of 50 units was $610 per unit. What will be the cost of assembling 100 additional units? (*Hint:* The general form of the learning curve function is $y = ax^{-l}$, where y is the average cost per unit for x cumulative units, x is the cumulative units produced, a is the cost of the first unit, and l is the improvement factor.)

31. **Assumptions of Statistical Regression**
Exhibit 3-13 shows the cumulative volume of activity and cumulative labor costs for a particular product.
    When we fit a line to these data, the residuals—that is, $TC_{act} - TC_{est}$—behave as shown in Figure 3-11, where the first residual plotted is the residual of the first observation made, the second residual is the residual of the second observation made, and so on.

(a) State the normal assumptions underlying the use of a regression model for cost estimation.
(b) From your analysis of the residuals, which of the assumptions appears to be violated? State your reasons.
(c) What particular problem, resulting from applying linear regression to cost accounting data, does your analysis suggest?
(d) What type of algebraic term and/or transformation would you incorporate

---

[27] Based on a problem from C.A. Theodore, *Applied Mathematics: An Introduction*. Homewood, Ill.: Irwin, 1965, p. 272.

EXHIBIT 3-13_____

Cumulative Volume of Activity	Cumulative Costs	Cumulative Volume of Activity	Cumulative Costs
78	63	434	211
103	78	454	219
126	93	488	231
163	103	522	238
188	119	577	252
201	120	599	262
215	135	626	276
239	137	664	284
304	167	684	288
337	169	731	299
348	180	766	311
400	198	803	326

FIGURE 3-11 _____

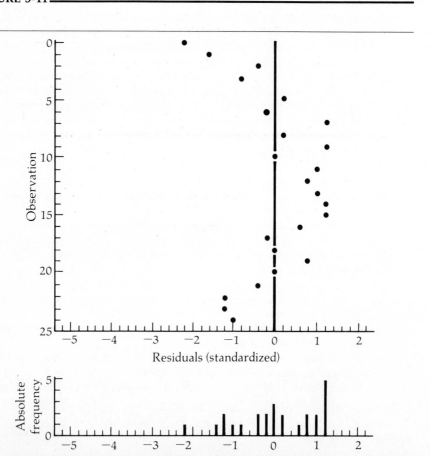

in the regression equation to incorporate the problem suggested by the residual plots?

*32. **Inflation and Statistical Regression Assumptions**
Ralph's Trap is a regression problem. Ralph manages a firm in which the quarterly overhead is

$$\text{Overhead} = \$40,000 + \$10\text{DLH} + \epsilon$$

where DLH is direct labor hours and ϵ is a normally distributed error term with a zero mean and a $6,000 standard deviation.

This model is stated in *real* terms. During the most recent eight quarters the inflation rate has been 6 percent per quarter. Actual data are displayed below.

Period (P)	Actual Overhead (OVHD)	DL Hours (DLH)	DL Dollars (DL$)	Deflated Overhead in Period 1 $ (OVHD/1)
1	108,154	5,500	55,000	108,154
2	97,226	5,500	58,300	91,694
3	90,100	4,000	44,800	80,482
4	95,090	4,700	55,930	79,903
5	123,166	5,300	66,780	97,743
6	125,818	5,700	76,380	93,857
7	125,893	5,400	76,680	88,699
8	156,241	5,900	88,500	103,927

Ralph gives these data to a local consultant to find the overhead curve. The consultant runs the following regressions. (Note that all five variables are used.)

CORRELATION MATRIX

	P	OVHD	DLH	DL$	OVDH/P
P	1.00				
OVHD	.82	1.00			
DLH	.38	.74	1.00		
DL$	.87	.95	.78	1.00	
OVHD/1	.04	.60	.77	.44	1.00

MODEL 1

$$\text{OVHD} = -\$23,270 + 26.39 \text{ DLH}$$
$$(52,162) \qquad (9.88)$$
$$-.4 \qquad\qquad 2.7 \qquad\qquad r^2 = .47$$

MODEL 2

$$\text{OVHD} = -\$3,849 + 5,623P + 17.86\text{DLH}$$
$$(29,854) \quad (1,509) \qquad (6.0)$$
$$-.1 \qquad\quad 3.7 \qquad\quad 3.0 \qquad r^2 = .83$$

MODEL 3
$$\text{OVHD} = \underset{\substack{(13,143)\\1.6}}{20,815} + \underset{\substack{(.20)\\7.3}}{1.45\text{DL\$}} \qquad r^2 = .88$$

MODEL 4
$$\text{OVHD}/1 = \underset{\substack{(22,919)\\1.2}}{26,651} + \underset{\substack{(4.34)\\2.9}}{12.65\text{DLH}} \qquad r^2 = .52$$

Required (a) Carefully explain each of the regressions.

(b) Which regression would you recommend for cost estimation purposes? Why?

4
Cost–Volume–Profit Analyses

T he purpose of this chapter is to focus on the firm's short-run decisions and their associated information problem. These decisions are typically referred to as "cost–volume–profit" (CVP) decisions, because the focal point in the analysis is usually some alteration in volume and its cost and profit consequences.

A common assumption in the various types of CVP analyses is that the firm (department, division, or whatever decision unit is involved) commits itself to holding various forms of capacity for at least another operating period. Capacity may be held in the form of plants, buildings, equipment, and managerial and other skilled labor (both manufacturing and nonmanufacturing). Inventories that will be carried over from one period to another may also be classified as a capacity.

The commitment to hold capacities results in the incurrence of fixed capacity costs. These costs may be current cash outlays or allocations of prior period outlays. Examples of the former are salaries for managerial and other skilled personnel, taxes and insurance on properties owned (plant, buildings, equipment, and inventories), rentals or lease payments on fixed contracts, and interest and principal payments on existing debts, assuming that the debts will be kept outstanding to finance activities of the decision unit. Examples of fixed costs that are allocations of prior period outlays are depreciation on fixed tangible assets and allocations of patent costs and other intangible assets (such as advertising and research). Very often, fixed costs represented by cash outlays are quite significant in comparison with the noncash fixed costs, and this is now recognized to be an important factor in CVP analyses under uncertainty.

Moreover, it is important to recognize at the outset that this interpretation of the class of decision problems and associated cost and revenue structures requires a fair degree of delicacy. Basically, the decision problem at hand involves alterations that are in some sense "close" to what the firm is presently doing. The product mix may be altered, a product line may be dropped, a subcontracted component may be internally manufactured. But in each case the overall level of operations is not dramatically altered. This allows us to approximate the cost and revenue structures with reasonably accurate but easy to use (usually linear) cost and revenue functions. Thus, what is meant by a fixed cost here must be interpreted in terms of this approximation of the firm's cost function in the neighborhood of its current level of activity.

The chapter is organized as follows. We begin with a brief review of the certainty-assuming economic model of a single-product firm. This familiar model is then approximated with linear cost and revenue functions. From this, we can approximately analyze small changes in the firm's output and factor decisions, and we can rationalize the accountant's break-even model. We then expand on this theme by focusing on three related, short-run decision problems.

Finally, two important assumptions are analyzed. One is that a single output is involved. Relaxing this assumption extends our analysis to the problem of allocating a set of capacities to alternative mixes of outputs. The other assumption is the formal introduction of uncertainty.

The Short-Run (Deterministic) Economic Model

Figure 4-1 displays a numerical example of the nonlinear revenue and nonlinear cost curves typically assumed in the economist's model of a short-run output problem. In this particular example, the revenue curve is nonlinear under the assumption that the decision unit sells its output in an imperfect market wherein additional units of output can be sold only as the output's price is reduced. The cost function is nonlinear to reflect increased economies of scale, up to a point, followed by diseconomies. Note that a single period, with no inventories (either beginning or ending), is being assumed here.

It may be helpful to review some terminology. The firm's (economic) marginal cost is the derivative of TC(x) with respect to x:

$$\frac{d\,TC(x)}{dx} = MC(x) = 6x^2 - 40x + 100$$

The (economic) fixed cost is the cost at $x = 0$:

$$TC(x = 0) = 200$$

And the (economic) variable cost is $TC(x) - TC(0)$. Similarly, the (economic) marginal revenue is the derivative of $TR(x)$ with respect to x:

$$\frac{d\,TR(x)}{dx} = MR(x) = 200 - 30x$$

Suppose the firm knows the illustrated revenue and cost functions and seeks the output quantity that will produce maximal profit. We readily locate this quantity by examining the firm's profit function of $\pi(x) = TR(x) - TC(x)$:

$$\pi(x) = (200x - 15x^2) - (2x^3 - 20x^2 + 100x + 200)$$

Taking the derivative, $d\pi(x)/dx$, and setting it equal to zero provides the familiar "marginal revenue equals marginal cost" rule:

$$\frac{d\pi(x)}{dx} = 0 = (200 - 30x) - (6x^2 - 40x + 100)$$

or

$$MR(x) = 200 - 30x = MC(x) = 6x^2 - 40x + 100$$

This provides a solution of $x^* = 5$, assuming $x \geq 0$. (You should check second-order conditions to ensure that a maximum and not a minimum has been located by this procedure.) The firm will experience a revenue of $TR(5) = \$625$, a cost of $TC(5) = \$450$, and a maximal profit of $\pi(5) = \$175$.

This model for the short-run capacity allocation problem is deterministic in the sense that the decision maker is assumed to possess complete knowledge of the revenue and cost functions over the entire range of feasible outputs. Unfortunately, such knowledge is not generally available for an operating unit, either because there are no opportunities to obtain sample evidence on revenue and cost functions over all ranges of output or because it is simply too costly to do so. For example, decision units rarely operate at a zero level of capacity; therefore, knowledge of what the level of fixed (capacity) costs would be at that level of output can only be estimated. Similarly, it is costly to run tests to determine maximum sales levels for different prices. Recall from our discussion in Chapter 3 the difficulty of obtaining a set of cost observations over anything beyond a restricted range. Indeed, these are often insufficient even to determine whether the cost function is linear or nonlinear. The typical assumption is that decision units make some estimate of a probable range of output levels for a restricted set of possible prices—for example, based upon what occurred in the most recent past period, adjusted for anticipated changes in economic factors. Then they estimate a cost function for that relevant range of possible output levels. This permits decision units to

FIGURE 4-1 _____

Nonlinear revenue and cost curves.

Revenue function: $TR(x) = 200x - 15x^2$
Cost function: $TC(x) = 2x^3 - 20x^2 + 100x + 200$

x	TR(x)	TC(x)	$\pi(x) = TR(x) - TC(x)$
0	$ 0	$ 200	−$200
1	185	282	−97
2	340	336	4
3	465	374	91
4	560	408	152
5	625	450	175
6	660	512	148
7	665	606	59
8	640	744	−104
9	585	938	−353
10	500	1,200	−700

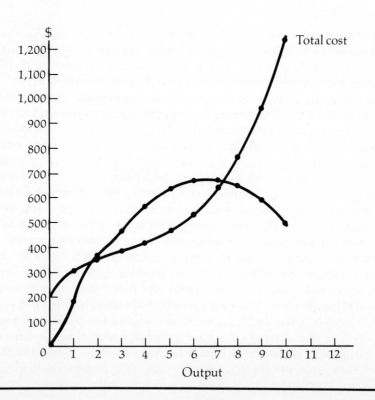

estimate profits at different outputs, given some estimate of the revenue and cost functions appropriate for the range of output levels most likely to occur in the next operating period. The revenue and cost functions are generally assumed to be linear, but only within restricted ranges of operations.

The Short-Run (Deterministic) Accounting Model

Expansion on this important theme will allow us to develop and rationalize the simplified accounting counterpart to this economic analysis. Suppose the firm tentatively selects an output level of 5 units (by coincidence the optimal output just determined). The firm expects a total revenue of $625, or average revenue of $125 per unit. It also anticipates a total cost of $450, implying an average cost of $90 per unit.

Now focus more closely on the cost. Some estimate of variability is also desirable; suppose for the sake of illustration that the firm uses

$$TC \cong 350 + 20x$$

as graphed in Figure 4-2.

Precisely how this approximation is developed is not important at this juncture. It might represent an entirely subjective estimate. Alternatively, the account classification method might have been employed, using an output of $x = 5$, and thus an estimated total variable cost of $100, so that $TC(5) = 350 + 20(5) = 450. The important question is one of interpretation. We have specified an approximate cost curve of

$$TC \cong F + vx$$
$$= \$350 + \$20x$$

Quite literally, F, the fixed cost, is the intercept of the approximation, and v, the variable cost, is the slope of the approximation. No other significance is warranted or contemplated. Moreover, there is no guarantee that this approximation is accurate or useful for any level of output outside of the contemplated neighborhood of somewhere close to $x = 5$ (again, see Figure 4-2).

If we combine the two linear approximations, we obtain the so-called break-even model depicted in Figure 4-3(a) and (b). Notice, in particular, that the revenue line displays a slope of $125/unit with a zero intercept, while the cost line displays a slope of $20/unit with a nonzero intercept. Moreover, by construction, the profit at 5 units is $175.

Several comments are in order. First and foremost, this should be interpreted as a simplified representation of a commitment to produce and sell,

FIGURE 4-2

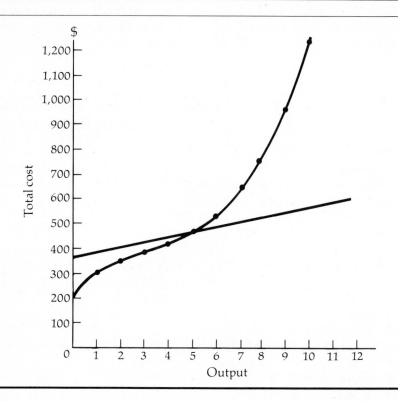

at an average price per unit *(p)* of $125, an output of 5 units. And in the neighborhood of 5 units we approximate the total cost with a fixed component of $350 and a variable component of $20 per unit. At no point did we suggest or even contemplate production of, say, 10 units at a total revenue of ($125)(10) = $1,250 and a total cost of $350 + ($20)(10) = $550. This is surely inconsistent with the firm's revenue and cost structure. Rather, we offer the linear model as an apparently useful approximation to the firm's cost and revenue structure *in the neighborhood* of a particular level of output. For a small change, we model revenue as increasing at the rate of $125 per unit and cost as increasing at the rate of $20 per unit. We refer to the intercept of the cost approximation as the fixed cost and the slope as the variable cost per unit throughout the text. *It is imperative that you carry along this qualifying interpretation.*

Second, taken in literal terms, we have a model with the following structure:

$$TR = px$$
$$TC = F + vx$$

FIGURE 4-3

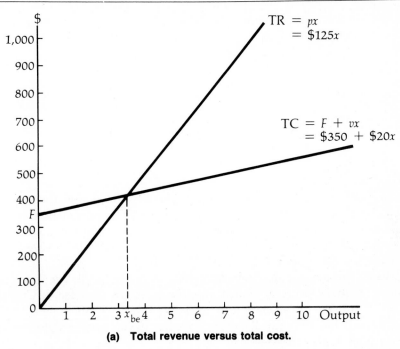

(a) Total revenue versus total cost.

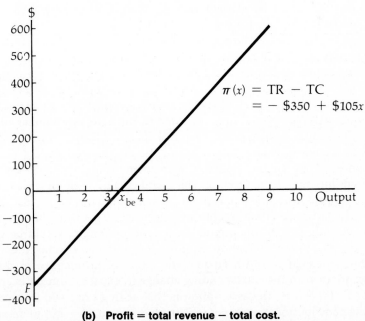

(b) Profit = total revenue − total cost.

(though there is no reason why the TR approximation should not also have a nonzero intercept term, called fixed revenue). About the only question one could ask of such a stark model is the break-even point, or the point at which TR and TC are equal:

$$TR = TC$$
$$px = F + vx$$
$$(p - v)x = F$$

or

$$x_{be} = \frac{F}{(p - v)}$$

The firm will break even when its output equals its fixed cost (the intercept in its linear cost approximation) divided by its contribution margin of price less variable cost (the slope of the TR approximation less the slope of the TC approximation). For our numerical example, we have a break-even point of $350/(125 - 20) = 350/105 = 3.33$.

Third, the linear approximation depicted in the break-even model is actually a central feature of control reporting. As we shall see in Chapters 5, 6, and 7, a major consideration in assessing a decision unit's performance is how well it has performed relative to what it was predicted to perform using such an approximation.

Finally, it should be evident that changes proposed by management may be usefully displayed with this model. These changes might include an increase or decrease in the selling price per unit or a substitution of one factor for another that increases the intercept and lowers the slope of the linear cost approximation. In addition to changing the dollar figures of the variables involved, changes in prices and fixed expenditures can affect expected units of output and sales. To illustrate, management might contemplate increasing advertising expenditures in order to increase the number of units sold at a particular selling price. The anticipated effect on profit could be graphed as shown in Figure 4-4(a), where the dashed line reflects the effect of the contemplated action. Similarly, management might wish to assess the effect of adding more labor (another shift) and cutting back on leased capacities, which would lower the intercept but increase the slope of the cost approximation. The latter would be graphed as a decrease in the contribution margin per unit, because $(p - v)$, the original contribution margin, would be greater than $(p - v')$, the new contribution margin. The combined effect of this change is illustrated in Figure 4-4(b). Finally, the effect of an increase or decrease in selling prices with the corresponding change in expected output is graphed in Figure 4-4(c). There, the assumption is that selling price will be increased, raising the contribution margin per unit from $(p - v)$ to $(p' - v)$, but decreasing expected units of output from x to x'.

————————————FIGURE 4-4

Effect of various changes in the cost structure on the break-even point.

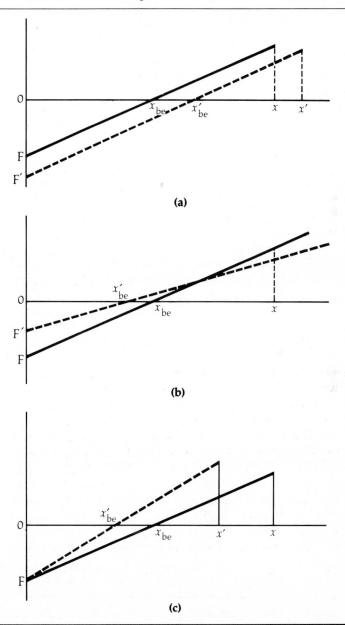

(a)

(b)

(c)

Extension to the Multiproduct Firm

It is obvious that break-even analysis is a rather crude attempt to give some structure to the effect of changing output levels and contribution margins on profit, assuming some fixed level of capacity. Problems of nonlinearity, discontinuities in the cost curve, and uncertainty in parameter estimates are all waved away. The crudeness is even more apparent when we consider that most firms produce more than one product or service, so that any revenue or cost curve depicted for such a firm would be a weighted average of prices and variable costs for all output types.

A ready example is provided by discussions of what is required to achieve profitability in the airline industry. It is common to express this requirement in terms of the percentage of seating capacity that must be sold *on average* for the airline to break even or achieve a certain level of profit. Yet, we know that the average variable cost per passenger mile for a modern, "wide-body" aircraft is not the same as the average cost for smaller and older types of aircraft, nor are their fixed costs the same. Similarly, the mix of prices for tickets sold on each aircraft will also vary, being composed of first class, coach, and discount fares, and this mix could differ across different routes. Still, on a year-to-year basis it may (and apparently does) prove useful for top management to initially ignore these variations and merely compare averages over time and averages across major routes. The alternative is to explicitly model the multiproduct structure, a topic discussed later in this chapter.

REVIEW PROBLEMS 1, 2, and 3

1. Figure 4-5 represents a cost–volume–profit graph, as depicted earlier in Figure 4-3(b). Complete the following statements:

   (a) Line BB' represents _____.
   (b) The horizontal axis AE represents _____, and the vertical axis AF represents _____.

FIGURE 4-5

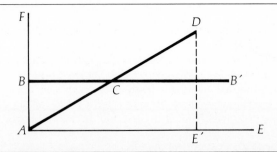

    (c)   Point C represents _____.
    (d)   The distance DE' divided by the distance AE' is _____.

2.   *Calculation of Break-Even Points*
    The NMN Company produces a single product for distribution to
    wholesalers. The product has a list price of $10 per unit. Variable
    costs of production are $5 per unit, and fixed costs of production
    are $50,000 per year. The distribution of the product results in addi-
    tional costs of $0.90 per unit (variable) and $11,500 per year (fixed).

    (a)   What is the expected break-even point?
    (b)   Suppose the NMN Company predicts sales of $200,000 for the
          year. What is the expected profit (assuming sales and production
          are equal)?
    (c)   While NMN does not set prices for its output, the company
          does have some idea about the effects on demand of changes
          in price, advertising, competitors' actions, and so on. Assume
          that a 5 percent decrease in price will increase total volume by
          15 percent (in units), that an additional expenditure of $7,500
          on advertising will further increase total volume by 5 percent,
          but that the increased production will result in an increase in
          variable costs of production by $.10 per unit in excess of 21,000
          units. Maximum practical capacity is 25,000 units. What effect
          will these changes have on net profit?
    (d)   Suppose, instead, that NMN can also expand its sales by 20
          percent (in volume) by offering its wholesalers a rebate of 1
          percent on all the units they purchase and an advertising allow-
          ance of $20,000. Is this a better alternative than (c)?

    Instead of making predictions about the volume expected, management
    has asked you to determine the following:
    (e)   At what volume of output would the contemplated changes in
          (c) yield the same profit as in (b)?
    (f)   At what volume of output would the contemplated changes in
          (d) yield the same profit as in (b)?

3.[1] In its October 31, 1969, issue, *Time* commented on American Motors'
    acquisition of the Jeep Division. Part of the story was devoted to
    the recollection of how, when new management took over in 1967,
    "AMC's future seemed so shaky that its creditors, a consortium of
    24 banks headed by Chase Manhattan, examined the books every
    ten days. The new chiefs trimmed costs by $20 million annually to
    cut the break-even point [from 350,000] to 250,000 cars a year."

---

[1] Prepared by David·O. Green.

Required (a) From this fragmentary report, and assuming that the "cost trimming" was with fixed costs exclusively, indicate

  (1) the per-unit contribution
  (2) total fixed costs for the year
  (3) the loss that would have occurred had the old pattern of costs been continued and unit sales were 300,000
  (4) the expected profit if 400,000 units will be sold next year

(b) Prepare a list of the three most important assumptions you have employed in reaching your answers to (a).

Three Analogous CVP Decisions

Our discussion to this point has dealt with the traditional topic of cost–volume–profit analysis, which we interpret as a highly simplified but apparently useful representation of cost and revenue consequences of small changes in operating decisions. We stress the approximating nature of the representation.

This type of analysis is important, because it is a building block in more sophisticated analyses,[2] as well as being directly applicable to any decision problem involving the utilization of fixed capacities. In subsequent chapters, we will see how precisely the same idea is used to estimate cost and revenue consequences of various proposals to alter fixed facilities or inventory policies. And beyond that we will see the same approximations used in performance evaluation. In the present section we address three analogous CVP decision problems and their associated information problems.

At this point, it will be useful to distinguish between two extreme types of productive processes: job-order and continuous. Job-order processing is characterized by a diversity of orders that can be worked on with the same set of productive capacities. Each order is somewhat different from any other, and the basic decision unit (therefore the costing unit) is the individual job or specific lot of production. Some common types of job-order firms are furniture manufacturing, construction, heavy machinery production, machinery repair, printing, public accounting, advertising, and shipbuilding. In each, the nature of the inputs will vary according to the specific kind of job being produced.

In contrast, the output of a continuous processing facility is considered homogeneous. There are no substantive economic differences among individual units. As a result, fewer products and processing technologies are typically involved. Three important types of continuous processing firms are chemical

---

[2] Lest the sceptic feel that linear approximation is useless, two points should be considered. Quite clearly, a natural extension is the use of nonlinear (and presumably more accurate) approximations. Moreover, the formal theory of optimization can be developed from this perspective.

plants, oil refineries, and automobile manufacturers. We may also consider banks, insurance companies, and laboratories as continuous processing firms, given a specific product line.

In many respects, the previous section on CVP analysis is more descriptive of its use in continuous processing than in job-order firms. Recall that we assumed relatively constant contribution margins as output was continuously varied in a specific limited range. This implies a relatively homogeneous output. In contrast, a job-order firm may be working on a completely diversified set of orders, with each order constituting a separate product. For example, it is not uncommon for an airframe manufacturer to speak in terms of a break-even point for each type of aircraft it produces. Then the job, rather than the process, becomes the costing unit.

Adding or Dropping a Product

Consider, now, a classic question of whether an identified product should be added or dropped. If uncertainty is not an issue, we could state a simple rule: The decision unit will add (drop) a product if the incremental revenues from the product are greater (less) than the incremental costs of producing and distributing the product. In general, the incremental costs consist of the incremental cash outlay costs plus the opportunity costs of using the given capacities to produce the product. The opportunity costs will be positive if the capacities could be diverted from the product in question and used to produce another product.

The question of whether to add a product under conditions of fixed capacity generally arises in job-shop operations, where a decision to bid on a new order constitutes a decision to add a new product (the order). The capacity needed to work on the new order is available to the decision unit, and the question is whether to devote the capacity to the new order, to devote it to other products (other orders), or to let it remain idle.

The decision of whether to add a new product in a continuous processing operation is less common, because the capacity needed to produce the new product may have to be acquired through additional investments. If that is the case, the analysis will likely rely on capital budgeting techniques, such as a discounting model, to resolve the decision (see Chapter 14). The same rule would hold if the decision to drop a product would result in the liquidation of long-lived capacities, such as the sale of fixed assets. Liquidation of long-lived capacities reduces cash flows—revenues and cash costs—of time periods beyond the immediate operating period.[3] In short, the decision to add or drop a product can be treated as a short-run, cost–volume–profit decision only if the level of capacities held does not vary with the decision.

---

[3] The decision by a railroad to liquidate passenger rail service is the type of decision that goes beyond the immediate operating period, because the railroad contemplates a liquidation of certain fixed assets in the process (such as rail cars and stations).

With these admonitions before us, suppose that a firm is considering whether to accept or to reject an offer from a customer for a one-time production of a special project. The offered price is $50,000. Analysis indicates that the product will not displace any capacity currently in use. No opportunity costs are involved, and the only question is whether incremental labor, material, and overhead costs are less than the offered price of $50,000.

To sort this out, the firm will most likely work with an approximation to its cost curve in the neighborhood of the current production level. Suppose it is estimated that production of the special project will require the purchase of material costing $18,000 and that labor requirements will be $10,000. Overhead is known to vary with direct labor dollars at a rate of $2 of overhead per direct labor dollar. No changes in the intercept or slope of the overhead approximation are anticipated if the offer is accepted. We therefore arrive at the following summary analysis:

Incremental revenue			
(Selling price)	=		$50,000
Incremental material cost	=	$18,000	
Incremental labor cost	=	10,000	
Incremental overhead cost	=	20,000	
Total incremental cost	=		48,000
Incremental profit	=		$ 2,000

which indicates the offer should be accepted.

Our conventional analysis becomes somewhat more complicated if we admit to an opportunity cost. Suppose processing capacity is in short supply and acceptance of this offer will necessitate reducing the production of another product. Assume the incremental profit on the displaced product is $5,000. Then, *if* the offer is accepted, the firm will gain $2,000 in direct incremental profit, but will forego $5,000 in incremental profit on the displaced product. Thus, the net gain is −$3,000. We readily interpret this as an incremental analysis in which an opportunity cost is associated with the use of fixed facilities:

Incremental revenue	=		$50,000
Incremental material cost	=	$18,000	
Incremental labor cost	=	10,000	
Incremental overhead cost	=	20,000	
Opportunity cost of fixed facilities	=	5,000	
Total incremental cost	=		$53,000
Incremental profit	=		−$ 3,000

Finally, suppose uncertainty is present. The firm may not know its material, labor, or overhead costs with certainty, or it may not know the profitability of a displaced product or opportunity. Uncertainty complicates the analysis in two important respects: Additional information may be quite valuable, and aversion to risk may be an important consideration in the decision. Risk aversion complicates the analysis, because the riskiness of the decision must now be assessed. And this may be more involved than just assessing possible incremental profit consequences, probabilities, and so on. For example, the proposed product may have important diversification qualities, such as its demand may vary inversely with the demand of other products. These considerations take us away from incremental analysis and call for a simultaneous analysis of the entire set of short-run decisions.

Information considerations, though, arise irrespective of the firm's attitude toward risk. Returning to our original example in which no opportunity cost is present, suppose the material and overhead cost estimates are fairly reliable, but the labor cost is open to question. Management decides to regard the material and overhead costs as certain ($18,000 for the former and a slope of $2 overhead per direct labor dollar for the latter). Engineers agree that the labor cost will be somewhere between $8,000 and $12,000. For the sake of analysis, suppose we focus on three discrete possibilities of $8,000, $10,000, and $12,000. Assume that the three events are equally likely and that the firm analyzes such small additions to its product line on an expected incremental profit or contribution basis. The analysis would then be done in the following fashion:

	Labor Cost of $8,000	Labor Cost of $10,000	Labor Cost of $12,000
Selling price	$50,000	$50,000	$50,000
Incremental material cost	$18,000	$18,000	$18,000
Incremental labor cost	8,000	10,000	12,000
Incremental overhead cost	16,000	20,000	24,000
Total incremental cost	$42,000	$48,000	$54,000
Incremental profit	$ 8,000	$ 2,000	−$ 4,000

This can be readily displayed in matrix form (see Exhibit 4-1). The *expected* incremental profit is

$$\frac{1}{3}(\$8,000) + \frac{1}{3}(\$2,000) + \frac{1}{3}(-\$4,000) = \$2,000$$

and the firm will, therefore, accept the offer.

Suppose, however, that an engineering study can be commissioned. The study will be definitive: It will reveal the actual labor cost. How much would our firm pay for such a study? Quite clearly, if the labor cost turns out to be $8,000 or $10,000 the offer will be accepted; if it turns out to be $12,000

EXHIBIT 4-1————————————————————————————————————

Incremental Profit Matrix

	Labor Cost of $8,000	Labor Cost of $10,000	Labor Cost of $12,000
Accept offer	$8,000	$2,000	−$4,000
Reject offer	0	0	0

the offer will be rejected. For a price, the firm can guarantee no loss on the special project venture. Its expected incremental profit would then be

$$\frac{1}{3}\,(\$8,000) + \frac{1}{3}\,(\$2,000) + \frac{1}{3}\,(0) = \$3,333.33$$

The firm will, therefore, pay up to

$$\$3,333.33 - \$2,000 = \$1,333.33$$

for the definitive engineering study. [Notice that $\$1,333.33 = \frac{1}{3}\,(\$4,000)$.]

An even more interesting version of this problem arises when the firm is bidding on the special project. It will submit a bid, as will its competitors. The customer will accept, say, the lowest bid, and the firm therefore acquires the "product" only if it submits the lowest bid. Cost analysis is important here for two reasons. First, the firm presumably would not submit a bid below its incremental cost. To do so would subject the firm to a possible loss, whereas no bid guarantees neither loss nor gain. (Remember, though, that the project may carry beneficial externalities for other projects, such as when engineering skills acquired on one project spill over into other projects. If this is the case, the incremental cost estimation can be extremely difficult.) Second, cost analysis may tell the firm something about its competitors and what bids they are likely to submit. Indeed, the bidding problem is now modeled by more sophisticated firms as a noncooperative game in which various firms compete to obtain the maximal contribution that the market will bear.[4]

Adding or dropping a product is thus a variation on the CVP theme of approximating revenue and cost consequences of small changes in the firm's activities. Generally, the critical estimates in decisions to add or drop a product are the estimates of the incremental costs of producing and distribut-

---

[4] This already complex situation becomes more complex if we admit that another bid opportunity *may* materialize in the future. If the present project is successfully bid for, its implementation will preclude the subsequent project. Again, there is an opportunity cost, but one that is even more subtle than the use of management's time or of a fixed facility on another currently identified project.

ing the product. If the product is a new order, there will likely be uncertainty about the required outlays for materials, labor, and incremental overhead, as well as the opportunity costs of devoting the capacities to the new order. Even if the order calls for an output that the decision unit has previously produced, there will likely be uncertainty about the incremental overhead costs associated with the order and the opportunity costs of the capacities. Remember that many overhead items rise in discrete steps (semifixed costs), making it difficult to determine their new level should a specific order be accepted.

The opportunity cost of using capacity to produce a particular product is difficult to estimate, because the estimation requires knowledge of future opportunities that will be available. If a decision unit currently has idle capacity, adding a product that uses only an incidental amount of this capacity probably will not incur an opportunity cost. (If no future opportunities will have to be rejected because of a new project, then the new project has zero opportunity cost.) If the product will use a significant amount of capacity, however, then it is more likely that acceptance will require the decision unit to reject future profitable opportunities. The difficulty lies in being able to predict which, if any, future opportunities will have to be rejected.[5]

If there is uncertainty about the incremental costs when a product is added, there must also be uncertainty about the reduction in costs if a current product is dropped. Quite often, the simplifying assumption is made that the incremental costs can be approximated by the variable costs of production and distribution, with some adjustment for changes in significant step costs— for example, supervision or setup costs. If the spread between the revenue per unit and the total variable cost per unit—the contribution margin—is relatively large, there will be a margin of safety to absorb overestimates or underestimates of changes in semifixed costs and the opportunity costs of devoting capacities to the product. Once the incremental outlay costs have been classified into variable and relatively fixed items, the same types of break-even and profit analyses illustrated earlier may be used to assess the effect of different volume levels on profit.

Finally, it is important to remember that we are dealing with "small" changes here. If small changes are analyzed without regard to risk aversion, incremental costs and their expected values are an appropriate method of analysis. But if aversion to risk cannot be ignored, the focus on incremental analysis is problematic. Diversification across projects becomes an important consideration, as does the relationship between scale of operations and the degree of risk aversion; we must then proceed with a thorough analysis of *all* projects and not proceed on an incremental basis.

---

[5] In the absence of specific knowledge of future opportunities, many managers will require the new product to earn a satisfactory percentage return, in addition to requiring total revenues to absorb all of the product's costs. This effectively forces each product to earn at least the average rate of return over all projects normally accepted by the decision unit.

Making or Buying a Unit

A very similar picture emerges when a firm has capacities available that it can use to manufacture a subunit rather than to purchase the subunit from an outside supplier. This is often a decision that can be made each operating period, with the decision being resolved in favor of making the unit in some periods and purchasing it in others. Again, if uncertainty can be ignored, the firm will manufacture the unit if the incremental costs of manufacturing are less than the incremental costs of purchasing. The incremental costs of manufacturing are the incremental outlay costs plus the opportunity costs of devoting the capacities to the subunit. The latter will be zero if the capacities would otherwise stand idle and positive if the capacities devoted to the subunit could be used to manufacture another profitable product (that is, a main product or another type of subunit).

Our earlier comments on uncertainty also apply here. A major element of uncertainty, however, may be the quality or delivery reliability of the outside supplier. If so, assessment of the risks involved as well as the value of information will entail specification of how the firm might respond to inadequate quality or late delivery. In one extreme, production schedules may be maintained with in-house production of the required factor. The other extreme is interruption of the existing production schedule, which entails an opportunity cost of one form or another.

To Sell Now or to Process Further

A third variation on this theme concerns whether to sell a product at an intermediate stage or process it further. Whether to add more chapters on decision analysis in an accounting text is a ready example. Another is whether to sell semiconductor chips or retain them for use in component assemblies. De facto, the question is whether to add a product, and all that was said earlier continues to apply. For example, if uncertainty is not significant, we expect the decision unit will process a product further rather than sell it immediately if the incremental revenues from processing exceed the incremental costs of processing. The incremental revenues are measured by the difference between the selling price of the unit after processing and the selling price if sold immediately times the number of units to be processed, that is, $(p_{\text{later}} - p_{\text{now}})$ (total units). The incremental costs are the incremental outlay costs of processing and the opportunity costs of using the capacities to process the product.

Summary

The three situations described in this section rely on the basic assumptions of CVP analysis: A decision unit intends to hold a set of capacities during the subsequent operating period. We represent the cost structure with a linear approximation that typically (though not necessarily) exhibits a nontrivial fixed intercept. And the net result is to expect choices that favor short-run utilization of the fixed facilities. It is important to recognize, however, that our discussion to this point also assumes only two available choices (drop or not, add or not, make or buy, further process or not). When the alternatives are more complex, we must abandon our simple rules in favor of more systematic analysis. This situation is discussed in the following review problems.

Review Problems 4 and 5

4. Specialty Products makes products to customer order. Though the current period's production has been set, a customer has inquired about the production of a particular product. The required materials will cost $5,000. Forty hours of direct labor will be required (at an average cost of $15/hour). Moreover, overhead is approximated by the following linear equation:

$$\text{Overhead} \cong \$200,000 + \$18 \cdot \text{DLH}$$

where DLH denotes total direct labor hours.

Required (a) Estimate the incremental cost of producing this product assuming no opportunity costs are present.

(b) Estimate the incremental cost of producing this product assuming labor is in short supply and overtime production will be used. Overtime entails a premium payment of an additional $8 per direct labor hour.

(c) Estimate the incremental cost of producing this product assuming that machine capacity is in short supply and that, if accepted, a related product with a contribution margin of $4,000 will be displaced. No overtime is involved.

(d) Suppose no overtime or opportunity cost issues are present. Variable overhead is, however, uncertain. The slope of the overhead approximation is either $10, $18, or $26 per direct labor hour. Assume the three slopes are equally likely. The customer has offered to pay $10,000. How much will the firm pay to learn the actual variable overhead before accepting or rejecting this offer? (Assume risk neutrality.)

(e) Why is the calculated payment in (d) above likely to understate the value of learning the variable overhead?

5. ***To Sell Now or to Process Further***
Assume management has 6,000 hours of capacity it can use to convert product A into a finished item. Each finished unit, product B, consumes 3 hours of processing time.

The variable costs of processing are estimated as $1/unit. Special setup costs are $3,000 for each run. Product A could be sold now for $5/unit, or it could be processed further and sold, as product B, for $8/unit.

(a) Should the product be sold now or processed further?
(b) What is the minimum selling price of product B at which the firm would be indifferent between processing further or selling now?
(c) How many units of A must be processed into product B and sold later for the firm to break even on the *decision* to process further?

Short-Run Multiproduct Models:
Linear Programing Extensions
of CVP Analysis

We now discuss a linear programing extension of the previous analysis. This is done for several reasons. Linear programing formulations of short-run capacity utilization problems are very common. Moreover, with suppression of uncertainty and use of linear cost and revenue approximations, linear programing may be viewed as the multiproduct extension of the traditional CVP analysis.[6] Finally, the exercise of systematically analyzing *all* of the firm's short-run production (and sales) options will provide added insight into our use of opportunity costs.

Consider a firm that may produce products x_1 and x_2. We approximate its total cost by

$$TC = 800 + 12x_1 + 5x_2$$

and its total revenue by

$$TR = 15x_1 + 7x_2$$

The profit is, therefore,

$$\pi = (15 - 12)x_1 + (7 - 5)x_2 - 800$$

---

[6] This relationship is spelled out more clearly in R.K. Jaedicke, "Improving Break-Even Analysis by Linear Programming Techniques," *N.A.A. Bull.*, March 1961, and A. Charnes, W.W. Cooper, and Y. Ijiri, "Breakeven Budgeting and Programming to Goals," *J. Accounting Research*, Spring 1963.

Maximizing profit is equivalent to maximizing contribution to profit (price less variable cost) multiplied by the number of units:

$$\pi + 800 = (15 - 12)x_1 + (7 - 5)x_2$$
$$= 3x_1 + 2x_2$$

The only catch is that the firm has an available capacity of 500 hours. Each output unit of x_1 requires 2 hours of capacity, and each output unit of x_2 requires 1 hour of this capacity. Thus, the firm can produce 250 units of x_1, 500 units of x_2, or various linear combinations of x_1 and x_2, provided that $2x_1 + 1x_2 \leq 500$ hours and x_1 and x_2 are nonnegative. In more precise terms, we formulate the problem as

$$\begin{array}{ll} \text{Maximize} & 3x_1 + 2x_2 \\ x_1, x_2 & \\ \text{subject to} & 2x_1 + x_2 \leq 500 \\ & x_1, x_2 \geq 0 \end{array} \qquad [4\text{--}1]$$

This problem is simple enough that it may be solved by comparing *relative* contribution margins. We note that a unit of x_1 uses 2 hours of the scarce resource and returns \$3 in contribution margin. Stated alternatively, x_1 returns \$1.50 per hour of capacity used. However, x_2 returns \$2 per hour of capacity used; therefore, x_2 is relatively more profitable than x_1. Because all the relationships in the problem are linear, it follows that the firm should produce 500 units of x_2 and no units of x_1 (that is, every unit of x_1 produced forces the firm to forego two units of x_2; the net effect is a loss of \$1 of contribution margin). Five hundred units of x_2 yields a total contribution margin of \$1,000. This is the maximum contribution margin possible, given the statement of the problem.

This problem can also be solved using graphic techniques. Let the horizontal axis in Figure 4-6 represent the output of x_1 and the vertical axis represent the output of x_2. The feasible set of production schedules then consists of all points on or below the line $x_1 + x_2 = 500$, provided $x_1 \geq 0$ and $x_2 \geq 0$. This is the shaded region in the figure. The dashed lines represent equal amounts of total contribution margin resulting from combinations of outputs of x_1 and x_2. For example, 300 units of x_2 yields the same total contribution margin (\$600) as 200 units of x_1. Similarly, 500 units of x_2 yields the same total contribution margin (\$1,000) as 333 units of x_1. However, 333 units of x_1 is not feasible, because this output would require 666 hours of capacity. Hence, the maximum contribution margin possible is \$1,000, achieved by producing 500 units of x_2. Note that the optimal solution occurs

FIGURE 4-6 _____

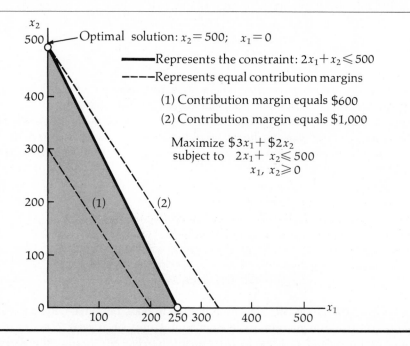

at a point where the total contribution margin line (in this case, CM = $1,000) touches an extreme point of the feasible region.

Now return to our earlier discussion of opportunity cost. We modeled the firm's decision problem in Equation [4-1] with no mention or use whatever of an opportunity cost notion. The reason is quite simple. The model systematically searches all opportunities; we do not need to control for alternative uses of the facilities, because the model searches over *all* possible (feasible) uses. But suppose we focus on the two obvious extreme points of $x_1 = 250$, $x_2 = 0$ and $x_1 = 0$, $x_2 = 500$. Clearly, with positive contribution margins, the solution will always be one of these. (In the limit of indifference between the two extremes, we would regard any combination of these extremes as acceptable.) Now suppose we further specialize the question to: Should we select product x_1? (For example, should we add product x_1, or should we drop product x_2?) Using the prescription and data given previously, we would have

$$
\begin{array}{lr}
\text{Incremental profit from } x_1 & = \$ \quad 750 \\
\text{Less opportunity cost } (500)(\$2) & = -1{,}000 \\
\hline
& -\$250
\end{array}
$$

The idea is rejected. Conversely, we may ask the question: Should we select product x_2. This provides

$$\begin{array}{ll} \text{Incremental profit from } x_2 & = \$1{,}000 \\ \text{Less opportunity cost } (250)(\$3) = & -750 \\ \hline & \$\ \ 250 \end{array}$$

and the idea is accepted. *We use the opportunity cost notion in our modeling when we implicitly, rather than explicitly, search over all available alternatives. A fully formulated model would not entail any assessment of opportunity cost.*

Further notice here, in this simple example, that the best use of the available output is to produce $x_2 = 500$, yielding a "return" of $2 per unit of capacity. This $2 datum is the "shadow price," "dual variable," or opportunity cost of the fixed capacity when it is used optimally. It provides the (instantaneous) change in total contribution margin per unit change in the available capacity. Thus, if we divert one unit from this optimal scheme, we forego $2.

Our ability to generate insights becomes more difficult as we add variables and constraints, but the basic principle remains. A systematic analysis of all alternatives does not require any expression of opportunity cost. No desirable alternatives will be rejected. To illustrate, suppose now that a second constraint is imposed on the problem. The outputs x_1 and x_2 must pass through a second production department, which is constrained according to $1.5x_1 + 2x_2 \le 480$ hours. This constraint implies that either of the two extremes, 320 units of x_1 or 240 units of x_2, may be produced in the second department. When this constraint is coupled with the previous one shown in Figure 4-6, the feasible region is modified as shown in Figure 4-7. In turn, the optimal solution changes to $x_1 = 208$ and $x_2 = 84$.

The consequences of diverting the fixed facilities away from this optimal solution are more difficult to assess, because any alteration in either capacity will be optimally responded to by altering both x_1 and x_2. It is, however, possible to show that the shadow price on the first capacity is $1.20 per unit, while that on the second is $.40 per unit. (You can verify this, in our simple situation, by re-solving the model for 499 units of the first capacity and 480 of the second and then for 500 of the first and 479 of the second.)

Sensitivity of Solution to Accounting Estimation Errors

The linear programing solution just obtained relies on estimates of the contribution margins of x_1 and x_2 and their technical coefficients of production. The latter are basically engineering data. However, contribution margins are measured using accounting estimates of product variable costs along with

FIGURE 4-7

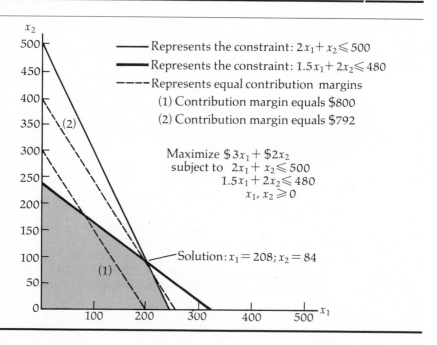

estimates of the revenue per unit of output. These accounting measurements are subject to error, and our concern now is the extent to which we can assess the significance of these errors.

The significance of measurement errors in contribution margins may be assessed in part by analyzing the sensitivity of the linear programing solution to changes in contribution margins. If the solution is sensitive to small changes, it may be profitable to obtain more reliable estimates of variable costs and revenue. To illustrate, suppose that past data indicate that the actual variable costs of product x_2 fluctuate in such a manner that its contribution margin may fall anywhere in the range of $1 to $3 (unlikely, perhaps, but useful for illustrative purposes).

Referring to Figure 4-7, we note that if x_2's contribution margin is $1, while x_1's remains at $3, the new optimal solution will become $x_1 = 250$ and $x_2 = 0$. Total contribution margin would be $3(250) + $2(0) = $750. However, if x_2's contribution margin were $3, the new optimal solution would be the same as the original one—that is, $x_1 = 208$ and $x_2 = 84$—but with a revised total contribution margin of $3(208) + $3(84) = $876.[7]

---

[7] For each case, we draw new equal contribution margin lines to reflect the revised relationships. Thus, the first change yields equal contribution margin lines with a slope of $-3/1 = -3$, whereas the second results in a slope of $-3/3 = -1$. The original lines have a slope of $-3/2$.

These "sensitivity" results can be interpreted as follows. If the estimator knew with certainty that x_2's contribution margin would be $1 during the next operating period, the decision unit would revise its production plan and produce 250 units of x_1 and 0 units of x_2. In contrast, no revision would be necessary were the actual contribution margin of x_2 to increase to $3.

Note, however, that the estimator does not know for sure the contribution margin of x_2 for the next operating period. Instead, the estimator relies on a best estimate, which we assume is $2. Suppose, then, that the original production plan is implemented and actual output is $x_1 = 208$ and $x_2 = 84$. Assume now that the actual contribution margin of x_2 drops to $1, so that the decision unit obtains only $3(208) + $1(84) = $708. Recall that if x_2's contribution margin dropped to $1, the optimal solution was $x_1 = 250$ and $x_2 = 0$, yielding a total contribution margin of $3(250) = $750. Hence, the cost of not knowing in advance the actual contribution margin of x_2 is simply $750 - $708 = $42 (that is, the optimal value of the objective function minus the actual value).

In turn, a more systematic application of these common sensitivity procedures will provide an expected value of perfect information orientation. Suppose, to illustrate, that the contribution margin for x_2 will be $CM_2 = $1, $2, or $3, with respective probabilities of .25, .50, and .25. If no additional information is available, the estimator will proceed by assuming the contribution margin is $2, solving the indicated linear program, and implementing the $x_1 = 208$, $x_2 = 84$ solution. Hence, the *expected* contribution total will be

$$208(\$3) + .25(84)(\$1) + .50(84)(\$2) + .25(84)(\$3) = \$792$$

Now consider the acquisition of perfect information (Exhibit 4-2). If the contribution margin for x_2 turns out to be $1, the optimal solution is $x_1 = 250$ and $x_2 = 0$. If the contribution is $2, the optimal solution is $x_1 = 208$ and $x_2 = 84$. For a $3 contribution, the best solution is again $x_1 = 208$ and $x_2 = 84$. The *expected* contribution margin is therefore

$$.25[250(\$3) + 0(\$1)] + .50[208(\$3) + 84(\$2)] + .25[208(\$3) + 84(\$3)]$$
$$= .25[\$750] + .50[\$792] + .25[\$876]$$
$$= \$802.50$$

Hence, the expected value of perfect information is

$$\$802.50 - \$792 = \$10.50$$

Further notice that the expected value of perfect information calculation can be produced by directly focusing on the expected cost of CM_2 estimation errors. Recall that if we estimate $CM_2 = \$2$ and instead we obtain $CM_2 =$

EXHIBIT 4-2_____

EVPI Calculations

	EVENT		
	$CM_2 = \$1$	$CM_2 = \$2$	$CM_2 = \$3$
Optimal contribution margin	$750	$792	$876
Actual contribution margin under $x_1 = 208$, $x_2 = 84$	708	792	876
Cost of estimation error	$ 42	$ 0	$ 0

$1, the cost is $42. Estimating $CM_2 = \$2$ when we obtain $CM_2 = \$2$ or $CM_2 = \$3$ results in zero cost, because the optimal solution is undisturbed:

$$.25(\$42) + .5(\$0) + .25(\$0) = \$10.50$$

These calculations are summarized in Exhibit 4-2.

The difficulty with this illustration, and with sensitivity analysis in general, is that the selection of the estimate(s) to vary and the ranges in which their observed values might vary are generally based on ad hoc procedures. The estimator must decide whether sensitivity analyses should be performed on the contribution margins, the contribution margin components separately (that is, the individual revenue and cost estimates), the disaggregated costs, the technological constraints, or various combinations of these. The latter would be appropriate if sources of variability are correlated, in which case joint probability functions must be assessed. The selection process can become so complex that formal methods of sensitivity analyses are too costly to develop. Fortunately, fairly common computer-based methods for performing sensitivity analyses have proved useful, and the previous illustration should be viewed as a simplified approach to the problem and its relationship to the more fundamental value of information calculation.

REVIEW PROBLEMS 6 and 7 _____

6. **Whether to Make or to Buy and Opportunity Costs**
   The M Company produces a line of iron products using several sub-assemblies and parts. Many of these parts and components can be either produced or purchased from outside suppliers. Cost data for four parts are listed below.

	#11	#12	#13	#14
Material cost per unit	$1.00	$2.00	$5.00	$3.00
Variable labor per unit	.50	1.00	3.00	1.00
Overhead (variable only) per unit	.25	.50	1.50	.50
Total cost per unit	$1.75	$3.50	$9.50	$4.50
Machine hours required per unit	½	1	4	½

The purchase prices of the parts vary somewhat from month to month, depending on the available capacities of the outside producers. The estimates of prices and the quantities of units needed during the next production period are given below. Assume that the capacity of the producing department is 500,000 machine hours, but only 30 percent of the capacity is to be used for producing parts 11, 12, 13, and 14 in total. Also assume that for any part, a portion of the requirement could be purchased.

Part	Units Required	Outside Prices
#11	100,000	$ 2.00
#12	80,000	5.00
#13	15,000	14.00
#14	100,000	4.25

Required (a) In the absence of a constraint on machine hours available for producing parts, which would be produced and which would be purchased?

(b) Given the constraint of 150,000 hours, how much of each part should be purchased and how much should be produced?

(c) Explain your answer to (b) in terms of outlay and opportunity costs.

7. *Cost Estimation with Linear Programing Models*
A firm has just opened a new facility to produce products x_1 and x_2. Using aggregate data, you obtain two estimates of variable costs per unit for each product. The two equations for each product are:

$$\text{A estimates} \quad VC_{x_1} = 6(x_1)$$
$$VC_{x_2} = 7(x_2)$$
$$\text{B estimates} \quad VC_{x_1} = 4(x_1)$$
$$VC_{x_2} = 8(x_2)$$

The selling price for a unit of x_1 is $19; that of x_2 is $22. Each product is processed through departments #1 and #2. The estimated hourly requirements for each product and total capacity available are:

	x_1	x_2	Total Capacity (in hours)
Department #1	1 hr	1 hr	400
Department #2	1 hr	2 hrs	500

(a) Using a graphical approach, what is the optimal output if the A estimates for each product are used?

(b) The optimal solution if the B set of estimates are used would be:

$$x_1 = 400 \qquad x_2 = 0$$

with an expected contribution margin of $6,000.

    (1)   Verify this solution using the graphical approach.

    (2)   Assume you select the B estimates as the "true" estimates and order 400 units of x_1 to be produced. Using your answer from (a) above, what would be the cost of estimation errors if the A estimates were the actual ones?

  (c) Suppose you assess .50 probability that either set of estimates is correct. Without additional information, you will implement the solution in (b). How much would you pay to learn the correct cost figures before selecting your solution?

The following section, as indicated by the asterisk, discusses important but more technically sophisticated material.

*Uncertainty and CVP Analysis

We conclude our survey of CVP analysis with a closer look at uncertainty. Surely there is no need to motivate the presence of uncertainty. The real difficulty is deciding what to do about it. Questions of the value of additional information arise here; we have made repeated reference to and analysis of this theme because of its fundamental importance in our study of the firm's information problem. Questions of the decision unit's attitude toward risk also arise here. We have mentioned this as well, but have assumed a neutral attitude toward risk and made only veiled references to the complexity of formalizing a nonneutral attitude. Our purpose here is to say a bit more on this topic.

Notice at the outset, however, that our goals are rather modest. One reason is that all of CVP analysis is related to small changes, and we have considerable sympathy with initially analyzing such changes in a risk-neutral manner.[8] Second, and more important, is a lack of normative theory to guide us. The difficulty lies in specifying the firm's and not the individual's attitude toward risk.

Recall that the chapter began with a review of the classical theory of the firm. Profit maximization was assumed; this is normatively correct in the usual, pristine setting of economic analysis. The firm's owners want management to maximize profit. We then extended this to incremental analysis and, without justification, to maximization of *expected* profit (or expected incremental profit) for small changes. Formally admitting to uncertainty raises the deep and vexing question of what the firm's attitude toward risk should be. This would be easy enough to address if a market existed in which to evaluate risks. A market price (yes, profit) orientation would develop and

---

    [8] See R. Howard, "Proximal Decision Analysis," *Management Science,* May 1971, for extensive analysis and application of this point.

"cost of risk" would merely be another item in our accounting of the decision unit's costs. Unfortunately, markets are *not* this perfect. There are no market prices by which we are able to evaluate all of the firm's possible activities. And economic theory presently regards the firm's objectives in such a setting as an open question. At this point, we often view the firm as catering to a particular clientele and speak more or less casually of its attitude toward risk. But exactly how this comes about and relates to the individuals' risk attitudes remains a mystery, except in specialized cases.

Having entered the abyss, suppose our decision unit is risk-averse. In general, it rejects actuarially fair profit gambles. How do we now extend CVP analysis to accommodate such an attitude? Two considerations arise. One deals with portfolio effects and the other with assessing the probability distribution of profit consequences.

Portfolio Considerations

Incremental analysis is a parsimonious approach to profit or expected profit maximization, because the decision unit need only examine differences in the revenue and cost totals. Suppose, however, a small change is contemplated, but the decision unit is also risk-averse in evaluating small changes. In general, the risk assessment will depend on the scale of operations (unless constant risk aversion is assumed). This risk assessment will also depend on the small change's diversification potential. For example, the decision unit may be more risk-averse when it is near the break-even point than when considerable positive profits are assured. The implication is that total and not incremental analysis is essential (unless we continually adjust the risk attitude for the scale of operations). Hence, fixed costs are now important, because the attitude toward risk depends on the level of fixed costs.

A very simple example will illustrate this point. A decision unit must decide whether to accept or reject a special order. Acceptance will provide an *incremental* gain of $10,000 or loss of $5,000, with equal probability. The expected gain is, therefore, $2,500. Suppose the decision unit is risk-averse, with a utility function for profit given by $\sqrt{x}$ for $x \geq 0$.

Carefully examine Figure 4-8 before proceeding. The $\sqrt{x}$ utility function for profit indicates that the firm is indifferent between a guaranteed profit of $10,000 and a venture in which the profit will be $0 with probability .50 or $40,000 with probability .50:

$$\sqrt{\$10,000} = .50\sqrt{\$0} + .50\sqrt{\$40,000} = \$100$$

Fair gambles are rejected here. (Indeed, the $0, $40,000 gamble here has an expected value of $20,000, which is considerably greater than $10,000.) We use the utility function to represent the firm's attitude toward risk. One ven-

FIGURE 4-8 _____

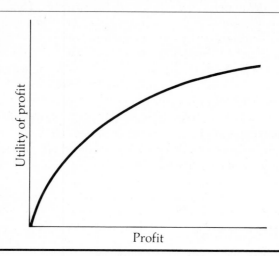

ture is better than another if the expected value of utility from the one is greater than from the other.

At present, the decision unit enjoys a guaranteed profit of $150,000. Hence, the expected value of the utility of the special order if accepted would be

$$.50 \sqrt{\$150,000 + \$10,000} + .50 \sqrt{\$150,000 - \$5,000} = \$390.39$$

If rejected, the utility measure would be $\sqrt{\$150,000} = \$387.30$. The expected utility analysis indicates that the project will be accepted.

But suppose the firm enjoys a guaranteed profit of only $5,000. Acceptance would then provide

$$.50 \sqrt{\$5,000 + \$10,000} + .50 \sqrt{\$5,000 - \$5,000} = \$61.24$$

which compares unfavorably with the rejection measure of $\sqrt{\$5,000} = \$70.71$. Here, the decision unit will reject the project, because it is too risky. In other words, the decision unit's attitude toward risk depends on its scale of operations. We can analyze this choice in incremental terms if we specify a utility for incremental profit of $\sqrt{\$150,000 + z}$ in the first case and $\sqrt{\$5,000 + z}$ in the second, where z denotes incremental profit, or we can focus on total profit consequences.

Of course, the analysis becomes more complex if we admit that the present profit level is also uncertain. Using the $\sqrt{x}$ utility function as before, suppose the present profit anticipations are $20,000 and $5,000 with equal probability. Now what about the special order? If the present and proposed projects are *independent*, the expected utility with the new project is

$$.25 \sqrt{\$20,000 + \$10,000} + .25 \sqrt{\$20,000 - \$5,000}$$
$$+ .25 \sqrt{\$5,000 + \$10,000} + .25 \sqrt{\$5,000 - \$5,000} = \$104.54$$

Without the new project, the expected utility is

$$.50 \sqrt{\$20,000} + .50 \sqrt{\$5,000} = \$106.07$$

Suppose instead that the two projects are perfectly correlated in the sense that if one returns the higher profit, the other does also. The expected utility with the new project is now

$$.50 \sqrt{\$20,000 + \$10,000} + .50 \sqrt{\$5,000 - \$5,000} = \$86.60$$

On the other hand, if the two projects are perfectly negatively correlated in the sense that low profit in one is accompanied by high profit in the other, the resulting diversification makes the project desirable:

$$.50 \sqrt{\$20,000 - \$5,000} + .50 \sqrt{\$5,000 + \$10,000} = \$122.47$$

This is why portfolio considerations become important under conditions of risk aversion.

It is important, then, to understand that insights obtained under conditions of risk neutrality do not necessarily extend to the case of risk aversion. Our ability to analyze projects on an incremental basis becomes limited here, as does our ability to ignore fixed costs. For example, under an assumption of decreasing absolute risk aversion, an increase in the level of fixed costs can lead to a decrease in what would otherwise be the optimal level of output.[9] Recall, though, that in the certainty (equivalent) model, a change in fixed costs would not affect the optimal output.

Probability Distributions

It is a relatively simple matter to analyze possible cost and revenue conse-quences when we confine ourselves to a small number of possible outcomes. Allowing the number of possible outcomes to increase (and become un-bounded as with a normal distribution) raises the question of producing and using summary statistics for the probability distribution of revenue, cost, and profit. With risk neutrality, of course, we care only about the mean of

---

[9] See A. Sandmo, "On the Theory of the Competitive Firm," *Amer. Econ. Rev.*, March 1971, and H.E. Leland, "Theory of the Firm Facing Uncertain Demand," *Amer. Econ. Rev.*, June 1972. The former deals with a competitive firm, whereas the latter deals with monopolistic firms. A comment by I. Bernhardt on Sandmo's analysis, and Sandmo's reply, appear in the March 1972 issue of the *American Economic Rev.* Also see R.H. Day, D.J. Aigner, and K.R. Smith, "Safety Margins and Profit Maximization in the Theory of the Firm," *J. Pol. Econ.*, Nov.–Dec. 1971.

this distribution. Risk aversion, though, requires that we look beyond the mean. In normative choice theory, we would rely on the expectation of the utility function with respect to this distribution. Complexity dictates, however, that we focus on a more simplified approach, based essentially on summary measures of the profit probability distribution.

Jaedicke and Robichek were among the first to advocate such an approach.[10] Basically, they expanded the CVP model to accommodate normal probability distributions and summarized output decisions in terms of the mean and variance of the resulting profit distribution.

In subsequent publications by others, criticisms have been levied against Jaedicke and Robichek for their simplified, and perhaps erroneous, assumptions about the distributions of their random variables, especially profit, which is a derived variable.[11] More important, though, is the assumption that the most useful summary statistics are the means and variances of the profit distributions of individual alternatives. In this regard, two criticisms of the basic approach particularly warrant our attention.

In the first, Johnson and Simik criticize the approach, because it fails to recognize that the choice of products (or lines) to produce is actually a portfolio choice, rather than a single-product choice.[12] If the products are not completely independent, then the total firm's profit variance will depend on the covariance among the profits of the various product lines.[13] If the

---

[10] R.K. Jaedicke and A.A. Robichek, "Information for Production and Marketing Decisions," *Accounting Rev.*, Oct. 1964.

[11] See, for example, J.E. Hilliard and R.A. Leitch, "Cost–Volume–Profit Analysis under Uncertainty: A Log Normal Approach," *Accounting Rev.*, Jan. 1975, as well as some of their references.

[12] G. Johnson and S. Simik, "Multiproduct C.V.P. Analysis under Uncertainty," *J. Accounting Research*, Autumn 1971.

[13] Recall that an estimate of the mean of a random variable, X, is

$$\bar{X} = \sum_{i=1}^{N} \left(\frac{X_i}{N} \right)$$

where X_i represents observed values of X and N is the number of observations. The variance around the mean may be estimated as

$$\sigma_x^2 = \frac{\sum_{i=1}^{N} (X_i - \bar{X})^2}{N-1}$$

The standard deviation is the square root of σ_x^2:

$$\sigma_x = \sqrt{\sum_{i=1}^{N} \frac{(X_i - \bar{X})^2}{N-1}}$$

The covariance between two random variables, X and Y, is the *expected value* of the product $[X - E(X)][Y - E(Y)]$:

$$E[X - E(X)][Y - E(Y)]$$

profits of products are positively correlated, then the total variance (and standard deviation) of profits will increase; if these profits are negatively correlated, the total variance will decrease. This is the diversification issue addressed earlier.

Magee,[14] on the other hand, focuses on capital asset pricing theory to question the relevance of variance as an appropriate summary statistic for assessing risk. Under his approach, "the essential variables for the manager's short-run decision problem are not the expected value and variance of profit, but, rather, the expected value of profit *and the covariance of profit with the return on the market portfolio.*" Covariance with the assets in the economy—not variance—is the risk measure implied by the capital asset pricing model.

In short, it is a natural progression to move from linear approximation and point estimates of the cost and revenue consequences in small changes, to introducing probability distributions over possible consequences, and then on to summarizing these probability distributions with one or two summary measures. These summary measures are sufficient for normative analysis in specialized settings. But in general we interpret them as possibly cost-effective ways for dealing with uncertainty in CVP analysis.

Conclusion

Our objective in this chapter has been to illustrate the nature of information problems associated with the classical short-run allocation problem: Given a fixed set of resources, what actions will lead to their most desirable utilization? We began with the economist's nonlinear profit-maximization model, which provides a more general analysis of the interaction between a firm's revenue and cost functions and output than the accountant's linear model. The accountant's linear model was then viewed as an approximate expression of management's commitments to input and output decisions that are consistent with the nonlinear profit-maximization model.

This approximation was then explored further, as the basic building block in the firm's analysis of short-run allocation alternatives. Single-project

---

where E is the expectations operator. An estimate of the covariance is

$$\frac{\sum_{i=1}^{N} (X_i - \bar{X})(Y_i - \bar{Y})}{N-1}$$

The terms $\bar{X}$ and $\bar{Y}$ are the means of X and Y, respectively. The total variance of a two-variable portfolio would be

$$\sigma_P^2 = \sigma_X^2 + \sigma_Y^2 + 2\,\mathrm{Cov}(X,Y)$$

[14] R.P. Magee, "Cost–Volume–Profit Analysis, Uncertainty and Capital Market Equilibrium," *J. Accounting Research,* Autumn 1975.

considerations, such as adding or dropping a product, making or buying a subcomponent, and selling or further processing a product, were examined. Multiple-project considerations were then addressed. Finally, formal incorporation of uncertainty and risk-aversion considerations were examined.

Supplementary Readings

Articles

Adar, Z., A. Barnea, and B. Lev, "A Comprehensive Cost–Volume–Profit Analysis under Uncertainty," *Accounting Rev.,* Jan. 1977.

Charnes, A., W.W. Cooper, and Y. Ijiri, "Breakeven Budgeting and Programming to Goals," *J. Accounting Research,* Spring 1963.

Devine, C.T., "Boundaries and Potentials of Reporting on Profit–Volume Relationships," *N.A.A. Bull.,* Jan. 1961.

Dillon, R.D. and J.F. Nash, "The True Relevance of Relevant Costs," *Accounting Rev.,* Jan. 1978.

Jaedicke, R.K., "Improving Break-Even Analysis by Linear Programming Techniques," *N.A.A. Bull.,* March 1961.

Jaedicke, R.K. and A.A. Robichek, "Cost–Volume–Profit Analysis Under Uncertainty," *Accounting Rev.,* Oct. 1964.

Jensen, R., "Sensitivity Analysis and Integer Linear Programming," *Accounting Rev.,* July 1968.

Johnson, G. and S. Simik, "Multiproduct C.V.P. Analysis Under Uncertainty," *J. Accounting Research,* Autumn 1971.

Books

Demski, J.S., *Information Analysis.* Reading, Mass.: Addison-Wesley, 1980.

Demski, J.S. and G.A. Feltham, *Cost Determination: A Conceptual Approach.* Ames, Iowa: Iowa State Univ. Press, 1976.

Eppen, G.E. and F.J. Gould, *Quantitative Concepts for Management.* Englewood Cliffs, N.J.: Prentice-Hall, 1979.

Wagner, H.M., *Principles of Operations Research.* Englewood Cliffs, N.J.: Prentice-Hall, 1975.

Questions and Problems

1. Compare and contrast the economist's short-run model of the firm with the accountant's break-even chart.

2. Given: π = profit
   p = selling price per unit
   b = variable costs per unit
   a = fixed costs

(a) What is the equation for the break-even point in units of output? In dollars of sales?

(b) Suppose management has a target of π. What is the equation for determining the necessary output to achieve this target profit (in units or dollars)?

3. What effect would the following changes have on the break-even point and expected profit?

(a) an increase in fixed costs
(b) an increase in wage rates
(c) an increase in selling prices
(d) an expansion of volume by 10 percent over the expected volume
(e) an increase in rentals paid on leased equipment

4. Break-even analysis, the determination of make-or-buy policies, the decision to process a unit further, and the determination of an optimal sales mix are characteristic of the same type of general problem. Discuss.

5. Assume product A has a contribution margin of $5 and product B has one of $1. Total fixed costs are $10,000. Without any additional information on sales mix(es), discuss the problem involved in trying to use break-even analysis for such a multiproduct firm. What combinations of outputs of A and B will yield a break-even point for this firm? (*Hint:* There are many more possible combinations than just a few.)

6.[15] The *Wall Street Journal* (February 11, 1970) reported on Chrysler Corporation's performance for the year 1969. Among other items, the story pointed out that Chrysler had boosted its market share from 10 percent in 1962 to 18 percent in 1968. In 1969, however, countermeasures by Ford and General Motors, plus a 10 percent decline (that is, one million units) in total industry sales, created severe problems for Chrysler. In its (unsuccessful) efforts to maintain its market share and protect its profitability, Chrysler cut prices and increased advertising allowances, which reduced contribution by an average of $100 per unit compared to 1968. Working toward internal economies, cutbacks in technical and administrative staff permitted a 20 percent reduction in fixed costs for 1969 relative to 1968. Nonetheless, 1969 pre-tax profits were only $80 million on sales of 1.4 million units, whereas 1968 pre-tax profits were $300 million.

Required From these fragments, answer the following questions. (*Notice:* If you are "stuck," it is not difficult to solve these by "trial and error.")

(a) What was the fixed cost in 1968?
(b) What was the fixed cost in 1969?
(c) What was the per-unit contribution in 1968?
(d) What was the per-unit contribution in 1969?
(e) List major assumptions you have made and discuss them briefly.

---

[15] Prepared by David O. Green.

7. *Cost–Volume–Profit Graph*

The Tri-Products Company produces three main products: Alpha, Beta, and Gamma. The current budget calls for the production of 12,000 units of Alpha, 10,000 units of Beta, and 8,000 units of Gamma. The selling prices and the direct costs of producing the three products are summarized as follows:

	Alpha	Beta	Gamma
Selling price per unit	$20	$16	$10
Direct variable costs per unit	$ 8	$ 6	$ 5
Direct fixed costs	$25,000	$20,000	$10,000

In addition, the company estimates that other costs of production and distribution are $155,000 for the total volume of 30,000 units.

(a) Construct a cost–volume–profit graph that will illustrate to management the effect on profit of the output mix they have selected.

(b) The maximum (practical) capacity of Tri-Products is 33,000 units. The company's productive facilities are not completely flexible, so an expansion to 33,000 units may cause a change in the ratio of 12 : 10 : 8. Suppose the company believes that a $2 decrease in the price of Alpha will result in an increase in sales of 3,500 units. In order to achieve this output, the production of both Beta and Gamma will have to be reduced by 500 units each. Is the change profitable? (Use the cost–volume–profit graph to illustrate the new profit.)

(c) How practical is this type of sensitivity analysis for multiproduct firms?

8. *Multiple Products: Break-Even Analysis*

The David Company has prepared the following budget for the first quarter of 1982.

	Product A	Product B	Total
Output	50,000	100,000	150,000
Revenues	$100,000	$300,000	$400,000
Operating costs			
Materials	$ 25,000	$ 80,000	$105,000
Direct labor	30,000	80,000	110,000
Overhead[a]	32,500	90,000	122,500
Total costs	$ 87,500	$250,000	$337,500
Expected gross profit	$ 12,500	$ 50,000	$ 62,500

[a] Estimated at fixed costs plus 25 percent of direct labor.

Prepare a break-even analysis based upon expected sales from the David Company (see also Problem 9).

9. The following data reflect the actual operations for the David Company during the first quarter of 1982.

	Product A	Product B	Total
Output	56,000	104,000	160,000
Revenues (net)	$112,000	$312,000	$424,000
Operating costs			
Materials	$ 26,880	$ 85,280	$112,160
Direct labor	33,600	83,200	116,800
Overhead[a]	35,960	94,840	130,800
Total costs	$ 96,440	$263,320	$359,760
Gross profit	$ 15,560	$ 48,680	$ 64,240

[a] Fixed overhead was $100,400.

(a) What was the actual break-even point?

(b) Draft an explanation of these variances for management's consideration; that is, account for the difference between actual and expected profit in terms of changes in average revenue per unit of mix, average variable cost, fixed costs, and volume.

10. **Cost–Volume Behavior**

Executives are often quoted in print about what will happen to their profits if some event takes place. Each of the following hypothetical statements is of that type.

Analyze each statement, indicating briefly the nature of the cost–volume relationship that the executive apparently assumes must exist. Each statement is independent of all the others.

(a) "Last year our planes flew with 50 percent of their seats filled, and we had a small loss. In the coming year, I expect that we will better this figure by 5 or 10 percentage points, that is, 55 percent to 60 percent of the seats filled, and we will earn a normal return on our investment."

(b) "Our firm is in an industry whose profits fluctuate violently in response to small changes in sales volume (in units)."

(c) "The essence of a profitable operation in our industry is generating great volume. Only under that condition can a firm operate profitably."

(d) "Our profit was reduced, because prices were depressed in the industry."

(e) "Despite achieving the same level of sales (in dollars) as last year and a slight increase in volume, profits fell. This was clearly due to our failure to retain our share of the SuperDuper Widget market."

(f) "Management during the past year has invested in equipment that is expected to yield certain economies in production. It is expected that sales will be large enough to take full advantage of them."

(g) "While sales volume has grown quite rapidly during the past years, profits have not kept pace with management's estimates based upon the results of 1980 and 1981 operations."

11. **Application of the Break-Even Concept to a Choice Situation**

A recent advertising campaign stressed the economies involved in the operation of the Brand Z transistor radio. The economies were the result of using specialized batteries with longer battery lives. The following fictitious data are assumed to have resulted from tests of this brand of transistor radio and those of a competitor, Brand J:

	Brand Z	Brand J
Cost of radio, exclusive of batteries	$40.00	$15.00
Cost of batteries (per set)	$ 2.00	$ 1.20
Life of batteries	80 hours	40 hours

Answer the following questions. Each question is independent of the others, except as noted.

(a) Assuming the battery cost to be a linear variable cost rather than a step function, calculate the number of hours the radio must be used for the owner to be indifferent between choosing Brand J and Brand Z.

(b) How would you answer part (a) if the more realistic step function were assumed?

(c) How much would the consumer be willing to pay for Brand Z on sale (Brand J is still $15) if he expects the radio to last exactly 800 listening hours and then disintegrate?

(d) If Brand Z could be recharged by plugging it into a wall socket, thereby requiring no batteries to operate (and a negligible amount of electricity), how many hours would it have to be used before Brand Z is preferable to Brand J?

(e) If the customer will buy the higher-priced brand *only* if he feels that it will save him $10 on operating costs over its life, how many hours must he expect to use it? Assume a linear variable cost function.

12. ***Multiple Products Break-Even Analysis***

P. Kay, owner of the Chicago Sox baseball club, has secured your services as a consultant on certain managerial accounting problems. He submitted to you the following data, relevant to the Sox operation.

(1) The Sox current season ticket prices are $2, $3, and $4 for the bleacher, grandstand, and box seats, respectively. The visiting team receives $.75 from each bleacher ticket, $1.25 from each grandstand ticket, and $2 from each box seat ticket.

(2) The capacity of Kay Field is 7,500 bleacher seats, 30,000 grandstand seats, and 12,500 box seats.

(3) Attendance has always been in the same ratio as the capacities, that is, 1 bleacher customer to 4 grandstand customers to 5/3 box seat customers.

(4) The available cost data are as follows:

	Bleacher	Grandstand	Box Seat
Variable costs (per 500 admissions)			
Ticket printing	$ 1.00	$ 1.00	$ 2.00
Ticket taking	5.00	7.00	13.00
Ushers	4.00	7.00	10.00
Cleanup crew	25.00	30.00	35.00
Total variable cost (per 500 admissions)	$35.00	$45.00	$60.00

Fixed costs (reduced to a
per-home-game basis)

Depreciation on plant	$15,000
Ballplayers' salaries	35,000
Administrative expenses	10,000
Other	5,000
Total costs (per home game)	$65,000

(5) The Sox' share of the gate receipts when they are the visiting team equals their cash travel costs, and television revenues cover all other expenses.

Required (a) Calculate the Sox "break-even" attendance per game. What meaning would you attach to this number?

(b) If Kay raises the ticket price for box seats to $5.50, what is the effect on the break-even point? (Assume the visiting team still receives $2.) What reservations, if any, do you have on this analysis?

(c) Kay is thinking of reclassifying some grandstand seats as reserved seats and charging $4 apiece for them. The variable costs per 500 would increase to $55.00 for these seats. The visiting team will receive $1. Briefly, would you recommend this? Why or why not?

(d) Kay is curious about the advisability of securing a "winning team," that is, one above .500. He estimates that it would cost $30,000 more per game and guarantees that all box and bleacher seats would be sold for every game. However, only an average of 65 percent of the grandstand seats would be sold. Using these facts, calculate the break-even point per game. What do you think—as an accountant, not a baseball fan—of this investment opportunity?

13. **Dropping a Product**

The president of Eastern Company wants guidance on the advisability of eliminating product C, one of the company's three similar products, or investing in new machinery to reduce the cost of product C in the hope of reversing product C's operating loss sustained in the previous year. The three similar products are manufactured in a single plant in about the same amount of floor space, and the markets in which they are sold are very competitive. Exhibit 4-3 is the condensed statement of operating income for the company and for product C for the previous year.

Answer the following questions. Disregard income taxes.

(a) Prepare a schedule showing the contribution of product C to the recovery of fixed costs and expenses (marginal income) for the previous year. Assume that each element of cost and expense is entirely fixed or variable within the relevant range and that the change in inventory levels has been negligible.

(b) Assume that the variable costs and expenses of product C totaled $297,500 and that its fixed costs and expenses amounted to $75,100. Prepare a schedule computing the break-even point of product C in terms of annual dollar sales volume. Sales for the year amounted to $350,000.

EXHIBIT 4-3

	All Three Products	Product C
Sales	$2,800,150	$350,000
Cost of sales		
Raw materials	$ 565,000	$ 80,000
Labor		
Direct	1,250,000	150,000
Indirect	55,000	18,000
Fringe	195,750	25,200
Royalties (1% of product C sales)	3,500	3,500
Maintenance and repairs	6,000	2,000
Factory supplies	15,000	2,100
Depreciation (straight-line)	25,200	7,100
Electrical power	25,000	3,000
Scrap and spoilage	4,300	600
Total cost of sales	$2,144,750	$291,500
Gross profit	$ 655,400	$ 58,500
Selling, general, and administrative expenses		
Sales commissions	$ 120,000	$ 15,000
Officers' salaries	32,000	10,500
Other wages and salaries	14,000	5,300
Fringe benefits (15% of wages, salaries, and commissions)	24,900	4,620
Delivery expense	79,500	10,000
Advertising expense	195,100	26,000
Miscellaneous fixed expenses	31,900	10,630
Total selling, general, and administrative expenses	$ 497,400	$ 82,050
Operating income (loss)	$ 158,000	$ (23,550)

(c) The direct labor costs of product C could have been reduced by $75,000 and the indirect labor costs by $4,000 by investing an additional $340,000 (financed with 5 percent bonds) in machinery with a ten-year life and an estimated salvage value of $30,000 at the end of the period. However, the company would have been liable for total severance pay costs of $18,000 (to be amortized over a five-year period), and electrical power costs would have increased $500 annually.

Assuming the information given above in part (b), prepare a schedule computing the break-even point of product C in terms of annual dollar sales volume if the additional machinery had been purchased and installed at the beginning of the year.

[AICPA adapted]

14. *Make-or-Buy Decision*
P.K. Igley hires you to evaluate a report submitted to him. It concerns Mr. Igley's desire to have the printing of scorecards for the Chicago Bruins done by an

outside firm for $.05 each instead of by his gum factory's printing department. The report is reproduced below.

To: Mr. P.K. Igley
Re: Outside printing of scorecards
Decision: Outside printing saves $4,000. Accept the offer.
I have based my decision on the following cost data, which are available at the plant. No data are available on the market value of the gum wrappers, because they are a component of final product. Instead, I have found that like items are generally available at $1 per 10,000.

	Gum Wrappers (100,000,000 Units)	Scorecards (500,000 Units)	Total
Paper	$ 1,000	$ 5,000	$ 6,000
Ink	2,000	1,000	3,000
Labor (machine operators)	3,000	12,000	15,000
Department overhead (all variable costs)	500	2,000	2,500
Machinery depreciation	5,000	5,000	10,000
General plant costs	1,000	4,000	5,000
	$12,500	$29,000	$41,500

The ultimate sales value of the scorecards is $.10 each, but a commission of $.02 per scorecard is paid to the vendor. The scorecards and the gum wrappers are both printed on a single standard press. The cutting of the large sheets into individual wrappers and scorecards is done on another machine by changing the cutting dies.

(a) Evaluate the report, indicating what figures you feel are inappropriate, are irrelevant, or may merit inquiry, and why.
(b) Indicate how you would analyze this problem. Be sure to indicate what other available data you would find useful. Be as specific as you can.

15. **Processing a Unit Through Additional Departments**
A joint processing company is characterized by the fact that during a specified time period a fixed ratio of products is produced from a single department. These products will often require additional processing through separate departments. The profitability of processing these units further, however, may depend upon the alternatives available to the firm at the time of split-off, or when they emerge from the initial production department. We do not consider how the firm may proceed to determine the ratio of joint products to produce initially, since it is a complex programing problem. We can consider some of the secondary problems, however, such as the following:

Assume the Acme Company produces in a joint process, say process X, two main products and a so-called by-product. The by-product may be sold now for $5.15 per gallon less discounts and shipping costs, which average about 1 percent of this price. Alternatively, the by-product may be processed further through process Y, after which it can be sold for $7.50 per gallon, net. One of

EXHIBIT 4-4

Output (gallons of either the main products or the by-product)	20,000	30,000	40,000	50,000[a]
Materials				
Main product	$30,000	$45,000	$60,000	$75,000
By-product	10,000	15,000	20,000	25,000
Direct labor ($\frac{1}{5}$ of an hour @ $6 for each product)	24,000	36,000	48,000	60,500
Indirect overhead (semivariable)	15,000	17,000	19,000	21,100
Fixed costs	10,000	10,000	10,000	10,450

[a] Costs are discontinuous at an output of approximately 48,500 gallons. In other words, we have two cost functions: one for the range up to 48,500 and one for the range beyond.

the main products must also be processed through process Y. The total capacity of process Y is 50,000 gallons a month, regardless of which product is worked on. For either product, the cost of process Y at different outputs are as given in Exhibit 4-4.

(a) The company has 35,000 gallons of its main product and 18,000 gallons of its by-product. Given that the firm wishes to process 35,000 gallons of the main product, determine whether the company should sell all of its 18,000 gallons of the by-product now or process whatever it can through process Y. Explain.

(b) Suppose the company has 35,000 gallons of main product and 25,000 gallons of the by-product that it must either process or sell. The demand for the finished by-product has increased, so the new price available is $8 per gallon, net. Discuss how this new price complicates the determination of the output mix of the main product and the by-product in process Y.

16. *CVP Analysis with Uncertainty*
   A. The Wing Manufacturing Corporation produces a chemical compound, product X, which deteriorates and must be discarded if it is not sold by the end of the month during which it is produced. The total variable cost of the manufactured compound, product X, is $50 per unit, and its selling price is $80 per unit. Wing can purchase the same compound from a competing company at $80 per unit plus $10 freight per unit. Management has estimated that failure to fill orders would result in the loss of 80 percent of customers placing orders for the compound. Wing has manufactured and sold product X for the past 20 months. Demand for the product has been irregular, and at present there is no consistent sales trend. During this period monthly sales have been as follows:

Units Sold per Month	Number of Months
8,000	5
9,000	12
10,000	3

Required (a) Compute the probability of sales of product X of 8,000, 9,000, or 10,000 units in any month.

(b) Compute what the contribution margin would be if 9,000 units of product X were ordered and either 8,000, 9,000, or 10,000 units were manufactured in that same month (with additional units, if necessary, being purchased).

(c) Compute the average monthly contribution margin that Wing can expect if 9,000 units of product X are manufactured every month and all sales orders are filled.

B. In the production of product X, Wing uses a primary ingredient, K-1. This ingredient is purchased from an outside supplier at a cost of $24 per unit of compound. It is estimated that there is a 70 percent chance that the supplier of K-1 may be shut down by a strike for an indefinite period. A substitute ingredient, K-2, is available at $36 per unit of compound, but Wing must contact this alternative source immediately to secure sufficient quantities. A firm purchase contract for either material must now be made for production of the primary ingredient next month. If an order were placed for K-1 and a strike occurred, Wing would be released from the contract and management would purchase the chemical compound from its competitor. Assume that 9,000 units are to be manufactured and all sales orders are to be filled.

Required (a) Compute the monthly contribution margin from sales of 8,000, 9,000, and 10,000 units if the substitute ingredient, K-2, is ordered.

(b) Prepare a schedule computing the average monthly contribution margin that Wing should expect if the primary ingredient, K-1, is ordered with the existing probability of a strike at the supplier. Assume that the expected average monthly contribution margin from manufacturing will be $130,000 using the primary ingredient and the expected average monthly loss from purchasing product X from the competitor (in case of a strike) will be $45,000.

[AICPA adapted]

17. *Linear Programing, Break-Even, and Sensitivity Analyses*
The data in Exhibit 4-5 represent the operating results of a cycle company for the year 1980 and the first quarter of 1981.

Assume the following for 1982:
(1) Sales of cycles will be limited as follows:

| luxury cycles | 1.20 million |
| off-road cycles | .60 million |

(These limits reflect expectations on prices, advertising, competitors' actions, and so on.)
(2) The company has two main facilities, engine blocks and frames, that are

EXHIBIT 4-5————————————————————————————————————

	1980	1981 (1st Quarter)
Units sold	1,320,000	375,000
Net sales (in millions)	$3,168.00	$937.50
Operating costs (in millions)		
Variable factory costs	$1,900.80	$581.25
Fixed factory costs	690.00	181.25
Variable selling and administrative costs	47.54	18.76
Fixed selling and administrative costs	78.00	22.00
	$2,716.34	$803.26
Net operating income (before taxes)	$ 451.66	$134.24

used in the production of both cycles. The capacities of these facilities are limited as follows, where x_1 = luxury cycles and x_2 = off-road cycles:

$$.8x_1 + .5x_2 \le 1.00 \text{ million} \qquad [4\text{-}2]$$
$$.5x_1 + 1x_2 \le .90 \text{ million} \qquad [4\text{-}3]$$

(3) Each unit of x_1 contributes $970, and each unit of x_2 contributes $890.

(4) Total fixed costs are expected to be $814.80 million.

Required (a) Find the break-even point in dollars for the year 1980.

    (b) Determine the number of units that will have to be sold in 1981 to break even.

    (c) Will the company be able to break even in 1982?

    (d) Are there different break-even points for the year? Explain.

    (e) What is the best output combination for this firm, and how much operating profit will the company report?

    (f) How much would the firm be willing to pay to expand the facilities shown in Equation [4-2] from 1.00 to 1.10 million, and those in Equation [4-3] from .90 to 1.00 million? (*Hint:* The easiest way to determine the answer is to use the graphical solution to test the sensitivity of the optimal decision to an increase in each of the facilities. Then take the change in the total contribution margin that results.)

    (g) Assess the effects of a reduction in the contribution margins of x_1 to $400. Do the same for a reduction in the contribution margin of x_2 to $550. [*Hint:* Use the graphical solution as in (f).]

18. **Cost–Volume–Profit Analysis: L.P. Extensions**
The Wiley Company produces two main products, X and Y. A budget has been prepared for the next operating period (see Exhibit 4-6) that indicates the preliminary profit figures for the two products.

    (a) The management of the corporation wants to know how many units of X and Y must be sold to break even. The controller responds that such a calculation would be meaningless for a multiproduct firm. Calculate the

_____ EXHIBIT 4-6

	X	Y
Sales in units	50,000	40,000
Price per unit	$10	$7.50
Revenue	$500,000	$300,000
Costs		
Direct variable	$150,000	$ 90,000
Variable overhead	95,000	55,000
Fixed factory overhead related to products	50,000	20,000
Selling and administrative (variable)	50,000	30,000
	$345,000	$195,000
Profit by products	$155,000	$105,000

Total profit	$260,000
General overhead	120,000
Net profit	$140,000

expected break-even point for this profit plan, and indicate your reasons for agreeing or disagreeing with the controller.

(b) The sales manager suggests that additional advertising of $30,000 should be spent on product X to increase its sales to 60,000 units. His argument is that the added contribution from 10,000 additional units of product X will more than cover this increased cost. In fact, the sales manager believes that additional ways should be sought to increase the sale of product X since it is more profitable than product Y.

The controller counters that this is not true, because product X uses more scarce capacity than product Y. This fact would show up clearly if the general fixed overhead were allocated to the two products on the basis of the machine hours needed to process a unit of each. You learn that product X requires $1\frac{1}{3}$ hours and product Y requires 1 hour of processing time. On the basis of this criterion, which product is more "profitable"? Explain. Under what condition(s) would the contribution from the additional 10,000 units of X be sufficient to cover the advertising cost?

(c) Suppose that product X contributes an average of $3 per unit and product Y contributes $2.50 per unit to general overhead.

The production of X and Y is constrained by the capacities of two departments as follows:

$$\tfrac{2}{3}X + \tfrac{1}{4}Y \le 50,000 \text{ hours} \qquad [4\text{-}4]$$
$$\tfrac{1}{2}X + \tfrac{3}{4}Y \le 52,500 \text{ hours} \qquad [4\text{-}5]$$

Using a graphic approach, show how these facilities should be allocated to the two products. What is the total contribution margin from your solution?

(d) Suppose the Wiley Company could expand the capacities of both departments by 5,000 hours at a cost of $15,000 per operating cycle. Should these facilities be expanded? Explain.

(e) Discuss how the accountant could use a linear programing model to assess the impact of possible errors in some of the estimates of the variables in this problem. For example, what would the cost of such errors be and how much would be paid to avoid such errors?

(f)   Discuss the role of opportunity costs for your analyses in (b) and (c) above.

19.   *Contribution Analysis: Multiproducts and Linear Programing*
The Marcie Company, your client, has asked your assistance in determining an economical sales and production mix of their products for 1982. The company manufactures a line of dolls and a doll dress sewing kit.

The company's sales department provides the following data:

Item	Estimated Demand for 1982 (Units)	Established Net Price (Units)
Laurie	50,000	$5.20
Debbie	42,000	2.40
Sarah	35,000	8.50
Kathy	40,000	4.00
Sewing kit	325,000[a]	3.00

[a] Includes direct and indirect sales.

To promote sales of the sewing kit, there is a 15 percent reduction in the established net price for a kit purchased at the same time that a Marcie Company doll is purchased. From accounting records, you develop the following data:

(1)   The production requirements *per unit* are as follows:

Item	Material	Labor
Laurie	$1.40	$ .80
Debbie	.70	.50
Sarah	2.69	1.40
Kathy	1.00	1.00
Sewing kit	.60	.40

(2)   The labor rate of $4 per hour is expected to continue without change in 1982. The plant has an effective capacity of 60,000 labor hours per year on a single-shift basis. Present equipment can produce all of the products.
(3)   The total fixed costs for 1982 will be $100,000. Variable overhead costs will be equivalent to 50 percent of direct labor costs.
(4)   The company has a small inventory of its products that can be ignored.

Required   (a)   Prepare a schedule computing the contribution margin of each product.
(b)   Prepare a schedule computing the contribution to profit of a unit of each product per labor hour expended on the product.
(c)   Prepare a schedule computing the total labor hours required to produce the estimated sales units for 1982. Indicate the item and number of units that you would recommend be increased (or decreased) in production to attain the company's effective productive capacity.

(d) Formulate this problem as a linear programing problem. Assume each doll is sold with a sewing kit.

[AICPA adapted]

20. **Effect of Changes on Profitability**

This problem (adapted from an old—1965—CPA Examination) is a classic illustration of the difficulty we encounter in confining CVP analysis to a single-period setting. In particular, a seemingly innocent question about capacity changes will likely entail changes in cash flows for a number of periods, and at that point we must recognize these additional cash flows (eventually using techniques to be discussed in Chapter 14).

The president of Beth Corporation, which manufactures tape decks and sells them to producers of sound reproduction systems, anticipates a 10 percent wage increase on January 1 of next year for the manufacturing employees (variable labor). He expects no other changes in costs. Overhead will not change as a result of the wage increase. The president has asked you to assist him in developing reasonable product strategy for next year.

Below are the current year data assembled for your analysis:

Current selling price per unit	$120.00
Variable cost per unit	
Material	$ 40.00
Labor	15.00
Overhead	10.00
Total variable cost per unit	$ 65.00
Annual volume of sales	5,000 units
Fixed costs	$60,000

Provide the following information for the president, using cost–volume–profit analysis:

(a) What increase in the selling price is necessary to cover the 10 percent wage increase and still maintain the current net income?

(b) How many tape decks must be sold to maintain the current net income if the sales price remains at $120 and the 10 percent wage increase goes into effect?

(c) The president believes that an additional $400,000 of machinery (to be depreciated at 10 percent annually) will increase present capacity (5,300 units) by 30 percent. If all tape decks produced can be sold at the present price and the wage increase goes into effect, how does the estimated net income before capacity is increased compare with the estimated net income after capacity is increased? Prepare computations of estimated net income before and after the expansion.

(d) Continuing with the 30 percent capacity expansion proposal, suppose the additional variable costs require cash expenditures. The net cash inflow from the expansion will then be $85,065. Further, suppose this same additional inflow will exist for 10 consecutive years. At a 20 percent market interest rate, we would have to pay $356,590 for such a stream of inflows. Compare this datum with the expansion's cost.

[AICPA adapted]

21. *Cost–Volume–Profit with Three Products*

Ruidoso Ski Lodge operates a ski shop, restaurant, and lodge during the 120-day ski season from November 15 to March 15. The proprietor is thinking of changing his operations and keeping the lodge open all year.

Results of operations for the year that ended March 15, 1981, were as given in Exhibit 4-7.

Other information is as follows:

(1) The lodge has 100 rooms, and the rate from November 15 to March 15 is $30 per day for one person. The occupancy rate from November 15 to March 15 is 90 percent.
(2) Ski shop and restaurant sales vary in direct proportion to room occupancy.
(3) For the ski shop and restaurant, cost of goods sold, supplies, and utilities vary in direct proportion to sales. For the lodge, supplies and utilities vary in direct proportion to room occupancy.
(4) The ski shop, restaurant, and lodge are located in the same building. Depreciation on the building is charged to the lodge. The ski shop and restaurant are charged with depreciation only on equipment. The full cost of the restaurant equipment became fully depreciated on March 15, 1981, but the equipment has a remaining useful life of three years. The equipment can be sold now for $1,200, but will be worthless in three years. All depreciation is computed by the straight-line method.
(5) Insurance premiums are for annual coverage for public liability and fire insurance on the building and equipment. All building insurance is charged to the lodge.

EXHIBIT 4-7 ——

	SKI SHOP		RESTAURANT		LODGE	
	Amount	Percent	Amount	Percent	Amount	Percent
Revenue	$54,000	100%	$80,000	100%	$324,000	100%
Costs						
Costs of goods sold	$29,700	55%	$48,000	60%		
Supplies	2,700	5	8,000	10	$ 22,680	7%
Utilities	540	1	2,400	3	6,480	2
Salaries	3,240	6	24,000	30	97,200	30
Insurance	1,620	3	1,600	2	29,160	9
Property taxes on building	1,080	2	3,200	4	19,440	6
Depreciation	2,160	4	4,000	5	84,240	26
Total costs	$41,040	76%	$91,200	114%	$259,200	80%
Net income (loss)	$12,960	24%	($11,200)	(14%)	$ 64,800	20%

(6) Salaries are the minimum necessary to keep each facility open and are for the ski season only, except for the lodge security guard, who is paid $5,400 per year.

Two alternatives are being considered for the future operation of Ruidoso Ski Lodge:

(i) The proprietor believes that during the ski season the restaurant should be closed, because "it does not have enough revenue to cover its out-of-pocket costs." It is estimated that lodge occupancy would drop to 80 percent of capacity if the restaurant were closed during the ski season. The space utilized by the restaurant would be used as a lounge for lodge guests.

(ii) The proprietor is thinking of keeping the lodge open from March 15 to November 15. The ski shop would be converted into a gift shop if the lodge should be operated during this period, with conversion costs of $2,000 in March and $2,000 in November each year. It is estimated that revenues from the gift shop would be the same per room occupied as revenues from the ski shop, that variable costs would be in the same ratio to revenues, and that all other costs would be the same for the gift shop as for the ski shop. The occupancy rate of the lodge at a room rate of $20 per day is estimated at 50 percent during the period from March 15 to November 15 whether or not the restaurant is operated.

Determine which of the two alternatives is preferable.

[AICPA adapted]

22. *Linear Programing with Service Departments*

Ralph, our itinerant manager, has now become the manager of a two-product firm (Latent Products) and is considering how best to display his managerial skills. His initial action is to obtain a thorough analysis of the firm's cost structure. The following monthly data are developed (where X_1 and X_2 denote production and sale of the first and second products, respectively):

Cost Element	Fixed Costs	Approximate Variable Costs
Building	$500	—
Central administration	$800	—
Production administration	$100	$0.10 per equivalent DLH of production
Marketing	$200	$1.72X_1 + $3.02X_2
Power	$375	$0.02 per kilowatt-hour
Maintenance	$145	$4.00 per maintenance unit[a]
Production Department 1 overhead	$300	$0.90 per DLH in Department 1
Production Department 2 overhead	$480	$1.40 per DLH in Department 2

[a] For reasons known only to Ralph, a "maintenance unit," the measure of maintenance activity, is equal to ¼ hour of maintenance work.

MISCELLANEOUS PRODUCT STATISTICS

	Product 1	Product 2
Selling price	$51	$70
Direct materials cost	$10	$ 8
Required DLHs in Department 1	1 hr.	1 hr.
Required DLHs in Department 2	1 hr.	2 hrs.

MISCELLANEOUS PRODUCTION DEPARTMENT STATISTICS

	Department 1	Department 2
Capacity	400	500
Power consumption per DLH	9 kilowatt-hour	20 kilowatt-hour
Maintenance consumption per DLH	.1 unit	.2 unit
Direct labor cost per hour	10	15

Required (a) Determine the incremental cost per unit of each product.
(b) Determine an optimal output schedule.
(c) Determine the full[16] and variable cost per unit, given the schedule determined in (b).

23. *Linear Programing with Uncertain Estimates*
(Refer to Problem 22.) For purposes of answering the following questions, you should assume Ralph's problem has the form

$$\text{Maximize} \quad \alpha x_1 + 12x_2$$
$$\text{subject to} \quad x_1 + \ \ x_2 \le \beta$$
$$x_1 + 2x_2 \le 500$$
$$x_1, x_2 \ge 0$$

With $\alpha = 10$ and $\beta = 400$, we have the same setting as in Problem 22, where the optimal solution is $x_1{}^* = 300$ and $x_2{}^* = 100$.

Required (a) Suppose β equals 400 and α is either 6, 10, or 14, with respective probabilities of .25, .50, and .25. Without additional information, a value of $\alpha = 10$ will be assumed. What is the expected value of perfect information on α? (Assume Ralph is risk-neutral.)
(b) Suppose α equals 10 and β is either 350, 400, or 450, with respective probabilities of 1/3, 1/3, and 1/3. Without additional information, a value of $\beta = 400$ will be assumed. What is the expected value of perfect information on β? (Again assume Ralph is risk-neutral.)

---

[16] For full-cost assessment purposes, central administration cost is treated as a period expense (as is marketing cost), but the building cost is allocated on the basis of floor space used (10 percent to central administration, 7 percent to production administration, 5 percent to marketing, 5 percent to power, 3 percent to maintenance, 30 percent to Department 1, and 40 percent to Department 2).

24. ***Regression Analysis and Linear Programing*** [17]

In November 1981, the Springfield Manufacturing Company was in the process of preparing its budget for 1982. As the first step, it prepared a pro forma income statement for 1981 based on the first 10 months' operations and revised plans for the last 2 months. This income statement, in condensed form, was as follows:

Sales		$3,063,000
Materials	$1,105,000	
Labor	343,000	
Factory overhead	858,000	
Selling and administrative	459,000	2,765,000
Net income before income taxes		$ 298,000

These results were better than expected, and operations were close to capacity, but Springfield's management was not convinced that demand would remain at present levels and hence had not planned any increase in plant capacity. Its equipment was specialized and made to its order; over a year lead-time was necessary on all plant additions.

Springfield produces three products. Sales have been broken down by product, as follows:

	A	B	C
Units produced	100,000	40,000	20,000
Selling price	$20.63	$10.00	$30.00
Sales by product	$2,063,000	$400,000	$600,000
Total sales		$3,063,000	

Management has ordered a profit analysis for each product and has available the following information:

	A	B	C
Materials	$ 6.00	$ 4.00	$17.25
Labor	2.33	1.00	3.50
Factory overhead	5.83	2.50	8.75
Selling and administrative	3.09	1.50	4.50
Total costs	$17.25	$ 9.00	$34.00
Selling price	20.63	10.00	30.00
Profit	$ 3.38	$ 1.00	$ (4.00)

Factory overhead has been applied on the basis of direct labor cost at a rate of 250 percent; management feels that approximately a quarter of the overhead is variable and that it varies primarily with labor cost. Selling and administrative costs have been allocated on the basis of sales at the rate of 15 percent; approximately one-half of these costs are variable, and they vary primarily with sales in dollars.

As the first step in the planning process, the sales department has been

---

[17] Based on a problem originally prepared by Carl Nelson.

asked to make estimates of what it could sell. These estimates have been reviewed by the firm's consulting economist and by top management. They are as follows:

A	130,000 units
B	50,000 units
C	50,000 units

Production of these quantities is impossible. Each product requires the use of machines in each of two departments. Department 1 has a practical capacity of 75,000 machine hours, and Department 2 has a practical capacity of 60,000 machine hours. The industrial engineering department has concluded that these capacities cannot be increased without the purchase of additional equipment. The production rates for the two departments are:

	A	B	C
Department 1	2 per hour	4 per hour	4 per hour
Department 2[18]	3 per hour	8 per hour	4/3 per hour

The following solutions to the limited production problem have been rejected: (1) subcontracting the production out to other firms, which is considered to be unprofitable because of problems of maintaining quality, (2) operating a second shift, which is impossible because of shortage of labor, (3) operating overtime, which would create problems because a large number of employees are "moonlighting" and would therefore refuse to work more than the normal 40-hour week. Price increases have also been rejected; although they would result in higher profits this year, the long-run competitive position of the firm would be weakened, resulting in lower profits in the future.

The treasurer then suggested that product C has been carried at a loss too long and that now was the time to eliminate it from the product line. If all facilities are used to produce A and B, profits would be increased.

The sales manager objected to this solution because of the need to carry a full line. In addition, he maintains that there is a group of customers who have provided and will continue to provide a solid base for the firm's activities, and these customers' needs must be met. He provided a list of the customers and their estimated purchases (in units), which total as follows:

A	80,000 units
B	32,000 units
C	12,000 units

It was impossible to verify these contentions, but they appeared to be reasonable. They also served to narrow the bounds of the problem, so that the president concurred.

The treasurer reluctantly acquiesced, but maintained that the remaining capacity should be used to produce A and B. Because A produced about 3.4 times as much profit as B, he suggested that the production of A (in excess of

---

[18] Thus, A requires $\frac{1}{3}$ hour of machine time in Department 2. Rounding is an issue to avoid, so use a coefficient of .333 for analysis discussion purposes.

the 80,000 minimum set by the sales manager) be 3.4 times that of B (in excess of the 32,000 minimum set by the sales manager).

The production manager made some quick calculations and said that this would result in budgeted production and sales of approximately:

A	122,000 units
B	44,000 units
C	12,000 units

The treasurer then made a calculation of what profits would be, as follows:

	A	B	C
Units produced	122,000	44,000	12,000
Profit (loss) per unit	$3.38	$1.00	($4.00)
Profit (loss) by product	$412,360	$44,000	($48,000)
Total profit		$408,360	

As this would represent a substantial increase over the current year, there was a general feeling of self-satisfaction. Before final approval was given, however, the president said that he would like to have his new assistant check over the figures. Somewhat piqued, the treasurer agreed and at that point the group adjourned.

The next day the above information was submitted to you as your first assignment on your new job as the president's assistant. *Prepare an analysis showing the president what he should do.* Table 4-8 presents additional cost-related data that are available in the accounting records.

25. **Estimation Errors**[19]

(Refer to Problem 24.) The managers of Springfield are uncertain about some of the predictions they made in arriving at their production plans for 1982. You are to determine the cost of the following possible prediction errors if they were to occur and if the production plans were based on the predictions in the Springfield Manufacturing Company. The errors in each section are to be analyzed separately. Also, to save you some work in parts (3) and (4), notice that the capacity constraints are stated in terms of machine hours. The ratio of direct labor hours to machine hours is considerably less than one in each department. And the average direct labor cost *per machine hour* is $2 in Department 1 and $4 in Department 2.

(1) The selling price of product A may actually be $21.63 instead of the predicted magnitude of $20.63.
(2) The material cost of producing product B may actually be $5 instead of the predicted magnitude of $4.
(3) The production rate in Department 1 for product C may actually be 3 per hour instead of the predicted magnitude of 4 per hour.

---

[19] Prepared by Gerald Feltham.

TABLE 4-8

Accounting Data for the First 10 Months of 1981

Month	LABOR COST			OVERHEAD			Sales Revenue	Selling and Administrative Expense
	Dept. 1	Dept. 2	Total	Dept. 1	Dept. 2	Total		
1	$ 14,000	$ 14,600	$ 28,600	$ 31,512	$ 34,638	$ 66,150	$ 275,000	$ 39,900
2	13,500	12,500	26,000	29,825	33,487	63,312	240,000	37,400
3	12,200	11,800	24,000	29,450	33,133	62,583	230,000	36,950
4	13,200	13,800	27,000	31,025	33,854	64,879	260,000	38,800
5	13,800	13,200	27,000	31,437	34,381	65,818	270,000	39,700
6	12,300	11,700	24,000	29,675	32,962	62,637	230,000	37,200
7	11,500	11,500	23,000	29,325	32,321	61,646	220,000	36,200
8	14,500	13,500	28,000	31,400	34,208	65,608	270,000	39,050
9	12,000	13,000	25,000	30,950	33,591	64,541	255,000	38,750
10	11,700	11,300	23,000	29,262	32,485	61,747	220,000	36,300
Total	$128,700	$126,900	$255,000	$303,861	$335,060	$638,921	$2,470,000	$380,250

(4) The production rate in Department 2 for product C may actually be 2 per hour instead of 4/3 per hour.

(5) Major repairs to the machinery in Department 2 may reduce its capacity to 55,000 hours.

If the planned production is infeasible, Springfield's production staff usually cuts back the production with smallest profit, subject to the restriction that the production of any product must be sufficient to satisfy the demands of the customers whose needs must be met. (Here, profit is as determined by the original profit analysis in Problem 24: $3.38 for A, $1.00 for B, and a loss of $4.00 for C.)

26. *Contribution Calculations with Probabilities*

Commercial Products Corporation, an audit client, requested your assistance in determining the potential loss on a binding purchase contract that will be in effect at the end of the corporation's fiscal year. The corporation produces a chemical compound that deteriorates and must be discarded if it is not sold by the end of the month during which it is produced.

The total variable cost of the manufactured compound is $25 per unit, and it is sold for $40 per unit. The compound can be purchased from a vertically integrated competitor at $40 per unit plus $5 freight per unit. It is estimated that failure to fill orders would result in the complete loss of 8 out of 10 customers placing orders for the compound.

The corporation has sold the compound for the past 30 months. Demand has been irregular, and there is no sales trend. During this period, sales per month have been:

Units Sold per Month	Number of Months[a]
4,000	6
5,000	15
6,000	9

[a] Occurred in random sequence.

(a) For each of the following, prepare a schedule (with supporting computations in good form) of the

(1) probability of sales of 4,000, 5,000, or 6,000 units in any month.

(2) contribution to income if sales of 4,000, 5,000, or 6,000 units are made in one month and 4,000, 5,000, or 6,000 units are manufactured for sale in the same month. Assume all sales orders are filled.

(3) average monthly contribution to income the corporation should expect over the long run if 5,000 units are manufactured every month and all sales orders are filled.

(b) The cost of the primary ingredient used to manufacture the compound is $12 per unit of compound. It is estimated that there is a 60 percent chance that the primary ingredient supplier's plant may be shut down by a strike for an indefinite period. A substitute ingredient is available at $18 per unit of compound, but the corporation must contract immediately to purchase the substitute, or it will be unavailable when needed. A firm purchase contract for either the primary or the substitute ingredient must now be made with one of the suppliers for production next month. If an order were placed for the primary ingredient and a strike should occur, the corporation would be released from the contract and management would purchase the compound from the competitor.

Assume that 5,000 units are to be manufactured, and all sales orders are to be filled.

(1) Compute the monthly contribution to income from sales of 4,000, 5,000, and 6,000 units if the substitute ingredient is ordered.
(2) Prepare a schedule computing the average monthly contribution to income the corporation should expect if the primary ingredient is ordered with the existing probability of a strike at the supplier's plant. Assume that the expected average contribution to income from manufacturing will be $65,000 using the primary ingredient or $35,000 using the substitute, and the expected average monthly loss from purchasing from the competitor will be $25,000.
(3) Should management order the primary or substitute ingredient during the anticipated strike period (under the assumptions stated in (b)2), above]? Why or why not?
(4) Should management purchase the compound from the competitor to fill sales orders when the orders cannot be otherwise filled? Why or why not?

[AICPA adapted]

27. *Linear Programing Analysis and Assessing the Value of Perfect Information*
Assume a manager of a firm must determine an allocation of the capacities of two departments, given certain constraints. After extensive soul-searching, you (as an accountant) have assembled the following estimates:

	Product X	Product Y
Selling price	$10.00	$8.00
Upper demand levels for these prices	20,000	18,000
Variable production costs	$5.00	$4.00
Variable selling costs	$1.00	$.50
Fixed costs		
Capacity requirements	½ hr, Dept. 1	¼ hr, Dept. 1
	1 hr, Dept. 2	1 hr, Dept. 2
Capacity available	Dept. 1, 12,000 hr	Dept. 2, 30,000 hr

Objective: Maximize the total contribution margin, TCM.

(a) If the manager uses a linear programing approach, what mix of output will he produce?

(b) Suppose you have developed 95 percent confidence levels for the variable production costs of both X and Y as follows: Probability is 95 percent that (1) true variable production costs of X will fall in the interval $4.50 \leq VC_X \leq $5.50 and (2) true variable production costs of Y will fall in the interval $2.00 \leq VC_Y \leq $6.00.

Assess the sensitivity of the solution in (a), first, to the *upper* limit of the change in the costs of X and then to the *lower* limit of the change in the costs of Y.

(c) The value of perfect information about the outcomes of future events is usually measured in terms of the loss incurred through forecast errors. Suppose the capacity in Department 1 is measured in machine hours and the requirement of ½ hour for each unit of X is the average time over prior periods. In reviewing the past observations, you note that there were a number of periods—about 20 percent of the observations—when the time required was ¾ hour. On the assumption that there are no variable costs associated with machine operations (that is, variable production costs will remain at $5.00), how would the solution change if the coefficient for X were ¾ instead of ½?

(d) Assume that the original solution in (a), above, was X = 17,500 and Y = 12,500 (not the correct answer), and that the department attempted to produce this combination of output rather than switching to your solution in (c). If the actual time for producing X in Department 1 increases to ¾ hour, this production plan would not be feasible. Actual output would drop to X_{act} = 12,500 and Y_{act} = 10,500. What is the expected opportunity cost of not knowing in advance that X would consume ¾ hour instead of ½ hour?

28. **Summary Measures**[20]

Assume a firm produces a single product, X_1. Management is contemplating the addition of two other products, X_2 and X_3. All three products have the same expected demand, $\bar{X}_j$ contribution margin, and fixed expenses, but the probability distribution of demand for each has a different variance. Relevant data are:

Product X_j	Expected Demand $\bar{X}_j$	Demand Variance $(\sigma_{X_j})^2$	Contribution Margin CM_j	Fixed Expenses f_j
1	500	$(60)^2$	$125	$58,000
2	500	$(40)^2$	125	58,000
3	500	$(20)^2$	125	58,000

(a) For a risk-averse manager, which individual product would be preferred, assuming their covariances are zero?

(b) Given that CM_j and f_j are constants, what is the expected profit (total contribution less fixed expenses) for product X_1 above? For all three products

---

[20] Based on Johnson and Simik, "Multiproduct C.V.P. Analysis."

together? The variance for any one product is merely $(CM_j)^2 \sigma_{x_j}^2$. What is the variance of the profit of each product?

(c) If profit, which we denote by π, is normally distributed, then the distribution of profit could be shown as a bell-shaped curve centered on $E(\pi)$, with approximately 68 percent of the area under the curve located within the interval $E(\pi) \pm 1 \sigma_\pi$, where σ_π denotes the standard deviation of the π distribution. Similarly, since the curve is symmetrical, 50 percent of the area is above the mean and 50 percent is below. Using these properties, and appropriate tables, we can ask the question: What is the cumulative probability that π will exceed some number in the distribution, once the number is expressed in standard deviations from the *mean*, $E(\pi)$? For example, what is the probability $\pi_{x_1} \geq 0$? Let z be a standardized normal variable (as in Table 4-9). Then asking for the probability that $\pi_{x_1} \geq 0$ is the same as asking for the probability that $z = [0 - E(\pi_{x_1})]/\sigma_{\pi_{x_1}} \geq 0$. Using Table 4-2, we thus conclude the probability that $\pi_{x_1} \geq 0$ (or $z \geq -.6$) is .7257.

(1) What is the probability that $\pi_{x_2} \leq 0$?

(2) What is the probability $\pi_{x_2} \geq 1,500$ and $\pi_{x_3} \geq 3,000$? Similarly, what is the probability that $\pi_{x_2} \leq 1,500$ and $\pi_{x_3} \leq 3,000$?

(3) The covariance between X_1 and X_2 may be calculated as $2\rho_{1,2}\,\sigma_{x_1}\,\sigma_{x_2}$, where $\rho_{1,2}$ is the correlation coefficient between X_1 and X_2. The variance of π_{x_1,x_2}, or $(\sigma_{x_1,x_2})^2$, is equal to $(CM_{x_1})^2(\sigma_{x_1})^2 + (CM_{x_2})^2(\sigma_{x_2})^2 + 2\rho_{1,2}\sigma_{x_1}\sigma_{x_2}(CM_{x_1})(CM_{x_2})$. Calculate the variance and its square root, assuming $\rho_{1,2} = 0.7$.

*29. In Problem 28, you were asked to compute the variance of the profit distribution, $(\sigma_{x_1,x_2})^2$, and its square root, σ_{x_1,x_2}, assuming that output X_2 was added to the firm's output portfolio and that the correlation coefficient of demand of the two products was 0.7. Assume your answer for σ_{x_1,x_2} was 11,500 (not correct). A similar calculation for products X_1 and X_3, or σ_{x_1,x_3}, would yield 943,000 (rounded off). If the firm added both products to X_1, the expected profit $E(\pi_{x_1,x_2,x_3})$ would be 13,500. In all cases, $\rho_{ij} = 0.7$. The standard deviation of profit, σ_{x_1,x_2,x_3}, would be the square root of the variance, which would be equal to

$$(\sigma_{x_1,x_2,x_3})^2 = (CM_{x_1})^2(\sigma_{x_1})^2 + (CM_{x_2})^2(\sigma_{x_2})^2 + (CM_{x_3})^2(\sigma_{x_3})^2$$
$$+ 2\rho_{1,2}\,\sigma_{x_1}\,\sigma_{x_2}(CM_{x_1})(CM_{x_2}) + 2\rho_{1,3}\,\sigma_{x_1}\,\sigma_{x_3}(CM_{x_1})(CM_{x_3})$$
$$+ 2\rho_{2,3}\sigma_{x_2}\sigma_{x_3}(CM_{x_2})(CM_{x_3}) \cong (13,205)^2$$

Required (a) (1) What is the probability the firm will achieve a total profit equal to or greater than zero, given that all three products are produced?

(2) What is the probability that total profit will equal or exceed $13,500? That it will equal or exceed $15,000?

(3) What is the probability that actual profit will be equal to or less than −$1,500?

(b) Assume $\rho_{x_1,x_2} = \rho_{x_1,x_3} = -0.7$ and $\rho_{x_2,x_3} = +0.7$.

(1) What will be the standard deviation of profit if X_1 and X_2 are produced? If X_1 and X_3 are produced?

———————————————————————————————— **TABLE 4-9**

Normal Distribution Function

$$F(z) = \frac{1}{\sqrt{2\pi}} \int_{-\infty}^{z} e^{-1/2\, t^2}\, dt$$

z	.00	.01	.02	.03	.04	.05	.06	.07	.08	.09
.0	.5000	.5040	.5080	.5120	.5160	.5199	.5239	.5279	.5319	.5359
.1	.5398	.5438	.5478	.5517	.5557	.5596	.5636	.5675	.5714	.5753
.2	.5793	.5832	.5871	.5910	.5948	.5987	.6026	.6064	.6103	.6141
.3	.6179	.6217	.6255	.6293	.6331	.6368	.6406	.6443	.6480	.6517
.4	.6554	.6591	.6628	.6664	.6700	.6736	.6772	.6808	.6844	.6879
.5	6915	.6950	.6985	.7019	.7054	.7088	.7123	.7157	.7190	.7224
.6	.7257	.7291	.7324	.7357	.7389	.7422	.7454	.7486	.7517	.7549
.7	.7580	.7611	.7642	.7673	.7704	.7734	.7764	.7794	.7823	.7852
.8	.7881	.7910	.7939	.7967	.7995	.8023	.8051	.8078	.8106	.8133
.9	.8159	.8186	.8212	.8238	.8264	.8289	.8315	.8340	.8365	.8389
1.0	.8413	.8438	.8461	.8485	.8508	.8531	.8554	.8577	.8599	.8621
1.1	.8643	.8665	.8686	.8708	.8729	.8749	.8770	.8790	.8810	.8830
1.2	.8849	.8869	.8888	.8907	.8925	.8944	.8962	.8980	.8997	.9015
1.3	.9032	.9049	.9066	.9082	.9099	.9115	.9131	.9147	.9162	.9177
1.4	.9192	.9207	.9222	.9236	.9251	.9265	.9279	.9292	.9306	.9319
1.5	.9332	.9345	.9357	.9370	.9382	.9394	.9406	.9418	.9429	.9441
1.6	.9452	.9463	.9474	.9484	.9495	.9505	.9515	.9525	.9535	.9545
1.7	.9554	.9564	.9573	.9582	.9591	.9599	.9608	.9616	.9625	.9633
1.8	.9641	.9649	.9656	.9664	.9671	.9678	.9686	.9693	.9699	.9706
1.9	.9713	.9719	.9726	.9732	.9738	.9744	.9750	.9756	.9761	.9767
2.0	.9772	.9778	.9783	.9788	.9793	.9798	.9803	.9808	.9812	.9817
2.1	.9821	.9826	.9830	.9834	.9838	.9842	.9846	.9850	.9854	.9857
2.2	.9861	.9864	.9868	.9871	.9875	.9878	.9881	.9884	.9887	.9890
2.3	.9893	.9896	.9898	.9901	.9904	.9906	.9909	.9911	.9913	.9916
2.4	.9918	.9920	.9922	.9925	.9927	.9929	.9931	.9932	.9934	.9936
2.5	.9938	.9940	.9941	.9943	.9945	.9946	.9948	.9949	.9951	.9952
2.6	.9953	.9955	.9956	.9957	.9959	.9960	.9961	.9962	.9963	.9964
2.7	.9965	.9966	.9967	.9968	.9969	.9970	.9971	.9972	.9973	.9974
2.8	.9974	.9975	.9976	.9977	.9977	.9978	.9979	.9979	.9980	.9981
2.9	.9981	.9982	.9982	.9983	.9984	.9984	.9985	.9985	.9986	.9986
3.0	.9987	.9987	.9987	.9988	.9988	.9989	.9989	.9989	.9990	.9990
3.1	.9990	.9991	.9991	.9991	.9992	.9992	.9992	.9992	.9993	.9993
3.2	.9993	.9993	.9994	.9994	.9994	.9994	.9994	.9995	.9995	.9995
3.3	.9995	.9995	.9995	.9996	.9996	.9996	.9996	.9996	.9996	.9997
3.4	.9997	.9997	.9997	.9997	.9997	.9997	.9997	.9997	.9997	.9998

SOURCE: Taken from G. Hadley, *Introduction to Probability & Statistical Decision Theory.* San Francisco, Calif.: Holden-Day, 1967.

(2) If both X_2 and X_3 are added, the standard deviation of profits drops to $1,620. How does this affect assessments of the probabilities that the firm will achieve a total profit equal to or in excess of $0, $5,000, and $15,000?

(c) List some of the limitations of the type of calculations above, paying attention to such matters as

(1) risk–return trade-offs for a firm.

(2) probability distributions of demand, selling prices, variable costs, and profits.

(3) assessments of correlation between product demands.

5
Performance Evaluation Systems

Our study of the use of accounting data in the internal management of a firm now expands to explicitly recognize that a large number of employees is typically present. Two problems emerge: First, except under theoretically ideal conditions, motivating the various individuals to provide the desired labor services is a difficult, subtle, and poorly understood problem. Second, even with ideal motivation, there remains the problem of coordinating the activities of the various individuals.

The study of these two problems is typically structured around the idea of a management control system. Control is often defined as the process by which management ensures that the performance of operating personnel conforms to the plans and expectations of the firm. Our objection to this definition is that it implies too narrow a scope for a control system. Performance should not be forced to conform to original expectations unless those expectations continue to reflect optimal actions. It is conceivable that unanticipated events will signal the need for or desirability of a change in the plan. Any viable control system should facilitate rather than restrict adaptation to unexpected events.

Accordingly, we will view control as a system or process in which expectations and actual performance are compared and the comparisons serve as a basis for determining the proper responses to operating results. These responses include taking corrective action at the planning or decision-making level as well as at the performance level.

Note that, from an accounting perspective, the common theme in studies of control systems is the idea of _performance evaluation_. Accordingly, we structure our study of these topics around the central theme of how to design systems to evaluate performance. Basic ideas and their relationship to our conceptual cost and value-of-information models are discussed first. Then we present a discussion of pragmatic considerations in the design of evaluation systems, followed by a discussion of the use of explicit standards of performance.

167

Performance Evaluation

The idea of performance evaluation is simple enough: At the time of choosing among alternatives, we make a provision to retrospectively analyze the choice and/or its outcome. A simple cost measurement system provides a ready illustration. A firm is offered a chance to manufacture a special order; whether to accept or reject the offer is the choice at hand. Suppose the firm accepts the offer and begins production. At this point, performance evaluation begins; costs are accumulated in a job-order cost system. After the order has been completed and delivered, the job-order cost system provides a measure of the cost of producing the special order. This is performance evaluation.

Of course, designing, implementing, and maintaining a performance evaluation system is costly. Inevitably, then, we must ask whether the system is worth its cost. In turn, this brings us to the basic question of why we engage in such evaluations.

Uses of Performance Evaluation

To explore this question, first consider a firm consisting of a single person and a single decision. Once the decision is made and the outcome realized, the firm will liquidate, never to appear again. It is difficult to envision such an example, but deciding on a method of liquidation prior to retiring to the beach comes close enough. Suppose two choices are available: a sealed-bid auction, with the highest bidder acquiring the firm, or an auction in which the participants bid in sequence, as in an art or cattle auction. Why might the proprietor commit resources for an after-the-fact evaluation of his choice between these two liquidation options? Of course, he might decide to do so if he contemplated a similar decision situation in the future. But this is, by assumption, his final decision. There is no benefit whatsoever to possessing this information, and he surely would not spend his money to obtain it.

Suppose, however, that the proprietor was not contemplating liquidation. Instead, the choice involves the introduction of a new product, or whether to accept an offer to manufacture a special product. Similar choice problems are contemplated in the future. Thus, he now would be interested in evaluating the current decision and/or outcome to the extent that such evaluation might help him improve the quality of future decisions. This is, in fact, the theme that was conceptualized in Chapter 1 and pursued in Chapter 4. Our interest in an evaluation rests directly on its ability to help us improve our decision making in the future.

Now, return to the terminal decision involving liquidation. This is the final decision, and there is nothing to improve upon beyond this final act. But suppose this final choice has been delegated to a manager or agent. Performance evaluation now becomes of interest, because it may help motivate the manager to make a decision that is in the proprietor's best interest. The manager may see the world differently or have different tastes. He might, for example, have a strong personal interest in acquiring experience with sealed-bid auctions even though a sequential auction would be in the proprietor's best interest. Evaluation information might, therefore, be used to help control the manager's decision, even though this is the final decision in the firm's existence. But this use is somewhat indirect. The proprietor pays the manager for his services. Precisely what services have been provided is generally difficult to sort out, and it is here that evaluation information becomes important. The manager's reward is designed to depend on the performance evaluation, so that his interests become as closely aligned with the proprietor's as is feasible (or desirable). Many refer to the idyllic state of complete alignment as *goal congruence.* Figure 5-1, outlined for the special order example, summarizes the basic idea:

Three points should be noted before we proceed. First, we have identified two components to the motivation exercise: evaluation and reward. While the evaluation side is usually stressed in accounting, it is important to keep both components in our thinking. Very often, an incentive arrangement is actually a substitute for an elaborate evaluation system. Rather than finding massive amounts of detail on a division manager's activities, we typically see bonus arrangements that depend on aggregate results such as divisional profit, divisional profit divided by divisional assets (return on investment), market share, and so on. Second, the notion of reward should be interpreted

_____FIGURE 5-1

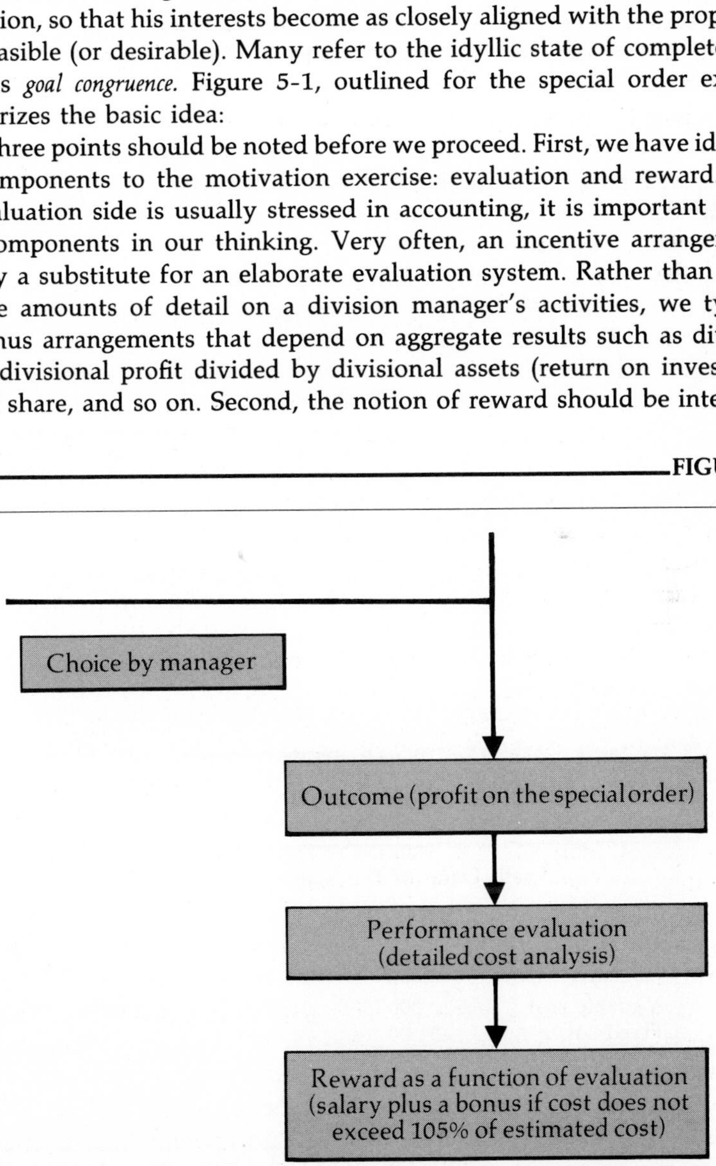

Choice by manager

Outcome (profit on the special order)

Performance evaluation
(detailed cost analysis)

Reward as a function of evaluation
(salary plus a bonus if cost does not
exceed 105% of estimated cost)

in a broad context, extending far beyond cash payments. Various nonpecuniary factors, such as the work environment, commute schedule, and promotion possibilities, are ready examples. Third, this information is useful even when the firm is engaging in its final decision. No subsequent decision will be affected. Its sole purpose at this point is to provide a basis for rewarding the manager so that the manager—when focusing on his personal rewards—will behave in a manner consistent with the proprietor's desires.

Finally, suppose we have many managers and the prospect of many related decision opportunities as time unfolds. The performance evaluation information is now potentially useful as part of the motivation structure, for improving future choices, and for assisting central management in its role of managing the managers, the firm's control system, and so on. Analysis of this more ambitious setting will be postponed until later chapters; for the moment, we will concentrate on the case of a single manager.

Before proceeding to explore various implications of our basic model in Figure 5-1, a numerical example might be helpful. Suppose a division has been approached to supply a required subcomponent to Master Casters. The incremental cost of supplying x units of this subcomponent is known to be

$$\text{Cost} = \$45,000 + \$10x$$

consisting of initial tooling costs of $45,000 and production costs of direct materials, direct labor, and variable overhead totaling $10 per unit. Master Casters is willing to pay $50 per unit. The only catch is that demand is uncertain. Our division will be called upon to produce 1,000, 1,500, or 2,000 units, with respective probabilities of .25, .50, and .25. Relevant profit calculations are summarized in Exhibit 5-1. Notice that the *expected* profit is

$$.25(-\$5,000) + .50(\$15,000) + .25(\$35,000) = \$15,000$$

Now suppose the manager of our division traditionally receives a bonus of 10 percent of the *income* on these special contracts. If income is measured as in Exhibit 5-1, he faces bonus possibilities of −$500, $1,500, and $3,500

EXHIBIT 5-1_____

Profit Data for the Special Order

Demand	1,000	1,500	2,000
Revenue	$50,000	$75,000	$100,000
Variable cost	$10,000	$15,000	$ 20,000
Fixed cost	45,000	45,000	45,000
Total cost	$55,000	$60,000	$ 65,000
Profit	$(5,000)	$15,000	$ 35,000

_____ EXHIBIT 5-2

Absorption Cost Income for the Special Order

Demand	1,000	1,500	2,000
Revenue	$50,000	$75,000	$100,000
Variable cost	$10,000	$15,000	$ 20,000
Average fixed cost @ $30/unit	30,000	45,000	60,000
Total cost	$40,000	$60,000	$ 80,000
Income	$10,000	$15,000	$ 20,000

with respective probabilities of .25, .50, and .25. Suppose, instead, that income is measured under a full (absorption) costing system, wherein fixed costs are allocated to units of output. We might use an "anticipated" production volume of 1,500 units for this purpose, thereby implying a unit cost of $10 + $45,000/1,500 units = $40/unit. This implies the income measures in Exhibit 5-2, where we further assume no adjustment is made for production that differs from the "anticipated" 1,500 units. (In more precise terms, the manager is to be held responsible for production costs based on an average fixed cost datum, but not for any "volume variance.") Notice, now that here the division manager faces bonus possibilities of $1,000, $1,500, and $2,000, with respective probabilities of .25, .50, and .25. In both cases, the expected bonus is $1,500. But the bonus based on the Exhibit 5-1 measure is decidedly more risky. As such, it is conceivable that the division manager could be sufficiently averse to risk that he would _reject_ the offer in the context of Exhibit 5-1 but _accept_ it in the context of Exhibit 5-2.

Several points are in order. First, this example is worthy of study, because it illustrates in a simplistic setting the manner in which evaluation data are used as a basis for determining rewards and how this provides a vehicle for motivating the manager.[1] Second, the example illustrates the important distinction between absorption and variable costing income measures in terms of variability of the resulting measure. Both will eventually average out to the same measure, but the absorption costing measure tends to reduce a manager's risk, which may be an important consideration in motivating the manager to make decisions that are consistent with those desired by the firm in general. Third, with the 10 percent bonus arrangement in place, the question of choice between the evaluation measures in Exhibit 5-1 and 5-2 revolves around the desires of the firm. If the firm wants contracts with this risk–return structure accepted, absorption costing should be used. If not, the variable costing system should be used.

_____

[1] A fuller, more complex discussion of _optimal_ evaluation–incentive structures is available in J. Demski, _Information Analysis,_ Reading, Mass.: Addison-Wesley, 1980, Ch. 6.

Decision Control and Operational Control

Now consider a less artificial setting in which the firm not only wants to improve the quality of its decision making in the future but also is concerned with motivating its managers. These two control concerns give rise to two broad control categories: decision control and operational control. Decision control is the application of the control process to particular decisions of management and evaluation of the results relative to management's expectations. One example of decision control would be evaluation of the profitability of a special order accepted by management during a time of excess capacity. The questions likely to be asked in such a setting would include:

(1) How did the actual contribution of the order compare to its expected contribution?
(2) Did production conditions (such as new orders and available capacity) conform to management's expectations?

Thus, decision control can be viewed as the evaluation of actions selected by management from among a set of possible actions, with an overall concern of improving the quality of such selections in the future.

In contrast, operational control is concerned with the efficiency with which tasks are performed. It is concerned with the extent to which the expected level of performance was achieved in the implementation phase of any decision. Operational control is much more frequently discussed than decision control, because the operations of any organization at the lower levels are usually better understood by management than the decision-making process. Most of the techniques discussed in subsequent chapters may also apply to decision control, but it is important to recognize that they have their origins and greatest use in operational control.

The decision–operational dichotomy is, to some degree, an artificial one. In any organization, the two facets of management interact to affect the actual level of the organization's performance. Thus, a "good" decision poorly executed can look "bad" in an aggregate assessment of what has occurred. Conversely, good operational management can make marginal decisions achieve favorable results.

Considerations in the Design of Performance Evaluation Systems

As we see, then, it is a fairly straightforward exercise to extend our thinking about the use of accounting data in the management of an organization to include performance evaluation. In turn, we regard these evaluation systems as desirable to the extent that they provide a basis for improving the organization's performance, in terms of operational or decision control. This is, of course, more easily said than accomplished, and it is important, therefore, to reinforce our conceptual model with a brief look at pragmatic considerations in the design of performance evaluation systems.

The Importance of Behavioral Science

One set of considerations deals with human behavior, individually or in a group. We have sketched a model of superior–subordinate relations and the use of performance evaluation therein, but the behavior of the subordinate under any particular evaluation–reward scheme remains an open question. And it is at this point that behavioral science becomes important.

Unfortunately, the behavioral sciences present us with a wide diversity of individual and group models of behavior. This is exemplified in the works of (1) Maslow;[2] (2) McGregor[3] and Ouchi;[4] (3) Simon,[5] Cyert and March,[6] Williamson[7] and Ouchi;[8] (4) Herzberg;[9] (5) Skinner;[10] and (6) Vroom.[11] Even synthesizing these works is a task well beyond the reach of an introductory textbook.[12] Instead, we offer a summarization in terms of what these theories do not assume. Although this may appear perverse, it is important to understand that there is no single model that is universally acknowledged to explain human behavior. At the same time, however, we have learned to view control

---

[2] A complete exposition of Maslow's work is presented in A.H. Maslow, *Eupsychian Management: A Journal*. Homewood, Ill.: Irwin, 1965.

[3] McGregor's writings are most frequently characterized by the positions taken in his book *The Human Side of Enterprise*. New York: McGraw-Hill, 1960.

[4] In recent contrast with McGregor's famous labels of authoritarian (Theory X) and participative (Theory Y) views of the management process, we have Ouchi's Theory Z. See W. Ouchi and A. Jaeger, "Type Z Organization: Stability in the Midst of Mobility," *Academy of Management Rev.*, 1978.

[5] H. Simon, "Theories of Bounded Rationality," in C. McGuire and R. Radner, eds., *Decision and Organization*. Amsterdam: North-Holland, 1972.

[6] R. Cyert and J. March, *A Behavioral Theory of the Firm*. Englewood Cliffs, N.J.: Prentice-Hall, 1963.

[7] O. Williamson, M. Wachter, and J. Harris, "Understanding the Employment Relation: The Analysis of Idiosyncratic Exchange," *Bell J. of Econ.*, Spring 1975.

[8] W. Ouchi, "A Conceptual Framework for the Design of Organizational Control Mechanisms," *Management Science*, Sept. 1979.

[9] F. Herzberg, B. Mausner, and B. Snyderman, *The Motivation to Work*. New York: Wiley, 1959.

[10] The work of Skinner in learning theory is not discussed in the context of control as the works of the other writers are. However, see his *Science and Human Behavior*. New York: Free Press, 1953.

[11] V. Vroom, *Work and Motivation*. New York: Wiley, 1964. A recent application of the expectancy model is presented by J. Ronen and J. Livingstone, "An Expectancy Theory Approach to the Motivational Impact of Budgets," *Accounting Rev.*, Oct. 1975.

[12] See H. Rush, *Behavioral Science, Concepts and Management Applications*. New York: National Industrial Conference Board, 1969; E. Caplan, *Management Accounting and Behavioral Science*. Reading, Mass.: Addison-Wesley, 1971; or B. Kolasa, *Introduction to Behavioral Science for Business*. New York: Wiley, 1969.

problems with a vastly less mechanical perspective than that of automatic control (as exemplified by the design of computerized aircraft landing systems).

Specifically, then, behavioral models do *not* assume that

(1) absolute authority rests in a superior relative to his subordinate,
(2) the superior's knowledge of the process being controlled is significantly greater than that of the subordinate's,
(3) "perfect" communication exists between superior and subordinate,
(4) the subordinate is indifferent to the task assigned him and must be motivated to perform that task through various incentives.

Rather, the literature in the behavioral sciences argues that such presumptions are inappropriate.

The assumption that a superior has absolute authority implies not only that he has adequate power to achieve his ends vis-à-vis a subordinate, but also that the subordinate is powerless against him. Such a characterization denies the potential for conflict in an organization. And we know that superior–subordinate conflict does exist. Moreover, when such conflict exists, it is common for the subordinates as a group to gain concessions from their superiors in the form of lowered production quotas, fringe benefits, and other factors that can raise the cost of achieving a given level of activity. No control system can be enforced without at least the acquiescence of the controlled.

The assumptions about knowledge and communication are related. One reason is that if reliable, undistorted communication of information by the subordinates to the superior exists, then the superior knows all that his subordinates know about the process as well as other data gleaned from more privileged sources. Though it is rarely made explicit, the implication is that the superior is also better able to utilize the data than the subordinates. Moreover, assumptions of perfect communication and perfect knowledge imply that the subordinate is willing and able to convey his knowledge free of noise to his superior. Ignoring, for the moment, any problems in information processing between subordinates and superior, this assumption is reasonable only in the absence of conflict. It requires that the subordinates have no desire to withhold or bias the data they communicate.[13] But selective communication of information and "misinformation" in a superior–subordinate hierarchy is a weapon in intergroup conflict. Indeed, motivating the honest communication of private information is the very essence of the control problem. The superior cannot, by assumption, observe the subordinate's private information and, therefore, cannot monitor his communication. How, then, do

---

[13] For examples of this behavior, see A. Lowe and R. Shaw, "An Analysis of Managerial Biasing: Evidence from a Company's Budgeting Process," *J. Management Studies,* Oct. 1968, and J. Fendrock, "Crisis in Conscience at Quasar," *Harvard Bus. Rev.,* March–April 1968.

we ensure that, say, bad news is brought forward in a timely fashion? This is a major dilemma in, for example, the use of audit committees or the maintenance of compliance with the Foreign Corrupt Practices Act.

The assumption about task indifference rules out numerous nonpecuniary dimensions to the work environment. Labor economists refer to the notion of "consumption at work." Friendships, challenge, office decor, computing equipment, structure—all may be important concerns that help shape the subordinate's behavior. Indifference is hardly to be expected.

Two final points conclude our observations here. First, any control system can have attendant dysfunctional consequences. The prospect of being evaluated affects the behavior of the person in question. Consider the simple case of evaluating a subordinate by comparing his production cost with some norm or standard production cost. By employing this particular standard, the superior is informing the subordinate that the cost indicator is important, and thus the subordinate's attention may be directed to it. As a result, he may concentrate on tasks that improve this indicator and ignore tasks previously considered important. To the extent that the change in behavior is in the desired direction, the indicator and its use have achieved their purpose. However, if the introduction of the indicator has caused the subordinate to alter his behavior in a manner that the superior feels is undesirable, the indicator and its use have had a dysfunctional effect. The indicator itself has become the object of the subordinate's goal-oriented behavior rather than merely a convenient representation of the organization's goal. For example, if a production cost indicator is applied to a division manager's performance, it may replace the notion of maximum profitability for him. In striving to reduce costs, the subordinate may lose sight of the overriding goal, profits. As a result, he may forego opportunities, because he is preoccupied with a subgoal. In any case, the establishment and use of indicators can have negative as well as positive effects on subordinate behavior.

Second, people acting individually or as a group may behave according to general rules. However, exactly how each person will react to any given factor is not known. Some individuals function best in a structured situation; others do not. Some prefer a precise statement of goals; others would prefer to shape their own. Each individual produces best in the environment that best fits his or her personal wants and needs. Thus, the ultimate problem is that we must speak in generalities, and we cannot prescribe a single control system that is ideal for all organizations.

The Relationship Between Organization Design and Control Systems

Another set of considerations in the design of performance evaluation systems is the organization structure, or design, at hand. To be sure, the organization design will, in part, reflect evaluation difficulties. For example, the current interest in a matrix form of organization of shared responsibility reflects evaluation difficulties in clearly delineating the responsibility of each individual in the organization. Similarly, merger is one possible solution to the control of external effects imposed by one firm or division on another, as in the classic case of the honey and apple farmers.

On the other hand, the firm's performance evaluation system will reflect the individual decision-making or authority units within an organization. Typically, these authority units are arranged in a hierarchical fashion with authority flowing from the top downward. For example, the president or chief administrative officer has authority over all the activities of the organization. Reporting to him would be a set of vice-presidents, or their equivalent, who have control over managers of individual departments or functions, and so on down the line. (This typical hierarchical arrangement is purposely "blurred" in the matrix organization.) In general, the accountant designs his evaluation system so that it is consistent with the organizational structure and organizational philosophy of the firm.

Evaluation systems are present in some form at all levels of a large organization. The greater the degree to which authority has been delegated, the greater the motivation for the man delegating the authority to be aware of and to evaluate the individual acting on his behalf. Thus, we would expect the relationship between the president and his vice-presidents to reflect many of the same control characteristics we would observe in the relationship between any supervisor and his subordinates. However, there will be differences in the form that each characteristic takes. In the case of the president and vice-presidents, the specific acts to be performed are much less standardized. A vice-president is usually given authority to define the manner in which he will accomplish his function. Consequently, his performance is usually evaluated in broad terms. For example, a vice-president in charge of production would be evaluated by the overall efficiency of his production departments, as characterized by unit costs, quality control, and so on. In contrast, a supervisor might be evaluated in terms of the material and labor costs of a specific kind of output. It is also likely that the vice-president's performance would be evaluated over longer periods of time, partly because his decisions have greater long-run implications. To illustrate, the results of a decision to change production schedules may not affect productivity for several time periods, whereas the effect of a supervisor's decision to change workers on one type of machine will be reflected in the next production run.[14]

In decision control, performance indicators lose their precision mainly because there is uncertainty about what constitutes optimal performance by the individuals responsible for various activities. This is well illustrated by research and development. Basic research is conducted under conditions of

---

[14] This notion of the time it takes for an individual's decision to affect the organization has been used, on occasion, to define the levels within an organization.

extreme uncertainty and may lead to highly profitable new products or to nothing. But the outcome of current expenditures for research will not be known until some future period. The question, then, is how should the expenditure decisions made in the current period by someone in charge of research be evaluated? Ideally, the performance of an individual in charge of an activity should be evaluated by comparing the amount of resources consumed to produce a certain number of units of "good output" with some standard. In the case of research, "good output" could be new products or even new knowledge. But since we do not expect to observe any good output in the current period from current outlays, some other means of evaluation must be instituted to assess the performance of the person in charge of research during the current period.

This problem is a common one at higher levels of an organization, as well as in many service organizations. As we shall discuss later, one approach to this problem is to evaluate the decision processes of managers rather than the results of their decisions.

Characteristics of Effective Performance Evaluation Systems

Performance evaluation, then, is intimately related to the firm's quest for improved quality in its decision making. This is easy enough to state, but how are we to judge whether one evaluation system is superior to another? Extending our cost and value-of-information model in Chapter 1 will allow us to formalize the basic idea. But the implied analysis is extensive and, as a result, more pragmatic guides are commonly used. Typical examples are:

(1) Congruence of the evaluation measure with the firm's goal
(2) Measurement error
(3) Timeliness
(4) Cost
(5) Behavioral effects

Others have given different names to some of these properties, but the intended meaning is usually the same. In the following paragraphs, we discuss each of these properties and indicate why, other things being equal, each might be desirable.

Congruence with Goals.   Ideally, top management should operationalize the firm's goals, so that the performance indicator conveyed to any subordinate will be such that if he maximizes this indicator, he will also maximize his contribution to the goals of the organization. This is difficult to achieve.

Consider the following example of the return on investment (ROI), or ratio of profit to total assets, a common performance indicator that is discussed in greater detail in Chapter 10. The ROI is a surrogate that operationalizes top management's exhortation to the division manager to use the division's assets efficiently. It is possible that, in maximizing his own division's rate of return, however, the manager will make less than his maximum possible contribution to the net cash inflows of the firm. For example, he may reject opportunities that would lower his division's rate of return from, say, 25 percent to 22 percent, even though their return would still be above the firmwide return of, for example, 15 percent. This highlights one difficulty in using a performance indicator that is a surrogate: Efforts of a well-intentioned manager may lead to results that are less than optimal for the organization as a whole. Because of measurement problems, however, most performance indicators do deviate to some degree from perfect congruence with the organization's goals.[15]

Moreover, the idea of maximizing a performance indicator denies the presence of risk in all but the most ideal situations. For example, a firm might evaluate its salespeople on the basis of the expected present value of the contracts sold. Suppose the customers vary in riskiness and the implied rate of return varies with the risk. Adopting a conventional present value[16] measure with a fixed rate, say 12 percent, will make the most risky contracts appear to be the most desirable at the time of evaluation, and this will, no doubt, result in the riskiest of contracts being acquired.

Congruence of the evaluation measure with the firm's goal (or goals), in other words, may contain a fair degree of subtlety. Seeking a maximal contribution, even if well measured, may best be viewed in terms of seeking the best risk–return tradeoff, and at evaluation time we are likely to see only the actual outcome. More will be said about this later.

Measurement Error.   When a property is measured, it is possible for the measuring technique to lead to two types of errors. One is bias. Bias exists when the reported measurement systematically differs in one direction from the true value of the variable. For example, a worker reporting his own time working on various tasks may report that nearly all of his time is spent on productive activities and that little, if any, is spent on nonproductive tasks. The resulting data are biased in a known direction, but probably not by a known amount. Faced with such a situation, management can infer that the reported activity is no more efficient than as shown in the worker's report and probably is less so. Because of the bias inherent in the measurement process, however, management cannot be confident that a favorable performance report really reflects efficient work. The measurement bias could be obscuring the actual state of the worker's performance.

The second error potentially present in the measurement of any perfor-

---

[15] See V.F. Ridgway, "Dysfunctional Consequences of Performance Measurements," *Administrative Science Quarterly*, Sept. 1956.

[16] Present value concepts are discussed in Chapter 14.

mance refers to unsystematic (random) differences between repeated measures of the property of a given event. Again using the example of the worker who is expected to report his time by jobs, we can see that even the most honest and diligent of workers will make only relatively accurate estimates of the time per job. Factors such as rounding to the nearest minute, inability to punch in and out precisely at the start and finish of a job, and various distractions may all alter the reported time from trial to trial.

Measurement error is potentially harmful in a performance evaluation system for two reasons. First, the manager cannot be as sure of the underlying state of performance as he would like to be. When the variability is high, or the bias is unknown, he runs a greater risk of misevaluating performance because of noise added to the data by the measurement process. The second problem is that the subordinate may recognize this and note inequities that arise when what he feels are equally good performances are accorded different ratings.

Timeliness and Costs.   A simple measure may be prepared and reported quickly at relatively little cost. A more sophisticated measure usually requires greater time for preparation and results in greater cost. It is easy to see that, within reasonable limits, timeliness and cost effectiveness are desirable. Moreover, expenditures on the development and reporting of the performance indicators (like other properties of the control system) must be justified by expected benefits. It would be futile for management to invest thousands of dollars to develop a reporting system that makes hourly reports possible if the new system could save only a few hundred dollars a year.

Behavioral Effects.   The design of any evaluation process should consider the impact of the message on the receiver. A performance indicator, as part of the reporting process, affects the performer. It is traditional to assume that accounting reports are neutral, that their presence does not alter the behavior of the recipient, except to the extent that the data contained in the report aid in decision making. There is substantial evidence that this is not the case. The writing of Ridgway cited earlier discusses how the performance indicator refocuses the attention of the subordinate.[17] (It may also refocus the attention of the superior.) Similarly, Stedry found in laboratory studies, as users of Skinnerian methods found in the field, that the manner in which the data are presented can affect behavior.[18] And more recently, Hopwood has documented the importance of the manner in which the supervisor uses evaluation data.[19] In short, timely, errorless, congruent measures are not enough.

---

[17] Ridgway, "Disfunctional Consequences."

[18] See A. Stedry, *Budget Control and Cost Behavior.* Englewood Cliffs, N.J.: Prentice-Hall, 1960, and "Where Skinner's Theories Work," *Business Week,* Dec. 2, 1972.

[19] A. Hopwood, "An Empirical Study of the Role of Accounting Data in Performance Evaluation," *J. Accounting Research Supp.,* 1972.

An interesting example of this is given by the experience of one firm in dealing with absenteeism.[20] By shortening the reporting period from a month to a week, absenteeism was reduced from 11 percent to about 6 percent. The cause of the decline was simply the redirecting of the workers' attention from one long period to four shorter ones. Management found that, once the worker had been absent once during a period, the likelihood of another absence later in the period was quite high. By shortening the period, management reduced the opportunity for further absences by simply reducing the number of days in a period. Thus, under the one-month period, a worker absent early in a period might miss several additional days later in the month. With the weekly periods, however, the worker had a clean start each week and was less likely to stay home for trivial reasons.

In sum, the evaluation system is desirable to the extent that (1) in conjunction with the rewards based thereon, it provides a vehicle for motivating good decision making by subordinates and (2) it provides a basis for learning and for improving decision making in future periods. Characteristics such as congruence, measurement error, timeliness, cost, and behavioral effects may help the firm analyze the design of its evaluation system. But this is not an easy task for which well-laid-out recipes exist.

Standards of Performance

A final observation on the generally murky topic of performance evaluation concerns the use (and misuse) of *standards of performance.* Quite simply, the idea is to base the evaluation on performance relative to some norm. We will refer to this norm as a *standard,* or standard of performance. But you should be aware that in accounting circles the term has a fairly precise meaning, which will be discussed in more detail in Chapter 6.

If standards of performance are part of the evaluation process, we have the following sequence of events in this process:

(1) Defining the goal(s) of some unit of activity (for example, produce 10,000 widgets).
(2) Establishing specific performance standards for each act required to accomplish these goals (for example, each widget should require one pound of wood).
(3) Communicating the goals and the standards of the activity to the person designated to be responsible for directing the process being controlled.
(4) Performing the activity under the direction of the responsibility head.

---

[20] "Where Skinner's Theories Work."

FIGURE 5-2

A formal control system.

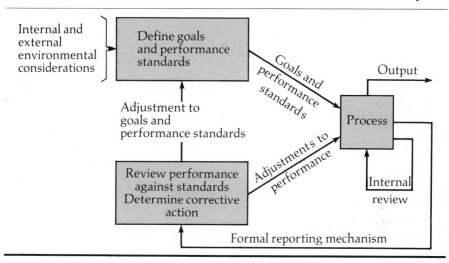

(5) Recording the results of performance and comparing them with the previously established standards.

(6) Communicating, through a report of performance compared against standards, with the person responsible for the operation of the activity and analyzing any deviation from the standards.

The goals and standards may be set by top management, with or without the participation of the responsibility head. Figure 5–2 illustrates these steps in diagrammatic form.

Note that the sequence of steps is shown explicitly for the evaluation and control of only one activity or process. Other systems would exist for each of the various processes, departments, or activities. Furthermore, within the box labeled "Process," several subcontrol systems could also exist. For example, assume that the process represents a division of a firm. The output goals for this division are probably set by central management and communicated to the division head, who determines the activities that are necessary to accomplish the goals set for him and the standards for each. The standards for each activity are then communicated to the supervisors held responsible for the various activities. Each supervisor will then outline the appropriate goals and performance standards for the personnel working for him. This hierarchy continues to all levels where control via a systematic process exists.

The six steps outlined previously provide a detailed framework within which any control system can be examined. For convenience, they can be compressed into three steps:

(1) The standard-setting phase of the system consists of steps 1, 2, and 3 (determining goals, and establishing and communicating standards).

(2) The operating phase consists only of step 4 (performing the activity).

(3) The feedback phase consists of steps 5 and 6 (recording and communicating the results).

The Standard-Setting Phase

Setting standards of performance is a difficult and poorly understood task. Three classes of problems are present: (1) What aspects of performance should be highlighted against a performance norm? (2) Who should set these standards? (3) What level of performance should the standards require?

Controllable Aspects of Performance. The usual answer to the first question rests on the notion of controllability. The manager's evaluation should be confined to those aspects of performance that he can directly influence in the time period under consideration. The idea is that without an ability to directly influence, say, revenue, the manager cannot (indeed, should not) be held responsible for revenue. And if his influence does not show up in current period revenue, he cannot be held responsible for that segment of the revenue stream.

As such, the controllability criterion rests on a notion of "fairness." But remember that this is a simplistic, pragmatic approach to the problem. The firm attempts to motivate the manager through judicious choice of performance indicators and rewards structured thereon. So the real question is what performance indicators are useful in this regard. In turn, the firm is trying to use the indicators to infer the quality of the manager's behavior.

As a first cut at the problem, controllability has a lot to recommend it. If the manager cannot influence the price of raw materials, then this particular cost item presumably tells us nothing about the manager's behavior. But this is not entirely clear. The price may be uncertain, and one of the manager's tasks is to deal with such factor price uncertainty as best he can. If so, it is important to use price in evaluating him. To do otherwise invites behavior that ignores the uncertainty. Similarly, two branch managers may be compared, even though the two managers have no influence whatever on each other's performances. The reason is that common elements of uncertainty affect both branches, and the performance of one branch manager is useful in inferring the behavior of the other.

Moreover, financial aspects of performance are not the only ones that are important. Number of units produced, number of defective units produced, market share, speeches to civic industries, number of new customers, employee turnover, debris in the parking lot, and so on have all been used in manager evaluation. The manager can control, say, employee turnover, and at the margin this statistic is useful in inferring his behavior.

Controllability, then, is a key idea in deciding what aspects of firm performance to use in evaluating a given manager's performance. But recognizing the underlying issues also indicates that an appropriately tempered rather than overly zealous approach to its implementation is important.[21]

Participation in Standard-Setting.   The second question in the standard-setting phase concerns who should set the standards, that is, who should determine which aspects of firm performance to use in evaluating the manager (and what norms or standards should be used in the evaluation). One extreme is autocratic decree by top management; the other is autocratic decree by the manager. Both are naive in the sense that the manager can always quit and reenter the labor market and the firm can always replace the manager. So the real question is (again) one of degree; both parties are involved in one way or another.

One way to view the role of participation is in terms of providing the subordinate a "richer" task that permits information to flow from the subordinate to the superior, and vice versa. The use of participation in the setting of standards was analyzed in this manner by Becker and Green.[21] They stressed that participation by itself does not necessarily lead to improved performance; other conditions conducive to increased productivity must also be present. Their arguments can be stated briefly as follows. If greater interaction of individuals within the management process leads to greater group cohesiveness, and if this cohesiveness plus some incentive to produce at either a higher or lower level are positively correlated, then participation can induce higher or lower levels of performance. If participation at an upper level generates a positive attitude on the part of supervisors, then they in turn will try to induce higher individual and group aspirations in their subordinates, which will lead to higher levels of production.

The complexity of these interactions indicates that increased participation in setting the standard can lead to either increased or decreased levels of performance. Poorer performance can result when the participative standard-setting process appears to conflict with the leadership styles usually found in the organization. This is particularly true of the authoritarian method of supervision, where the supervisor or manager imposes standards on his subordinates. In a basically authoritarian setting, any attempts at participation,

---

[21] We are, of course, hinting at difficult evaluation questions in a world of uncertainty. See J. Demski, "Uncertainty and Evaluation Based on Controllable Performance," *J. Accounting Research,* Autumn 1976; Ronen and Livingstone, "An Expectancy Theory Approach"; J. Demski and G. Feltham, "Economic Incentives in Budgetary Control Systems," *Accounting Rev.* (April 1978); and B. Holmstrom, "Moral Hazard and Observability," *Bell J. of Econ.* Spring 1979.

[21] S. Becker and D. Green, "Budgeting and Employee Behavior," *J. Bus.,* Oct. 1962, and "Budgeting and Employee Behavior: A Rejoinder to a Reply," *J. Bus.,* April 1964.

regardless of good intentions, are usually interpreted by the subordinate as insincere or manipulative.

Another way to view the role of participation is in terms of private information. If the superior and subordinate are equally cognizant of all aspects of the production setting, the only issue is striking a performance bargain that all parties can live with. This is not an easy task, but the important thing to note is that a strong flavor of negotiation surrounds the question at this point.

Contrast this with the case in which the subordinate possesses superior production information. He, for example, better knows his local market, his cost-savings opportunities, and so on. A major purpose of the standard-setting phase is to bring this information to bear on the firm's decision making. But will the subordinate capitalize on his superior information by withholding some of it or creating "slack" in his performance norms? That is, nontrivial participation is engaged in so as to provide a vehicle for bringing this superior information to bear.

This is precisely the idea of the currently popular "management by objectives" (MBO) approach to evaluation. The superior and subordinate negotiate a set of goals, and the subsequent evaluation is based on these negotiated goals. And it is no accident that a good arrangement for negotiation between differentially informed parties takes a similar form. Suppose you want to purchase a used car and acknowledge that the current owner knows whether the car is a lemon. One way to utilize the owner's information is to make two offers: one with and one without a warranty. The owner's acceptance of one over the other may reveal whether the car is a lemon. And judiciously setting the two offers will guarantee that you do not overpay for the car, regardless of its quality. In a similar vein, the MBO negotiation can be viewed in terms of a menu of budgets being offered, with the better informed subordinate selecting one, thereby revealing his information and committing himself to its use.

Participation in standard-setting, then, is not an issue of presence or absence. In the sense that there is a labor market, we always have some degree of participation. And viewed as a matter of degree, we link its use to behavioral considerations and the subordinate's private possession of important information.

Tight Versus Loose Standards. The final question in the standard-setting phase concerns the level at which the standard should be set. Here, as with controllability and participation, we offer an ambiguous answer, because practice varies and our limited theories are consistent with a wide spectrum of answers.

To understand the role of the standard, it is important to recognize that the subordinate might psychologically identify with the standard and derive satisfaction from favorable performance relative to it. Moreover, his explicit rewards are also likely to depend on his performance relative to the standard. A "low" or "loose" standard might, in other words, be associated with a nontrivial failure penalty and a "high" or "tight" standard with a nontrivial success bonus. Bonus arrangements in professional sports provide an excellent source of examples, with specific standards varying from quite loose to extremely tight.

On the other hand, the typical recommendation is that the standards of performance should be reasonably attainable. If they are too low, superior performance may be discouraged, and if they are too high, reasonable performance may even be discouraged.

A classic study intended to assess the impact of standards on subordinate behavior was conducted by Stedry.[23] He developed a model of subordinate behavior based on standards of varying degrees of difficulty. His results highlighted (1) the importance of acceptance by the subordinates of the standards set for them and (2) the relationship between the level of difficulty of the standard and the level of performance actually achieved.

In Stedry's study, two groups were given the same performance test. One group was given the standard first, then asked to set their own goals for their performance in the subsequent period. The second group was asked to indicate their goals before they knew the standard the experimenter set for them. He found that the students who set their goals first set higher goals and performed better than those who were told the experimenter's standards first. In addition, the students whose standards were attainable performed significantly better than those given very difficult standards.

Apparently, the worker whose standard is set by management at a lower level than his personal goal lowers his "aspiration level" to conform to that goal. In effect, the worker performs up to the level of the external standard. This can be significantly below his abilities and even below what he might have done in the absence of the imposed standard.

One of the inferences drawn from Stedry's findings is the possible desirability of actively varying the standard and performance reports according to the psychological characteristics of the individual being controlled. There is little question that the skills of individuals and their reactions to deviations between their performance and the standard vary. For example, one individual may react to a large deviation by improving subsequent performance, but another may react to the same deviation by losing all initiative to improve performance. A central issue, then, is whether these and similar characteristics ought to be taken into account in the design of the organization's control system.

Record-keeping problems would abound with the use of highly personalized and formal evaluation mechanisms. But this is only part of the difficulty. For example, suppose several individuals performing similar tasks discovered

---

[23] Stedry, *Budget Control and Cost Behavior.*

that each had a different standard. Could management justify the situation in terms of the differences in their skills (as in bonus clauses in professional sports)? Would an individual controlled by a tight standard feel that the overall system was fair? These are difficult questions, and it is important to remember that an issue such as the use of personalized standards cannot be divorced from the intended use of the performance standard. Here, the relationship between the standard and the reward structure is important. Thus, depending on circumstances, personalities, and implicit and explicit rewards, we would expect to see tight performance standards, loose performance standards, and reasonably attainable performance standards. Similarly, in dealing with a group of individuals, we would expect personalized evaluation–reward structures if skill and effort differences were important, readily discernible, and marketable. Otherwise we would expect more homogeneous treatment, as in the internal labor market structures of, say, large CPA firms.

The Feedback Process

Feedback, or reporting on performance relative to standards (refer to Figure 5-2), fulfills two functions. One is to inform all interested parties of the results of the previous period's activities. The other is to provide information on possible trouble spots. Note that feedback does not seek to establish blame for an unfavorable act. This is significant, for it reinforces the basic tenet underlying the evaluation system—the purpose is to improve decision-making. Too great an emphasis on blame can actually frustrate the intended purpose of the system.

Feedback as Data for Decisions. During the current operating period, all parties to the evaluation system will have an idea about how operations are progressing. The closer the individual is to the activity, the better his knowledge of that activity is likely to be. The subordinate will know more than his supervisor about the current state of the activities for which he is responsible. Similarly, his supervisor is expected to be more aware of the details of the activities than is a supervisor who is two layers removed from the activities.

The subordinate's knowledge is based on two factors. One is that these activities are his primary concern and occupy a far greater proportion of his time than of his superiors. The second is that he is physically present and can observe the activities, keeping an informal information system (either written or mental) concerning them. During the period, he is a potential source of information for the superior.

The subordinate's knowledge of what is occurring during an operating period permits him to react and make any necessary adjustments during the period. It also means that he is capable of adapting his own behavior to the new situation. This can be advantageous to the organization. If the subordinate does not accept the standard being used to evaluate him, however, he is in a position to ultimately frustrate the organization's pursuit of its goals. Piece-rate workers, suspicious that management will increase the required rate if they exceed the standard by too large an amount, have been known to restrict their work to modest levels.

Similarly, managers who are falling behind in their quota can adapt their behavior to meet the standard for its own sake. For example, managers in Russia during the 1950s and 1960s were reputed to regularly "storm" at the end of a period. (Storming is producing large quantities so as to meet the standard rather than the demand.) Nail plant managers whose quotas were set in tons of nails per month produced large quantities of spikes at the end of those months in which production had lagged, because it was easier to produce one spike than an equal weight in smaller nails. The manager thereby met his production quota, but it is unlikely that his performance was as valuable to the central planners as it would have been under a lower quota with a more desirable assortment of nail sizes.[24]

Feedback as Data for Evaluation. It is obvious that the format used to report performance data will direct the superior's attention to particular facets of the subordinate's behavior and performance. At its best, the report permits both parties to focus on key issues. Unfortunately, to be successful, this usually requires a peerlike relationship between the superior and subordinate. Except for unusual situations, any inquiry by the superior into the cause of an unfavorable deviation from a performance indicator is likely to be perceived as threatening by the subordinate. Thus, he will do the best he can to protect himself by explaining the problem in the way most favorable to him.

Ideally, the evaluation phase should be dispassionate and nonhostile. But assessment is ultimately involved with questions of the subordinate's career, welfare, and position, which are issues that cannot be taken lightly. The potential for superior–subordinate conflict is surely nontrivial.[25] To alleviate this threat, many organizations have encouraged self-control by the subordinate. The standard is set in a way that leads to goal congruence between the subordinate and the organization. Subsequently, the primary responsibility for change rests with the subordinate, and his superior is concerned over the longer run not only with what problems he faced but also with whether he resolved them efficiently. Thus, the superior is not involved intimately or frequently with the subordinate, and some of the potential for conflict is removed. Every management adopting such an approach, however, must recognize that benefits can be secured only at the risk of permitting other problems to go undetected.

---

[24] Another version of this phenomenon is documented by Zimmerman in a government-sponsored research agency. See J. Zimmerman, "Budget Uncertainty and the Allocation Decision in a Nonprofit Organization," *J. Accounting Research,* Autumn 1976.

[25] A. Brief, R. Aldag, and M. Van Swell, "Moderators of the Relationships Between Self and Superior's Evaluation of Job Performance," *J. Occupational Psychology,* July 1977.

Management Audits

A more recent approach to evaluation is the "management (or managerial) audit"; its purpose is to evaluate the manner in which the manager has performed his job. The emphasis is on observing the procedures he followed rather than on focusing entirely on the results he achieved. Obviously, the presence of an observer who will somehow pass judgment will affect a manager's performance. One early study of these effects sheds some light on this problem. It was found that managers whose performances had been audited conformed to firm policy more readily when told that their work would be audited again than did a group of managers who had not previously been audited.[26] Presumably, the audited managers realized the potential impact on them of a deviation from the firm's policy. They therefore adhered to the policy, even in the face of more efficient alternatives.

Internal audits have long been used to ensure that certain policies and procedures are being followed and to verify the financial transactions of the firm. Recently, they have been extended to include an examination of the efficiency of managers. Such managerial audits are used to determine whether the managers used the best principles of management in carrying out their responsibilities. Different forms of managerial audits are performed in organizations on a routine basis. For example, the review of a capital budgeting decision by a central committee is a form of managerial audit. Similarly, a review of a surgeon's operation by a hospital staff may have as its purpose the determination of whether the proper diagnostic and operating procedures were followed. The assumption behind the use of managerial audits is that the specific outcomes of some types of decisions do not adequately reflect the efficiency of the individual who made the decision. The individual's efficiency depends also on the reasonableness of his or her decision, given the information available at the time the decision had to be made.

The managerial audit might also include an examination of the procedures used in such activities as estimating costs and revenues, making inventory decisions, and choosing output mixes. Indeed, the managerial audit may represent the only means of control over activities with performance levels that are difficult to evaluate. As an example, it may be more feasible to control capital expenditures by reviewing the decision process itself than by looking at the specific outcomes achieved. In fact, the outcomes of many capital budgeting decisions—that is, the degree to which actual cash flows parallel projected cash flows—may not even be observable. The actual cash flows from one decision commingle with those of other decisions, so that specific cash flows are no longer identifiable. Similar comments apply to evaluating a man-

---

[26] See N. Churchill, W. Cooper, and T. Sainsbury, "Laboratory and Field Studies on the Behavioral Effects of Audits," in C. Bonini, R. Jaedicke, and H. Wagner, eds., *Management Controls.* New York: McGraw-Hill, 1964.

ager's response in the face of nontrivially risky options. Top management seeks the desired risk–return trade-off. This will be obvious from actual outcomes only after a long period of time. Hence, the interest in a "management audit" as an evaluation device increases.

Conclusion

In this chapter we have described some general aspects of performance evaluation systems and the problems involved in implementing them. Performance evaluation systems are useful in providing information to improve the quality of future decisions and in providing information as a basis for motivating subordinates to make desired current period decisions. As such, they are an essential component of the firm's control system.

There are many unsolved problems concerning the proper design of evaluation systems. Most of these center on motivational effects of control procedures, which are always present in situations in which it is necessary for one individual to review and evaluate the performance of another. Although these problems are not yet resolved, an awareness of their origin may facilitate the implementation of formal systems of control.

This chapter's general discussion should serve as a frame of reference for studying the specific mechanics of designing accounting systems for control. In Chapter 6, we discuss the mechanics of setting standards for performance. On a number of occasions we shall find it useful to refer back to issues raised in this chapter.

Supplementary Readings

Articles

Arrow, K., "Control in Large Organizations," *Management Science,* April 1964.

Benston, G., "The Role of the Firm's Accounting System for Motivation," *Accounting Rev.,* April 1963.

Blocher, E., "Performance Effects of Different Audit Staff Assignment Strategies," *Accounting Rev.,* July 1979.

Devine, C., "Observations on Internal Controls," in S. Zeff *et al.,* eds., *Essays in Honor of William A. Paton.* Ann Arbor, Mich.: University of Michigan, 1979.

Kaye, S. and G. Stern, "Executive Compensation: Price vs. Pride," *Directors & Boards,* Fall 1977.

Schiff, M. and A. Lewin, "The Impact of People on Budgets," *Accounting Rev.,* April 1970.

Shavell, S., "Risk Sharing and Incentives in the Principal and Agent Relationship," *Bell J. of Econ.,* Spring 1979.

Books

Argyris, C., *The Impact of Budgets on People.* New York: The Controllers Foundation, 1952.

Coombs, C., R. Dawes, and A. Tversky, *Mathematical Psychology: An Elementary Introduction.* Englewood Cliffs, N.J.: Prentice-Hall, 1970.

Dalton, G.W. and P.R. Lawrence, *Motivation and Control in Organizations.* Homewood, Ill.: Irwin, 1971.

Dalton, M., *Men Who Manage.* New York: Wiley, 1959.

George, A., *Presidential Decisionmaking in Foreign Policy: The Effective Use of Information and Advice.* Boulder, Col.: Westview Press, 1980.

Hopwood, A., *Accounting and Human Behavior.* London: Haymarket Publishing Ltd., 1974.

Itami, H., *Adaptive Behavior: Management Control and Information Analysis.* Sarasota, Fla.: American Accounting Association, 1977.

Lawler, E. and J. Rhode, *Information and Control in Organizations.* Pacific Palisades, Ca.: Goodyear, 1976.

Newman, W. and E. Warren, *The Process of Management,* Engelwood Cliffs, N.J.: Prentice-Hall, 1977.

Pfeffer, J., *Organizational Design.* Arlington Heights, Ill.: AHM Publishing, 1978.

Swieringa, R. and R. Moncur, *Some Effects of Participative Budgeting on Managerial Behavior.* New York: NAA, 1975.

Williamson, O., *Markets and Hierarchies: Analysis and Antitrust Implications.* New York: The Free Press, 1975.

*Questions and Problems*_____

1. Performance evaluation systems are not confined to workers or operating foremen; they affect management as well. In what ways would the manager-oriented evaluation system differ from the worker-oriented system? Is there a performance evaluation system for the chairman and his board of directors in the large, publicly held corporation? For the board's audit committee?

2. Suppose you owned a taxicab and planned to drive it one more week, then retire.
    (a) Of what use would performance evaluation be in this final week?
    (b) Suppose you hired an agent to drive the taxicab during the final week. Of what use would performance evaluation now be during this final week? How do you reconcile your answer with that in part (a)?

3. (a) How would you attempt to control expenditures in a firm's research and development department? Indicate the role of planning in the control process.
    (b) Given the control system you suggested in part (a) of this question, how would you channel your activities if you were now head of the research and development department?

4. Reconsider your answer in part (a) of Question 3 above. Does it possess the characteristics of a "good" performance evaluation system?

5. It is sometimes suggested that there is a control system in which no feedback loop is present. Do you think such a system could exist in industry? Do you think it would be desirable?

6. Is the organization chart (manual) sufficient information on which to base a firm's responsibility accounting and control systems?

7. In Figure 5–2 there is a loop for internal reporting and adjustment. How does this informal step fit into the formal control system? Under what conditions is this loop important?

8. Define controllability. What is its relevance in the design of performance evaluation systems?

9. What is the accounting system's role in the firm's control system?

10. **Nonfinancial Performance Measures**[27]
Fast-food chains employ a variety of performance evaluation measures. An outlet manager might, for example, be evaluated in terms of sales revenue, contribution margin (sales less variable expense), employee training activities, and a service index. The service index, in turn, is compiled by auditors who spot-check the outlet and rate it in terms of, say, cleanliness, product quality, service quality, and so on. Discuss the reasons for such an approach to manager evaluation. Do you feel such an approach is fair? Do you think the evaluation scheme would change through time as the food chain grows in size?

11. **Decision-Operational Evaluation**
A popular approach to cost control is to classify cost items into committed, discretionary, and engineered categories. The committed category consists of cost items for decisions that are not subject to review during the current period. (For example, the cost associated with plant and equipment.) The discretionary category consists of costs that arise from periodic appropriation decisions (such as research and development) and bear no particular relationship to short-run operating decisions during the current period. The engineered category consists of costs that arise from short-run operating decisions (typically in "well engineered" fashion, as exemplified by requisite number of production supervisors, component assemblies, or other factors). Discuss this approach to performance evaluation in terms of the model presented in this chapter.

12. **Behavioral Aspects of Goal Setting**
The results of Stedry's study suggest that the best control system is the one that gets the best results, such as lowest costs. To illustrate, if you tell a worker his standard is 5 hours, knowing it will take him longer to perform the task, and he does it in 10 hours, that is a better system than one where he is told to perform the task in 11 hours, and he does it in 10¼ hours.

(a) Do you agree or disagree with this definition of a good control system? Why or why not?

(b) Do you think performance under the first system would continue to be superior to the second over several periods? Why or why not?

---

[27] Based on W. Sasser and S. Pettway, "Case of Big Mac's Pay Plans," *Harvard Bus. Rev.* July–August 1974.

13. **Effects of an Incentive Scheme**

Modern Management, Inc., has recently installed a new incentive system for Cly-Ent Company's foremen. The plan consists of a bonus of $200 for each week the performance of the foreman's department is up to the standard quota and $10 per unit on the favorable variance, that is, the amount by which his department exceeds the production quota. The data for eight weeks before the plan is instituted are shown below.

	1	2	3	4	5	6	7	8
Actual	10,200	10,000	10,900	10,500	11,600	12,000	11,900	12,200
Quota	10,000	10,500	10,500	11,500	11,000	11,800	12,000	12,000
Variance[a]	200F	500U	400F	1,000U	600F	200F	100U	200F

[a] F denotes favorable; U denotes unfavorable.

Given the above information, answer the following:

(a) How has Cly-Ent apparently been setting the production quota in the past?
(b) How would you behave as foreman to maximize your own income from the incentive system?
(c) What change would you make in the new system to make it more effective? Why?

14. **Effects of Compensation Scheme on Costs**

Major Manufacturer, usually called 2M, has developed a new formula for an appetite appeaser. Until recently, it has been sold only in 2M's traditional market, New England, where it was quite successful. As a result of this consumer acceptance, 2M market tested it in large segments of the South. The results exceeded 2M's expectations. They are now going into national distribution.

Modern Management, Inc., developed a commission plan for 2M's salespeople that is outlined below.

New England region:
$200 per month plus 2 percent of sales as commission. (Commissions average about $1,500 per month.)
Southern region:
$50 per month plus 5 percent of sales as commission. (Commissions average about $1,400 per month.)
Remainder of the country:
$200 per month plus 3 percent of sales as commission plus $25 for each new customer. (Three percent is the industry's normal rate of commission.)

After three months of operations under this system, the cost data are being reviewed by 2M's management. They are not concerned about the wage and commission payments to the salespeople but rather about the difference in the expenses they have incurred. As the comptroller put it, "New England-based salespeople turn in expense vouchers with only the usual travel, food, and a few phone calls on it. The Southerners are traveling more than they used to and have started to show some entertainment expenses. But it's the others that bother me! Too much travel, phone, and lunches. They are way out of line with the other two regions."

(a) Discuss whether the incentive system is affecting cost behavior.
(b) Discuss whether you consider the incentive system appropriate.

15. **Intergroup Conflict and the Control System**
Dalton found in one firm that managers were able to manipulate the records, so that they subverted the system.[28] The various lower-level managers united in their own best interest, against the system.

(a) What does this imply for the design and implementation of management control systems?
(b) Do any of the points you raised in part (a) also apply to control systems for workers?

16. **Effect of an Incentive System on Worker Behavior**
The president of Taylor School Supply Company, a wholesaler, presents you with a comparison of distribution costs for two salesmen and wants to know if you think the salesmen's compensation plan is working to the detriment of the company. He supplies you with the following data:

	SALESMEN	
	McKinney	**Sim**
Gross sales	$247,000	$142,000
Sales returns	17,000	2,000
Cost of goods sold	180,000	85,000
Reimbursed expenses (e.g., entertainment)	5,500	2,100
Other direct charges (e.g, samples distributed)	4,000	450
Commission rate on gross sales dollars	5%	5%

(a) A salesman's compensation plan encourages him to work to increase the measure of performance to which his compensation is related. List the questionable sales practices by a salesman that might be encouraged by basing commissions on gross sales.
(b) What evidence that the compensation plan may be working to the detriment of the company can be found in the data? What other information might the president obtain before reaching definite conclusions about this particular situation? Why?

[AICPA adapted]

17. **Decentralization and Decisions**
The Ajax division of Gunnco Corporation, which is operating at capacity, has been asked by the Defco division of Gunnco to supply it with electrical fitting number 1726. Ajax sells this part to its regular customers for $7.50 each. Defco,

---

[28] See M. Dalton, *Men Who Manage*, Ch. 3.

which is operating at 50 percent capacity, is willing to pay $5.00 each for the fitting. Defco uses the fittings in a brake unit it is producing for a commercial airplane manufacturer on the basis of cost plus a fixed fee.

Ajax has a variable cost of $4.25 for producing fitting number 1726. The cost of the brake unit being built by Defco is as follows:

Purchased parts, outside vendors	$22.50
Ajax fitting 1726	5.00
Other variable costs	14.00
Fixed overhead and administration	8.00
	$49.50

Defco's management believes that if it must pay more than $5.00 for the part, it cannot retain the contracts.

The company uses return on investment and dollar profits in the measurement of division and division manager performance.

(a) Assume that you are the division controller of Ajax. Would you recommend that Ajax supply fitting 1726 to Defco? (Ignore any income tax issues.) Why or why not?

(b) Would it be to the short-run economic advantage of the Gunnco Corporation for the Ajax division to supply Defco division with fitting 1726 at $5.00 each? (Ignore any income tax issues.) Explain your answer.

(c) Discuss the organizational and manager behavior difficulties, if any, inherent in this situation. As the Gunnco controller, what would you advise the Gunnco Corporation president to do in this situation?

[ICMA adapted]

18. **Timely Calculation of Incentives**

An automobile dealer had been paying his new car salesmen on the total profit in a deal. They received $25 plus 20 percent of any profit above the $100 minimum the dealer required. On new car sales without a trade-in, the calculation was simple, and the system functioned smoothly. Selling price less all costs including taxes and transportation was the gross profit. That figure less $100 was the basis for calculating the bonus. However, the plan has led to some questions when a trade-in, especially a newer model, is taken. Profit is not calculated until the trade-in is finally disposed of and cash received. Thus, if a 1976 model is traded in on a new 1982 car, that 1976 car must be considered part of the deal in calculating the profit. If the 1976 car is subsequently sold for cash and a 1968 car, the profit on the new car sale is still incomplete. Only if the 1968 car is finally sold for cash is the profit on the 1982 model calculated. An example is given in Exhibit 5-3.

There has been some grumbling among the salesmen, because the system takes too long before the bonus is calculated and received. Management is therefore interested in analyzing and, if necessary, revising the plan.

——————————————————————————————EXHIBIT 5-3

Auto Sold	Cash	Trade-in
1982 model	$12,000	1976 model
1976 model	8,500	1968 model
1968 model	500	none
Total value of sale	$21,000	
Less cost of 1982 model	10,000	
Gross profit	$11,000	
Less minimum profit	100	
Bonus base	$10,900	
Bonus (20% × $10,900)	$ 2,180	

(a) Advise them about the strengths and weaknesses of their present plan.
(b) Propose at least one alternative plan and discuss its strengths and weaknesses.

19. *Risk and Incentive Computations*

Ralph has hired a manager, named Ralf, to run his firm. To see how things will work, Ralph poses the following situation. Suppose, in his absence, Ralf is called on to decide whether to accept or reject an offer to supply a unique customer with a special product. The precise quantity is presently unknown, but it will be either 500, 1,000, or 2,000 units and respective sales revenue less variable production costs will be $200, $1,000 or $2,500. Fixed production costs of $1,000 will also be incurred if the offer is accepted. Both Ralf and Ralph assign respective probabilities of .3, .4, and .3 for the 500, 1,000, or 2,000 unit demand events.

Further suppose that Ralf receives 10 percent of the net income he generates by accepting such orders. Ralph may choose between two possible job-order income measures. He may measure the income at incremental contribution margin less fixed cost, or he may measure the income at incremental contribution margin less a unitized fixed cost of $.50 per unit of demand. Any volume variance in this full-cost measure is taken "below the line" and is not attributed to Ralf. The alternative income measures are displayed below.

JOB-ORDER INCOME MEASUREMENT DATA

	500	1,000	2,000
Demand	500	1,000	2,000
Probability	.3	.4	.3
Incremental contribution margin	$ 200	$1,000	$2,500
Fixed cost	1,000	1,000	1,000
Direct cost income	−800	0	1,500
Full-cost income (with a normal volume of 2,000 units)	−50	500	1,500

Required Analyze this problem from Ralf's point of view. How will he behave under each measure and which would he prefer?

*20. **Incentives, Expected Utility, and Nonpecuniary Returns**

Ralph is now analyzing some delegation problems. He is risk-neutral in this scenario (that is, he evaluates options via the expected value of *his* income) and has signed a "cost-plus" contract with his cousin Rolf for production of a special subcomponent. Rolf is risk-averse and has agreed to implement a production method of Ralph's choosing (since Ralph absorbs all the risk via the cost-plus contract).

The cost will be

$$F - 10as + a^2$$

where s is some uncertain state, with expected value $\bar{s}$, and a is the production method in question. Naturally, Ralph wants $a^* = 5\bar{s}$ implemented, and the contract calls for a payment of π plus the actual cost. Rolf is both risk- and work-averse, with a utility function of $(x - a)^{1/2}$, where x is *his* net income.

(a) What is the expected utility of Ralph and Rolf under this arrangement?

(b) Suppose Ralph can only observe the total cost actually incurred. (He cannot observe the actual state or Ralph's act.) Also suppose Ralph is certain that the utility determined in part (a) is sufficient to compensate Rolf. How much, assuming use of the above π plus actual cost payment scheme, would Ralph pay to observe Rolf? (Answer: $25\bar{s}^2$.)

*21. **Incentives and Timing of Payment**

Ralph works, as manager, for an owner. The firm in question has been approached by a customer and asked to supply 200 units of a special product, 50 in the first period and 150 in the second period. Available production capacity is 100 units in each period. The offered price is $160 per unit, and the incremental cost *each period* is estimated to be

$$5,000 + 80q$$

or

$$5,000 + 120q$$

where q denotes the production quantity and the 5,000 cost is straight-line depreciation of a $10,000 investment that will be required if the offer is accepted. Thus, if the offer is accepted and if the low-cost event results, the cash flow will be $x = -\$10,000$ in the first period and $z = \$16,000$ in the second period (versus $x = -\$14,000$ and $z = \$12,000$ if the high-cost event results). The two events are equally likely (and low cost in period 1 implies low cost in period 2).

By tradition, Ralph receives 10 percent of the income (not cash flow) generated each period by such special orders. Let x_1 and z_1 denote, respectively, first and second period incremental cash flow to Ralph. His utility measure is

$$u_1(x_1, z_1) = (350 + x_1)^{1/4}(350 + z_1)^{1/4}$$

Similarly, the owner's preferences for an incremental cash flow of $x_0 = x - x_1$ in the first period and $z_0 = z - z_1$ in the second period are represented by

$$u(x_0, z_0) = (15,000 + x_0 + .95 z_0)^{1/2}$$

The owner has two available methods for measuring the income from the special order. The first, a conventional direct-cost measure, will not inventory any fixed costs, while the second, a conventional full-cost measure, will. (If, for example, the low-cost event occurs, the periodic variable cost measures will be −$1,000 and $7,000, while the periodic full-cost measures will be $1,500 and $4,500.) Which performance measurement method should the owner employ? Explain in one brief sentence the reason for this choice.

6
Budgets and Standards for Control

In Chapter 5 the broad outlines of the performance evaluation process were presented. That chapter focused upon the dual functions of performance information: evaluation of decisions and motivation of the agent in the (simplistic) two-person system. In this chapter we will discuss the various ways accountants organize data in reports to facilitate evaluation and motivation as well as examine the various details of the techniques used.

The techniques usually used are called budgets. These are formal, quantitative statements of anticipated resource flows. An example would be a profit budget for the ensuing year. When budgets are coordinated with the accounting system that reports on actual events in such a way that individual manager responsibility is highlighted, we have a *responsibility accounting system*. The name, responsibility accounting, emphasizes the role of budgets in formally delegating resources and responsibility for performing activities and in stressing accountability for the level of performance.

Responsibility accounting concepts were first introduced in Chapter 2, where we defined controllable and uncontrollable costs. Aggregating costs according to the activity responsible for their incurrence focuses both the superior's and the subordinate's attention on who is responsible for which costs. The addition of yardsticks against which performance can be assessed gives a clearer picture of how the subordinate has performed.

Responsibility Accounting

Responsibility accounting systems vary from organization to organization simply because no two organizations delegate responsibility for decision making and decision implementation in exactly the same way. However, as discussed in Chapter 5, certain basic notions are present in any performance evaluation

199

system. The added complication at this point is the presence of more than a single manager or agent. We therefore associate *some* of the firm's activities with each manager and proceed as indicated in Chapter 5. The responsibility accounting procedure thus consists of:

(1) *Identification* of decision points within the organization.
(2) *Matching* of decision and individuals so that decision authority and decision responsibility are aligned.
(3) *Allocation* of resources for performance of the tasks at the various identified points.
(4) *Selection* of measures of performance or performance standards.
(5) *Observation* of the decision maker's actual performance and comparison with the performance standard.

It should be readily apparent that these notions or guides are not always met exactly. For example, no firm would try to identify *all* decision points. The cost of system design, planning, and control would exceed the benefits for many decisions. The same cost–benefit criterion stressed in Chapter 1 applies in the design of responsibility accounting systems. Thus, we really are speaking about the identification of those decision points in any organization that are critical in its operations. Once those points are selected, they are matched with the individual responsible for them. We then proceed, in steps 4 and 5, as in the single manager case discussed in Chapter 5.

Cost Control

Most control systems are based upon responsibility accounting with the focus on *cost control*. This is accomplished by focusing on the consumption of direct materials, direct labor, and overhead and on the individual managers to whom the various consumption responsibilities have been assigned. Quite naturally, responsibility accounting can and often does focus on more than cost control, but this will be deferred until later. For the moment, we envision a setting in which central management has made a set of decisions and the managers to be evaluated are responsible for efficiently implementing these decisions.

Exhibit 6-1 illustrates the relationship between the "pyramid of control" and responsibility accounting reports. All the responsibility units, called centers, are concerned with controlling the use of resources or, in accounting terminology, costs. As a result, they are called *cost centers*. (Other managers are evaluated on other dimensions: profitability, return on investment, or services rendered. These are called profit centers, investment centers, and service centers. In this chapter the primary focus will be on cost centers and cost control.)

In Exhibit 6-1 we have assumed that all costs are controllable by the manager who incurs them. This enables us to avoid showing any uncontrol-

EXHIBIT 6-1

The Pyramid Effect of Controllability

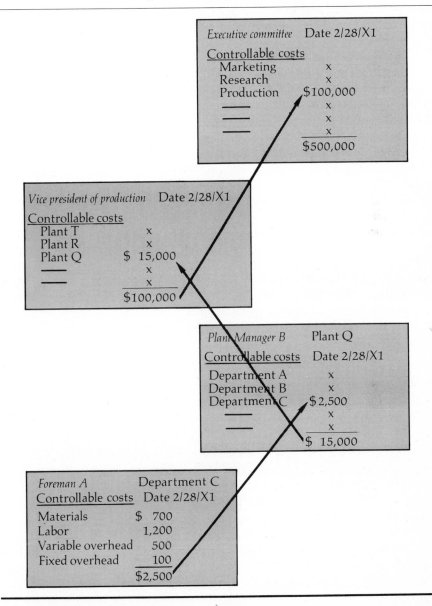

Executive committee Date 2/28/X1

Controllable costs
Marketing	x
Research	x
Production	$100,000
——	x
——	x
——	x
	$500,000

Vice president of production Date 2/28/X1

Controllable costs
Plant T	x
Plant R	x
Plant Q	$ 15,000
——	x
——	x
	$100,000

Plant Manager B Plant Q

Controllable costs Date 2/28/X1
Department A	x
Department B	x
Department C	$2,500
——	x
——	x
	$ 15,000

Foreman A Department C
Controllable costs Date 2/28/X1
Materials	$ 700
Labor	1,200
Variable overhead	500
Fixed overhead	100
	$2,500

lable costs among the various items. Later in the chapter, when we discuss budgets, this assumption must be relaxed. For the moment, however, we may assume that a direct focus on who controls which cost elements leads to the pyramid structure in Exhibit 6-1.

The detailed costs are included for Foreman A, who runs Department

C. If these costs are his expected or targeted costs for some period, say March, 1981, we would call them budgeted costs and call the report a *budget*. If they are the actual costs incurred during a period, say the month of February, we would call them actual costs and call the report a *statement of actual costs*.

The arrows linking one report to another as we progress up the pyramid show how each prior report is included in the next one. All of the detail of Foreman A's activities in Department C are summarized in Plant Manager B's report by the $2,500 total. If Manager B wants more data on Department C, he can call for the detailed report, or perhaps retrieve it automatically via a computer terminal. It will usually be the case in our discussion that data will be more heavily aggregated as we go up the organization chart. Again, this does not mean that the detailed data are unavailable to higher levels of management; rather, it reflects that they may not be routinely reported. Should a manager spot a problem, he or an assistant can secure the data as required.

In summary, the responsibility accounting system facilitates organizational control by first coordinating the scope of each report with the boundary of the decision-making unit or the authority of the decision maker. Then, within that framework it stresses controllable costs. In the next section the standard against which the past period's performance is compared is added to the responsibility accounting system.

Budgets

In order to perform his required tasks, each manager must know the level of resources—the mix as well as the total level—allotted to him. If Foreman A in Exhibit 6-1 is in charge of the Cleaning Department, he would expect to know before the start of the period what Plant Manager B expects of him (his "goal") and the various resources he is expected to use in order to achieve this goal. These expectations are likely to be formalized in a budget.

The key to understanding budgets is to return to the linear cost model employed in Chapters 2, 3, and 4:

$$TC = a + bx$$

where x is some measure of activity, a is the intercept (or fixed cost), and b is the slope (or variable cost). We begin with some activity variable(s) and then express the expected or targeted cost, TC, as a function of that activity variable, in whatever detail is desired. This is a budget in its most simple form.

To illustrate, suppose we focus on Department C in Exhibit 6-1. This is a cleaning department; the activity measure is square feet of floor space to be cleaned. Exhibit 6-2 is an example of the foreman's budget when his department is expected to clean 50,000 square feet during the month of June.

_____ EXHIBIT 6-2

Cleaning Department
Budget
June 1981

Account	Expected Cost
Labor	$40,000
Electricity	5,000
Equipment rental	2,000
Maintenance supplies	1,000
(cleaners, rags, etc.)	
Total	$48,000

Expected square feet cleaned in June: 50,000

Static Budgets

A budget of the type shown in Exhibit 6-2 is called a _static budget._ A static (cost) budget is a proposed level of resource consumption for a specific level of activity. A budget of this type will be sufficient for Foreman A to plan his activities in June and for Plant Manager B to evaluate A's performance if one or both of the following are true:

(1) The preponderance of the department's costs are fixed costs, implying that the total departmental cleaning cost is largely insensitive to the activity level in the department.
(2) Plant manager B is able to accurately predict the monthly activity in the department and thus know the expected cleaning cost _for the level of activity._

Should the preponderence of the costs be fixed relative to our measure of activity—square feet cleaned—cleaning 54,000 square feet would have no effect on A's need for resources. He should still be able to stay within his budget. Naturally, as the level of activity actually experienced goes further and further beyond the 50,000 square foot level, the risk that the budget may be inappropriate increases. Recall from Chapter 4 that the fixed cost is actually the intercept in a linear approximation to the cost curve. And we naturally expect that as activity (square feet cleaned) increases, the $48,000 datum in Exhibit 6-2 will become less and less accurate. Still, over the relevant range, the budget will aid Foreman A in planning his activities, for he knows the level of spending Manager B anticipates. Conversely, B has a basis against which to evaluate A.

Even if all costs are essentially fixed relative to the level of activity, some potential for managerial discretion is possible. For example, assuming that the foreman of the maintenance and cleanup crews has some flexibility

EXHIBIT 6-3——

**Cleaning Department
Performance Report
June 1981**

Account	Actual	Budget	Difference[a]
Labor	$38,500	$40,000	($1,500)
Electricity	6,000	5,000	1,000
Equipment rental	2,900	2,000	900
Maintenance supplies	980	1,000	(20)
Total	$48,380	$48,000	$ 380

Square feet actually cleaned: 54,000

[a] Parentheses indicate that the actual outlay was *less* than the budgeted amount.

in how he does the job, he might decide to rent more machines and use less labor because he feels the trade-off will reduce costs.

Exhibit 6-3 compares the actual results with the budget. Note that the *total* cost is essentially the same as the budget. Foreman A spent $380 more than the budget allowed. However, he spent less on labor and more on equipment rentals and electricity. In this case the two differences almost canceled out each other. If the cost center head has discretion, management will usually report not only on the total budgeted and actual costs but also on the item-by-item costs for both. By disclosing the differences between budgeted and actual costs on an item-by-item basis, A's activities are reported in greater detail to Manager B, giving B a better understanding of what has happened. This need not give A and B the same level of knowledge about A's actions during June. However, it does tell A in advance that B will be checking on what B feels are the most important aspects of running the Cleaning Department. This should result in a more rational allocation of effort by A. Such a plan is consistent with the discussion in Chapter 5.

Flexible Budgets

If, in fact, the cleaning department's labor costs are largely variable and not fixed in the activity range under consideration, it is critical that accurate estimates are available concerning the expected level of activity. Even small variations in activity could destroy the usefulness of the comparison of actual to budgeted costs found on the performance report. If Foreman A's department does 54,000 square feet of cleaning, his labor costs now would be expected to exceed the budgeted $40,000 figure. The problem is that we do not know by how much. Under such a set of circumstances—variable labor costs and

4,000 square feet more work done than budgeted—our intuition might suggest that the foreman did a very good job in June: He cleaned 8 percent more square feet at an overall added cost of less than 1 percent more than budgeted.

The difficulty is that we know a target cost for $x = 50,000$ square feet and an actual cost for $x = 54,000$ square feet. Whether performance is above or below expectations depends critically on those expectations. Suppose the targeted cost is

$$TC = \$3,250 + \$.895x$$

which implies a budget of $48,000 at $x = 50,000$ and $51,580 at $x = 54,000$. This is the idea of a *flexible budget*. We focus on the cost–volume relationship at hand and define the manager's responsibility in terms of the budgeted cost *for the activity variables achieved*. If $\hat{x}$ square feet are cleaned, the performance norm is $\$3,250 + \$.895\hat{x}$. The foreman is responsible for this amount, but not for $\hat{x}$. In a sense, he is called upon to efficiently provide whatever cleaning services are demanded. (The question of whether $\hat{x}$ should be an item of evaluation is somewhat subtle. Eventually, we will consider a manager with, say, profit responsibility and the task of selecting $\hat{x}$ or living with whatever $\hat{x}$ the market forces provide. This is where such a question is examined. For the moment, you should concentrate on the flexible budget idea of treating $\hat{x}$ as an independent variable.)

Exhibit 6-4 shows a flexible budget that might have given rise to a budget of $48,000 for 50,000 square feet cleaned. Note that each cost item has a particular cost–volume equation associated with it. As you might expect, some are strictly fixed (rental cost) or strictly variable (labor), but others are mixed.

The total budget for any volume can be calculated either by using the total budget equation or by calculating each item separately, as shown in the third column of Exhibit 6-4. These costs are what Foreman A would use to plan his activities for a given volume and against which his performance would be evaluated.

_____ EXHIBIT 6-4

Cleaning Department
Flexible Budget
June 1981

(x = square feet cleaned)		$x = 50,000$
Labor	$.80x$	$40,000
Electricity	$1,000 + \$.08x$	5,000
Equipment rental	$2,000	2,000
Maintenance supplies	$ 250 + \$.015x$	1,000
Total	$3,250 + \$.895x$	$48,000

EXHIBIT 6-5_____

Cleaning Department
Cost Report
July 1981

Account	Actual	Budget	Difference
Labor	$47,500	$48,000	($500)
Electricity	5,900	5,800	100
Equipment rental	2,000	2,000	0
Maintenance supplies	1,200	1,150	50
Total	$56,600	$56,950	($350)

Square feet cleaned: 60,000

Exhibit 6-5 shows the typical cost report that Foreman A might receive. Here the Cleaning Department did 60,000 square feet of cleaning. The cost report, which compares A's performance to the budget for 60,000 square feet, reports A's overall performance and his utilization of broad categories of resources. If it were economically desirable, the report could detail the labor costs by category (or even by person) and the supplies by type.

REVIEW PROBLEM 1 _____

Using the flexible budget data in Exhibit 6-4, calculate the budget for the Cleaning Department at 75,000 square feet and fill in the performance report shown below. Then calculate the difference between budgeted costs and actual costs.

Cleaning Department
Performance Report
July 1981

Account	Actual	Budget	Difference
Labor	$62,000	_____	_____
Electricity	6,500	_____	_____
Equipment rental	2,100	_____	_____
Maintenance supplies	1,255	_____	_____
Total	$71,855	$70,375	$

Square feet cleaned: 75,000

Using Flexible Budgets

From the previous section it should be apparent that the decision to use a flexible budget rather than a static budget approach is not trivial. The situations where managers can forecast the period's volume of activity with any accuracy are few, and except for a relatively small proportion of costs (measured either by dollar amount or number of accounts), cost categories exhibit a significant degree of variability. In the language of Chapter 2, very few costs are strictly fixed over the relevant range; most exhibit some variability. Thus the use of static budgets for all departmental resources—materials, labor, and overhead—is not usually feasible if the budget is expected to effectively achieve its dual purposes of aiding in planning and evaluation.

In contrast to materials and labor, overhead costs often do exhibit a high degree of fixity. For rather large shifts in volume, only small changes in total cost are expected. Thus some firms will retain static budgets for overhead while using flexible budgets for materials and labor. Because we have implicitly assumed that we have a good understanding of cost–volume behavior, the use of a flexible budgets approach is advantageous to management. For the present we will continue to assume a high degree of knowledge about our firm's cost function and turn to the problem of setting the standards that compose budgets.

Setting Standards

The budget just examined is an aggregate representation of cost incurrence. Typically, many factor inputs are involved, and when we construct the budget by aggregating individual factor considerations, we deal with "per unit" resource consumptions rather than a total. Performance norms at the per unit level are called _standards_.

Consider a very simplistic setting in which a firm produces widgets. Three factors of production are involved: direct materials (DM), direct labor (DL), and overhead ($\hat{O}$). The budget would then consist of

$$TC = DM + DL + \hat{O}$$

Now let q denote the number of widgets produced. Envisioning linear estimating equations, we might then have

$$DM = a + m \cdot q$$
$$DL = b + l \cdot q$$
$$\hat{O} = F + v \cdot q$$

which imply

$$TC = a + b + F + (m + l + v) \cdot q$$

In turn, we usually assume $a = b = 0$. With this added assumption, m would be the standard materials cost, l the standard labor cost, F the standard fixed cost, and v the standard variable overhead cost. In addition, $m + l + v$ would be the standard variable product cost and $m + l + v + F/\hat{q}$ would be the standard full (or absorption) cost *at volume $\hat{q}$.*

Viewed in this (simplistic) manner, the question of determining a budget is broken down into subquestions of determining m, l, v, and F. In Chapter 5 we raised the issue of how tight a standard should be so as to elicit the best possible performance from the subordinate. This question was inextricably intertwined with the nature of the reward structure. In this chapter we will assume that management has articulated a policy of setting standards at a level attainable through reasonable effort by subordinates possessing the requisite degree of skills.

However, once the tightness issue is resolved, the question still remains of how one estimates the individual standards. As we noted in Chapter 3, there are numerous ways of estimating cost. They differed on many dimensions—cost, accuracy, timeliness, and so forth. It is important to keep this in mind, because a measure of a manager's performance against some formal standard *could* reflect an error in the standard, as well as other possible causes.

Standards for Production Activities

Standards can be developed for the three major functions of most organizations: production, distribution, and administration. It should be obvious from earlier statements, however, that the precision of the standards will vary from activity to activity. In general, more precise standards can be determined for production than for distribution and administration, for two reasons. First, the quality and amount of output from production processes can be measured with greater precision. Second, production processes tend to be more standardized than those of distribution and administration. This provides a more stable relationship, over time, between specific inputs and outputs. We will now illustrate the standard setting process for production.

Materials Standard

As stated earlier, many of the activities required in the production of a physical output can be controlled by reasonably accurate standards. The primary output (or activity) variable for production is the number of units produced. The inputs required to produce a given level of output, especially in the case of direct materials, are generally determined by the technology of the process. Although production processes are not completely inflexible, typically there are only particular grades of materials that can be used to produce a particular product. Because there are technological limits on the kinds and amounts of inputs needed to produce a specified number of outputs, it is usually possible for the engineer and the accountant to establish accurate standards for the direct cost of producing units of output.

The setting of the standard cost for direct materials is an important part of any production department's budget. Raw materials are a significant portion of departmental cost. In setting these standards, management usually makes three determinations:

(1) The size of the lots of output for which cost standards will be set.
(2) The proper handling of spoilage during production where spoilage is part of the normal process of production.
(3) The cost per unit of input that management should expect to pay.

The size of the costing unit for the center's output can range from one unit to thousands of units of output. The exact size chosen will depend upon the characteristics of the production process and of the output. For example, while cars are produced in large numbers, the individual car is the costing unit. In contrast, a special fastener may be produced in smaller quantities, but costed in lots of 500. In this case, the cost per automobile is large, while the cost per individual fastener probably was too small to be meaningful to report. Once the size of the costing unit is set, engineering estimates normally are used to set the *quantities* of raw materials required. The engineering estimates will reflect the technical requirements of the process.

One factor influencing the level of the materials standard is the amount of waste or spoilage permitted by the standard. This is labeled "normal" waste or spoilage since the standard allows for it. Normal waste can result from many causes, some of which are independent of the subordinate's actions or abilities. An example is a raw material that contains a flaw or is of an odd size, such as the end piece of a bolt of cloth that is less than the amount needed for a run of the pattern-cutting equipment. This waste occurs because the patterns do not permit use of the entire sheet of cloth, rendering part of the sheet useless. Ideally, the standard allows for the amount of such waste that is unavoidable.

Spoilage also depends on the abilities and motivation of the workers. In many jobs some degree of human error is expected, given the skills of the people hired to perform the task. The higher the skill levels of the workers for that job, the lower the number of defectives we might expect. Of course, holding the skill level constant, we would expect better performance as the worker's reward is related to the quality of his performance. For our purposes, we will assume that the standard allows for the amount of spoilage that occurs when the worker performs the task with reasonable care.

EXHIBIT 6-6

Ajax Widgets
Bill of Materials
Electronic Widget

Part	Quantity	Unit Cost	Total Cost
Wire: Copper #13	12 ft	$ .12/ft	$1.44
Steel: ASTM #43	0.5 ft²	.72/ft²	.36
Resistor: 12 KΩ	7	.10	.70
Tubes: 12CB7	2	1.40	2.80
12AUX7	2	1.70	3.40
6B6	1	.90	.90
			$9.60

Setting a Standard Using Spoilage.   Exhibit 6-6 shows a bill of materials for an electronic widget. The quantity column shows the amounts of the various parts needed for its production. The standard quantity for copper wire reflects an allowance for waste. The engineers estimated that end pieces in the rolls of copper wire usually are too short to be used and must be discarded as waste. This had the effect of adding 0.5–foot of wire to each unit.

Similarly, the engineers recognized that the copper wire is extremely fine and difficult to handle. As a result, the wire often breaks during assembly. After discussing the problem with the production manager, it was decided that achieving the desired volume for the product would require the workers to assemble 10 units per hour. At that rate, they concluded, the careful worker would break the wire about once every eleven parts. To allow for this spoilage, another foot was added to the standard.

Thus it is possible, at least crudely, to disaggregate the standard for copper wire into three parts. These are about 10.5 feet required to do the job, 0.5 foot waste averaged over the good production, and 1 foot per part that is allowed for the occasional broken wire. If the workers are able to reduce waste or spoilage, they will use on the average less wire than the standard allows.

Setting the Materials Price Standard.   The worker could be evaluated on the engineering standards shown in the quantity column of Exhibit 6-6. However, usually these quantities are reduced to monetary units by costing them at a *standard price*. Thus Exhibit 6-6 shows a cost of $1.44 for the copper wire and $m = \$9.60$ as the materials standard for an electronic widget.

There are three reasons why the standard is expressed in monetary as well as physical units:

(1) Someone is responsible for the acquisition of the materials, and therefore a price standard will be set.

(2) Most records for the department will be kept in monetary terms.
(3) Managers may be able to choose among materials to find the least cost mix in producing widgets of acceptable quality.

The first reason reflects the usefulness of setting a price standard in order to measure the purchasing unit's performance. Typically that function is performed by the purchasing department rather than by the production departments. We will discuss the evaluation of the purchasing department later in this chapter.

The second reason reflects the assumed need to tie all of the reports back to the accounting system. Since those records are kept in monetary terms, the performance report will eventually be summarized in monetary terms. Note that while Exhibit 6-4 did not include physical quantities, there is no reason why it should not. Exhibit 6-7 is an example of a more detailed performance report on the operations of the electronic widget manufacturing department. It contains all of the data the superior would normally seek to evaluate the subordinate's performance and the data the subordinate uses to learn from past successes (and failures) in planning for the coming period.

The third reason is by far the most important to management. If the manager has any choice among inputs (for example, using different types of steel for the base plate), the standard should allow him to shift from the prescribed material to the alternative so long as the quality of the product is not affected. The standard price offers a starting point in this analysis. As relative prices change, the desired input may change, and, of course, so will the standard.

In turn, this raises an additional question of how often these standards should be changed. With inflationary pressures affecting the costs of most materials, firms may revise their price standards much more frequently than

———————————————————————————EXHIBIT 6-7

Ajax Widgets: Assembly Department
Performance Report
January 1982

	QUANTITY			COST		
Part	Actual	Standard	Difference	Actual	Standard	Difference
Wire: Copper #13	124,000 ft	120,000 ft	4,000 ft	$14,880	$14,400	$ 480
Steel: ASTM #43	4,900 ft^2	5,000 ft^2	(100 ft^2)	3,528	3,600	(72)
Resistor: 12 KΩ	69,000	70,000	(1,000)	6,900	7,000	(100)
Tubes: 12CB7	20,100	20,000	100	28,140	28,000	140
12AUX7	20,400	20,000	400	34,680	34,000	680
6B6	10,000	10,000	0	9,000	9,000	0
Total				$97,128	$96,000	$1,128
Production: 10,000 widgets						

before. How frequently the standards should be updated will vary with the item in question. Three possible events could trigger a change in the price standard:

(1) A periodic, planned review indicates that a change in the price standard is desirable.

(2) A cost overrun (or underrun) leads the investigator to ascertain a nontransitory change in the price of a material.

(3) A frequently changing price makes it desirable to index the price standard to some freely available market price for the commodity.

The first two points can be illustrated by the price standard for the electronic widget. If the prices of the tubes are relatively stable, those prices will be unchanged until the next periodic review unless an investigation of poor performance by the purchasing department reveals a significant and permanent change in the price of a tube.

In the case of copper wire, the price may fluctuate. Therefore, the firm may periodically check the price of copper in the metal market and make an appropriate change in the standard. Then at certain predetermined dates, a more comprehensive review can be undertaken. This procedure may be useful in retaining reasonable price standards in times of volatile prices.

Under each set of circumstances, management will review the price standard as frequently as is merited by the relative costs and benefits. Chapter 8 discusses this issue in the context of variance investigation.

Labor Standards

Similar comments can be made about the importance of labor standards. Indeed, because labor skills are more flexible than the qualities of materials, there are even greater opportunities for substituting one type of labor for another in the production of a particular kind of output. The difference between the standard labor cost of producing an output and the actual labor cost incurred is often the best measure of the effort expended by department heads. Implicit in this assumption is the belief that department heads are able to substitute different degrees of labor skills at a net benefit to the firm and to motivate higher levels of performance. The amount of labor used in a particular process, as compared to the standard amount that should have been used, is also a primary measure of the ability of department heads to obtain cooperation from their employees.

Labor standards are an important evaluative device in the control of direct labor. However, labor standards are also important in planning. If permanent changes take place in either the required use of labor or the rates paid for different labor skills, the firm may be motivated to change its input or output decisions and to substitute, say, more capital for labor.

——————————————————————————————————EXHIBIT 6-8

Ajax Widget
Direct Labor Standards
Electronic Widget

Activity	Hours	Rate	Total Cost
Soldering	0.5	$ 9.00	$4.50
Assembly	0.3	7.50	2.25
Finishing	0.1	8.75	.875
Checking	0.1	11.25	1.125
	1.0		$8.75

Generally, the relationships between labor inputs and physical outputs are stable over time, so that labor standards can be established by engineering studies.[1] However, if the production process is less predictable, a less formal method of setting labor standards will likely be employed. As one alternative, the standard may be based upon the average of past experiences. It should be noted that such a standard will not represent what the cost of an activity *should* be. It will only reflect an average of the past efficiency of the firm.

The actual determination of a wage rate standard may be quite complex, depending on the diversity of the payment plans used by the organization. In addition, the process is complicated by the number and extent of the ranges of pay scales within the firm. For this reason, standard wage rates are usually averages of several pay scales. Thus, a firm may have five wage rate standards, which cover 25 or so different wage scales. A further complicating factor is the effect of any fringe benefits that are linked to labor cost. Should the wage rate standard be adjusted to include fringe benefits and special payments to labor? As a rule, fringe benefits are included in the labor price standard, while special payments are classified as overhead and included within the overhead budget.

An example of a labor standard appears in Exhibit 6-8, with $l = \$8.75$. In examining Exhibit 6-8, one could draw the conclusion that there exists a single salary scale for each job classification. For example, one might assume that all assemblers earn $7.50 per hour. In fact, however, we would expect the assemblers with the greatest experience and seniority to earn more than $7.50 and those with the least experience to earn less than that. The $7.50 datum, then, is only the average cost for labor in assembling the electronic widgets. If we investigate further we might find that the assemblers fit into two categories, junior and senior, where the senior assemblers are those with more than three years of experience. Exhibit 6-9 summarizes the calculations that were made to arrive at the standard labor rate for assemblers. Note that this rate is an average. Since we are keeping records of the cost of the

---

[1] An excellent discussion of industrial engineering procedures is available in R. Barnes, *Motion and Time Study Design and Measurement of Work.* New York: Wiley, 1980.

EXHIBIT 6-9

Ajax Widget
Standard Labor Cost
Assembler

Classification	Rate	Percent	Portion
Junior	$6.50	60%	$3.90
Senior	9.00	40	3.60
	Standard rate per hour		$7.50

entire production, variations in batches from the 60–40 percent mix will tend to average out.

Overhead Cost Standards

Thus far we have discussed the standard materials and labor costs of producing an electronic widget. Exhibit 6-6 showed the cost of materials and 6-8 showed the cost of labor. The indicated standard cost of producing an electronic widget is $m = \$9.60$ for materials and $l = \$8.75$ for labor. Overhead remains to be specified.

The first task in developing an overhead standard is to classify overhead costs by cost centers in a manner consistent with the firm's responsibility accounting structure. Any errors of classification will affect the accuracy of the various cost center standards and budgets, although they may not affect what the total overhead costs should be for the firm.

After the overhead costs have been assigned to the various cost centers, the budgeted amounts of each overhead cost are determined relative to different output levels. Given the amorphous nature of overhead, this is typically approached in the manner outlined in Chapter 3. On the other hand, some knowledge of individual overhead elements may be available. For example, standards for overhead cost items that are known not to vary with volume changes, regardless of the output base used, can be set at the known, fixed amounts. (Of course, determining what this fixed amount should be may be problematic.)

Standards for known semifixed overhead cost elements are slightly more difficult to establish. Since these costs are discontinuous at particular output levels, a different budgeted amount might be set for each point of discontinuity. For example, if supervision costs are $10,000 for each 5,000 units of the output variable, then a separate budget or standard might be set for each range: $10,000 for the first 5,000 units, $20,000 for 5,001–10,000 units, and so on.

More complex procedures are involved in setting standards for variable and semivariable costs. In general, these standards are based on the estimating techniques discussed in Chapter 3. Recall that the essential steps involve a selection of some output base and a method for determining the association between the cost item and whatever output base is used. Different kinds of costs are expected to vary with different independent variables. Thus, indirect labor might vary with direct labor hours, whereas maintenance costs might vary with machine hours. The extent to which the most representative base should be used depends on the significance of the overhead items. Insignificant items may be pooled and associated with a single output variable. However, an effort should be made to find the output base (or bases) that provides the best explanation of the variability of each major overhead item.

In a single-product firm, it is likely that the variability of each such overhead element will eventually be tied to units of output. Even so, they may be individually associated with intervening variables. Some may depend on labor hours, some on labor dollars, some on machine activity, and so on. If all of these variables were mechanically related to output, then output would be a suitable independent variable. But suppose the relationship is

_____EXHIBIT 6-10

Ajax Widget
Flexible Budget for Manufacturing Overhead
Output Range: 200,000–400,000 Direct Labor Hours

Volume (in direct labor hours)	200,000	300,000	350,000	400,000
Percent of capacity	40%	60%	70%	80%
Controllable				
Variable costs				
Electricity[a]	$ 20,000	$ 30,000	$ 35,000	$ 40,000
Water[b]	10,000	15,000	17,500	20,000
Semivariable				
Indirect labor[c]	$ 50,000	$ 70,000	$ 80,000	$ 90,000
Miscellaneous[d]	15,000	20,000	22,500	25,000
Fixed and semifixed				
Supervision	$ 5,000	$ 5,000	$ 6,500	$ 6,500
Group insurance	600	600	600	600
Uncontrollable				
Depreciation	$ 1,000	$ 1,000	$ 1,000	$ 1,000
Rent and taxes	1,500	1,500	1,500	1,500
Total budgeted costs	$103,100[e]	$143,100[e]	$164,600[f]	$184,600[f]

[a] $TC = \$.10$ (direct labor hours)
[b] $TC = \$.05$ (direct labor hours)
[c] $TC = \$10,000 + \$.20$ (direct labor hours)
[d] $TC = \$ 5,000 + \$.05$ (direct labor hours)
[e] $TC = \$23,100 + \$.40$ (direct labor hours)
[f] $TC = \$24,600 + \$.40$ (direct labor hours)

less than mechanical. Efficient use of labor would then save on overhead elements that vary with labor. How much of this type of subtle dependence to search for and reveal in the overhead standard is difficult to sort out. Moreover, with a multiproduct firm we would most likely work with a universal independent variable such as direct labor hours or dollars.

In our continuing example, suppose the primary activity variable is direct labor hours. In that case, a flexible overhead budget such as the one in Exhibit 6-10 might be prepared. The estimating equations given in the footnotes can be used to budget the respective costs for output levels that fall within the range of 200,000 to 400,000 direct labor hours. Thus, for activity in the neighborhood of 300,000 direct labor hours, standard fixed overhead would be $F = \$23,100$ and standard variable overhead per direct labor hour would be $.40. In turn, with each widget requiring one hour of direct labor (see Exhibit 6-8), this implies a variable standard overhead of $v = \$.40$ per widget.

Standards for Product Costs

Frequently, management is also interested in standard product cost. These estimates may be useful in planning analyses. Moreover, many cost accumulation systems use standard costs because of the resultant savings in bookkeeping costs. (Any minor differences between actual and standard would be written off during the period; significant differences would be prorated between cost of goods sold and ending inventory.) It is, therefore, important to understand how these individual standards for cost centers are aggregated into firm-wide product standards.

The first step in the procedure is to determine how the overhead costs of a department vary with units of output. This may be a simple task, since the independent variable (for example, labor hours) may already be standardized on a per-unit-of-output basis. For example, as already noted, the electronic widget in Exhibit 6-11 requires 1 hour of direct labor. The product standard for indirect labor would then be $10,000 + \$.20q$, where q represents the number of electronic widgets produced during the period. The other overhead cost elements for Department LB would be handled in a similar manner, implying $v = \$.40$ per widget. We therefore have, in the neighborhood of 400,000 units, a standard variable cost of $m + l + v = \$18.75$ per widget, coupled with a standard fixed cost of $24,600. Alternatively, in the neighborhood of 300,000 units, the fixed cost standard is $23,100.

This is the basic manner in which standard product costs are developed. Complications are provided by the existence of service centers whose costs must also be reflected in the standard. But notice that our standard depends on an estimate of volume. Moreover, any attempt to create a fixed or absorption standard cost depends on a specific volume "target."

EXHIBIT 6-11

Ajax Widget
Production Costs for Department LB

Cost Item	Variable Rate per Unit	Fixed Cost
Electricity	$.10[a]	—
Water	.05[b]	—
Indirect labor	.20	$10,000[c]
Miscellaneous	.05	5,000[d]
Supervision	—	6,500[e]
Group insurance	—	600
Depreciation	—	1,000
Rent and taxes	—	1,500
	$.40	$24,600

[a] See footnote a, Exhibit 6-10.
[b] See footnote b, Exhibit 6-10.
[c] See footnote c, Exhibit 6-10.
[d] See footnote d, Exhibit 6-10.
[e] Assuming output will be about 80 percent of capacity.

Selecting the Proper Volume

Selecting the proper volume is no easy matter. Standards reflect linear approximations in some neighborhood of activity, so in many respects the volume question concerns what neighborhood of activity the standards should reflect.

Three alternatives are maximal, expected, and normal volume. Maximal, practical volume is usually rejected as being inconsistent with volume expectations. Expected volume directly answers this objection, but at the expense of having to deal with year-to-year changes in volume. A cyclical demand and production pattern could, for example, have dramatic changes in year-to-year standard product cost. The answer is to use an average volume over several periods. This is the idea of *normal volume.* If the firm's capacity were optimally determined (under conditions of certainty), we would interpret normal volume as the point of maximum efficiency for the size of the plant owned by the firm. But it is best interpreted as an average volume the firm expects to achieve over a several year period.

Suppose, now, that we have a standard fixed cost of $1,000,000 with a maximal volume of 500,000, expected volume of 425,000, and normal volume of 450,000 units. Even if the standard fixed cost is the same at all three volumes, the average fixed cost per unit of output will be different:

Maximal volume $\qquad$ Expected volume $\qquad$ Normal volume

$$\frac{\$1,000,000}{500,000} = \$2.00 \qquad \frac{\$1,000,000}{425,000} = \$2.353 \qquad \frac{\$1,000,000}{450,000} = \$2.222$$

In any event, normal volume is the typical choice. It speaks to the issue of being related to actual expectations and adopts an average point of view, thereby alleviating year-to-year changes in (at least) the full standard product cost. In other words, we typically begin with a cost estimation of

$$Cost = F + (m + l + v) \cdot q$$

EXHIBIT 6-12 ───

Ajax Widget
Standard Cost
Electronic Widget

Material				
Wire: Copper #13	12 ft	@	$ .12/ft	$1.44
Steel: ASTM #43	0.5 ft²	@	.72/ft²	.36
Resistors: 12 KΩ	7	@	.10	.70
Tubes: 12 CB7	2	@	1.40	2.80
12 AUX7	2	@	1.70	3.40
6B6	1	@	.90	.90
Total materials cost				$ 9.60
Labor				
Soldering	0.5 hour	@	$ 9.00	$4.50
Assembly	0.3 hour	@	7.50	2.25
Finishing	0.1 hour	@	8.75	.875
Checking	0.1 hour	@	11.25	1.125
Total labor cost				8.75
Overhead				
Variable				
Electricity				$.10
Water				.05
Indirect labor				.20
Miscellaneous				.05
Total variable overhead cost				.40
Fixed				
Indirect labor			$10,000	
Miscellaneous			5,000	
Supervision			6,500	
Group insurance			600	
Depreciation			1,000	
Rent and taxes			1,500	
Total fixed overhead			$24,600	.07[a]
Total unit cost				$18.82

[a] Fixed cost per unit is expected fixed cost ÷ expected volume: $24,600 ÷ 350,000 = $.0703.

for some range of activity. Already we have considerably specified or relied upon a neighborhood of activity for which the estimate is useful. Beyond this, construction of a full standard cost relies on a specific estimate of normal volume, $\hat{q}$:

$$\text{Standard full cost} = \frac{\text{Cost at } \hat{q}}{\hat{q}}$$

$$= \frac{F + (m + l + v) \cdot \hat{q}}{\hat{q}}$$

$$= \frac{F}{\hat{q}} + (m + l + v)$$

Exhibit 6-12, using a normal volume of $\hat{q} = 350,000$ units, summarizes these computations for our continuing example.

Additional Considerations in Setting and Interpreting Production Standards

It is, of course, much easier to read or write about production standards than it is to actually set them. Hence, it is vital that the student not acquire a false impression of the ease or accuracy with which these standards are set. Remember, for example, that we are dealing with linear approximations. The typical labor standard, based on a linear model, cannot accommodate learning. If learning is present, the efficient amount of labor will depend on the length of the production run as well as on the total number of units produced. Thus, when a particular job involves a longer-than-average run, the nature of the standard (assumed to be a linear variable) produces a bias toward a favorable variance. Conversely, for shorter-than-average runs, the bias is toward an unfavorable variance. Both of these variances are essentially independent of supervisory performance. (Obviously, if the learning phenomenon is significantly distortive of the linear model, we would expect the firm to use a nonlinear labor cost model.)

We do not mean to suggest that learning invalidates a linear model, but only to emphasize that the standard is an approximation.[2] Similarly, use of elementary inventory techniques (discussed in Chapter 16) implies a nonlinear material cost model. Typically, though, we rely on direct materials standards that are based on linear approximations.

---

[2] For a fuller discussion, see E. Summer and G. Welsch, "How Learning Curve Models Can be Applied to Profit Planning." *Management Services,* March–April 1970; W. Morse "Reporting Production Costs That Follow the Learning Curve Phenomenon," *Accounting Rev.* Oct. 1972; and N. Baloff and J. Kennelly, "Accounting Implications of Product and Process Start-ups," *J. Accounting Research,* Autumn 1967.

Similar comments apply to the overhead standards. Aside from the linearity issue, we typically employ a single independent variable in the overhead model. Multiple independent variables may be important, but expediency usually dictates use of a single variable. Again, then, the message is one of caution in the interpretation of the standards.

A final point concerns the interpretation of the standard product cost measure. We have a basic standard product cost model of

$$\text{Cost} = F + (m + l + v) \cdot q$$

However, the accounting profession is committed to the inclusion of all manufacturing overhead costs in the costs of production and then into inventory for published financial statements. This view, called full or absorption costing, holds that the fixed overhead costs represent service potentials that must be accumulated in the production cost accounts until the goods are finished and sold. This idea, called "costs attach," requires the proration of fixed costs over production during the period. The net result is to emphasize a cost model, using a normal volume of $\hat{q}$, of the following form:

$$\widehat{\text{Cost}} = \left[\frac{F}{\hat{q}} + (m + l + v) \right] \cdot q$$

It is important not to confuse the two models.

REVIEW PROBLEM 2

Marston Manufacturing produces a single product: souvenir English flags that are sold to tourists. The flags are made in a small shop run by the owner and several employees. The process and costs of producing the flags are described below.

Flag. The flag itself is purchased from a supplier on preprinted bolts of cloth. Each bolt has 1,000 flags printed on it. However, because of the nature of the printing process, about 10 percent are normally unusable. They are blurred, printed too close to the edge, or printed on a defect in the cloth. Thus Mr. Marston expects to cut only 900 flags from each bolt of cloth.

Cutting. All flags are cut by hand. Mr. Marston has carefully observed the process and decided that 180 flags can be cut per hour.

Poles. The flag poles are plain wooden poles 10 inches in length. Mr. Marston buys them cut to the proper size. Breakage is negligible.

Assembly. The cut flags are stapled to the poles using a specially designed bench and stapler. This can be done at the rate of 200 flags an hour.

Costs.

  Cloth: $54 per bolt.
  Poles: $1 per 100 poles.

Labor: All work is done by part-time labor at the rate of $3.60 per hour.

Overhead: Mr. Marston has supplied you with his budgeted costs for two levels of activity. Use the high–low approach to estimate the fixed and variable portions of the costs. It takes one-half machine hour to assemble 100 flags. Normal volume is 900 stapler machine hours.

	750 Machine Hours	960 Machine Hours
Building rent	$2,400	$ 2,400
Utilities	3,500	3,920
Supplies	750	960
Fringe benefits	1,500	1,920
Depreciation	1,000	1,000
	$9,150	$10,200

Develop a standard cost per 100 flags for Mr. Marston.

REVIEW PROBLEM 3

Using the data in Review Problem 2, what change would occur in the materials cost standard if Mr. Marston decided to allow for normal spoilage of 10 flags per bolt in cutting and 3 broken poles per 100 in assembling? Assume that the poles break before a flag is attached and that no additional flags are lost during assembly.

Standards for Nonproduction Costs

As management searches for new ways in which to control costs, areas such as distribution and administration appear promising. In general, it has been discovered that while standards can be set for some of these costs, it is difficult to do so in many other areas. This is because many of these activities are not well understood and because precise output measures often do not exist. Thus, as you might expect, greater use is made of static budgets than is the case for production costs.

The use of static budgets to control distribution and administrative costs suggests that either the costs are essentially fixed or that we have an inadequate knowledge of the production function for the cost items within these categories. In fact, both of these reasons characterize many distribution and administrative cost categories. Many of the costs are discretionary; that is, the amount expended on an activity is determined by the judgment of an individual (or group) rather than being significantly affected by a production function linking the level of organization or departmental activity and the implicit need for a given level of inputs.

Distribution Standards

It is often convenient to discuss distribution costs under the broad classifications of order-obtaining and order-filling costs. Order-obtaining costs represent all the activities necessary to obtain a sales order. The more important of these activities are advertising, promotion, sales representatives' calls and contacts with customers, and order-taking. Order-filling costs represent the activities of storage, packing and shipping, billing, and collections.

Intuitively, we would expect that a measure of good output could be obtained more easily for order-filling costs than for order-obtaining costs. For example, we can easily determine the amount of direct labor and materials required to store, pack, ship, and bill orders. We should also be able to relate changes in order-filling overhead to changes in the number of orders filled. Thus, standards should not be difficult to determine, in theory at least, for this category of costs. Practical difficulties may arise if different amounts of labor, materials, and overhead costs are incurred as different types of orders are filled, but this should not be a serious problem.

More serious difficulties arise when standards for order-obtaining costs are to be determined. Order-obtaining costs are those incurred primarily to increase present and future sales. Since *future* sales cannot (by definition) be observed in the current period, it is not possible to measure the quantity of output of advertising or sales representatives' calls. These costs are usually controlled under some total budget commitment for such activities. That is, the personnel involved in these activities submit proposals for advertising and contracts with customers for the coming period; the level of activity is set; and the expected costs of achieving this level are estimated.

Examples of order-obtaining and order-filling budgets are found in Exhibits 6-13 and 6-14. In Exhibit 6-13 the budget reflects the expected total cost for various items. Some, such as warehousing, are probably fixed costs; the others are probably variable or semivariable costs. The point is that cost equations estimating total cost per operation may be ascertainable by management. In that case, standards comparable to those of production departments may be feasible. For example, the packing division may be subject to a flexible budget of say, $1,000 + $.08 per unit shipped. If so, then management can readily appraise the efficiency of performance for levels other than the projected volume of 50,000 units.

In contrast, the discretionary costs in Exhibit 6-14 (television and radio costs) can be altered at the choice of management. To control these costs, management might compare the cost paid for television programing to the

EXHIBIT 6-13

Order-Filling Budget:
Ajax Widget
Shipping and Receiving Budget
January 1982

Operation	Output Variable	Total Expense	Units	Average Cost per Unit	PRODUCT 1		PRODUCT 2	
					Units	Cost	Units	Cost
Packing[a]	Units	$ 5,000	50,000	$ .10	10,000	$1,000	40,000	$ 4,000
Warehousing[b]	Floor space (ft²)	20,000	40,000	.50	5,000	2,500	35,000	17,500
Stamping[a]	Units	700	7,000	.10	2,000	200	5,000	500
Loading[a]	Weight	2,000	200,000	.01	100,000	1,000	100,000	1,000
Unloading[a]	Weight	500	50,000	.01	40,000	400	10,000	100
Receiving[a]	Labor hours	300	150	2.00	100	200	50	100
Total		$28,500				$5,300		$23,200

[a] These activity costs are variable with the output of the departments, but it may be difficult to correlate them with activity.
[b] Unless storage space is purchased, the expense is primarily fixed from period to period, given the operating range (in units) expected during the period. Allocation represents the accountant's proration of costs among alternatives.

Order-Obtaining Budget:
Ajax Widget
Advertising Budget
January 1982

EXHIBIT 6-14

Media	Output Variable	Total Expense	Units	Average Cost per Unit	AREA 1		AREA 2	
					Units	Cost	Units	Cost
Direct mail	Pieces	$ 1,000,000	10,000,000	$ .10	7,000,000	$ 700,000	3,000,000	$ 300,000
Television[a]		10,000,000				5,000,000		5,000,000
Radio[a]		100,000						100,000
Newspaper	Column inches	5,000,000	5,000,000	1.00	1,000,000	1,000,000	4,000,000	4,000,000
Dealer promotion[b]	Participating dealers	25,000	2,500	10.00	2,000	20,000	500	5,000
Total		$16,125,000				$6,720,000		$9,405,000

[a] These expenses are fixed by managerial policy during the operating period.
[b] These expenses are not fixed, but are difficult to correlate with an output variable.

EXHIBIT 6-15

Ajax Widget
R & D Budget
First Quarter 1982

Facility[a]	Output Variable	Total Expense	Units	Unit Cost	Project 1		Project 2	
					Units	Cost	Units	Cost
Engineering	Labor hours	$10,000	1,000	$10	700	$ 7,000	300	$ 3,000
Drafting	Labor hours	8,000	4,000	2	3,000	6,000	1,000	2,000
Computer[b]	Computer minutes	20,000	2,000	10	1,000	10,000	1,000	10,000
Shop	Labor hours	12,000	6,000	2	1,000	2,000	5,000	10,000
Materials	Dollar values	15,000				7,000		8,000
Lab	Labor hours	3,000	1,000	3	200	600	800	2,400
Total		$68,000				$32,600		$35,400

[a] Most activities are committed at the beginning of the operating period. Allocation really indicates where effort will be directed during the period, not the manner in which expense varies.
[b] If purchased from an outside service, this facility is strictly variable; otherwise, it is difficult to specify the variable cost rate.

results of a marketing survey that indicated how many people purchased electronic widgets as a result of the television commercials. Such analyses are an important part of periodic assessments of the effectiveness of such programs, but are of little help in setting budgets for future periods.

Administration Budgets

Much of the foregoing discussion also applies to the control process for administrative costs. Except for clerical and minor routine activities, it is practically impossible to measure the output of administration activities in the same period the associated costs are incurred. The best example is provided by the research and development department whose budget is shown in Exhibit 6-15. Note that the various categories of expenses have been assigned to projects. In turn, these projections may be compared with actual counterparts, say by requiring personnel in the department to record the times and materials spent on each of the projects. But the time spent does not indicate whether engineering, drafting, and so on produced "good" or "bad" results. The same could be said for most administrative functions.

The limited degree of control that is possible in administration and distribution activities raises the question of whether the budget actually serves as a standard of performance. If a manager is given a budget that authorizes so much research activity for Project 1 and so much for Project 2, or so much advertising for Medium A or Medium B, and so forth, there is an incentive for the manager to follow the allocation procedure exactly as prescribed in the budget.[3] Indeed, *not* spending these amounts may be regarded as poor performance. This is quite different from the manager being told that he has to achieve a certain quality improvement in a product or a certain increase in sales with a budgeted amount of funds. The lack of conventional performance measures in distribution and administration activities is a bothersome area in accounting, and several of the problems at the end of this chapter explore some alternatives to the fixed-budget approach.

Summary

This chapter discussed the techniques that accountants use to translate the goals of the managerial control system into realities. Responsibility accounting was defined as a system of budgets intended to relate the use of resources and the authority to use them by means of a series of formal documents called budgets.

---

[3] See J. Zimmerman, "Budget Uncertainty and the Allocation Decision in A Nonprofit Organization" *J. Accounting Research* Autumn 1977.

The budgets reflected the allocation of resources available to achieve the responsible unit's goals. Some budgets allocated a fixed bundle of resources, while others were formulated to allow greater amounts of resources when activity rises and fewer amounts when activity falls. The former, called static budgets, are most commonly found in those areas of operations where costs are fixed with respect to activities or where the manager has significant discretion over the level of costs and output measures are lacking. The latter, called flexible budgets, are used when cost levels are directly related to some available measure of activity. These budgets permit the manager to anticipate the effects of changes in activity levels on costs. This facilitates use of the data in various decisions and in controlling operations.

Within these budgets, the individual cost elements are controlled by standards. The standards for variable costs consist of a standard *quantity* per unit of output and a standard *price* for the inputs utilized. Standards are most typically found in measuring the performance of production departments. This is because the firm usually has a better understanding of these production functions.

It is, however, important to remember that the use of budgets and standards is subject to the usual cost versus value test. The implication is that the standards (and budgets) are less than perfect. Linear approximations abound, as do aggregations across less than homogeneous cost elements. Moreover, the controllability criterion is central to much of these procedures, even though it too is an approximation to what management might find useful in designing performance evaluation systems.

Supplementary Readings——————————

Articles

Anthony, P. "Functional Cost Accounting for Data Processing Centers," *Management Accounting,* Oct. 1976.

Baloff, N. and J. Kennelly. "Accounting Implications of Product and Process Start-ups," *J. Accounting Research,* Autumn 1975.

Bruns, W. and J. Waterhouse. "Budgetary Control and Organization Structure," *J. Accounting Research,* Autumn 1975.

Ferrara, W. "Responsibility Accounting—A Basic Control Concept," *N.A.A. Bulletin,* Sept. 1964.

Finney, J. "Costing in a Data Processing Department," *Management Accounting,* Oct. 1974.

Hirschmann, W. "Profits from the Learning Curve," *Harvard Business Rev.,* Jan.–Feb. 1964.

Livingstone, J. "Organization Goals and Budget Process," *Abacus,* June 1975.

*Questions and Problems*_____

1. What is a responsibility accounting system? How does the emphasis on such a system fit in with the discussion of performance evaluation in Chapter 5?
2. Sports contracts often have bonus clauses. Examples are a bonus based on a baseball pitcher's "earned run average," a football punter's average "hang time," and an ice hockey player's total of goals scored less goals scored by opponent while said player is on the ice. Are these standards? Discuss.
3. What purposes must a standard serve? Does the same type of standard (one that represents "ideal" conditions, one that represents "normal" conditions, one that represents "current" conditions, or one that is merely an average of past performance) best serve all these purposes?
4. What is the relationship between

    (a) responsibility accounting and the total control system?
    (b) departmental profit reports and the total control system?
    (c) analysis of actual versus budgeted results and the total control system?

5. Some accountants have suggested that a particular firm's budget for research and development and advertising activities should bear some relationship to the average amounts expended for these activities by other firms in the same industry. Discuss the validity and feasibility of developing such standards from industry data.
6. In setting the standard price for raw materials, an accountant discovered that some producers offer substantial quantity discounts for their products. Other products have seasonal fluctuations in price. Still others have price variations according to brands. The latter may reflect an aura of quality—such as a name brand in the consumer market—or a difference in the nature of the commodity. How would you attempt to allow for these factors in

    (a) setting the standard price for record-keeping?
    (b) comparing actual and standard performance in evaluating the purchasing agent?

7. A foreman has stated, "In any firm covered by a union contract—and that's most now—it is silly to set a standard price for labor. The contract does that. It tells us what to pay." If the foreman is correct, what information does a variation from labor's standard price communicate to management?
8. In many respects, the problem of setting standards for administration departments (credit, typing pool, purchasing, and so on) is equivalent to the problem of developing flexible budgets for manufacturing departments. The only difference is in the output measure used as a basis for the standard. Discuss.
9. A large, multioffice insurance firm sets standards for overhead costs in its offices by regressing cost data for all offices of comparable size against several independent variables. Those independent variables that were significant became the basis for the calculation of the standard cost. The cost calculated from the equation was used as the standard. Comment on the desirability of developing standards in this manner.

10. *Nature of Responsibility Accounting*

An important concept in management accounting is that of responsibility accounting.

(a) What are the conditions that must exist for there to be effective responsibility accounting?

(b) What benefits are said to result from responsibility accounting?

(c) Listed below are three charges found on the monthly report of a division that manufactures and sells products primarily to outside companies. Division performance is evaluated by the use of return on investment, that is, the ratio of profit to total assets. You are to state which, if any, of the following charges are consistent with the responsibility accounting concept. Support each answer with a brief explanation.

(1) A charge for general corporation administration at 10 percent of division sales.

(2) A charge for the use of the corporate computer facility. The charge is determined by taking actual annual computer department costs and allocating an amount to each user based on the ratio of departmental hours of use to total corporate hours of use.

(3) A charge for goods purchased from another division. The charge is based upon the competitive market price for the goods.

[ICMA adapted]

11. *The Behavioral Impact of Budgets*

The flexible budget is a very common instrument used by many businesses. While it usually is thought to be an important and necessary tool for management, it has been subject to some criticism from managers and researchers studying organizations and human behavior.

(a) Describe and discuss the benefits of budgeting from the behavioral point of view.

(b) Describe and discuss the criticisms leveled at the budgeting processes from the behavioral point of view.

(c) What solutions are recommended to overcome the criticism described in part (b)?

[ICMA adapted]

12. *Responsibility Accounting in Banks*

One large multiple-service bank divided its various areas into three separate profit centers: checking accounts, savings accounts, and loans. Each center was expected to show a contribution over its own controllable operating costs. Services such as checking were priced accordingly. After the system had been in effect for several periods, the head of the checking accounts units complained that the system was unfair to him.

(a) On what basis was he probably objecting?

(b) Did he have a valid objection?

(c) What could be done about it?

13. **Definition of Responsibility for Accounting Purposes**

At the suggestion of the personnel department, several of a firm's management trainees have been placed on the production line for a month. It was felt that the experience would be valuable to them. However, because of various important rush orders, all of them were assigned to a single department. They spent the month of January working there. At the end of the month, the head of that department received the monthly performance report, a portion of which is shown below. He was furious: "It isn't my fault those trainees can't work," he said, and he demanded an explanation from accounting. Do you feel his claim is valid? How can this problem be solved if the personnel department contemplates continued assignment of trainees to him for a month of factory duty as part of their training program?

Alpha Company
Department A Performance Report
January 1982

Account	Actual	Standard	Variance
:	:	:	:
Rework	$10,000	$8,500	$—1,500
Waste	5,000	4,000	—1,000
:	:	:	:

14. **Source of Responsibility**

After receiving her first cost report since becoming department head in ready-to-wear, Ann Gree is shocked to see an item called vacation pay. "Why should I be responsible for that?" she exclaims. "They aren't working for me during vacation time. Someone must have goofed this time." Did someone goof? If so, why? If not, why not?

15. **Defining Responsibility Units**

Day-Get's, a major discount department store, has found that a good reputation in the sale and servicing of large and small household appliances aids in drawing potential customers to their stores. As a result, their pricing, service, and exchange policies on appliances have been quite liberal. They are known to meet any price and to give good service on appliances they sell. Management is now about to institute a responsibility accounting system. Some question has arisen over the appropriateness of the profit center concept for sales and service departments. These are two separate departments under different managers.

(a) Discuss the desirability of considering the sales department and the service department (1) as separate profit centers and (2) as a single profit center.
(b) From management's point of view, would a profit-oriented system be desirable for these departments?

16. **Classify Costs for Control Purposes**

Based upon the following information, decide whether the cost should be considered controllable or noncontrollable on the contribution report for a firm's grinding department.

Electricity. The electricity in this department is used for lighting the department and running the machines.

Water. Water is used in clean-up.

Maintenance costs. All repairs of the machines (except for an extraordinary situation) are done by a group of mechanics under the control of a maintenance foreman. The hourly maintenance rate is set by dividing expected repair hours into expected total costs of the maintenance department. The grinding department's maintenance cost is calculated by multiplying the hours maintenance works in grinding by the rate per hour.

Floor space. The depreciation on the building is divided by its square footage to yield a rate per square foot. The grinding department is charged for the floor space it uses.

Plant administrative costs. The total cost of running the plant manager's office is prorated equally among the firm's three operating departments.

17. ***Responsibility Accounting in the Distribution Function***

In recent years, distribution expenses of the Avey Company have increased more than other expenditures. For more effective control, the company plans to provide each local manager with an income statement for his or her territory showing monthly and year-to-date amounts for the current and the previous year. Each sales office is supervised by a local manager; sales orders are forwarded to the main office and filled from a central warehouse; billing and collections are also centrally processed. Expenses are first classified by function and then allocated to each territory in the following ways:

Function	Allocation Basis
Sales salaries	Actual
Other selling expenses	Relative sales dollars
Warehousing	Relative sales dollars
Packing and shipping	Weight of package
Billing and collections	Number of billings
General administration	Equally

(a) What are the objectives of profit analysis by sales territories in income statements?

(b) Discuss the effectiveness of Avey Company's comparative income statements by sales territories as a tool for planning and control. Include in your answer additional factors that should be considered and changes that might be desirable for effective planning by management and for evaluation of the local sales managers.

(c) Compare the degree of control that can be achieved over production costs and distribution costs, and explain why the degree of control differs.

(d) Criticize Avey Company's allocation and/or inclusion of (1) other selling expenses, (2) warehousing expense, and (3) general administration expense.

[AICPA adapted]

18. ***Implementation of a Control System***

Harden Company retained Finch and Associates, an engineering consulting firm, to establish direct labor standards. None had existed at Harden before. After a complete study of the work process, the consultants recommended a labor standard of one unit every 30 minutes, or 16 units per 8-hour day.

Harden's vice-president for production thought that this standard was too tight and that the employees would be unable to attain it. He believed a labor standard of 40 minutes per unit, or 12 units per 8-hour day, would be more realistic and more reasonable. Unfortunately, a search of the files found no historical data capable of shedding any light on the conflict.

The president of Harden believed that a high standard should be set to motivate the workers, but also felt that adequate information for planning and control must be available to management. To this end, he suggested that two standards be set:

(1) All reports to the labor force would stress the 30 minute/16 unit standard.

(2) All reports to management would use the 40 minute/12 unit standard.

The president's plan was adopted. The labor force was given the new standard. The vice-president for production met with the work crews to explain the plan. At the same time he announced a wage increase to bring Harden's nonunion labor force in line with unionized plants in the area.

In the first six months of the plan, the following results were reported:

	Jan.	Feb.	Mar.	Apr.	May	June
Production (units)	5,100	5,000	4,700	4,500	4,300	4,400
Direct labor hours	3,000	2,900	2,900	3,000	3,000	3,100
Variance from:						
30-minute standard:	$1,350U	$1,200U	$1,650U	$2,250U	$2,550U	$2,700U
40-minute standard:	$1,200F	$1,300F	$700F	0	$400U	$500U

Where U = unfavorable and F = favorable.

During the same period, raw materials quality, labor mix, and plant facilities were essentially unchanged.

Evaluate Harden's decision to employ dual standards in their evaluation process.

[ICMA adapted]

19. **Preparing a Flexible Budget: High–Low**

Roher, Inc., has been using little in the area of budgeting for planning and control. However, a recent business school graduate has indicated to management that flexible budgeting might be useful. He has asked for your help with this task. Exhibit 6-16 gives the best data available. In setting the budget, use the high–low approach to estimate cost variability. Use machine hours as a measure of activity. The normal range of activity is 60,000 to 80,000 machine hours per quarter.

(a) Calculate the flexible overhead budget for a range of 60,000 to 80,000 machine hours.

(b) Would you suggest this budget be used if the firm contemplated operations

_____Exhibit 6-16

	Q₁	Q₂	Q₃	Q₄
Electricity for lighting and operating machines	$25,000	$36,000	$30,000	$32,000
Repairs of machines	15,000	21,750	18,000	19,600
Cleanup crews for machining scraps	24,000	31,000	28,000	29,000
Lubricants and preventive maintenance	1,030	1,500	1,200	1,310
Departmental supervisor	6,000	6,000	6,000	6,000
Rent	3,000	3,000	3,000	3,000
Machine hours worked	50,000	75,000	60,000	65,000

of 45,000 to 60,000 machine hours? Indicate why your answer in part (a) is or is not acceptable for the new range.
(c) Indicate two uses for the flexible budget.

20. **Preparing a Flexible Budget: High–Low**
Rohrer, Lyon & Rohrer have recently gone into the production of cigarette filters for sale to the major cigarette manufacturers. Until they hired you, they followed the procedure of estimating the budget for manufacturing overhead by estimating the level of each cost at each of the anticipated volumes (a so-called static budget). These estimates, given in Exhibit 6-17, were for the most part accurate. However, their preparation was time-consuming and therefore expensive. You have been asked to develop as efficient a flexible budget system as possible for them, using the high–low approach to estimate variable costs. Assume that, in general, over-head varies with direct labor hours.
(a) Indicate how you would deal with each of the cost categories in developing your flexible budget system.
(b) Prepare the actual budget formulas for management.
(c) In conversing with the management of RL&R, you find that the firm was operating on the last few months of an old lease. Beginning in January—it is now late November—the rent will rise from $750 per month to $1,000 per month. Similarly, a new wage contract will give the supervisors, quality

_____Exhibit 6-17

	Jan.–Feb.	Mar.–Apr.	May–June	July–Aug.	Sept.–Oct.
Rent	$ 1,500	$ 1,500	$ 1,500	$ 1,500	$ 1,500
Supervisors	4,800	4,800	7,200	7,200	7,200
Quality control	2,000	2,000	2,000	3,000	3,000
Machine repairs	900	750	1,000	1,200	1,300
Heat and light	220	200	190	190	210
Power	6,000	4,500	7,000	9,800	10,000
Indirect labor	20,000	17,000	35,000	44,500	47,000
Supplies	500	450	600	700	725
Direct labor, hours	40,000	25,000	50,000	75,000	80,000

Exhibit 6-18

Period	Cost (in $1,000s)	Machine Hours (in 1,000s)
1	$25	33
2	23	37
3	27	40
4	28	45
5	29	46
6	30	50
7	33	55
8	33	60
9	38	68
10	35	70
11	38	75
12	39	79

control personnel, and those workers classified as indirect labor a 10 percent salary increase on December 1 of each of the next two years. Does this alter your answer to part (b)?

(d) Indicate briefly the relative strengths and weaknesses of the flexible budget relative to the static procedure previously employed for planning and control.

21. **Least Squares and Flexible Budgets**
The total of all the overhead costs for Cub, Inc., is as given in Exhibit 6-18. The plant manager feels that overhead varies with machine hours.

(a) Use the least squares techniques (Chapter 3) to calculate an equation from the data in Exhibit 6-18 to estimate overhead cost behavior for planning operations. Do you feel that the equation will assist in the planning of operations?

(b) Assume that you used multiple regression techniques and developed a cost equation such as overhead cost $= \$10,560 + \$1.10 \cdot \text{DLH} + \$.75 \cdot \text{MH}$, where DLH is direct labor hours and MH is machine hours. How would you explain the economic significance of this equation to a management used to seeing equations with only a single measure of activity?

22. **Constructing the Flexible Budget**
The following data are the best estimates of Comet Engineering's industrial engineers about cost behavior. It is assumed that all costs are linear between any two levels of activity.

	VOLUME			
Account	40,000 hr	60,000 hr	80,000 hr	100,000 hr
Supervision	$15,000	$15,000	$20,000	$ 20,000
Quality control	5,000	10,000	15,000	15,000
Power	10,000	15,000	20,000	30,000
Maintenance	20,000	30,000	30,000	35,000
Overtime	0	0	5,000	10,000
	$50,000	$70,000	$90,000	$110,000

Using the high–low method on total cost, the firm has developed a flexible budget line of $10,000 + $1 per hour. Is it better to use total costs than to use the individual items in developing a flexible budget?

23. **Standards for Sales and Administration Services**
Indicate an output measure (or measures) that could serve as a basis for setting standards to control each of the following departments or activities. Where appropriate, indicate whether these standards should be adjusted for variation in the types of services involved. (For example, the standard for receiving materials might vary depending on the size, shape, or weight of the item received.)

(a) Credit and collections
(b) Stenographic services
(c) Mailroom
(d) Receiving department (raw materials and supplies)
(e) Shipping department (finished goods)
(f) Payroll department
(g) Purchasing department
(h) Warehouse
(i) Expense allowances for salespeople
(j) Billing department
(k) Accounting department

24. **Development and Use of Flexible Budgets**
Department A is one of 15 departments in a plant and is involved in the production of all of the six products manufactured. The department is highly mechanized. Flexible budgets are utilized throughout the factory in planning and controlling costs, but here the focus is upon the application of flexible budgets only in Department A. The following data, covering a time span of approximately six months, were taken from the various budgets, accounting records, and performance reports (only representative items and amounts are utilized here).

On March 15, 1981, the following variable budget was approved for the department; it will be used throughout the 1982 fiscal year, which begins July 1, 1981. This variable budget was developed through the cooperative efforts of the department manager, his supervisor, and certain staff members from the budget department.

1982 Flexible Budget
Department A

Controllable costs	Fixed Amount per Month	Variable Rate per Direct Machine Hour
Employee salaries	$ 9,000	—
Indirect wages	18,000	$.07
Indirect materials	—	.09
Other costs	6,000	.03
	$33,000	$.19

On May 5, 1981 the sales plan and the production budget for 1982 were completed. In order to continue preparation of the annual profit plan (which was detailed by month), the production budget was based on planned activity for each of the factory departments. The planned activity for Department A for the 12 months ending June 30, 1982, was

	Year	July	Aug.	Sept.	Other
Planned output in direct machine hours	325,000	22,000	25,000	29,000	249,000

On August 31, 1981, the manager of Department A was informed that his planned output for September had been revised to 34,000 direct machine hours. He expressed some doubt as to whether this volume could be attained. At the end of September 1981, the accounting records provided the following actual data for the month for the department:

Actual output in direct machine hours	33,000
Actual controllable costs incurred	
Employee salaries	$ 9,300
Indirect wages	20,500
Indirect materials	2,850
Other costs	7,510
Total costs	$40,160

(a) Why were direct machine hours a good measure of volume in the budget for this department? How should one determine the range of the activity base to which the variable rates per direct machine hour are relevant? Explain.

(b) Explain and illustrate how the flexible budget can be utilized

    (1) in budgeting costs when the annual sales plan and production budget are completed (about May 5, 1981, or shortly thereafter).

    (2) in budgeting a cost revision based upon a revised production budget (about August 31, 1981, or shortly thereafter).

    (3) in preparing a cost performance report for September 1981.

[AICPA adapted]

25. **Standard Product Cost**

Yates Enterprises makes two products, x and y. Each requires 4 pounds of a specialized material that is available at (a standard price of) $14 per pound. Engineering studies reveal that x requires 8 hours of direct labor, while y requires 6 hours. The current labor cost (an average) is $15 per hour. The controller estimates the firm's overhead with the following monthly flexible budget: overhead = $58,000 + $12·DLH, where DLH denotes direct labor hours.

Required (a) Construct standard (variable) product cost measures for x and y.

    (b) Assuming Yates averages 1,000 direct labor hours per month, construct standard full product cost measures for x and y.

26. *Product Cost and Overhead Budget* [4]

Ralph's firm produces two products (Product 1 and Product 2). There are two departments in the firm: shaping and finishing. Both products require 1 unit of raw material and 1 hour of direct labor in the shaping department. Product 1 requires 1 direct labor hour in the finishing department, while Product 2 requires 2 hours. Because of the physical characteristics of the departments, full capacity in each is 300 DLH (shaping) and 500 DLH (finishing).

If all available capacity is used to produce Product 1, unit cost on an absorption (full cost) basis (with no under- or over-absorbed overhead) is:

Raw materials	$10
Direct labor	20
Factory overhead	30

If all available capacity is used to produce Product 2, unit cost on an absorption basis (with no under- or over-absorbed overhead) is:

Raw materials	$10
Direct labor	30
Factory overhead	42

Selling price for Product 1 is $80; for Product 2, it is $110. Factory overhead is a linear function of the total DLH in the firm as a whole. Determine each product's contribution margin.

27. *Standard Product Cost*

Consider a production department with the following standard cost specifications:

Direct materials:	3 pounds at $10 per pound	= $30
Direct labor:	2 hours at $22 per hour	= $44

In addition, manufacturing overhead is budgeted at

$$OVHD = F + \$1 \cdot DM\$ + \$20 \cdot DLH$$

where DM$ is total *direct material dollars* and DLH is total *direct labor hours*. Moreover, F follows a classic step cost pattern:

$$F = \$10,000 \text{ if } \quad 0 \leq Z \leq \$7,000$$
$$F = \$20,000 \text{ if } \quad \$7,000 < Z \leq \$14,000$$
$$F = \$30,000 \text{ if } \$14,000 < Z \leq \$21,000$$

where Z is *total variable overhead.*

We now focus on a particular period in which 240 units were scheduled for production. (Treat this as *normal* volume for costing purposes.)

Required (a) Compute the standard variable cost per unit.
(b) Compute the standard full cost per unit.

---

[4] Contributed by John Fellingham, a Ralph convert.

(c) With a multiple-product firm, the fixed manufacturing cost allocation would be difficult here because of the use of multiple independent variables. How might you accomplish such allocation?

28. **Comparing Budget and Actual**

Dana Products has developed a flexible budget for its factory overhead. The accounting department uses the following equations to estimate the monthly costs in terms of machine hours (m.h.). These are:

Item	Equation
Electricity	\$.10 m.h.
Water	\$.05 m.h.
Indirect labor	\$10,000 + \$.20 m.h.
Supervisory labor	\$ 6,000
Insurance	\$ 600
Depreciation	\$ 1,000
Rent and taxes	\$ 1,500
Total budget equation	\$19,100 + \$.35 m.h.

During the past month, 100,000 machine hours were worked. The actual costs incurred are noted below:

Item	Cost
Electricity	\$12,000
Water	4,500
Indirect labor	31,500
Supervisory labor	6,400
Insurance	600
Depreciation	1,000
Rent and taxes	1,500
	\$57,500

Prepare a detailed (item-by-item) budget report for Dana Products' factory overhead comparing budgeted cost for 100,000 machine hours with the actual costs. Why do you think the cost of insurance, depreciation, and rent were right at budget?

29. **Comparing Budget to Actual**

Leah Lady's Cosmetics sells beauty products door to door. All its salespeople work on commission. The regional offices advertise, handle deliveries, and follow up on customers to see if they are satisfied. After an analysis of the costs by a cost analyst from central headquarters, the Woods Hole regional office developed the following flexible sales expense budget. All variable and semivariable costs are a function of the volume of sales measured in dollars, S. The equations per month are:

Item	Equation
Commissions	$.25S
Delivery equipment cost	$ 500 + $.10S
Telephone	$ 50 + $.05S
Office staff	$1,000 + $.01S
Advertising	$ 400
Total budget equation	$1,950 + $.41S

During August sales in the Woods Hole region were $60,000. Actual costs were:

Item	Actual cost
Commissions	$15,000
Delivery equipment cost	7,500
Telephone	3,100
Office staff	1,500
Advertising	350
	$27,450

Prepare a statement comparing Leah's budgeted August marketing costs with the actual costs on an item-by-item basis. In comparing actual to budget, how "fixed" do you think advertising really is?

30. **Use of Multiple Bases in a Flexible Budget**
Referring to the previous problem, one member of the central office's cost analysis team suggested that some of the marketing costs incurred by Leah Lady's Cosmetics are more truly related to the number of sales (n), not the dollar volume of sales (S). He suggested the following flexible budget:

Item	Equation		
Commissions		$.25S	
Delivery equipment cost	$ 675		+$1.00n
Telephone	50		+$ .10n
Office staff	400		+$ .10n
Advertising	400		
Total budget equation	$1,525	+ $.25S	+$1.20n

During August the sales force made 6,000 sales to generate the $60,000 of sales.

Using the actual cost data in Problem 29, prepare a statement comparing Leah's budgeted August marketing costs with the actual marketing costs on an item-by-item basis. When does the use of two bases merit consideration by management?

31. **Performance Targets in a Service Unit**
Bell Systems has embarked on an experimental approach to measuring the output of its accounts receivable clerks. Since there is no price that can be put on their services and the clerks do three or four different tasks, Bell has devised a point system. Each task has a point value based upon the expected time to perform

it. Departments and clerks are given a monthly quota of points to earn. The points are:

Activity	Point Value
Open new account	2
Answer phone inquiry about an account	2
Correct an error in an account	3

When the system was established, a goal of an average of 5 points per worker per hour was established. This standard has not been changed. During January, the Accounts Receivable Department had 8 clerks who worked a total of 20 eight-hour days. During January the department actually handled 100 new accounts, 200 inquiries, and 75 errors.

Calculate the budget in points for the Accounts Receivable Department. (Your budget will consist solely of the statement "x points.") Compare the actual work measured in points to the budget. What does the difference between actual and budget mean to the department head?

32. ***Comprehensive Problem: Comparing Actual to Budget***
The Kimberly–Robinson Company produces small pumps for air conditioners at several different plants. The business has decided to experiment with a flexible budgeting approach at its Red Wing plant. The standards for the various costs were developed in late 1981. The budget data developed are shown below:

Material	6 pounds @ $1.50	$ 9.00 per unit
Labor	2 hours @ $9.00	18.00 per unit
Indirect Labor		4.00 per unit
Indirect Materials		.50 per unit
Total variable costs per unit		$31.50 per unit
Fixed costs (per month)		
Depreciation		$ 6,000
Supervision		9,000
		$15,000

During January 1982 the Red Wing plant produced 4,100 pumps and incurred the following costs:

Material (25,000 pounds)	$ 37,500
Labor (8,300 hours)	74,700
Indirect labor	16,900
Indirect materials	8,000
Depreciation	6,000
Supervision	9,000
Total	$152,100

Prepare a detailed statement comparing the Red Wing plant's flexible budget for 4,100 units with its actual costs.

33. *Learning Curves and Cost Standards*[5]

An 80 percent learning curve has been found to be applicable to production in the MLT Company plant. This indicates that labor hours per unit will reduce by the fixed percentage of 80 percent every time the quantity of output is doubled. To illustrate, assume that the time to produce the first 100 units is 100 hours. For an output of 200 units, the labor hours will be $0.80 \times 100 = 80$ hours per 100 units. Doubling output to 400 units reduces the number of labor hours per 100 units of 64 (that is, $0.80 \times 80 = 64$), and so on. The number of total hours needed will increase from 100 to 160 to 256 for outputs of 100, 200, and 400 units, respectively. Note that the incremental number of hours used to expand production from 100 to 200 units is only 60 hours.

(a) Discuss how learning curve techniques may be used in setting standards for decision making and control.

(b) Suppose a firm has a production run of 3,200 units. What would be the change in hours per 100 units if the run were expanded to 6,400 units? Indicate the marginal change in total hours if the run were increased to 6,400 units. (Use the 80 percent rate.)

(c) The relationship between average labor hours per unit and cumulative output is a power function of the form $y = ax^{-l}$, where $y =$ number of hours per unit, $a =$ number of hours for the first unit, $x =$ output, and l is the learning exponent. For an 80 percent learning curve, $l = 0.3219$[6].

For example, if we let $a = 100$ and $x =$ the output expressed as a multiple of 100, $y_{200} = 100(2)^{-0.3219}$. This equation can be solved by taking logarithms of both sides. Hence:

$$\log y_{200} = \log 100 + (-0.3219)(\log 2)$$

or

$$\log y_{200} = 2.0 + (-0.3219)(.3010)$$
$$= 1.903108$$

Therefore:

$$y_{200} = 80 \text{ (approximately)}$$

Suppose the firm above has a chance to bid on a contract that will raise its total output from 200 to 500 units. What will be the increase in standard labor hours required if the contract is accepted ($\log 5.0 = .69897$ and $\log 59.57 = 1.77500$)?

---

[5] The following problem is based on Marvin L. Taylor's article, "The Learning Curve— A Basic Cost Projection Tool," *N.A.A. Bull.* Feb. 1961, pp. 21–26. The basic concepts underlying the material in this problem were discussed in Chapter 3.

[6] See C.A. Theodore, *Applied Mathematics: An Introduction.* Homewood, Ill.: Irwin, 1965, p. 272.

Comparison of Budget with Actual Performance

In Chapter 5 we examined the control process, focusing upon the role of controls[1] in directing and motivating efficient performance and in facilitating evaluation. Budgets and standards, the focus of Chapter 6, stressed the relationship between the knowledge of cost–volume relations and the feasibility of designing a formal system of controls for an organization. Here we continue this basic theme with a study of how budgeted and actual results are compared. We will emphasize cost control in our discussion, though the same techniques are and will be applied to more elaborate settings. Our purpose, though, is to expose these techniques, and cost control is a sufficiently rich setting.

In broad terms, then, the purpose of this chapter is to describe the framework within which a budget (and its underlying standards) and the actual costs are brought together. Specifically, the focus is how managers can use these data to highlight the relationships between the level of performance and some intuitively plausible factors affecting performance. This comparison of actual costs to budgeted costs is called variance analysis. (Accountants often use the term "accounting variances" to avoid confusion with the statistical term "analysis of variance.")

The steps described in this chapter take place within a broader context. It is worthwhile to stress that context so as to keep the materials in perspective. In a cost control setting, these steps are:

(1) The organization develops (static or flexible) budgets to analyze and implement its overall plan of operations for the period.

(2) These data are communicated to the manager responsible for the various activities.

(3) These budgets and underlying standards provide information to the managers about the performance their superiors expect of them.

---

[1] Some writers use the singular "control" to describe the process and the plural "controls" to designate the techniques. That convention is being used in this material as well.

243

(4) At the end of the period, actual costs and the budget are compared via a performance report.
(5) The performance report is typically intended to highlight any deviations from the underlying standards due to differences in quantity of input used or price paid for it.
(6) Any deviation of sufficient size is investigated so as to facilitate proper corrective action.

The focus of this chapter is on step (5), the measurement process. Chapter 8 will discuss the investigation decision.

Our attention within the measurement process is on two basic issues. One is how the accountant measures the differences between actual costs and standard costs. The second is what can be learned from these reports. In both instances, it should be remembered that these measures are starting points for investigations for gathering yet additional information. A large deviation is the basis for initiating concern, rather than the basis for drawing any final conclusions. It must be remembered that the variances are indicators or clues, not conclusions.

The Measurement Process

Once the standards have been set and performance recorded, management is interested in an evaluation of that performance. For this reason, data are collected that compare actual costs to the respective standards. These reports are called *variance reports*. The form of the calculations is the same regardless of the activity being analyzed. In this section we will discuss the framework used, and in later sections we will apply that framework to specific though typical evaluation settings.

Single-Factor Analysis

Suppose we have a single-product firm and have developed a flexible cost budget consisting of direct materials (DM), direct labor (DL), and manufacturing overhead (OVHD) components. Let q be the number of units produced and x the independent variable used in the overhead budget. We then have the following budget components:

$$DM = m \cdot q$$
$$DL = l \cdot q$$
$$OVHD = F + v \cdot x$$

where m is the standard direct materials cost per unit of output, l is the standard direct labor cost per unit of output, F is the standard fixed (intercept) overhead, and v is the standard variable (slope) overhead *per unit of x*. (In turn, if x is, say, machine hours and h denotes the standard machine hours per unit of output, the overhead budget could be expressed in terms of $F + v \cdot h \cdot q$.)

Now suppose $\hat{q}$ units are actually produced, with actual direct materials cost of $\widehat{DM}$, actual direct labor cost of $\widehat{DL}$, and actual manufacturing overhead of $\widehat{OVHD}$:

$$\widehat{TC} = \widehat{DM} + \widehat{DL} + \widehat{OVHD}$$

with a static budget approach, we would now contrast $\widehat{TC}$ with

$$TC = DM + DL + OVHD$$

at some prespecified q and x. Alternatively, with a flexible budget approach, we would contrast $\widehat{TC}$ with TC^b at the actual level of output, $\hat{q}$, and the actual level of the overhead model's independent variable, $\hat{x}$:

$$TC^b = m \cdot \hat{q} + l \cdot \hat{q} + F + v \cdot \hat{x}$$

A further issue here is the relationship between $\hat{x}$ and $\hat{q}$. This will eventually be addressed, but for the moment we concentrate on the identified comparison.

With these specifications before us, the most direct way to proceed with the budget–actual comparison is to merely compare $\widehat{TC}$ with TC^b. The net result, then, is a cost overrun ($\widehat{TC} > TC^b$), underrun ($\widehat{TC} < TC^b$), or no deviation ($TC = TC^b$). In a cost-reporting system, the overrun is typically denoted as an *unfavorable (U)* variance, while the underrun is denoted as a *favorable (F)* variance. In turn, we could decompose the comparison by focusing on individual "line items" in the budget: $\widehat{DM}$ versus DM^b, $\widehat{DL}$ versus DL^b, and $\widehat{OVHD}$ versus $OVHD^b$. This is, however, a highly aggregate view of the budget–actual comparison activity. We would expect to have a number of responsibility centers, each characterized by components of this budget structure and their respective actual cost counterparts. And here the comparison activity would be approached on a responsibility center basis.

Recall our original example of a flexible budget in Chapter 6, the Cleaning Department in Exhibit 6-4. Exhibit 7-1 shows a budget versus actual performance report for this department. The first column reports the actual costs incurred during the month. The second column is the flexible budget for $\hat{x} = 70,000$ square feet cleaned. The third column is the difference between the first two columns.

From Exhibit 7-1 we learn that, overall, the manager of the department was very close to his budget. The difference of $1,200 is less than 2 percent of his total budget at 70,000 square feet. However, individual items varied by different relative amounts and in opposite directions. To understand the

EXHIBIT 7-1_____

Cleaning Department
Performance Report
June 1981

Account	Actual	Budget	Variance
Labor	$55,500	$56,000	$ 500F
Electricity	7,700	6,600	1,100U
Equipment rental	2,200	2,000	200U
Maintenance supplies	1,700	1,300	400U
Total	$67,100	$65,900	$1,200$U$

Volume: 70,000 square feet cleaned
Budget: $TC^b = F + v \cdot x = \$3,250 + \$.895(70,000) = \$65,900$

_____

department's performance better, we next examine the performance report on an item-by-item basis.

For example, the equipment rental budget of $2,000 represents the projected cost for the machines the department rents. Since the standard must be set before the start of the period, it is not surprising that the actual rental payments can differ from the standard. In Exhibit 7-1 the amount paid exceeded the standard by $200. If we assume that the equipment rental contracts set a flat rate per month and the manager cannot vary the quantity of equipment rented, the $200 can be attributed to only one cause—paying more than the standard. (While it is tempting to conclude that inefficiency exists, the unfavorable variance does *not* say the manager was inefficient. The variance may be the result of an incorrect standard or an uncontrollable and unpredictable event, such as unanticipated inflation.) The ability to compare actual cost with budget cost and calculate the only one relevant variance is what we have labeled the single-factor model. This approach is simplistic, for it suggests the presence of only one cause. However, some cases do conform to this model, such as when the manager is able to affect price *or* quantity, but not both. An example would be insurance costs when the coverage is already specified.

Two-Factor Analysis

The rental of equipment also can be used to illustrate the situation where two factors are possible sources of deviations from the budget. In explaining the behavior of a cost item, the total cost is often viewed as a function of both the *quantity* of an item used and the *price per unit* paid for that item. To illustrate, let us further assume that the machines are rented at a rate of $5 per hour. Each time a machine is turned on, a clock starts to run. At regular intervals, the firm owning the machines reads the meters and bills the user. For 70,000 square feet, the Cleaning Department is expected to run their

EXHIBIT 7-2 ───────────────────────────────

Block Diagram of Unfavorable Hours

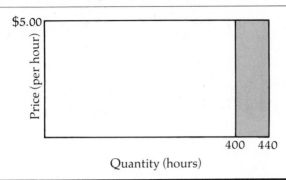

equipment 400 hours (400 hours at $5 per hour = $2,000). Further recall from the budget displayed in Exhibit 6-4 that equipment rental is regarded as a fixed cost. The $5 per hour construction therefore implies that the department should employ 400 equipment hours for any cleaning task in the relevant range covered by the indicated budget.

In any event, we now have an equipment rental cost overrun of $2,200 − $2,000 = $200. Regardless of whether the rental is treated as a fixed or variable cost, knowing the underlying prices and quantities allows us to decompose the cost overrun into price and quantity components. Viewed in this manner, there are an infinite number of ways the manager could exceed his budget by $200: all (feasible) combinations of price and quantity whose product equals $2200. Suppose the manager pays the rental standard price of $5 per hour, but uses 440 hours, or 40 hours in excess of the standard. Exhibit 7-2 illustrates this situation. The unshaded rectangle whose height is the standard price of $5 and whose length is the standard quantity of 400 hours represents the budgeted performance of $2,000. The larger rectangle (shaded and unshaded) whose height is also $5 but whose length is 440 hours represents the actual cost of $2,200. The shaded area represents their difference, the unfavorable variance shown in Exhibit 7-1: 40 hours at $5 per hour.

Exhibit 7-3 graphs the opposite situation where the price standard is exceeded, but the quantity standard is met exactly. The actual price is $5.50 per hour, while the actual quantity is 400 hours, implying an actual cost of ($5.50)(400) = $2200. The shaded area again represents the $200 unfavorable variance.

Now consider a situation where the actual quantity is 434 hours and the actual price is $5.07 per hour [with ($5.07)(434) ≅ $2200]. Exhibit 7-4 shows a block diagram for this possibility. The variances are shown as three rectangles. The first rectangle (I) is the quantity variance, for it represents the cost of the 34 extra hours *if they were acquired at the standard price*. The second

EXHIBIT 7-3 _____

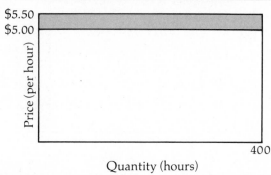

Block Diagram of Unfavorable Price

rectangle (II) is the price variance, for it measures the added cost of acquiring the *standard quantity of services* at the actual price of $5.07. The third rectangle (III) is the result of both the price paid and quantity used varying from the standards in the same period. Altogether, the three rectangles represent the total variance.

Some writers and many practitioners find the third rectangle (usually

EXHIBIT 7-4 _____

Block Diagram with Joint Variance

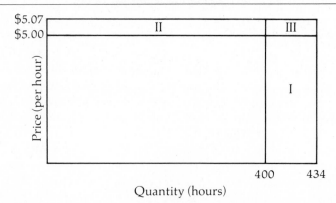

I (Quantity variance): 34 hours x $5 per hour $=$ $170 U
II (Price variance): $.07 per hour x 400 hours $=$ 28 U
III (Joint variance): $.07 per hour x 34 hours $=$ 2 U[a]
Total variance: $200 U
[a] Rounded off so that the total will equal $200.

_____ EXHIBIT 7-5

Block Diagram with Only Two Causes

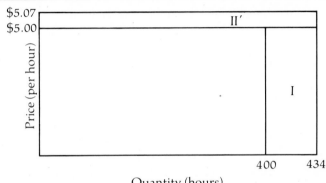

I (Quantity variance): 34 hours x $5 per hour = $170U
II' (Price variance): $.07 per hour x 434 hours =   30U[a]
                                                  $200

[a] Rounded off so that the total will equal $200.

called the joint variance) a bit awkward. It combines the effects of two causes, so it is not obvious to which cause it should be attributed nor why it occurred. As a result, the joint variance is usually arbitrarily assigned to one cause or the other. We will make the assumption commonly made in practice: The joint variance is assumed to be part of the price variance. Exhibit 7-5 shows this diagramatically and provides the appropriate calculations. Note that the total variance and the variance I are still the same and that variance II' is the sum of variances II and III in Exhibit 7-4.

    We call this procedure a two-factor analysis because the attempt is to decompose the difference between actual and budget into two factors. This, as well as all more complicated factor analyses, relies on a very simple device. Using the rental price and quantity as an illustration, let P denote the standard price and Q the standard quantity. Also denote their actual counterparts by $\hat{P}$ and $\hat{Q}$. This budget versus actual comparison of the Cleaning Department's rental cost compares $P \cdot Q$ with $\hat{P} \cdot \hat{Q}$. A single-factor comparison reports

$$P \cdot Q - \hat{P} \cdot \hat{Q}$$

A two-factor comparison _subdivides_ this difference by also computing $P \cdot \hat{Q}$:

$$P \cdot Q - \hat{P} \cdot \hat{Q} = P \cdot Q - P \cdot \hat{Q} + P \cdot \hat{Q} - \hat{P} \cdot \hat{Q}$$
$$= (P \cdot Q - P \cdot \hat{Q}) + (P \cdot \hat{Q} - \hat{P} \cdot \hat{Q})$$
$$= P(Q - \hat{Q}) + \hat{Q}(P - \hat{P})$$

The first term is the *quantity variance*, while the second is the *price variance* (see Exhibit 7-5). Notice in particular that the technique reflects an attempt to move from $P \cdot Q$ to $\hat{P} \cdot \hat{Q}$ by varying one factor at a time. Variance analysis procedures can be extremely complex, but in each and every case they rest on this simple device of inserting an intermediate computation and thereby decomposing or subdividing the total difference. The remainder of the chapter is merely an exploitation of this simple device.

REVIEW PROBLEM 1

A sales manager has been given a sales quota for his sales force. It is expected that the salespeople will achieve a volume of $100,000. Management based its estimates on expected sales of 100,000 widgets at an average price of $1.00 per widget. During 1981, 150,000 widgets are actually sold at an average price of $1.25 each. Thus total sales are $187,500.

(a) Draw a block diagram similar to Exhibit 7-4 for these data. Label the three variances—price, quantity, and joint.
(b) Redraw the figure, showing only the price and quantity variances. Assume the joint variance to be part of the price variance.
(c) Calculate each variance in parts (a) and (b).
(d) What is the relevance of the calculations in part (c)?

Part (d) of the Review Problem focuses attention on the critical aspect of the variance calculation process. How can management use these data? At the same time it stresses the interrelatedness of the price and quantity variance. Thus, while what we are trying to control is the level of the sales manager's effort, we can only observe the outcome. In this case, that outcome is described in detail in the answer to part (c). Total sales, the average selling price, and total units sold all exceeded our standard. Thus, in the absence of strong contrary evidence outside our analysis, we might infer that the sales manager had exerted at least satisfactory effort.

Because we are attempting to assess the manager's effort, it can be misleading to look at either the quantity sold variance or the price attained variance separately. The sales manager is assumed to be allocating the effort among various activities, leading to the best performance on the goal set for him, dollar value of sales. In this context, the price and quantities are only instrumental in achieving this end. What they do contribute to our analysis is a better insight into how the sales manager attained his goal. It should also be apparent that exceeding the budget does not necessarily imply superior performance. The standards might be erroneously low. Alternatively, an unexpected jump in demand (and market price) may have occurred. Further analysis could reveal that the firm actually lost ground in the widget market. Again, variances are precursors to acquisition of additional performance information; they are *not* a basis on which to draw firm conclusions.

Calculation of Cost Variances in a Production Setting

We now examine the manner in which the two-factor model is used in the analysis of production cost. To illustrate the calculations, we will use data for Beeball, Inc. Direct material is budgeted at $10 per unit of output. The $10 datum reflects a standard quantity of 2 pounds per unit and a standard price of $5 per pound. Thus for output quantity q we have:

$$DM = \$10q$$

Direct labor is budgeted at $6 per unit of output. This reflects a standard quantity of ½ hour per unit of output and a standard price (or wage rate) of $12 per hour:

$$DL = \$6q$$

The overhead budget uses *direct labor hours* as an independent variable, with a slope or variable component of $8 per direct labor hour and an intercept or fixed component of $36,200 per month:

$$OVHD = \$36,200 + \$8 \cdot DLH$$

where DLH denotes direct labor hours.

Beeball is a single-product firm. It manufactures paddle balls and uses a product lot of 100 units as its quantity measure, q. The standard variable cost of q is calculated by converting the overhead model to units of output and then combining the material, labor, and overhead budgets. We know that the standard direct labor quantity per unit of output is ½ hour, or DLH $= \frac{1}{2}q$. (This was used in constructing the DL budget.) We therefore have

$$
\begin{aligned}
OVHD &= \$36,200 + \$8 \cdot DLH \\
&= \$36,200 + \$8 \cdot (\tfrac{1}{2}q) \\
&= \$36,200 + \$4q
\end{aligned}
$$

Hence, the production-cost flexible budget is

$$
\begin{aligned}
TC &= DM + DL + OVHD \\
&= \$10q + \$6q + \$36,200 + \$4q \\
&= \$36,200 + \$20q
\end{aligned}
$$

We summarize these calculations with the specification of the standard costs for a lot of 100 paddleballs:

Material (2 pounds at $5 per pound)	$10
Labor (½ hour at $12 per hour)	6
Variable overhead (½ labor hour at $8 per hour)	4
	$20

In addition, since we are dealing with variable product cost, we specify a fixed manufacturing overhead standard of $36,200 per period.

Now suppose during the month of January that $q = 17,900$ lots are manufactured at a total cost of $398,072. Additional data are

Materials used: 35,600 pounds costing	$182,272
Labor used: 9,000 hours costing	109,000
Variable overhead	71,100
Fixed overhead	35,700
Total	$398,072

This provides the preliminary (one-factor) analysis shown in Exhibit 7-6. Our goal, now, is to generate additional insight into these events by applying the two-factor model to each of the cost components.

Direct Material Variance

From the above calculation we know that overall the use of material was in excess of the standard by an amount of $3,272. The question is why. Did someone buy material that was too expensive? Did the price rise during the period? Did someone not properly supervise the consumption of material? The total variance does not provide any insight that might help in answering any of these questions. It could even obscure the fact that two conflicting situations occurred. For example, the firm may have been very careful in its use of the material, but was using material that was too expensive. So as to begin to find out what did happen, we subdivide the total variance into the price and quantity variances. Application of the two-factor analysis provides:

EXHIBIT 7-6——————————————————————————————————————

Single-Factor Analysis of Beeball, Inc.

Cost Element	Actual Cost	Budget (at $q = $ 17,900)	Variance
Direct material	$182,272	$179,000	$3,272$U$
Direct labor	109,000	107,400	1,600U
Overhead			
Variable	71,100	71,600	500F
Fixed	35,700	36,200	500F
	$398,072	$394,200	$3,872$U$

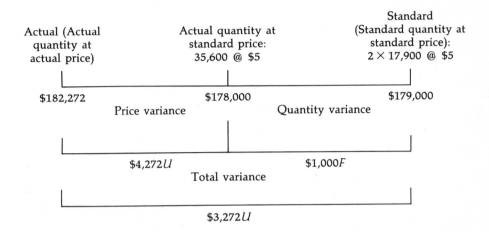

Actual (Actual quantity at actual price)

$182,272

Actual quantity at standard price: 35,600 @ $5

$178,000

Price variance

Standard (Standard quantity at standard price): 2 × 17,900 @ $5

$179,000

Quantity variance

$4,272U

$1,000F

Total variance

$3,272U

The calculations show that the total variance is the result of netting two variances: a small favorable quantity variance and a larger, unfavorable price variance. The manager now is in a better position to proceed with his investigation of what occurred during the month of January.

Note that in calculating the direct material variances, we used the actual price of the material actually used. But suppose materials are inventoried before their use in production. The previous procedure then focuses on the actual price of the materials *transferred* from storage into production during the period. An alternative procedure is to maintain the direct-material inventory account *at standard price.* This has several advantages, and is in fact the way most firms implement these procedures. Notice that with such a procedure the inventory account need not be concerned with multiple prices; all items are logged in at a given standard price (thereby lowering bookkeeping costs). We are also in a position to record the material-price variance at the time of acquisition (or order-placement in the ultimate accrual system) rather than at the time of use in production. Systematic reporting of price changes is thereby accomplished on a more timely basis. This also provides for a more timely evaluation of the purchasing function. If price changes were unanticipated or if purchasing were unusually resourceful (or lax), the system reports the price variance at the earliest possible time. In short, carrying the inventory at the standard price and identifying the material-price variance at the time of purchase provides a reporting system that is easier to interpret and more timely.

This does, of course, alter the way we implement the two-factor analysis. Suppose that Beeball, Inc., actually acquired 40,000 pounds of raw material at an average price of $5.10 per pound during the month of January, a total of $204,000. We would then report, under our modified procedure, the following variances:

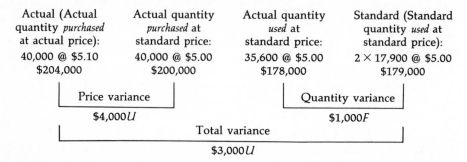

| Actual (Actual quantity *purchased* at actual price): 40,000 @ $5.10 $204,000 | Actual quantity *purchased* at standard price: 40,000 @ $5.00 $200,000 | Actual quantity *used* at standard price: 35,600 @ $5.00 $178,000 | Standard (Standard quantity *used* at standard price): 2 × 17,900 @ $5.00 $179,000 |

Price variance $4,000U

Quantity variance $1,000F

Total variance $3,000U

Notice that the quantity variance remains exactly the same as in the original analysis, but that the price variance is computed in terms of actual purchases and the price paid for those purchases. Since all materials purchased will not usually be used during the period they are purchased, the quantities and costs involved in the calculation of the two variances usually differ. In the Beeball example, 40,000 pounds were purchased and only 35,600 pounds were used. Moreover, some of the materials utilized must have been acquired in prior periods. The average price of the current purchase was $5.10 per pound, while the average cost per pound of the material used was $5.12.

A subtle distinction between these two systems arises when we compute the total direct-material cost for the period in question. If price variances are isolated at the time of use, this is simply actual use at actual price, or 35,600 @ $5.12 = $182,272. But if price variances are isolated at the time of purchase, the total direct-material cost is actual use at standard price *plus* the price variance *on purchases*, or 35,600 @ $5.00 + 4,000 = $182,000. Either way, we deal with actual use at standard price plus the price variance. But the price variance is recognized at a different point. (You should restate our one-factor analysis in Exhibit 7-6 to be consistent with this early isolation procedure. Material cost would then total $182,000. The total of all costs would be $397,800 and the total of all variances would be $3,600U.)

In practice, most standard cost systems do, as we mentioned, separate the timing of the calculation of price and quantity variances. This appears reasonable and is the method we shall emphasize. However, for the sake of permitting diversity, our illustrations and problems do include both forms.

A remaining consideration here concerns how we might interpret the price and quantity variances that emerge from the two-factor analysis. Basically, in the Beeball illustration we have decomposed a total direct-material cost overrun into price and quantity subcomponents. We often interpret the quantity variance as saying something about the efficiency of the production process and treat it as the responsibility of the manager in question. The price variance, in turn, is often treated as beyond the manager's control and is instead considered indicative of market forces, performance of the purchasing manager, or accuracy of the price standard. Although it may be tempting to advocate this position, we must recall from Chapter 5 that performance evaluation is a more delicate matter. The price may be beyond the production manager's control, but he may have the ability to alter the mix of various factors in response to changes in their relative prices. If so, the price variance might be useful in evaluating his performance; moreover, several variances might be related, such as when a material price increases and labor is substituted for material. (Indeed, more elaborate procedures may be implemented in an attempt to analyze the mix-change question.) We caution the student, in other words, not to adopt a simplistic view of who should be responsible for which variance or how the variances should be interpreted.

Direct Labor Variances

Direct labor variances follow in exactly the same manner as direct material variances. We do not inventory labor, so the question of when to isolate the price variance is moot. The quantity purchased is the quantity used.

Application of the two-factor analysis to the direct labor cost in our Beeball, Inc., example provides:

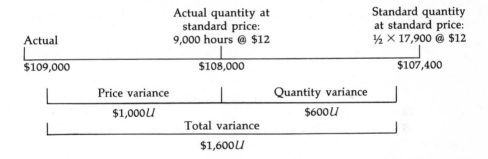

	Actual quantity at standard price: 9,000 hours @ $12	Standard quantity at standard price: ½ × 17,900 @ $12
Actual		
$109,000	$108,000	$107,400

Price variance	Quantity variance
$1,000 U	$600 U
Total variance	
$1,600 U	

Our original (single-factor) analysis in Exhibit 7-6 revealed an actual direct-labor cost of $109,000, a flexible budget allowance (at $q = 17,900$) of $107,400, and a cost overrun or unfavorable variance of $1,600 U. In turn, the two-factor procedure decomposes this $1,600 datum into price ($1,000 U) and quantity ($600 U) components. By convention, we often term the price variance a (wage) rate variance and the quantity variance an efficiency variance. But rather than insist on precise labels, we stress the conceptual identity between the decomposition procedures used in the material and in the labor analyses.

The question of assigning responsibility for the variances is similar to that in direct materials analysis. The price variance is unlikely to be controllable by the production manager, but substitution possibilities may be present. So, as before, we caution against a simplistic view that only the quantity variance is useful in evaluating the production manager or that the variances can be interpreted in isolation from each other.

REVIEW PROBLEM 2 —————————————————————————

Assume that during the year the Alphazee Co. produced 55,000 units. The standard cost per unit for materials and labor is as follows:

Raw materials	3 pounds per unit @ $3 per pound	$ 9.00
Direct labor	2 hours per unit @ $5.50 per hour	11.00

During the period, the company's actual materials and labor costs were:

Raw materials purchases (200,000 pounds)	$587,000
Raw materials used	163,000 pounds
Direct labor costs (112,000 hours worked)	$604,800

(a) Calculate the variances for raw materials and direct labor from these data. You can calculate the materials price variance only at time of purchase.

(b) Assume that the 163,000 pounds put into process had been acquired at a cost of $498,780. Now calculate the raw materials variances using "materials used" for the price variance.

Overhead Variances

The final analyses concern overhead. Recall that the flexible budget for Beeball, Inc., is

$$OVHD = \$36,200 + \$8 \cdot DLH$$

and that actual fixed overhead totaled $35,700, while actual variable overhead totaled $71,100 for the month of January. Our one-factor analysis in Exhibit 7-6 revealed a budget (at $q = 17,900$) of $71,600 for variable and $36,200 for fixed overhead, implying a favorable variable overhead variance of $500 and a favorable fixed overhead variance of $500. We now decompose these totals into price and quantity components.

Beyond this, the technique is exactly the same as before. The only point to observe is the somewhat troublesome question of specifying the "quantity" of overhead. This is done through judicious use of the independent variable (or variables) in the flexible overhead budget. For the flexible overhead budget used by Beeball, Inc., we use direct labor hours as a quantity variable. This implies that actual direct labor hours is the basis for measuring "actual quantity at standard price," while standard direct labor hours is the basis for measuring "standard quantity at standard price." It further implies that all fixed cost variances are price variances; by definition, the "quantity" does not vary with the independent variable in the flexible budget. This provides the following analysis, where we separately track the fixed and variable components:

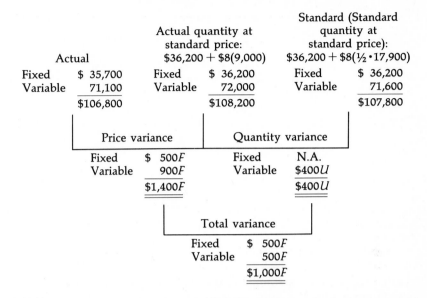

	Actual		Actual quantity at standard price: $36,200 + $8(9,000)		Standard (Standard quantity at standard price): $36,200 + $8(½·17,900)
Fixed	$ 35,700	Fixed	$ 36,200	Fixed	$ 36,200
Variable	71,100	Variable	72,000	Variable	71,600
	$106,800		$108,200		$107,800

	Price variance		Quantity variance	
Fixed	$ 500F	Fixed	N.A.
Variable	900F	Variable	$400U
	$1,400F		$400U

	Total variance	
Fixed	$ 500F
Variable	500F
	$1,000F

Notice that the variable overhead variance is the result of offsetting larger ones. This is why managers pursue the analysis of these variances beyond the total variance wherever it may be meaningful. If either or both of these components are significant, they give a different picture than the total variance did.

In our two-factor analysis of the variable overhead costs, the subdivision is based on use of the independent variable with which overhead costs are assumed to vary: direct labor hours. Each hour of direct labor is assumed to incur $8 of variable overhead cost. This means that the individual responsible for the efficient use of direct labor indirectly influences the amount of variable overhead. This interpretation is available whenever overhead varies with some factor other than units produced. Thus, the impact on the firm of its efficiency in utilizing inputs cannot be completely assessed until the overhead costs are measured. In the Beeball case, 50 extra direct labor hours implies a direct labor quantity variance of $12 × 50 = $600U *and* a variable overhead quantity variance of $8 × 50 = $400U. This suggests that an effective variance reporting system would communicate to the manager in charge of an input any indirect costs and benefits resulting from his decisions. In the case of Beeball, knowing the overhead efficiency variance aids the manager in assessing the impact of his decisions and aids others in evaluating his performance.

The fixed overhead analysis is more straightforward. There can, by definition, be no quantity variance here. There is only one relevant cause possible for a deviation from the budget: paying more or less than the standard amount.

EXHIBIT 7-7——

Two-Factor Analysis of Beeball, Inc.

Cost Element	Actual	Budget	Price Variance	Quantity Variance	Total Variance
Direct material[a]	$182,000	$179,000	$4,000$U$	$1,000$F$	$3,000$U$
Direct labor	109,000	107,400	1,000U	600U	1,600U
Overhead					
Fixed	35,700	36,200	500F	N.A.	500F
Variable	71,100	71,600	900F	400U	500F
	$397,800	$394,200	$3,600$U$	$ 0	$3,600$U$

[a] If the direct material price variance is based on use rather than purchase, the material total and price variance would each be $272 higher.

Thus, we identify only a price variance for fixed overhead. The quantity variance is not applicable (N.A.).[2]

Note that we have continued to use the price and quantity terminology in order to emphasize the conceptual identity of *all* of these computations. Common terminology is to call the overhead price components "spending" variances and the quantity component an "efficiency" variance. You should also note that, in practice, a number of subcomponents of the overhead cost might be identified and separately analyzed. How much detail to display initially (versus to be able to construct upon request or not at all) is a situation-specific question. More detail is more informative in a technical sense, but also more difficult to deal with. So we expect to see important subcomponents identified and analyzed, but this would be far short of the massive detail available in the firm's chart of accounts.

Finally, all that we said earlier (by way of caution) in terms of interpreting and assigning responsibility for individual variances applies here as well. It is, however, important to recognize that numerous overhead items may be the result of interdepartmental allocations (discussed in Chapters 9 and 10), which may or may not be useful in evaluating the manager in question. For example, a portion of the fixed overhead might be an allocation of some fixed central expense over which the production manager has no control (or responsibility) whatsoever.

In any event, this is how the two-factor analysis is applied in a manufac-

———————————

[2] A subtle point is present here. We are focusing on a model of Overhead = $F + vx$, and treating x as a quantity measure. Technically, then, variation in v or the quantity measure will affect variable overhead, but variation in the quantity measure does not affect fixed overhead. So in this analysis we ascribe the fixed overhead variance totally to the price component. But now suppose we further investigate the fixed price variance of $500. We may, in fact, subdivide this datum by focusing on prices and quantities of fixed facilities, just as was illustrated for the budget in Exhibit 7-1. The quantity measure is, of course, now quite different from x, but the factoring concept is identical.

turing cost setting. In each case (with the exception of fixed overhead), we subdivide the total variance into price and quantity components. For the case in which the material price variance is isolated at the time of purchase, on page 258 we have the summarization of our calculations for Beeball, Inc., in Exhibit 7-7.

REVIEW PROBLEM 3 ——

Given below are the data on Alphazee Co.'s overhead costs and standards:

Standard costs:
    Variable overhead ($2 per direct labor hour) $4/unit
    Fixed overhead $464,000/period
Actual costs:
    Variable overhead (112,000 direct labor hours) $229,600
    Fixed overhead $465,500
    Actual production   55,000 units

Calculate variable and fixed overhead variances.

Full Product Cost and the Volume Variance

The analysis illustrated above exploits an identified cost model of

$$TC = \$36{,}200 + \$20q$$

The flexible budget comparison is consistent with a variable product costing system in which the standard variable cost is $20 per unit of output (with a 100-unit production run) and the standard fixed manufacturing overhead is not allocated to individual units of output. Full costing systems are often used in business; thus there is a discrepancy between the previous analysis and the product cost totals that are entered in the firm's accounts.

To illustrate, return to the Beeball example and suppose the normal volume for allocating fixed manufacturing overhead is $\hat{q} = 18{,}100$ units. Then:

$$\frac{\$36{,}200}{18{,}100} + \$20 = \$2 + \$20 = \$22 \text{ per unit}$$

Since $q = 17{,}900$ was actually produced, the standard full cost would be

$$17{,}900 \times \$22 = \$393{,}800$$

In a standard full cost system, the standard cost of production would be recorded at this amount. (Think in terms of a transfer of 17,900 units at $22 each to finished goods inventory.) But the actual cost incurred would total $397,800, implying a variance of $397,800 - $393,800 = $4,000$U$. We have already explained $3,600$U$ of this total, and we can complete the comparison with a "plug" figure of 400U$.

This "plug" figure is typically called a volume variance. Originally we used a budget of $36,200 + $20q$. But in a full cost system the "budget" becomes $22q$. The difference between the two at $q = 17,900$ is:

$$\$36,200 + \$20(17,900) - \$22(17,900) = \$394,200 - \$393,800 = \$400$$

Notice, in particular, that normal volume is $\hat{q} = 18,100$, while $q = 17,900$ was actually achieved. The volume variance is the difference between these quantities multiplied by the average fixed cost of $2 per unit (per lot, in this case).

It may be tempting to search for an economic interpretation of this variance. The variance is zero only if $\hat{q} = q$. Otherwise any difference between $\hat{q}$ and q is "costed" at the average fixed cost per unit of q. It is, however, the difference between the cost model at hand ($36,200 + $20q$) and its full cost counterpart ($22q$). And it arises *solely* because of the use of a full product cost measure. In this sense it is a "plug" or reconciliation datum.

On the other hand, management may be interested in a comparison of output with some budgeted output. If so, physical units or extension of these variance techniques to an analysis of actual and budgeted profit appears to be much more informative.

In sum, use of a standard cost system in conjunction with full product cost measures introduces a type of volume variance. This variance is the difference between normal volume (18,100 lots, in this case) and actual production (17,900 lots) weighted by the standard fixed cost per unit (or [18,100 − 17,900] [$2] = 400U$).

The labeling of this variance is probably inappropriate, to say the least. We readily acknowledge the possibility that a planned production quantity set at the beginning of a period may become outdated and have to be revised. Thus, even if normal volume is interpreted as planned production, the dollar volume variance or the units volume variance may not reflect any unfavorable event unless the failure to meet the production quota was caused by inefficiencies on the part of the production department. More important, even if the planned amount should have been produced, the dollar amount of the volume variance may not measure the cost incurred by the firm's failure to meet its quota. If our firm should have produced 18,100 instead of 17,900 lots, for example, the cost of such a short fall would appear better measured in lost sales or some similar measure of opportunity cost. Weighting these 200 lots by the fixed overhead standard cost is nothing more than a convenient bookkeeping device that is required to meet the demands of external accounting. In Chapter 11, we will discuss an alternative method of external reporting that eliminates the fixed overhead per unit standard from the accounting system.

REVIEW PROBLEM 4 ──────────────────────────────

Return to Review Problem 3 and assume Alphazee Co. uses a full cost system. Normal volume is 116,000 direct labor hours. (This reflects the firm's normal annual production quantity of 58,000 units.) Calculate the standard full cost per unit of output and the volume variance.

REVIEW PROBLEM 5 ──────────────────────────────

Suppose a firm has an overhead budget of

$$\widehat{OVHD} = F + vx$$

where x is some independent variable. Display on a graph a situation in which both the fixed and variable price variances (a spending variance) are unfavorable, the quantity (or efficiency) variance is favorable, and the volume variance is favorable. Be certain to carefully label each variance.

Overhead Variances: Alternative Methods

In the previous section the overhead costs were discussed in terms of fixed and variable components. All calculations were made separately as if the two categories were distinct. These assumptions are, at best, useful approximations in most organizations. As a result, not all firms find it useful to retain the sharp dichotomy between fixed and variable costs in the responsibility accounting and reporting. Instead, these firms combine the variable and fixed price variances into a single variance.

To illustrate, suppose that the overhead cost model for the firm can be expressed as OVHD = $120,000 + $5x$, where x represents direct labor hours. Actual time worked was 55,000 hours. However, the standard time allowed for the output achieved was 50,000 hours. Actual overhead costs were $410,000. The variances are calculated as follows:

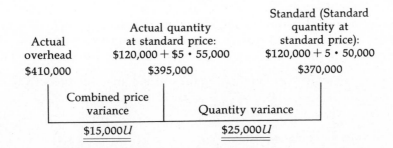

Actual overhead $410,000	Actual quantity at standard price: $120,000 + $5 \cdot 55,000$ $395,000	Standard (Standard quantity at standard price): $120,000 + 5 \cdot 50,000$ $370,000
	Combined price variance $15,000U$	Quantity variance $25,000U$

In short, we follow the same procedure as before, except that we do not subdivide the price variance into fixed and variable components. (You should replicate this analysis for the Beeball, Inc., case.)

As emphasized in Chapter 3, the overhead model, $120,000 + $5x$, can be obtained by using any of several estimation techniques. The usual caveats concerning errors in the estimates of the intercept and slope should be recalled. In the planning stages, we would probably be most concerned with the slope estimate. However, for purposes of control we must concentrate on the total, since that is the only datum we have available in this example. The presence of these mixed items complicates variance analysis, since we must now combine variable and fixed variances into a single overall analysis. On the other hand, it does not force a distinction that management feels is either irrelevant or difficult to obtain. And for this reason, numerous firms treat overhead analysis in this manner.

Other methods have been suggested in practice by various authors writing in this area.[3] One approach commonly found in practice combines the price and quantity variances calculated above. (A volume variance is also typical.) The rationale behind combining the two operating variances is that the manager's effort is expended in utilizing the resources efficiently. Since opportunity for a variety of trade-offs may exist, only one operating variance is meaningful. In short, some firms use a one-factor analysis of overhead, feeling that the subdivision into two factors is too elaborate for an initial analysis.

Use of Variance Data

Up to this point our focus has been on the calculations of the variances. Yet that is only the first step in the process. Variances are calculated to serve a variety of specific uses. They help to

(1) evaluate the accuracy of the planning process.
(2) summarize a prior period's activities for superiors removed from the process.
(3) assess the effort expended by subordinates.
(4) indicate if further data or investigation may be useful.

It is, therefore, important to reflect on the use and interpretation of variances.

---

[3] A four-way analysis is described by D. Solomons in "Flexible Budgets and the Analysis of Overhead Variances," *Management International* 1961; reprinted in H. Anton and P. Firmin, eds., *Contemporary Issues in Cost Accounting*.

Direct Materials Variances

How might a raw material *price* variance be interpreted? There are a variety of possible causal explanations. For example:

(1) The variance may result from the nature of the market in which the materials are acquired. Some random fluctuations are expected.

(2) The use of a formal price standard might imply that reasonable diligence will produce a supplier of the quantity needed at a price very close to the standard. Therefore any deviations from the price standard beyond that described in (1) represents efficient or inefficient performance.

(3) An unfavorable price variance might represent the purchase of material that is of higher quality than the average quality assumed in the standard price. If this is the case, we might then expect to observe a favorable quantity variance when these materials are used.

(4) The environment has proven to be different from that assumed when the standard was set. Thus, there has been a general price increase for the type of material used, resulting in an unfavorable variance. If the new price is expected to persist, it may signal the desirability of changing the input decisions of the firm, or at least call for a change in the standard.

(5) On occasion, the demands of production can cause purchasing to buy more units than usual or buy at an irregular time. We would usually expect these "forced" purchases to result in an unfavorable variance, since purchasing would not have the time to select a source of supply.

These are only a few of the possible reasons for a price variance. An investigation of the cause of the variance would be undertaken if the expected benefits are greater than the expected costs of searching for the causes. For example, if the variance is a random deviation as in possibility (1), the probability is high that no corrective action can be taken. Hence, no direct benefit would be obtained from an investigation to determine the cause. On the other hand, possibility (4) could lead to new operating decisions that would eliminate further unfavorable price variances and/or reduce operating costs.

The purchasing agent is usually considered responsible for the price variance on raw materials, since he or she makes the final selection of the sources of materials. Like most managerial positions, this position is not one of complete autonomy, and so the price variance will not always be an accurate or useful measure of the purchasing department's efficiency. Very few agents are given complete freedom to speculate in prices of materials. More typically, the purchasing department's activities are restricted by both the operating requirements of the firm and market conditions. For example, the typical purchasing department is usually constrained to buy only those items for which it has a request or purchase order. At that time it may bargain to secure the best price. The price on another material the firm uses regularly may be favorable, but the purchasing department is powerless to act without an authorization. As a result, potential savings may be lost, and a chance for the purchasing department to record a sizeable favorable variance goes unrealized. Despite this, most firms use production schedules as the primary basis for stocking inventories and discourage their purchasing departments from speculating. For these and other reasons, many purchasing departments are in fact price-takers, and their price variance may be more indicative of the state of the market than of the department's performance.

Even if purchasing departments are given some discretion, the price variance is only one measure of performance. Other factors, such as the ability to have the proper quantity of materials on hand at the proper time, are not reflected in the price variance. Similarly, the costs of storage and handling are excluded from the calculation even though the purchase terms (for example, delivery date) can affect the price paid. In the absence of control system costs, the control system for the raw materials acquisition function (purchasing) would attempt to measure all the relevant aspects. While the purchasing department would then be assessed on the variance on storage time, shortages, and so forth, as well as on the price variance, the costs and problems of implementing such a system are usually prohibitive. Instead, a series of judgmental evaluations usually replaces a standard monetary measure.

A materials *quantity* variance also might reflect any one of several possible causes. For example:

(1) The variance could be a random fluctuation in performance. That is, the standard for usage is the mean of average usage over time; randomness is expected. If this is the case, the variance presumably has no significance.

(2) The variance might indicate that this period's operations were more or less efficient than the standard.

(3) The quality of the materials may have been higher than that used in setting the usage standard. This could follow an unfavorable price variance.

(4) There may have been a permanent change in the technological coefficients of producing this output. This could signal the desirability of reviewing operating decisions concerning the amount of output produced or the type of materials used in its production.

Other explanations could require information concerning the labor variances as well if the same individual is responsible for the utilization of both resources. Also observe that even if the purchasing department is assumed to be responsible for a price variance, substitution possibilities imply that the production manager is expected to respond to uncontrollable price changes. Here price and quantity variances would then be important in evaluating the production manager.

Direct Labor Variances

Much of what was said about the general interpretation of materials variances can also be applied to labor variances. The scope of the possible explanations will depend upon the allocation of authority. In many cases the foreman, by supervising the workers (the labor quantity variance), is indirectly controlling the efficiency with which the raw materials are used. In these cases the two variances may be related, so that the foreman can trade one resource for another.

It is, however, important to bear in mind the precision with which the standard has been set. For raw materials, an aura of precision is often present. Automated production processes give the standard-setter a smooth (low-variability) process to monitor and measure, and they allow the formulation of a standard with slight random fluctuation. Many more problems may be present in the case of labor, thereby inducing added fluctuations in the process. If so, the labor standard is a less precise one. For example, machines may occasionally break down, or workers may frequently be absent. Either factor may leave a supervisor no choice but to use a less than optimal mix of workers. The resulting variance is one that management must be careful in interpreting.

Overhead Variances

The discussion in Chapter 3 indicates that it is difficult to determine precise overhead standards. The possibility of errors in the standards should be kept in mind as a constant qualification of any statement made about them. Since overhead cost variances are often viewed as a group, it is important to discuss their relevance to one another and to be aware of the common factors affecting all of them.

The variable overhead quantity variance, for example, aids management in measuring the total cost of other decisions. That is, since overhead cost is usually viewed as a function of some other activity, its level is considered a function of other decisions. In our earlier example, variable overhead cost was a function of direct labor hours. Thus, any decision that altered the direct labor hours would also affect the level of variable overhead. For example, if a department head is assigned a large number of trainees in his work force, he will have not only an unfavorable labor quantity variance but also, as a result of the same decision, an unfavorable variable overhead quantity variance. Other examples could be offered to illustrate the same point: The variable overhead quantity variance is the result of decisions reflected in other variances such as the labor or materials quantity variance. Because of this, in analyzing various combinations of variances, management must look elsewhere for causes and use the variable overhead quantity variance only to assess the full effects of a decision or event.

The underlying nature of the overhead cost function can also be a source of difficulty. Step costs illustrate our point. Assume an overhead cost that increases by \$500 for each 500 units of output. If we join the steps with a line that touches each step at its initial point, we will obtain the cost equation TC = \$500 + \$1x. This is an accurate measurement of the standard only at the points where the line touches a step cost. For example, at an output of 600 units, the cost estimate is \$500 + \$1 (600) = \$1,100, but the expected cost for an output of 600 units is only \$1,000. Thus, our standard will overestimate the cost at every output except 500, 1,000, 1,500, and so on. If we join the steps at their endpoints, the opposite type of error will result. That is, our estimate will be TC = 0 + \$1x, which will underestimate the standard except at the points where the cost is discontinuous. No linear model is entirely accurate, and it is unlikely that a more sophisticated model will be sufficiently useful to justify its cost.

In short, overhead variances may reflect randomness, unintended estimation errors, significant management decisions, superior or inferior performance, and conscious simplifying assumptions. This is the most amorphous of the three production cost categories and therefore requires the most delicacy in interpretation and use.

Disposition of Production Cost Variances

A final question in our study of variance analysis techniques concerns the treatment of these techniques in a firm's accounts. One of the reasons for using a standard product cost system is simply that it is much less expensive than other accounting systems. Of course, cost measurement can hardly be expected to be precise; thus, the standards are sufficient if they are not too far removed from actual cost.

Suppose, then, that the variances are "minor" in total. In this case the firm will merely expense them at the end of the period in question. If instead the variances are not "minor" in total, then the accounting profession requires an adjustment to ending inventories and cost of goods sold that will reflect the major discrepancy between standard and actual product cost. In other words, the accounting profession demands actual product cost measures. Standard costs are sufficient if they are "close" or if their use does not alter the firm's financial reports in a material way; otherwise an end-of-period adjustment is called for.

Summary of Production Variances

In the foregoing pages, we have discussed the application of the various models used to create data inputs for the evaluation and decision-making process. We could have applied the same techniques to other cost categories as well but did not do so for two reasons. First, the production setting is the most common one. Second, there is little to be gained from repetition of the same models with new names. However, this chapter and Chapter 8 provide a framework within which most cost situations can be analyzed to aid the decision maker as long as meaningful standards can be set. Standards and variances in a nonmanufacturing setting are derived and used in basically the same way as those in manufacturing.

Our discussion so far has identified a number of variances and shown how they may be calculated. How these variances are actually used is generally left to the discretion of managers. On the other hand, we reiterate that any such variances are merely clues, or indicators, of whether additional investigation is worthwhile; they are not explanations of performance.

Calculation of Profit Variances

A little thought should convince you that the exact same subdivision concept is useful in the analysis of revenues and profit. We might contrast this year's with last year's profit and decompose the difference into selling price changes, sales quantity changes, and cost changes. The possibilities are endless. But the technique is always the same.

We can illustrate this with a return to our Beeball, Inc., production cost example. Recall the production cost variances summarized in Exhibit 7-7. Beeball, Inc., had planned to manufacture and sell $q = 18,100$ lots during the month of January. Suppose it anticipated a selling price of $50 per lot, a manufacturing cost of $\$36,200 + \$20q$, a marketing cost (all fixed) of $75,000, and an administrative cost (all fixed) of $50,000. Assume that the number of lots actually produced and sold was 17,900, with a total revenue of $912,900, a total manufacturing cost of $397,800, a total marketing cost of $73,000, and a total administrative cost of $54,000.

A single-factor analysis provides us with the data in Exhibit 7-8:

EXHIBIT 7-8————————————————————————————

Single-Factor Analysis of Beeball, Inc., Income

	Actual	Planned	Variance
Revenue	$912,900	$905,000	$7,900F
Costs			
Manufacturing cost	$397,800[a]	$398,200	400F
Marketing	73,000	75,000	2,000F
Administration	54,000	50,000	4,000U
	$388,100	$381,800	$6,300F

[a] Taken from Exhibit 7-7.

The profit plan was exceeded by $6,300. A more detailed picture is provided by inserting an intermediate calculation of actual quantity at standard selling price and cost, as in Exhibit 7-9:

EXHIBIT 7-9————————————————————————————

Two-Factor Analysis of Beeball, Inc., Income

	Actual	Actual quantity (17,900) at standard price and cost	Planned quantity (18,100) at standard price and cost
Revenue	$912,900	$895,000	$905,000
Costs			
Manufacturing cost	$397,800	$394,200	$398,200
Marketing	73,000	75,000	75,000
Administration	54,000	50,000	50,000
	$388,100	$375,800[a]	$381,800

Price/Cost variance	Quantity variance
$12,300F	$6,000U

[a] 375,800 = revenue less cost = $50(17,900) − $36,200 − $20(17,900) − $75,000 − $50,000.

The quantity variance is the shift from 18,100 to 17,900 lots, evaluated at the contribution margin of selling price less variable cost = $50 − $20 = $30, that is, $30(18,100 − 17,900) = $6,000U. You should carefully contrast this with our earlier discussion of the (fixed cost-induced) volume variance.

The price/cost variance, in turn, consists of an increase in the average selling price ($912,900 − $895,000 = $17,900), coupled by slight shifts in marketing ($2,000*F*) and administration ($4,000*U*) and by a manufacturing cost overrun (given $q = 17,900$) of $3,600*U*. This latter variance is precisely the manufacturing cost variance we analyzed earlier (recall Exhibit 7-7).

In other words, the subdivision technique finds application well beyond the narrow confines of manufacturing cost analysis. In all cases we subdivide a difference through insertion of intermediate calculations. On the other hand, the mechanical aspects can become overwhelming, as when we recognize multiple products, inventories, alternative production techniques, and so on. Partly for this reason, we do not pursue the topic further. But in the main, we stop here because all that follows is a direct application of the same basic idea.

A final example may reinforce this important point. Exhibit 7-10 shows a comparison of a condensed income statement with the budget. (Much of the detail in the expense category has been omitted, for it adds little insight into the *process.*)

Several facts emerge from examining Exhibit 7-11. One is that the key factor in the improved profit performance is the increase in dollar volume of sales. These revenues more than covered any added expenses. While we cannot be certain from these data, it would appear that the increase in gross profits may result from a 25 percent increase in volume.

Exhibit 7-10 also shows the relative variability of some costs. Despite the large increase in volume, there was virtually no shift in administrative costs. These costs were fixed, as we would assume, and their level bears little relationship to the volume of activities.

Marketing costs increased by about 16 percent in response to the 25 percent increase in volume. It therefore appears that the increase in volume

EXHIBIT 7-10

Alpha Company
Income Statement Analysis:
Actual to Budget

	Actual	Budget	Difference
Sales	$100,000	$72,000	$28,000
Less: Cost of goods sold	80,000	60,000	20,000
Gross margin	$ 20,000	$12,000	$ 8,000
Less: Marketing costs[a]	$ 7,000	$ 6,000	$ 1,000
Less: General and administrative[a]	8,000	7,500	500
Operating profit	$ 5,000	($ 1,500)	$ 6,500
Less: Interest charges	500	500	0
Net profit	$ 4,500	($ 2,000)	$ 6,500

[a] These accounts are the aggregate of the budgets and actual for many items. The individual items were omitted here for clarity.

EXHIBIT 7-11———————————————————————————————————

Two-Factor Analysis of Alpha Co. Income

Revenue		
(1)	Quantity effect	
	Forecast sales at forecast price (8,000 @ $9.00)	$ 72,000
	Actual sales at forecast price (10,000 @ $9.00)	90,000
		$ 18,000
(2)	Price effect	
	Actual sales at forecast price (10,000 @ $9.00)	$ 90,000
	Actual sales at actual price (10,000 @ $10.00)	100,000
		$ 10,000
(3)	Total revenue effect: (1) + (2)	$ 28,000
Cost of Goods Sold		
(4)	Quantity effect	
	Forecast sales at forecast cost (8,000 @ $7.50)	$ 60,000
	Actual sales at forecast cost (10,000 @ $7.50)	75,000
		$ 15,000
(5)	Cost effect	
	Actual sales at forecast cost (10,000 @ $7.50)	$ 75,000
	·Actual sales at actual cost (10,000 @ $8.00)	80,000
		$ 5,000
(6)	Total cost effect: (4) + (5)	$ 20,000
Net Effect on Gross Margin		
(3) + (6)		$ 8,000

was not accomplished through a massive increase in marketing costs. This does not mean that marketing did not help. The extra $1,000 may have been critical. Rather, it implies that marketing may have been quite efficient. If management is interested in assessing the effectiveness of the marketing function, they will have to examine the elements of the marketing costs, their intended effects, and the sales levels actually experienced.

We could analyze the income statement expense accounts in greater detail. Which administrative costs were up? Were any below the budgeted level? A similar analysis could be performed on the marketing data. The purpose of probing further would be twofold:

(1) to ascertain who may be responsible for "good" or "bad" performance.
(2) to ascertain where to direct our cost control efforts.

The first purpose is a traditional cost control situation. We cannot be sure of who can affect the organization's performance until we have isolated the area of inferior or superior performance. If administrative costs include several

_____EXHIBIT 7-12

Data for Review Problem
Warwick Products
Statement of Operations
January 1 to June 30, 1981

Accounts	Actual	Budget	Difference
Sales	$275,000[a]	$180,000[b]	$ _____
Less: Cost of sales	212,500	105,000[c]	_____
Gross profit	$ 62,500	$ 75,000	_____
Administrative expense	20,000	18,000	_____
Marketing expense	30,000	25,000	_____
	$ 12,500	$ 32,000	$ _____

[a] Actual selling price of $11 per unit; actual units of 25,000.
[b] Planned selling price of $12 per unit; planned units of 15,000.
[c] Planned fixed manufacturing cost of $20,000.

different types of expenditures controlled by different managers, we would want to know how each is doing. The individual manager, not the administrative cost, is the unit of control. And even if a single manager controlled all the administrative costs, we would want to know how each cost element is faring. Without these data, we might direct our efforts in the wrong directions.

REVIEW PROBLEM 6 _____

During the past year, Warwick Products has instituted a system that projects the company's income statement for the coming year. The first six months of data under the new system are now available (see Exhibit 7-12). Management is eager to see what it can learn from the new system.

(a) Fill in the variance column in the exhibit.
(b) Calculate price and quantity variances for sales.
(c) Calculate price and quantity variances for cost of goods sold.
(d) During this period, Warwick Products has made a concerted effort to expand its volume by cutting its price. The price was lowered from $12 to $11 (see Exhibit 7-12). The increase in production costs was the result of an unanticipated rise in petroleum distillates, a key ingredient. Do you think the price cut was a profitable idea?

_____ Conclusion

In this chapter, we have illustrated how budget versus actual comparisons can be measured, decomposed, and interpreted by management. The function of these procedures is to assist management in ascertaining the problem areas and potential causes of variances. In the context of the control process diagram (refer to Figure 5-2 p.181), this material is concerned with the comparison function of the feedback loop.

The greatest portion of the chapter was devoted to the analysis of production costs, because in most organizations that task is well structured and amenable to formal control procedures. However, the techniques could be applied in the administrative or marketing areas if management thought standards of performance could be set in those areas. Although standard costs are usually associated with manufacturing firms in mass production industries, more and more nonmanufacturing firms are finding that they can develop meaningful and useful standards for their operations. For example, many service organizations such as CPA firms now use formal budget procedures and standards.

The use of revenues as a subject for analysis by the same techniques is included to highlight two points. First, the usefulness of these techniques is not limited to the traditional area of production. Second, the standard need not be one set as an indicator of good performance. It may simply be performance in a prior period. In such a case, the analysis attempts to show why the two revenue figures differed without any pejorative implications.

Finally, it is important to remember that we have explored and hinted at use of a single technique: decomposition of a total. In complicated settings, different ways of measuring particular variances will be observed. But the technique is always the same. Differences arise from the manner in which the intermediate cost and profit calculations are defined.

Appendix A
Some Topics in Cost Accounting

This chapter dealt extensively with those topics with which a manager should be familiar if he is to understand the data he receives from the accounting department. However, no mention was made of how these data are entered into the accounting records by the accounting department or of other mechanical aspects of the accounting task. In this appendix, we will illustrate the journal entries needed to record the operating events and the disposition of variances. The data used are the variances calculated in Review Problems 2 and 3. (We shall not repeat the calculations.) In addition, sales of 50,000 units at $50 each, or a total of $2,500,000, have been assumed, so that a gross profit statement can be shown. Note that the time of purchase is used to calculate the raw materials price variance.

Accounting entries to record the operations of the period:
(A)	Raw materials control	$ 600,000	
	Materials price variance (2)[a]	13,000	
	Accounts payable		$ 587,000

(B)	Work-in-process	$ 495,000	
	Raw materials control		$ 489,000
	Materials quantity variance (2)		6,000
(C)	Work-in-process	$ 605,000	
	Labor quantity variance (2)	11,000	
	Labor price variance (2)		$ 11,200
	Wages payable		604,800
(D)	Work-in-process	$ 660,000	
	Variable overhead price variance (3)	5,600	
	Variable overhead quantity variance (3)	4,000	
	Fixed overhead price variance (3)	1,500	
	Fixed overhead volume variance (4)	24,000	
	Manufacturing cost control[b]		$ 695,100
(E)	Finished goods (55,000 units @ $32)	$1,760,000	
	Work-in-process		$1,760,000

[a] All numbers refer to the Review Problem.
[b] It is assumed that all overhead items are initially debited to manufacturing control. Corresponding credits would be to payables and assets (for example, cash).

Since all inventory accounts (materials, work-in-process, and finished goods) are carried at standard cost, the following entries would be made to record all the effects of sales of 50,000 units at $50 each:

(F)	Accounts receivable (or cash)	$2,500,000	
	Sales		$2,500,000
(G)	Cost of goods sold (50,000 units @ $32)	$1,600,000	
	Finished goods		$1,600,000

Finally, the net variance of $15,900 must be disposed of. The method below transfers all of it to cost of goods sold. An alternative method would prorate the net variance to the cost of goods sold, finished goods, and, if appropriate, work-in-process. Allocating all the net variances to cost of goods sold, we have:

(H)	Cost of goods sold	$15,900	
	Materials quantity variance	6,000	
	Labor price variance	11,200	
	Materials price variance	13,000	
	Labor quantity variance		$11,000
	Variable overhead price variance		5,600
	Variable overhead quantity variance		4,000
	Fixed overhead price variance		1,500
	Fixed overhead volume variance		24,000

These entries would give rise to a gross profit statement for the company, as illustrated in Exhibit 7-13.

EXHIBIT 7-13————————————————————————————————————

Alphazee Co.
Statement of Gross Profit

Sales		$2,500,000
Less: Cost of goods sold at standard	$1,600,000	
Adjustment for periodic variances (net)	15,900	1,646,800
Gross profit on sales		$ 884,100

Appendix B————————————————————————————
Flexible Materials Proportions:
Mix and Yield Variances

In the text sections that discussed the analysis of materials costs, the implicit assumption was made that the product required particular inputs in fixed proportion. Adding more of one raw material does not reduce the amount of a second raw material that is required. For example, using more bakelite in the handle of a tea kettle does not conserve on the amount of metal required to form the kettle portion. In the case of products involving nonflexible materials proportions, all the economies achieved (or diseconomies experienced) are reflected in the materials quantity variance. The units of raw material over or under standard are multiplied by the standard price to measure the monetary amounts involved. Thus, in the tea kettle example the following summary data might be reported:

Materials quantity variances	
Bakelite	$1,000F
Stainless steel	150U
Copper	900U
Total materials quantity variances	$ 50U

These data reflect the manager's performance in supervising the utilization of each item as well as his or her overall performance in the area.

What is important to our understanding of these variances is that (aside from any time constraints on the manager) the manager could improve the usage of copper without affecting the usage of bakelite. Each of the material quantity variances is independent of the other.

In direct contrast, some products permit variability in the proportions of the raw materials inputs. In these cases a reduction in the utilization of one material results in greater utilization of another. Thus the materials quantity variances are not independent and the total materials variance reflects the net effect of the manager's efforts. For example, a firm blending gasahol has the following variance report:

Materials quantity variances	
Gasoline	$1,000F
Alcohol	1,200U
Total materials quantity variance	$ 200U

In this case any improvement in the efficiency with which alcohol is used could reduce the favorable gasoline variance. This is because the saving on gasoline inputs may have been accomplished by using more alcohol.

To deal with this problem, accountants divide the total quantity variance into two components. One, called a *yield* variance, measures the efficiency with which the physical quantities of materials are utilized, independently of type. They are costed at a weighted average price for all the materials used. The other, called a *mix* variance, measures the effects of altering the proportions (of, say, gasoline and alcohol) from those shown in the standard. This is accomplished by measuring the difference in cost of each type of raw material from the weighted average cost and multiplying this by the quantity used or saved.

Each of these variances is illustrated in the following cases. We will use the following basic data in all cases. It takes 1 pound of A and 0.5 pound of B to produce one unit of output. The standard materials costs are:

	Cost per Unit		Mix Ratio	Weighted Average Price per Pound
A	(1 pound @ $1)	$1.00	$\frac{2}{3}$	$\frac{2}{3} \times \$1 = \$.67$
B	(0.5 pound @ $.70)	.35	$\frac{1}{3}$	$\frac{1}{3} \times \$.70 = \$.23$
		$1.35		$.90

In all three cases, 5,000 units of product were produced. Note that $1.35, the cost per unit, may also be expressed as 1.5 pounds at $.90 per pound.

Case A: No Mix Variance—Quantity Variance Reflects Difference from Standard Yield

Suppose that materials actually used in producing 5,000 units were as follows:

Material A	6,000 pounds
Material B	3,000 pounds
	9,000 pounds

In this case, the ratio of A to B (6,000 : 3,000) is the same as the standard mix of 2 : 1. Thus, any quantity variance will reflect only a change in the yield. We first calculate the normal quantity variance.

Standard quantities of materials allowed
    Good units produced   5,000
    Standard quantity of A required
      (5,000 units @ 1 pound per unit)   5,000 pounds
    Standard quantity of B required
      (5,000 units @ .5 pound per unit)   2,500 pounds
    Total materials allowed   7,500 pounds
Quantity variance (normal procedures)
    Material A $(6,000 - 5,000)(\$1.00)$ $\$1,000U$
    Material B $(3,000 - 2,500)(\$.70)$ $350U$
                      $\$1,350U$

Because there was no change in proportion and, therefore, no mix variance, this example could stop with the calculation of the traditional quantity variances. However, in order to illustrate the calculation of a yield variance, we will continue with the example.

In this calculation, it is assumed that we are equally concerned with inefficiency in using either A or B. Thus all pounds over standard (whether A or B) are costed at the weighted average price. Consistent with the fungibility of inputs assumed earlier, we are basically concerned with the *total* yield variance and not separate variances for A and B.

The total yield variance is the difference between the actual number of pounds used (9,000 pounds) and the standard pounds allowed (7,500 pounds) times the weighted average price per pound for the standard mix ($.90). This is

$$(9,000 - 7,500)(\$.90) = 1,500 \times \$.90 = \$1,350U$$

or using individual variances:

Σ(Actual quantity of material $-$ Standard quantity of material)
$$\times \text{Weighted average price (WAP)}$$
$$= (6,000 - 5,000)(\$.90) + (3,000 - 2,500)(\$.90) = 1,500 \ (\$.90) = \$1,350U$$

(Material A WAP) + (Material B WAP)

Notice in particular here that we have *defined* a yield variance in a particular manner (based upon total weight valued at a weighted average price). If the total of yield plus mix variances is to equal the conventional quantity variance, this construction also defines the mix variances. This is explored in the next case.

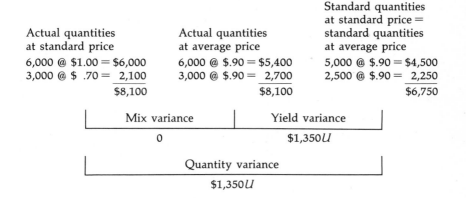

Actual quantities at standard price	Actual quantities at average price	Standard quantities at standard price = standard quantities at average price
6,000 @ $1.00 = $6,000	6,000 @ $.90 = $5,400	5,000 @ $.90 = $4,500
3,000 @ $ .70 = 2,100	3,000 @ $.90 = 2,700	2,500 @ $.90 = 2,250
$8,100	$8,100	$6,750

Mix variance	Yield variance
0	$1,350U

Quantity variance
$1,350U

Case B: Mix Variance—No Total Yield Variance

In Case B, to produce 5,000 units of output, actual materials used were

Material A	5,500 pounds
Material B	2,000 pounds
	7,500 pounds

The standard amount of materials for 5,000 units of output is, as in Case A, 7,500 pounds (1.5 pounds × 5,000). Therefore, the total yield variance is zero (7,500 − 7,500 = 0). We also can arrive at this by calculating the yield variances for A and B separately.

Yield variance for A (5,500 − 5,000)($.90)	$450U
Yield variance for B (2,000 − 2,500)($.90)	$450F
Total yield variance	0

In other words, there was a substitution of 500 additional pounds of Material A for 500 pounds of Material B. This was a perfect substitution in terms of pounds, and if each type of material were priced the same, the firm would be indifferent about the substitution. However, 500 pounds more of A at $1 per pound costs the firm $500, whereas the cost of B saved was 500 × $.70 = $350. Thus, this new mix resulted in a cost increase of $150. The mix variance reflects this and can be calculated as follows:

Σ(Actual pounds of material − Standard pounds of material)
    × (Standard price − Standard average price of materials) = Mix variance

As for the yield variance, the mix variance can be calculated for each material. Taken alone, however, these numbers are of even less significance to the managers than the separate yield variances. The calculations are:

Material A $(5,500 - 5,000)(\$1.00 - \$.90) = 500(\$.10)$ $\$\ 50U$
Material B $(2,000 - 2,500)(\$\ .70 - \$.90) = 500(\$.20)$ $\$100U$
Total mix variance $\$150U$

Note that since the yield variance is zero, the entire quantity variance of $(5,500 - 5,000)(\$1.00) + (2,000 - 2,500)(\$.70) = \$500 - \$350 = \$150$ is attributable to a mix variance.

Case C: Both Mix and Yield Variances

We now assume that actual materials uses were

Material A	6,000 lb
Material B	2,000 lb
	8,000 lb

First, we calculate the normal quantity variance:

Quantity variance for A $(6,000 - 5,000)(\$1.00)$ $\$1,000U$
Quantity variance for B $(2,000 - 2,500)(\$\ .70)$ $350F$
Total quantity variance $\$\ 650U$

Then, we calculate the mix variance:

Mix variance for A $(6,000 - 5,000)(\$1.00 - \$.90)$ $\$100U$
Mix variance for B $(2,000 - 2,500)(\$\ .70 - \$.90)$ $100U$
Total mix variance $\$200U$

Finally, we calculate the yield variance:

Yield variance for A $(6,000 - 5,000)(\$.90)$ $\$900U$
Yield variance for B $(2,000 - 2,500)(\$.90)$ $450F$
Total yield variance $450U$

Total mix and yield variances $= \$200U + \$450U = \$650U$

Though perhaps overbearing in appearance, these calculations are easy to explain. We are dividing the usual quantity variance into yield and mix components. Defining one variance automatically defines the other. If, for example, we define the yield variance as above, we would have:

Quantity variance	$\$650U$
Less yield variance	$\$450U$
Equals mix variance	$\$200U$

It is, in fact, a simple exercise to verify that the defined mix and yield variances total to the original quantity variance.

Indeed, further insight is available if we merely focus on *total* monetary amounts; then we have the familiar diagram:

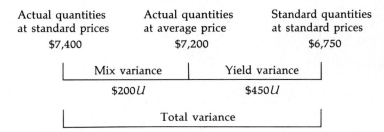

Actual quantities at standard prices	Actual quantities at average price	Standard quantities at standard prices
$7,400	$7,200	$6,750

Mix variance	Yield variance
200U$	450U$

Total variance

All variance procedures exhibit this theme of decomposing a total amount. Here the procedures are aimed at exploring cost effects of trade-offs between material inputs for a given product. Eventually, of course, we would link this to price variances and perhaps even to sales, sales mix, and so on. Several of the referenced articles explore these themes. We do not for two reasons. First, the conceptual nature of any such scheme is identical to what we have presented. Second, the precise scheme employed appears to be quite situation-specific, providing yet another example of our cost and value of analysis theme.

Supplementary Readings

Articles

Banks, C., "Applying Standard Costs to Recycled Products: The Automobile Tire," *Management Accounting*, Aug. 1976.

Demski, J., "An Accounting System Structured on a Linear Programming Model," *Accounting Rev.*, Oct. 1976.

Frank, W., and R. Manes, "A Standard Cost Application of Matrix Algebra," *Accounting Rev.*, Oct. 1967.

Hasseldine, C., "Mix and Yield Variances," *Accounting Rev.*, July 1967.

Hicks, J., "The Application of Exponential Smoothing to Standard Cost Systems," *Management Accounting*, Sept. 1978.

Hobbes, J., "Volume-Mix-Price/Cost Budget Variance Analysis: A Proper Approach," *Accounting Rev.*, Oct. 1964.

Horngren, C., "A Contribution Margin Approach to the Analysis of Capacity Utilization," *Accounting Rev.*, April 1967.

Malcolm, R., "Sales Variances: A Further Look," *Management Advisor*, March–April 1971.

Rockness, H., J. Bazley and L. Nikolani, "Variance Analysis for Pollution Control," *Management Accounting*, Jan. 1977.

Ronen, J., "Capacity and Operating Variances: An Ex Post Approach," *J. Accounting Research*, Autumn 1970.

Samuels, J., "Opportunity Costing: An Application of Mathematical Programming," *J. Accounting Research*, Autumn 1965.

Shank, J., and N. Churchill, "Variance Analysis: A Management-Oriented Approach," *Accounting Rev.,* Oct. 1977.

Solomons, D., "Flexible Budgets and the Analysis of Overhead Variances," *Management International,* 1961.

Wolk, H., and A. Hillman, "Materials Mix and Yield Variances: A Suggested Improvement," *Accounting Rev.,* July 1972.

Zannetos, Z., "On the Mathematics of Variance Analysis," *Accounting Rev.,* July 1963.

Questions and Problems

1. *Materials Variances*

   In making widgets, Super Widget, Inc., uses two basic raw materials, A and B. The records on their purchase and usage during January are shown below, followed by raw materials standards.

	PURCHASES		USAGE	
Material	Units	Actual Cost	Units	Actual Cost
A	10,000 pounds	$11,000	18,000 pounds	$17,500
B	8,000 pounds	$79,000	6,100 pounds	$61,000

Material	Standard Quantity	Standard Price	Total
A	9 pounds	$1 per pound	$9
B	3 pounds	$10 per pound	$30

   Production for January: 2,000 good widgets

   (a) From the above data, calculate the following materials variances:
   - (1) Price variance at time of purchase for A.
   - (2) Price variance at time of purchase for B.
   - (3) Price variance at time of use for A.
   - (4) Price variance at time of use for B.
   - (5) Quantity variance for A.
   - (6) Quantity variance for B.

   (b) How do you reconcile the figures you calculate for (1) and (3) and for (2) and (4)?

2. *Materials Variances*

   From the data below, calculate the required variances. In all cases, 1,000 good units were produced during the period.

	STANDARD PER UNIT		ACTUAL TOTAL	
Material	Quantity	Price	Quantity	Cost
A	2 feet	$2 foot	1,990 feet	$ 3,950
B	3 yards	$5/yard	2,890 yards	14,500
C	1 pound	$4/pound	1,125 pounds	4,450
D	2 tons	$100/ton	2,100 tons	211,000

3. *Analysis of Reported Materials Variances*

By-the-Book, Inc., calculates its materials variance at the time of purchase and holds the head of purchasing responsible. During the past period, he had a total variance of $4,000 unfavorable. He feels this is ludicrous. "Those people in accounting don't understand the real world. I had to special order that paint for finishing because of that rush defense order. I always get the requisitions late from Smith in scheduling. That costs money, too. If I had known that he'd need those casings, I would have bought them two months ago for much less. All in all, they changed a small favorable variance into a bad one!" Does he have a legitimate cause for complaint? If so, why, and what can be done? If not, why not?

4. *Adjusted Price Variance*

Gage, the new controller, wants you to revise the purchasing department's variance calculation. These are the details he gives you regarding purchasing's large favorable variances: "During the past six months, I have noted that purchasing has had four large favorable variances and two near zero. The latter were in periods when purchasing did little but production was still high. While I am pleased with this performance, I find that we have a four or five months' supply of many of our basic inputs. This is disquieting. Can you design a standard cost system for me that will aid in assessing what is happening?" What kind of system can you devise that will bring about the reconciliation Mr. Gage wants?

5. *Analyzing Reports*

The general manager has been looking at a report of material costs for the previous period, as shown below.

	Standard	Actual	Variance
1,000 units of product, material cost	$50,000	$51,350	$1,350$U$

He comments: "This variance does not seem to be large enough to be worried about. Here are the standards—can you see anything to concern us?"

Material A: 20 units @ $1.50 per unit	$30.00
Material B: 10 units @ $2.00 per unit	20.00
Materials cost per unit of product	$50.00

Usage records show that 25,000 units of A and 10,050 units of B were used during the period (use the figures for any price variance calculations needed). From the limited amount of information available to you, either support or argue against the general manager's position.

6. *Significance of Total Labor Cost*

From his analysis shown below, the head of the finishing department feels that both of his foremen are doing equally good jobs. Comment on whether this conclusion is justified. Note that he has only total labor costs.

Foreman	Actual Direct Labor Cost	Standard Cost
A	$20,000	$20,000
B	20,000	20,000

7. *Calculation of Direct Labor Variances*
Calculate the direct labor variances from the data below.

STANDARD		ACTUAL	
Hours per Unit	Rate per Hour	Hours (total)	Cost (total)
1.00	$10	4,010	$40,010
0.50	10	1,980	19,750
0.25	10	970	9,900
0.20	10	890	9,000

In all cases, good output was 4,000.

8. *Calculation of Direct Labor Variances*
From the data below, calculate the price and quantity variances for each case.

STANDARD (PER UNIT)		ACTUAL		
Hours	Rate per Hour	Total Hours	Total Cost	Units Produced
0.5	$30	1,200	$37,200	2,500
1.5	5	1,500	8,200	980
0.2	15	2,000	29,000	10,500

9. *Evaluation of Performance by Direct Labor Variances*
A foreman complains that the trouble he is having with labor variances is that "Jones in personnel doesn't like me, and he's buddies with Haight, who does the scheduling of workers. I think he gives me the dogs, and them the good workers. Anyway, here, take a look at these three performance reports. I'm Department C."

	ACTUAL RESULTS		
Department	Good Units Produced	Direct Labor Hours	Total Labor Cost
A	4,100	1,300	$16,500
B	4,000	1,500	18,750
C	4,200	1,200	16,800

Labor standards per unit are $13 per hour and 20 minutes per unit.

(a) Comment on the above data, supporting your analysis with calculations where possible.
(b) Is the foreman likely to be responsible for the labor rate variance?

10. **Calculating and Graphing Expected Fixed Overhead Standards**

(a) For each set of data below, calculate the standard fixed cost per machine hour and the standard fixed cost per unit.

	Estimated Fixed Cost	Expected Standard Machine Hours	Machine Hours per Unit
(1)	$100,000	20,000 hours	2 hours
(2)	100,000	25,000 hours	2 hours
(3)	100,000	30,000 hours	3 hours
(4)	100,000	50,000 hours	6 hours

(b) Graph the estimated fixed cost of $100,000 as it actually responds to changes in volume. On the same graph, show how the standard per hour rate makes it appear to respond to changes in volume using the data of (1) in part (a).

(c) At what volume do the two lines in the graph intersect? Why?

11. **Relating Fixed Overhead to Product Overhead Standards**
For each of the following sets of data, fill in the empty cell in the table.

	Expected Fixed Cost	Expected Volume	Standard Rate	Allocation Base per Unit	Standard Fixed Cost per Unit
(a)	$ 50,000	10,000 labor hours	$5.00	3 labor hours	_____
(b)	80,000	12,000 labor hours	6.67	_____	$20.00
(c)	80,000	_____	5.00	5 machine hours	25.00
(d)	_____	12,500 machine hours	8.00	1 machine hour	8.00
(e)	_____	10,000 machine hours	_____	2 machine hours	10.00
(f)	100,000	_____	5.00	_____	12.50
(g)	15,000	_____	1.00	10 machine hours	_____
(h)	108,000	12,000 machine hours	_____	_____	0.90

12. **Overhead Variances: Graphic Representation**
Figure 7-1 plots total standard overhead, *OA*, against volume and total monthly budget for overhead, *BC*. Actual overhead costs are plotted for months 1, 2, 3, and 4.

(a) In which of the four periods would the total overhead variance be unfavorable?

(b) For which periods would a favorable volume variance appear?

(c) In which of the four periods was the largest dollar figure added to the inventory accounts?

(d) In which period or periods, if any, was overhead overabsorbed?

13. **Overhead Variance—Graphic Representation**

(a) Indicate the areas of favorable and unfavorable spending (price) variances in Figure 7-2(a). Where would the spending variance be zero?

FIGURE 7-1

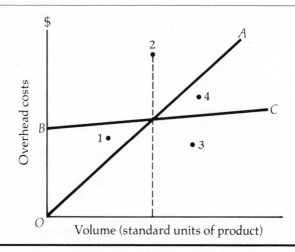

(b) Assuming a volume of standard production V_1 in Figure 7-2(a), locate the areas of favorable and unfavorable efficiency (quantity) variances.

(c) Indicate the areas of the fixed overhead favorable and unfavorable spending (price) variance in Figure 7-2(b).

(d) Indicate the areas of the favorable and unfavorable volume variance in Figure 7-2(b).

(e) Locate any volume V_3 in Figure 7-2(c) so that the volume variance is unfavorable. Locate a second point for the actual costs so that the following variances apply in each instance.

FIGURE 7-2

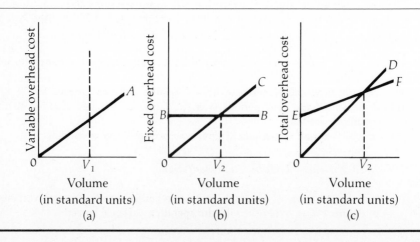

Case	Total Spending Variance	Efficiency Variance
1	Favorable	Favorable
2	Favorable	Unfavorable
3	Unfavorable	Favorable
4	Unfavorable	Unfavorable

(f)   What is the significance of volume V_2 in Figure 7-2(c)? Why would V_2 be the same amount in both Figure 7-2(b) (fixed costs only) and Figure 7-2(c) (total overhead costs) for any given department?

14.   *Calculating Overhead Variances*
X. Ample and Son manufacture parts for a major automobile manufacturer. The following data on actual performance and standards for overhead were gathered during the early part of the firm's production for the next model year.

Standard costs
 Variable $1.10 per unit (2 machine hours at $.55)
 Fixed $ .25 per unit (2 machine hours at $.125)
 Normal volume   200,000 machine hours

Actual costs
 Variable $98,500
 Fixed $26,000
Actual production   95,000 units
Actual machine hours   191,000 hours

Using these data, calculate the total overhead variance and all fixed and variable overhead variances.

15.   *Calculating Overhead Variances*
The following standard is used by Ex Company for costing the work done in its grinding department. Each standard unit requires 3 hours of machine time.

Variable overhead $1.00 per machine hour
Fixed overhead   5.00 per machine hour
Total overhead $6.00 per machine hour

Normal volume is 15,000 machine hours. During the most recent period, the following data were reported:

Volume: 5,200 good units of work completed
15,600 machine hours worked
Variable costs $15,800
Fixed costs   77,800
Total costs $93,600

(a)   Calculate expected fixed costs.
(b)   Calculate all overhead variances for fixed and variable costs.

16. *Calculation of Materials and Labor Variances with Journal Entries*
   Minny's Soda Pop, Inc., has set up the following standards for materials and
   direct labor for a vat of syrup:

Material:	10 pounds @ $3.00	$30.00
Direct labor:	4 hours @ $12.50	$50.00

   Assume that 10,000 vats were budgeted for the period and 9,810 vats were actually
   produced. Actual costs were

Materials:	98,073 pounds	$294,430
Direct labor:	39,399 hours	$488,548

   During the period, purchases amounted to 100,000 pounds at a total cost of
   $301,193.

   (a) Give all journal entries to record the above data.
   (b) Calculate all material and labor variances.
   (c) Comment on each of the variances as to most probable cause.

17. *Calculating All Variances*
   The following information relates to the operation of Ace Gum Company. The
   standard costs for one pound of refined, unflavored chicle are as follows:

Raw materials		
Chicle: 1.5 pound @ $.10 per pound		$ .15
Other chemicals: 0.1 pound at $.50 per pound		.05
		$ .20
Direct labor: ½ hour @ $5 per hour		$2.50
Overhead costs (per direct labor hour)		
Variable overhead		
Miscellaneous compounds	$.01	
Spoilage	.02	
Cleanup	.02	
Testing for quality	.03	
	$.08 per direct labor hour	.04
Fixed overhead		
Depreciation $1,000		
Supervisory 600		
$1,600	$.02 per direct labor hour	.01
Standard cost per pound		$2.75

   During the period, the department produced 130,000 pounds of refined, unflavored chicle. The relevant data are

Raw materials
  Chicle: 200,000 pounds
  Chemical: 12,000 pounds
Direct labor: 75,000 direct labor hours $345,000
Overhead costs
Variable overhead
  Miscellaneous compounds $ 1,410
  Spoilage 1,000
  Cleanup 950
  Testing for quality 1,400
  $ 4,760

Fixed overhead
  Depreciation $ 800
  Supervisory 1,200
  $ 2,000

During the period, purchases were
  Chicle: 250,000 pounds for $24,600
  Chemicals: 15,000 pounds for $9,000

(a) What is the expected volume of direct labor hours that would be worked during the period?
(b) Give all relevant variances for materials, labor, and each overhead item.
(c) Does the pattern of variances suggest any potential explanation?

18. *Journal Entries*
Using the data found in Problem 17, make all the required journal entries to reflect both operations and the calculation of variances.

19. *Calculating All Variances*
Assume the following data:

Materials
  Brume: 4 pounds @ $.15 per pound $ .60
  Buckram: 8 yards @ $.50 per yard 4.00 $ 4.60
Direct labor: 4 hours @ $7.50
  per direct labor hour 30.00
Variable overhead: 4 hours @ $.75
  per direct labor hour 3.00
  Inspection $.10
  Rework $.20
  Repair $.30
  Trucking $.15
Fixed overhead: 4 hour @ $5.00 20.00
  Supervision $2,000
  Depreciation $3,000
  Plant guards $5,000
Total standard unit cost $57.60

Actual cost data for the past month were as follows:

Materials		
Brume: 2,070 pounds	$ 289.80	
Buckram: 3,980 yards	2,029.80	$ 2,319.60
Direct labor: 2,010 hours @ $7.60		$15,276.00
Variable overhead		
Inspection	$ 400.00	
Rework	200.00	
Repair	900.00	
Trucking	500.00	$ 2,000.00
Fixed overhead		
Supervision	$2,000.00	
Depreciation	3,000.00	
Plant guards	7,500.00	$12,500.00
Total actual costs		$32,095.60

Note: The number of units produced equaled the normal volume.

(a) Calculate all relevant variances.
(b) Comment on possible causes of variances.

20. *Journal Entries*
Using the data given in Problem 19, make all the required journal entries to reflect both operations and the calculation of variances.

21. *Calculating All Variances*
The Carberg Corporation manufactures and sells a single product. The cost system used by the company is a standard cost system. The standard cost per unit of product is shown below:

Material: 1 pound plastic @ $2.00	$ 2.00
Direct labor: 1.6 hours @ $4.00	6.40
Variable overhead cost	3.00
Fixed overhead cost	1.45
	$12.85

The overhead cost per unit was calculated from the following annual overhead cost budget for a 60,000-unit volume:

Variable overhead cost	
Indirect labor: 30,000 hours @ $4.00	$120,000
Supplies (oil): 60,000 gallons @ $.50	30,000
Allocated variable service department costs	30,000
Total variable overhead cost	$180,000
Fixed overhead cost	
Supervision	$ 27,000
Depreciation	45,000
Other fixed costs	15,000
Total fixed overhead cost	$ 87,000

The actual costs of the manufacturing department for November, when 5,000 units were produced, are given below:

Material	5,300 pounds @ $2.00	$10,600
Direct labor	8,200 hours @ $4.10	33,620
Indirect labor	2,400 hours @ $4.10	9,840
Supplies (oil)	6,000 gallons @ $ .55	3,300
Allocated variable service department costs		$ 3,200
Supervision		2,475
Depreciation		3,750
Other		1,250
Total		$68,035

The purchasing department normally buys about the same quantity as is used in production during a month. In November, 5,200 pounds were purchased at a price of $2.10 per pound.

(a) Calculate variances from standard costs for: materials, direct labor, and overhead.

(b) The company has divided its responsibilities such that the purchasing department is responsible for the price at which materials and supplies are purchased. The manufacturing department is responsible for the quantities of materials used. Does this division of responsibilities solve the conflict between price and quantity variances? Explain your answer.

[ICMA adapted]

22. **Reconstruction of Standards: Different Standard Units for Material and Labor**
Loude and Cleare manufacture metal products for the home. One of these is a step stool for the kitchen. The stool is made of metal and has plastic treads and upholstery. During February, a fire in Loude's office destroyed the only copy of the master set of standards for the stool. All of the data available on operations for January are shown below.

Production materials: 750 standard units	
Labor and overhead: 600 standard units	
Materials issued	
Metal	7,500 pounds
Plastic	1,550 pounds
Cost	
Metal	$4,125
Plastic	$1,627.50
Direct labor	$9,500
Actual overhead	
Fixed	$3,280
Variable	$1,975
Direct labor hours worked	2,500

Variances
Materials

Metal	Price:	$375U	Efficiency: $ 0
Plastic	Price:	$ 77.50U	Efficiency: $ 50U
Direct labor	Rate:	$500F	Efficiency: $400U
Variable overhead	Total:	$175U	
Fixed overhead	Budget:	$ 20F	Capacity: $300F

(a) Reconstruct the firm's standard cost sheet for the stool and the number of units budgeted.
(b) Indicate any interrelationships you note in the above variances.

23. **Calculate Variances: Some Variances Given**

Ace Company produces various types of house and industrial paints. The basic processes for all paints are essentially similar. New equipment has just been installed in Department 1, and the company has not accumulated sufficient data for the determination of a standard cost per unit for that department. Department 2, however, is controlled by a formal standard cost system. Standard costs for Department 2 are provided below, along with the actual costs during the current period.

Department 2

Units of production: 11,500
Standard costs (per unit)

Costs assigned from Department 1	$ 10.00
Direct material: 2 pounds @ $.75 per pound	1.50
Direct labor: 2 hours @ $3.25 per hour	6.50
Variable overhead: 2 hours @ $1.80 per hour	3.60
Fixed overhead: 2 hours @ $2.25 per hour	4.50
Total	$ 26.10

Activities During the Period

Direct materials usage variance	$ 112.50U
Direct labor, actual costs	79,625.00
Variable overhead efficiency variance	450.00F
Fixed overhead, actual costs	55,000.00
Average prices of materials	.80/pound
Total overhead, actual costs	96,500.00
Actual output (equals normal output)	11,500.00

(a) Calculate the amount of materials issued and the total price variance for materials issued.
(b) Calculate the labor variances, both rate and efficiency.
(c) Calculate the variable overhead variances, both efficiency and spending.
(d) What was the budgeted fixed overhead?
(e) What were the fixed overhead budget and volume variances?
(f) Discuss the interrelationships between the various efficiency and price variances by indicating the possible sources of these variances and how they interact.

24. **Calculate All Variances**

The following represent the standard costs of processing Product A through Department I:

MATERIALS

No.	Description	Quantity per Unit	Price	Standard Cost per Unit
180	Processed oil	2 gallons	$.80	$1.60
190	Supplementary	1 gallon	$.40	.40
				$2.00 per unit

Spoilage and wastage allowance for A (7½%)   .15 per unit
Standard materials cost per unit $2.15 per unit

DIRECT LABOR

Pay Grade	Actual Base	Standard (Average)
11	$3.00	¼($3) + ½(3.20) + ¼(3.60)
12	$3.20	= $.75 + $1.60 + $.90
13	$3.60	= $3.25 per hour

The standard usage of labor, on the average, is 2 hours. Therefore, the standard direct labor cost is 2($3.25) = $6.50.

Standards for overhead are based on a flexible budget. A summary of this budget is reproduced below (based on monthly allocations).

	18,000 hr	20,000 hr	22,000 hr	24,000 hr
Indirect materials and labor	$ 5,400	$ 6,000	$ 6,600	$ 7,200
Maintenance and miscellaneous variables	9,200	10,000	10,800	11,600
Supervision	15,000	20,000	20,000	25,000
Depreciation	20,000	20,000	20,000	20,000
Miscellaneous fixed	2,000	2,000	2,000	2,000
	$51,600	$58,000	$59,400	$65,800

Normal volume: 22,000 hour
Variable overhead rate: $.70 per hour
Fixed overhead budget (based on 20,000 hour): $44,000
Fixed overhead rate: $2.00 per hour

Actual results for Department I were as follows:

Good units of work: 10,000 units
Costs
   Materials $43,600
   Labor   61,050
Overhead
   Material $ 5,735
   Maintenance and miscellaneous variables   9,500
   Supervision   20,500
   Depreciation   20,000
   Miscellaneous fixed   2,000
   Actual hours worked   18,500 hours
   Actual purchases
      22,000 gallons of 180 and 11,000 gallons of 190 $24,200

(a) Find the variances for materials, labor, and overhead.
(b) Show how the variable and fixed overhead rates were calculated.
(c) Discuss the economic significance of the prime cost variances.
(d) Discuss when and why a firm would allow for a standard amount of waste in setting its standard. If it did not, how could such waste be handled?

25. **Journal Entries**
Using the data in Problem 24, make all journal entries necessary to record standard costs of operation and all variances.

26. **Interpretation of Standard Cost Variances**
The Fillep Co. operates a standard cost system. The variances for each department are calculated and reported to the department manager. It is expected that the manager will use the information to improve his operations and recognize that it is used in turn by his superiors when they are evaluating his performance.
   John Smith was recently appointed manager of the assembly department of the company. He has complained that the system as designed is disadvantageous to his department. Included among the variances charged to the departments is one for rejected units. The inspection occurs after the unit has been assembled. The inspectors attempt to identify the cause of the rejection so that the department where the error occurred can be charged with it, but some errors cannot be easily identified with a department. These are totaled and apportioned to the departments according to the number of identified errors. The variance for rejected units in each department is a combination of the errors caused by the department plus a portion of the unidentified causes of rejects.

(a) Is John Smith's claim valid? Explain the reasons for your answer.
(b) What would you recommend the company do to solve its problem with John Smith and his complaint?

[AICPA adapted]

27. **Interpretation of Labor Variances**
The Clark Company has a contract with a labor union that guarantees a minimum wage of $500 per month to each direct labor employee having at least 12 years of service. One hundred employees currently qualify for coverage. All direct labor employees are paid $5.00 per hour.
   The direct labor budget for 1974 was based on the annual usage of 400,000 hours of direct labor at $5.00, or a total of $2,000,000. Of this amount, $50,000 (100 employees × $500 per month or $600,000 for the year) was regarded as fixed. Thus, the budget for any given month was determined by the formula $50,000 plus the quantity $3.50 times direct labor hours worked.
   Data on performance for the first three months of 1974 follow:

	January	February	March
Direct labor hours worked	22,000	32,000	42,000
Direct labor costs budgeted	$127,000	$162,000	$197,000
Direct labor costs incurred	110,000	160,000	210,000
Variance	$ 17,000F	$ 2,000F	$ 13,000U

The factory manager was perplexed by the results, which showed favorable variances when production was low and unfavorable variances when production was high, because he believed his control over labor costs was consistently good.

(a) How did Clark Company arrive at the rate of $3.50 per hour?
(b) Explain the variances using cost–volume behavior.
(c) Does this direct labor budget provide a basis for controlling direct labor cost? Explain, indicating changes that might be made to improve control over direct labor cost and to facilitate performance evaluation of direct labor employees.

[AICPA adapted]

28. *Overhead Variances with Two Independent Variables*
Stern Corp. is a multiproduct firm that supplies component parts to the automobile industry. One of its production departments has a monthly overhead budget with two independent variables:

$$\widehat{OVHD} = \$98,000 + \$14 \cdot MH + \$37 \cdot DLH$$

where MH denotes machine hours and DLH denotes direct labor hours. During a recent month, machine hours totaled 5,100 and direct labor hours totaled 2,020. Overhead totaled $254,240. Stern uses a standard system, with the following standards for the three products (A, B, and C) manufactured in this department:

Product	Standard Labor Time	Standard Machine Time
A	4.0 hours	8 hours
B	2.0 hours	5 hours
C	3.5 hours	6 hours

Total production was:

Product	Units
A	150
B	500
C	200

Analyze the department's overhead for the month in question.

29. *Variance Analysis: Sales*
Inglewood Waters sets quotas for their sales representatives and then supplies management with monthly performance reports so that they can evaluate the sales representatives' performances. The data below relate to one of their top salespeople, John Smith.

	Actual	Standard
Sales volume	$45,000	$40,000
Customers	300	200

(a) What is Mr. Smith's total sales variance for the period?
(b) How did his average sale per customer compare with the standard implied in the above data?
(c) How did his number of sales compare with his quota or standard?
(d) Draw up a schedule using the data in parts (b) and (c) to explain the total variance calculated in (a).
(e) If you were assessing Mr. Smith's performance, what other data might you request concerning his performance during the month?

30. **Interpretation of Sales Variances**
Mr. Smith (Problem 29) made 400 calls on customers during the month. The standard number a salesperson is expected to make is 500 calls. As a manager, how would you interpret the fact that he made 100 fewer customer calls than were expected of him?

31. **Calculation of Profit Variance**
During the first quarter of 1981, Lotta Kola Company found profits at a new all-time high of $140,000. Management is ecstatic, but now they must explain the reason for this to the financial press. As the accountant, you are given the task. The first-quarter data for 1980 and 1981 are shown below.

	1980	1981
Sales	$600,000	$1,000,000
Less: Cost of sales	450,000	700,000
Gross profit	$150,000	$ 300,000
Less: Other costs	160,000	160,000
Profit (Loss)	$(10,000)	$ 140,000
Volume	15,000,000 units	20,000,000 units

Draw up a report explaining the increase in profits over the first quarter of 1980.

32. **Calculation of Profit Variances**
XYZ Electronics began a comprehensive budgeting process last year for the first time. The projected 1981 income statement was the first output from the process. Management now wants to relate the actual 1981 results to their forecast. The forecast and the actual first quarter results are given below.

	Forecast	Actual
Sales	$180,000	$250,000
Less: Cost of sales	135,000	175,000
Gross margin	$ 45,000	$ 75,000
Less: Administrative costs	20,000	30,000
Profit	$ 25,000	$ 45,000
Volume	900 units	1,000 units

(a) Prepare a report explaining why profit exceeded the forecast.

(b) At the meeting where the report is presented, one board member asks for more information on the causes of the difference between actual cost of sales and forecast cost of sales and between actual and forecast administrative costs. How could a standard cost system aid you in providing the answer to his questions?

33. **Profit Variances**

You have acquired the following data for the calendar years 1980 and 1981 for Celebration, Inc.:

	1980		1981		Dollar Increase
Sales	$750,000	100%	$840,000	100%	$90,000
Cost of goods sold	495,000	66	560,000	66⅔	65,000
Gross margin	$225,000	34%	$280,000	33⅓%	$25,000
Unit selling price	$10		$12		

Prepare a statement in good form that analyzes the variations in sales and cost of goods sold between 1980 and 1981.

[AICPA adapted]

34. **Discussion of Variances and Disposition of Variances**

Last year, Crowley Corporation adopted a standard cost system. Labor standards were set on the basis of time studies and prevailing wage rates. Materials standards were determined from materials specifications and prices then in effect. In determining its standard for overhead, Crowley estimated that a total of 6,000,000 finished units would be produced during the next five years to satisfy demand for its product. The five-year period was selected to average out seasonal and cyclical fluctuations and allow for sales trends. By dividing the annual average of 1,200,000 units into the total annual budgeted overhead, a standard cost was developed for manufacturing overhead.

On June 30, 1981, the end of the current fiscal year, a partial trial balance revealed the following:

Materials price variance	$25,000F
Materials quantity variance	9,000U
Labor rate variance	30,000U
Labor efficiency variance	7,500U
Controllable overhead variance	2,000U
Noncontrollable (capacity) overhead variance	75,000U

Standards were set at the beginning of the year and have remained unchanged. All inventories are priced at standard cost.

(a) What conclusions can be drawn from each of the six variances shown in Crowley's trial balance?

(b) Give the theoretical justification for each of the following methods of accounting for the net amount of all standard cost variances for year-end financial reporting:

(1) Including the net variance on the income statement as another income or expense item.

(2) Allocating the net variance among inventories and cost of goods sold.

(3) Allocating the net variance entirely to cost of goods sold.

[AICPA adapted]

35. *Variance Analysis Review*[4]

Ralph has been hired as a consultant by Ferris Manufacturing Co. To make his analysis and recommendations, Ralph requires actual direct manufacturing cost data. Ferris uses a standard absorption cost system. Their cost of goods sold was calculated as follows:

Cost of goods sold:	
Beginning inventory, finished goods	$ 75,000
Cost of goods manufactured	2,600,000
Less ending inventory, finished goods	(90,000)
	$2,585,000

Beginning and ending inventory are at standard cost. Cost of goods manufactured includes the manufacturing cost variances for the period.

	Price or Spending Variance	Efficiency Variance
Direct materials	$17,000$U$	$ 20,000U
Direct labor	52,500U	105,000U
Variable factory overhead	35,000F	60,000U

	Production Volume Variance	Budget Variance
Fixed factory overhead	$40,000$F$	$20,500$U$

Total manufacturing cost variances: $200,000$U$

The standard costs for one unit of output are:

	Standard Input Quantity	Standard Input Price
Direct materials	2 pounds	$2 per pound
Direct labor	2 hours	$7 per hour
Factory overhead	2 hours	$6 per hour

Total standard cost for one unit of output is $30. Ralph assumes (as you may) that the direct labor and variable factory overhead variances are calculated using direct labor hours as the input quantity measure.

---

[4] Contributed by John Fellingham.

Compute the following:

(a) Actual cost of direct materials used for the period.
(b) Actual cost of direct labor.
(c) Actual cost of variable factory overhead.
(d) Actual cost of fixed factory overhead.

*36. **Mix and Yield Variances**
Morewood Products produces a glue that works especially well on plastic. The glue is made from scrap plastic and K-toner. However, the proportions are not rigidly fixed. The production manager will alter the mix within the boundaries set by the formula, according to his judgment and the availability of good scrap plastic.

The standard formula that is most efficient and the standard prices for scrap plastic and K-toner are as follows:

Scrap plastic (2 pounds)	$.20
K-toner (2 pounds)	.30
Standard cost per pint	$.50

During July, 1982, production data were

Scrap plastic (1,800 pounds)	$198
K-toner (2,100 pounds)	330
Total material costs	$528
Production 1,000 pints	

(a) Calculate whatever variances are necessary to explain the manager's choice of proportion for plastic and K-toner.
(b) How would your answer in part (a) differ if the two materials were not substitutable?
(c) How would you interpret the variances if you knew that
  (1) No good scrap plastic was available.
  (2) The manager was informed by purchasing that scrap was skyrocketing in price.
  (3) Conditions were normal, and both K-toner and scrap plastic were available in ample quantities and at about standard prices.

*37. **Mix and Yield Variances**
Kontrol makes a special insect repellent that appears to have the same potency as DDT but fewer side effects. The formula requires a blending of Kanta, Beta, and inert ingredients. Listed below are the data for Department 1, which blends Kanta.

Kanta is made from Materials X and Y. The department manager can vary the ratio of X to Y within limited bounds to minimize cost, meet market conditions, and so forth. However, the management has set a standard for

Kanta that reflects an expected level of good performance over the year. The standard for materials for 1,000 pounds of Kanta is

	Quantity	Price	Total Cost
X	500 pounds	$.12 per pound	$ 60.00
Y	500 pounds	$.15 per pound	75.00
	Total cost per 1,000-pound batch		$135.00

During the last week, actual data for Department 1 were

X	6,000 pounds	$ 660.00
Y	4,500 pounds	900.00
		$1,560.00

Yield: 10 batches of 1,000 pounds each

Required (a) Calculate the total variance on Kanta.

(b) Calculate the mix and yield variance.

(c) Given the manager's need to adjust the ratio to meet varying conditions, how should an unfavorable variance in part (a) be interpreted?

(d) The manager attempted to explain an unfavorable variance in part (a) by saying, "I shifted from Y to X because the X was of lower quality and would require extra processing time." How would you evaluate him?

(e) If the manager shifted from Y to X because of their prices, how would you evaluate his decision?

*38. **Nonlinear Cost Analysis**

Quadratic Ralph manages a single-product firm with a nonlinear (and, in fact, quadratic) cost curve. At the start of a recent month he made the following predictions:

Selling price per unit	$ 51
Direct Material	
Price per pound	$ 5
Pounds per unit of final product	1 pound
Scrap per unit of final product	.2 pound
(That is, 1.2 pounds are required per unit of final product.)	
Direct Labor	
Price per hour	$ 10
Hours per unit of final product	2 hours
Maintenance	
Fixed cost	$100
Variable cost per unit of final product	1
Central administration cost	$200
(all fixed)	
Manufacturing overhead	
Fixed	$500
Variable per labor hour	2
Variable per (labor hour)^2	.025

[Thus, for 50 labor hours the predicted overhead is $500 + 2(50) + .025(2,500)$].

Required (a) Using these predictions, determine a total cost curve, as a function of units produced, for Quadratic Ralph's firm.

(b) Plot your curve in a graph and consider the point at which 100 units are produced. What is the full cost per unit, variable cost per unit, and marginal cost at that point?

(c) Now compute total cost at 90 units and at 110 units and take the average of the nonfixed components. Adding the fixed cost intercept of 800, you have constructed a linear approximation of the nonlinear cost curve. State the linear cost approximation equation and plot it on your graph in (b).

(d) Using the *correct* cost curve, determine the optimal production quantity. (The answer is $q = 100$.)

(e) Suppose at the *end* of this month, we compile the following statistics:

Actual production and sales	$ 100
Sales price	$ 51
Direct material	
Actual purchases	200 pounds
Actual price per pound	$ 4
Total usage	150 pounds
Direct labor	
Actual usage	230 hours
Actual price per hour	$ 10.1
Total maintenance cost	$ 220
Total central administration cost	$ 180
Total manufacturing overhead	$2,200

What net income was predicted at the start of the month? What net income was actually earned during the month? Factor the difference between these two figures into as many variances as you feel are relevant. (Note: You should use the nonlinear cost curve in answering these questions.)

(f) Repeat (e) above using the approximate linear cost curve developed in (d) above.

(g) Which variances differ between (e) and (f) and why do they differ?

*39. **Comprehensive Planning Analysis**
This is a continuation of the saga begun in Ralph's LP (A), Problem 22 in Chapter 4. Following implementation of the output schedule determined in (A), 270 of the first product and 110 of the second are produced and sold. Ralph also collects the following data pertaining to the cost actually incurred in each production and service department. (No interdepartmental allocations are present in these data.)

	Department 1	Department 2
Actual DL hours	396	468
Actual DL cost	$4,100	$6,800
Actual overhead		
Fixed	$290	$560
Variable	$307	$710
Actual power consumption	3,700 KWH	10,300 KWH
Actual maintenance consumption	37 units	100 units
DM purchases[a]	590 pounds	120 pounds
Standard cost per pound	$5.00	$8.00
Actual cost per pound	$6.00	$7.40
Actual DM consumption	530 pounds	100 pounds

Actual building cost	$500
Actual central administration cost	$800
Actual production administration cost	$200
Actual power cost	$750
Actual maintenance cost	$800

[a] A different material is used for each of the two products. The material for the first product is used in Department 1, and the material for the second product is used in Department 2.

Required Using the actual cost data as well as the budget(s) developed in (A), analyze the performance of Ralph's firm during the month under consideration. You may assume that the anticipated product selling prices and marketing costs did, in fact, result.

Before beginning, it is probably wise to remember the task at hand. The budgeted profit is $1,300 and the actual is $688.40. First decompose this into shifts in the output schedule (180U$) and selling price and cost changes (431.60U$). Next decompose the latter into direct material, direct labor, production overhead, and so on. Finally, further decompose the material, labor, overhead, power, and maintenance into price and quantity components.

Assessing the Significance of Standard Cost Variances

In Chapter 7, we illustrated the mechanics of calculating standard cost variances and discussed how these variances may be viewed as signals that certain aspects of performance have deviated from the specific expectations used to formulate plans of operations. Our purpose in this chapter is to consider some of the methods used to assess whether the observed variances are significant enough to warrant investigation. Such investigation produces yet additional information, and the generic question is whether, at some cost, this information production is worthwhile. We begin by discussing the setting in which such a decision problem might arise and what the possible benefits of producing the additional information might be. Following this, we review several methods of analyzing the information production question, varying from Bayesian analysis to application of classical statistics approaches that find favor in quality control settings.

The Basic Problem

Obviously, variances can have significance only if they can be related to the decision problems of management. In order to assess their significance, we now must be more explicit in defining the relationship between standard cost variances and management's decision problems. Materials, labor, and overhead costs are controlled because they are input variables to many of management's operating decisions. For example, material prices and quantities, labor rates and hours worked, and variable overhead costs are used in cost–volume–profit decisions (Chapter 4) and in estimates of the cash flows for capital budgeting decisions (Chapter 14). Similarly, the variable costs of acquiring and storing inventories are inputs to inventory models, whether the models are deterministic or probabilistic (Chapter 16). Fixed overhead costs

301

are controlled, at least at standard levels, in order to gain some insight into the costs of providing capacities for products and services.

Standard costs are basically estimates of what costs are expected to be under various operating conditions. Since an accountant cannot specify exactly what will happen in the future, we would expect a certain amount of variation around these standard costs; that is, we would expect actual costs to vary around these standards. As an illustration, a labor standard of 2 hours per unit of output might be the average time spent by a worker who possesses an average degree of the skills required for the job. If we recorded the times spent on this job by this worker and others with a similar degree of skills, we would not be surprised if the times spent on a unit of output varied slightly, say, between 1 hour and 50 minutes and 2 hours and 10 minutes. The causes of the ±10-minute variances are many, and they are difficult (and costly) to specify. Therefore, the firm's management may be willing to tolerate these small variations in labor time. The same would be the case with respect to any other standard, except, of course, where even very small differences are deemed crucial. A certain amount of variance from standard is considered a reflection of random events that are beyond anyone's control.

Now suppose that, in a study of the same job, a labor time of 2 hours ±25 minutes is observed. Should this variance be "investigated"? It surely is significant in the sense of exceeding the ±10-minute limits that have been established for the random component. But investigation is costly: It takes time away from other managerial activities and may even interrupt the ongoing productive process. Thus the basic question is whether the investigation benefits are expected to exceed these costs.

As a basis for exploring this question, consider a firm that faces the following simple linear programing problem:

$$\text{Maximize} \quad TCM = \$3X_1 + \$2X_2$$

$$\text{subject to} \quad 2X_1 + \quad 1X_2 \leq 12{,}000 \text{ hour (Department I)}$$

$$1/2\,X_1 + 1X_2 \leq \ \ 6{,}000 \text{ hour (Department II)}$$

$$X_1, X_2 \geq 0$$

The specific standards for X_1 and X_2 are given in Exhibit 8-1.

The optimal solution to this problem is $X_1 = X_2 = 4{,}000$ units. Total contribution margin with this output is $\$3(4{,}000) + \$2(4{,}000) = \$20{,}000$.[1]

Suppose that an unfavorable variance of $3 per unit is observed in

---

[1] The specific methods for obtaining this solution have little relevance in this section, which deals with random versus nonrandom variances. However, the student should review the section on linear programing in Chapter 4 before continuing with the discussion of decision significance.

_____ EXHIBIT 8-1

	X_1			X_2
Revenue per unit		$75.50		$73.00
Variable costs				
Department I				
Raw materials	(1 lb @ $10/lb)	$10.00	(1½ lb @ $10/lb)	$15.00
Direct labor	(2 hr @ $14/hr)	28.00	(1 hr @ $14/hr)	14.00
Variable overhead	(2 hr @ $8/hr)	16.00	(1 hr @ $8/hr)	8.00
Department II				
Raw materials	(1 lb @ $6/lb)	6.00	(1½ lb @ $6/lb)	9.00
Direct labor	(½ hr @ $15/hr)	7.50	(1 hr @ $15/hr)	15.00
Variable overhead	(½ hr @ $10/hr)	5.00	(1 hr @ $10/hr)	10.00
Total variable cost per unit		$72.50		$71.00
Contribution margin per unit		$ 3.00		$ 2.00

Department I for the material used in producing X_1. That is, actual material costs are $13 per unit of output instead of $10. Also suppose that the variance originates in the quantity used and not in the price. The question now is whether this variance should be investigated and, if so, how we might respond to the results of the investigation.

Before proceeding, let us examine the problem in order to clarify some of the assumptions that are often made in the various approaches taken. First, of course, we can expect to incur some investigation costs, because both the person initiating the investigation and the person responsible for controlling the process will have to devote time to the process of investigation. These costs may vary with the type of variance being investigated; that is, the time required to investigate might depend on the source of the variance. However, we assume that the total cost of investigation, C, is constant and known. Second, an investigation may be completely successful, partially successful, or a complete failure. That is, we may or may not be able to identify the cause of the variance with precision. In the discussions that follow, we assume that the investigation is a complete success. Third, if the process is not investigated, the variance may persist or it may disappear in the next operating period, indicating that the process has moved back into control without any intervention. We assume that if a process that is out of control is not investigated, the observed variance will continue into the next operating period. Finally, to keep things simple we also assume the decision problem in Exhibit 8-1 will operate for only one more period into the future. This makes the investigation problem at hand sufficiently interesting without adding the (real) complication of not investigating the process and thereby gathering additional information prior to making a subsequent investigation.

Given these assumptions, we expect to incur costs C if we investigate. But what about the benefits?

The Benefits of Investigation

Suppose we have just observed the $3 per unit unfavorable materials variance in Department I. If no response is offered, the exact same production schedule will be implemented next period. This assumption is not very realistic, but it does allow us to discuss the conceptual issue at hand without becoming swamped in detail.

One possible outcome of an investigation is to discover that the variance arose from a specific decision of the department's manager. For example, he might have assigned workers to specific tasks in such a way that the materials quantity standard could not be met. Once revealed by investigation, this assignment could be corrected and the firm would expect to save $3(4,000) = $12,000 next period by ensuring production in conformity with the standard. (Conversely, if the variance was favorable, we might expect the manager to attain the same efficiency next period. The benefits then become more difficult to estimate because the production schedule may be altered in response to the newly found efficiency.)

A second possible outcome of an investigation is to discover that the variance arose from an error in the accounting system. Here no production gains are possible, because no change in the firm's economic structure is implied. Thus, in our simplified setting, the investigation benefits are nil in this case.

A third possible outcome of an investigation is to discover that the variance arose from uncontrollable randomness in the process. This is just part of the economic facts of life in the firm and nothing can be done. Moreover, nothing is implied about altering next period's standards or plans. Again, then, the investigation benefits are nil.

A fourth possible outcome of the investigation is to discover that the original standard was incorrect. Learning may have occurred, presumed production techniques may not be feasible,[2] and so on. This implies that the direct materials standard in Department I for product X_1 should be 1.3 pounds @ $10 per pound = $13 per unit. Reflecting back on the data in Exhibit 8-1, this implies a contribution margin of $0 per unit for product X_1. With this new information, the firm's simple programing problem for next period becomes:

$$\begin{array}{ll} \text{Maximize} & \text{TCM} = \$0X_1 + \$2X_2 \\ \text{subject to} & 2X_1 + 1X_2 \leq 12{,}000 \text{ hour} \\ & 1/2\,X_1 + 1X_2 \leq 6{,}000 \text{ hour} \\ & X_1, X_2 \geq 0 \end{array}$$

This has an optimal solution of $X_1 = 0$ and $X_2 = 6,000$ units. The total contribution margin would be $0(0) + $2(6,000) = $12,000. Without investiga-

---

[2] See J. Demski, "An Accounting System Structured on a Linear Programming Model," *Accounting Rev.*, October 1967, for an analysis of one particular such case.

tion, the original schedule of $X_1 = X_2 = 4{,}000$ units would be implemented and the contribution margin would be $\$0(4{,}000) + \$2(4{,}000) = \$8{,}000$. Thus the benefits from investigation in this case would be $\$12{,}000 - \$8{,}000 = \$4{,}000$. In effect, this investigation benefit arises from the fact that the variance (a) is due to sources beyond the control of the firm and (b) shifts the optimal solution to the point where it benefits the firm to revise its original production schedule.

We might define a variance as being decision-significant if it leads the firm to modify the original decision. In any event, it should be clear that the decision-significance of a variance can be assessed by analyzing the sensitivity of decisions to observed variances. For example, using some of the techniques described in Chapter 4, we can analyze how sensitive our decision is to changes in the costs and revenues of each product, via their effect on the contribution margin, as well as to changes in the resource requirements of each. Similarly, if our firm used a formal inventory model to guide its inventory decisions, we could evaluate the sensitivity of these decisions to variances from standards set for purchase order or setup costs, storage costs, and stock-out costs.

To illustrate using our linear programing problem, the original decision to produce 4,000 units of each product would remain optimal if the contribution margin of X_1 remained within the range $\$1.00 \leq CM_{X1} \leq \$4.00$, assuming $CM_{X2} = \$2.00$. Notice then that *if* the unfavorable materials quantity variance had totaled $\$1.00$ per unit and *if* it were determined to be the result of an error in the original standard, the investigation benefit would be nil because the optimal decision would not shift. (The range for the contribution margin of X_2 is $\$1.50 \leq CM_{X2} \leq \$6.00$, with CM_{X1} held constant. Ranges could also be established for the other variables of the problem.)

Return now to the basic story in our example of a $\$3$ per unit unfavorable materials quantity variance in Department I for product X_1. Depending on the underlying cause of the variance, the implied investigation benefits are $\$12{,}000$, $\$4{,}000$, or $\$0$. The precise benefit will not be known until the investigation is performed. In the language of Chapter 1, the investigation produces new information. In addition, the benefits might arise from operational or decision control considerations. In our particular example, an operational consideration arises when the variance is caused by the department manager's decisions and can be corrected. The decision control consideration arises when the variance is the result of an incorrectly specified standard; correction in its turn alters the firm's optimal decision. Also observe that the variance reported by the accounting system, $\$12{,}000$ in this case, may or may not equal the investigation benefit.[3]

With the benefit structure thus identified ($\$12{,}000$, $\$4{,}000$, or $\$0$), the next question is whether the benefits, when compared with the investigation

---

[3] This is discussed at length in Demski, "An Accounting System Structured on a Linear Programming Model."

cost (C), warrant an investigation. If C = 0, the answer is surely yes, while
if C = $80,000, it is surely no. But what if C = $6,000?

Should We Investigate?

Collecting our numerous (and debatable) assumptions, we face the decision
problem posed in Figure 8–1. An unfavorable materials quantity variance
of $12,000 has been observed and the question is whether, given this observa-
tion, we should intervene in the process. The difficulty is that the variance

FIGURE 8-1

Investigation decision.

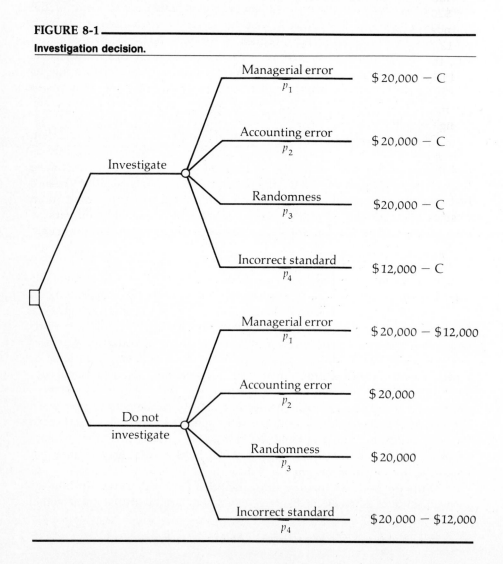

observation is not definitive. We remain uncertain as to the benefits from investigation.

More precisely, two choices are available: investigate or do not investigate. And one of four conceivable states is present: managerial error, accounting error, randomness, or incorrect standard. If the managerial error is present, investigation (at cost C) will ensure a next-period contribution margin of $20,000 − C. Lack of investigation will allow a repetition of the error, implying a contribution margin of $20,000 − $12,000 = $8,000. (This provides an investigation benefit of $12,000.) The accounting error and randomness states will provide a next-period expected contribution of $20,000 − C if we investigate and $20,000 if we do not. Finally, the incorrect standard state can be adapted to under investigation, thereby raising the anticipated contribution margin to $12,000 − C. Since lack of investigation does not provide for such adaptation, the contribution margin in that case is $20,000 − $12,000 = $8,000 (and the benefit is $12,000 − $8,000 = $4,000).

Now suppose, for convenience, that maximization of expected contribution margin is an appropriate decision criterion (that is, risk neutrality). Designating the respective state probabilities p_1, p_2, p_3, and p_4, we have the following:

$$(E(TCM/investigate) = p_1(\$20,000 − C) + p_2(\$20,000 − C) \\ + p_3(\$20,000 − C) + p_4(\$12,000 − C)$$

or, since the probabilities add to one:

$$E(TCM/investigate) = p_1(\$20,000) + p_2(\$20,000) \\ + p_3(\$20,000) + p_4(\$12,000) − C$$

and

$$E(TCM/not\ investigate) = p_1(\$8,000) + p_2(\$20,000) \\ + p_3(\$20,000) + p_4(\$8,000)$$

Expected benefits exceed or are equal to investigate cost if

$$p_1(\$20,000 − \$8,000) + p_2(\$20,000 − \$20,000) + p_3(\$20,000 − \$20,000) \\ + p_4(\$12,000 − \$8,000) = p_1(\$12,000) + p_4(\$4,000) \geq C \quad [8–1]$$

The value p_1 is the probability of a managerial error given the observed variance; p_4 is the probability of a standard error given the observed variance. In this sense the variance is a precursor to investigation, a source of information but not a definitive identifier of the underlying cause or state. Now, one way to proceed with the analysis is to subjectively assess p_1 and p_4 at this point and implement the decision rule given in [8–1].

Use of Prior Probabilities

A more systematic approach is to exploit prior probabilities and Bayesian revision in light of the observed variance (as was done in Chapter 1). This has considerable intuitive appeal because it permits the investigator to use his prior knowledge of the process systematically to evaluate the results of the "sample" taken from the process. Remember that p_1 is the probability of a managerial error *given* the observed $12,000 U$ materials quantity variance. And we could let it go at this, except for the fact that this entails a nontrivial amount of analysis.

To appreciate this, suppose the accounting system never fails ($p_2 = 0$), so the only possibilities are a control failure ($p_1 > 0$), randomness ($p_3 > 0$), or an incorrect standard ($p_4 > 0$). To proceed, we require a joint probability assessment of the various events and materials usages. For example, the mean of the process might be .7, 1.0, or 1.3 pounds per unit. Randomness might add $\pm.3$ to the mean, and the odds on a control failure might be 1 in 7. Our simple, naive model is becoming rather complex.[4] Indeed, the difficulty

---

[4] For the strong of heart, we might have the following joint probabilities:

	Mean = .7			Mean = 1.0			Mean = 1.3		
	Actual quantity			Actual quantity			Actual quantity		
	.4	.7	1.0	.7	1.0	1.3	1.0	1.3	1.6
No control error	.1	.8	.1	.1	.8	.1	.1	.8	.1
Control error	0	0	1	0	0	1	0	0	1

Further assume that the three means are equally likely and that the probability of a control error is .125 (also let the mean and error events be independent).

Now an actual quantity of 1.3 has been observed. This implies that either the mean is 1.0 (as assumed) and a control error was present, the mean is 1.0 and no control error was present, or the mean is 1.3 and neither control error nor randomness was present. Using Bayes' Rule, we find:

$$\text{Probability of a control error given 1.3} = \frac{1(.125)(\tfrac{1}{3})}{1(.125)(\tfrac{1}{3}) + .1(.875)(\tfrac{1}{3}) + .8(.875)(\tfrac{1}{3})}$$

$$= .137$$

$$\text{Probability of randomness given 1.3} = \frac{.1(.875)(\tfrac{1}{3})}{1(.125)(\tfrac{1}{3}) + .1(.875)(\tfrac{1}{3}) + .8(.875)(\tfrac{1}{3})}$$

$$= .096$$

$$\text{Probability of the mean} = 1.3 \text{ given 1.3} = \frac{.8(.875)(\tfrac{1}{3})}{1(.125)(\tfrac{1}{3}) + .1(.875)(\tfrac{1}{3}) + .8(.875)(\tfrac{1}{3})}$$

$$= .767$$

is even more apparent when we admit to numerous variances that are interdependent in various ways. As a result, use of prior probabilities in a full-blown decision analysis is generally regarded as impractical. Simplified assessment procedures therefore become of interest.

The Percentage Rule

Probably the simplest rule we could follow is to investigate a variance if its magnitude is greater than or equal to some fixed percentage of the standard. For example, we might adopt the familiar "materiality" rule of accounting and investigate the process if the variance exceeds some percentage of the standard cost—often 10 percent. This would imply that it is sufficiently likely that any variance that is less than our cutoff is unlikely to yield nontrivial investigation benefits. In contrast, any variance in excess of this cutoff would be judged significant, and our expectation would be that an investigation would lead to nontrivial benefits.

This procedure has the apparent advantage of avoiding any explicit concern with estimating benefits and their respective probabilities. But the critical question of where to set the investigation limit can only be analyzed by assessing these quantities. To explore this, suppose the error is attributable either to randomness or to a managerial failure. No accounting or standard-setting errors are possible. The investigation benefit is 0 if the deviation is caused by randomness, and it is B if the deviation is rooted in a managerial failure. Let P be the probability the error is one of randomness. The basic investigation model in [8–1] then calls for investigation when

$$(1 - P)B \geq C \qquad [8\text{–}2]$$

where $p_1 = 1 - P$.

This inequality can be manipulated to determine the critical value of P below which point the expected benefits from investigation would not warrant an investigation:

$$B - PB - C \geq 0$$

Therefore:

$$PB \leq B - C$$

$$P \leq \frac{B - C}{B}$$

Thus we should investigate the process only if the ratio $(B - C)/B$ is greater than or equal to the probability, P, that the error is not a managerial one. Alternatively, we should investigate any variance for which the conditional probability of randomness is less than or equal to $(B - C)/B$. This provides the link between decision theory and the percentage rule.[5]

Of course, the critical investigation limit is likely to be subjectively determined. A somewhat more sophisticated approach is rooted in traditional quality control procedures.

Statistical Quality Control

In its most simple form, statistical quality control consists in the determination of confidence limits for random variation around a standard based on the mean value of observations and some estimate of the variability around this mean value. Statistical theory tells us that if random samples of observations from a stable process are large enough—say, 30 or more—the mean values of these samples are normally distributed around the true mean of the process, μ. The mean values of the samples are denoted $\overline{X}_1$. If the process is stable, the average of these averages, denoted by $\overline{\overline{X}}$, is an unbiased estimate of the true mean, μ.

The variability of the distribution of a random variable is usually measured by the statistical variance, which is the expected value of the sum of the squared deviations of the random variable from its mean. The variance of the process will be denoted by σ_x^2. The variance of the distribution of the sample means around $\overline{\overline{X}}$ is equal to the variance of the process divided by the sample size, or

$$\sigma_{\overline{x}}^2 = \frac{\sigma_x^2}{n}$$

where n is the sample size. If the variance of the process is not known, which is typically the case, an estimate of the variance can be obtained from the sample variance:

$$s^2 = \frac{\Sigma \, (X - \overline{X})^2}{n - 1}$$

To look more closely at these procedures, refer back to our earlier illustration and assume the only possible causes of a variance are randomness or a managerial error. Further assume that the materials standard of $10 is the average of the sample averages of observations from the process when the process is assumed to be running according to standard. In other words, $\overline{\overline{X}} = \$10$. Assume also that our observation of actual material costs of $13

---

[5] This link is explored much more thoroughly in a more complicated setting in D. Dittman and P. Prakash, "Cost Variance Investigation: Markovian Control of Markov Processes," *J. of Accounting Research,* Spring 1978.

per unit is an average of the costs during the most recent sample taken of material costs (for example, a sample over the most recent lot of units produced). Collecting the observations from the samples when the process is running smoothly, we estimate the variance of the averages as $4.[6,7]

Since the averages of our samples are assumed to be distributed normally, with a mean of $\overline{\overline{X}}$ (= $10), we can use the properties of the normal curve to make statements about the probability that we would observe a variance of +$3 or more given that the process is running normally. More specifically, if the sample averages have a variance of $4, the standard deviation (the square root of the variance) is $\sigma_{\overline{x}}$ = $2. Hence, the standard cost variance of $3 is 1.5 standard deviations above the mean. The probability of observing a value 1.5 or more standard deviations above the mean of a normal distribution is approximately .0668. This does not mean that the probability of the process running normally is only .0668. Rather, it indicates that there is merely a low probability that a cost variance of $3 will be generated by a process whose mean is $10 with a standard deviation of $2.

In practice, statistical control limits may be set so that the probability of observing a sample average outside the limits is less than 1 percent. The limits for a 1 percent cutoff would be

$$\overline{\overline{X}} - 2.57\sigma_{\overline{x}} < \overline{X} < \overline{\overline{X}} + 2.57\sigma_{\overline{x}}$$

That is, the area under the normal curve over this interval contains 99 percent of the distribution. The probability of observing a sample average less than 2.57 standard deviations below the mean is only .005; similarly, the probability of observing a sample average more than 2.57 standard deviations above the mean is only .005. Hence, if a sample average falls outside these limits, the investigator is virtually certain that the process is no longer running according to the standards. In our example, a cost variance of about ±$5.10 would set the upper and lower limits for the control chart, and the investigator would always investigate a standard cost variance that exceeds ±$5.10.

Of course, this limit has been established without explicit consideration of possible benefits. Here, traditional statistical procedures—such as those employed in cost estimation in Chapter 3 or in quality control—speak in

---

[6] It is not necessary to go into the details of such a calculation, since statistical quality control can be implemented using only the range of values observed in the samples of observations. See, for example, A.J. Duncan, *Quality Control and Industrial Statistics,* 4th ed., Homewood, Ill.: Irwin, 1974. An illustrative setting and conversion chart are given in Problem 14 at the end of this chapter.

[7] A subtle but important point arises here. In our two-period setting, the sample with a cost overrun average of $13 per unit is the *only* information at hand. With more periods, we would be interested in earlier-period samples as well. One way to do this, in the classical statistics tradition, is to focus on the sum of the average over- and underruns during this history, the so-called "cusum" technique. See R. Kaplan, "The Significance and Investigation of Cost Variances: Survey and Extensions," *J. of Accounting Research,* Autumn 1975.

terms of the costs of Type I and Type II errors. If an investigation is made only when the observation is outside these control limits, the investigator runs the risk of not investigating a process when actually there exists a nontrivial investigation benefit. This is a Type II error. Alternatively, if he investigates the process often enough, there will be times when he investigates it even though there is no investigation benefit. This is a Type I error.

It is also important to reflect on the importance of the distributional assumptions underlying sampling theory. Generally, the distribution of the sample averages approaches normality as the sample size increases. The approximation is usually good for sample sizes of 30 or more observations. But this is a relatively large number of observations to obtain, and so control charts are more often based on sample sizes of fewer than 30 observations. If we know that the distribution of the observations being sampled is normal, control charts can be constructed from small samples using the t distribution.[8]

However, suppose we do not know the nature of the distribution of the observations being sampled. We can still construct control limits using Chebyshev's inequality, which allows us to state that at least $1 - (1/t^2)$ of *any* set of finite numbers must fall between the mean plus or minus t standard deviations.[9] For example, if we set t equal to 2, 75 percent of a set of numbers will fall within 2 standard deviations of the mean of that set, regardless of its distribution.[10] Of course, if the distribution were normal, we would expect about 95 percent of the set to fall within 2 standard deviations of the mean.

The subject of statistical control is complex, and we cannot review all the possible techniques. For example, control limits can also be established for the variability of the standard—the variance—using similar sampling assumptions.[11] Rather than go into these, we consider instead some of the practical problems of implementing statistical control charts.

Implementing Control Charts

The first point to consider is what kinds of standards we might control with the aid of control charts. Recall that material and labor standards are products of two factors: a standard price and a standard quantity. Each of these factors may be a random variable, and each may be distributed normally. However, their product may not be normal.[12]

---

[8] See any elementary text on statistics, such as J. Freund and F. Williams, *Elementary Business Statistics: The Modern Approach*, 3rd ed., Englewood Cliffs, N.J.: Prentice-Hall, 1977.

[9] See Freund and Williams.

[10] Chebyshev's inequality was first recommended in the accounting literature by Z. Zannetos, "Standard Costs as a First Step to Probabilistic Control: A Theoretical Justification, an Extension and Implications," *Accounting Rev.*, April 1964.

[11] The variability of the standard may reflect changes in the mix of workers or the mix of materials used. That is, monitoring the variability of a standard may signal management that the level of workers' skills or the quality of the materials mix could be changing.

[12] See, for example, G. Johnson and S. Simik II, "Multiproduct C–V–P Analysis under Uncertainty," *J. of Accounting Research*, Autumn 1971.

Overhead costs present another problem. The standard cost for either a single item of overhead or for total overhead may be represented as a linear function: $TC = a + bx$. The actual costs may be related to this standard through an error term, e: that is, $TC_{act} = a + bx + e$. Recall from Chapter 3 that if certain distributional assumptions hold for this error term, we can calculate confidence limits for an estimate of overhead costs for a given value of x.[13] However, in most practical situations, we would not expect to have a large number of observations available to estimate the parameters of the equation.[14] As a consequence, the standard errors for our equation (including the errors for individual parameter values, a and b) would probably be large. This leads to wide confidence belts for 90 percent or 95 percent confidence levels.

Moreover, the use of prior-period results becomes an issue here as well. We typically have, that is, a series of observations on the process. Combining this with the question of investigation benefits causes Kaplan, in concluding a review of this literature, to remark:

> My bias therefore is to first implement a procedure that systematically and sensibly processes the current data with all prior observations. . . . With this as a benchmark, I would then attempt to develop models that are closer to being "right" from a cost-benefit analysis. As more experience and data develop from such a process, I would then feel more comfortable about directly modeling the underlying stochastic process and implementing procedures which are optimal for that particular stochastic process.[15]

In short, we ultimately seek a practical way of balancing the costs and benefits of investigation.

Important Caveats

Our basic theme, then, is one of stressing the importance of the problem of investigating variances and its connection to the basic cost- and value-of-information orientation in this textbook. It is important to remember, however, that we have merely presented the most elementary of analyses of this class of issues. This, in turn, causes us to conclude the chapter with two important caveats.

Economic Considerations

We have considerably simplified the setting, focusing on a two-period model (now and later) and a single variance, in order to explore the rudiments of

---

[13] For ordinary least squares, we assume the error term is normally distributed with a constant variance and zero serial correlation.

[14] See Chapter 3.

[15] Kaplan, p. 358.

the investigation decision. Extensions of this theme to include numerous future periods, different stochastic models of randomness, and different test procedures have been reported in the literature.[16] With numerous periods, for example, we are able to process a *sequence* of observations and focus on the question of when this sequence warrants investigation.

More recently, the literature has addressed the question of how well simplified investigation rules, such as the percentage rule, perform in relation to more sophisticated decision analyses. Here the results are quite encouraging, indicating that highly simplified procedures may function quite well in complex settings.[17] This, in turn, lends support to the typical case in practice in which subjective assessment is relied upon.

Behavioral Considerations

Another class of simplifications concerns human behavior. For better or worse, most of our thinking on the variance investigation question has its roots in the quality control literature. Somehow the process periodically goes out of control and we gather sample information to guide the intervention decision. An apt analogy is monitoring and periodic replacement of a cutting tool on an automatic screw machine.

Difficulties emerge with this view, especially if you reflect back on the material in Chapter 5. First of all, investigation is unlikely to be a clinical affair: A manager is going to be involved (on the receiving end). And the implied "management by exception" orientation here has long been recognized as a potential source of motivation difficulties because of the tendency for investigations to emphasize failures of one kind or another. In short, the investigation may impose nonpecuniary costs on the departmental supervisor.

Second is the issue of reaction. The automatic machine is, except in the wildest of Kafka's fantasies, an inanimate (indeed, impersonable) machine. Its behavior is unaffected by the presence of monitors. But the mere presence of an investigation mechanism can be expected to influence human behavior. Thus the idea of controlling a particular stochastic process is inappropriate. The stochastic process depends on the controls applied! The probability of a cost overrun will, in general, depend on the investigation policy at hand.

This is an important point. The diagram in Figure 8–1 treats the various probabilities as parameters to be specified in implementing the decision rule in [1]. Remember, however, that the diligence and care used in making and implementing decisions may be affected by the investigation policy. Examina-

---

[16] Kaplan's survey paper should be consulted.

[17] See R. Magee, "A Simulation Analysis of Alternative Cost Variance Investigation Models," *Accounting Rev.*, July 1976; D. Dittman and P. Prakash, "Cost Variance Investigation: Markovian Control versus Optimal Control," *Accounting Rev.*, April 1979; and F. Jacobs, "An Evaluation of the Effectiveness of Some Cost Variance Investigation Models," *J. of Accounting Research*, Spring 1978.

tion policy is thought to influence studying behavior. The IRS's audit policy is thought to influence taxable income reporting (and generation). To the extent that this phenomenon is important, our model remains misspecified.

More serious modeling will, of course, allow us to address these economic and behavioral considerations. The trick is to analyze the problem as an explicit multiperson problem. This is the subject of game theory. While tantalizing in promise, the theory is presently too complex *and* too inadequate to give us much practical guidance here.[18]

Another concern, regardless of our modeling sophistication, is that in one way or another any practical model here will provide for only a simplified analysis of the decision problem at hand. This raises the question of comparative advantage. Individuals are not expert at judgment tasks. They may, for example, see "trends" in data when they are not present, and vice versa. Models, in turn, respond only with constructive patterns; they are the product of the model builder's skill and imagination. The judicious analysis, in other words, will complement but not replace the analyst. This is, of course, consistent with every other use of model building that we examine in this text.[19]

Conclusion

We have outlined some of the procedures that may be used to assess the significance of standard cost variances. In one way or another, the assessment question entails a choice of whether to investigate or produce additional information. The variances, in other words, are precursors to an investigation decision. All models used to determine when a process should be investigated operate from the premise that a certain amount of variation around the standards may be tolerated. The amount of variation to be tolerated depends on the benefits expected from an investigation and the costs of investigating the process. In some cases, these benefits and costs are not made explicit (for example, in the use of control charts); in others, they are formally incorporated within the significance models.

It is, however, much easier to talk in terms of costs and benefits than it is to advance practical models in this area. For this reason we find this chapter the most disconcerting to present. The topic is deep, subtle, and fascinating. Terribly complex models have been offered in the literature, yet each assumes away apparently important aspects of the investigation problem.

---

[18] It is, however, possible to produce a game theory solution in which only extreme variances are investigated. See S. Baiman and J. Demski, "Variance Analysis Procedures as Motivation Devices," *Management Science*, Aug. 1980, and "Economically Optimal Performance Evaluation and Control Systems," *J. of Accounting Research Supplement*, 1980.

[19] See P. Keen and M. Scott-Morton, *Decision Support Systems: An Organizational Perspective*, Reading, Mass.: Addison-Wesley, 1978, and W. Wright, "Financial Information Processing Models: An Empirical Study," *Accounting Rev.*, July 1977.

Rather than present an encyclopedia of the many models, we have chosen to display their basic spirit and shortcomings. We hope this helps the student construct a conceptualization of the investigation problem that is far richer than that with which the chapter was entered. But that is all we have to offer.

Few firms, to our knowledge, follow formal procedures in investigating variances. In part, this reflects the complexity of even simple models. But it also reflects the inadequacy of these models. Moreover, we must also recognize that the formal accounting system is not the only control device within a firm. Many of the day-to-day operating decisions can be made on the basis of direct observation of the physical relationships between inputs and desired outputs. Formal accounting systems are beneficial primarily to managers who are at least one step removed from the physical processes of production. These managers can rely to some extent on the ability of subordinates to control their own processes. The accounting system, then, is more a check on the willingness of the subordinates to achieve operating control and their success in doing so.

Supplementary Readings

Articles

Baiman, S. and J. Demski, "Economically Optimal Performance Evaluation and Control Systems," *J. of Accounting Research Supplement,* 1980.

Demski, J., "Optimizing the Search for Cost Deviation Sources," *Management Science,* April 1970.

Dittman, D. and P. Prakash, "Cost Variance Investigation: Markovian Control versus Optimal Control," *Accounting Rev.,* April 1979.

Dopuch, N., J. Birnberg, and J. Demski, "An Extension of Standard Cost Variance Analysis," *Accounting Rev.,* July 1967.

Gonedes, N., "Accounting for Managerial Control," *J. of Accounting Research,* Spring 1970.

Johnson, G., and S. Simik II, "Multiproduct C–V–P Analysis under Uncertainty," *J. of Accounting Research,* Autumn 1971.

Kaplan, R., "The Significance and Investigation of Cost Variances: Survey and Extensions," *J. of Accounting Research,* Autumn 1975.

Lev, B., "An Information Theory Analysis of Budget Variances," *Accounting Rev.,* Oct. 1969.

Magee, R., "The Usefulness of Commonality Information in Cost Control Decisions," *Accounting Rev.,* Oct. 1977.

Magee, R., "A Simulation Analysis of Alternative Cost Variance Investigation Models," *Accounting Rev.,* July 1976.

Ronen, J., "Nonaggregation vs. Disaggregation of Variances," *Accounting Rev.,* Jan. 1974.

Theil, H., "How to Worry About Increased Expenditures," *Accounting Rev.*, Jan. 1969.

Zannetos, Z., "Standard Costs as a First Step to Probabilistic Control: A Theoretical Justification, an Extension and Implications," *Accounting Rev.*, April 1964.

Books

Bowker, A.H. and G.J. Lieberman, *Engineering Statistics.* Englewood Cliffs, N.J.: Prentice-Hall, 1972.

Duncan, A.J., *Quality Control and Industrial Statistics,* 4th ed. Homewood, Ill.: Irwin, 1974.

Freund, J.E., and F.J. Williams, *Elementary Business Statistics: The Modern Approach,* 4th ed. Englewood Cliffs, N.J.: Prentice-Hall, 1982.

Grant, E.L., and R. L. Leavenworth, *Statistical Quality Control,* 4th ed. New York: McGraw-Hill, 1972.

Lapin, L.L., *Statistics for Modern Business Decisions,* 3rd ed. New York: Harcourt Brace Jovanovich, 1981.

Solomons, David, ed., *Studies in Cost Analysis,* 2nd ed. Homewood, Ill.: Irwin, 1968.

Questions and Problems

1. It has often been said that accountants fail to assess the significance of variances. How would you define "significance" within the context of variance analysis?

2. If the accounting system were designed to control the parameters of formal decision models, such as an allocation model, what changes would you anticipate in the types of standards that would be included in the system?

3. Statistical quality control[20] relies heavily on sampling theory as the basis for estimating the parameters of a universe in which we are interested. The assumption that the distribution of the means of samples is approximately normal with mean μ and variance $\sigma_{\bar{x}}^2 = \sigma^2/n$ is based on the central limit theorem. To illustrate the nature of the theorem, suppose we wish to draw slips of paper from a bowl containing 122 slips, with 2 slips marked -3.0, 2 marked -2.9, etc., up to 2 slips marked $+3.0$. The slips are drawn in such a way that each has the same probability, 1/122, of being selected. That is, a slip is drawn, its number is recorded, and then it is returned to the bowl again before the process is repeated. Suppose we drew 1,000 samples of 4 slips each (using the procedure outlined) and recorded the average of the numbers observed for each sample. The distribution of these means should be symmetric, with the peak of the curve at $\bar{\bar{X}} = 0$ (the mean of the population). Hence, sample means drawn from a uniform distribution take on the normal distribution. Note, however, that the experiment consists essentially of selecting a series of independent random variables that are considered to be identically distributed. More specifically, each draw can be viewed as a random variable that can take on values from -3.0 to $+3.0$, with the probability of obtaining -3.0, -2.9, -2.8, . . . , 2.8, 2.9, 3.0 = 1/122. Discuss whether these conditions would be expected to hold if we viewed the population as consisting of

---

[20] This problem is adapted from E. Grant, *Statistical Quality Control.* New York: McGraw-Hill, 1964, pp. 75–77.

(a) Tensile strength in pounds of a yarn, with a sample taken each run.
(b) Weight in ounces of the contents of detergent containers, with every 50th container being weighed.
(c) The dimensions of a manufactured part during a month, a year, and two years of operations, with each lot being sampled.
(d) Direct labor costs per unit during the month of April in a seasonal business, with a sample taken each day.
(e) Indirect supplies costs during April, with the cost standardized on the basis of direct labor and a sample taken each day.
(f) Prices of steel used as a raw material, sampled over a time period.
(g) Consumption of steel during the first six months of the year, sampled each week and at each production run.
(h) Contribution margin for Product A in a multiproduct firm, sampled over time.

4. Consider the investigation decision that was portrayed in Figure 8–1. List all of the important assumptions in this portrayal.

5. It is claimed that the basic idea in cost variance investigation is one of *inference*. The process is either "in control" or "out of control." We cannot tell whether the process is "in control" merely by observing the associated cost variances. So we use cost variance reports to infer if the process is in control. This idea of inference is not the same as the investigation acts that are taken subsequent to such inference. Comment on this view, paying careful attention to the models surveyed in the chapter.

6. Evaluating the appropriateness of the decision models used by a firm may be accomplished in part by reviewing the magnitude and frequency of variances reported over time. Suppose the firm uses a linear programing model to guide allocation decisions. What types of variances would we observe if a nonlinear model—for example, one in which a nonlinear objective function is maximized subject to linear constraints—were more appropriate to the operating conditions of the firm?

7. **Investigation of a Variance**
Suppose the standard for a particular cost is $1,000, which represents the mean or average amount expected. Based on prior observations of this cost, it is determined that the normal curve may be used to describe its frequency distribution. The standard deviation for the item is $75.

As indicated in this chapter in the section dealing with cost control charts, the decision to investigate a variance from a standard should be based on the comparison between the expected benefits (net) from investigation and the costs of investigating the variance; that is, if $C \le B(1 - P)$, the decision is to investigate.

(a) Suppose that an unfavorable variance of $85 is observed. The benefits obtained from an investigation would consist in an adjustment in performance equal to about 50 percent of the variance. It costs the company $35 to investigate a variance. You are asked to give your advice as to whether this variance should be investigated, since the normal curve indicates that the probability of observing an unfavorable variance of $85 is approximately 0.13.

(b) Suppose the variance is a favorable one of $85. The probability of observing this variance is also 0.13. Should this variance be investigated? Why or why not?

8. **Control of Linear Programing Models**
Assume that a firm's allocation problem can be expressed as follows ($C_1 = \$4$; $C_2 = \$5$):

$$\text{Maximize} \quad C_1X_1 + C_2X_2$$

$$\text{subject to} \quad 5X_1 + 4X_2 \leq 180 \quad [1]$$

$$4X_1 + 8X_2 \leq 240 \quad [2]$$

$$X_1, X_2 \geq 0$$

(a) Using a graphic technique, determine the amount of the increase in C_2 that could serve as the basis for assessing the significance of positive variances in C_2.
(b) Repeat (a) but for a negative variance (a decrease) in C_2.
(c) What other factor(s) should be considered before the firm can make a decision to shift to new policies?

9. Using the data in Problem 8, determine the significance of a 25 percent increase or decrease in constraint [1]. Use the graphic technique.

10. Combinations of changes that could affect the optimal solution to the linear programing problem (Problem 8) are likely to occur when a permanent change takes place in the labor requirements needed to produce a particular product. For example, suppose the data for X_1 in [1] and [2] reflect the expected times and costs for a relatively new method of production. The standard set for X_1 allowed for 5 hours of direct labor at a cost of $15. The actual times recorded indicate that the standard does not allow sufficient time to work the product in the first department. The variances recorded by the accountant average to ½ hour per unit (unfavorable).

(a) Compute the significance of this variance relative to the optimal decisions of the firm.
(b) Discuss the difficulty of trying to establish significance limits for multiple changes such as these.

11. **Unrecorded Variances**
It is important to reflect on a strong "transactions" bias in accounting reports: Accounting systems record what happened, not what might have happened. To reinforce this important observation, consider a simple linear program where two products are present (X_1 and X_2) and a single constraint is operative:

$$\text{Maximize TCM} = 15X_1 + 20X_2$$

$$\text{subject to} \quad X_1 + 2X_2 \leq 1{,}000$$

$$X_1, X_2 \geq 0$$

(a) Determine an optimal solution.
(b) Suppose your solution is implemented and all goes as planned, except product X_1 experiences a \$3 per unit unfavorable materials price variance. This is an error in the original standard. What variance will the accounting system report and what is the investigation benefit?
(c) Repeat (b) assuming the unfavorable price variance is \$8 per unit of X_1.
(d) Suppose all goes as planned, except that a favorable materials price variance for product X_2 of \$12 per unit occurs. What variance will the accounting system report? What is the benefit of discovering and responding to this "variance"?

12. **Sampling Theory**
Suppose we have a set of numbers that represent the outcomes of a trial or a process. If the numbers are distributed normally with mean μ and variance σ^2, then we can assess the probability of observing any particular number from the distribution. For example, if we let X represent the possible outcomes:

$$P(\mu - 1.96\sigma < X < \mu + 1.96\sigma) = 0.95$$

and

$$P(\mu - 2.57\sigma < X < \mu + 2.57\sigma) = 0.99$$

Similarly, if X is normal with mean μ and variance σ^2, then the distribution of averages of samples drawn from X is also normal with mean μ and variance σ^2/n, where n represents the number of items in the sample, so that

$$P(\overline{X} - 1.96\sigma/\sqrt{n} < \mu < \overline{X} + 1.96\sigma/\sqrt{n}) = 0.95$$

and

$$P(\overline{X} - 2.57\sigma/\sqrt{n} < \mu < \overline{X} + 2.57\sigma/\sqrt{n}) = 0.99$$

Assume that for the specification of a manufactured part, $\sigma = 0.03$ inch, but the mean is unknown. The manufacturer wants to set up a control limit for the true mean of the part, based on a sample of 16 items.

(a) Determine 99 percent confidence limits for this part.
(b) Determine 99 percent confidence limits based on Chebyshev's inequality using the same information. [Note: The inequality states that $1 - (1/t^2)$ of the distribution lies between $\overline{X} \pm t\sigma$; $t > 1$.]
(c) Compare the limits obtained in (a) and (b), and indicate when Chebyshev's inequality might be used.

13. **Theory of Runs**
A process is considered to be out of control if either the observations fall outside the specified limits or the number of successive observations above or below

some specified average is excessive. As one basis for determining what is excessive, we can use the binomial distribution in which we define an observation above or below the average as a success (or failure). The assumption is that the probability that an observation will be above or below the average is $\frac{1}{2}$. Consequently, we would expect a run of 5 observations above the average only $(\frac{1}{2})^5 = \frac{1}{32} = 3.13$ percent of the time.

(a) What is the probability that we would observe a run of 5 observations below the average?

(b) The probability of observing a run of 7 observations over the average is $\frac{1}{128} \approx 0.008$; similarly, the probability of observing 9 out of 10 observations above the average is 0.0098. Based on your own intuition, what length of runs would you consider excessive?

14. **$\bar{X}$ and $\bar{R}$ Charts**

Generally, control charts are based upon averages ($\bar{X}$'s) and their average ($\bar{\bar{X}}$). Assume a firm takes 20 samples of 5 items each. Letting $\bar{X}_i$ represent the average of the 5 items on the ith sample:

$$\bar{\bar{X}} = \frac{\sum\limits_{i=1}^{20} \bar{X}_i}{20}$$

Similarly, the range of the distribution is often used because the standard deviation of the process is not known and/or the range is easier to calculate. The control limits for ranges (that is, the difference between the highest and lowest values for each sample) are based on the relationship between their distribution and the distribution of the standard deviation. Tables have been prepared to facilitate the necessary computation (see Exhibit 8–2).[21]

Upper control limit for $\bar{X} = \bar{\bar{X}} + A_2\bar{R}$
Lower control limit for $\bar{X} = \bar{\bar{X}} - A_2\bar{R}$
Upper control limit for $R = D_4\bar{R}$
Lower control limit for $R = D_3\bar{R}$

These factors are based on $\bar{\bar{X}} \pm 3\sigma$.

(a) Given the data in Exhibit 8–3 on page 323, determine upper and lower limits for $\bar{X}$ and R that can be used as the basis for control charts for these statistics. (The observations have been rounded off.)

(b) Plot the $\bar{X}$'s on a chart, and indicate whether any points seem out of order.

(c) Suppose the second sample had an average of 138. Would your answer to (b) change?

---

[21] Taken from E. Grant, *Statistical Quality Control*, 3rd ed. New York: McGraw-Hill, 1964, p. 562.

EXHIBIT 8–2

Factors for Controlling the Mean and Range of a Standard

Number of Observations in Each Sample	A_2 Factor for $\bar{X}$ Chart	Factors for R Chart	
		Lower Limit D_3	Upper Limit D_4
2	1.88	0	3.27
3	1.02	0	2.57
4	.73	0	2.28
5	.58	0	2.11
6	.48	0	2.00
7	.42	.08	1.92
8	.37	.14	1.86
9	.34	.18	1.82
10	.31	.22	1.78
11	.29	.26	1.74
12	.27	.28	1.72
13	.25	.31	1.69
14	.24	.33	1.67
15	.22	.35	1.65

15. **Revision of Probabilities in Cost Control**

This problem concerns probability revision in light of actual cost observations. You have taken a simplified view and consider the production process either "in" or "out" of control. The possible cost outcomes and associated probabilities are as follows:

	PROBABILITIES	
Observed Average Cost	In Control	Out of Control
$3.50	.004	
4.00	.054	
4.50	.242	.004
5.00	.400	.054
5.50	.242	.242
6.00	.054	.400
6.50	.004	.242
7.00		.054
7.50		.004

The cost of investigating the process is $100 (to cover lost time of the investigator and the department head). If the process is out of control, an investigation will lead to a savings of 200 times the accounting variance per production run of this item. (The standard is clearly $5.00.)

(a) Calculate the in-control probability, P_c, below which it would pay to investigate the process. [Set $B = 200x$, and solve for $P_c = f(x)$.]

_____ EXHIBIT 8–3

Sample Number	Measurement of Each Item—Drawn Each Two Hours					Average $\bar{X}$	Range R
1	141	146	143	142	140	142.4	6
2	138	144	137	148	139	141.2	11
3	139	140	136	135	136	137.2	5
4	140	133	140	142	138	138.6	9
5	142	134	142	140	140	139.6	8
6	144	141	138	136	134	138.6	10
7	143	149	144	142	143	144.2	6
8	140	142	141	135	141	139.8	7
9	137	137	143	144	145	141.2	8
10	135	147	145	139	136	140.4	10

$$\bar{\bar{X}} = 140.3 \qquad \bar{R} = 8.0$$

(b) At the time the next production run is initiated, the probability P that the process is in control is .80. The average cost observed for the run is $5.50. Determine the revised probability of the process being in control.

(c) Suppose instead that an actual cost of $6.00 was observed. Compute the revised probability that the process is still in control given the prior probability = .80.

(d) Should the process be investigated if the observed cost was $5.50? If the observed cost was $6.00? Explain.

16. **Investigation Benefits and EVPI Calculations**
Consider the following linear program in which a firm is seeking to schedule two products, X_1 and X_2, so as to maximize its contribution margin:

$$\begin{aligned} \text{Maximize} \quad & \alpha X_1 + 12 X_2 \\ \text{subject to} \quad & X_1 + X_2 \leq \beta \\ & X_1 + 2 X_2 \leq 500 \\ & X_1, X_2 \geq 0 \end{aligned}$$

Note that with $\alpha = 10$ and $\beta = 400$ we have $X_1^* = 300$ and $X_2^* = 100$.

Required (a) Suppose $\beta = 400$ and α is either 6, 10, or 14, with respective probabilities of .25, .50, and .25. Without additional information, a value of $\alpha = 10$ will be assumed. What is the expected value of perfect information on α? (Assume risk neutrality.)

(b) How does this value of information calculation relate to variance investigation benefits?

(c) Suppose $\alpha = 10$ and β is either 350, 400, or 450, with respective probabilities of $\frac{1}{3}$, $\frac{1}{3}$, and $\frac{1}{3}$. Without additional information, a value of $\beta = 400$ will be assumed. What is the expected value of perfect information on β? (Again assume risk neutrality.)

*17. **Control of Inventory Models**
Advanced Manufacturing has adopted the general EOQ model with no stockouts (Chapter 16) as the basis for controlling its inventory of raw materials purchases. The following standards were used to implement the system:

$$C_p = \$8$$
$$C_s = 1\tfrac{1}{2}\% \text{ per month per unit price}$$

In addition, it was estimated that 4,000 units would be needed during the coming year. The expected price per unit during the next year is $5.50. This price was arrived at by extrapolating the trend in prices during the last few years.

(a) Determine an optimal inventory policy.
(b) Evaluate the effect of ±20 percent errors in the estimated price per unit. (Recall that the standard formulas require an expression of storage costs in dollars per unit per year.) Does a 20 percent error seem significant from the standpoint of its effect on inventory policies?

*18. **Performance versus Decision Evaluation**
Suppose that under the conditions specified in Problem 17, the actual prices incurred by the firm are approximately 20 percent higher than anticipated. Also assume that a 20 percent increase in purchase prices does not significantly affect the firm's inventory policies (regardless of your answer to Problem 17). Finally, assume that the standard deviation for the distribution of prices described in Problem 17 is $.60 and that the distribution is symmetric. Would you consider the 20 percent increase significant for performance evaluation? Why or why not?

*19. **Information Measures**[22]
Assume a firm establishes a budget for its five divisions[23] as follows:

	Budget	Percentage
Division A	$ 350	35%
Division B	200	20
Division C	200	20
Division D	150	15
Division E	100	10
Total	$1,000	100%

Actual expenditures were

	Amount	Percentage
Division A	$ 420	35 %
Division B	210	17½

---

[22] Based on an example taken from H. Theil's article, "How to Worry about Increased Expenditures," *Accounting Rev.*, Jan. 1969.

[23] Note that we could disaggregate the budget of each division into department budgets.

	Amount	Percentage
Division C	270	22½
Division D	150	12½
Division E	150	12½
Total	$1,200	100 %

(a) Suppose a manager used a 10 percent rule to establish the significance of variances from the budget. Which division(s) would be investigated?

(b) Theil's information measure, I, for this firm would be calculated as follows:

$$I = .350 \log_2 \left(\frac{.350}{.350}\right) + .175 \log_2 \left(\frac{.175}{.200}\right) + .225 \log_2 \left(\frac{.225}{.200}\right)$$

$$+ .125 \log_2 \left(\frac{.125}{.150}\right) + .125 \log_2 \left(\frac{.125}{.100}\right)$$

$$= .350(.000) + .175(-.19) + .225(.17) + .125(-.26) + .125(.32)$$

$$= 0 + (-.0333) + (.0383) + (-.0325) + (.040)$$

$$= .0125 \text{ bits}[24]$$

(1) Discuss how the total information measure may be used to evaluate the entire budget variance of $200 unfavorable.

(2) Give an interpretation to each individual component of the I measure.

(3) If we label the budgeted and actual percentages p_i and q_i, $I = \Sigma \ q_i \log(q_i/p_i)$. Evaluate this method of variance analysis against, say, the percentage rule.

---

[24] Bits are the units of measurement when logarithms are taken to the base 2; if natural logarithms are used, the unit of measurement is a "nit."

Cost Allocations: Joint Products and Service Departments

In early chapters we stressed the cost measurement techniques that would be most useful to management in planning and controlling the firm's operations. Aside from issues of overhead measurement, cost allocation issues did not arise. These issues do, however, extend beyond questions of overhead measurement. In this chapter we examine allocation considerations in general and then look carefully at two cost measurement problems traditionally associated with allocation questions. The first is the case of joint products in which a particular process yields two or more different types of outputs in some (more or less) fixed ratio. In the traditional literature, this is often referred to as *the* joint costing problem. The second is the case of a service department in which the output of a particular department is consumed by one or more other departments within the organization. This service department problem differs from the joint costing problem in that the outputs of service departments may not be distributed to other departments in any fixed ratio.

Our purpose in examining these settings is strictly managerial. We therefore concentrate entirely on the use of cost allocations within the firm. External reporting considerations, which concern inventory valuation, are deferred until Chapter 11.

Cost Allocation

In a broad, general sense, cost allocation concerns the division of a total cost among two or more products, departments, divisions, or whatnot. Thus it is intimately associated with joint production, broadly interpreted. And in this sense, depreciation of manufacturing equipment is the ultimate example. In the extreme case it is joint with respect to time periods, different product lines, and individual units of each product line in each period.

For any particular allocation problem, there may be numerous procedures that could be employed and quite different "answers" that can be expected. Needless to say, heated controversies may result. For example, a typical product line such as ready-to-eat cereals at General Foods can show trivial or amazingly large profitability depending on the cost allocation procedures employed.

To better understand these difficulties, we will look at a simple model of the process of allocation, the reasons for allocation, and the use of criteria to guide the allocation process.[1]

The Allocation Process

The process of cost allocation can be viewed in terms of identifying (1) a *total cost* to be allocated, (2) a *set of cost objects* to which the total cost is to be allocated, and (3) an *allocation base* or method of relating the cost to the objects. In our study of overhead measurement for short-run planning purposes, for example, the total cost was the firm's overhead for the period in question, the set of cost objects was the firm's output, and the allocation base was a regression-based function relating overhead to some independent variable such as direct labor hours. (And direct labor hours, in turn, were related to the firm's output.)

Notice that the description does not require that the total cost be divided among the objects. This would imply that the sum of the allocations would precisely equal the total, and there is no reason to insist on such tidiness. Indeed, we are already familiar with numerous instances in which fixed overhead is *not* allocated to the firm's product, thereby implying that total overhead exceeds the sum of the allocation. Also notice that numerous total cost "pools" may be involved, with each being allocated to divisions or products using a different allocation base. In general, two "pools" can be grouped together if they are to be allocated in direct proportions with the same allocation base. Such "pools" are termed homogeneous. But we will not explore this complication in the ensuing discussion.

The Demand for Allocations

Suppose we have identified a total cost to be allocated to a set of products. The remaining task in implementing the just-described process is to choose an allocation base. To properly address this, however, we must focus on the reason for the allocation. That is, allocation methods are not good or

---

[1] Here we provide a brief sketch of the general problem of allocation. Much deeper treatments can be found in A. Thomas, *The Allocation Problem: Part Two*, Sarasota, Florida: American Accounting Assoc., 1974 and *A Behavioural Analysis of Joint-Cost Allocation and Transfer Pricing*, Stipes Publishing Co., 1980; Y. Ijiri, *Theory of Accounting Measurement*, Sarasota, Florida: American Accounting Assoc., 1975; J. Demski and G. Feltham, *Cost Determination: A Conceptual Approach*, Ames, Iowa: Iowa State University Press, 1976; J. Zimmerman, "The Costs and Benefits of Allocation," *Accounting Rev.*, July 1979, and J. Demski, "Cost Allocation Games," in S. Moriarity (ed.), *Joint Cost Allocations*, Norman, Ok.: Center for Economic and Management Research, 1981.

bad, and a universal allocation base does not exist. As with any other kind of information, then, the key to usefulness is the use to which the information might be put.

Decomposition Demand

To understand this setting, suppose we consider a firm that combines three factors of production, denoted f_1, f_2, and f_3, to produce two products, X_1 and X_2. To specify the productive possibilities, let $T(f_1, f_2, f_3)$ be the set of possible output combinations that are feasible if f_1, f_2, and f_3 are made available. The schedule denoted (X_1, X_2) is then feasible when f_1, f_2, and f_3 are acquired if (X_1, X_2) is one of the elements that make up $T(f_1, f_2, f_3)$. We denote this, using familiar set terminology, via

$$(X_1, X_2) \in T(f_1, f_2, f_3)$$

Further assume each factor is acquired in a perfect market, with per unit price P_i. Also let the revenue from sale of any (X_1, X_2) combination be $R(X_1, X_2)$. Under these admittedly abstract conditions, our firm would maximize its profit with the following fairly obvious programing problem:

$$\text{Maximize} \quad R(X_1, X_2) - [P_1 f_1 + P_2 f_2 + P_3 f_3] \qquad [9\text{--}1]$$
$$X_1, X_2, f_1, f_2, f_3$$
$$\text{subject to} \quad (X_1, X_2) \in T(f_1, f_2, f_3)$$

Notice that factors and output are to be determined.

An equivalent way to proceed is to focus directly on the output, its revenue, and *its* cost. To do this we define the cost of the output schedule (X_1, X_2), denoted by $C(X_1, X_2)$, with the following construction:

$$C(X_1, X_2) = \text{minimum} \quad P_1 f_1 + P_2 f_2 + P_3 f_3 \qquad [9\text{--}2]$$
$$f_1, f_2, f_3$$
$$\text{subject to} \quad (X_1, X_2) \in T(f_1, f_2, f_3)$$

And we then locate the maximum profit with

$$\text{Maximize} \quad R(X_1, X_2) - C(X_1, X_2) \qquad [9\text{--}3]$$
$$X_1, X_2$$

Carefully contrast the two models. The initial version in [9–1] *directly* focuses on outputs and inputs. The version in [9–3] *directly* focuses only on outputs. The inputs are addressed in an indirect manner by construction of the output cost function. Notice that decomposition of the problem into selecting efficient factor combinations followed by selecting profit maximizing output creates a demand for output cost measurement. This interest in product cost arises solely because of the problem formulation in [9–3]. It does not arise in the formulation in [9–1].

Typically, of course, we think and analyze business problems in terms of revenues and costs associated with products. Indeed, we often go further and do this on a product-by-product basis. In our abstract example, this would entail (perhaps) approximating the revenue and cost functions so that they assume a *separable* form:

$$R(X_1, X_2) \cong R_1(X_1) + R_2(X_2)$$

and

$$C(X_1, X_2) \cong C_1(X_1) + C_2(X_2)$$

We also might have constants in either expression, interpreted as "fixed" revenue or cost.

We will ignore allocation demands for financial reporting, tax measurement, and cost justification[2] and concentrate on demands that arise totally within the firm. Within this narrower setting, the demand for cost allocation appears to arise from decision decomposition, motivation, and coordination concerns. Decomposition arises when we take the firm's overall decision problem and decompose it into a series of subproblems that are easier to analyze. For example, the variable overhead allocation in a linear programing model actually surrogates for the myriad of activities in the overhead area, such as personnel management, production scheduling, materials handling, and so on. Motivation considerations arise when, for example, we employ a responsibility accounting structure and base the allocation of the firm's costs among its managers on the basis of controllability. Similarly, coordination issues occur when at least two managers are involved and their activities are interdependent in one way or another. Here allocation issues arise when we attempt to control for this interdependency via some allocation. For example, two managers may place demands on a service facility and the marginal cost of supplying one may depend on the demands of the other. The motivation demand has been discussed in Chapter 5 and the coordination demand will be discussed at length in Chapter 10. We therefore confine the present chapter to decomposition demand. And in any event, the motivation and coordination demands are based upon an initial decomposition of the firm's

---

[2] Cost-based pricing in government procurement is an interesting process that, due to regulation of cost measurement by the Cost Accounting Standards Board, has resulted in a set of cost accounting standards that must be used by defense contractors in any form of negotiated contract. A more theoretical analysis is presented in Demski and Feltham.

decision problem among its managers. (This is, in fact, intimately associated with the use of linear approximation, discussed in Chapter 4.)

Consider then a formulation in which, say, Product 1 is to be analyzed via $R_1(X_1) - C_1(X_1)$. What is $C_1(X_1)$? Surely the answer is "the cost of X_1." But its geneology is very important. We have moved from the model in [9–1], where no product cost measurement was demanded, to the model in [9–3], where a combined product cost was demanded, to this version, in which the cost of a particular product is being demanded. This is the subject of cost allocation. We think in terms of "assigning" $P_1f_1 + P_2f_2 + P_3f_3$ to X_1 and X_2 in order to construct $C_i(X_i)$. But a heavy burden is being placed on this assignment procedure: We want to do it in such a manner that the firm comes sufficiently close to locating an optimal combination of inputs and outputs without ever formulating the complete problem in all of its detail.

A simple example may be helpful. Suppose we have a linear production relationship in which f_1 denotes labor, f_2 denotes material, and f_3 denotes leased capital. One unit of each factor is combined to produce X_1 and two units of each are combined to produce X_2. To distinguish factor assignments, let $f_i = (f_{1i}, f_{2i})$, where f_{1i} is the amount of factor i used in production of X_1. Finally, no more than a total of 50 combined units of output is feasible. Problem [9–1] is now expressed as[3]

$$\text{Maximize} \quad R(X_1, X_2) - P_1f_1 - P_2f_2 - P_3f_3 \qquad [9\text{–}1A]$$
$$X_1, X_2, f_1, f_2, f_3$$
$$\text{subject to} \qquad X_1 \leq f_{1i} \ i = 1, 2, 3$$
$$X_2 \leq 2f_{2i} \ i = 1, 2, 3$$
$$X_1 + X_2 \leq 50$$
$$X_1, X_2, f_1, f_2, f_3 \geq 0$$

The product cost function, thanks to our linear production assumption, is trivial. We would never acquire too many units of any factor. One of each is required for each unit of X_1 and two of each are required for each unit of X_2. So problem [9–2] provides

$$C(X_1, X_2) = [P_1 + P_2 + P_3]X_1 + 2[P_1 + P_2 + P_3]X_2 \qquad [9\text{–}2A]$$

where

$$X_1 + X_2 \leq 50 \quad \text{and} \quad X_1, X_2 \geq 0$$

Finally, suppose $R(X_1, X_2)$ is also linear: $R(X_1, X_2) = \bar{P}_1X_1 + \bar{P}_2X_2$. With this useful assumption, the formulation in [9–3] provides the linear program:

---

[3] To completely specify the $T(f_1, f_2, f_3)$ function we would have to specify feasible factor combinations in the model in [9–1].

Maximize $\qquad [\bar{P}_1 - P_1 - P_2 - P_3]X_1 + [\bar{P}_2 - 2P_1 - 2P_2 - 2P_3]X_2$ $\qquad$ [9–3A]
X_1, X_2

subject to $\qquad X_1 + X_2 \leq 50$

$\qquad\qquad X_1, X_2 \geq 0$

Indeed, $[\bar{P}_1 - P_1 - P_2 - P_3]$ is the contribution margin of X_1, while $[\bar{P}_1 - 2P_1 - 2P_2 - 2P_3]$ is that of X_2.

The point of all this is to remind you that you already know a great deal about the topic of cost allocation. We typically formulate problems of this nature in terms of contribution margin. This familiar procedure rests on a decomposition in which various factor specifications have been decided and controlled for through the contribution margin specification. Our more extensive study of cost allocation continues this basic theme. Note that we could re-express the model in [9–3A] to focus entirely on X_1 by use of the opportunity cost theme explored in Chapter 4.

We now apply these basic ideas to the joint-product setting.

Joint Products

The term "joint products" refers to more than one output (product) produced from a single set of inputs (such as raw material and labor factors) in a predetermined ratio. Typical of the joint product industries are petroleum refining, meat packing, dairies, chemicals, and sawmills. Each of these takes a single set of inputs and produces several outputs in somewhat fixed proportions.

For some joint-product industries, the ratio is fixed by the nature and quality of the input. For example, a packer can buy animals that have various proportions of select cuts of meat. When he has selected a given animal, nothing he does during the processing of the animal can alter the proportion of select to inexpensive cuts of meat. The proportion is fixed by the input. In other joint-product situations, the product mix may be varied, but only through additional processing. For example, the mix of gasoline and oil products from crude oil can be altered if management is willing to incur the added costs of modifying the process. However, even in these situations the extent to which the mix can be changed is limited.

Figure 9-1 illustrates the variety of forms the joint-product situation can take. In this diagram, there are three joint processes (in Departments 1, 2, and 5). As the multiple products leave each process to move along their separate ways, they are said to pass through a *split-off point*, a point at which they become separately identifiable products. An asterisk (*) identifies each splitoff point in the figure. Initially, inputs A are processed through Department 1, and Products X and Y emerge in some fixed ratio. For example, this might represent the input of crude oils and the joint input of naphthas

FIGURE 9-1

Schematic diagram for joint-product decisions.

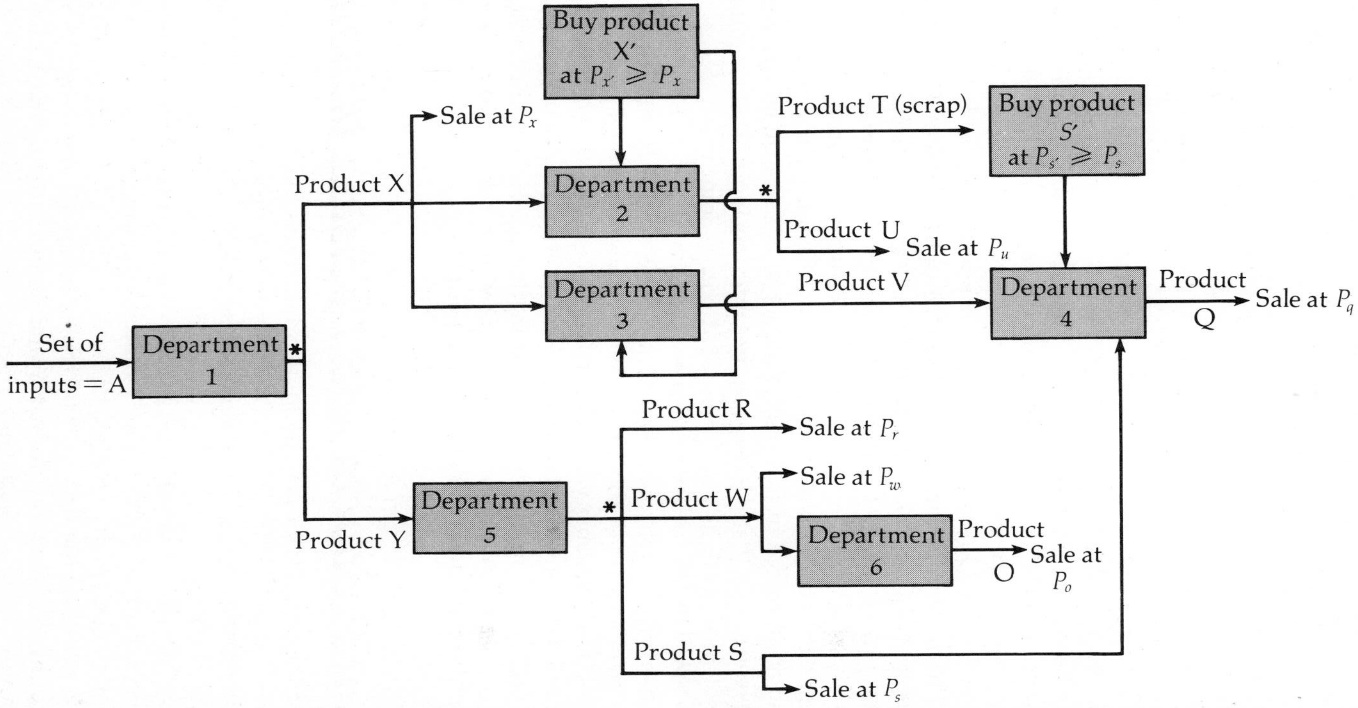

and oils. For the sake of simplicity, output ratios and related input ratios have been omitted from the figure.

After the initial point of splitoff in Department 1, each product presents its own set of alternatives. Product X may be (1) sold to other refineries, (2) processed further, through Department 2 (reforming), or (3) processed through Departments 3 and 4 to become part of a blended gasoline. Either Product X or Product X' (purchased from outside) may be processed through Department 2, where it serves as an input for joint products of a very special type, Products U (reformed gasoline) and T (scrap). Scrap is a commercially valueless output whose disposition may actually cost the firm money. When the units of X are processed through Departments 3 and 4, only a single product results: Q (some blend, such as premium).

Product Y must be processed further in Department 5, where it becomes the input for three joint products, R, W, and S. Product R must be sold and cannot be processed further by this firm (although it may be a raw material for some other firm). Product W may be sold or processed further through Department 6 (to become Product O, lubricating oil). Product S may be sold or processed further, with Product V, in Department 4 to yield Product Q (a blend). Note that while Q requires multiple inputs that are joint products, it is not the nature of the process that creates joint cost problems. The firm could purchase all of its requirements of X and S externally (inputs X' and S'). Then production of Q would not involve the traditional joint costing problems. The price of the purchased raw materials would probably be greater than the net realizable value that could be secured for the firm's own units of X and S if they were sold, because selling entails some out-of-pocket costs that reduce net revenues below market price. Furthermore, added costs such as freight and handling may be incurred when X' and S' are purchased, raising the total outlay above the market price.

Joint Products and Decision Making

One of the complexities of any joint-product situation, as illustrated in Figure 9-1, has to do with the interrelationships among various products and between various processes. The firm's demand for Products X and S is closely related to management's decision to produce other commodities (such as Y). Thus, only by following a systematic procedure can the entire network be optimized. Moreover, Figure 9-1 deliberately omits certain other issues that many managements must resolve. For example, is it possible to store Y at reasonable cost? If not, then the firm may be forced to curtail its production of Product X once the demands for Product Y and its derivative products are met. But, if Y can be stored at reasonable cost, additional X may be produced as long as production can be justified relative to all pertinent costs, including storage. The consideration of inventories increases the complexity of the problem.

Similarly, many managers in joint-product firms face bottlenecks in their plants. A bottleneck exists whenever the capacity of one function prevents the firm from producing additional units of output for which there is a market. Bottlenecks complicate a manager's decision making, because a change in one product can have cascading effects on the entire system. Bottlenecks are of particular concern for managers who revise their production plans during the period. The greater the number of potential bottlenecks (constraints), the greater the likelihood that the entire plan must be revised to accommodate revision of the schedule for a single product.

Quite clearly, one way to proceed is to model the entire setting in a formal programing model.[4] Typically, though, numerous choices are made in a more decomposed manner. This raises the question of decomposition strategy and the importance of allocating the joint production cost. (In Figure 9-1, this is illustrated by the cost in Department 1 of producing X and Y.) We will explore this theme next, making the important assumption that management is operating under certainty and seeks to maximize total contribution margin. This allows us to proceed in incremental terms: Further processing is warranted if incremental revenue exceeds incremental cost.

Stages in Decision Making

The first decision problem concerning joint products occurs at the initial point of the operating cycle (Department 1 in Figure 9-1), prior to the splitoff of the joint products, X and Y. In our example, the firm wishes to decide whether to process any A at all. The basic question facing management at the start of each period is, "Does the incremental cash inflow from the products exceed the incremental cash outflow required to acquire and process A?" As one possibility, management could compare the expected revenue from X, R, W, and S with the cash outflows to acquire A and run Departments 1 and 5. The cash inflows from X, R, W, and S are determined by using the prices P_x, R_r, P_w, and P_s and the related quantities Q_x, Q_r, Q_w, and Q_s. Note that referring *solely* to the values of X and Y is insufficient, since Product Y has no market as an end product and must be processed further for sale.

The decision can be made without considering the benefits of processing X, W, and S through Departments 2, 3, 4, and 6. However, if the sale of X, R, W, and S yield cash inflows that are insufficient to cover the cash outflows for input A and the processing costs of Departments 1 and 5, management will want to analyze the entire decision tree before determining if any A should be processed at the existing prices. This is a more complex decision

---

[4] Formal programing models are often used in these settings. See G. Eppen and F. Gould, *Quantitative Concepts for Management: Decision Making Without Algorithms* (Englewood Cliffs, N.J.: Prentice-Hall, 1979), and H. Wagner, *Principles of Operations Research* (Englewood Cliffs, N.J.: Prentice-Hall, 1975). Also see R. Hartley, "Decision Making with Joint Products," *Accounting Rev.*, Oct. 1971.

than the initial problem and requires many more estimates. We assume that management performs this analysis only in rare instances. (You should reflect on the cost-benefit analysis implicit in this assumption.)

When X, R, W, and S are produced, a second set of decisions must be made. All products except R may be processed further in an attempt to increase the total contribution margin of the firm. The principle of incremental analysis should be applied as before. However, the complexities in the application of this principle vary. For W, the comparison is simply between the incremental cash inflow from W after it is processed minus the cash outflows from additional processing compared to W's present market value. For X and S, the alternatives are more complicated. For example, all of S and X can be sold, or S can be sold and X processed to yield U and T (scrap). Alternatively, S and X can both be processed to yield Q. The complexity of the problem is now fairly obvious. A complete analysis would have to incorporate the simultaneous effects of these decisions on the available capacities of the different processes. The number of possible combinations of outputs is too great to discuss, let alone evaluate, if we are to maintain a cost-benefit perspective.

Continuing with the discussion, we see that the firm can make another decision if its initial analysis indicates that it should not process any A. Management can buy X' and S' (at $P_{x'}$ and $P_{s'}$, respectively) from other producers and process them through Departments 3 and 4 to produce Product Q. While this might require paying a premium over the net cost of producing X and S internally, such a decision may be desirable. This decision would permit the firm to shut down Departments 1, 2, and 5 at some cost saving but would result in the loss of revenues from R, W, and U. It is possible that the saving in costs from shutting down these departments and not purchasing A is great enough to make the contemplated course of action (the ultimate production of Q) desirable.

One decision that management may have the opportunity to make (omitted from Figure 9-1) concerns the ratio in which the joint products should be produced. Assuming that some flexibility exists, the manager would produce more X (or Y) up to the point where opportunity costs equal incremental revenue. For example, the opportunity cost of producing more W and less R is the sum of the sales value of the units of R given up and the added cost of processing incurred in Department 5 to achieve this. The incremental cash flow from the added units of Product W is the net cash flow received from immediate sale of W or from the sale of Product O after W is processed through Department 6.

REVIEW PROBLEM 1

A firm makes a variety of products from a single input, as illustrated in Figure 9-1. Four decision problems follow. In all cases, assume that we can obtain a value for Y directly rather than by reference to R, W, or S.

(a) *Decision to Process Any Input at All*

Data:

Cost of initial input, A	$100 per unit
Cost of processing A in Department 1	$50
Output of X and Y from 1 unit of A	10 units of X and
	30 units of Y
Market value of X	$8 per unit $(= P_x)$
Net realizable value of Y	$4 per unit $(= V_y)$

(b) *Decision to Process Product X Through Department 2 Only*

Data:

Market value of X	$8 per unit $(= P_x)$
Market value of U	$25 per unit $(= P_u)$
Market value of T	$0
Output of T and U from 10 units of X	5 units of U and
	3 units of T
Processing costs of Department 2	$60

(c) *Decision to Process X to Produce Q Assuming S Has Been Produced*

Market value of X	$8 per unit $(= P_x)$
Market value of S	$1 per unit $(= P_s)$
Market value of Q	$10 per unit $(= P_q)$
Output of Q from 10 X and 20 S	45 units
Processing costs—Department 3	$120
Processing costs—Department 4	$90

(d) *Decision to Manufacture Q with Outside-Purchased Units of X and S*

Data:

All data per above (C) except	
Cost to purchase X	$15 per unit $(= P_{x'})$
Cost to purchase S	$5 per unit $(= P_{s'})$

The decisions outlined in the Review Problem are not conceptually different from the cost–volume–profit problems discussed in Chapter 4, particularly the decision to process further or to sell. The firm in all instances strives to maximize total contribution margin. The only difference is in the complexity of the situation and the variety of alternatives that can be interrelated.

The Role of Cost Allocation in Joint-Product Decision Making

In our discussion of joint-product decision making, no mention whatsoever was made of joint cost allocation. This is no accident; for purposes of deciding whether to process any input or whether to engage in additional processing beyond the splitoff point, *allocated joint costs are not required.*

To appreciate this fully, let us greatly simplify the setting in Figure 9-1 and assume that Y can be sold for a price of P_y and that X can be sold for a price of P_x or processed through Department 2 and sold for a price $\hat{P}_x$. Further assume the incremental processing cost in Department 2 is C_2 per unit processed and the incremental processing cost in Department 1 is C_1 per unit of A processed. Department 1 has a capacity of $\bar{A}$ units; Department 2 has no capacity constraint; and X and Y are produced in a fixed proportion of one X and one Y for each unit of A processed.

A linear programing model of the firm's problem is

$$\text{Maximize TCM} = P_y Y + P_x X_1 + (\hat{P}_x - C_2)X_2 - C_1 A$$
$$\text{subject to} \quad A \leq \bar{A}$$
$$Y \leq A$$
$$X_1 + X_2 \leq A$$
$$A, Y, X_1, X_2 \geq 0$$

where X_1 denotes units of X sold immediately and X_2 denotes units processed through Department 2. Also, the first constraint reflects the available capacity in Department 1 and the other two reflect availability of X and Y given the units of A processed. We assume that excess units of X or Y can be freely disposed of.

We further assume P_y, P_x, and $(\hat{P}_x - C_2)$ all are greater than zero. Then the optimal solution clearly has either $A^* = 0$ or $A^* = \bar{A}$, where the asterisk denotes the optimal solution. Equally clear is

$$Y^* = A^*$$
$$X_2^* = A^* - X_1^*$$

and

$$X_1^* = \begin{cases} A^* & \text{if} \quad P_x > (\hat{P}_x - C_2) \\ 0 & \text{otherwise} \end{cases}$$

Now observe the manner in which we are able to decompose this overall problem into subproblems. First, for any value of $X = A$, what is the best choice between immediately selling or processing X through Department 2? The answer is obvious:

$$X_1 = \begin{cases} A & \text{if} \quad P_x > (\hat{P}_x - C_2) \\ 0 & \text{otherwise} \end{cases}$$

and

$$X_2 = A - X_1$$

In other words, Product X is sold immediately if the sales price P_x exceeds the net realizable value of further processing, $(\hat{P}_x - C_2)$.

Suppose further processing is optimal. The input choice is then equally clear:

$$A^* = \begin{cases} \bar{A} & \text{if} \quad P_y + (\hat{P}_x - C_2) > C_1 \\ 0 & \text{otherwise} \end{cases}$$

By exploiting the linear technology, constraints, and cost and revenue structure, we have decomposed the problem in a manner that allows for optimal choice on a step-by-step basis. And no allocation of the joint cost in Department 1 whatsoever is involved. This is precisely what we did in the earlier examples. And this is why we stated that allocated joint costs are not required here. In fact, their use may lead to incorrect choices.

To illustrate, assume $P_x = \$500$, $\hat{P}_x = \$900$, $C_2 = \$300$, and $C_1 = \$1600$. Further assume a separate manager is in charge of Department 2. With $P_x = \$500 < (\hat{P}_x - C_2) = \$600$, the units of X should be further processed. But suppose C_1 were split equally between X and Y. If the manager in Department 2 were to accept X for further processing, the accounting system would assign him a cost of \$800 per unit of X_2. His apparent contribution margin would then be $(\hat{P}_x - C_2) - \$800 = -\$200$, and he would not choose to process.

A rather different situation arises when some intermediate department is considering an increase in the amount it processes. For example, what is the cost of increasing X? Here we might have a situation in which Department 1 is producing at capacity but is able to alter the mix to less Y and more X. To explore this choice by focusing on the costs and benefits of altering X, we must assess the opportunity cost of decreased Y. This can be done in the manner just illustrated, though with considerable complication, by using the dual variables from the completely laid-out programing problem.[5] And at this point the joint cost allocation might provide a viable approximation to the opportunity cost datum. But notice that the question is not one of further processing a given product, but one of altering the availability of that product. A similar exercise arises in service departments, and we will defer further discussion to that setting.

The important point to dwell on here is that the typical decision problem of how to process joint products is devoid of joint cost allocation issues. The demand for joint cost allocation is nil here. (A possible exception is variation in the amount of such joint products.) Yet joint products are often inventoried, and financial and tax reporting *require* an allocation of the joint cost. The usual procedures and their extension to byproducts will be discussed in Chapter 11. We turn now to an important variation on this theme provided by service departments.

---

[5] See R. Weil, "Allocating Joint Costs," *American Economic Rev.*, Dec. 1968.

REVIEW PROBLEM 2

A firm processes input A into products X and Y. The processing cost consists of fixed overhead of $50,000, direct labor of $800 per unit of A processed, variable overhead of $1,200 per unit of A processed, and direct material of $2,000 per unit of A processed. Each unit of A that is processed results in 2 units of X and 1 unit of Y. Current capacity is 100 units of A. Each unit of X is sold for $4,000 and each unit of Y is sold for $1,500.

Management is considering installation of a new department that will process units of Y into an equal number of units of Z. Each unit of Z sells for $5,000. The new department's incremental cost structure will consist of fixed overhead of $50,000 and direct labor of $900 per unit, variable overhead of $1,350 per unit, and $850 direct material per unit (in addition to the input of Y). Should the Y units be further processed?

Service Departments

Service departments, as their name implies, exist to provide services of various kinds to other units of the organization. As such, they may provide assistance to production departments, managing departments, and other service departments. It is even possible that a service department may utilize a portion of the services it produces. These departments do not participate directly in the production of the output of the firm, and therefore their costs are indirect costs of operations rather than direct product costs. Such costs are allocated to production or management cost centers as part of the cost accounting process.

In many ways, the allocation of common costs of service departments is similar to the allocation of joint costs. However, there are three important differences between the two types of costs. First, of course, service department costs reflect services provided to other departments rather than direct product costs. Second, because the transactions between departments are internal, no market prices may exist. As a result, service department costs are usually allocated using an index of activity instead of a market value. Third, and most important, the consuming department often determines the quantity of service supplied.

In this section we consider four topics: the allocation of service department costs in support of output decisions, make or buy considerations in obtaining these services, the complication of reciprocal service arrangements, and the control of service costs. As such, our orientation reflects earlier discussions in the chapter. We concentrate on allocations that support decomposition of the firm's decision problem. Financial and tax reporting considerations are not addressed.

Output Decisions

The basic problem in dealing with service departments when decomposed output decisions are under consideration is to assess the service costs associated with the output alternatives. In the absence of capacity constraints and reciprocal arrangements, this is no different than the variable-cost-of-overhead theme developed in Chapter 4.

Suppose our firm produces two products, X and Y. Nothing out of the ordinary is involved, except that each product is produced in its own department and a single service center provides some service to each department. The service department's cost structure is given by

$$\text{Service cost} = F + vS$$

where S is units of service, F is a fixed cost, and v is the variable cost per unit of service. We also let $S = S_x + S_y$, where S_x is the number of units provided to the department that produces X, and S_y is the number of units provided to the department that produces Y. We also assume that for any combination of X and Y, we must have $S_x \geq X$ and $S_y \geq Y$. Quite clearly, the minimum cost solution entails $S_x = X$ and $S_y = Y$.

Now suppose the product X manager has been approached to fill a special order of 10 units. He wants to compare the offered price with the incremental cost to the firm. The latter consists of the incremental production cost in his department (materials, labor, and overhead) and the incremental service cost. The latter is surely $10v$.

Now observe that if we allocate the variable service cost to the two departments, the allocation will control for the need to pick up implied variations in S. This is the reason for allocating variable service costs to consuming departments.

Several points are in order. First, if fixed service costs are also allocated, we *overstate* the cost in this case just as in the case of fixed factory overhead. Second, we should distinguish the case of service units directly metered from that in which they are not. If, in fact, units of service are observed, we face a transfer pricing problem and techniques that will be discussed in Chapter 10 are applicable. A more common case is that in which S is not directly observed. Instead, the service cost is estimated as a function of some activity measure in each department, such as units produced or direct labor hours. In the above example, we would then have

$$\text{Service cost} = F + v(X + Y)$$

Third, the decomposition objective becomes more complicated when the service department's capacity is binding.

To clarify, suppose the service department is producing at capacity when the special order of 10 extra units of X is presented. If extra units of service can be subcontracted at a price of $v' > v$ per unit and if the extra demand will be so accommodated, the relevant service cost is clearly $10v'$.

If no subcontracting is available, then the only way to produce the extra 10 units of X is to decrease S_y by 10 units and thereby decrease Y production by 10 units (since $S_y \geq Y$). Assuming no adverse market effects, the relevant service cost is now $10 \cdot CM_y$, where CM_y is the contribution margin of product Y exclusive of *any* service cost allocation. (Notice that this is really a question of whether to process S into X or into Y, with the S cost being irrelevant to the choice.)

This is easy enough to sort out in a textbook with two products and one service department. But consider the case of numerous products and services. Here one might argue that a full cost allocation of $v + F/\bar{S}$, where $\bar{S}$ is the service department's capacity, provides a useful approximation to v' or CM_y. Whether this is true obviously depends on a myriad of considerations, but the argument is not without merit. Observe, however, that we are *not* advocating fixed cost allocation. We are pointing out that in some circumstances such a procedure may provide a more useful cost figure. Exactly when this is the case is, however, too subtle a topic for an introductory text.[6]

Make or Buy Decisions

Another common decision problem in the service department setting is whether to internally produce or externally acquire a service. This offers no special difficulty if reciprocal service arrangements are absent. Return to the previous example and suppose $\hat{S}$ total units of service are being demanded. The cost is

$$\text{Service cost} = F + v\hat{S}$$

Suppose that outside acquisition is available at $v' > v$ per unit and that the fixed cost can be driven to zero with this outside purchase. The purchase cost then becomes

$$v'\hat{S}$$

Thus purchase is warranted if $v'\hat{S} < F + v\hat{S}$. Of course, making these estimates is not easy. More important, though, is the fact that altering the marginal cost may alter demand. This is a familiar story in computing services, for

---

[6] See J. Demski and G. Feltham, *Cost Determination: A Conceptual Approach,* for an extensive discussion of this topic.

example. Originally the firm has a "small" machine that is taxed to capacity and probably even does some outside subcontracting. Then a larger machine is purchased, initial demand is well below capacity, variable cost allocation is resorted to, and demand suddenly triples.

This concludes our survey of service department cost allocation in the support of output decisions. Numerous practical details, such as those centering around estimation of the service department's cost function or those involved in passing the allocations through the firm's chart of accounts, are present here. But they do not differ in any appreciable way from our earlier discussion of manufacturing overhead. Hence they are not pursued at this point. Instead we examine the complications of having reciprocal service departments.

REVIEW PROBLEM 3 _____

Zelt Corporation makes numerous products. One, product X, is sought by a new customer. He wants 10 units and is willing to pay $2,000 per unit. Standard product cost is:

Direct labor	$ 500
Direct material	800
Variable overhead	750
	$2,050

Variable overhead is allocated at a rate of 150 percent of standard direct labor dollars. Included in the variable overhead allocation is a maintenance component. Maintenance has the following flexible budget:

$$\text{Cost} = \$18,000 + \$50M$$

where M denotes units of maintenance. Moreover, M varies at the approximate rate of $M = (.01)(\text{direct labor dollars})$.

Required   (a) Present an analysis of the special offer that explicitly accounts for maintenance.

        (b) Discuss the relationship between your analysis and the $2,050 standard variable cost datum.

Reciprocal Services

Existence of more than one service department does not alter any of the previous statements, though the situation becomes more complex when service departments provide services to one another as well as to production departments. This has, in fact, been a source of confusion in the literature, so we pause to examine it in this section.

_____EXHIBIT 9–1

Reciprocal Allocation Example

	Variable Cost Per Unit Exclusive of Any Service Input	Required Per Unit Usage of	
		Service A	Service B
Service A	$ 100	0	½
Service B	$ 250	1	0
Output X	$1,000	2	1
Output Y	$2,000	1	2

Again consider a firm with two products, X and Y. Each is produced in its own division. Now, however, two services, A and B, are also internally produced. The difficulty is that service A is required to produce service B and vice versa. Specific technical requirements and cost functions are listed in Exhibit 9–1.

Thus each unit of service A costs $100 plus ½ unit of service B; each unit of final output X costs $1,000 plus 2 units of service A and 1 unit of service B. All costs are variable in this example.

Two questions emerge. What does an extra unit of X or Y cost, and how much can be saved by subcontracting the services to an outsider? Both questions revolve around the cost of the services and, due to their decomposed nature, both entail allocations.

The incremental or variable cost of X turns out to be $2,600 and that of Y turns out to be $3,850. Also (remembering that no fixed costs are involved), production of A should be subcontracted for any price below $450 per unit.

One way to see this is to focus on the minimum cost schedule to produce a given level of output. (Recall the model in [2].) Suppose that 100 units of X and 100 units of Y are required. Then we must have at least 300 units of each service available for the producing departments. We therefore formulate the minimum service cost problem as

$$\text{Minimize} \quad \$100A + \$250B$$
$$\text{subject to} \quad A - B \geq 300$$
$$- \tfrac{1}{2}A + B \geq 300$$
$$A, B \geq \quad 0$$

In particular, 300 units of A must be available for output X and Y and each unit of B requires one unit of A. Hence $A \geq 300 + B$. The B constraint is similar: $B \geq 300 + \tfrac{1}{2}A$.

The solution to this linear program is readily found to be $A^* = 1,200$ and $B^* = 900$, with a minimum service cost of \$345,000. Moreover, the shadow price on the A availability constraint is \$450 and that on the B availability constraint is \$700. Thus the marginal cost of expanding the availability of service to the producing department is \$450 for A and \$700 for B. Hence the (incremental) cost of one additional unit of X is \$1,000 + 2(\$450) + 1(\$700) = \$2,600.

Another way to see this is to re-solve the above service cost minimization problem for 101 units of X and 100 units of Y. The difference between the two minimum cost levels would then be the incremental service cost of producing one additional unit of X. Here we require 302 units of A and 301 units of B in production. Hence, we have

$$\text{Minimize} \quad \$100A + \$250B$$

$$\begin{aligned} \text{subject to} \quad A - B &\geq 302 \\ -\tfrac{1}{2}A + B &\geq 301 \\ A, B &\geq 0 \end{aligned}$$

The solution is $A^* = 1,206$ and $B^* = 904$, with a minimum cost of \$346,600. Hence the incremental service cost here is \$346,600 − \$345,000 = \$1,600. And the incremental cost of X is therefore \$1,600 + \$1,000 = \$2,600.

Yet another way to see this is with an allocation of the service costs to X and Y. Clearly X requires 2 units of A and 1 unit of B. What is the unit cost of A and B? Here we focus on the reciprocal structure and solve simultaneous equations:

$$C_A = \$100 + \tfrac{1}{2}C_B$$

$$C_B = \$250 + C_A$$

The unit cost of A, denoted C_A, is \$100 plus (recognizing B consumption) $\tfrac{1}{2}$ the unit cost of B. Similarly, the unit cost of B, denoted C_B, is \$250 plus the unit cost of A. In short, each cost consists of a direct component and an allocated component. And the solution is readily determined:

$$C_B = \$250 + C_A$$

$$= \$250 + (\$100 + \tfrac{1}{2}\,C_B)$$

or

$$\tfrac{1}{2}\,C_B = \$350$$

$$C_B = \$700$$

and

$$C_A = \$100 + \tfrac{1}{2}\,C_B = \$100 + \tfrac{1}{2}\,(\$700)$$

$$= \$450$$

Notice that the purpose of the allocation is to substitute for solving the A and B schedule problem by decomposing the firm's problem into concern over X and Y. For example, the incremental (and variable) cost of X is $1,000 + $2C_A$ + $1C_B$ = $1,000 + 2($450) + 1($700) = $2,600.

It is at this point that confusion might arise. Suppose our firm produces 100 of X and 100 of Y. (Recall that this implies $A^* = 1,200$ and $B^* = 900$.) The department producing A will incur a direct cost of 1,200($100) = $120,000 and an allocated cost of $\frac{1}{2}$(1,200)($700) = $420,000, for a total cost of $540,000. Similarly, the department producing B will incur a direct cost of 900($250) = $225,000 and an allocated cost of 900($450) = $405,000, for a total cost of $630,000. Thus the total of direct and allocated costs associated with the two service departments is $1,170,000. Yet the total service cost is surely 1,200($100) + 900($250) = $345,000.

When the allocations are completed, however, each service center account will net to zero and the total allocated to the X and Y departments will be 300($450) + 300($700) = $345,000. [The A department, with a total cost of $540,000, is allocated via 900($450) = $405,000 to the B department and 300 ($450) = $135,000 to the X and Y departments.] No "over" or "double" counting is involved. Use of A imposes a cost via B and vice versa. Decomposing the problem requires that the allocation control for this externality, and the proper cost measures therefore exceed the direct service production costs.

Now consider the question of acquiring A from an outside subcontractor. This will save the direct cost in the department producing A as well as reduce the required production of B. Let P be the external purchase price, A_i be internally produced units of A, and A_e be externally acquired units. For the basic case of $X = Y = 100$ units, our minimum service cost problem becomes

$$\text{Minimize} \qquad \$100A_i + PA_e + \$250B$$
$$\text{subject to} \qquad A_i + A_e - B \geq 300$$
$$-\tfrac{1}{2}A_i + B \geq 300$$
$$A_i, A_e, B \geq \quad 0$$

Here, the total $A = A_i + A_e \geq 300 + B$. But since A_e consumes no internal service, $B \geq 300 + \frac{1}{2}A_i$.

The solution is clearly $A_i^* = 1,200$, $A_e^* = 0$, and $B^* = 900$ at a cost of $345,000 or $A_i^* = 0$, $A_e^* = 600$, and $B^* = 300$ at a cost of $75,000 + 600P$. And the firm will acquire the A service externally if $345,000 > $75,000 + 600P, or $P < ($345,000 - $75,000)/600 = $450, which should hardly come as a surprise. Moreover, any such move will save a total of $270,000 - 600P = 600($450 - P)$. This has the ready interpretation of a per unit saving of ($450 - P)$ and 600 units being acquired if the savings are available. Further note that all of this insight is available without resorting to any cost allocation whatsoever. The cost allocations arise when we decompose the problem.

In turn, an allocation approach focuses on the costs of A and B in the production of X and Y. As previously shown, this implies $C_A = \$450$ and $C_B = \$700$. Hence, any external offer to produce A at less than $450 is attractive.[7]

Simplified Procedures

With numerous services and products, and extensive reciprocal service arrangements, a simplified allocation procedure is often sought. One way to do this is to totally ignore reciprocal arrangements. In our basic example in Exhibit 9–1, with $X = Y = 100$ units, this would entail use of cost figures of $\hat{C}_A = 1,200(\$100)/300 = \$400$ and $\hat{C}_B = 900(\$250)/300 = \$750$. The allocated total would be "correct," and all that can be said is that the resulting approximation may or may not be good enough. For obvious reasons, this is called the *direct method* of allocation.

Another alternative, termed the *step method,* is a compromise between recognizing and ignoring the reciprocal arrangements. Here we rank the service departments in terms of the importance of reciprocal arrangements and then allocate the respective costs in sequence. To illustrate, service A is more important in the production of service B than vice versa in the sense that 75 percent of A goes to the department producing B, while only 67 percent of B goes to the department producing A. So we initially allocate the direct cost in producing A to the production departments and to the department producing B, using the cost figure of $\hat{C}_A = \$100$. The total cost to be allocated in the department producing B is now $900(\$250) + 900(\$100) = \$315,000$, and the implied unit cost when these costs are allocated to the producing departments (but *not* back to the A department) is $\hat{C}_B = \$1,050$.

Note that the step method requires that we first rank the service departments according to the amounts of service provided to the other departments. Once a service department's costs have been allocated, that department is eliminated from further consideration, and the allocation percentages are based on the relative amounts of services consumed by the remaining departments.

Another alternative would be to rank the service departments according to their direct costs, and then to allocate the costs of the service department that incurred the highest direct costs to the departments that used its services, then the department with the next highest direct costs, and so on. Either method, however, will produce questionable allocations simply because we eliminate each department from further assignments of costs after its costs have been allocated, even though that department may have received services from departments whose costs are allocated at a later point in the sequence.

---

[7] Formal use of matrix algebra in analyzing allocation problems has been suggested in the literature. Any serious look at the ability of matrix algebra to provide insight into allocation should begin with R. Kaplan, "Variable and Self Service Costs in Reciprocal Allocation Models," *Accounting Rev.,* Oct. 1973. Also see R. Capettini and G. Salamon, "Internal versus External Acquisition of Services When Reciprocal Services Exist," *Accounting Rev.,* July 1977.

Control of Service Departments

The control of service department costs is not significantly different from cost control in any other cost center. Standard costs for labor and materials, and flexible budgets for overhead costs, may be used to control any service department for which we can measure output. In those cases in which output cannot be measured accurately (the personnel department, for example), management may have to control the departments through fixed budgets.

The only other consideration at this point is whether cost allocations should be based on the standard costs of the service department or whether the actual costs should be allocated. The usual argument here is that no department receiving the services of a service department should be charged for any inefficiencies or given credit for any efficiencies of a particular service department. Hence, the methods we have described in the preceding sections should be used to allocate only the standard variable and standard fixed costs to production departments.

As discussed in Chapter 5, however, this prescription is slightly naive in the sense that it de facto insures the user against any cost variations in the service department. If this is desirable, then the prescription makes sense. But if the user should be responding to the existence of cost variations in the service department, management may want to consider allocating actual rather than standard costs. Thus, existence of uncertainty tempers the usual argument.

*Cost Allocation Criteria*_____

Our discussion of cost allocation has emphasized internal, managerial use of the resulting cost figures in a decomposed or piecemeal approach to decision making. We have repeatedly stressed and illustrated the fundamental point that cost allocations serve to "couple" the decomposed parts; therefore, no allocation is essential in the absence of decomposition.

It is, we admit, easier to explicate such a position than to implement it. The proper allocation can be readily ascertained in a textbook, but real-world complexities typically require a more simplified approach. We stop short of implementing the "perfect" allocation scheme, and we even stop short of analyzing the full implication of one allocation scheme versus another. This latter tack is the subject of cost allocation criteria.

How does the firm (or its accountant) choose between two allocation schemes (such as alternative sequencing in implementing the step down approach)? Ideally we would focus on the merits of the eventual decisions. But this is a costly exercise. As a result, allocation criteria are invoked, just as criteria were invoked to simplify the design of performance evaluation systems for motivation purposes in Chapter 5.

In this regard, fairness and equity are often treated as primary criteria. That is, each product should bear a "fair" share of the firm's overhead. Does this mean a product should be dropped if it has a positive contribution margin but one that is not large enough to absorb a "fair" share of fixed overhead? This appears illogical, unless management is uninterested in profits. Pushed to the extremes, fairness and equity appear to be either without content or to describe any allocation that produces an optimal decision. Either way they seem too general to offer much help.

More specific criteria include benefits received and causality.[8] Benefits received has more of an economic orientation in that the idea is to allocate the total cost in proportion to the benefits received by each object. And an allocation method is desirable to the extent that it accomplishes this. For decision-making purposes, however, we must remember that the essence of an allocation problem is an attempt to decompose a joint problem into subcomponents. Alterations in one of a set of joint products should be done in a manner that is cognizant of important effects on the other products. Allocating the joint cost in proportion to benefits is unlikely to portray the benefit-cost trade-offs at hand.

A similar comment applies to the causality criterion, in which an object is allocated the joint cost it caused to be incurred. In the extreme, alterations in one product might drastically change the joint cost total and benefit all of the products. But under the causality criterion such an alteration would impose total incremental cost on an activity that generates only a fraction of the anticipated benefits. Again, this is unlikely to portray the benefit-cost trade-offs at hand.

To conclude, allocation criteria serve the useful purpose of simplifying the design of a cost allocation system, but except in special cases they cannot be relied upon to produce perfect answers. They arise because management foregoes an explicit or implicit analysis of the precise demand for allocation. It appears that a better understanding of what the allocation criteria are surrogating for in the analysis will lead to improved design of allocation systems.

Summary

Though reasons are varied (and some are beyond the scope of an introductory managerial accounting text), we stress the importance of linking any concern over cost allocations to the demand for those allocations. One particular source of demand, decomposing a complex decision problem, was analyzed. Here joint cost allocation was seen to be inessential in a joint product setting where

---

[8] Another criterion is "ability to bear." The basic idea is that other, more desirable criteria are too difficult to implement, so expediency of some sort is invoked. How this relates to the decomposition demand is difficult to ascertain.

further processing of an intermediate product was at issue. But this is not the case in a typical service center setting in which production decisions alter the optimal activity (and therefore cost) in the service facility.

On more abstract grounds, it is important to recognize that cost allocations need not be arbitrary or useless. We emphasize precisely the opposite. Decomposition of complex problems creates a demand for cost allocation. In complex settings, allocation issues are important and difficult to resolve. Understanding their source is, we feel, essential to enlightened resolution.

Supplementary Readings

Articles

Bierman, H., Jr., "Inventory Valuation: The Uses of Market Prices," *Accounting Rev.,* Oct. 1967.

Capettini, R. and G. Salamon, "Internal versus External Acquisition of Services When Reciprocal Services Exist," *Accounting Rev.,* July 1977.

Hamlen, S., W. Hamlen, and J. Tschirhart, "The Use of Core Theory in Evaluating Joint Cost Allocation Schemes," *Accounting Rev.,* July 1977.

Hartley, R., "Decision Making with Joint Products," *Accounting Rev.,* Oct. 1971.

Itami, H. and R. Kaplan, "An Activity Analysis Approach to Unit Costing with Multiple Interactive Products," *Management Science,* Aug. 1980.

Jaedicke, R.K., "Marketing Cost Analysis—a Reply," *N.A.A. Bull.,* July 1962.

Kaplan, R., "Variable and Self Service Costs in Reciprocal Allocation Models, *Accounting Rev.,* Oct. 1973.

Kaplan R., and G.L. Thompson, "Overhead Allocation via Mathematical Programming Models," *Accounting Rev.,* April 1971.

Weil, R., "Allocating Joint Costs," *American Economic Rev.,* Dec. 1968.

Zimmerman, J., "The Costs and Benefits of Allocations," *Accounting Rev.,* July 1979.

Books

Davidson, S., and R. Weil, eds., *Handbook of Cost Accounting.* New York: McGraw-Hill, 1978.

Demski, J., and G. Feltham, *Cost Determination: A Conceptual Approach.* Ames, Iowa: Iowa State Univ. Press, 1976.

Thomas, A., *A Behavioural Analysis of Joint-Cost Allocation and Transfer Pricing.* Champaign, Ill.: Stipes, 1980.

Questions and Problems

1. Define cost allocation.
2. Describe the cost allocation process. Is the allocation of manufacturing overhead portrayed by your description? Explain.

3. What is meant by the terminology "demand for allocation"?

4. The state of California regulates commuter train prices by (in part) allocating rail bed costs between freight and commuter uses. Attempts are made to establish "fair" allocations. Comment on this practice.

5. Many contend that cost allocations are arbitrary. Do you agree? Explain.

6. A student poses the following question: "Earlier we learned that allocated costs usually are irrelevant for decisions. However, from the discussion in Chapter 9, it now appears that at least a portion of the service department's allocated costs may be relevant for decision making. Why the change in policy?" Explain to the student what the difference is, if there is one, or why none exists.

7. Discuss the statement, "The purpose of allocating joint costs is to permit management to assess the profitability of different joint products."

8. Define joint costs and joint products as normally used by accountants.

9. What is meant by a common cost? In what way are common costs and joint costs alike?

10. If Department A requires two different raw materials in order to yield two outputs, that is, 1 A and 2 B yield 1 C and 1 D, could we consider this a joint cost problem?

11. Assume that a department head is in charge of a process that has some flexibility. By twisting knobs and setting timers he can change the ratio of A to B from 3:1 to 1.5:2 per unit of input. Is it possible to set standard costs for the output of such a process? (*Hint:* See Chapter 7's appendix on mix and yield variances.)

12. *Use of Joint Costs in Decision Making*
The Harbison Company manufactures two sizes of plate glass, which are produced simultaneously in the same manufacturing process. Since the small sheets of plate glass are cut from large sheets that have flaws in them, the joint costs are allocated equally to each good sheet, large and small, produced. The difference in after–split-off costs for large and small sheets is due to material.

The company decided to increase its efforts to sell the large sheets because they produced a larger gross margin than the small sheets. Accordingly, the amount of the fixed advertising budget devoted to large sheets was increased and the amount devoted to small sheets was decreased. However, no changes in sales prices were made.

By midyear, the production scheduling department had increased the monthly production of large sheets in order to stay above the minimum inventory level. However, it also had cut back the monthly production of small sheets because the inventory ceiling had been reached.

At the end of the year, the net result of the change in product mix was a decrease of $112,000 in gross margin. Although sales of large sheets had increased 34,500 units, sales of small sheets had decreased 40,200 units.

Identify the mistake that the Harbison Company made in deciding to change its product mix, and explain why it caused a smaller gross margin for the year.

[AICPA adapted]

13. *Joint Products and Prices of Inputs*
The Southern Cottonseed Company has the capacity to produce 20,000 tons of cottonseed per year. The yield of a ton of cottonseed is as follows:

Product	Average Yield per Ton	Average Selling Price per Trade Unit
Oil	300 pounds	$ .15 per pound
Meal	600 pounds	50.00 per ton
Hulls	800 pounds	20.00 per ton
Lint	100 pounds	3.00 per cwt
Waste	200 pounds	—

At these selling prices the company can sell its entire output for the year. Processing costs are as follows (excluding cottonseed costs):

> Variable: $9 per ton of cottonseed put into process
> Fixed: $108,000 per year
> Marketing (all variable): $20 per ton sold
> Administrative (all fixed): $90,000 per year

Last year, the company had to pay an average of $32 per ton for cottonseed.

(a) What is the break-even point for Southern Cottonseed, assuming that the prices of cottonseed will remain at $32 during the coming year?

(b) What is the maximum price the company can pay for a ton of cottonseed? Maximum price is defined as the amount that would result in losses no greater when operating than when closed down. Assume that all fixed costs listed above would continue unchanged if the company did shut down its plant.

(c) The stockholders' equity in the business is $950,000. Management estimates that a 20 percent return before taxes is a fair rate of return to earn on stockholders' equity. Compute the maximum price the company can pay for a ton of cottonseed in order to realize 20 percent on the stockholders' investment.

[AICPA adapted]

14. *Joint Product Decision Making*

Crush Incorporated produces three products, X, Y, and Z. In Department 1, inputs are combined to produce X and intermediate product W in fixed proportion of 2X to 1W. Capacity is limited to 400 such "bundles." Department 1's flexible budget reports $1,000 in fixed cost and a variable cost of $200 per "bundle." Product X sells on the open market for $50 per unit. Product W can be converted into Y at no cost and sold for $100 per unit. It can also be processed into Z. This is done in Department 2, where each unit of W so processed yields 4Z. The flexible budget for Department 2 is $2,000 fixed plus $80 per unit of W processed, exclusive of the cost of W. Product Z sells on the open market for $60 per unit and Department 2 has no binding capacity constraint. This budget is felt to be sufficiently accurate for any processing between 0 and 500 units of W.

(a) Suppose Department 1 operates at capacity. Should W be processed into Y?

(b) Should Department 1 operate at capacity?

(c) Formulate a linear program to answer the questions in (a) and (b).

(d) Suppose Crush is asked to supply 10 units of Y by a desperate customer. Determine the minimum price that Crush would demand.

(e) Answer part (d) above by using the linear program (appropriately modified) that you constructed in part (c).

(f) Contrast the importance of opportunity cost calculation in parts (d) and (e).

15. *Mechanics of Service Department Cost Allocation*
Zowie Books sells paperback books of two types. Culture Books (hereafter called C Books) are intended for the college bookstores and better department store book departments. Enjoyable Books (E Books) are devoted to current fiction. Many of the functions and costs of the two lines are separate because of their totally different markets. However, some of the firm's costs are related to servicing both lines of books (that is, they are costs common to both C and E Books). The jointly used departments are advertising design, sales, and office staff.

During the past period these departments incurred the following costs:

Advertising design	$ 4,300
Sales	6,800
Office staff	3,000
	$14,100

These costs must be allocated to C Books and E Books for purposes of ascertaining the two managing editors' bonuses, which are related to profits.

Operating data for the past period are as follows:

	C Books	E Books	Advertising Design	Sales	Office Staff
Size of departmental staff	2	8	5	10	5
Layouts requested	10	30	0	4	6
Hours spent on this function by sales force	60	90	10	20	10

(a) Allocate the departmental costs to C Books and E Books, ignoring any reciprocal relationships. The allocation is made according to dollar volume of sales. Sales for C Books were $12,000, and sales for E Books were $36,000.

(b) Allocate these costs in steps, ignoring any reciprocal relationships. Allocate advertising first, then sales, and finally office staff.

16. *Allocation of Service Department Costs*
H & B are producing Little League bats under their highly successful H & B label. The techniques are highly automated and consist of two steps, shaping and finishing, which are carried out in separate departments. H & B have three other departments. One is their own power plant, which supplies power to all parts of the firm both for running machinery and for heat, light, and air condition-

EXHIBIT 9-2

	To					
From	Shaping	Finishing	Power	Accounting	Repair	Total
Shaping department	100%	—	—	—	—	100%
Finishing department	—	100%	—	—	—	100%
Power station	30%	30%	—	10%	30%	100%
Accounting department	20%	40%	20%	—	20%	100%
Repair and service crew	50%	20%	20%	10%	—	100%
Cost	$40,000	$35,000	$10,000	$4,500	$9,500	

ing. The second is the accounting department. The third consists of the firm's repair crew, who are skilled at servicing everything from air conditioners and typewriters to heavy equipment.

The accounting department has calculated the total variable costs for each department shown in Exhibit 9-2. The various service department heads have estimated as best they can the services rendered by their departments to the other four units.

(a) Allocate the service department costs sequentially, and determine the total cost for the shaping and finishing departments. Allocate the power station first, then the accounting department, and finally the repair crew.

(b) Solve this problem algebraically for the service departments.

17. *Service Department Costs and Business Decisions*
Ace Card Company is concerned with the profitability of its toys and games division. Ace went into this market during the 1950's when the toy market was quite profitable. Lately, however, the entire market has changed from children's games to more active toys. Thus, the line has not been showing a profit above its full costs.

Realizing that profit and contribution to divisional costs are different concepts, the president has requested that you prepare an analysis of the division's operations. The data below reflect all you could gather about the division's operations.

(a) Production costs for 1981 were as follows for the toys and games division.

Raw materials		$ 25,000
Labor		50,000
Overhead		
Power	$12,000	
Indirect labor (cleanup)	8,000	
Repair and maintenance	5,000	
Depreciation	30,000	55,000
Total production costs		$130,000

(b) Production during 1981 was 200,000 games.
(c) Service department costs for 1981 were as follows:

Power Department

Variable costs	$10,000
Fixed costs	50,000
Total costs	$60,000

Repair and Maintenance Department

Variable costs	$36,000
Fixed costs	24,000
Total costs	$60,000

(d) Of the various service department costs, the division was allocated its share on a pro rata basis with other operating departments. No reciprocal relationships exist among the various service departments. The indirect (cleanup) charges were for employees in the toys and games division.
(e) All labor can be transferred to other divisions that are now shorthanded. In fact, management feels that this would relieve a production bottleneck in these departments and add another $10,000 to the company's net cash flow.
(f) Sales during the next few years are projected at 180,000 units at $.50 per unit.
(g) After discussing the problem with the head of the repair and maintenance department, it appears that the repair crews will not need to replace $2,000 worth of tools that are used on machines found solely in the toy and game division. These tools had a life of about one year and were charged to the fixed expenses of the repair and maintenance department.
(h) Assume that the scrap value of the machinery is only enough to cover the costs of winding up the division.

Analyze these data, and indicate whether the department should be retained.

18. **Effects of Allocation**

Carla Products has recently revamped its operating systems to increase efficiency. One of the most controversial changes involves the repair and maintenance function. Until the revision, each of the four departments had its own repair crew that worked exclusively for the department manager. Now there is one central repair crew under the direction of a foreman who schedules the repairmen, supervises their work, and is responsible for their performance.

The costs of the department are allocated at the end of each period by first dividing total actual costs by total actual hours worked to determine the rate per hour. The hours worked in each department are then multiplied by this standard rate to arrive at each department's repair cost.

One department head feels that this system is costing him more than the old system and the following dialogue occurs:

Head, Department A: I don't like the new system. My costs for repairs are up.

President, Carla Products: That doesn't make sense. My reports show that *total* repair and maintenance is down from $10,000 last week to $7,500. Did you use more than before?

Head: No, my hours of repair work are down from 65 hours for this week last year to 45 hours this year.

President: That doesn't seem right. Is it due to inflation?

Controller: No, . . .

(a) Finish the controller's answer, explaining how this could happen.

(b) How does the new organization of the repair and maintenance function lead to altered behavior by the department heads?

(c) How could this problem and the department head's be alleviated by altering the allocation scheme rather than the organization of Carla Products?

19. ***Various Bases for Allocating Service Department Costs***

Thrift-Shops, Inc., operates a chain of three food stores in a state that recently enacted legislation permitting municipalities within the state to levy an income tax on corporations operating within their respective municipalities. The legislation established a uniform tax rate that the municipalities may levy, and regulations that provide that the tax is to be computed on income derived within the taxing municipality after a reasonable and consistent allocation of general overhead expenses. General overhead expenses were not allocated to individual stores previously, but they must be allocated now to compute the taxes.

Each of the municipalities in which Thrift-Shops, Inc., operates a store has levied the corporate income tax as provided by state legislation, and management is considering two plans for allocating general overhead expenses to the stores. The 1980 operating results before general overhead and taxes for each store were as shown below.

	Ashville	Burns	Clinton	Total
Sales (net)	$416,000	$353,600	$270,400	$1,040,000

General overhead expenses in 1980 were as follows:

Warehousing and delivery expenses		
Warehouse depreciation	$20,000	
Warehouse operations	30,000	
Delivery expenses	40,000	$ 90,000
Central office expenses		
Advertising	18,000	
Central office salaries	37,000	
Other central office expenses	28,000	83,000
Total general overhead		$173,000

Additional information includes: (1) Delivery expenses vary with distance and number of deliveries. The distances from the warehouse to each store and the number of deliveries made in 1980 were as follows:

Store	Miles	Number of Deliveries
Ashville	120	140
Burns	200	64
Clinton	100	104

(2) All advertising is prepared by the central office and is distributed in the areas in which stores are located.

For each of the following two plans for allocating general overhead expenses, compute the income of each store that would be subject to the municipal levy on corporation income.

(a) *Plan 1:* Allocate all general overhead expenses on the basis of sales volume.
(b) *Plan 2:* First, allocate central office salaries and other central office expenses evenly to warehouse operations and each store. Second, allocate the resulting warehouse operations expenses, warehouse depreciation, and advertising to each store on the basis of sales volume. Third, allocate delivery expenses to each store on the basis of delivery miles times number of deliveries.

[AICPA adapted]

20. *Service Cost Allocation and Decomposition*
Ralph's firm produces two products, X and Y. Current demand is 200 of X and 100 of Y. Production capacity is 300X and 200Y. X is produced in Department I and Y is produced in Department II. Cost data are:

	Dept. I	Dept. II
Direct labor per unit of output	$100	$200
Direct material per unit of output	$400	$200
Variable overhead per dollar of direct labor	$2.50	$4.00

In addition, each unit of output in either department requires two units of service A and two units of service B. These services are produced in two service departments with respective variable costs of $300 and $500 per unit.

(a) Formulate a linear program to find the minimum cost method of producing $X = 200$ and $Y = 100$. Be certain to include A and B as decision variables.
(b) Modify your analysis, by allocating service costs to X and Y so as to drop A and B from explicit consideration in your model.

21. *Reciprocal Service Costs and Decomposition*
Repeat Problem 20, except that each unit of service A requires ½ unit of B and each unit of service B requires ½ unit of A.

22. *Service Department Cost Allocation*

Assume the following distribution of service department services:

Services of ↓	Used by →	S_1	S_2	P_1	P_2	Total
S_1		—	600	300	100	1,000 hours
S_2		200	—	100	700	1,000 hours

Variable costs	$4,000	$10,000
Fixed costs	2,000	4,000

The output of P_1 and P_2 are sold outside for $15 and $20, respectively. The average variable costs per unit incurred directly in P_1 and P_2 are $10 and $12, respectively. Both P_1 and P_2 produced 2,000 units of output.

(a) Ignoring fixed costs, set up the equations and solve the allocation problem, *recognizing the reciprocal relationships between S_1 and S_2.*

(b) If done correctly, you could then obtain the following solution: $S_1 = 6,818.18$ and $S_2 = 14,090.91$. As you will note, the total $(S_1 + S_2) = (6,818.18 + 14,090.91)$ exceeds the 14,000 variable costs incurred by S_1 and S_2. After adjusting for the "double accounting" problem, what are the adjusted amounts to be changed to P_1 and P_2? Show the solution as follows:

	P_1	P_2	Average cost per hour of service to P_1 and P_2
S_1 to:	_____	_____	_____
S_2 to:	_____	_____	_____
Total	_____	_____	_____

(c) Calculate the net contribution (that is, contribution after service department costs) of P_1 and P_2.

	P_1	P_2
Contribution over the department's variable costs	_____	_____
Less service department costs from B above	_____	_____
Net contribution	_____	_____

(d) Using the method in (b) above, the average variable cost per hour of service from S_1 would be 6.82; that for services received from S_2 would be 14.09. Suppose the production departments could buy (from outside firms) the same types of services as those provided by S_1 and S_2. The prices are PO_1 and PO_2 for S_1 and S_2 services, respectively. When should the production departments buy outside?

(e) Verify your answer above by constructing a linear program in which no service cost allocation is present.

*23. **Matrix Algebra Allocation: Multiple Choice**
A manufacturer's plant has two service departments (designated below as S_1 and S_2) and three production departments (designated below as P_1, P_2, and P_3) and wishes to allocate all factory overhead to production departments. The company makes the distribution of overhead from service departments to production departments on a reciprocal basis, recognizing the fact that services of one service department are utilized by another. Data regarding costs and allocation percentages are as follows:

Service Dept.	S_1	S_2	P_1	P_2	P_3
			Percentages to Be Allocated to Departments		
S_1	0%	10%	20%	40%	30%
S_2	20	0	50	10	20

Overhead to Be Allocated

$98,000	$117,600	$1,400,000	$2,100,000	$640,000

Matrix algebra is to be used in the allocation process. The amount of overhead to be allocated to the service departments is expressed in two simultaneous equations as follows:

$$S_1 = \$\,98{,}000 + .20S_2 \quad \text{or} \quad S_1 - .20S_2 = \$\,98{,}000$$
$$S_2 = \$117{,}600 + .10S_1 \quad \text{or} \quad S_2 - .10S_1 = \$117{,}600$$

(a) The system of simultaneous equations above may be stated in matrix form as follows:

(1)
$$\overset{A}{\begin{bmatrix} 1 & -.20 \\ -.10 & 1 \end{bmatrix}} \overset{S}{\begin{bmatrix} S_1 \\ S_2 \end{bmatrix}} = \overset{b}{\begin{bmatrix} 98{,}000 \\ 117{,}600 \end{bmatrix}}$$

(2)
$$\overset{A}{\begin{bmatrix} 1 & 98{,}000 & 1 \\ -.20 & 117{,}600 & -.10 \end{bmatrix}} \overset{S}{\begin{bmatrix} S_1 \\ S_2 \end{bmatrix}} = \overset{b}{\begin{bmatrix} 98{,}000 \\ 117{,}600 \end{bmatrix}}$$

(3)
$$\overset{A}{\begin{bmatrix} 1 & S_1 & 1 \\ -.20 & S_2 & -.10 \end{bmatrix}} \overset{S}{\begin{bmatrix} S_1 \\ S_2 \end{bmatrix}} = \overset{b}{\begin{bmatrix} 98{,}000 \\ 117{,}600 \end{bmatrix}}$$

(4)
$$\overset{A}{\begin{bmatrix} 1 & 1 & S_1 \\ -.20 & -.10 & S_2 \end{bmatrix}} \overset{S}{\begin{bmatrix} S_1 \\ S_2 \end{bmatrix}} = \overset{b}{\begin{bmatrix} 98{,}000 \\ 117{,}600 \end{bmatrix}}$$

(b) For the correct matrix A in (a), there exists a unique inverse matrix A^{-1}. Multiplication of the matrix A^{-1} by the matrix A produces
  (1) the matrix A.
  (2) another inverse matrix.
  (3) the correct solution to the system.
  (4) an identity matrix.

(c) Without being prejudiced by your previous answers, assume that the correct matrix form in (a) is

$$\begin{matrix} A & S & b \\ \begin{bmatrix} 1 & -.20 \\ -.10 & 1 \end{bmatrix} & \begin{bmatrix} S_1 \\ S_2 \end{bmatrix} = & \begin{bmatrix} 98,000 \\ 117,600 \end{bmatrix} \end{matrix}$$

Then the correct inverse matrix A^{-1} is

  (1) $\begin{bmatrix} 1/.98 & .20/.98 \\ .10/.98 & 1/.98 \end{bmatrix}$

  (2) $\begin{bmatrix} 1/.98 & 1/.98 \\ .20/.98 & .10/.98 \end{bmatrix}$

  (3) $\begin{bmatrix} 1/.30 & .20/.30 \\ .10/.30 & 1/.30 \end{bmatrix}$

  (4) $\begin{bmatrix} 1/.98 & -1/.98 \\ -.20/.98 & .10/.98 \end{bmatrix}$

(d) The total amount of overhead allocated to Department S_1 after receiving the allocation from Department S_2 is
  (1) $141,779.
  (2) $124,000.
  (3) $121,520.
  (4) $117,600.

(e) The total amount of overhead allocated to Department S_2 after receiving the allocation from Department S_1 is
  (1) $392,000.
  (2) $220,000.
  (3) $130,000.
  (4) $127,400.

(f) Without being prejudiced by your previous answers, assume that the answer to (d) is $100,000 and to (e), $150,000; then the total amount of overhead allocated to production Department P_1 would be
  (1) $1,508,104.
  (2) $1,495,000.
  (3) $1,489,800.
  (4) $108,104.

[AICPA adapted]

*24. **Allocation Decisions and Joint Cost Allocations**[9]

(a) Bierman advocates use of the (net) marginal revenue of each joint product as the basis for allocating joint costs in inventory valuation. His justification is simply that these values are the ones used in allocating the services of the joint process.

Using his illustration, assume that a process produces two products, X and Y, in equal proportions. For each unit of raw material R used in the process, the firm receives one unit each of Products X and Y. A unit of R costs $10; the joint variable costs of processing R are $5 per unit. Each unit of X and Y requires additional processing costs of $5 and $2, respectively.

Also assume the total revenue function for the firm can be expressed as follows:

$$TR_{x,y} = \frac{Q_x}{2}(50 - Q_x) + Q_y(25 - 2Q_y)$$

where Q_x and Q_y represent the quantity of each product sold. Accordingly, the profit function for the firm is

$$\pi_{x,y,r} = \frac{Q_x}{2}(50 - Q_x) + Q_y(25 - 2Q_y) - 15(Q_r) - 5(Q_x) - 2(Q_y)$$

The restriction on this firm is that Q_x (or Q_y) must not exceed Q_r.

The optimal solution to the firm's output problem may be found by differentiating the firm's profit function with respect to Q_x and Q_y, providing the restrictions above are observed. The latter can be taken into account by the use of Lagrangian multipliers.[10] That is, we first subtract the constraints $\lambda_1 (Q_x - Q_y - 0)$ and $\lambda_2 (Q_y - Q_r - 0)$ from the profit function and then take partial derivatives of π with respect to Q_x, Q_y, Q_r, λ_1, and λ_2 and set each equal to 0. We determine the values of Q_x, Q_y, Q_r, λ_1, and λ_2 that satisfy these equations and determine whether λ is nonnegative (≥ 0). If it is, the resulting solution is optimal. If $\lambda < 0$, we can ignore the respective constraint.

Hence:

$$\pi(Q_x, Q_y, Q_r, \lambda_1, \lambda_2) = \frac{Q_x}{2}(50 - Q_x) + Q_y(25 - 2Q_y)$$

$$- 15Q_r - 5Q_x - 2Q_y - \lambda_1(Q_x - Q_r) - \lambda_2(Q_y - Q_r)$$

---

[9] This problem is adapted from one illustrated in Harold Bierman, Jr., "Inventory Valuation: The Uses of Market Prices," *Accounting Rev.*, Oct. 1967.

[10] For a discussion of this approach, see Roman Weil, Jr., "Allocating Joint Costs," *American Economics Rev.*, Dec. 1968.

Solution

$$\frac{\partial \pi}{\partial Q_x} = 25 - Q_x - 5 - \lambda_1 = 0$$

$$\frac{\partial \pi}{\partial Q_y} = 25 - 4Q_y - 2 - \lambda_2 = 0$$

$$\frac{\partial \pi}{\partial Q_r} = -15 + \lambda_1 + \lambda_2 = 0$$

$$\frac{\partial \pi}{\partial \lambda_1} = -Q_x + Q_r = 0$$

$$\frac{\partial \pi}{\partial \lambda_2} = -Q_y + Q_r = 0$$

Since $Q_x = Q_r = Q_y$, we obtain the following solution:

$$Q_x = 5.6$$
$$Q_y = 5.6$$
$$Q_r = 5.6$$
$$\lambda_1 = 14.4$$
$$\lambda_2 = 0.6$$

The values $\lambda_1 = 14.4$ and $\lambda_2 = 0.6$ represent the opportunity costs of restricting the output of X and Y accordingly. For example, if Q_x is increased by 0.01 to 5.61, the net contribution from the output of X will increase from

$$\$25(5.6) - \$5(5.6) - \$(5.6)^2/2 = \$96.32$$

to

$$\$25(5.61) - \$5(5.61) - \$(5.61)^2/2 = \$96.464$$

This is an increase of $.144, which is approximately equal to $14.4(.01). Discuss the use of this technique for joint-product costing. What are the limitations of using opportunity costs in cost allocations? (Recall from Chapter 4 that opportunity costs are also available from linear programming solutions.)

(b) What would happen to your analysis if uncertainty were omitted?

*25. **Strategic Choice of Allocation Method***

Consider a firm with two production divisions and one service center. Each division must select labor quantity of "low" or "high," and capital quantity of "small" or "large." The capital is provided by a service center which has the following cost structure:

Division 1 Demand	Division 2 Demand	Service Center Cost
small	small	$100
small	large	150
large	small	150
large	large	400

Each division's net expected cash flow, exclusive of the service cost, is given by:

		DIVISION'S CHOICE	
Labor	Capital	Division 1	Division 2
low	small	$300	$ 300
low	large	500	600
high	small	600	400
high	large	700	1,800

Thus, if Division 1 uses *low* labor and *large* capital, its cash flow will be $500. If Division 2 uses *high* labor and *large* capital, its cash flow will be $1,800. The joint capital demand (large from each) will cost the service center $400, and the firm's net cash flow will be: $500 + 1,800 - 400 = $1,900. Before proceeding, you should verify that the maximal expected profit is $2,250. (Do this now.)

The task is to find an allocation that will allow us to separate Division 1 from Division 2. The difficulty is that the marginal cost of either division's service depends on the service demanded by the other. To see this more clearly, construct a table in which the *net realizable value* method is used to allocate the joint cost:

Division 1 Choice	Division 2 Choice	Service Cost	Division 1 Allocation	Division 2 Allocation
.	.	.	.	.
.	.	.	.	.
.	.	.	.	.

For example, if each division picks *low–small,* the service cost will be $100. The net realizable value allocation will then be $\left(\dfrac{300}{300 + 300}\right) 100 = 50$ to each division. (And in general the allocation method works in this simple setting by assigning the service center cost on the basis of the relative cash flow in each of the two divisions.)

Now, take your table (which should have 16 rows) and for each "Division 1 Choice" select as an allocation the *worst* of the allocations in the table that is consistent with the particular division's choice. This would be $215 for Division 1 if *it* selects high–large; $182 if *it* selects low–large; etc.) Once you have done this, verify that such a procedure allows you to myopically locate the optional firm-wide choice. In particular, for each choice by Division 1 you now have a cost allocation independent of the other's choice. Netting this against the division 1 expected cash flow should lead you to the optimal choice.

What is going on? (*Hint:* read the problem's title.) Give a thoughtful one-paragraph answer.

*26. *Cost Allocation Demands*

Our study of cost allocation has stressed the basic point that formulation of a precise reason for producing the cost allocation is a necessary precursor to understanding how the allocation should be accomplished (as well as used). And in this chapter, we have stressed the use of cost allocation in decomposing complex choice problems into smaller, presumably more manageable subproblems. Viewed in this manner, the cost allocations "couple" the decomposed subproblems. Other uses are, of course, possible; and it is the purpose of this final exercise to move your thinking in that direction.

Consider a simple organization context similar to that stressed in Chapter 5. Two managers are involved; each runs his own separate division. The two divisions are, in fact, totally separate. The two managers have, however, agreed to jointly share some service center, such as legal counsel, an internal accounting group, a computer facility, and so on. At present, each manager is evaluated on the basis of the accounting income of his respective division; any centrally incurred expenses (or revenues) are quite immaterial. Quite naturally, acquisition of the central shared facility will produce some cost datum. So we might envision three evaluation measures: income in the first division, income in the second division, and the cost of the shared facility. At this point, we must confront the question of allocating the cost of the shared facility between the two divisions.

The firm's accountant, a well known advocate of cost allocation, naturally insists that the allocation should be accomplished in some conventional manner. A local curmudgeon, on the other hand, asks why not base each manager's evaluation on his division income and the *total* of the shared facility. Suppose the local accountant is correct. Why might this be the case? Conversely, suppose the curmudgeon is correct. Why might this be the case? (This is somewhat subtle.)

10
Decentralization and Transfer Pricing

The purpose of this chapter is to examine the accounting problems encountered in the preparation of performance reports for decentralized segments of the firm. In many respects, this is but an application of the performance reporting techniques studied in earlier chapters. We seek to evaluate managerial performance as well as the performance of the division or segments themselves. On the other hand, the design of performance reporting systems for decentralized segments should not be viewed as entirely straightforward. This problem is, in fact, distinguished from our earlier study in two important respects. First, it is decidedly more *complex*. Evaluating a geographically removed manager who makes numerous investment as well as operating decisions is vastly more complex than evaluating a local manager who makes operating decisions only. Second, the problem also entails elements of *coordination*. Except in a pure conglomerate of several (or numerous) completely independent divisions, the various segments will be interdependent in one way or another. They may share some common resource, such as a large computing facility or centralized management of cash balances; or they may transfer products among themselves, as when one segment produces a semiconductor chip used as a subcomponent by a second segment, whose final product is marketed by a third segment. Either way, management faces the problem of coordinating the segments, and transfer prices are often involved here.

Initially, we explore some of the organization design issues that arise in such a setting. With this background we then organize the discussion of the performance reporting problems that arise out of decentralized operations around three distinct organizational settings:

(1) Limited decentralization, with one segment forced to transfer all of its outputs internally to another segment.

365

(2) Complete decentralization, with the segment dealing with outsiders only.

(3) Combinations of 1 and 2, where the segment may deal with insiders and outsiders.

Basic Issues

Perhaps the best way to enter this topic is to admit that our subject firm is "large" in two important respects. Decisions are implemented by a nontrivial number of managers; each manager knows something of importance that the others do not. We might, for example, have a large manufacturing facility coupled with regional marketing groups. The manufacturing manager has superior cost information, while each marketing manager has superior market information. This implies, of course, that any concerns over use of this manager-specific information must be addressed within a setting of productive uncertainty: Information is not an interesting subject in a world of certainty.

Bringing this information to bear on the decisions that lead to coordinated behavior among the managers in question is the basic issue to be resolved. This has important parallels with our earlier discussion of cost allocation in which a complex decision problem was decomposed into a series of smaller decision problems. Here, too, the firm's decision problem may be decomposed. But we face the added problem of factoring in the motivations of the various managers. Will they, for example, completely share their private information during the annual budget preparation? The phenomenon of organizational slack[1] suggests not. Thus, we must simultaneously worry about devising a coordination mechanism and a set of incentives for the managers that will motivate them to operate within the mechanism. This is, in fact, the topic of organization design.

One extreme organization design is *decentralization.* Here the important coordination decisions such as production and marketing schedules are delegated to the managers in possession of important information. Indeed, numerous motives are typically present here: Communication costs are minimized (both in terms of explicit costs as well as the time it takes to respond to the local environment), managers acquire important training by engaging in nontrivial decision-making activity, and managers enjoy important nonpecuniary returns associated with the exercise of decision-making authority. Of course, all large firms would be completely decentralized if this was the entire story. But decentralization is not costless. Despite the best incentive schemes available, managers may not make and implement the choices desired by central management or by the firm's shareholders. As discussed in Chapter

---

[1] See M. Schiff and A. Lewin, "The Impact of People on Budgets," *Accounting Rev.,* April 1970.

5, they may have differing tastes for risk–return trade-offs or differing preferences for nonpecuniary versus monetary returns. Moreover, decentralization does not imply that all information will be channeled into the managers' decisions. It may be too costly to engage in elaborate communication, even if the managers are well motivated.[2]

The other extreme form of organization design is complete *centralization*. Here central management makes all of the important coordination decisions. Each manager communicates private information to "center" and, in turn, implements center-chosen activities.[3] Here, center's tastes are paramount in the decision-making process. But the communication may be costly and cumbersome, implying that less than full communication will be engineered into the design. And we also must address the question of whether managers can be relied upon to honestly commmunicate and to implement the assigned decisions. In short, neither extreme approach to organization design is without its costs. We should expect to see actual designs somewhere in between, as well as dependent on the firm's particular circumstances.

It is also important to recognize that particular approaches to performance evaluation are not necessarily associated with particular approaches to organization design. In broad terms we might consider cost, profit, or investment centers for the evaluation of managers. Whether a manager should be evaluated in terms of cost, cost and revenue, or cost, revenue, and assets employed is often framed in terms of what variables are subject to the manager's control. But, as discussed at length in Chapter 5, controllability is a simplified approach to performance evaluation. The underlying question is the information content of the variable in question. For example, suppose the revenue variable tells center something about a manager's performance, either directly because revenue is influenced by the manager or indirectly because revenue is influenced by economic conditions to which the manager should be responding. In this case we would expect revenue to be used in the evaluation of that manager.

Thus, decentralization and profit centers are not necessarily coexistent; that is, one may exist without the other. Top management might make all critical decisions but evaluate a manager in terms of profit achieved given those decisions. Similarly, a manager might have considerable latitude in choice of production method so long as he meets a centrally determined production quota. In other words, the most desirable type of evaluation measure cannot be determined by knowing whether the segment manager has little or considerable discretion in managing the segment.

---

[2] A theory of organizational structure based on the economies of information processing has been developed by a number of authors. See K. Arrow, *Limits of Organization.* New York: Norton, 1974; S. Becker and G. Gordon, "An Entrepreneurial Theory of Formal Organization, Part I," *Administrative Science Quarterly,* Dec. 1966, esp. pp. 331–35; O. Williamson, *Markets and Hierarchies: Analysis and Antitrust Implications.* New York: The Free Press, 1975.

[3] This focus on "center" is convenient but begs the deep question of what the firm's goals should be. Without the appropriate, nearly pristine, market conditions, this is an open question.

Finally, we should reflect on the importance of transfer prices for a moment before proceeding. An accounting system will record physical movements across departments, segments, or divisions regardless of the organization design at hand. But the purpose of such recording depends critically upon this design. Under decentralization, the accounting price at which a marketing division is charged for transferred-in manufactured product may convey important cost information. Conversely, the price paid the manufacturing division may convey important demand information. With centralization, however, the accounting treatment conveys no such information and is probably more geared to the satisfaction of external reporting requirements (as we will discuss in Chapter 11). On the other hand, a more mixed approach based on intermanager negotiation will likely reflect risk-sharing dimensions.[4] Thus you should not expect to see transfer pricing arrangements that reflect any uniform policy across firms. Their nature will likely vary with the environment and with the specific approach to coordination that the firm adopts.[5]

Limited Decentralization with Internal Transfers

We begin with a simple firm that has very limited decentralized authority and then consider how the reporting process becomes more complicated as more decision authority is delegated to lower level managers. Initially, suppose the firm has two departments—a production department and a distribution department—and produces only one product. Units produced are transferred directly from the production department to the distribution department to be sold to outsiders.

To set the stage further, initially suppose that top management knows the cost structure in each department as well as the price in the output market. As an illustration, let the price in the output market be $P = \$1,000$ per unit, the total cost in the producing department be

$$C_p = \$6,000 + \$80q + \$4q^2$$

and the total cost in the distribution department be

$$C_d = \$4,000 + \$20q + q^2$$

---

[4] See C. Kanodia, "Risk Sharing Transfer Price Systems under Uncertainty," *J. of Accounting Research,* Spring 1979.

[5] Indeed, survey data suggest nontrivial use of variable cost, full cost, full cost plus a markup, market and negotiation approaches. See R. Vancil, *Decentralization: Management Ambiguity by Design.* Dow Jones-Irwin, Homewood, Ill.; 1979, or R. Tang, *Transfer Pricing Practices in the United States and Japan.* New York: Praeger, 1979.

FIGURE 10-1

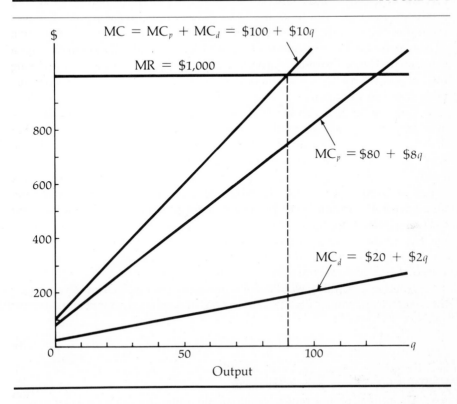

where q denotes total production (and sales). Further assume that no other costs or revenues are present and that top management wants to maximize the firm's profit. Quite clearly, the profit associated with q units is

$$\$1,000q - C_p - C_d = \$1,000q - \$10,000 - \$100q - \$5q^2$$

We locate the optimal output by setting marginal revenue equal to marginal cost:

$$MR = \$1,000 = MC = \$100 + \$10q$$

which implies an optimal output of $q^* = 90$ units and a maximum profit of $\$30,500$.[6] A graphical portrayal is presented in Figure 10–1.

In such a case, top management—knowing the firm's entire cost and

---

[6] More directly, we have $\max_q \pi = \$1,000q - \$10,000 - \$100q - 5q^2$, which provides a first order condition of $d\pi/dq = 0 = \$1,000 - \$100 - \$10q$ and a second order condition of $d^2\pi/dq^2 = -10 < 0$.

revenue structure—easily determines how many units of output should be produced and sold. The responsibilities of each department would therefore be limited to meeting the production and sales quotas, at the standard cost of production and at the standard cost of distribution and the standard selling price, respectively. There is, in other words, no economic advantage in allowing the department managers to influence or set the production and sales schedule under these assumptions.

The situation may change, however, if we assume the departmental managers have information that is not possessed by top management. Each manager may, for example, know the precise cost function in his department, while top management has only an imprecise fix on the respective cost structures. The problem is then one of collecting all of this information so that it can be used to determine the firm's optimal output and sales schedule. One possibility would be to have each manager convey his information to top management and then have top management determine the optimal schedule. For example, each manager might communicate his marginal cost and top management would then determine the optimal schedule by equating marginal cost and marginal revenue.

Another possibility would be a transfer pricing mechanism. The production department could offer to sell to the distribution department any quantity of products at its marginal cost. In turn, the distribution department could offer to purchase any quantity at marginal revenue less marginal distribution cost. This would allow each department to equate the *firm's* marginal cost and marginal revenue. In short, coordination of the departments would be accomplished with a price mechanism.

To appreciate this, return to our simple numerical example. Let T denote the price paid by the distribution department to the production department. Then the production department's local problem is

$$\text{Max } Tq - C_p = Tq - \$6{,}000 - \$80q - 4q^2 \qquad [10\text{-}1]$$

Setting the *department's* marginal revenue equal to its marginal cost, we obtain

$$\text{MR}_p = T = \text{MC}_p = \$80 + \$8q \qquad [10\text{-}2]$$

Similarly, the distribution department's local problem, recognizing the payment of Tq to the production department, is

$$\text{Max } \$1{,}000q - \$4{,}000 - \$20q - q^2 - Tq \qquad [10\text{-}3]$$

Setting this department's marginal revenue equal to its marginal cost, we obtain

$$\text{MR}_d = \$1{,}000 = \text{MC}_d + T = \$20 + \$2q + T \qquad [10\text{-}4]$$

Recall, now, that the optimal schedule is characterized by the *firm's* marginal revenue equaling the *firm's* marginal cost:

$$MR = \$1,000 = MC = \$100 + \$10q$$

Setting $T = \$800$ will allow the above mechanism to reproduce this result. (You should verify that with $T = \$800$ both departments select a quantity schedule of $q^* = 90$ units.)

This is, of course, no accident. Each department, in making its decision, should evaluate the decision from the firm's standpoint. The function of the transfer price T is to "price out" the secondary consequences of each department's decision. Consider the production department. The marginal cost of production is $\$80 + \$8q$. The marginal benefit to the firm is the marginal revenue less the marginal distribution cost: $\$1,000 - \$20 - \$2q$. We therefore establish a marginal revenue schedule *for the production department* of $\$1000 - \$20 - \$2q$. It equates its marginal cost with this (internal) marginal revenue:

$$(\$80 + \$8q) = \$1,000 - \$20 - \$2q$$

and selects $q = 90$, implying $T = \$1,000 - \$20 - \$2(90) = \$800$.

Similarly, the net marginal benefit of output distribution experienced by the distribution division is $\$1,000 - \$20 - \$2q$, while the secondary marginal cost to the firm is the marginal production cost of $\$80 + \$8q$. By transferring output to the distribution department at $T = \$80 + \$8q$, we again reproduce the firm-wide analysis:

$$\$1,000 = \$20 + \$2q + (\$80 + \$8q)$$

which implies $q^* = 90$ and $T = \$800$.

In sum, this is the basic argument in Hirshleifer's classic paper on transfer pricing.[7] We employ a pricing mechanism such that each department, seeking to maximize its local, departmental profit reproduces an evaluation of its decision that mirrors a firm-wide analysis. The merits of a price system have, in other words, been reproduced within the firm. And in the case of one department transferring all of its output to a second department, this procedure results in a transfer at the first department's marginal cost. Indeed, if you reflect on this, you will notice that a transfer based on anything other than marginal cost will distort the output decision in this case. (Why?)

Thus, with critical information dispersed among the managers, top management may solicit the information (as in a participative budgeting procedure) and make the output decision in a centralized fashion. Alternatively, it may decentralize the decision with an appropriate transfer-pricing mechanism. (Of

---

[7] J. Hirshleifer, "On the Economics of Transfer Pricing," *J. of Business*, July 1956.

course, other alternatives are also present, such as when, for cost reasons, only some of the information is solicited.)

If top management makes the choice, the production department is responsible for its production cost, while the distribution division is responsible for its distribution cost and the selling price. Both departments are also responsible for sending accurate estimates to top management. Alternatively, if the transfer-pricing arrangement is employed, both departments are responsible for their local, departmental profits.

Which extreme form is more desirable is a situation-specific issue. Suppose, to illustrate, that we further complicate the setting by considering a firm with a single production department that supplies two or more distribution departments. Further suppose the output of the production department consists of services, such as repairs and maintenance, computer processing, or planning and scheduling. From the firm's standpoint, the departments that use these services should continue to acquire them up to the point where the marginal cost of providing an additional unit of service exceeds the marginal benefit from the service. The individual managers can likely assess the benefits of these services better than top management. If the production department has sufficient capacity to satisfy the demand of all the departments that use its services, then the marginal cost of producing the service would consist of the marginal out-of-pocket costs of production. And employing a transfer-pricing arrangement in which the service is priced at marginal cost appears to be a straightforward solution here. Indeed, as a practical matter, the marginal cost can often be approximated by a standard (average) variable cost of producing the service. Assuming that the production department operates within a fairly constant output range, the standard variable costs of production could serve as the transfer price in this type of situation. (Recall our interdepartmental cost allocation discussion in Chapter 9.)

Centralizing the service decision, on the other hand, would necessitate that each consuming department inform top management of the marginal benefit provided by the service in the department. Top management, in turn, would determine the optimal service consumption for each department and communicate the resulting schedule.

Now consider the effect of introducing a constraint on the capacity of the production department. For example, suppose a number of departments desire the services of the production department and the total demand for services exceeds the short-run supply. The cost of providing services to any one department will now exceed the production department's marginal costs by the amount of the opportunity costs incurred whenever other departments cannot obtain the services they desire. The firm would wish to allocate the services of the production department on the basis of the highest net returns—benefits less out-of-pocket and opportunity costs. But the net returns would depend on the relative values attached to the services by the different demanding departments. Top management, then, might solicit information regarding benefits from each of the consuming departments and then make the allocation (with the same programing model discussed in Chapter 4). Alternatively, it might implement a transfer-pricing arrangement by allowing the managers to work within a system of negotiation and bidding or by prescribing a specific pricing rule such as some measure of cost. Whether the involved communication associated with the centralization approach is more or less costly than the departmental time and effort associated with the latter two approaches is problematic. Compare this with the no-constraint case, in which the marginal production cost is generally well known and a variable-cost transfer policy is easy to establish, relative to communication and centralized choice of each department's allocation.

The point, then, is that a transfer price policy may or may not be a critical part of a well-thought-out approach to organization design. But the student should also recognize that we have analyzed the most simple setting and touched on only the more obvious organization cost questions. To appreciate this point, notice that the above pricing arrangement of transferring at marginal cost presumes a goal of profit maximization as well as knowledge of the marginal cost. Suppose uncertainty is present, and the marginal cost or marginal revenue cannot be determined. Setting the optimal production schedule must therefore be attentive to risk–return trade-offs. The pricing arrangement becomes decidedly more complex here,[8] and the firm may employ a crude cost-plus arrangement instead of a complex, difficult-to-administer pricing arrangement.[9] Moreover, the above discussion has presented a set of rules that will lead to profit maximization but has not addressed the incentives of the department managers to follow these rules. If top management makes the choice, relying on department managers to communicate cost and/or demand information, the procedure is vulnerable to gaming by the department managers. Cost standards may be set too high, or sales quotas set too low, because top management is unlikely to have any reliable method of auditing the managers' forecasts.[10] Similar comments apply to the transfer-pricing arrangement. It may be in the department manager's self-interest to distort, say, his alleged marginal cost in order to ensure a more favorable price. Moreover, the rules sketched above require the participants to ignore their influence on the transfer price. Yet, for example, the production manager could behave as a monopolist by recognizing that his production quantity affects the transfer price. This would increase the production department's profit, but would decrease the firm's profit.

Finally, the entire analysis is based on the assumption that the manager

---

[8] Kanodia, "Risk Sharing Transfer Price Systems under Uncertainty."

[9] This appears to be the case in cost-plus contracting. See J. Demski and G. Feltham, *Cost Determination: A Conceptual Approach.* Ames, Iowa: Iowa State University Press, 1976, particularly Ch. 8.

[10] This problem has been dealt with using the terminology of creating "slack" in a budget. See, for example, Schiff and Lewin, "The Impact of People on Budgets."

will maximize his evaluation measure, or under uncertainty, his behavior will depend on the uncertainty manifest in the evaluation measure. But existence of nonpecuniary returns (such as good colleagues and leisure) clouds this relationship.

Both schemes, then, are vulnerable on incentive grounds. However, it is possible in limited circumstances to construct incentive structures such that it is always in the manager's self-interest to communicate honestly in the centralized case or follow the pricing rules in the transfer-pricing case. But these are specialized circumstances, and we conclude that most organizational arrangements are vulnerable at some point on this score.[11]

The picture that emerges, in other words, is that the proper or best reporting system is both tied to the organization design at hand and quite difficult to sort out. Moving to the opposite extreme, in which the segments are fully independent and autonomous, reveals yet another dimension to the reporting design problem. In this case each segment is akin to a separate firm and the reporting question therefore takes on the usual aspects of (external) financial reporting in general. The only difference is that regulatory considerations are irrelevant, except in terms of honoring these requirements in the firm's financial reports. For example, compliance with the Foreign Corrupt Practices Act is likely to influence the firm's internal reporting.[12]

Complete Decentralization

To explore this case, we now assume the firm is organized as a pure conglomerate. The firm consists of several divisions. Each is managed by a relatively autonomous manager who makes operating and investment decisions. And the various divisions are independent: No services are shared, no interdivisional transfers occur, and the cost and revenue structures of each division are totally unaffected by decisions in the other segments of the firm. This

---

[11] The precise vulnerability is difficult to pin down. Under very specialized conditions under which the managers seek to maximize their divisional profit measures, honest reporting and full use of the information may be possible. See M. Loeb and W. Magot, "Soviet Success Indicators and the Evaluation of Divisional Management," *J. of Accounting Research*, Spring 1978, or J. Ronen and G. McKinney, "Transfer Pricing for Divisional Autonomy," *J. of Accounting Research*, Spring 1970. A closer look at these ideas is available in J. Green and J. Laffont, *Incentives in Public Decision-Making*. New York: North-Holland, 1979.

But under less stringent circumstances, honest communication may be inconsistent with full use of the information. Plea bargaining is a ready example. See R. Myerson, "Incentive Compatibility and the Bargaining Problem," *Econometrica*, Jan. 1979.

Finally, careful selection and socialization may considerably dampen these noncooperative tendencies. See W. Ouchi, "A Conceptual Framework for the Design of Organizational Control Mechanisms," *Management Science*, Sept. 1979.

[12] The Foreign Concept Practices Act of 1977 requires that a firm whose securities are registered with the SEC install and maintain a system of internal accounting control in order to maintain the integrity of the accounting records.

is, of course, an extreme idealization, but it is useful for the exploration at hand.

In particular, such a setting illustrates a set of evaluation difficulties. The managers will be evaluated as a basis for ensuring proper motivation in managing their divisions. Also, top management is likely to periodically evaluate its investment in the divisions and its choice of managers. In designing a system to accomplish these objectives, the evaluation principles discussed in conjunction with responsibility centers continue to apply. But the resultant techniques differ. In particular, top management cannot rely on conventional standard cost systems for such divisions because they would then have to decide on the types, amounts, and combinations of the inputs needed for each division. The level of detail would be overwhelming. We have already admitted that top management is not able to make operating decisions for its divisions as efficiently as the divisional managers; otherwise there would be little economic motivation for completely decentralizing the firm's operations. Instead of trying to evaluate individual operating and investment decisions of the divisions, top management must shift its evaluation to more global measures of performance, such as the net profit earned by divisions compared against their asset holdings or major line items in a budget.

The importance of this point must be stressed. The information cost assumptions that are consistent with decentralization are inconsistent with the application of minutely detailed standard cost principles. As a result, a substantively more aggregate, less refined evaluation mechanism is employed here. Actual decentralized reporting practices are often maligned in academic circles, where it is argued that the resulting evaluations are inconsistent with good decision making. But a cost- and value-of-information perspective recognizes the extant procedures as a first-stage reporting mechanism. Specialized, more costly studies are available if the "preliminary" data warrant their production. This is, of course, consistent with the value-of-information discussion in Chapter 1.

In any event, design of the divisional reporting systems that will adequately support a decentralized organization is a difficult task. The manager has investment and operating responsibility, and top management is also interested in evaluating the division apart from its manager.[13] Though both objectives warrant separate evaluation measures, we typically observe a single evaluation mechanism being employed, which is consistent with costly information production. The common element is, of course, investment. If this is linked to an analysis of investment decisions, it is only natural to expect the reporting to reflect a return-on-investment orientation. But even admitting such an orientation, the reporting alternatives remain bewildering in number.

---

[13] Evaluating a division per se is easiest in this case, because the divisions are largely independent. Abandoning a division in our "forced" transfer setting in the previous section would liquidate the firm.

Measurement Problems in Rate-of-Return Calculations

As any student of financial reporting is aware, measurement of income and assets opens a Pandora's box of measurement questions. Inventory measurement is a ready example. If our decentralized division does not use standard costs to control its own operations, then it must make assumptions about the proper valuation of inventories. Prices of materials will likely fluctuate across purchases, and the accountant must determine the prices to be assigned to materials put into work-in-process and to materials still in inventory. (This is the familiar inventory problem of LIFO versus FIFO versus weighted average.) The accountant faces a similar problem in assigning values to finished goods inventory, assuming that the total costs of manufacturing vary over batches of finished goods transferred from work-in-process. (Alternatively, use of a standard cost system raises the issue of how to dispose of the resulting variances.)

Profit is measured as revenues realized during a period less cost of sales, less selling and administrative expenses. Cost of sales, recall, includes the costs of raw materials, direct labor, and variable and perhaps fixed overhead. We have already briefly commented on the problems involved in deciding how and whether to allocate fixed overhead to products and will address this question again in Chapter 11. But consider another accounting issue associated with fixed overhead: the amount of depreciation of plant and equipment to be charged during the period. Depreciation methods are generally thought to rely on assumptions about the pattern of benefits obtained from fixed assets, including estimated holding periods and estimates of end-of-life salvage values. Much literature has appeared concerning the "proper" depreciation method for long-lived assets. In general, the belief is that depreciation should reflect the decline in the discounted value of the net receipts attributable to the asset,[14] assuming, of course, the requisite assumptions to justify a discounting procedure are present. (Refer to our discussion in Chapter 14.) In practice, these assumptions are unlikely to be met, and traditional straight-line or accelerated depreciation models are chosen on largely subjective grounds.[15]

Finally, the profit figure reported by a division will be influenced by the method of accounting used to record such expenditures as advertising, research and development, and major repairs. If these expenditure items are not first recorded as assets and then depreciated in a systematic way (another

---

[14] In effect, we would use capital budgeting techniques to assign a value to the asset at different points in time—say, at the time of purchase and each subsequent year. Depreciation would be the decline in the value of the asset from year to year. One of the earliest proponents of the discounted method of analysis of depreciation is H. Anton; see his "Depreciation, Cost Allocation and Investment Decisions," *Accounting Research,* April 1956.

[15] The surrogate approach is recommended by I. Reynolds, "Selecting the Proper Depreciation Method," *Accounting Rev.,* April 1961. The approach is illustrated in Problem 34 at the end of this chapter.

depreciation problem), a divisional manager may be able to influence his reported profit from one period to the next arbitrarily through timing of expenditures. For example, he can show a higher profit in any one period by cutting back on such expenditures. Of course, in the process he forgoes the benefits of these "assets," but he may be willing to do so in a current period, hoping to make up for it in a subsequent period of higher revenues.

Return on Investment versus Residual Income

Granting agreement on the measurement of the decentralized division's income and assets, we next address their relationship. One approach is to focus on a rate of return or ROI calculation: income ÷ assets. Another is to focus on a residual income calculation: income less (required rate of return) × assets.[16] Both are simple enough and are, in fact, derivatives of competing approaches to analyzing investment decisions. ROI is linked to an internal rate of return model, while residual income is linked to a present value model. Both models are discussed at length in Chapter 14. The important point to understand here is that full knowledge of their parentage does not resolve the issue of which is a superior accounting technique. The reason is straightforward. As we discuss in Chapter 14, present value analysis is normatively correct in a world of perfect markets and certainty. Moreover, it is fairly easy to provide examples where the internal rate of return and present value models conflict. Case closed? Not quite, because such an ideal world of certainty and perfect markets exists only in the economics literature. Hence, in the world of application we do not know which model is superior. We do not, in a world of uncertainty and less than perfect markets, have a completely defensible normative model of how the firm should make investment decisions. Hence we cannot distinguish between ROI and residual income on the basis of appeal to a normative model of firm behavior.[17]

Price-Level Changes

Another question concerning these calculations is whether the investment base and subsequent cost allocations should be adjusted for changes in general and/or specific price levels.[18] The case for recognition of specific price changes is put forth by the advocates of replacement cost or exit value reporting systems. The replacement cost is designed to reflect the current price of equiva-

---

[16] The former is more popular. See J. Reece and W. Cool, "Measuring Investment Center Performance," *Harvard Business Rev.,* May–June 1978.

[17] Further note that the question of an appropriate rate of return must also be addressed. Risk adjustment is one consideration; price level changes is another.

[18] Recall that with our firm consisting of several independent (sub) firms, divisional reporting becomes almost indistinguishable from financial reporting. Price-level recognition is an excellent example. See R. Vancil and R. Weil, *Replacement Cost Accounting: Readings on Concepts, Uses and Methods.* Glen Ridge, N.J.: Horton and Daughters, 1976.

lent capacity (such as the current price of the same used automobile in terms of age, mileage, maintenance history, and so on). The exit value is designed to reflect the current price for which the asset could be sold. Of course, if perfect asset markets existed, the two prices would be identical and known to all parties.

In general terms, recognition of price changes in the firm's products and factors of production is critical to the firm's success, and it is on this score that these proposals appear to draw their favor. For example, in comparing divisional performances, top management must be aware of the possibility that one division may report a higher rate of return or residual income than another simply because its assets were purchased in prior periods, when the prices were substantially lower. Similarly, the evaluation of the division managers ought to be sensitive to the manager's response to changing specific prices of the division's product and factors of production.

But whether replacement or exit value reporting is a good answer to the evaluation problems associated with changing prices is problematic. The precise manner in which either measure would or should be used in the evaluation process if unclear. This is in part due to the fact that such measures are difficult to produce. Prices change for a variety of reasons, including technological change. New assets are rarely exact equivalents of old assets; and without an active second-hand market, the approximation of the current value (replacement or exit) becomes difficult. And whether managers should be responsible for price changes also poses a difficult question. Managers are generally not responsible for the price changes, but at the same time, top management wants to motivate them to respond to these changes as well as to probable future changes.[19]

It is also important to recognize that formal incorporation in the accounting procedures is but one approach to recognition of changing prices. The use of budgets is another. Evaluation relative to a budget based on historical cost procedures (perhaps supplemented) can be accomplished in a way that is sensitive to price changes. Thus, it is not essential that a firm adopt some form of explicit current value accounting for its evaluation system to be cognizant of changing prices.[20]

Finally, a separate issue here is whether recognition should be given to changes in general prices. Given that the firm deals in markets for its specific factors and products, the usefulness of general price level adjustments in evaluating its divisions and managers is difficult to pin down. The usual argument is that time series comparisons are facilitated if general movements in the price level are removed from the comparison.

---

[19] See R. Magee, "Accounting Measurement and Employment Contracts: Current Value Reporting," *Bell J. of Economics,* Spring 1978.

[20] This is discussed in C. Horngren, "Budgets, Respect, and Inflation," *J. of Accountancy,* March 1980.

Further note that when dealing with general versus specific price changes, it is important to distinguish between anticipated and unanticipated changes. For example, if the real rate of return is 6 percent and an 8 percent inflation rate is expected, the nominal rate of return will be $(1.06)(1.08) - 1 = 14.5\%$. Historical procedures will reveal a 14.5 percent return here, and one can readily adjust this to a real return by knowing the anticipated inflation rate: $1.145 \div 1.08 - 1 = 6\%$. But price level adjusting the historical depreciation actually double counts the price level effect, because it has already been anticipated.[21]

In any event, there is no such thing as a *true* accounting income of a firm or division. The rate of return or residual income calculations are, at best, benchmarks for evaluation; neither is a complete standard of evaluation.

Internal and External Transactions

We now turn to the case in which producing and demanding segments can deal both with each other and with outsiders. One extreme approach here is to have no transactions with outsiders; the other extreme is to decouple the segments by dealing only with outsiders. Both situations have been discussed, and the case at hand is actually a blending of these extremes.

In particular, transfer prices are again one possible approach to coordination of the activities of the various segments. In an ideal setting, the prices should drive each manager, looking only at his segment's evaluation measure, to make decisions that are optimal from top management's perspective. And if the segment managers possess superior information, transferring this information to top management and allowing top management to make the critical decisions is an alternative organization design strategy.

To keep the discussion within bounds, we again consider a production and a distribution division, as in our earlier discussion of transfer pricing. The added dimension is that an external market exists for the production division's output. Thus, this division may sell in the outside market or to the distribution division. And the distribution division may purchase its product requirements from the production division or from outside sources. Suppose that this intermediate market is perfect: Unlimited quantities can be bought and sold at a known, constant price per unit. Establishing a transfer price (assuming no transactions costs) at any amount other than this price in the intermediate market would then be questionable. The distribution division will purchase from the production division if and only if the transfer price is no greater than the market price. And the production division will

[21] See H. Bierman, "Discounted Cash Flows, Price Level Adjustments and Expectations," *Accounting Rev.*, Oct. 1971; and W. Beaver, "Accounting for Inflation in an Efficient Market," contained in a 1979 supplement to the *International J. of Accounting* entitled *The Impact of Inflation on Accounting: A Global View*.

FIGURE 10-2

Demand and marginal revenue curves for the production division.

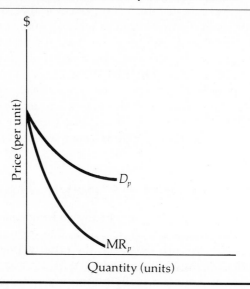

Quantity (units)

sell to the marketing division if and only if the transfer price is at least as high as the intermediate market price.[22]

Alternatively, suppose the intermediate market is imperfect. Transaction costs may be present,[23] or the market price may depend on the quantity. With imperfect competition, the optimal solution from the perspective of the profit-maximizing firm is to act in the manner of a classical discriminating monopolist. Taking the extreme case of imperfect intermediate and final markets, we briefly review Hirshleifer's classic analysis.[24] Three of his graphs, with slight modifications, are shown here. Figure 10-2 illustrates the demand and marginal revenue curves for units sold by the production division to outside firms. Figure 10-3 illustrates how the marginal revenue curve (MR_d) and the marginal cost curve (MC_d) for the distribution division are used to derive its net marginal revenue curve (nMR). The nMR curve is the difference between the marginal revenue curve and the marginal distribution cost curve. Figure 10-4 consolidates the information from Figures 10-2 and 10-3 and illustrates the three points of equilibrium. The equilibrium for the firm occurs at the point where the total marginal revenue curve ($MR_t = MR_p + nMR$)

---

[22] Note that with a perfect intermediate market, top management is totally indifferent toward transactions between the two departments. Hence the actual transfer price is irrelevant so long as both managers have complete freedom to operate in the intermediate market.

[23] See J. Gould, "Pricing in Firms When There Are Costs of Using an Outside Market," *J. of Business,* Jan. 1964.

[24] J. Hirshleifer, "On the Economics of Transfer Pricing."

FIGURE 10-3

Derivation of the distribution division's net marginal revenue curve.

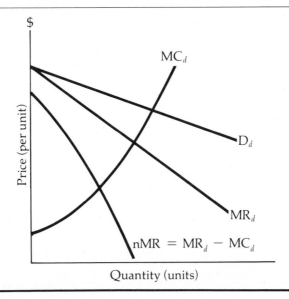

intersects the marginal cost of production curve (MC_p). This gives a price
of A, which also becomes the transfer price. Units will be sold to outside
firms as long as the marginal revenue from outside sales is greater than the
price A. According to Figure 10-4, the total quantity sold to outside firms
is measured by the distance OM on the horizontal axis, since this is the
output at which the marginal revenue from outside sales MR_p is equal to
the transfer price A. (Note that a higher price, B, is charged externally.) Prior
to that point the production division can sell its output externally for a marginal revenue higher than A. Similarly, the distribution division will purchase
units from the production division up to the point where the net marginal
revenue from the sale of the product is equal to the cost of the product, or
the price A. This is represented by the distance OD on the horizontal axis.
The total output of the firm is measured by the distance OR and is equal
to $OM + OD$.

These graphs are meant to illustrate the nature of the profit-maximizing
solution as well as reinforce our earlier discussion of the importance of information processing. If top management knows the demand and cost structure
in each division and market, it surely is capable of setting the production
schedules. But if it has only a vague idea, while the local managers have
superior information, the coordination problem is one of bringing this dispersed information to bear on the decision at hand. Top management may
then centralize the decision and rely on its managers to transfer their information. Alternatively, it may decentralize by encouraging free-form negotiation

FIGURE 10-4 _____

Equilibrium conditions for production and distribution divisions.

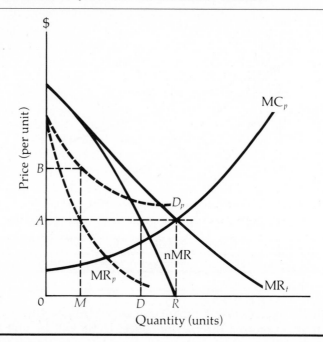

between the two department managers or by structuring their interactions with an appropriate pricing policy. Each solution, observe, is akin to a type of solution employed by society in general for controlling external effects. Centralization is the same as the use of quantity controls, such as air pollution standards. Reliance on negotiation is akin to merger, as when two neighbors jointly build a fence separating their yards; the transfer price arrangement is similar to the use of taxes and subsidies, as in the taxation of alcoholic beverages. In short, the use of transfer prices is but one approach to coordinating segments in the firm. No approach is perfect, and each raises incentive difficulties. We therefore expect to see different approaches used in different circumstances, as well as mixtures of the various approaches used within a single firm.

Two additional complications should be mentioned. First, the analysis of the optimal pricing arrangement portrayed in the previous graphs assumes that once the available information is collected, the firm is operating in a world of certainty. If uncertainty prevails, the proper attitude toward risk becomes an added dimension in the analysis. Recall, for example, that while a transfer price policy based on actual cost plus some predetermined profit is difficult to rationalize in the context just discussed, it does have risk-sharing implications that may be critical in obtaining the desired degree of risk-taking behavior on the part of the managers.[25]

Second, evaluation of the segments also becomes more complicated in this setting. If the firm is a conglomerate, each segment stands alone and the evaluation problem has strong parallels with financial reporting. Similarly, if no intermediate market is present, the segments are actually a unit, and separating them for evaluation purposes makes little sense since one cannot exist without the other. But in the mixed case at hand, unless the intermediate market is perfect, the segments are interdependent. Attempts to evaluate them separately, therefore, give rise to familiar allocation difficulties.

Most firms, for example, maintain centralized control of cash. How, then, is working capital to be associated with each division? Presumably, economies of scale in cash management result in the central cash pool being less than the total would be were cash decentralized. The same difficulty arises with any shared assets or liabilities in the firm. Identification of income provides a similar pattern. If we relax the pure conglomerate assumption, jointly produced revenues or jointly incurred costs raise all too familiar problems of precisely identifying a division's share. The fixed cost of any common service is an obvious example.[26]

Accounting Implications of Transfer Prices

The transfer price problem generally involves issues in organization design and economics. However, the topic is important to the accountant, since he or she is responsible for providing performance reports for the different segments of the firm. Indeed, the standard cost of a unit of output in a centralized firm may be viewed as a transfer price of the unit as it proceeds from one department to another. This accounting price represents what the cost of the unit will be to each succeeding department. The difference between the price of entry (the standard cost of input) and the price of exit (the standard

---

[25] Further observe that a cost-plus arrangement is a form of insurance. While this may be desirable, it also may lessen cost control incentives. Once again, perfect solutions are in the realm of fiction. See J. Demski and G. Feltham, "Economic Incentives in Budgetary Control Systems," *Accounting Rev.*, April 1978.

[26] Other aspects of this problem can be found in W.J. Vatter, "Does the Rate of Return Measure Business Efficiency?" *N.A.A. Bull.*, Jan. 1959; J. Dearden, "The Case Against ROI Control," *Harvard Business Rev.*, May–June 1967; and J. Ronen and G. McKinney, "Transfer Pricing for Divisional Autonomy," *J. of Accounting Research*, Spring 1970. Further observe that game theoretic ideas have been advanced here. See M. Shubik, "Incentives, Decentralized Control, the Assignment of Joint Costs and Transfer Pricing," *Management Science*, April 1962, and A. Roth and R. Verrecchia, "The Shapley Value as Applied to Cost Allocation: A Re-Interpretation," *J. of Accounting Research*, Spring 1979.

cost of output) may be viewed as a measure of the value added within each department. A comparison of this measure with the costs incurred by the department may be used as the basis for evaluating the department's efficiency.

No matter what transfer price is used, the accountant should always attempt to determine whether the price is consistent with the objectives of decentralization. The price should encourage divisional or departmental managers to make decisions that are optimal from the perspective of the firm as a whole. This perspective can be used to assess the conditions under which different prices—variable cost per unit, full cost per unit, market price, and so on—can be expected to function well in a decentralization environment.

We do not offer a precise principle, such as transfer at outlay plus opportunity cost. One reason is that such prescription seems too simplistic; a second reason is its problematic nature under uncertainty. Here risk may be important, and we must recognize the risk-taking attitudes of the managers. Under typical conditions, the notion of opportunity cost becomes vague because the managers may be placed in a risky position. Foregone use of the productive capacity is not, then, likely to be viewed with any degree of unanimity among the individuals involved. The net result is a manager-specific assessment. A third reason for not presenting a more precise principle concerns private information. The very definition of the best foregone use must be sensitive to the information at hand. For example, in a basically noncooperative setting, central management may commit itself to underutilizing manager-specific information as part of the scheme to ensure honest communication. Cost budgets may not be automatically revised when the manager reports on improved production methods, or a profit budget need not be automatically revised when a new market is developed. Best use, in other words, is a terribly subtle issue.

With this in mind, recall that if a production department supplies one distribution department with a single output, with no outside market and under conditions of certainty, use of the marginal cost of production as the transfer price will lead to profit maximization (unless the scheme is "gamed"). Within certain output ranges, the variable cost per unit is a good approximation of the marginal cost of production. In these cases the transfer price for interdepartmental transfers could be set at the standard variable cost per unit. However, it is difficult in this setting to specify normal operating conditions under which full cost or "full cost plus" per unit is a suitable basis for the transfer price. This condition might, however, be encountered in multiproduct firms under uncertainty, where the cost of producing one type of output must include the well-defined opportunity cost of not producing another type. Similarly, risk considerations may dictate such an approach.

As indicated earlier, market prices are important in setting transfer prices whenever the buying and selling divisions have the alternative of dealing with outside firms. If the outside markets are reasonably competitive, the observed market price of the unit being transferred is a reasonable transfer price.

Negotiated prices have been considered as a basis for transfer prices primarily when market prices do not exist for units transferred. Negotiation, presumably, relies on those who are most informed to set the production-sales schedules and to divide the resulting profit. This is somewhat akin to merging the divisions and, therefore, raises the issue of whether the transaction cost of the negotiation itself will be excessive. For example, some firms have resorted to internal "courts" to settle negotiation disputes. An added concern is the behavioral dimension in negotiation and the fear that more "skillful" negotiators distort the solution to their advantage and the firm's disadvantage. Nevertheless, negotiation may be the superior alternative in situations involving demand and supply interdependencies.[27]

Our discussion seems to suggest that a transfer pricing system works best when central management is well informed or when the production department has the alternative of selling its output in a competitive market. Otherwise, complications arise that make it difficult to define the optimal decisions of divisional heads as measured in terms of the firm's overall profit. In other words, it is difficult to specify an internal pricing policy when the center is poorly informed, when complex interactions between divisions exist, or when these divisions operate in less than perfectly competitive markets. Under such conditions, top management must balance any information economies it may achieve against the losses incurred because decision heads must base their decisions on less than optimal transfer prices. If internal transactions are an insignificant percentage of the total transactions of divisions, then top management may be willing to rely on the imperfect transfer pricing system rather than involving itself in internal disputes, even though analytically optimal decisions will not always result. (Note again the implied cost-benefit analysis.) If the opposite condition exists, top management may wish to centralize internal divisional transactions to reduce the cost of dysfunctional decisions, assuming appropriate communication incentives. Indeed, we would expect to see a mixed approach, categorizing the transfers in this or a similar manner.

Legal Considerations

The firm may be required to allocate costs to products and functions in order to justify prices quoted to government units for work performed under government contracts (such as in federal procurement or in the medical industry). A similar situation develops when transfer prices are used as the basis for tax computations for divisions located in different states or countries. In general, the firm would prefer to report a low profit for a division that operates in a relatively high tax locality, while the government in the high tax locality

---

[27] See D. Watson and J. Baumler, "Transfer Pricing: A Behavioral Context," *Accounting Rev.*, April 1975, and Roth and Verrecchia, "The Shapley Value as Applied to Cost Allocation."

would prefer just the opposite. If an impasse arises, the courts may have to establish an appropriate transfer price—just as we see top management adjudicating transfer price disputes for management control purposes.

The tax issue centers, of course, on acceptable cost allocation techniques.[28] Here the parallel with cost plus contracting should be noted. A government unit is willing to accept as a price its share of the total cost incurred by a firm in working on a government product plus some fee. This has led to a number of controversies regarding what costs are appropriate for inclusion in the base and what the government unit's proper share of this cost base is. As a result, the Cost Accounting Standards Board was created and given the responsibility for defining appropriate accounting procedures in this area.[29]

A Comment on Linear Programing

A linear programing model of the firm's activities represents a system of interdependencies among a set of outputs and their demands for resources. We might even imagine that the set of outputs represents a group of decentralized distribution divisions that are competing for a set of resources in short supply. If this were the case, the firm might wish to use the shadow prices as transfer prices.

To illustrate, consider the simple problem of

$$\text{Maximize} \quad z = \$3x_1 + \$3x_2$$

$$\text{subject to} \quad 2x_1 + 4x_2 \leq 6 = b_1$$
$$5x_1 + 3x_2 \leq 8 = b_2$$

which has a solution of $x_1 = x_2 = 1$, along with dual variables or shadow prices of \$3/7 for each constraint.

We note that it takes 2 units of b_1 and 5 units of b_2 to produce 1 unit of output of x_1. The contribution margin of x_1 is \$3. If we charged \$3/7 for each required unit of b_1 and b_2, it would cost $2(\$3/7) + 5(\$3/7) = \$21/7 = \$3$ to produce a unit of x_1. Similarly, it would cost $4(\$3/7) + 3(\$3/7) = \$21/7 = \$3$ to produce a unit of x_2. In other words, the charge for resources

---

[28] For example, Section 482 of the Internal Revenue Code allows the government to allocate costs among divisions so as to reflect their "true taxable income." See I. Sharau, "Transfer Pricing—Diversity of Goals and Practices," *J. of Accountancy*, April 1974; and S. Davidson and R. Weil, eds. *Handbook of Cost Accounting*. New York: McGraw Hill, 1978, Ch. 23, "Tax Considerations in Cost Accounting."

[29] The background for the Board's formation and the problems facing it are outlined in *Report on the Feasibility of Applying Uniform Cost-Accounting Standards to Negotiated Defense Contracts*. Washington, D.C.: GPO, 1970. The eventual list of regulations covers such diverse items as home office expense, interest expense, use of standard costs, and deferred compensation.

equals the contribution margin for each of the products that should be produced.

Suppose a divisional manager must decide which products to finish for distribution. He knows the contribution margin of each, and the charge for scarce resources is calculated in the manner illustrated above. This manager should produce any output whose contribution margin covers the charge for scarce resources, that is, breaks even. Thus, he has sufficient information to determine which products he should finish and which he should not. In this respect, shadow prices of the scarce resources serve as transfer prices that can yield an optimal allocation of a firm's scarce resources.

Our problem is trivial in the sense that we are dealing with only two types of output, x_1 and x_2. However, it is sufficient to illustrate the major problem inherent in the use of shadow prices as a basis for transfer-pricing solutions. The prices of $3/7 for each unit of scarce resources tell the divisional manager only which units of output should be produced; they do not indicate how much of each is called for in the optimal solution. The solution is $x_1 = x_2 = 1$, but the divisional manager has no information concerning these amounts.

Thus, the prices themselves—even if known—cannot be relied upon to coordinate the divisions. More information is required. One alternative is use of *nonlinear* price schedules. Otherwise we conclude that the use of linear programing models within a firm suggests a movement away from decentralization toward more centralization.[30]

Conclusion

The topic of decentralization and transfer pricing is too complex to be exhausted in one chapter. Indeed, entire books have been devoted to it.[31] We have tried to summarize the relationship between organization design and accounting performance reports. Many of the difficulties encountered by the accountant in providing useful, cost-effective data for evaluating department and division managers stem from the numerous interactions among responsibility heads. That is, with a pure conglomerate the reporting question is similar to financial reporting in general. But with interdependencies among the segments, the reporting question becomes more complex. And the type of reporting appears to depend critically on the organization structure at hand.

---

[30] See G.B. Dantzig and P. Wolfe, "Decomposition Principle for Linear Programs," *Operations Research,* Jan.–Feb. 1960, and N. Dopuch and D. Drake, "Accounting Implications of a Mathematical Programming Approach to the Transfer Price Problem," *J. of Accounting Research,* Spring 1964.

[31] D. Solomons, *Divisional Performance: Measurement and Control.* New York: Financial Executives Research Foundation, 1965, and R. Vancil. *Decentralization.*

Supplementary Readings

Articles

Abdel-Khalik, A. R., and E. Lusk, "Transfer Pricing—A Synthesis," *Accounting Rev.,* Jan. 1974.

Arrow, K., "Control in Large Organizations," *Management Science,* April 1964.

Dearden, J., "The Case Against ROI Control," *Harvard Business Rev.,* May–June 1967.

Dopuch, N., and D.F. Drake, "Accounting Implications of a Mathematical Programming Approach to the Transfer Price Problem," *J. of Accounting Research,* Spring 1964.

Gould, J., "Pricing in Firms When There Are Costs of Using an Outside Market," *J. of Business,* Jan. 1964.

Hirshleifer, J., "Economics of the Divisionalized Firm," *J. of Business,* April 1957.

Hirshleifer, J., "On the Economics of Transfer Pricing," *J. of Business,* July 1956.

Jennegren, L.P., "Decentralization on the Basis of Price Schedules in Linear Decomposable Resource-Allocation Problems," *J. of Financial and Quantitative Analysis,* Jan. 1972.

Loeb, M. and W. Magot, "Soviet Success Indicators and the Evaluation of Divisional Management," *J. of Accounting Research,* Spring 1978.

Pondy, L., "Toward a Theory of Internal Resource Allocation," in J. Livingstone and S. Gunn, eds., *Accounting for Social Goals: Budgeting and Analysis of Nonmarket Projects.* New York: Harper and Row, 1974.

Ronen, J., and G. McKinney, "Transfer Pricing for Divisional Autonomy," *J. of Accounting Research,* Spring 1970.

Shubik, M., "Incentives, Decentralized Control, the Assignment of Joint Costs and Transfer Pricing," *Management Science,* April 1962.

Vatter, W.J., "Does the Rate of Return Measure Business Efficiency?" *N.A.A. Bull.* Jan. 1959.

Watson, D. and J. Baumler, "Transfer Pricing: A Behavioral Context," *Accounting Rev.,* April 1975.

Books

Anthony, R., and J. Dearden, *Management Control Systems,* 4th ed. Homewood, Ill.: Irwin, 1980.

Arrow, K., *Limits of Organization.* New York: Norton, 1974.

Bierman, H., Jr., and T. Dyckman, *Managerial Cost Accounting.* New York: McGraw-Hill, 1971, Ch. 11.

Solomons, D., *Divisional Performance: Measurement and Control.* New York: Financial Executives Research Foundation, 1965.

Thomas, A., *A Behavioural Analysis of Joint-Cost Allocation and Transfer Pricing.* Champaign, Ill.: Stipes, 1980.

Tomkins, C., *Financial Planning in Divisional Companies.* London: Haymarket Publishing, 1973.

Vancil, R. *Decentralization: Management Ambiguity by Design.* Homewood, Ill.: Dow Jones–Irwin, 1979.

Questions and Problems

1. Discuss the relationship between organizational design and performance reports.
2. What are some reasons other than those that are strictly economic in nature that might encourage decentralization?
3. In his classic article on responsibility accounting, Gordon states:

> A related problem in the design of a responsibility accounting system arises when a sub-firm manager is not charged with all the costs consequent upon his decisions in an area where he has authority. For instance, a plant manager under a standard cost system may have authority to decide when an item of inventory should be replenished and how large the production run should be. Long runs and stable plant output will have a favorable impact on his costs, but interest and other costs of carrying inventory, write-downs due to obsolescence, and stockout losses commonly do not appear in his cost report. . . .
>
> The problem here is that the individual high enough in the organization to consider all costs may not have the information necessary to make an informed decision. The main concern of management science has of course been the development of inventory control models, computer programs, etc., which allow informed production and inventory decisions on a centralized basis.[32]

   Discuss this statement, relating your comments to the effects on control systems brought about by the introduction of formal decision models.
4. Under what conditions would the variable costs of production measure the outlay plus opportunity costs of transferring a unit from the supplying division to the buying division?

5. ***Cost-Plus and Suboptimization***
   A company has two decentralized divisions: Seller and Buyer. The Seller division is the only source of supply of a major input for the Buyer unit. The standard costs for a representative range of production for the Seller unit are given in Exhibit 10-1.
   Both the Seller and Buyer divisions are treated as profit centers, although the output of the Seller division is "sold" internally only. The Seller division sells its output at a price determined by adding a 25 percent markup to its standard cost per unit. The normal volume is set at 100,000 units. In the past few years, the actual volume has averaged closer to 95,000 units.

   (a) Calculate the transfer price used by the Seller division, assuming that 100,000 units is used as the basis for determining the standard cost per unit.
   (b) Suppose that the Seller division's actual overhead costs at an output of 95,000 units were $365,250. Calculate the overhead variances for this divi-

---

[32] M. Gordon, "Toward a Theory of Responsibility Accounting Systems," *N.A.A. Bull.*, Dec. 1963.

EXHIBIT 10-1

Output, units	90,000	95,000	100,000	105,000
Direct materials and labor	$720,000	$760,000	$800,000	$840,000
Overhead				
Supplies	$ 45,000	$ 47,500	$ 50,000	$ 52,500
Handling costs	22,500	23,750	25,000	26,250
Indirect labor	80,000	83,000	86,000	89,000
Insurance and taxes	25,000	28,000	28,000	31,000
Lease rentals	35,000	35,000	38,000	38,000
Depreciation	100,000	100,000	100,000	100,000
Miscellaneous	48,000	48,000	48,000	53,000
Total overhead costs	$355,500	$365,250	$375,000	$389,750

sion, and indicate how this system of pricing is affected by deviations from a normal volume.

(c) Suppose that the Buyer unit can obtain an order for an additional 10,000 units (present rate of activity is set at 95,000 units) at a net marginal revenue of $11.50 per unit. The transfer price normally set by the Seller division is $15 per unit [regardless of your answer to part (a)]. The Buyer division asks the Seller division to cut this transfer price to $10.50. The Seller division refuses to do so. You are asked to prepare a report to indicate (1) whether the order should be accepted and (2) at what price the units should be transferred.

6. **Rationalization of Cost-Plus Pricing**

Refer to the situation in the previous problem. What reasons might top management have for employing this cost-plus pricing arrangement?

7. **Internal Transfers at Standard Cost**

A firm has two decentralized divisions, say, production and marketing. All output of the production division is transferred to the marketing division. The production division operates under a standard cost system with the following standards:

Direct material per unit	$48
Direct labor per unit	$97
Variable overhead per unit	$143
Fixed overhead per month	$800,000

During a recent month the actual variable cost averaged $327 per unit, which is the price charged the distribution division (and credited to the production division).

The marketing division manager has objected to being charged for the cost overrun and has suggested that transfers be priced at standard variable cost of production. Evaluate the marketing manager's recommendation.

8. **Peak-Load Pricing and Sharing Fixed Costs**

Two divisions in a large firm (A and B) pooled resources to acquire a large computing facility that they both share. They originally agreed to each pay half of the facility's cost, and both parties were happy with the arrangement for several years. But nothing lasts forever, especially interdivisional happiness.

In recent times, each division's demand for computing has grown to the point where the total capacity is inadequate for such a casual arrangement. More specifically, the divisions have been forced to negotiate the scheduling of access to the central facility. In turn, this has weakened the attractiveness of the sharing formula, because a 50–50 split, the managers argue, is not reflective of the service each receives.

The proposed solution is a "tiered" pricing system in which the time of month is divided into "busy" and "slack" times. During "slack" times, the user would pay variable computing cost, while during "busy" times the user would pay a substantial surcharge. (The surcharge would be varied so as to keep demand in line with capacity.) Finally, at the end of each month, any remaining cost of the shared facility (total monthly cost less charges to A and B) would be split between A and B in proportion to their billings for the month. It is anticipated that this remaining cost will total several million dollars per month.

Evaluate the proposed pricing arrangement. (Assume, for purposes of analysis, that the demand is not large enough to warrant subcontracting with an outside supplier; at the same time it is too large to warrant separate facilities.)

9. *Cost-Plus Internal Pricing and Merchandise Writedowns*
Sears, Roebuck & Co. employed, until recently, what they termed the "599 Account." A centralized purchasing group would purchase merchandise for all of the stores and then internally transfer the merchandise at some transfer price. The 599 Account accumulted surcharges on these transfers:

> A Sears buyer agrees to buy an ashtray, say, from a manufacturer for $1. But the buyer charges the Sears store managers not $1, but $1.20; the buyer puts the extra $.20 into a kitty. Currently, the rate of overbilling ranges from about 10% to 20%, averaging 15%.[33]

This fund, or 599 Account, was then used to pay for central advertising, for fixed costs of acquisitions (such as acquiring a designer item), and for markdowns. If, for example, a store manager felt he had to mark down some item, the markdown would be absorbed by the 599 Account. And with time, markdowns became the primary drain on the Account.

Should Sears, in your opinion, have abandoned this internal pricing procedure? (*Hint:* Be careful to sort out the objectives that led to the procedure as well as the implications of abandoning it and pricing at acquisition cost.)

10. *Internal Transfers at Marginal Cost*
Suppose a decentralized firm has a production (P) and a distribution (D) division. No intermediate market exists, and the final product market is perfect, with a known selling price of $500 per unit. Letting q denote the joint production–distribution quantity, the production cost is

$$C_p = \$500 + \$90q + q^2$$

---

[33] *Wall Street Journal*, Dec. 27, 1978.

and the distribution cost is

$$C_D = \$5,000 + \$10q + q^2$$

(a) Locate a profit-maximizing schedule.
(b) Determine the marginal cost in each division.
(c) Determine a transfer price T and associated division profit measures such that each manager maximizing the divisional measure will produce the solution in (a) above.

11. **Asset measurement**
Suppose it is possible to measure the "value" and "costs" of output for a department. This would permit a calculation of the net income of the department, the numerator of the rate of return. What are some common problems the accountant will encounter in trying to calculate the investments (assets) of the department, assuming that the department is not physically separated from the firm? Try to envision which assets would be invested in a specific department.

12. **Accelerated versus Straight-Line Depreciation and Rate of Return**
A division is contemplating an investment in an asset that promises to return revenues minus cash expenses over four years as follows:

	Year 1	Year 2	Year 3	Year 4
Net receipts	$1,000	$750	$500	$250

The asset costs $2,075 and has a zero salvage value at the end of Year 4. Ignoring taxes and assuming no other assets and no other revenues and expenses, compute the accounting rate of return for each year on this asset using

(a) straight-line depreciation.
(b) accelerated depreciation using the sum-of-the-years'-digits method.

In your calculations, use the net book value of the asset as of the beginning of each year (original cost − accumulated depreciation). Which method of depreciation seems more reasonable for this asset? Why? (The next two problems may provide some additional insight into your choice.)

13. **Gross versus Net Assets**
Assuming that the assets and income of a firm can be allocated to different departments, would you recommend the use of gross assets or net assets (asset cost − accumulated depreciation) in rate-of-return calculations? Illustrate using the data in Problem 12.

14. **ROI**
Improvements in rate of return may come about through improvements in income margins and/or more efficient utilization of the capital invested in a division.

This is reflected in the basic relationship:

$$\frac{\text{Income}}{\text{Sales}} \times \frac{\text{Sales}}{\text{Capital}} = \frac{\text{Income}}{\text{Capital}} = \text{Rate of return}$$

For example, assume that a division earns 25 percent on sales of $1,000,000 (100,000 units at $10). Capital invested is also $1,000,000.

$$\text{Rate of return} = \frac{250,000}{1,000,000} \times \frac{1,000,000}{1,000,000} = 25\%$$

Suppose that if the division increases its sales price by 10 percent, its output decreases to 90,000 units. Variable costs are $5 a unit. The reduction in units will allow the division to cut its investment by $30,000 and fixed costs by $3,000. Calculate the new profit margin, investment turnover, and rate of return.

15. **Dysfunctional Behavior**[34]
A profitable division is expected to report the following income statement, assuming that no additional investments will be made:

Year ended 12/31/81

Sales	$1,000,000
Variable costs	$500,000
Fixed costs	300,000
Total costs	$800,000
Income	$200,000
Capital	$667,000
Rate of return	30.0%

The company as a whole has been reporting a rate of return of 20 percent.
Assume that the profitable division is contemplating the following investment:

Outlay	$150,000
Expected sales	$200,000
Variable costs	45% of sales
Fixed costs	$75,000

(a) As the division manager, would you accept or reject the proposal? Why?
(b) How might this firm avoid similar kinds of problems in the future?

16. **Divisional Reporting**
A divisional profit and loss statement is presented in Exhibit 10-2. It has been said that such allocations of corporate costs make the divisional manager cognizant of the corporation's costs that must be absorbed by divisional profits. Moreover,

---

[34] This problem is adapted from M. Backer, "Additional Considerations in Return on Investment Analysis," *N.A.A. Bull.*, Jan. 1962.

EXHIBIT 10-2

	Actual	Profit Plan	Variance
Gross sales	$1,500,000	$1,200,000	$300,000
Returns	100,000	50,000	(50,000)
Net sales	$1,400,000	$1,150,000	$250,000
Variable cost of sales	840,000	635,000	205,000
Contribution	$ 560,000	$ 515,000	$ 45,000
Fixed costs			
Manufacturing	$ 120,000	$ 110,000	$ (10,000)
Selling and administrative	75,000	60,000	(15,000)
Engineering	35,000	35,000	—
Other	10,000	5,000	(5,000)
Total	$ 240,000	$ 210,000	$ (30,000)
Operating income	$ 320,000	$ 305,000	$ 15,000
Allocations of corporate costs	120,000	120,000	—
Net earnings	$ 200,000	$ 185,000	$ 15,000

the division heads are usually allowed to participate in the determination of these allocations. Discuss this policy of allocation as well as the report itself as a basis for evaluating divisional managers. If the corporate costs must be allocated, what would be a good basis (if any) for determining these allocations?

17. *ROI and Allocation*[35]

A company using rate of return as the basis for divisional evaluation had a problem in allocating assets and costs, since the company was organized by product groups rather than by geographical location. The procedures for allocating common assets and costs were as follows:

> Cash—based on monthly forecasts of costs and expenses for each profit center.
> Receivables—based on sales volumes, adjusted for ages and discounts.
> Inventories—based on proportions of material content in products.
> Fixed assets—based on relative usage of facilities as determined by long-run sales forecasts of product lines.
> Prepaid expenses—same as inventories and fixed assets.
> Fixed costs—based on long-run product mixes (variable costs are related directly to product lines).

Evaluate these bases in terms of their effects on different product lines, assuming that the different lines have varying profit margins.

18. *Current Assets and ROI*

The inclusion of inventories in the investment base of a division has been criticized, even though there is no question that the division manager has control

---

[35] This problem is adapted from "Experience with Return on Capital to Appraise Management Performance," Accounting Research Report No. 14, *N.A.A. Bull.*, Feb. 1962, Sec. 3.

over the inventories, because (1) the required rate of return on inventory motivates the manager to hold less inventory than normal, assuming that the rate of return required by the division is greater than the actual storage cost, and (2) the fluctuations in inventory levels will be accentuated, since managers will avoid holding high levels of inventory.

(a) Discuss the possible side effects on inventory policies brought about by the inclusion of inventories in rate-of-return calculations.

(b) Adverse side effects were also noted in the inclusion of accounts receivable in the investment base. Can you indicate any of these?

19. **Residual Income**[36]

Some companies encourage divisions to strive for a target income rather than a rate of return on assets used. Of course, absolute amounts of net income are deficient as indicators of success, since they fail to allow for differences in the productivity of capital. It is possible to overcome this deficiency by charging divisions a cost of capital expressed as a percentage against capital used. To illustrate the technique and the different results achieved, consider two divisions, R and S, which report the following investments and income:

	R	S
Net income	$ 24,000	$15,000
Investments in assets	$150,000	$75,000
Rate of return	16%	20%

(a) If a company charges each division 10 percent on capital employed, which division will report the highest "residual" income?

(b) Which division would you consider the most efficient? Why?

20. **ROI and Price Level Changes**

Two division managers have been quarreling about their relative performances for the past year. The manager of Division B claims that his performance was better even though the rate of return earned for his division was less than that earned by Division A. His argument is that the use of historical asset values gives Division A an advantage, since its fixed assets are older and therefore do not reflect the increases in prices of fixed assets during the past few years. The purchase price of their assets did rise about 40 percent between the time Division A acquired its assets (three years ago) and the time Division B acquired its assets (one year ago). Division A counters that the prices paid by Division B for its assets actually reflect savings in variable costs, since Division B's assets are more efficient than Division A's.

Suppose that the price level increased by 10 percent during the time span under dispute.

(a) Using the data below, calculate the rate of return of each division using historical costs and "adjusted" costs; assume straight-line depreciation for

---

[36] This problem was adapted from D. Solomons, *Divisional Performance: Measurement and Control.* New York: Financial Executives Research Foundation, 1965, p. 63.

each asset. In calculating the rate of return, use the gross assets held by each division.

	Division A	Division B
Current assets (net)	$12,000	$15,000
Fixed assets	$50,000	$70,000
Less: Depreciation	30,000	14,000
Net book value	$20,000	$56,000
Sales (at $10 each)	$75,000	$85,000
Variable costs	48,750	51,850
Fixed costs (depreciation only)	10,000	14,000

(b) Would you recommend the use of replacement costs for rate-of-return calculations? If the accountant did try to measure replacement costs, do you believe he would be able to separate the increases in prices due to technology changes from those due to changes in price levels of assets?

21. *ROI on Total Assets versus Net Worth*
The Trading Company is decentralized by divisions that operate relatively independently of one another. These divisions have complete authority to make their own operating and short-run financing decisions. Divisions may petition the central office for permission to issue long-term bonds, but the final decision to issue the bonds is made by the central office. Once the bonds are issued, they are allocated to the petitioning division, where they appear on the division's balance sheet.

Exhibits 10-3 and 10-4 are statements submitted to the central office by Divisions C and D.

(a) Calculate the rate of return for each division using
(1) gross assets and controllable operating income.
(2) gross assets minus current liabilities and controllable income adjusted for interest.

EXHIBIT 10-3

Income Statement Entries
for Divisions C and D
for Year Ended 12/31/81

	C	D
Sales: Variable costs	$100,000	$125,000
Fixed operating expenses	60,000	75,000
Controllable operating income	$ 40,000	$ 50,000
Interest paid by divisions	870	1,590
Controllable income	$ 39,130	$ 48,410
Costs of central office allocated		
by various measures of activity	10,000	14,000
Net income	$ 29,130	$ 34,410

_____EXHIBIT 10-4

**Balance Sheet Entries
for Divisions C and D
for Year Ended 12/31/81**

	C	D
Current assets	$ 20,000	$ 34,000
Current liabilities	(14,000)	(28,000)
Net working capital	$ 6,000	$ 6,000
Fixed assets		
Original cost	$100,000	$115,000
Accumulated depreciation	50,000	55,000
Net fixed assets	$ 50,000	$ 60,000
Total net assets	$ 56,000	$ 66,000
Long-term debt: 20 year, 6%		
(semiannual)	(15,000)	(25,000)
Net worth	$ 41,000	$ 41,000

(3) net worth and net income.

(4) the asset and income figures you think would be the most meaningful.

(b) Evaluate each of measures (1)–(4) in part (a), indicating their advantages and disadvantages.

22. *Alternative Depreciation Policies and ROI*

The effects on income of using alternative accounting methods may "wash out" over time. As an illustration, assume a division intends to acquire a total of five identical assets, costing $1,500 each and lasting for five years (zero salvage). A new asset is purchased each year, and as each wears out a new replacement is obtained.

(a) Determine the total depreciation expense and net book value for this depreciation for Years 1 through 10 and thereafter using

(1) straight-line depreciation.

(2) sum-of-the-years'-digits depreciation.

(b) Does the statement hold true for the income effect under the two methods? How will the investment base be affected under the two methods?

23. *Alternative Accounting Policies for Intangibles*

A similar phenomenon to that observed in Problem 22 will develop in comparing the effect of adopting either of the two accounting policies concerning intangibles—that is, the recording of each year's expenditures as an expense versus the capitalization of expenditures as assets.

An accountant is contemplating whether to capitalize the research and development expenditures of a division or to record them as expenses as they are incurred. At best, these R&D expenditures will provide benefits over a three-year period.

The division manager prefers an immediate expensing of the item, arguing that if she spends a constant amount each year the net effect will be the same. The accountant looks at the past records and notes that R&D expenditures have averaged about $15,000 per year.

Using straight-line depreciation, compare the effects of using the two accounting policies for recording total R&D expense for Years 1–3 and thereafter. What effect is observed on the investment base under the two methods?

24. **Transfer Pricing Issues**
Regarding transfer pricing problems, the following comment was made:

> Where conditions such as the absence of a competitive market to guide interunit transfer pricing make it necessary to use other bases for pricing, decentralized responsibility for profits usually is not successfully maintained and other methods for measuring managerial performances must be used.[37]

(a) Why is a competitive market apparently necessary to maintain decentralized responsibility for profits?

(b) What is the most likely alternative to profit responsibility as a basis for evaluating managerial performances?

25. **Market Prices as Transfer Prices**
An important principle to observe in designing a transfer pricing system is to ensure that the resulting prices do not motivate the division manager to expand his profits at the expense of the company's total profit potential. Indicate a type of market situation in which a transfer price based on observed market prices might lead to divisional decisions that are not optimal from the standpoint of the firm.

26. **Negotiated Prices**
The following statement relates to internally negotiated prices: Whenever we have to price products that do not have an exact counterpart in the marketplace, we resort to a transfer price based on negotiations between the parties involved. Discuss this basis for setting transfer prices.

27. **Cost-Plus Transfer Prices**[38]
A company prepares monthly plant profit and loss statements that are used to evaluate their plant managers. As the basis for preparing these reports, the company determines the "value" of the manufactured output, which the plant managers then use as the price charged to the "merchandiser units." The merchandiser units have sales, service, and distribution facilities.

The "value" of the output is determined as follows:

---

[37] "Accounting for Intra-Company Transfers," *Research Series No. 30*, New York: National Association for Accountants, 1956, p. 9.

[38] This problem is adapted from R.A. Benson, "Pricing Interplant Transfers for Measuring Plant Operations," *N.A.A. Bull.*, Feb. 1963.

(1) From the final selling price of the product subtract the total cost, including selling and general expenses, in order to determine the product's margin.

(2) Divide the margin by total cost to determine the markup percentage of cost.

(3) Multiply the plant cost by the markup percentage to determine the plant margin.

(4) Plant margin plus plant cost equals the gross intracompany price, which is then adjusted for discounts and warranty costs.

Required (a) Discuss this set of procedures as a basis for measuring the value of outputs relative to the evaluation of plant and merchandiser managers.

(b) How might this intracompany price lead to nonoptimal decisions by plant managers? By merchandiser managers?

28. ***Alternative Measures of Performance***
One well-known diversified company evaluates its divisions on the basis of the following factors:

(1) Profitability

(2) Market position

(3) Productivity

(4) Product leadership

(5) Personnel development

(6) Employee attitudes

(7) Public responsibility

(8) Balance between short-range and long-range goals

Required (a) In your opinion, does an evaluation of factors (2)–(8) overlap the evaluation of profitability—that is, does not profitability encompass favorable results in these other areas? Explain.

(b) The evaluation of personnel development is based on such statistics as turnover rate, absenteeism, number of grievances, tardiness, and accident experience, as well as on a survey of the attitudes of the employees by groups. Does this type of evaluation assume something about the relationship between attitudes and productivity? Explain.

(c) Which of factors (2)–(7) might the accountant attempt to measure in terms of investment costs and appropriate expense writeoffs in order to reflect the periods in which the investment benefits would be realized?

(d) How would you as a manager of a division of this firm react to this scheme of evaluation?

29. ***Transfer Prices with Externalities***
Your local automobile dealership may be (and often is) thought of as a firm with three divisions: new auto sales, used auto sales, and repair services. Further note that there is generally an active used car market as well as an active service market.

(a) Discuss the strengths and weaknesses of various transfer pricing arrangements for such a firm.

(b) Contrast the transfer pricing arrangement with a cooperative arrangement in which the "divisions" are not distinguished and negotiation among the three managers is used to coordinate their activities.

30. **External versus Internal Transactions**

The production division of AMA manufactures and distributes Product Z, both to outsiders and to the finishing division. The price charged to the outside buyers is set at $5 per unit. Because the production division can save on distribution costs, its manager is willing to sell its output internally at a price of $4.25. The latest income statement reported by the production division showed the following:

Sales		
Outside	$500,000	
Finishing	85,000	$585,000
Variable costs of production		$360,000
Variable costs of distribution		72,000
Fixed costs		
Depreciation		60,000
Distribution		20,000
Total traceable costs		$512,000
Division's profit contribution		$ 73,000
Share of corporate expenses		20,000
Net income before taxes		$ 53,000

The finishing division has obtained an offer from an outside supplier who will ship 20,000 units of a product very similar to Z at a price of $3.75 per unit, F.O.B. destination. The manager of the finishing division threatens to accept the offer unless the production division lowers its price from $4.25 to $3.75. How should the manager of the production division react to this proposal under the assumption that

(a) additional units cannot be sold outside except at a reduced price of $4.25?

(b) additional units can be sold outside at a discounted price of $4.60 per unit?

31. **Imperfect Competition and the Optimal Transfer Price**

The XY Company has two divisions: X, the supply division, and Y, the finishing division. The output of X is sold to outside firms and to Division Y. The output of Y is sold to outsiders only. The expected revenues and costs of each division are reflected in the data in Exhibit 10-5.

(a) Assume that the manager of Division X is given the above information. What allocation of sales should be made between outside buyers and Division Y? Explain your answer.

(b) What transfer price should be quoted to the manager of Division Y to ensure that his "purchase" decisions will be consistent with your answer to part (a)?

EXHIBIT 10-5

| | PRODUCT X | | PRODUCT Y |
| | | | |
Output (Units)	Total Cost of Production and Administration (in $1,000's)	Revenue from Outside Sales (Net of Selling Expenses in $1,000's)	Net Marginal Revenue from Sales of Y: Total Revenue − Total Costs of Finishing (in $1,000's)
30	$125	$165	$75
40	150	220	75
50	175	275	70
60	201	329	63
70	228	383	55.5
80	255	435	47
90	283	486	39
100	312	535	30
110	342	581	
120	374	623	
130	408	663	
140	446		
150	486		
160	528		
170	572		
180	617		
190	664		

32. *Imperfect Markets and Interdivisional Trading*[39]

The Western division of the B company, in conjunction with the Eastern division, has just finished perfecting a new container for use in packaging its product. The Eastern division was reimbursed for its efforts in designing the container and was prepared to construct the container for Western at a price of $1,040 per 100 containers. The Western division would require about 20,000 containers a year.

The Western division also received bids for constructing the containers from two outside firms. Able Company quoted a price of $790 and Baker Company countered with a bid of $765 per 100 containers.

If Able's bid is accepted, it will subcontract part of its work to the Eastern division, paying $250 per 100 containers for the work performed by Eastern. Of this amount, $100 will be paid to the Northern division and $50 will be paid to the Southern division, both of whom would be participating with Eastern on this subcontract.

If Eastern receives the bid, it will purchase components from Northern at a price of $570 per 100 containers (the price quoted by Northern) as well as parts from Southern at a price of $75 per 100 containers. In addition, Southern will supply Northern with inputs valued (by Southern) at $122 per 100 containers.

The price of $122 quoted to Northern is the current competitive price for the parts it would receive from Southern. However, it is doubtful that this

[39] This problem was adapted from a case appearing in R. Anthony and J. Dearden, *Management Control Systems.* Homewood, Ill.: Irwin, 1976, pp. 296–98.

outside price would hold for the number of additional units Southern would be producing should Eastern receive the bid. The out-of-pocket costs of producing the parts for Northern would be approximately 82 percent of the price quoted. Similarly, only 80 percent of the $75 to be charged to Eastern represents out-of-pocket costs to Southern.

The $570 price quoted by Northern (to Eastern) is based on Northern's full cost to produce the components plus a markup of 20 percent on cost; this cost includes the $122 charge by Southern. Only 70 percent of the costs that would be incurred in the Northern division on this project would represent out-of-pocket costs. Northern does not have outside sales.

The 80 percent and 70 percent figures indicated above will also apply to the subcontracting work done by Southern and Northern should Able's bid be accepted.

The Western manager asks the Eastern manager if he is willing to drop his bid to meet those of Able and Baker. The Eastern manager indicates that he cannot lower the bid by more than $15, since this is the only markup he has added to his costs of $1,025 (which include the prices of components to be purchased from Southern and Northern). 75 percent of Eastern's direct costs represent out-of-pocket costs associated with its bid. (This figure also applies to any subcontracting work.)

The Eastern manager further points out that he could make at least 12 percent profit on his subcontracting work for Able (based on cost). Thus, he is unwilling to cut his price any lower than his full cost, which will still leave him with an opportunity cost of $10 in lost profit.

Draft a report to the Western manager, indicating the optimal bid from the standpoint of the company as a whole. In your report you should be careful to point out any assumptions you make regarding market prices, availability of capacity, and so forth.

33. *Linear Programing and Transfer Prices*
In this chapter it was noted that the use of "shadow prices" generated by a linear programing solution as the basis for establishing transfer prices ultimately eliminates the need to decentralize. That is, the calculation of the "shadow prices" by central management presumes sufficient information on their part to make all of the allocation decisions of the firm. As one writer indicates, "the use of programmed transfer prices does not . . . make it possible to preserve the autonomy of the divisions as profit centers while at the same time ensuring that, left to themselves, they will operate optimally from a corporate viewpoint."[40]

However, suppose that a multiproduct form is decentralized by products and that the various divisions are linked by a number of constraints on the resources of the firm. All the information on prices and costs in the various divisions is collected and processed by the division managers. In a sense, central management merely acts as a centralized computer service for these divisions, since all they receive is information on the contribution margins of the different products.

Assume that central management uses these contribution margins to gener-

---

[40] D. Solomons, *Divisional Performance*, pp. 196–97.

ate a linear programing solution to the firm's output problem. Discuss how this optimal plan might be used to evaluate the efficiency of the division managers.

*34. *Discounted Cash Flow Approach to Depreciation*
   (a) Using the cash flows from Problem 12, compute the present value of the $2,075 asset at the end of each year, including Year 0, using a 10 percent discount rate. How does the decline in the present value of the remaining receipts from one year to the next compare to the straight-line and accelerated (sum-of-the-years'-digits) methods of depreciation?
   (b) Suppose the net receipts for the four years were $655 each year. What depreciation method would be consistent with the decline in the present value of the asset from year to year? Use 10 percent as a discount rate, and round off as appropriate.
   (c) Suppose the net receipts were $771 each year. What would happen if we discounted these receipts at a 10 percent rate? What rate would be appropriate in this case? (Use tables at the end of Chapter 14.)

*35. *Annuity Depreciation, Residual Income, and Inflation*
   Suppose an asset is acquired at a cost of $50,000. It will last three years, with respective end-of-year cash inflows of $19,000, $27,000, and $23,600. All dollars are in nominal terms, and the nominal required rate of return is 18 percent. Also, the anticipated inflation rate is 9.26 percent, implying a required real rate of return of 8 percent.

Required: (a) Provide a nominal depreciation schedule such that the annual rate of return on the asset is 18 percent.
   (b) Construct the corresponding residual income measures for your schedule in part (a).
   (c) Convert your calculations in (a) to real terms and display a price level adjusted schedule that provides an annual rate of return of 8 percent.
   (d) Construct the corresponding residual income measures for your schedule in (c).

11
Financial versus Managerial Accounting: A Summary of Cost Allocation Issues

$\mathbf{A}$t several points in earlier chapters we alluded to the frequently occurring differences between the data required to meet financial reporting obligations and the data useful for managerial accounting decisions. For the most part, these conflicts arise from the fact that all manufacturing costs must be allocated to units of output in order for firms to comply with generally accepted accounting principles (GAAP). Deviations from GAAP result in qualified opinions and perhaps even disclaimers by the firm's CPAs. Moreover, some of the same principles are imposed by other regulatory agencies, such as the IRS, the Cost Accounting Standards Board, and the ICC.

Determining variable unit costs of output does not create problems, since this information is both useful to management and necessary for financial purposes. That is, the decision to accept or reject new orders in a job shop depends heavily on estimates of the variable costs of completing the orders, which often extend from analyses of past variable costs of similar jobs. In the same manner, accumulating variable costs by processes in process-type firms is useful in determining the level and mix of output of these processes. A conflict arises because of the need to assign fixed manufacturing overhead to jobs or to processes in order to reflect the total average unit costs of output produced in a particular accounting period. Based on these unit costs, total costs incurred are divided between the ending inventory balance and cost of goods sold. This calculation is a major determinant of a firm's income for an accounting period. Similar requirements apply to service department costs and joint manufacturing costs, which must be allocated to units of output as well.

This chapter reviews some of the issues involved in the financial accounting requirements regarding manufacturing costs. Be aware that similar rules are found in nonmanufacturing situations when costs are used as a basis for setting prices, for example, in cost-plus contracts or for insurance reim-

405

bursements in hospitals.[1] First we shall review the basic calculation of a fixed overhead rate and how a price and volume variance may be generated for fixed overhead costs, even for firms that do not use a standard cost system. We shall then discuss an alternative to full costing, which has led to the absorption costing versus direct costing controversy. Service department cost allocations and joint cost allocations are then discussed, emphasizing the distinctions between allocations for financial accounting purposes and those useful for managerial purposes. (The latter were discussed in Chapter 9.)

Fixed Overhead Allocations to Units of Output

In Chapter 6 we explained how fixed manufacturing overhead may be allocated to units of output in a standard costing system. Budgeted fixed overhead for the period is divided by a normal volume (expressed either in number of units or some independent variable such as the hours required to produce a normal number of units) to arrive at the rate of allocation. Treating fixed overhead in this manner may result in two variances—a spending or price variance because budgeted overhead did not equal actual fixed manufacturing overhead incurred or a volume variance because actual volume did not equal normal volume.

Strangely enough, a firm that does not use a standard cost system will produce essentially the same variances for fixed manufacturing overhead, although they are usually aggregated into a single variance called over- or underapplied. That is, in order to allocate fixed overhead to output in an actual costing system, the firm's accountant must estimate the total fixed overhead costs for the coming period and the level of output to be achieved (again, in units or some independent variable such as direct hours). If actual overhead incurred differs from the estimated amount or the actual level of output differs from the estimated volume of activity, the overhead allocated will not exactly equal the amount incurred, and either a price or a volume variance, or both, will occur.

To illustrate, assume that estimated fixed overhead for a period is $100,000 and expected output is 5,000 units. The fixed overhead rate is therefore $100,000/5,000 = $20 per unit.

During the period, actual overhead incurred is $100,000, but actual volume is only 4,900 units. The $100,000 in overhead costs incurred is accumulated in the overhead control account, but the amount applied to work-in-process is only $20 × 4,900 = $98,000. The excess of the amount incurred relative to the amount "applied" becomes $2,000 underapplied.

An overapplication would occur if actual production exceeded the base used to determine the overhead rate. For example, assume now that actual output was 5,200 units and actual overhead costs were $100,000. The amount

---

[1] Particular regulations will not be discussed.

applied would be $20 × 5,200 = $104,000, or $4,000 overapplied. These over- and underapplied overhead amounts are diagramed in Figure 11-1, assuming actual overhead costs equal the $100,000 estimate. The graph can also illustrate a spending (price) variance. In this case, we assume actual output equals 5,000 units but that actual overhead incurred is $98,000 or $104,000. In each case, overhead applied is 5,000 × $20 = $100,000.

This example is the simplest type of accounting problem associated with fixed manufacturing overhead allocations. Additional factors complicate the allocation procedure. They may include questions such as whether to use a single overhead rate for all departments or to use different rates based on each department's estimated overhead costs and estimated activity level. Later in this chapter we discuss the problem of allocating manufacturing service department costs to producing departments. This problem produces at least two levels of allocation questions—how to allocate service department costs to service department units of activity and how to allocate the service depart- ment's activity to producing departments. There is also the question of ac- counting for the over- and underapplied amounts over time. The general rule is to allow the over- and underapplied amounts to "ride" in a deferred account from one interim accounting period to the next (for example, from

_____**FIGURE 11-1**

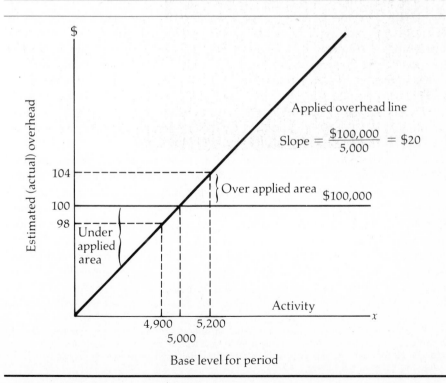

quarter to quarter) on the possibility that they may total zero for the fiscal period. At the end of the fiscal period any amount remaining would probably be included in cost of goods sold: Underapplied amounts would increase cost of goods sold and overapplied amounts would decrease it. If the over- or underapplied amounts are "material," however, the accountant might pro-rate them among work-in-process, finished goods, and cost of goods sold based on the relative proportions of applied amounts in each account.

Note that this discussion parallels the disposition of standard cost vari-ances in Chapter 7. This fact tends to confuse operating personnel in firms that do not use standard cost systems but nevertheless produce cost variances in the form of over- and underapplied overhead. Most operating personnel understand the accountant's concern over a budget variance, when actual overhead costs do not equal some estimated amount. People accustomed to dealing with actual costs, however, may not understand a volume variance produced when the actual volume of activity does not equal the estimated amount of activity for an accounting period. Such difficulties in interpreting the volume variance contributed considerably to the absorption costing versus direct costing controversy.

Direct versus Absorption Income

Accounting systems based on fixed cost allocations are called absorption (or full) cost systems. The term probably derives from the notion that fixed overhead is "absorbed" as output is produced. Direct (or variable) accounting systems do not apply fixed overhead allocations to production. This terminol-ogy is somewhat of a misnomer since absorption costing allocates *all* manufac-turing costs to units of output, fixed and variable, and direct costing allocates only variable manufacturing costs to units of output. Under both systems, selling and administrative costs are treated as period costs and are recorded directly on the income statement.

The issue here is the main effect of each system on the income reported by a firm or one of its decision units. If fixed overhead is allocated to units of output (absorption), it enters into the product cost datum, and therefore the valuation of the inventory balances of work-in-process and finished goods. If fixed overhead is not allocated to units of output (direct costing), the entire amount is treated as a period cost charged against the revenues reported for that period.[2] Given this difference in the accounting treatment of fixed overhead, the main effect of using either system is a function of whether production during an accounting period is equal to the sales of the period (in units). If production exceeds sales, the level of inventory will increase

---

[2] Variations for interim statements—such as allocating the total yearly overhead amount according to the proportion of sales recognized in each interim period—could produce a seasonal-ized charge for each interim period. However, the total fixed overhead for a year would be charged to the year's revenues.

and some of the fixed overhead incurred during the accounting period will not be charged to sales but will remain in the ending inventory account balance. If production is below sales, more fixed overhead than the amount actually incurred will be charged to sales since the inventory reduction will include prior period fixed overhead as a charge to current sales. This is a general rule: The difference between income recognized under absorption and income recognized under direct costing is actually equal to the amount of fixed overhead in ending inventory minus fixed overhead in beginning inventory. A positive sign in the answer means that absorption income exceeds direct costing income (fixed overhead in inventory increased over the period). This general rule is illustrated in Exhibits 11-1 and 11-2.

If a firm uses a standard fixed overhead rate and treats budget and volume variances as adjustments to cost of goods sold, the difference between absorption income and direct costing income is merely equal to the change in inventory (in units) multiplied by the fixed overhead rate; that is, (End-

_____EXHIBIT 11-1

Producers, Inc.—Eastern Division
Statement of Production Costs
Year Ended December 31, 1981
(Production: 10,000 units)

(A) ABSORPTION COSTING

	Total Cost	Cost per Unit
Direct costs		
Raw materials	$175,000	$17.50
Direct labor	400,000	40.00
Indirect costs		
Indirect labor	90,000	9.00
Indirect materials	12,500	1.25
Electricity	72,500	7.25
Maintenance	6,000	.60
Supervision and quality control	78,000	7.80
Depreciation—machinery	24,000	2.40
Depreciation—building	12,000	1.20
Totals	$870,000	$87.00

(B) DIRECT COSTING

	Total Cost	Cost per Unit
Direct variable costs		
Raw materials	$175,000	$17.50
Direct labor	400,000	40.00
Indirect variable costs		
Indirect labor	90,000	9.00
Indirect materials	12,500	1.25
Electricity	72,500	7.25
Totals	$750,000	$75.00

EXHIBIT 11-2——

Producers, Inc.—Eastern Division
Income Statement
Year Ended December 31, 1981

(A) ABSORPTION COSTING

Sales (8,000 units @ $125)	$1,000,000
Less: Cost of goods sold[a]	696,000
Gross profit	$ 304,000
Less: General and administrative expenses	
($100,000 variable; $60,000 fixed)	160,000
Net income	$ 144,000

(B) DIRECT COSTING

Sales	$1,000,000
Less: Cost of goods sold[b]	600,000
Manufacturing margin	$ 400,000
Less: Variable operating costs	100,000
Contribution margin to fixed costs	$ 300,000
Less: Fixed costs ($120,000 manufacturing overhead and	
$60,000 general and administrative expenses)	180,000
Net income	$ 120,000

[a] 8,000 units at $87 per unit as calculated in Exhibit 11-1. Inventory: 2,000 units at $87 per unit = $174,000.
[b] 8,000 units at $75 per unit as calculated in Exhibit 11-1. Inventory: 2,000 units at $75 per unit = $150,000.

ing inventory in units × Fixed overhead rate) − (Beginning inventory in units × Fixed overhead rate). If a firm is using an actual costing system, fixed overhead per unit rates will change from period to period to the extent that estimated fixed overhead and estimated volume change. This calculation is complicated by the fact that the change in fixed overhead in inventory during the period will depend on whether the firm uses FIFO, LIFO, or the average cost method for tracing manufacturing costs into and out of the inventory accounts. Equations for computing the differences between the two income methods for actual cost systems are provided in Appendix A.

Impact of Production on Income

Let us assume that a firm using standard fixed overhead rates wishes to assess the advantages and disadvantages of using absorption rather than direct costing (or vice versa). For purposes of illustration, the standard variable costs of production (direct materials plus direct labor plus variable overhead) are $25 per unit of output. Fixed factory overhead is $50,000 per period, and normal volume is 10,000 units, which gives us a fixed overhead rate of $5 per unit.

Because fixed overhead costs pass through the inventory accounts under absorption costing, the periodic income figure is affected both by total sales for the period and whether production in units is equal to sales in units. If at the end of a period production equals sales, *total* absorption income will equal *total* direct costing income.

To illustrate, we assume the following production and sales data. For each period, a unit of output sells for $40. Beginning inventory is zero.

	PERIOD				
	1	**2**	**3**	**4**	**Total**
Production (units)	10,000	12,000	12,000	10,000	44,000
Sales (units)	8,000	10,000	14,000	12,000	44,000
Absorption Income:					
Sales	$320,000	$400,000	$560,000	$480,000	$1,760,000
Cost of goods (at standard)	240,000	300,000	420,000	360,000	1,320,000
Volume Variance (favorable)	—	(10,000)	(10,000)	—	(20,000)
Income (gross)	$ 80,000	$110,000	$150,000	$120,000	$ 460,000
		50,000	70,000		
Fixed overhead		−10,000	−10,000		
charged to sales	40,000	40,000	60,000	60,000	200,000
Direct Costing Income:					
Sales	$320,000	$400,000	$560,000	$480,000	$1,760,000
Cost of sales:					
Variable	200,000	250,000	350,000	300,000	1,100,000
Fixed	50,000	50,000	50,000	50,000	200,000
Income from manufacturing	$ 70,000	$100,000	$160,000	$130,000	$ 460,000

Absorption costing anticipated the sales increase from period 1 to period 3 in the sense that absorption income was higher in periods 1 and 2 than direct costing income for the same periods. However, when production was less than sales (period 3, in anticipation of lower sales in period 4), direct costing income exceeded absorption income. Because total production for the four periods equals total sales, the total income under the two methods is equal.

Some years ago, Amerman[3] argued that because production tended to be smoother than sales, absorption income tended to be smoother than direct costing income. His conclusion was based on assumptions about inventory management, but the result may be an empirical fact as well. If so, managers

---

[3] G. Amerman, "Facts about Direct Costing for Profit Determination," *Accounting Research,* April 1954; reprinted in H.R. Anton and P.A. Firmin, eds., *Contemporary Issues in Cost Accounting,* 2nd ed. Boston: Houghton Mifflin, 1972.

may choose absorption income for their compensation plans in order to smooth their earnings over time.

On the other hand, the fact that absorption income may be increased merely by producing in excess of sales can give managers distorted short-term results. There is a story that a tractor firm in the Midwest was left with a large number of unsold units at the end of a period. A manager received a bonus for increasing that period's current (absorption) income, then left the firm in search of new challenges.

Absorption versus Direct Income for External Reporting

One of the advantages of using absorption costing internally is that the resulting accounting reports will be consistent with the rules of private and public accounting regulatory agencies (including the Financial Accounting Standards Board). We know of no accounting agency that has adopted direct costing as a preferred costing method, although direct costing may be accepted in certain situations (special tax conditions). Hence, a firm that is already using absorption costing need not maintain a separate set of records to conform to accounting methods dictated by a regulatory agency.

This may be a rather minor advantage. At the end of an accounting period, a firm that is using direct costing can easily adjust its records to report absorption costing income. The firm would simply adjust the inventory balances and cost of sales to reflect a change in the fixed costs in inventories that occurred because production did not equal sales.

To illustrate this point, we return to our earlier example and assume our firm uses direct costing internally but wishes to report absorption income externally at the end of each time period. Beginning inventory of period 1 is zero, so the fixed cost in beginning inventory is also zero. Ending inventory for period 1 is 2,000 units valued at $25 per unit (total variable costs). Ending inventory of fixed overhead should be 2,000 × $5 = $10,000. If we adjust inventory and cost of sales, our result will be an ending inventory balance of $50,000 + $10,000 = $60,000 and a cost of sales of $250,000 − $10,000 = $240,000, the amount shown for absorption costing.

At the end of period 2, inventory is 4,000 units with a direct costing value of $100,000 ($25 per unit). The ending inventory under absorption includes $20,000 fixed overhead (at $5 per unit). However, the inventory adjustment still has a balance of $10,000 carried over from period 1. A $10,000 adjustment will result in an inventory balance of $100,000 + $20,000 = $120,000 and (absorption) cost of sales of $300,000 − $10,000 = $290,000, the net amount shown for absorption cost of sales in period 2.

In period 3 production fell below sales, so the sign of the difference between absorption income and direct costing income changes. The ending inventory for period 3 contains 2,000 units × $25 = $50,000. The fixed cost in ending inventory should be $10,000, but the inventory adjustment now has a balance of $20,000. Reducing the adjustment by $10,000 gives us an absorption cost of sales of $400,000 + $10,000 = $410,000, the net cost of sales for period 3.[4]

Thus we can see why a direct costing firm does not need to maintain two sets of accounting records in order to convert its financial statements to absorption costing. It must, however, maintain an inventory adjustment account to adjust inventory for the amount of fixed overhead that should be deferred in an inventory account at the end of an accounting period. Because the record-keeping advantage of using absorption costing is a minor one,[5] firms probably use absorption for other reasons.

Theoretical Considerations

During the 1960s accounting theorists debated the theoretical superiority of either absorption or direct costing for income determination. Those in support of absorption relied on the "matching" principle so prevalent in historical accounting. (See reference Fess and Ferrara [1961]). The matching notion implied that all costs, fixed or variable, that benefit revenues recognized in a future period should be deferred until those revenues are recognized (that is, the inventory is sold). Those who favored direct costing also adopted the matching principle, but the costs they would allocate to future revenues were the costs that were "obviated" by producing in the current period rather than later. (See references, Green [1960] and Sorter and Horngren [1962].) Since fixed overhead costs incurred in a current period do not obviate fixed overhead costs in the future, they are not deferred.

The matching notion is an important consideration when choosing an accounting method for a firm's external reports. For the internal reports, however, the usefulness for decision making and performance evaluation is the relevant criterion. (Recall discussions on the usefulness of internal reports in Chapters 4, 5, and 6.)

Disclosure Formats for Internal Reports

Decisions regarding the use of capacities (see Chapter 4) and those concerning the acquisition or sale of capacities (see Chapter 14) often depend on estimates of incremental costs associated with different alternatives. A large portion of incremental costs for many of these alternatives includes variable costs—materials, labor, and variable overhead—particularly if these alternatives generate levels of output that fall within the range of capacity utilization used to obtain linear approximations of cost functions. Similarly, variable costs represent a large portion of the controllable costs that are examined during the evaluations of heads of responsibility units, particularly those managers who have not remained in their positions long enough to make decisions

---

[4] The adjustments in periods 1 and 2 require debits to the inventory adjustment account and credits to cost of sales. The adjusting entry in period 3 is the opposite.

[5] A firm on an actual cost absorption system would need more complex calculations, but the equations in Appendix I are not that unwieldly for adjusting direct to absorption costing.

EXHIBIT 11-3   Panel A _____

Producers, Inc.—Eastern Division
Income Statement
Year Ended December 31, 1981
(Modified Direct Costing)

Net sales (8,000 units @ $125)		$1,000,000
Less: Variable costs of goods sold[a]		600,000
Margin on sales		$ 400,000
Less: Variable divisional operating costs		100,000
Contribution to division period costs		$ 300,000
Less: Division period costs		180,000
Contribution to company overhead		$ 120,000
Less: Prorata share of company general and administrative costs		40,000
Net excess contribution		$ 80,000
Adjustment to absorption costing[b]		
Fixed charges to ending inventory		
6,000 units @ $12 overhead per unit	$72,000	
Less: Fixed charges to beginning inventory		
4,000 units @ $15 overhead per unit	60,000	12,000
Net profit—absorption costing		$ 92,000

[a] Assuming FIFO and variable costs of $75 per unit each period.
[b] Adjustment equals fixed overhead assigned to ending inventory *less* fixed overhead assigned to beginning inventory. If the sign were negative, the adjustment would be subtracted from direct costing income.

affecting capacity levels. Therefore, a number of reporting situations would benefit from distinguishing between costs on the basis of their variability with some activity measure, to the extent possible. The reporting framework under direct costing tends to be consistent with this objective. That is, the important issue is whether the excess of revenues over variable costs (the contribution margin) is sufficient to absorb total capacity costs. It is important to remember, however, that the direct (or variable) costing framework relies on a more refined (and more costly) analysis of the firm's cost structure. Individual firms should consider carefully whether this added cost is worthwhile.

A direct costing report is illustrated in Exhibit 11-3, panels A and B. There we assume that the fixed overhead rate is $15 in a prior period (part of beginning inventory), but only $12 in the current period (part of ending inventory). Variable costs are $75 in each period.

Variance Analysis—Absorption Costing versus Direct Costing

We have seen that the only difference between absorption and direct costing is the application of fixed overhead to units of output under absorption costing. A firm that uses standard costs for variable and fixed factors, therefore, will

————————————————————————————————EXHIBIT 11-3   Panel B

Producers, Inc.—Eastern Division
Income Statement
Year Ended December 31, 1981
(Absorption Costing)

Net sales (8,000 units @ $125)	$1,000,000
Less: Cost of goods sold[a]	708,000
Gross margin	$ 292,000
Less: Divisional selling and administrative costs[b]	160,000
Divisional contribution	$ 132,000
Less: Pro rata share of company general and administrative costs	40,000
Divisional profit	$ 92,000
Opening inventory (4,000 units @ $90)[c]	$ 360,000
Plus: Current production (10,000 units @ $87)[d]	870,000
Goods available for sale	$1,230,000
Less: Ending inventory (6,000 units @ $87)	522,000
Cost of goods sold	$ 708,000

[a] Assuming FIFO and variable cost of $75 per unit each period.
[b] Includes both the variable division costs and the managed division costs.
[c] $75 + $15.
[d] $75 + $12.

generate the same types of variances under each standard costing system except that the volume variance will be eliminated under direct costing. (Recall our discussion of the volume variance in Chapter 7.) That is, each standard cost system will generate price and quantity variances for materials, direct labor, and variable overhead and a spending (budget) variance for fixed overhead. But since fixed overhead is not assigned to output under direct costing, no volume variance will be required to resolve any difference between actual and normal volume.

Fundamentally, we can offer no preference for either absorption or direct costing for profit reporting. Direct costing reveals more of the cost structure, but absorption costing, with its charge for fixed overhead per unit, may provide a useful estimate of the long-run opportunity cost of using capacities—at least a closer estimate than direct costing, which imputes a zero opportunity cost for capacities. On the other hand, absorption costing may provide too high an estimate in the short run, when available capacities could be used for special orders, increased output levels, and additional products. There is utility in reporting variable and fixed costs separately. (There is also an added cost.) However, we should not assume that only the variable costs represent the "real" costs of production. A firm may trade fixed factors for variable factors or vice versa—for example, add more capacity and reduce shifts or increase shifts to avoid additional capacity. A profitable firm can generate revenues that exceed both types of costs. In short, we continue to regard a firm's best cost reporting system as a situation-specific question.

REVIEW PROBLEM 1 Part A

A.B.C. Electronics manufactures stereo earphones. An absorption costing income statement for A.B.C. appears below for the year 1981. A.B.C. uses a FIFO cost flow assumption for determining its cost of goods sold. Use these income statement data to:

(a) Calculate the direct costing standard cost per unit.
(b) Prepare a direct costing income statement.
(c) Determine the finished goods inventory balance on 12/31/81 under direct costing.
(d) Reconcile the differences between the absorption costing profit shown below and the direct costing profit calculated in (b) above.

A.B.C. Electronics
Absorption Costing Income Statement
Year Ended December 31, 1981

Sales		$1,000,000
Cost of goods sold[a]		600,000
Gross profit		$ 400,000
Operating expenses		
Selling[b]	$150,000	
Administrative[c]	200,000	350,000
Profit before taxes		$ 50,000

Inventory
January 1, 1981: 6,000 headsets
December 31, 1981: 2,000 headsets

[a] Standard cost per headset

Materials	$ 6.00
Labor	4.00
Variable overhead (50% of direct labor cost)	2.00
Fixed overhead[d]	3.00
	$15.00

[b] Selling costs are composed of $2 per unit variable cost and $70,000 per year fixed cost.
[c] All administrative costs are fixed. Assume there was no volume variance or any other standard cost variance in this period.
[d] Fixed costs are $108,000 per year.

REVIEW PROBLEM 1   Part B

Refer to the standard cost in A.B.C.'s absorption costing income statement. Assume that in the next period A.B.C. produced 40,000 units and sold 36,000. Acutal and standard manufacturing costs for production were as follows:

	Actual Costs	Standard Costs
Materials	$250,000	$240,000
Labor	164,000	160,000
Variable overhead	82,000	80,000
Fixed overhead	108,000	120,000
	$604,000	$600,000

(a) Compute the gross margin under absorption costing assuming all variances are charged (or credited) to cost of goods sold.

(b) What variances would be charged to sales under direct costing?

(c) Compute the difference in income for 1982 between absorption and direct costing, given your results in (a) and (b) above.

(d) How would cost of goods sold and ending inventory balances be affected if the firm carried its inventory at actual costs under a FIFO flow assumption?

Service Department Allocations

Generally accepted accounting principles require that all manufacturing service department costs—fixed or variable—be allocated to units of production. The procedure has two stages. First, costs are accumulated in accounts for the specific service departments, and then they are allocated to the producing departments as additional overhead.

Recall from Chapter 9 that we could develop a demand for allocating incremental service department costs to producing departments in order to assess the total incremental costs incurred when the activities of producing departments are varied among different alternatives. We often use variable costs as estimates of incremental costs. Therefore, we could then accept the rule to allocate variable service department costs to production since it would be consistent with management's purposes as well. The same cannot be said for fixed overhead.

In financial accounting, the purpose of service department allocations is simply to provide a basis for distributing manufacturing costs incurred between ending inventories and cost of goods sold. Consequently, the methods used to allocate costs can be less refined (simplified) without *materially* affecting the income reported by a firm for a particular accounting period. As we shall see in the following example, however, simplified rules may not be appropriate when the allocations are used as a basis for pricing or rate setting.

Assume that an organization consists of two production departments and two manufacturing service departments Data governing the activities of the service departments are summarized below.

Services of (in hours)	Hours Used By				Total	Costs of Service Department
	S_1	S_2	P_1	P_2		
S_1	—	600	300	100	1,000	$ 8,000
S_2	200	—	100	700	1,000	10,000

A. Allocate Service Department Costs Directly to Production Departments.

For the general purpose of allocating service costs to production, it is often practical to allocate service department costs directly to the producing departments, irrespective of the fact that the service departments also consume one another's services. The allocations are based on the fractions of services consumed *by each producing department* relative to the total amount provided to production.

In our example, P_1 and P_2 consumed 400 hours of S_1's services and 800 hours of S_2's. Their relative fractions are

	To	
Costs of	P_1	P_2
S_1	300/400	100/400
S_2	100/800	700/800

The total service cost allocations based on these fractions would result in [($8,000)300/400 + ($10,000)100/800] costs to P_1 and ($8,000)100/400 + ($10,000)700/800 costs to P_2, or $7,250 and $10,750, respectively (note the total of $18,000).

This so-called direct method is practical, but it can distort the relative costs of each producing department. It is clear that much of the activity of S_1 is for the benefit of S_2 (600/1,000 hours, or 60 percent of its services). Similarly, most of S_2's activity is for the benefit of P_2. Hence, much of the activity of S_1 is indirectly caused by P_2. In such situations we can obtain materially different allocations if we ignore reciprocal uses of services by the service departments, as above, or try to account for them in the allocations.

B. The Step Method of Recognizing Interdepartment Consumption.

A practical method for dealing with interdepartment transfers of services (reciprocal relationships) is the step method, which was popular before the advent of computers and calculators. As indicated in Chapter 9, the method allocates one service department's costs to the remaining service departments *and* to the producing departments on the basis of the relative amounts of services consumed by each. Then a second service department's costs, which include its own plus its allocation from the first department, are allocated to the remaining service departments and the producing departments. The procedure is repeated until all service department costs are allocated to the production departments only. The order of allocation may be based on the magnitude of the service department costs—for example, the department with the largest costs allocated first, the second largest second, and so on. Allocation order may also be determined on the basis of the pervasiveness of the services provided—that is, allocate the costs of the department serving the most service and producing departments first, then the costs of the department servicing the next largest number of departments, and so on.

Let us try both sequences in our example: (a) costs of S_1 first and then costs of S_2, and (b) costs of S_2 first and then costs of S_1. The following table shows the cost allocations for the first situation.

Costs of	Amount	\multicolumn{4}{c}{Allocated to}	Fractions
		S_1	S_2	P_1	P_2	
S_1	8,000	—	$4,800	$2,400	$ 800	$6/10, 3/10, 1/10$
S_2	14,800			1,850	12,950	$1/8, 7/8$
Totals				$4,250	$13,750	$18,000

Compared with the direct method, this allocation results in significantly different portions of costs being allocated to the producing departments. Although both methods are acceptable for financial accounting purposes, the parties affected might not be indifferent about them. For example, suppose P_1 produces commercial products and P_2 produces government products. If the government contract were based on a cost-plus formula, the firm would prefer the second allocation, since it might result in a higher price by being able to have more allocated costs reimbursed. At the same time, the government negotiators would probably prefer the first allocation. (Of course the basic issue would then be what to charge the customer and not how to allocate the cost.) If both departments produced commercial goods with prices independent of service cost allocations, the firm's total income might not be affected to the extent that the same total amount of service department costs remain in the inventories for each department.

Now consider the allocation of S_2 costs followed by those of S_1.

Costs of	Amount	Allocated to				Fractions
		S_1	S_2	P_1	P_2	
S_2	$10,000	$2,000		$1,000	$7,000	$\frac{2}{10}, \frac{1}{10}, \frac{7}{10}$
S_1	10,000			7,500	2,500	$\frac{3}{4}, \frac{1}{4}$
Total				$8,500	$9,500	$18,000

We obtained nearly the same result with the direct method, which suggests that the step method may not solve (or take proper account of) the reciprocity problem in all cases.

C. Algebraic Method. As illustrated in Chapter 9, it is possible to solve the service department cost allocation problem with a series of equations. (Matrix algebra can even be employed to advantage.) First, we set up the service department equations to reflect the extent to which they account for one another's activities.

$$S_1 = \$8,000 + \tfrac{2}{10}\, S_2$$

$$S_2 = \$10,000 + \tfrac{6}{10}\, S_1$$

Then we solve by substituting the first equation in the second.

$$S_2 = \$10,000 + \tfrac{6}{10}(\$8,000 + \tfrac{2}{10}\, S_2)$$

$$S_2 = \$10,000 + \$4,800 + \tfrac{12}{100}\, S_2$$

$$\tfrac{44}{50}\, S_2 = \$14,800$$

$$S_2 = \$16,818$$

We substitute this result back into the first equation to solve for S_1.

$$S_1 = \$8,000 + \tfrac{2}{10}\, S_2$$

$$= \$8,000 + \tfrac{2}{10}(\$16,818)$$

$$= \$8,000 + \$3,364$$

$$= \$11,364$$

Note that the sum of these two results, $16,818 + $11,364 = $28,182, clearly exceeds the total costs incurred ($18,000) by the two departments. This "double-accounting" problem reflects the fact that the costs incurred by the two service departments—$8,000 and $10,000—already include the cost of the services provided to each other. Our equations, therefore, represent inflated amounts of cost to be allocated to the production departments. The amount of the double charges is removed by allocating to the production departments only their percentage shares of the two solutions obtained above. That is, since P_1 and P_2 consumed $\frac{3}{10}$ and $\frac{1}{10}$ of S_1's services, respectively, they would be allocated $\frac{3}{10}(\$11,364)$ and $\frac{1}{10}(\$11,364)$ for S_1's services. Based on their relative shares of S_2's services, P_1 would receive $\frac{1}{10}(\$16,818)$ and P_2 would receive $\frac{7}{10}(\$16,818)$ as their allocations of S_2's costs. These calculations are summarized in the following table:

	Assigned to	
Costs of	P_1	P_2
S_1	$3,409	$ 1,136
S_2	1,682	11,773
	$5,091	$12,909
Total = $18,000		

We now have three different allocation methods that may be used for financial accounting purposes. Other proposals have been made, but they are basically variations of the algebraic method. As indicated earlier the different methods may not affect materially a firm's income figures, depending on what portion of these costs is allocated to the inventory balances of P_1 and P_2 and what portion goes to cost of sales. Of course, the choice of allocation methods should not be so cavalier when the information is used for managerial decisions. Generally, we can conclude (as in Chapter 9) that an algebraic approach applied to the variable service department costs is preferred for managerial decision making purposes. (In making this statement we ignore the cost of implementing the preferred procedure; otherwise a qualified remark would be in order.) Although both fixed and variable service department costs will be allocated for financial accounting purposes, we might argue that the algebraic method could be used here as well.

Suppose P_2 is a revenue-generating unit in a hospital that treats patients who have complex illnesses. The services of S_2 and its drawing on the services of S_1 result in heavy expenditures by each. Hence, the patients treated in P_2 are actually the source of much of the hospital's total service department costs. As a result, those patients who are treated in P_1 may not be willing to share the costs of S_1 and S_2 under the direct or step method but would prefer an allocation method that reflects the lower costs of services provided to P_1. The Cost Accounting Standards Board tends to follow the same principle. The Board has not limited its acceptance to a single method of cost allocations, but it has implied a preference for the algebraic method.[6]

If a firm is using internally an algebraic method for allocating its service departments' variable costs, the incremental costs of using the same method to allocate fixed costs in order to meet financial accounting requirements should be small. In the process, it might also achieve another advantage. Outside users of accounting data tend to accept financial statement figures more readily if they are based on the accounting methods used in a firm's internal accounting system. In cases when a firm consciously selects different accounting methods for different purposes, outside users are cautious about the results of the accounting methods. This seems to be especially true with the IRS.

Finally, we should recognize a common variation of the service department allocation question that occurs when a product passes through several production departments. Manufacturing overhead may be allocated on a department-by-department basis, or the overheads might be aggregated and a single firm-wide allocation used. Discussion of this question would precisely mirror all that we have said above: Usefulness for decision making and performance evaluation may or may not be consistent with external reporting requirements.

REVIEW PROBLEM 2
Service Department Costs _____

Assume the following service time relationships among two service departments and two production departments:

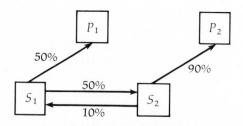

---

[6] Elaborate accounting rules prevail in cost-reimbursement settings such as government contracting and health insurance contracting in the United States. The Cost Accounting Standards Board issued 18 standards during its tenure. An excellent reference is H. Wright and J. Bedingfield, *Government Contract Accounting*. Washington, D.C.: GPO, 1979. Medicare accounting provisions can be found in Commerce Clearing House's *Social Security and Medicare Explained*. Finally a theoretical treatment of these issues would begin with a specification of the basic production and pricing questions at hand, as sketched in Chapter 9 for a simple setting. See J. Demski and G. Feltham, *Cost Determination: A Conceptual Approach*. Ames, Iowa: Iowa State Univ. Press, 1976.

Other production data include the following:

	P_1	P_2	S_1	S_2
Output (units, hours)	1,000	2,000	2,000	2,000
Variable costs	$10/unit	$10/unit	$10,000	$20,000
Fixed costs	$6,000	$8,000	$ 8,000	$10,000
Selling prices of "output"	$20/unit	$22/unit	?	?

(a) The firm's accountant wants the allocation of service department costs kept as simple as possible, because the only reason such costs are allocated is to meet financial accounting requirements. Therefore, she suggests that all the costs of S_1 be transferred directly to P_1 and all those of S_2 directly to P_2.

   Assume this is done. Determine the *average cost of the services* used by P_1 and P_2 and insert your answers in the following chart.

	P_1	P_2
Variable costs	_____	_____
Fixed costs	_____	_____
Average cost per hour of service received	_____	_____

(b) Repeat part (a) using the step method (allocate S_1's cost first).

	P_1	P_2
Variable costs	_____	_____
Fixed costs	_____	_____
Average cost per hour of service received	_____	_____

(c) Repeat part (a) using an algebraic approach to service department cost allocations.
We start with variable costs as follows:

$$S_1 = \$10,000 + \tfrac{1}{10} S_2$$
$$S_2 = \$20,000 + \tfrac{5}{10} S_1$$

and then repeat with fixed costs:

$$S_1 = \$8,000 + \tfrac{1}{10} S_2$$
$$S_2 = \$10,000 + \tfrac{5}{10} S_2$$

Our final allocations are the following:

	P_1	P_2
Variable costs	_____	_____
Fixed costs	_____	_____
Average cost per hour of services received	_____	_____

(d) Discuss the conditions under which it would be important to rely on an algebraic approach to service department cost allocations.

Joint Cost Allocations

In Chapter 9 we saw that allocations of the joint costs of producing two or more types of outputs in a relatively fixed ratio—for example, 2 units of A and 1 unit of B per standard amount of input costs—are typically not useful for managerial purposes. Joint manufacturing process costs, however, must be allocated to the different outputs in order to obtain acceptable inventory valuations for financial reporting purposes.

To illustrate some possible allocation methods, assume that a joint manufacturing process has produced 5,000 units of Product A and 3,000 units of Product B at a total cost of $40,000. The units of A and B have not been sold and must be recorded in their respective inventory accounts. Each unit of A sells for $6 net of any additional future costs of finishing and delivery. We call this the *net realizable value* per unit of A. The net realizable value of each unit of B is $10. Note that the total net realizable value of A is $6 × 5,000 units = $30,000, the same as the total net realizable value of B($10 × 3,000 units).

Suppose we tried to record the inventories of A and B at these values. We would acknowledge A inventory of $30,000 and B inventory of $30,000, but could only record a joint process cost of $40,000. The $20,000 excess is "unrealized" profit, which is generally not recorded in financial accounts. Exceptions might be made in the business of mining precious metals (like gold and silver) in which net realizable amounts are relatively certain of being realized. The general rule, however, is to record inventory of units at the historical or incurred costs. This means that regardless of the allocation method used, the sum of the recorded inventory values of A and B cannot exceed $40,000. Let us now consider some acceptable methods of allocating costs.

Unit Cost of Output

One option is merely to divide the joint process costs by the total number of units of output, in this case, $40,000/8,000 units = $5 per unit. Each unit of A and B would be entered into its respective inventory account at this average unit cost.

Suppose, then, that one-half of the output of each type of product was sold at the net realizable value. Our firm's income statement would appear as follows:

	A (2,500 Units)	B (1,500 Units)	Total
Sales	$15,000	$15,000	$30,000
Less cost of goods sold	12,500	7,500	20,000
Gross margin	$ 2,500	7,500	$10,000

This allocation method makes product B "look" three times as profitable as product A even though its total net realizable value is the same as A's. Such data might promote inappropriate profitability assessments.

Net Realizable Value

In order to avoid arbitrarily making one product of a joint process appear more profitable than another, accountants use a method of joint cost allocation based on the relative net realizable value of the *total* output of each product (not the relative net realizable value per unit). Earlier we calculated the total net realizable value of the output of the process, $60,000. The ratio of the net realizable value of each product's output to the total is $30,000/$60,000 for A and $30,000/$60,000 for B, or ½ for each. The $40,000 joint cost would be allocated to each output on the basis of this fraction, that is, $20,000 to each. Note though that the per unit cost of product A in inventory will be $20,000/5,000 = $4, whereas the per unit cost of B will be $20,000/3,000 = $6.67.

Again we assume that one-half the output of each product is sold at its net realizable value.

	A (2,500 Units)	B (1,500 Units)	Total
Sales	$15,000	$15,000	$30,000
Less cost of goods sold	10,000	10,000	20,000
	$ 5,000	$ 5,000	$10,000

This method does not distort the relative profitability of the total outputs of the two products as the unit cost allocation method does. Moreover, if we compare the profitability of each product on a per unit basis we observe the following:

	A	B
Profit per unit	$2.00	$3.33
$\dfrac{\text{Profit}}{\text{Net realizable value}}$	$\dfrac{\$2.00}{\$6.00} = .333$	$\dfrac{\$3.33}{\$10.00} = .333$

This result is considered "equitable," because the joint cost allocation does not favor the profit margin of one product at the expense of the other joint product(s).

Relative Total Weight

Another possible basis of joint cost allocation is the relative total weight method. To illustrate, suppose a unit of A weighs 3 pounds and a unit of B weighs 1 pound. The total weight of the output of A would be 15,000 pounds and the total weight of B would be 3,000 pounds, for a total of 18,000 pounds. Under this method of allocation, A's inventory of 5,000 units is recorded at $^{15}/_{18}(\$40,000) = \$33,333$, and B's inventory of 3,000 units is recorded at $^{3}/_{18}(\$40,000) = \$6,667$. Observe then that if one-half the output of each product were sold, A would show a loss—($15,000 − $16,667) = −$1,667—but B would show a nice profit—($15,000 − $3,333) = $11,667—with the total again being $10,000. As we can see, the relative total weight method suffers from the same potential problem as the relative number of units method.

The Case of By-Products

The joint cost problem is further complicated by the existence of by-products. By-products are joint-process outputs whose total net realizable value is considered immaterial, with the definition of immaterial following traditional accounting rules (small percentage of income or asset values). There are two basic methods for dealing with by-products. The first is not recording their output and treating the net selling values as additional revenue (or additional income) as these units are actually sold. If they are "sold" at negative values, the accountant would either increase the cost of goods sold of the main products or show these amounts as "other expense." The second approach is to reduce the joint cost by recording the value of the by-product output in an inventory account. The question is, at what per unit values?

The general rule is to record by-products at their net realizable value so that when they are eventually sold, and prices are as anticipated, the products will show a zero profit (zero loss). To illustrate, suppose the joint process in our example also makes a by-product, Z, whose selling price is $1 per unit. However, in order to sell Z the firm has to incur additional "disposal" costs of $.25 per unit. The process produced 500 units of Z along with the 5,000 units of A and 3,000 units of B.

The inventory of by-products would be recorded at 500 × .75 = $375, thereby reducing the joint process costs, which will then be allocated to the inventories of A and B as before (using the net realizable value, inventory A would receive ½ of $39,625 and inventory B would receive ½ of $39,625).

Of course, this whole system depends on the definition of a product as a by-product. If the definition does not apply, the product will have to be considered a main product and share in an allocation of the joint costs of the process producing it.

The Problem of Split-off Prices versus Final Prices

In our previous illustration we assumed that our main products were transferred to inventory to await sale at net prices of $6 and $10, respectively. Suppose the firm had the option to process each product further through separate processes after which they could be sold for $9 and $15, respectively, for A and B. The additional processing costs of A are $10,000, or an average of $2 per unit. B's additional processing costs are $9,000, or $3 per unit. How should the $40,000 joint processing costs be allocated to A and B so that they can be recorded in inventory at their point of separation—the split-off point?

There are two possibilities: One is to use the prices at the split-off point and the other is to use the net realizable value of each product on the assumption each will be processed further before sale. We might even compromise and state that the prices should be selected that best reflect management's intent—either to sell now or to process further.

Income If All Joint Products Are Sold

Joint cost allocations will not alter a firm's income if all joint products are sold in the period in which they are produced. For example, if all units of A and B are sold in the current period, the entire amount of costs allocated to each, regardless of the method, will pass through the inventory accounts and become part of cost of goods sold. Hence, the entire $40,000 of joint costs will be charged to cost of goods sold. The only effect of different allocation methods would be to shift the relative amounts of costs allocated to each output type, thus showing different product-line profitabilities. Because we cannot justify showing different levels of profitability of products by a joint process, any allocation of joint costs in such situations should not be taken seriously. There are exceptions here, if we can be more precise. Recall from our discussion in Chapter 9 that we should approach the allocation issue with the allocation's purpose *explicitly* defined. A joint cost allocation might be used, for example, for cost-plus pricing purposes. In this case, the joint cost allocation should be taken quite seriously: the price is based on it. The question of how to allocate the joint cost becomes a question of what price is to be paid.[7]

---

[7] Recent allocation literature has employed game theory to generate "optimal" allocations of joint costs. These "optimal" allocations may, in fact, look quite similar to those we could obtain with, say, the net realizable value method. Eventually, however, the notion of "optimality" must be linked to the purpose for producing the allocation. Otherwise we are able to present

REVIEW PROBLEM 3

Assume a joint process produces two main products and a by-product, referred to hereafter as A, B, and B$_p$, respectively. During a particular accounting period, 10,000 units of A, 5,000 units of B, and 1,000 units of B$_p$ were produced at a total cost of $80,000. Product A may be sold immediately at a price of $6 per unit or treated further through Process II, after which it will sell for $10 per unit. Processing costs for Process II are $15,000 for 10,000 units. Product B either must be processed further in Process III or scrapped. Additional costs in Process III are $3 per unit. Once processed, Product B can be sold for $8. The by-product, B$_p$, must be treated at a cost of $.75 per unit before it can be scrapped in order to conform to state pollution laws.

Required   (a)   Use the following methods to allocate the joint processing costs to A and B, including the negative value of B$_p$, so that B$_p$ will show a zero profit or loss when it is disposed of:
(1)   Net realizable values based on the final price of A.
(2)   Net realizable values based on the price of A at split-off.
(3)   Total units of output.
(b)   Suppose one-half of the total output of each product were sold. After further processing what will be the gross margin for the firm under (a)(1) above?
(c)   Suppose all of the output of each product were sold. What would be the gross margin for the firm under any method of allocation?

Conclusion

In this chapter we have surveyed the types of allocation problems encountered when costs must be assigned to units of output in order to conform with GAAP or other absorption costing regulations. Variations to the basic methods described in the chapter are illustrated in the problems that follow. Because this chapter may be used early in the course and not in the natural sequence, we were forced to repeat some of the discussion which appears elsewhere in the book. Also notice that, in contrast with Chapter 9, our discussion was basically procedural. The accounting community simply does not understand financial reporting well enough to offer a more conceptual treatment at this time.

In the next chapter we shall continue with actual cost systems and illustrate how costs are accumulated in job order and process costing systems. Knowing the basics of fixed cost allocations should make the material in the next chapter easier to follow.

---

only alternative procedures and their properties. See J. Demski, "Cost Allocation Games," in S. Moriarity, ed., *Joint Cost Allocations.* Norman, Okla.: Center for Economic and Management Analysis, 1981.

Appendix A
Absorption versus Direct Costing

EXHIBIT 11-4

Differences in Absorption (Full) and Direct Costing Income[a]

Notation is as follows:
  PF = income under absorption costing
  PD = income under direct costing
  FC = the current period's fixed manufacturing cost
  BF = the fixed manufacturing cost portion of the opening inventory
  OI = opening inventory quantity
  EI = ending inventory quantity
   S = quantity sold in the current period
   q = quantity produced in the current period
  SF = standard fixed cost per unit
FIFO = first in, first out
LIFO = last in, first out

Inventory Costing Method	Difference, PF − PD
Average actual	$\dfrac{EI}{EI+S}\left(\dfrac{FC}{S}-\dfrac{BF}{EI}\right)$
FIFO actual[b]	$EI\left(\dfrac{FC}{q}-\dfrac{BF}{EI}\right)$
LIFO actual with $S<q$	$(EI-OI)\dfrac{FC}{q}$
LIFO actual with $S>q$	$(EI-OI)\dfrac{BF}{OI}$
Standard costs	$SF(EI-OI)$

---

[a] Adapted from Y. Ijiri *et al.*, "The Effect of Inventory Costing Methods on Full and Direct Costing," *J. of Accounting Research*, Spring 1965, p. 71. The first two results may not be obvious, in which case the student should refer to the original paper for their derivations. The LIFO actual results may be explained as follows: (1) $q > S$, the amount of fixed costs carried over in inventories will be equal to the increase in units in inventory times the current year's fixed costs per unit. The product will be positive, indicating that PF > PD. (2) If $S > q$, fixed costs charged to sales will exceed the total amount of fixed costs incurred in the period by the amount released from beginning inventory. This will equal $(EI − OI)$ times the prior year's fixed cost per unit. In this case, the difference will be negative (i.e., EI < OI and PF < PD).
[b] Assumes sales exceed opening inventory; that is, $S > OI$.

Appendix B
Debits and Credits

Assume a firm has the following balances in its control accounts at the beginning of an accounting period.

Assets (other than inventory)	$20,000	Liabilities	$25,000
Raw materials	10,000	Owner's equity	50,000
Work-in-process	20,000		
Finished goods	25,000		
Totals	$75,000		$75,000

During the accounting period the following transactions took place:

(1)	Acquired raw materials on account		$ 30,000
(2)	Raw materials requisitioned by producing departments		25,000
(3)	Direct labor costs, credited to liabilities		30,000
(4)	Overhead costs incurred:		
	Amounts credited to liability accounts	$15,000	
	Amounts credited to asset accounts	6,000	
	Total incurred	$21,000	
(5)	Total applied		20,000
	Total current costs to work-in-process		$ 75,000
(6)	Cost of goods manufactured and charged to finished goods		$ 70,000
(7)	Ending inventory of finished goods		20,000
(8)	Sales revenues, cash and credit		125,000
(9)	Selling and administrative costs incurred (credit liabilities)		25,000
(10)	Liabilities paid at the end of the period		90,000
(11)	Under-applied amounts charged to cost of goods sold		1,000

Required   (a)   Open accounts for assets, liabilities, owners' equity, each type of inventory, cost of goods sold, overhead control, sales, and selling and administrative expenses.

(b)   Record beginning balances and the effects of transactions (1) through (11) in the accounts opened in (a) above (key entries by numbers).

(c)   Prepare an income statement covering the accounting period and a balance sheet for the end of the period.

Solution

Assets

B. Bal.	$ 20,000	$ 6,000	(4)
(8)	125,000	90,000	(10)

| E. Bal. | $ 49,000 | | |

Overhead Control

(4)	$ 21,000	$ 20,000	(5)
		1,000	(11)

| | 0 | | |

Raw Materials

B. Bal.	$ 10,000		
(1)	30,000	$ 25,000	(2)

| E. Bal. | $ 15,000 | | |

Liabilities

		$ 25,000	B. Bal.
		30,000	(1)
(10)	$ 90,000	30,000	(3)
		15,000	(4)
		25,000	(9)

| | | $ 35,000 | G. Bal. |

Owners' Equity

	$ 50,000	B. Bal.

Work-in-Process

B. Bal.	$ 20,000		
(2)	25,000		
(3)	30,000		
(5)	20,000	$ 70,000	(6)

| E. Bal. | $ 25,000 | | |

Sales

	$125,000	(8)

Cost of Goods Sold

(7)	$ 75,000	
(11)	1,000	

Finished Goods

B. Bal.	$ 25,000		
(6)	70,000	$ 75,000	(7)

| E. Bal. | $ 20,000 | | |

Selling & Administrative Costs

(9)	$ 25,000	

INCOME STATEMENT

Sales	$125,000
Cost of goods sold	76,000
Gross margin	$ 49,000
Less: Selling and administrative costs	25,000
Net income	$ 24,000

BALANCE SHEET

Assets	$ 49,000	Liabilities		$ 35,000
Raw materials	15,000	Owner's equity:		
Work-in-process	25,000	Beginning balance	$50,000	
Finished goods	20,000	Net income	24,000	74,000
Total	$109,000			$109,000

Supplementary Readings

Articles

Amerman, G., "Facts about Direct Costing for Profit Determination," *Accounting Research,* April 1954; reprinted in H.R. Anton and P.A. Firmin, eds., *Contemporary Issues in Cost Accounting,* 2nd ed. Boston: Houghton Mifflin, 1972.

Bierman, H., "Inventory Valuation: The Uses of Market Prices," *Accounting Rev.,* Oct. 1967. This paper illustrates a procedure of cost allocation based on the marginal revenue of the joint products.

Fess, P., and W. Ferrara, "The Period Cost Concept for Income Measurement—Can It Be Defended?" *Accounting Rev.,* Oct. 1961.

Fremgen, J., "The Direct Costing Controversy—An Identification of Issues," *Accounting Rev.,* Jan. 1964.

Green, D., "A Moral to the Direct Costing Controversy?" *J. of Business,* July 1960.

Ijiri, Y. et al., "The Effect of Inventory Costing Methods on Full and Direct Costing," *J. of Accounting Research,* Spring 1965.

Kaplan, R., "Variable and Self Service Costs in Reciprocal Allocation Models," *Accounting Rev.,* Oct. 1973.

Sorter, G., and C.T. Horngren, "Asset Recognition and Economic Attributes—A Relevant Costing Approach," *Accounting Rev.,* July 1962.

Weil, R., "Allocating Joint Costs," *American Economic Rev.,* Dec. 1968.

Other

Davidson, S., and R. Weil, eds., *Handbook of Cost Accounting.* New York: McGraw-Hill, 1978.

Questions and Problems

1. Define absorption (full) costing and direct (variable) costing.
2. It has been suggested that for many firms the shift from their present absorption costing methods to direct costing would have little impact on the financial statements. Explain why this could be the case.
3. Briefly compare the reason why LIFO and FIFO show different profits and the reason absorption costing and direct costing show different profits.
4. Explain briefly, but as analytically as you can, why the following statement is correct: "Profit under absorption costing reflects the effects of changes in sales and production. Direct costing reflects only changes in sales."
5. Define joint costs and joint products, as normally used by accountants, and distinguish between a joint product and a by-product.
6. Discuss the statement, "The purpose of allocating joint costs is to permit management to assess the profitability of different joint products."
7. Comment on the following: "The net realizable value method of allocating joint costs is the most realistic method the accountant has available for such allocations."
8. What is meant by the split-off point?
9. The relative sales values of joint products may be based either on the market prices of the products at the split-off point or on their net realizable values at split-off. Assuming prices exist at the split-off, which method would you use, and why?

10. **Form of Direct Costing Income Statement**
   XYZ, Inc., manufactures paint. During 1981 it produced 1,000,000 gallons and sold 990,000 gallons at $.30 per gallon. On January 1, 1981, its inventory of paint was 20,000 gallons, which was carried at $1,500 on direct costing and $3,000 on FIFO absorption. The costs for the year are shown in Exhibit 11–5. The entries in parentheses indicate how the firm classifies the product costs.

EXHIBIT 11–5

Account	Amount
Basic white (raw materials)	$15,000
Depreciation on mixers (overhead)	10,000
Heat and light (overhead)	5,000
Machine operators' wages (direct labor)	48,000
Managers' salaries	50,000
Office rental	6,000
Office workers' salaries	18,000
Pigments (raw materials)	14,000
Quality control personnel (overhead)	12,000
Rental on plant	12,000
Sales commissions	29,700
Supervisors' wages (overhead)	16,000
Thinner (raw materials)	1,000
Power (overhead)	2,000

(a) Draw up a direct costing income statement.
(b) Calculate the direct costing cost per gallon.
(c) Calculate the FIFO absorption cost per unit for the production of the period.

11. **Direct Costing and the Size of Contribution and Profits**

Chair-Makers, Inc., manufactures a single product, auditorium seats, in only one style. The color of the upholstery does not affect the cost. Each seat sells for $12 and incurs $6 variable cost to produce and $1 variable cost to sell. Fixed costs are $40,000. Of that figure, $10,000 are administrative and selling expenses and $30,000 are production costs.

(a) Compute the contribution margin per unit.
(b) Make up a direct costing income statement for a sales volume of 11,000 chairs.
(c) What is the effect on direct costing profit if production increases from 11,000 to 15,000 chairs and sales remain constant?

12. **Comparison of Direct Costing and Standard Absorption Costing Profits**

A.B.C., Inc., manufactures a single product, A-ite, that removes spots. A.B.C. sells it for $3 per gallon to various distributors, who package it under their own trade names. A.B.C. uses a standard cost system and allocates fixed costs over the expected normal volume of 25,000 gallons per year. All of the relevant data for the three years in which A.B.C. operated before going out of business are shown below. Assume that no inventory of A-ite was on hand at the start of 1979.

	1979	1980	1981
Units produced (gallons)	30,000	25,000	10,000
Units sold (gallons)	25,000	20,000	20,000
Variable cost per gallon	$1	$1	$1
Fixed costs per year	$50,000	$50,000	$50,000
Administrative and advertising expenses	$10,000	$10,000	$10,000

(a) Calculate the gross margin and net profit for each year assuming A.B.C. uses:
(1) Direct costing.
(2) Standard costs with the volume variance considered a period charge.
(3) Standard costs with the volume variance allocated between inventory and cost of goods sold.
(b) Comment on the causes of the annual differences.

13. **Conversion of FIFO Profit to Direct Costing Profit**

Alpha Products has been recording its inventory on a FIFO absorption costing basis. It is considering converting to a FIFO direct costing basis for internal purposes. The data for the first four years of Alpha's operations are given below.

	Year 1	Year 2	Year 3	Year 4
Absorption costing profits	$ 40,000	$ 30,000	$ 55,000	$100,000
Equivalent tons of production	2,500	2,500	3,000	3,500
Tons sold	2,000	2,500	2,500	3,500
Fixed costs	$100,000	$125,000	$105,000	$105,000

(a) Calculate the direct costing profit for each year. *Hint:* Calculate the fixed cost per unit of output for each period; then compute the change in fixed costs in inventory assuming a FIFO flow. For example, in Year 1 the change was a *plus* $40 × 500 units = $20,000. In Year 2 ending inventory would be 500 units but the fixed cost per unit would be $50 (or $125,000/2,500 units).

(b) Explain the difference between the total profits under FIFO absorption for the four-year period and the direct costing profit over the same period.

14. **Comparison of Absorption and Direct Costing: Multiple Choice**
The following annual flexible budget has been prepared for use in making decisions relating to Product X.

	100,000 Units	200,000 Units
Sales	$800,000	$1,600,000
Manufacturing costs		
Variable	$300,000	$ 600,000
Fixed	200,000	200,000
Total	$500,000	$ 800,000
Selling and other expenses		
Variable	$200,000	$ 400,000
Fixed	160,000	160,000
Total	$360,000	$ 560,000

Management predicts sales of 200,000 for the coming year, and that volume will be used for allocating fixed manufacturing costs to units of Product X.

All fixed costs are budgeted and incurred uniformly throughout the year and all costs incurred coincide with the budget. Over- and underapplied fixed manufacturing costs are deferred until year-end. Annual sales have the following seasonal pattern:

	Portion of Annual Sales
First quarter	10%
Second quarter	20
Third quarter	30
Fourth quarter	40
	100%

At the end of the first six months the following information is available:

Production completed	120,000 units
Sales	60,000 units

(a) The amount of fixed factory costs applied to Product X during the first six months under absorption costing would be
   (1) overapplied by $20,000.
   (2) equal to the fixed costs incurred.
   (3) underapplied by $40,000.
   (4) underapplied by $80,000.
   (5) none of the above.
(b) Reported net income (or loss) for the first six months under absorption costing would be
   (1) $160,000.
   (2) $80,000.
   (3) $40,000.
   (4) ($40,000).
   (5) none of the above.
(c) Reported net income (or loss) for the first six months under direct costing would be
   (1) $144,000.
   (2) $72,000.
   (3) $0.
   (4) ($36,000).
   (5) none of the above.
(d) Assuming that 90,000 units of Product X were sold during the first six months and that this is to be used as a basis, the revised budget estimate for the total number of units to be sold during this year would be
   (1) 360,000.
   (2) 240,000.
   (3) 200,000.
   (4) 120,000.
   (5) none of the above.

[AICPA adapted]

15. *Direct Costing and Decision Making*

(a) Your firm is about to convert to direct costing for internal reporting. One department head has been sold on it because it provides better data for decision making than the absorption costing data he has been receiving. He has given you a list of the decisions he must make frequently. Indicate to him when the direct costing data are correct for his purposes or, if they are inappropriate, where he will be misled.
   (1) When there is excess capacity, that is, idle machines, the department head calls the large buyers and solicits orders from them. They are

not usually customers of your firm, so they will demand a very good price.

(2) The department has two sections. One is filled with new equipment that is always running. The other consists of old, standby machines that can be used when demand is high and you can receive a high price for your product. The department head must decide whether to open the old section, run overtime, or reject a new order.

(3) Quite often, typically in the planning stage of the next model year, the department head is called upon to "cost out" the new model. That is, he must estimate its cost.

(4) Less frequently than in (3), he must make cost estimates on special projects for other departments that require use of his facilities.

(b) Based on your answers to part (a) of this question, under what general conditions does direct costing assist the internal decision maker?

16. **Effect of Changed Costs and Selling Price on Profit**
The Dawn Mining Company mines selum, a commonly used mineral. The company's report of operations is presented in Exhibit 11–6.

The following information pertains to the company's operations:

(1) The sales price of selum was increased from $8 per ton to $11 per ton on January 1, 1981.

(2) New mining machinery was placed in operation on January 1, 1981, that reduced the cost of mining from $9 per ton to $8.50 per ton.

(3) There was no change in ending inventories that were valued on the LIFO basis.

Required (a) Prepare an analysis that accounts for the change in the gross profit of the Dawn Mining Company. The analysis should account for the effects of the changes in price, volume, and volume–price factors on (1) sales and (2) cost of goods sold.

(b) Assume that the inventory was carried at FIFO and consisted of 10,000 tons at both the beginning and the end of the year. How would this alter the 1981 statement?

[AICPA adapted]

————————————————————————————— EXHIBIT 11–6

The Dawn Mining Company
Report of Operations
For the Years Ended December 31, 1980 and 1981

	1980	1981	Increase (decrease)
Net sales	$ 840,000	$891,000	$ 51,000
Cost of goods sold	945,000	688,500	(256,500)
Gross profit (loss)	$(105,000)	$202,500	$307,500

17. *Calculation of Direct Costing Profit from Absorption Profit Data*
Normal capacity of the Adams Company is 20,000 units per month, or 240,000 units per year. Standard variable cost per unit is: materials, $3.00; labor, $2.25; and overhead, $.75; or a total of $6.00 per unit. Standard fixed manufacturing expenses are $300,000 per year, or $25,000 per month. In the data given below, there is no variance except the volume variance. This was closed to profit each month as the absorption cost income statements were prepared. Thus, all inventories are stated at standard cost.

	Month 1	Month 2	Month 3	Month 4
Units produced	17,500	21,000	19,000	20,000
Units sold	17,500	18,000	21,000	16,500
Absorption cost profit	$40,000	$45,750	$51,500	$40,375

Using the given data, compute the direct costing profit for each month.

18. *Major Review Problem—Chapter 7 and Chapter 11: Comparison of Direct Costing and Absorption Costing with Standards and Variances*
Norwood Corporation is considering changing its method of inventory valuation from absorption costing to direct costing for internal reporting.

The corporation manufactures Gink. Marsh is added when processing starts, and labor and overhead are added uniformly during the manufacturing process. Production capacity is budgeted at 110,000 units of Gink annually. The standard costs per unit of Gink are

Marsh, 2 pounds	$3.00
Labor, 1 hour	6.00
Variable manufacturing overhead per labor hour	1.00
Fixed manufacturing overhead	1.10

A process cost system with standard costs is used. Variances from standard costs are now charged or credited to cost of goods sold.

Inventory data for 1981 follow:

	Jan. 1	Dec. 31
Marsh (pounds)	50,000	40,000
Work-in-process (units)		
⅖ processed	10,000	
⅓ processed		15,000
Finished goods (units)	20,000	12,000

During 1981, 220,000 pounds of Marsh were purchased at a cost of $680,000, and 230,000 pounds were transferred to work-in-process. They completed 110,000 units of Gink during the year. Conversion costs (labor and variable overhead) were $790,000 for the 112,000 direct labor hours worked in 1981. Actual fixed manufacturing overhead during the year was $121,000. Standard costs allowed would be based on the equivalent units of output for each category of costs. For materials this would be 110,000 less 10,000 beginning inventory (received materials last period) plus 15,000 ending inventory. For conversion costs the equivalent units would be 110,000 minus $\frac{2}{5}(10,000)$, the work done last period, plus $\frac{1}{3}(15,000) = 111,000$.

(a) Calculate the standard cost under direct costing.
(b) Calculate all the relevant variances from the above data under absorption costing and direct costing.
(c) Calculate the cost of goods sold under both absorption standard costing and direct standard costing.

[AICPA adapted]

19. *Estimated Overhead Costs and Overhead Rates*

Let us assume a company has two producing departments and three service departments. Estimated overhead costs and levels of activity expected for the period are summarized below

	P_1	P_2	S_1	S_2	S_3
Estimated over- head costs	$50,000	$60,000	$25,000	$30,000	$32,000
Activity levels (in hours)	10,000	15,000	5,000	10,000	8,000
Expected shares of service hours to P_1 and P_2			50%,50%	40%,60%	60%,40%
(no reciprocal relationships)					

(a) On the assumption that service department costs are charged to producing departments on the basis of departmental rates, what are the overhead rates for each of the service departments?
(b) Assuming service department costs are allocated to producing departments on the basis of the above rates, what is the combined overhead rate for P_1 and P_2?
(c) Suppose actual results were as follows:

	P_1	P_2	S_1	S_2	S_3
Actual overhead	$52,000	$60,000	$25,000	$28,000	$33,000
Actual hours	10,000	14,000	5,000	9,000	8,500
Actual shares of service hours			50%,50%	50%,50%	60%,40%

(1) Determine over- and underapplied amounts for the service departments.
(2) Determine over- and underapplied amounts for the producing departments. (Remember estimated service department costs were added to estimated producing department costs to determine overall rates for P_1 and P_2.)

20. *Inventory Valuation and Allocation Methods*
The Diversity Company processes certain raw materials into three products, A, B, and C. During the period the company produced the following outputs: 10,000 units of A, 15,000 units of B, and 7,500 units of C. Each unit of A and B weighs 2 pounds. One unit of C weighs 3 pounds. Additional processing costs for A and B are $1.00 and $.75 per unit, respectively, and selling prices are $2.25 and $1.50, respectively. One unit of C may be sold immediately for $2 minus selling costs of $.30 per unit, or it may be processed further to yield net revenues of $2.25 per unit (that is, revenues minus additional processing costs). Total processing costs incurred in the period were $10,000.

(a) Allocate the joint costs to products A, B, and C on the basis of:
    (1) Total units of output.
    (2) Total weight of output.
    (3) Relative sales values using (i) net realizable values based on final selling prices, and (ii) net realizable values based on market prices of the products at split-off (if available).
(b) Suppose that 2,000 units of A, 1,000 units of B, and 500 units of C remained unsold at the end of the accounting period. What average costs per unit should be assigned to inventories of A, B, and C under methods (1), (2), and (3) of part (a)? (Assume that A and B have been processed into their finished form.)

21. *Joint Product and By-Product Costs*
During 1981 the Juno Chemical Company started a new division whose operation consists of processing a mineral into commercial products, A, B, C, and D. Each product passes through identical processing operations. However, Product D is classified as a second, or reject, and is sold at a lower price.
The following information is available regarding the company's operations for 1981:

Sales (including Product D)	$24,480
Production costs	49,769
Selling costs allocated to division	1,224

	Products				
	A	**B**	**C**	**D**	**Total**
Quantity (tons)					
Beginning inventory	—	—	—	—	—
Production	305	137	22	170	634
Sales	132	83	10	60	285
Ending inventory	173	54	12	110	349
Sales price per ton (constant throughout the period)	$100	$100	$100	$ 33	—

(a) Compute the inventory valuation on December 31, 1981, under the net realizable value method of accounting at the lower of cost or market assuming all products are main products.

(b) Compute the inventory valuation on December 31, 1981, under the by-product method of accounting at the lower of cost or market on an individual item basis. The company has elected to recognize total income from by-products in the period in which the by-products are produced. No selling costs are assigned to the by-products.

[AICPA adapted]

22. **Complex Analysis of Joint Costs**
The Joint Products Company processes raw materials into products A, B, C, D, and E. Products A and B are produced in Process 1 in a 1:1 ratio. Product A then passes into Process 2, where it is processed into Products C and D. Product B is used in Process 3 to produce Product E.

Product A yields Products C and D in the ratio of 70:30. Product C is processed further in Process 4, after which it sells for a net of $4.50 per unit. Product D may be sold immediately at a net price of $3.60, or it may be processed further in Process 5, after which it can be sold at a net price of $5.20 per unit.

Product E is processed in Process 6, where normal spoilage of 5 percent occurs. Spoiled units are disposed of at a loss of $.50 per unit. Product E sells for $3.80 per unit (net).

The following costs were incurred during the latest accounting period:

	Costs	Units of Output
Process 1	$250,000	200,000
Process 2	75,000	100,000
Process 3	59,000	100,000
Process 4	65,000	70,000
Process 5	50,000	30,000
Process 6	48,500	95,000*

* Good units.

(a) Determine the amounts of joint costs that should be allocated to A and B and to C and D (use the market price at split-off) using the relative net realizable value method.
(b) Calculate the net income earned from the final sales of Product D. Is the company wise in processing D through Process 5? Explain.

23. **Joint Products with a By-Product**
Assume the following description of a firm producing several joint products and a by-product, X. Process I yields Products A, B, and C. A is sold immediately, but B and C are processed further as shown below.

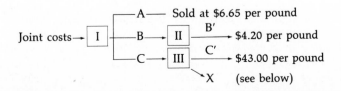

	Process I	Process II	Process III
Costs incurred	$45,640	$3,372	$24,640
Outputs produced	A—3,600 lbs.		
	B—2,800 lbs.	B'—2,660 lbs.	
	C—7,600 lbs.	(5% waste)	C'—1,440 lbs.
			X—$10,000 net

Required Using the net realizable value method, determine the amount of Process I costs that should be allocated to A, B, and C assuming that by-product X reduces the final processing costs of C'. (Round to three decimal places.)

24. *Projected Income Statements*
A single-product firm has developed the following revenue and cost estimates:

	Projected Cost per Unit
Direct material (all variable)	$30.00
Direct labor (all variable)	19.00
Manufacturing overhead:	
Variable cost	6.00
Fixed cost (based on 10,000	
units per month)	5.00
Selling, general, and administrative:	
Variable cost	4.00
Fixed cost (based on 10,000	
units per month)	2.80

The projected selling price is $80 per unit. The fixed costs remain fixed within the relevant range of 4,000 to 16,000 units of production.
Management has also projected the following data for the month of June 1982:

	Units
Beginning inventory	2,000
Production	9,000
Available	11,000
Sales	7,500
Ending inventory	3,500

Required Prepare projected income statements for June 1982 for management purposes under each of the following product-costing methods:

(a) Absorption costing with all variances charged to cost of goods sold each month.
(b) Direct (variable) costing.

[AICPA adapted]

25. **By-Product Accounting**

The Bi-Product Company produces two products, Main and Subsidiary, from the processing of special chemicals in one of the company's main plants. The joint costs of processing these products during the past period were $800,000.

Both Main and Subsidiary are processed further before they are sold. The additional costs of processing Main average $10 per unit, while the additional costs of processing Subsidiary average only $2 per unit. Main sells for $22 per unit (net), and Subsidiary sells for a net of $6 per unit. During the past period 100,000 units of Main and 80,000 units of Subsidiary were produced; 10,000 units of Main and 5,000 units of Subsidiary remain unsold.

(a) Prepare an income statement on the assumption that Subsidiary is treated as a by-product for each of the following cases:
   (1) Net revenues from by-product sales are treated as other revenue.
   (2) Net revenues from by-product sales are treated as a reduction of the cost of sales of the main product.
   (3) The net realizable value of Subsidiary is treated as a reduction of the costs of processing Main.
(b) Prepare an income statement assuming that Subsidiary is treated as a joint product.

26. **Process Costs and Joint Costs**

The MCB Corporation produces one principal product designated "Main-Line." Incidental to this production two additional products result—"Co-Line" and "By-Line." Material is started in Process 1; the three products come out of this process. "Main-Line" is processed further through Process 2; "Co-Line" is processed further through Process 3, and "By-Line" is sold without further processing. The following data for February of the current year are available:

(1) Material put in Process 1: $12,000.
(2) Conversion costs: Process 1, $8,000; Process 2, $4,000; Process 3, $300.
(3) There were no beginning or ending in-process inventories.
(4) Production and sales data are given in the following table:

	Quantity Produced	Quantity Sold	February Average Sales Price	Market Price at End of February
Main-Line	5,000	4,000	$6.00	$6.00
Co-Line	3,000	2,000	1.00	.90
By-Line	1,000	900	.50	.55

(5) Selling and administrative expenses are related to the quantity sold. It is estimated that next period's selling and administrative costs will be the same as February's actual costs, which were

Main-Line	$2,000
Co-Line	800
By-Line	36

(6) Standard net profit on Co-Line is 10 percent of sales.

(7) No profit or loss is recognized on By-Line sales.

Required (a) Compute the costs transferred from Process 1 to By-Line units during the period and the value of ending inventory of By-Line.

(b) Compute the costs transferred from Process 1 to Co-Line units during the period, the costs of finished units of Co-Line, and the value of the ending inventory of Co-Line.

(c) Compute the costs transferred from Process 1 to Main-Line during the period, the costs of finished units of Main-Line, and the value of the ending inventory of Main-Line.

(d) Copy and complete the following income statement:

	Main-Line	Co-Line	By-Line	Total
Sales				
Cost of goods sold				
Gross profit				
Selling and administrative expenses				
Net profit				

[AICPA adapted]

27. *Comprehensive Joint Product and By-Product Problem*

Amaco Chemical Company manufactures several products in its three departments. In Department 1, the raw materials amanic acid and bonyl hydroxide are used to produce Amanyl, Bonanyl, and Am-Salt. Amanyl is sold to other companies that use it as a raw material in the manufacture of stimulants. Bonanyl is not salable without further processing. Although Am-Salt is a commercial product for which there is a ready market, Amaco does not sell this product, preferring to submit it to further processing.

In Department 2, Bonanyl is processed into the marketable product, Bonanyl-X. The yield of Bonanyl-X from a unit of Bonanyl has remained constant for several months.

In Department 3, Am-Salt and the raw material colb are used to produce Colbanyl, a liquid propellant that is in great demand. As an inevitable part of this process, Demanyl is also produced. Demanyl was discarded as scrap until the discovery of its usefulness as a catalyst in the manufacture of glue; for two years Amaco has been able to sell all of its production of Demanyl.

In its financial statement, Amaco states inventory at the lower of cost (on a first in, first out basis) or market. Unit costs of the items most recently produced must therefore be computed. Costs allocated to Demanyl are computed so that after allowing for packaging and selling costs of $.04 per pound, no profit or loss will be recognized on sales of this product.

Selected data for October 1981 follow:

Raw Materials

	Pounds Used	Total Cost
Amanic acid	6,300	$5,670
Bonyl hydroxide	9,100	6,370
Colb	5,600	2,240

Conversion Costs (Labor and Overhead)

	Total Cost
Dept. 1	$33,600
Dept. 2	3,192
Dept. 3	22,400

Products	Pounds Produced	Sales Price per Pound
Amanyl	3,600	$ 6.65
Bonanyl	2,800	—
Am-Salt	7,600	6.30
Bonanyl-X	2,660	4.20
Colbanyl	1,400	43.00
Demanyl	9,800	.54

During October, the 2,800 pounds of Bonanyl were used to produce the 2,660 pounds of Bonanyl-X.

(a) Draw a diagram showing the flow of the various inputs, joint products, and by-products.
(b) How would you infer a value for the Bonanyl, which has no market value? Calculate a specific answer.
(c) Assume your answer to (b) was $3.00. Calculate a cost per pound for Amanyl, Bonanyl, and Am-Salt using the net sales value at point of split-off method.
(d) At what value is Demanyl shown in the inventory?
(e) Calculate the cost per pound of Colbanyl. Assume that your answer in (c) yielded a cost for Am-Salt of $3.40.

[AICPA adapted]

28. *Service Department Costs*
Assume the following flow of services:

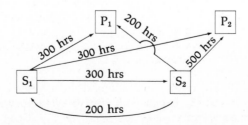

Other data:

	P_1	P_2	S_1	S_2
Selling prices	$20	$25	$0	$0
Average variable costs				
incurred in each department	$20,000	$24,000	$5,000	$12,000
"Units of output"	2,000	2,000	900 hrs	900 hrs

(a) Allocate service department costs to P_1 and P_2 directly, that is, ignore the reciprocal relationship between S_1 and S_2.
Show your answer as follows:

Allocated to

Costs of	P_1	P_2
S_1	_____	_____
S_2	_____	_____
Total	_____	_____

Taken with the production department's own costs, your allocations should have resulted in total variable costs per unit of production of $12.965 for P_1 and $17.535 for P_2.

(b) To recognize reciprocity, first solve for S_1 and S_2 in the following equations:

$$S_1 = 5,000 + \tfrac{2}{3} S_2$$
$$S_2 = 12,000 + \tfrac{1}{3} S_1$$

The approximate solutions would be

$$S_1 = 8,280.28$$
$$S_2 = 14,760.09$$

which exceed the $17,000 costs incurred—this is the double-counting problem. Make the necessary adjustments to these figures and allocate $17,000 to P_1 and P_2 based on this solution. Show your answers as follows (round off):

Allocated to

Costs of	P_1	P_2
S_1	_____	_____
S_2	_____	_____
Total	_____	_____

(c) Which allocation method is appropriate for evaluating the relative profitability of P_1 and P_2? Explain why the two methods give different hourly costs for S_1's and S_2's services.

29. *Allocation of Service Department Costs*
The following costs were incurred by three service departments, G, M, and C.

	G	M	C
Costs	$160,000	$200,000	$240,000

These departments provided services to two producing departments, P_1 and P_2, as well as to one another according to the following matrix:

		Provided to			
Services of	G	M	C	P_1	P_2
G	3%	2%	5%	50%	40%
M	1%	2%	3%	51%	43%
C	4%	1%	5%	55%	35%

Allocate service department costs to P_1 and P_2 using the
(a) Direct method (that is, ignore allocations to other service departments)
(b) Step method, allocating C's costs first, then M's, and then G's
(c) Reciprocal two-step approach described in the chapter, assuming you have a calculator handy. Solve the system of equations and then make the proper allocations to P_1 and P_2.

30. *Joint Cost Allocations*
The Harrison Corporation produces three products—Alpha, Beta, and Gamma. Alpha and Gamma are joint products while Beta is a by-product of Alpha. No joint cost is to be allocated to the by-product. The production processes for a given year are as follows:

(1) In Department One, 110,000 pounds of raw material, Rho, are processed at a total cost of $120,000. After processing in Department One, 60 percent of the units are transferred to Department Two and 40 percent of the units (now Gamma) are transferred to Department Three.
(2) In Department Two, the material is further processed at a total additional cost of $38,000. Seventy percent of the units (now Alpha) are transferred to Department Four and 30 percent emerge as Beta, the by-product, to be sold at $1.20 per pound. Selling expenses related to disposing of Beta are $8,100.
(3) In Department Four, Alpha is processed at a total additional cost of $23,660. After this processing, Alpha is ready for sale at $5 per pound.
(4) In Department Three, Gamma is processed at a total additional cost of $165,000. In this department, a normal loss of units of Gamma occurs which equals 10 percent of the output of Gamma. The remaining output of Gamma is then sold for $12 per pound.

Required (a) Prepare a schedule showing the allocation of the $120,000 joint cost between Alpha and Gamma using the relative sales value approach.

The net realizable value of Beta should be treated as an addition to the sales value of Alpha.

(b) Independent of your answer to part (a), assume that $102,000 of total joint costs were appropriately allocated to Alpha. Assume also that there were 48,000 pounds of Alpha and 20,000 pounds of Beta available to sell. Prepare a statement of gross margin for Alpha using the following facts:

    (1) During the year, sales of Alpha were 80 percent of the pounds available for sale. There was no beginning inventory.

    (2) The net realizable value of Beta available for sale is to be deducted from the cost of producing Alpha. The ending inventory of Alpha is to be based on the net cost of production.

    (3) All other cost, selling price, and selling expense data are those presented in the beginning of the problem.

[AICPA adapted]

31. *Joint Cost Allocations*

Vreeland, Inc., manufactures products X, Y, and Z from a joint process. Joint product costs were $60,000. Additional information is as follows:

| | | | Sales Values and Additional Costs if Processed Further | |
Product	Units Produced	Sales Value at Split-off	Sales Values	Additional Costs
X	6,000	$40,000	$55,000	$9,000
Y	4,000	35,000	45,000	7,000
Z	2,000	25,000	30,000	5,000

(a) Assuming that joint product costs are allocated using the physical measures (units produced) approach, determine the total costs allocated to Product X.

(b) Assuming that joint product costs are allocated using the relative sales value at split-off approach, determine the total costs allocated to Product Y.

[AICPA adapted]

32. *Joint Cost Allocations*

Superior Company manufactures Products A and B from a joint process that also yields a by-product, X. Superior accounts for the revenues from its by-product sales as a deduction from the cost of goods sold of its main products. Additional information is as follows:

Products

	A	B	X	Total
Units produced	15,000	9,000	6,000	30,000
Joint costs	?	?	?	$264,000
Sales value at split-off	$290,000	$150,000	$10,000	$450,000

Assuming that joint product costs are allocated using the relative sales value at split-off approach, determine the joint cost allocated to Product B.

[AICPA adapted]

12
Job Order and
Process Cost Systems

The purpose of this chapter is to examine the manner in which costs are accumulated, classified, and aggregated in order to determine the cost of goods sold or services rendered. Specifically, we shall discuss the two costing procedures commonly used to calculate actual costs of production—*job order costing* and *process costing*. Using job order costing, we compute the actual average costs of working on each job. In process costing, we accumulate the actual costs incurred by a particular process for a specified time period and then calculate an average cost per unit of output.

Actual, or historical, costs of operations are merely the characterizations of outcomes of previous decisions. Why, then, is a discussion of the techniques of generating such data relevant here? We have already provided much of the justification for generating the data in previous chapters, but the central points are worth mentioning here. First, historical cost data constitute part of the data base used for estimating the outcomes of future decisions. Second, these data constitute part of the data base employed in comparing outcomes with plans (standards) in control processes. A third use, which has not yet been discussed, is that historical cost data are often demanded by parties external to the organization. These external demands call for the data-generating techniques discussed here and in Chapter 11 even if the data are not directly useful in management decision making. We call this set of forces "environmental considerations."

Environmental Considerations

There are a number of environmental reasons why accountants must provide historical cost data. Various reports such as those filed with the Internal Revenue Service or the Securities and Exchange Commission are based on these

451

data. GAAP and CASB pronouncements are based on historical absorption cost measures.

Historical absorption cost accounting is also required to meet certain state and federal statutes. Under the Robinson–Patman Act, for example, a firm that practices price discrimination among classes of customers must be able to justify such action on the basis of cost behavior. Clearly, cost accounting data will be relevant for such purposes, and management may find that it is worth the expense to have these data available.[1]

Closely related to the use of cost data for Robinson–Patman compliance is its use for bids on contracts and in contract negotiations. When a potential buyer is dealing with a supplier, for example, the supplier may resort to cost data to bolster the argument that he cannot offer a better price. In some instances, contracts are written so that a selling price is related to actual costs, subject to incentive clauses and certain ceilings on cost. As noted earlier, this is a common practice in federal procurement. Similarly, Blue Cross determines its payments to hospitals based on the actual hospital costs.

Finally, historical cost data are becoming more important in labor negotiations. As both parties to these negotiations become more sophisticated, the demand for and the use of accounting data increase. Historical costs are often used by both sides to justify their positions on the profitability of a plant or the firm's ability to pay a given wage increase.

Providing such data is not required by law. From the provision that management bargain in good faith, however, the National Labor Relations Board has inferred the right of labor unions to seek various kinds of data from the firm. These data include

(1) Basic wage data.
(2) Aspects of business operations likely to affect an employee's pay or status.
(3) Data supporting the firm's contention that it is unable to meet the union's demands.

In each case the union must appeal to the NLRB for a ruling, and the board's rulings can be appealed to the courts. Thus the right of access is not unlimited and is subject to change as the board's or the court's philosophy changes.[2]

Cost Accounting

The role of the product cost accounting system is to determine the historical cost of the firm's output. It is really a subsystem within the firm's accounting system concerned with the collection and analysis of various data to facilitate

---

[1] However, good faith attempts to meet competition may be vastly more important than cost justification per se.

[2] See J. Palmer, *The Use of Accounting Information in Labor Negotiations,* New York: N.A.A., 1977, and B. Foley and K. Manders, *Accounting Information Disclosure and Collective Bargaining,* London: MacMillan, 1977.

measuring unit costs. Doing this requires that data be identified, classified, aggregated, and associated with particular cost units. For simplicity's sake our discussion will usually cover the issues of product costing in a manufacturing setting, although most points would be relevant for costing services as well.

Identification of cost data refers to the need to ascertain which events among the multitude facing the firm are relevant to the production of inventory. For the most part this task may be laborious but not difficult. For example, the issuance of materials from stores to the production line will probably be associated with the production of goods. Conversely, issuance of the same goods to the advertising department usually would not constitute a production cost. Numerous situations fall between these two extremes—for example, issuance of the same materials for use in repairing the building. Our concern will be with the rules used by the cost accountant to decide cases that fall between the two extremes. Most firms rely on a predetermined policy even for the more ambiguous cases.

Classification refers to the categorization of any cost element into the traditional cost accounting categories discussed in Chapter 2. The element may be a product or a period cost; if a product cost, it may be a direct cost (raw materials or labor) or an indirect cost (overhead). While both direct and indirect costs are charged to the cost of production, they are associated with production in different ways. The classification of product costs into different categories can result in different prorations of costs among products and different unit costs.

Aggregation is the accumulation of costs according to the traditional cost accounting categories and subcategories. As we have repeatedly emphasized, the number of primary cost categories is usually set at three (materials, labor, and manufacturing overhead) or four (materials, labor, variable manufacturing overhead, and fixed manufacturing overhead). Of course, numerous subcategories may be opened under each. For example, materials may include several types of raw materials.

Association, the final step in the inventory costing process, utilizes one of the traditional cost accounting techniques to relate the costs by category to the units of output. By doing this, the cost accountant completes the process of examining production transactions and reducing them to a useful set of summary data. The rules used in the association process are a major topic of this chapter. Particularly important are job order and process costing methods.

Job Order Cost Systems

As the name implies, job order cost systems are designed to associate the firm's production costs with specific jobs or lots of production. The primary characteristic of the outputs of manufacturing firms using job order cost systems is that no two orders are necessarily alike; all orders do not pass through the same manufacturing processes. Thus cost information is accumulated separately for each order or job. Further, the primary objective of a job order cost system is to properly associate direct materials, direct labor, and manufacturing overhead with each *job order*. Industries in which job order systems are used include furniture manufacturing, construction, heavy machinery production, machine shops, printing, public accounting, health care, consulting, and shipbuilding. In each of these industries, the specific types of inputs, including the amounts of overhead incurred, will vary with the type of job.

Job order accounting systems are not elaborate. The basic accounts consist of raw materials, direct labor, and overhead. An important feature of such a system is the maintenance of detailed subsidiary records that indicate allocations of raw materials, labor, and overhead to specific jobs. These records usually take the form of job tickets or cards.

We are all familiar with job order cost systems. They are common in consumer-oriented repair services. For example, the typical trip to have an automobile repaired results in receipt of a bill similar to a garage's or service station's job ticket. The parts required are usually listed separately on the order form, and the labor cost is shown elsewhere on the form. The two figures are added together to produce the bill.

Interestingly, the typical service station, garage, or auto body shop does not list any overhead on the bill. This does not mean you are not paying anything toward the business' overhead cost. Rather, the labor rate per hour used on your bill is calculated so as to include not only the mechanic's rate per hour (that is, direct labor), but also overhead and an allowance for profit. (The latter, of course, is not part of any costing system the garage would use for its own records.) Similarly, the required parts listing is not costed at the business' raw materials cost, but has been adjusted to reflect the "market" price, which includes various overhead items and a profit allowance.

In addition to the basic control accounts (raw materials, direct labor, and overhead), job order accounting systems must include a work-in-process account and a finished goods account. Again, these are supplemented by detailed subsidiary records, in the form of job cards or tickets, that are used to accumulate the costs separately for each job. Job cards or tickets circulate with the goods being produced; two examples of these tickets are given in Exhibits 12-1 and 12-2.

The job ticket in Exhibit 12-1 shows that $525 of materials were used on Job 1014. This amount, $525, is Bookstores Inc.'s *cost* for the quantity of materials actually used on the job. Similarly, the exhibit shows a labor cost of $264 for the two workers. This represents the wages actually earned by those workers and a pro rata share of their fringe benefits for the time actually spent on Job 1014.

Since the quantities of materials and labor shown on the ticket are the quantities actually used, the job ticket provides a basis for estimating the

_____EXHIBIT 12-1

Job 1014
Bookstores, Inc.

	Costs
Date started 5/2/82	
Date completed 5/4/82	
Materials	
1,000 board ft. #10A shelving	
@ $.50/board ft.	$500
500 ft. #3 stripping @ $.05/ft.	25
Direct labor	
John Carpenter: 12 hr. @ $12/hr.	144
A.Y. Helper: 10 hr. @ $12/hr.	120
Overhead	
Direct labor hours: 22 hr. @ $5/hr.	110
Total cost	$899

cost of doing an identical or similar job for another customer. In that same sense, the materials and labor costs are not _average_ costs for the period but are instead the actual costs of materials and labor used on that job.

The handling of the manufacturing overhead costs is directly opposite that of materials and labor. The use of these productive inputs is impossible (or not economically feasible) to trace to any given job. The costs are common to the productive activities of the period: that is, many jobs benefit simultaneously from overhead inputs. Thus the extent of the benefit to each of those jobs is not readily and economically measurable, if measurable at all. As an example, overtime production of a particular job results in payment of a labor premium. Because such production often benefits all jobs by de

_____EXHIBIT 12-2

Job 1015
Ultrasonic, Inc.

	Costs
Date started 5/17/82	
Date completed	
Materials	
50 board ft. #6 facing @ $.60/board ft.	$ 30
100 board ft. #20 veneer @ $1.00/board ft.	100
Direct labor	
A.N. Expert: 35 hr. @ $16/hr.	560
Overhead	
Direct labor hours: 35 hr. @ $5/hr.	175
Total cost	$865

facto increasing production capacity, the premium is typically allocated across all jobs rather than to the specific job in question.

As a result of such commonality of benefits, flowing from one cost to several jobs, cost accountants have had to develop techniques for allocating these costs to the various jobs upon which work was done during the period. The typical method utilizes one of the cost measurement techniques discussed in Chapter 3 or the nature of the production process to determine a reasonable basis for allocating a common overhead cost. For example, in the case of an automobile repair garage, the operating overhead cost could be allocated to the jobs based upon the number of direct labor hours worked on the jobs. If the overhead costs in January were $9,500 and mechanics charged 1,900 hours to their jobs, overhead would be charged to the jobs at a rate of $5 per direct labor hour ($9,500 ÷ 1,900 direct labor hours). This assumes that the cost accountant waits until the *end* of the accounting period to calculate the overhead per hour. In practice, however, many job order firms want the overhead cost per hour available *during* the period so that they can bill accordingly. The use of a predetermined overhead charging rate is illustrated in the following example.

Jones and Company makes fixtures for department stores. In some instances, several fixtures of the same kind are made, but an order usually consists of a variety of kinds and sizes of fixtures. Moreover, items made for one customer are seldom identical to those ordered by other customers. For these reasons, management has installed a job order cost system.

The operating period for the firm is one month. At the beginning of May, 1982, management estimated that 80,000 direct labor hours would be worked during that month. The estimate for the manufacturing overhead costs was based on an overhead flexible budget of $3.50(DLH) + $120,000, or $400,000 at $\hat{x} = 80,000$ direct labor hours. From this, an overhead application rate of $5 per direct labor hour was derived ($400,000/80,000 DLH); this rate was used to allocate both fixed and variable manufacturing overhead costs.

During the period (May, 1982), work was done on a large number of jobs, two of which are described in Exhibit 12-1 and 12-2. For simplicity, we assume that both jobs were started during the period in question. However, only Job 1014 for Bookstores, Inc., was completed during this period. Note that each job ticket was charged for the materials specifically requisitioned for that job. Job 1014 required large quantities of material, and the ticket reflects this cost. In contrast, Job 1015 required less total raw materials, although they were expensive. Similarly, each job ticket shows the direct labor hours actually worked, who worked them, and the appropriate hourly rate. Special skills were required for Job 1015, so more expensive labor was used. However, the same overhead rate was charged, because the rate was defined according to direct labor hours rather than total direct labor cost.

Because Job 1014 was started and completed during the period, the costs incurred become part of finished goods or goods sold, depending upon whether the job was billed to the customer. Since Job 1015 was not finished, its cost of $865 will be included in the balance of the work-in-process account at the end of the period, on May 31. The total cost includes not only the raw materials and direct labor costs already incurred, but also $175 of manufacturing overhead. In the next operating period (June), the additional costs incurred in completing Job 1015 will also be accumulated on the job ticket. If it is finished in June, the total cost will be transferred from the work-in-process account to the finished goods account for that month. This total cost figure will include all costs incurred in working on the job during both accounting periods.

Journal Entries

Because both the job order cost system discussed here and the process cost system, which is discussed next, are derivations of the firm's accrual accounting system for external reporting, we can conveniently show the way these events are portrayed in the accrual accounting double entry format.

The journal entries for job order accounting require little explanation except for the handling of manufacturing overhead. The journal entries for Job 1014 in the foregoing illustration are typical of those made for any job under a job order cost system. During the period when the job is actually being worked on, the journal entries with their subsidiary record references are as follows:[3]

Dr.	Work-in-process: Job 1014	$525	
Cr.	Raw material, #10A		$500
Cr.	Raw material, #3		$ 25
Dr.	Work-in-process: Job 1014	$264	
Cr.	Wages payable		$264
Dr.	Work-in-process: Job 1014	$110	
Cr.	Overhead, applied		$110

When the job is completed, the transfer from work-in-process to finished goods is shown by a debit to finished goods and a credit to work-in-process for the full amount of the job's cost:

Dr.	Finished goods	$899	
Cr.	Work-in-process: Job 1014		$899

Note that the journal entries charge the job for its share of the expected manufacturing overhead cost. All overhead charges made to work-in-process

---

[3] Raw materials, work-in-process, and overhead applied accounts are control accounts. The total amounts charged to the individual job reports should balance with the entries in these control accounts, obeying the usual accrual accounting control/subsidiary relationship.

during the period are accumulated as a credit balance in an account entitled "Overhead: Applied." At the end of the period, the amount of these charges made to production is compared against the manufacturing overhead costs actually incurred (debits). Any difference is disposed of either by allocating it among work-in-process, finished goods, and cost of goods sold or by including the entire amount in the period's cost of goods sold.

Briefly, the steps in the recording of manufacturing overhead are:

(1) All manufacturing overhead costs are debited to the "overhead, actual" account as they are incurred.

(2) The overhead charged (debited) to work-in-process is offset by a credit to the "overhead, applied" account.

(3) At the end of the period, the balances in these accounts are compared, and any differences are distributed in the same manner as standard cost variances, that is, to cost of goods sold or proportionately among cost of goods sold, finished goods, and work-in-process.

Thus, if Jones and Company actually incurred $390,000 in overhead costs for all of its jobs during May, the following entry would be made:

Dr.	Overhead, actual	$390,000	
Cr.	Various asset and liability accounts		$390,000

If 76,000 direct labor hours are worked during the period, $380,000 would be charged to production. This reflects an overhead application rate of $5 per direct labor hour multiplied by 76,000 hours.

Dr.	Work-in-process control	$380,000	
Cr.	Overhead, applied		$380,000

At the end of the period, both overhead accounts are closed. Assuming that any difference between actual and applied is charged to cost of goods sold, the journal entries are

Dr.	Overhead, applied	$380,000	
Dr.	Cost of goods sold	$ 10,000	
Cr.	Overhead, actual		$390,000

Alternatively, the debit of $10,000 may be made to a balance sheet account, under (over) applied overhead. The latter procedure is usually followed in interim reports. Whatever balance remains at the end of the year is then handled in the same manner as standard cost variances. It is either charged to cost of goods sold or prorated among work-in-process, finished goods, and cost of goods sold.

REVIEW PROBLEM 1

Carl's Car Customizing, Ltd., has developed a profitable business in customizing stock cars for clients who want to drive a car that is "different."
The relevant data for activities in February, 1982, are given below. In
answering the questions, we assume that Carl's bases its overhead rate
on *expected direct labor hours* and calculates an *estimated* overhead at the beginning of the year for use throughout 1982.

(1) The estimated number of direct labor hours for 1982 is 8,400 hours.
Expected overhead costs are:

Supplies	$ 8,000
Cleanup	10,900
Rework, waste, etc.	4,500
Utilities	10,200
	$33,600

(2) One job, a Cadillac, was started in January, 1982. During January,
the following direct costs were incurred on the Cadillac:

Materials	$ 1,000
Labor: 50 hr. @ $15/hr.	750
	$ 1,750

(3) During February, two other cars were brought in and work begun
on each. The costs associated with each of the three cars for the
month of February were:

	Cadillac	VW	Omni	Total
Materials	$100	$500	$1,200	$1,800
Labor (@ $15 per hour)	220 hr.	160 hr.	310 hr.	690 hr.

(4) During February, actual manufacturing overhead costs incurred were
$2,600.

(5) In February, the Cadillac and VW were completed.

Required (a) Calculate the overhead rate per direct labor hour for 1982.
(b) Calculate Carl's total cost to customize the Cadillac and
VW.
(c) Determine the dollar amount of work-in-process at the
end of February.
(d) Determine whether the overhead for February was over
or under applied and by how much.
(e) Determine the managerial significance, if any, of your
answer in part (d).

Process Cost Systems

The rationale behind keeping detailed records for each job in a job order costing system is that the jobs differ from one another and, in a relative sense, only a small number of jobs are involved in any given accounting period. In such situations, the data derived from the cost system justifies the added cost of bookkeeping.

However, suppose Carl's Car Customizing, Ltd., decides to change its style of operations. From now on, it will perform only one kind of work: that is, taking old VW's and placing imitation Rolls Royce chrome radiators on them. The radiator conversion is relatively inexpensive, and Carl's will charge $750. The firm expects a large volume of work. Moreover, the cost of materials, time, and so on varies little from one job to another. Therefore Mr. Carl suggests that there is little use for a detailed record of the cost of each job. Rather, during the month he can accumulate all of the material, labor, and overhead costs in separate accounts. At the end of the month he can divide each by the number of jobs done, to obtain the unit costs. If total materials are $1,500 in February, labor is $1,800, and overhead is $840, and 12 cars are customized, the unit costs are calculated as follows:

Materials ($1,500 ÷ 12 cars)	$125
Labor ($1,800 ÷ 12 cars)	150
Overhead ($840 ÷ 12 cars)	70
Cost per car	$345

In effect, what Carl's Car Customizing, Ltd., did was to switch from a job order cost system to a process cost system. Because conditions were appropriate, Mr. Carl reduced the company's bookkeeping costs without any significant loss of information.

As mentioned earlier, a process costing system is one where costs are accumulated by process or by department rather than by job. This can be done because the outputs are homogeneous and we may therefore assume that costs for each unit of output are the same as for other units. Not surprisingly, process costing is usually associated with continuous process or mass production industries.

The key assumption in the design of a process costing system is that all units of output passing through a particular process during a specified time period are alike in all economic respects. If this is true, then it makes sense to treat them equally for purposes of cost accounting. (Some firms may have several subsystems within their process costing systems to allow for differences between types of output. Such situations are beyond the focus of this chapter. Here, it is assumed we are discussing a single-product firm.)

Equivalent Unit Computation

Carl's calculated its cost per car by dividing each cost category by the number of cars customized. The firm started and completed 12 cars during February. But what if Carl's had started a 13th car during February and did not complete it? How would the costs be spread over production then? Twelve units would be too small to serve as a measure of work done and 13 would be too large. To avoid this problem, cost accountants prorate the costs over the work actually done during the period. If the car is 25 percent completed, the accountant might use 12.25 units to calculate the cost per unit for labor and overhead. However, all of the parts needed for the 13th car may already have been taken from stores. In that case the cost of materials would be the cost for 13 cars.

If we assume that all units receive "equal" treatment within a particular process, we can treat as equivalent the amount of effort expended to produce 10 units and the amount used to produce 100 units that are only 10 percent complete. In other words, we assume that a change in the percentage of completion of a unit requires the same average amount of economic effort regardless of its stage of progress through the process. This assumption is crucial to process costing, since it is used as the basis for determining the equivalent amount of work performed within a particular process during any accounting period.

For example, consider a paint manufacturing process with no beginning inventory.[4] During one time period, 1,000 gallons of paint start through the process and 800 gallons of finished product are turned out. The ending inventory of 200 gallons is estimated to be 40 percent processed. We assume that all inputs to this process (materials, labor, and overhead) are added uniformly throughout the process.

Under our assumption of uniform processing, the firm has therefore completed the equivalent of 880 units of output:

Work Done	Gallons
Completed	800
Plus: Equivalent completed units of work done on ending inventory[5]	
(40% × 200 gal.)	80
Total	880

---

[4] In some industries, such as canning, each new season or new batch of output commences without beginning inventories. These new batches may be viewed as projects, although they are hardly ever accounted for in this manner.

[5] Conventionally, units in process are defined by the units in which output is expressed—in this case, gallons of paint. Thus, the term "gallons" should be interpreted to mean "the amount of this input (materials, labor, overhead) associated with one gallon of final output."

More specifically, our assumption is that enough materials, labor, and overhead were added to the process during the period to start and complete 880 gallons of paint. To obtain the actual costs per equivalent unit, we divide the total of each input cost—direct materials, direct labor, and overhead—by 880 equivalent units. The sum of these is the average cost of each equivalent gallon of paint processed:

	Total Cost	Equivalent Units	Cost per Gallon
Direct materials	$ 440	880 gal.	$ .50
Direct labor	616	880 gal.	.70
Overhead	264	880 gal.	.30
Total	$1,320		$1.50

Addition of Costs at Discrete Points

The example just given is the simplest computation of equivalent units. A complication arises when some of the input costs of the process—generally the costs of raw materials—are incurred only at discrete points. For example, suppose that all raw materials used in the paint process are added at the beginning of the process; all other data are as before. Since all of the units have passed the point at which materials are added, all are 100 percent complete in terms of raw materials.

Equivalent units for materials would now be calculated as $100\% \times 800$ gal. $+ 100\% \times 200$ gal. $= 1,000$ gal. The computation for the other inputs (labor and overhead) remains at 880 units, for we still assume these inputs are added uniformly throughout the entire process. The costs per gallon under this assumption are as follows:

	Total Cost	Equivalent Units	Cost per Gallon
Direct materials	$ 440	1,000 gal.	$ .44
Direct labor	616	880 gal.	.70
Overhead	264	880 gal.	.30
Total	$1,320		$1.44

Note that the cost of raw materials now is spread over the full 1,000 units that were started. In the next period, when the 200 gallons of paint in process are completed, no additional outlays will be required for their raw materials. If in the next period the department completes only the final 200 gallons left over from the previous period, costs for the second period would be of the general form:

Direct materials	$ 0
Direct labor	84
Overhead	36
Total	$120

Beginning Inventories

Another type of complication arises when we consider the effect of beginning inventories. Consider a glue manufacturing process. During the month in question, 800 gallons are finished. At the beginning of the month, 200 gallons were carried over as inventory-in-process, estimated to be 30 percent complete with respect to all inputs. At the end of the month, 200 gallons—estimated to be 40 percent complete with respect to all inputs—remain in inventory. There are two common approaches to calculating equivalent units when beginning inventories exist. These are the FIFO and the weighted average methods.

The techniques are similar to the inventory techniques discussed in financial accounting. The weighted average approach is the easier of the two methods when viewed from the record keeper's point of view. Work-in-process costs are not segregated from current-period costs. As a result, the unit cost is the weighted average of costs for both periods.

In contrast, FIFO maintains two separate cost pools. One is the opening work-in-process costs; the other is the current period's costs. The FIFO method yields two different costs for units completed during the period. One is for the units in the opening work-in-process. This cost is a mixture of the current period's costs and the last period's costs. The other cost is the cost of goods on which work was done solely during the current period. Their costs are based entirely on the current period's costs. The two methods are described in the following pages.

FIFO Method.　　Because the FIFO (first in, first out) method retains one set of costs for the opening inventory and another set of costs for those units produced entirely in the current period, the per unit cost of output completed during the period will depend upon whether the output was started in this period or in a prior period.

Using the FIFO method of calculation for our glue example, we would compute the equivalent gallons processed as follows:

Work Done (FIFO)	Number of Gallons
Completed (100% × 800 gal.)	800
Plus: Equivalent units of ending work-in-process (40% × 200 gal.)	80
Total	880
Less: Work done on opening inventory in previous period (30% × 200 gal.)	(60)
Equivalent units for the period	820

Since the 800 gallons completed in this period include the 200 gallons in beginning inventory, we must subtract the equivalent amount of work done in the previous period to ascertain this period's equivalent units of output.

Alternatively, we could calculate the same number in the following fashion:

Work Done (FIFO)	Number of Gallons
Completed	800
Less: Opening work-in-process	(200)
Started and completed in this period (100% × 600 gal.)	600
Plus: Work done to complete opening work-in-process (70% × 200 gal.)	140
Work on ending work-in-process (40% × 200 gal.)	80
Total	820

The FIFO method is used when we are interested in separating the costs of completing the beginning inventory (200 gallons) from the costs that would be assigned to the 600 gallons started and completed within a single accounting period. For example, assume that costs assigned in the previous period for the units in the beginning inventory (30% × 200 gal. = 60 equivalent gal.) were as follows:

Item	Amount	Cost per Equivalent Unit
Direct materials	$ 60	$1.00
Direct labor	180	3.00
Variable overhead	90	1.50
Fixed overhead	120	2.00
Total costs	$450	$7.50

Equivalent units: 60
Cost per equivalent unit: $7.50

Assume further that the current period's costs allocated to the process (for 820 equivalent units) are as follows:

Item	Amount	Cost per Equivalent Unit
Direct materials	$ 902	$1.10
Direct labor	2,460	3.00
Variable overhead	1,312	1.60
Fixed overhead	1,763	2.15
Total costs	$6,437	$7.85

Equivalent units: 820
Cost per equivalent unit: $7.85

Under the FIFO method of calculating costs, we use the current period's equivalent units and the $7.85 cost per equivalent unit to allocate the current period's cost of production among the completion of the opening work-in-process, the units started and completed during the period, and the units of ending work-in-process. Using the $7.85 figure, we assign 140 × $7.85 =

$1,099 to the beginning inventory. This amount represents the cost in the current period of completing the 200 gallons of beginning inventory. The 600 gallons that were started and completed in the same period are costed at 600 × $7.85 = $4,710. Finally, the ending inventory of 200 gallons, which represents 80 gallons of equivalent work, is assigned a cost of 80 × $7.85 = $628. In short, we use the equivalent units of work done on each category as the basis for prorating the costs of the period. These allocations and the total costs are summarized below.

Inventory Category	Equivalent Units	Allocated Cost	Prior Period	Total
Opening inventory	140	$1,099	$450	$1,549
Started and completed	600	4,710	—	4,710
Ending inventory	80	628	—	628
Total period's costs		$6,437	$450	$6,887

Because the cost of the opening inventory and the cost of the units started and completed are calculated separately under the FIFO method, the cost of producing the units in the opening work-in-process inventory was $1,549. Of this amount, $450 was incurred in the previous period and $1,099 was incurred during the current period. The average cost per unit of opening inventory is calculated by dividing the sum of all the costs to start and complete those units by the number of units completed: $1,549/200 units = $7.745 per unit. The cost of units started and completed during the present period is $7.85 per unit, the current period's cost per equivalent unit.

Note that the cost of *this* period's *ending* work-in-process inventory, $628, will be the cost per unit of the *next* period's *opening* work-in-process inventory. That cost plus the costs incurred next period to complete the remaining 60 percent of the work will be aggregated to calculate the total cost of producing those units.

Weighted Average Method.   Process costing can also be carried out by the weighted average method, where the beginning inventory costs are combined with the current period's costs and the work done in prior periods is ignored. In effect, *all units finished during the accounting period are treated as if they were started and finished during that period.* Because the production costs from the current and prior periods are merged, the resulting cost per unit is a weighted average of at least two periods' costs. Using the same data as in the FIFO example, the equivalent units calculation under this method is as follows:

Work Done (weighted average)	Number of Gallons
Completed (100% × 800)	800
Plus: Equivalent units of work done on ending units of work-in-process (40% × 200 gal.)	80
	880

Note that the calculation is similar to the first calculation in the FIFO discussion, except that no adjustment is made for the work done in prior periods on the opening work-in-process. This is because the costs associated with that work have been treated as if they were incurred during the current period.

The calculation of cost per equivalent unit is as follows:

Item	Last Period	Current Period	Total Cost
Direct materials	$ 60	$ 902	$ 962
Direct labor	180	2,460	2,640
Variable overhead	90	1,312	1,402
Fixed overhead	120	1,763	1,883
Total costs	$450	$6,437	$6,887

Equivalent units: 880
Cost per equivalent unit: $7.826

The total cost of $6,887 would be assigned to just two categories, 800 units completed this period and sent to the next process or to finished goods and 200 units ending inventory, which are 40 percent complete. The assignment is again based on the equivalent units in each class.

$$\begin{array}{lll} \text{Completed} & 800 \times \$7.826 = & \$6,261 \\ \text{Ending inventory} & 80 \times \$7.826 = & \underline{626} \\ & & \$6,887 \end{array}$$

Evaluation of Methods.   We cannot choose one method over the other on the basis that one is more accurate. Both calculations produce average unit costs of production and as such reflect a series of cost allocations and assignments. We can only comment on the usefulness of each calculation relative to the amount of effort needed to obtain it. Certainly the weighted average method results in less clerical effort than the FIFO method. In addition, it is unlikely that the magnitude of difference that will result from using one method over the other will be large, assuming there has been no major change in price levels or in the manner of processing the units from one period to the next. Indeed, survey data indicate that the FIFO method is not generally used in practice.[6] However, it does continue to appear in professional accounting examinations.

The problems at the end of this chapter provide an arena for the exploration of these methods. An alternative (and common) technique is to employ a standard cost system. If the standards are moderately accurate, no material misstatement of the ending inventories and cost of goods sold will result. And the entire issue of handling beginning inventories is rendered moot.

---

[6] See R. Skinner, "Process Costing," *Abacus*, Dec. 1978.

This is, perhaps, the most vivid example of bookkeeping economies associated with the use of standard costs.

REVIEW PROBLEM 2 ——————————————————————————————

Hop's Wood Company produces a special outdoor lumber that is insect and weather resistant, but also has a very grainy, weatherbeaten look even when it is new. Their process requires certain kinds of logs to be cut into 24-foot lengths, called rods, then immersed for several hours in a chemical bath, and subsequently kiln dried. The only direct material involved is the log itself. The workers doing the cutting and supervising the chemical bath and kiln drying are considered direct labor. Further, for cost accounting purposes it is assumed that the direct labor costs are equal in each of the three phases. Thus cut logs are $\frac{1}{3}$ complete with respect to direct labor, and cut and treated 24-foot rods are $\frac{2}{3}$ complete with respect to direct labor. The same workers do all three jobs—cutting, bathing, and drying. The relevant data for April, 1981, are shown below:

(1) At the start of the period there were 900 rods cut and treated, ready for the kiln.

(2) During the month 42,200 rods were completed. In addition, a total of 600 rods were cut and ready for the chemical bath at the end of the month.

(3) Cost data for April are:

	April	Opening Inventory	Total
Direct materials (logs)	$125,700	$2,340	$128,040
Direct labor	83,600	1,155	84,755
Overhead	66,880	1,050	67,930
Total	$276,180	$4,545	$280,725

(4) Assume overhead costs are incurred at the same rate as direct labor costs.

Required[7] (a) Calculate the cost per rod for April using the weighted average approach.

(b) Calculate the total cost of ending work-in-process and finished goods.

——————————*Standard Product Cost Systems*

Use of a standard cost system is readily illustrated with a continuation of the previous glue manufacturing example. Suppose the standard cost per gallon (unit) of glue is specified as:

———————
[7] For the strong of heart, the FIFO finished good datum here is $278,205.

Direct materials	$1.00
Direct labor	3.00
Overhead (100% of direct labor)	3.00
	$7.00

The beginning inventory of 200 units, 30 percent complete as to all inputs, would be costed at 200(.30)($7.00) = $420. Units completed would be costed at 800($7.00) = $5,600, and the ending inventory would be costed at 200(.40)($7.00) = $560.

We are now in a position to apply standard cost variance analysis. Direct materials, direct labor, and overhead totaled $6,437 during the month in question. The number of equivalent units produced was 820, with the budget based on an absorption cost of 820($7.00) = $5,740. Single-factor analysis for the individual items provides the following data:

Item	Actual	Standard[a]	Variance
Direct materials	$ 902	$ 820	$ 82
Direct labor	2,460	2,460	0
Overhead	3,075	2,460	615
	$6,437	$5,740	$697

[a] Based on 820 equivalent units.

By expanding the amount of information, we could compute price and quantity variances for each item (as well as the fixed overhead volume variance, since absorption costing is being employed). But this would be repetitious. It is, however, important to note that what in Chapter 7 was called "actual costs" can now be thought of as "actual *process* costs."

It is also possible to employ standard costs using a job order costing system. However, it may be much more difficult and expensive, since the job order system was designed f situations where each job is unique. Still, because cost control is an important element in any profitable operation, standard cost methods (or pseudo standard cost methods) have been developed for job order systems.

As an example of the demand for these methods, consider a large construction project such as a building renovation. Before entering into a contract, a general contractor must set a budget for the project (see Exhibit 12–3). This budget, along with the contractor's knowledge of the likely bids from others, will form the basis for his bid. If the contractor is successful, the budget becomes the standard against which he will assess the performance of the project manager and the project manager's assistants.

The project's budget will consist of numerous subbudgets covering different elements of the job. Some may specify materials required and their price and quantity; others may specify the details of the expected labor costs. (see Exhibit 12–4).

_____EXHIBIT 12-3

E-Z Construction Company
Summary Budget: M. Hall Co. Renovation
January, 1981

Cost to gut second, third, and fourth floors	$ 200,000
New wiring for all floors	500,000
Costs to rebuild second, third, and fourth floors	2,000,000
Special equipment for the laboratory	800,000
	$3,500,000

Some job order firms perform numerous small jobs rather than a few large ones. Such firms may develop standards for each operation, provided the number of different basic operations is not too great. Thus, rather than utilizing readymade standards for an individual job, these firms develop standards for individual activities common to many of the jobs. The standards are then aggregated for the job standard.

This is the procedure followed in various industries where prices are quoted to customers based upon estimates of the number of hours to be

_____EXHIBIT 12-4

E-Z Construction Company
Budget: Renovation of Second Floor of
M. Hall Company
January, 1981

Materials			
Partitions			
200 – 8' × 12'		$30,000	
80 – 8' × 10' with doors		20,000	
80 – 8' × 6'		8,000	$ 58,000
Ceiling tiles and supports			40,000
Flooring			
Tile (400,000 squares @ $.25/square)			100,000
Carpet (30,000 sq. yd. @ $20/sq. yd.)			600,000
Total materials cost			$798,000
Labor			
Electricians	1,000 hr. @ $40/hr.		$ 40,000
Installers	1,000 hr. @ $30/hr.		30,000
Finishers	500 hr. @ $25/hr.		12,500
Floors installers	1,500 hr. @ $30/hr.		45,000
Plumbers	500 hr. @ $35/hr.		17,500
Foremen	400 hr. @ $50/hr.		20,000
Total labor costs			$165,000
Total cost			$963,000

worked and the amounts of materials needed. The estimator reduces what appear to be diverse tasks to a certain set of basic tasks that require known standard times. Some typical examples of this are auto body repair workshops, painting companies, and the construction industry.

Examples of nonmanufacturing firms that use a job order cost system with standard costs are the major public accounting firms. Most functions performed on an audit are common to all audits. Standard times are set for each function according to the firm's experience on previous engagements and are adjusted for any peculiar characteristics of the new audit.

Related Topics in Product Costing

Most cost accounting courses devote an extensive portion of the available time to problems of product costing. For the most part this material focuses on the problems of cost recordkeeping and how the systems just described— process costing and job order costing—can be adopted to meet different situations. This section briefly discusses two issues: interdepartmental transfer of goods and shrinkage and spoilage. The first item concerns the situation where one department's finished product is the raw material of another. The second concerns the problems facing the accountant when product units are lost through spoilage, shrinkage, or waste.

Units Transferred In

In many processes the output of the first stage is the input to the second stage. In Review Problem 2, which provided an example of process costing, each of the processes could have been handled by a separate department. In that case the logs cut into 24-foot rods are the output of Department 1 and the raw material of Department 2, the chemical bath department. The "wet" rods are the finished units of the chemical bath department and the inputs of Department 3, which does the kiln drying.

For cost accounting purposes, the units transferred into a department are accounted for in the same manner as any other material inputs. Their cost is determined by their cost in the prior department. Thus, in the case of the logs the materials cost for the cutting department is the purchase price of the logs. In the second department, the cost of the units transferred in reflects all of the first department's costs. Finally, the drying department's cost of units transferred in is the accumulated costs of the first two departments. Exhibit 12-5 shows this relationship in a simple situation, where none of the departments had any opening work-in-process. This highlights the manner in which the costs flow from one department to the next.

Our earlier comment on the economies associated with using standard product cost statistics applies here as well. Indeed, we have already illustrated

_____EXHIBIT 12-5

Flow of Costs Through Departments

	Cost	Equivalent Units	Cost per Unit
Department 1: Cutting			
Materials	$120,000	50,000	$2.40
Labor	30,000	50,000	.60
Total	$150,000		$3.00
Less: Transferred out	(150,000)	(50,000)	3.00
Ending inventory	0	0	
Department 2: Chemical Bathing			
Transferred in	$150,000	50,000	$3.00
Labor and overhead	60,000	40,000[a]	1.50
Total	$210,000		$4.50
Less: Transferred out	(135,000)	(30,000)	4.50
Ending inventory	$ 75,000	20,000	$3.75[b]

[a] Units Started and completed   30,000
    Work-in-process (20,000 units, 50% complete)   10,000
                                               40,000

[b] Cost of ending work-in-process:
    Materials (100% complete) $3.00
    Conversion costs ($\frac{1}{2} \times$ $1.50)   .75
    Cost per unit $3.75

	Cost	Equivalent Units	Cost per Unit
Department 3: Kiln Drying			
Transferred in	$135,000	30,000	$4.50
Labor and overhead	30,000	30,000[a]	1.00
Total	$165,000		$5.50
Transferred to finished goods	(165,000)	(30,000)	$5.50
Ending inventory	0	0	

[a] There was no ending inventory of work-in-process.

such a case, when we consider that accounting for beginning and ending inventories is a special type of interdepartmental or interstage transfer (namely, across time periods).

Spoilage and Lost Units

Most firms operate in an environment where some units of product are lost. Typically, this results from at least one of three causes: waste, evaporation, or spoilage.

Waste refers to the scrap that remains after materials have been processed, such as the end of a bolt of cloth or material trimmed from a panel to make it fit into place. In some instances, waste may be salvagable. For example, the holes cut from the center of a donut can be accumulated into a large ball and then recut into donuts. Eventually, some dough may be wasted, but it will be much less than the original amount. (Of course, the "holes" themselves might be sold, thereby eliminating the problem.)

Evaporation refers to shrinkage during processing. For example, a food processor may find that 100 gallons of tomato puree may yield only 95 gallons of tomato sauce when it is cooked prior to canning. Evaporation is any natural contraction in volume due to processing.

Spoilage is used to describe defective units. Breaking a cup during production or producing a cup whose shape is irregular would qualify as spoilage. Numerous products have defective units that are useless. However, for certain products the "spoiled" units still possesses significant economic value. "Blem" tires or factory seconds of clothing often can be sold at special prices.

It should be readily apparent that the accounting profession may be called upon to devise procedures that will reflect the costs associated with such phenomena. The issue is how to do it best. A variety of possibilities exist. Our purpose here is simply to illustrate the issues and provide an overview of the inherent problems. For convenience the term "spoilage" will be used as if it were synonymous with all three causes.

Consider a simple example. A manufacturer of high-quality art books produces 1,000 copies of a special work on the art of Bernard Buffet. A careful examination reveals that 100 of the books contain pages with serious flaws on them. Rather than allowing the spoiled books to be distributed and sold for less than the full price, they are destroyed, leaving only 900 books to be sold.

Costs of production for the books, along with three possible solutions to the cost allocation problem, are shown in Exhibit 12-6. Note that in the first solution, which allocates the cost to the 900 units, it is assumed implicitly that the cost of the 100 defective books should be absorbed by the 900 good ones. Perhaps because of the quality of art reproduction required, the manufacturer anticipates a spoilage rate of about 10 percent. In such a case, the cost of the defective units is inherent in producing good ones.

The second approach spreads the costs over all 1,000 books. These books are then split into two categories—the cost of good units and a $900 loss due to spoilage. The former will be charged to finished goods as the books are sold. The disposition for the latter remains an open question.

The third solution offers one possible approach to the cost of spoiled units. While the costs of materials and labor are calculated over 1,000 units, the cost of overhead—including spoilage—is allocated over 900 good units.

In the final analysis, the first and third method show the same total unit cost and charge the same total cost to finished goods. However, they

_____EXHIBIT 12-6

Various Approaches to Spoilage

Item	Cost	Production	Cost per Book
1. All costs averaged over good units:			
Materials	$1,800	900	$ 2.00
Labor	4,500	900	5.00
Overhead	2,700	900	3.00
Totals	$9,000		$10.00
2. Cost allocated to all books:			
Materials	$1,800	1,000	$ 1.80
Labor	4,500	1,000	4.50
Overhead	2,700	1,000	2.70
Totals	$9,000		$ 9.00
Cost of good units (900 @ $9.00)	$8,100		
Cost of spoilage (100 @ $9.00)	900		
	$9,000		

Item	Production	Unit Cost
3. Mixed approach to costing good units:		
Materials	1,000	$1.80
Labor	1,000	4.50
Overhead	900	3.00
Spoiled units	100	1.00[a]
Total		$10.00
Cost of good units (900 @ $10.00) $9,000		

[a] Cost of spoilage per unit = spoilage cost ÷ good units = $900 ÷ 900 units = $1.00 unit.

do reflect different amounts for the elements making the per unit cost. This raises the question of which data are potentially more useful.

One can only make conjectures, based upon certain assumptions. Since some spoilage is probably anticipated in "high quality" products such as this, some of the costs of the spoiled units might be included in the cost of good units. But how much? A typical answer is only the normal or anticipated level of spoilage.

The implied distinction between normal and abnormal has significance under the assumption that it is necessary to segregate costs of spoilage that are a normal part of production costs from those that are essentially losses due to inefficiencies. Suppose, for example, that under normal conditions we would expect 5 percent, or 50, of the art books to be defective. We would then expect to see, say, a $450 loss recognized, presuming such a distinction is important.

A further complication arises if the spoiled units have some resale value—that is, they may be sold at some positive net price (selling price less additional costs of disposal). The simplest procedure in this case would be to debit an inventory account for the net value of the spoiled units and credit the work-in-process account. A similar kind of accounting problem arose in Chapter 11, where we considered by-product accounting.

Conclusion

In this chapter, we have shown how the accountant associates the actual costs of production with particular units of output. The procedures used depend on the type of production process encountered. When a number of jobs of different types are produced, a job order cost system is used. When the outputs are homogeneous, a process cost system is used.

As we indicated, the primary purpose of actual costing systems is to comply with the demands of external parties—investors, regulating bodies, bargaining agents, and so on—for accounting information about a firm. For purposes of planning and control, management would like to design some type of standard costing system. The standards used in such a system may be based on the detailed procedures for setting standards and preparing budgets (discussed in earlier chapters) or they may be based on management's best estimates of what the various costs will be in the next operating period. In either case, a system of standard costs improves the basis for evaluating operating performances and simplifies the accounting records used for inventory accounting. Indeed, economies in bookkeeping may be a major impetus for the use of standard cost systems.

Supplementary Readings

Articles

Beckett, J., "A Study of the Principles of Allocating Costs," *Accounting Rev.*, July 1951.

Corcoran, A.W. "A Matrix Approach to Process Cost Accounting," *Management Accounting*, Nov. 1966.

Samuels, J., "Opportunity Costing: An Application of Mathematical Programming," *J. of Accounting Research*, Autumn 1965.

Van Cise, J., "The Robinson-Patman Act and the Accountant," *New York Certified Public Accountant*, May 1958; a discussion with a slightly different emphasis is in H. Taggart, "Cost Justification Under the Robinson-Patman Act," *J. of Accountancy*, June 1956.

Books

Palmer, J. *The Use of Accounting Information in Labor Negotiations.* New York; N.A.A., 1977.

Questions and Problems

1. The distinguishing characteristic of job order cost systems is the emphasis on the cost of individual orders or jobs as opposed to costs of entire departments or processes. What types of operations generally lend themselves to job order cost systems?

2. In general, process cost systems are suitable for continuous or mass production industries. In such industries, output consists of like units, with each unit being processed in the same manner. Discuss this statement, contrasting the type of cost data collected in process cost systems with that collected in job order cost systems.

3 Indicate whether you would expect to find the conditions stated in Problem 2 in the following types of firms:

(a)	a chemical firm	(g)	an automobile firm
(b)	a steel firm	(h)	a manufacturer of aircraft
(c)	a rubber firm	(i)	a petroleum firm
(d)	a textile firm	(j)	a manufacturer of bolts and
(e)	a manufacturer of home appliances		screws
(f)	an electric parts firm	(k)	a consulting firm

4. Explain why the calculation of overhead rates is part of the general problem of cost behavior analysis discussed in Chapter 3.

5. Discuss why the difference between the balance in the overhead cost control account and the balance in the overhead applied account may or may not be viewed as a standard cost variance.

6. Under what conditions might the FIFO method yield information useful in controlling operations?

7. Explain how the distinction between normal and abnormal spoilage reflects an extension of the principle of "management by exception."

8. *Job Order Costs*
   Benjie's Auto Repair works on vehicles for Rachel's Auto Rentals. Benjie estimates that during the year its mechanics will work 2,000 hours and total overhead will be $20,000. During the first week in January, Benjie's cost accountant recorded the following costs:

Job Number	Part	Cost
105	Transmission	$400
103	Front end kit	125
106	Rim	25
106	Tire	80
104	Tune-up package	20
105	Fluid	5
102	Brake lining	35

		JOB				
Worker	**Rate**	**102**	**103**	**104**	**105**	**106**
Murray	$12	4 hr.	5 hr.	10 hr.	15 hr.	2 hr.
Kramer	$15	—	10 hr.	8 hr.	4 hr.	—
Total hours		4 hr.	15 hr.	18 hr.	19 hr.	2 hr.

The departmental overhead is allocated according to expected annual hours and expected annual costs. Calculate the overhead rate and the cost of all jobs (#102–106) during this period.

9. *Application of Overhead in Job Order Costing*
The cost accountant for Phrank's Auto Repair accumulated $4,000 of overhead in the last week of January. During the same period Phrank's mechanics worked 180 hours on various jobs. Phrank is using a rate of $20 per labor hour to allocate overhead to the jobs.

(a) What is the overhead charged to the jobs?
(b) What is the overhead over or under applied in this week?
(c) Assume that the overhead was under applied by $400. Does that tell the service department's manager anything about the department's efficiency in controlling overhead cost?

10. *Defining Overhead*
Southern Pennsylvania College is in the midst of a major upheaval as it attempts to decide on which costs are to be included in the overhead costs charged on research contracts won by the college. The primary disagreement centers on the handling of the costs of the college's computer center.

Members of the physics department are leading a group that feels the computer center's costs should be included in the overhead account and allocated along with other costs such as heat, light, miscellaneous supplies, etc., as a fixed percentage of direct contract costs. In contrast, several social science departments want the computer center's costs included in the direct costs at some flat rate per hour based upon the center's expected costs.

(a) What do you think would be the effect on a physics department's contracts cost using their approach compared to the other plan?
(b) How do you feel a decision should be made on whether a cost is part of overhead? Use the computer center to illustrate your point.
(c) What are some comparable problems that could exist in an industrial setting?

11. *Job Order Costs*
The Specialty Company manufactures machine tools on special order. On February 1, 1982, the following balances appeared in the raw materials, work-in-process, and under (over) applied overhead accounts.

Raw materials control		$100,000
Work-in-process control		
Job 101	$60,000	
Job 103	50,000	
Job 107	25,000	$135,000
Under (over) applied overhead		$5,000 (debit)

The following transactions took place in the month of February:

(1) Production orders were issued for jobs 110, 111, and 112.
(2) Direct labor costs of $249,100 were incurred as follows. The hourly rates are averages for all workers.

Job 101	3,000 hours at $8.00/hr.	$ 24,000
Job 103	4,500 hours at 8.40/hr.	37,800
Job 107	5,000 hours at 8.40/hr.	42,000
Job 110	6,500 hours at 8.20/hr.	53,300
Job 111	6,000 hours at 8.00/hr.	48,000
Job 112	5,500 hours at 8.00/hr.	44,000
	30,500 hours	$249,100

(3) Materials and supplies purchased were $80,000.
(4) Materials were requisitioned as follows:

Job 101	$ 12,000
Job 103	14,000
Job 107	18,000
Job 110	23,000
Job 111	22,000
Job 112	17,000
Overhead control	10,000
Total	$116,000

(5) Indirect labor (including supervision) amounted to $75,000.
(6) Miscellaneous variable overhead costs were $23,000.
(7) Depreciation and other fixed overhead costs were $85,000.
(8) Overhead costs are charged to jobs at the rate of $6.50 per direct labor hour.
(9) The following jobs were finished and billed to the customers:

	Billed at
Job 101	$170,000
Job 103	185,000
Job 107	165,000

Required (a) Compute the costs of finishing jobs 101, 103, and 107. What is the gross profit rate on cost for each job?

(b) What are the ending balances of work-in-process and under (over) applied overhead?

(c) Discuss other bases for overhead allocation that the Specialty Company might use, including the possibility of using multiple rates. What techniques might the accountant use to develop multiple rates for overhead allocation?

12. *Job Order Costs and Contract Pricing*

The Estes Corporation was awarded a federal government fixed-price incentive contract that called for the construction and delivery of 10 digital computers within the next 12 months.

(1) Provisions of the contract included the following:
1. The total contract target price is $900,000, which includes a target cost of $775,000. The total adjusted price cannot exceed $1,100,000.
2. The total adjusted price is computed as follows:

When Total Adjusted Cost Is:	Allowance for Profit Is:
Equal to total target cost	Total target profit
Greater than total target cost	Total target profit less 20% of the excess of total adjusted cost over target cost
Less than total target cost	Total target profit plus 20% of the difference (total target cost—total adjusted cost)

(2) At the end of 6 months, the corporation submitted the following report to the government:

Costs Accumulated on the Contract

Direct materials	$150,000
Direct labor	165,000
Overhead	200,000
Total	$515,000

Estimated Costs to Complete Contract

Direct materials	$155,000
Direct labor	170,000
Overhead	215,000
Total	$540,000

(3) Five computers were completed and billed at the target price of $500,000.
(4) Past experience has shown that approximately 1½ percent of the allocated overhead costs are not allowed by government auditors as contract costs. No provision has been made for this disallowance. In addition to the 1½ percent disallowance, the following costs will not be allowed: (1) depreciation of $1,500 on equipment that was not used for work on the contract and (2) $5,000 of nonrecurring costs of training personnel.

(5) The Estes Corporation failed to take purchase discounts of $2,500 on materials charged to the contract. These "lost discounts" will be subtracted from the contract costs.

Required (a) Prepare a schedule computing the estimated total adjusted price (the final contract price) for the fixed-price incentive contract.

(b) Assume you are the cost accountant for the Estes Corporation. Justify charging the government contract with such common costs as depreciation on the factory, rent on equipment, supervisory personnel, maintenance and repairs on equipment, and general administrative costs.

[AICPA adapted]

13. ***Standard Job Order Costing with Variance Calculations***
Vogue Fashions, Inc., manufactures ladies' blouses of one quality, produced in lots to fill each special order from its customers, comprised of department stores located in various cities. Vogue sews the particular stores' labels on the blouses. The standard costs per dozen blouses are:

Direct materials	24 yards @ $1.10	$26.40
Direct labor	3 hours @ $4.90	14.70
Manufacturing overhead	3 hours @ $4.00	12.00
Standard cost per dozen		$53.10

During June, 1981, Vogue worked on three orders, for which the month's job cost records disclose the following:

Lot No.	Units in Lot	Material Used	Hours Worked
22	1,000 dozen	24,100 yards	2,980
23	1,700 dozen	40,440 yards	5,130
24	1,200 dozen	28,825 yards	2,890

The following information is also available:
(1) Vogue purchased 95,000 yards of material during June at a cost of $106,400. The materials price variance is recorded when goods are purchased. All inventories are carried at standard cost.
(2) Direct labor during June amounted to $55,000. According to payroll records, production employees were paid $5.00 per hour.
(3) Manufacturing overhead during June amounted to $45,600.
(4) A total of $576,000 was budgeted for manufacturing overhead for the year 1981, based on estimated production at the plant's normal capacity of 48,000 dozen blouses annually. Manufacturing overhead at this level of production is 40 percent fixed and 60 percent variable. Manufacturing overhead is applied on the basis of direct labor hours.
(5) There was no work in process at the beginning of June. During June, lots

22 and 23 were completed. All material was issued for lot 24, which was 80 percent completed as to direct labor.

Required (a) Prepare a schedule showing the computation of standard cost of lots 22, 23, and 24 for June, 1981.

(b) Prepare a schedule showing the computation of the materials price variance for June, 1981. Indicate whether the variance is favorable or unfavorable.

(c) Prepare a schedule showing, for each lot produced during June, 1981, computations of the
1. Materials quantity variance in yards.
2. Labor efficiency variance in hours.
3. Labor rate variance in dollars.
Indicate whether each variance is favorable or unfavorable.

(d) Prepare a schedule showing computations of the total controllable and noncontrollable (volume) manufacturing overhead variances for June, 1981. Indicate whether the variances are favorable or unfavorable.

[AICPA adapted]

14. *Job Order Costing: Comprehensive Review*

The Custer Manufacturing Corporation, which uses a job order cost system, produces various plastic parts for the aircraft industry. On October 9, 1981, production was started on job number 487 for 100 front bubbles (windshields) for commercial helicopters.

Production of the bubbles begins in the Fabricating Department where sheets of plastic (purchased as raw material) are melted down and poured into molds. The molds are then placed in a special temperature and humidity room to harden the plastic. The hardened plastic bubbles are then removed from the molds and hand worked to remove imperfections.

After fabrication the bubbles are transferred to the Testing Department, where each bubble must meet rigid specifications. Bubbles that fail the tests are scrapped, and there is no salvage value.

Bubbles passing the tests are transferred to the Assembly Department, where they are inserted into metal frames. The frames, purchased from vendors, require no work prior to installing the bubbles.

The assembled unit is then transferred to the Shipping Department for crating and shipment. Crating material is relatively expensive and most of the work is done by hand.

The following information concerning job number 487 is available as of December 31, 1981 (the information is correct as stated):

(1) Direct materials charged to the job:
(a) 1,000 sq. ft. of plastic at $12.75 per sq. ft. was charged to the Fabricating Department. This amount was to meet all plastic material requirements of the job assuming no spoilage.

(b) 74 metal frames at $408.52 each were charged to the Assembly Department.

(c) Packing material for 40 units at $75 per unit was charged to the Shipping Department.

(2) Direct-labor charges through December 31, 1981, were as follows:

	Total	Per Unit
Fabricating Department	$1,424	$16
Testing Department	444	6
Assembly Department	612	12
Shipping Department	256	8
	$2,736	

(3) Differences between actual and applied manufacturing overhead for the year ended December 31, 1981, were immaterial. Manufacturing overhead is charged to the four production departments by various allocation methods, all of which you approve.

Manufacturing overhead charged to the Fabricating Department is allocated to jobs on the basis of heat-room hours; the other production departments allocate manufacturing overhead to jobs on the basis of direct-labor dollars charged to each job within the department. The following reflects the manufacturing overhead rates for the year ended December 31, 1981:

	Rate Per Unit
Fabricating Department	$.45 per hour
Testing Department	.68 per direct-labor dollar
Assembly Department	.38 per direct-labor dollar
Shipping Department	.25 per direct-labor dollar

(4) Job number 487 used 855 heat-room hours during the year ended December 31, 1981.

(5) Following is the physical inventory for job number 487 as of December 31, 1981:

Fabricating Department:
(a) 50 sq. ft. of plastic sheet
(b) 8 hardened bubbles, ¼ complete as to direct labor
(c) 4 complete bubbles
Testing Department
(a) 15 bubbles, which failed testing when ⅖ of testing was complete, no others failed
(b) 7 bubbles complete as to testing
Assembly Department:
(a) 13 frames with no direct labor
(b) 15 bubbles and frames, ⅓ complete as to direct labor
(c) 3 complete bubbles and frames
Shipping Department:
(a) 9 complete units, ⅔ complete as to packing material, ⅓ complete as to direct labor

(b) 10 complete units, 100 percent complete as to packing material, 50 percent complete as to direct labor

(c) 1 unit complete for shipping was dropped off the loading docks; there is no salvage

(d) 23 units were shipped prior to December 31, 1981

(e) No inventory of packing materials in the shipping department at December 31, 1981

(6) Following is a schedule of equivalent units in production by department for job number 487 as of December 31, 1981:

Custer Manufacturing Corporation
Schedule of Equivalent Units in
Production for Job Number 487
December 31, 1981

FABRICATING DEPARTMENT (UNITS)

| | | Bubbles | | |
	Plastic (sq. ft.)	Materials	Labor	Overhead
Transferred in from raw materials	1,000	—	—	—
Production to date	(950)	95	89	95
Transferred out to other departments	—	(83)	(83)	(83)
Spoilage	—	—	—	—
Balance at December 31, 1981	50	12	6	12

TESTING DEPARTMENT (UNITS)

| | Bubbles | | |
	Transferred in	Labor	Overhead
Transferred in from other departments	83	—	—
Production to date	—	74	74
Transferred out to other departments	(61)	(61)	(61)
Spoilage	(15)	(6)	(6)
Balance at December 31, 1981	7	7	7

ASSEMBLY DEPARTMENT (UNITS)

	Transferred in	Frames	Labor	Over-head
Transferred in from raw materials	—	74	—	—

ASSEMBLY DEPARTMENT (UNITS)

	Transferred in	Frames	Labor	Over-head
Transferred in from other departments	61	—	—	—
Production to date	—	—	51	51
Transferred out to other departments	(43)	(43)	(43)	(43)
Balance at December 31, 1981	18	31	8	8

SHIPPING DEPARTMENT (UNITS)

	Transferred in	Packing Material	Labor	Over-head
Transferred in from raw materials	—	40	—	—
Transferred in from other departments	43	—	—	—
Production to date	—	—	32	32
Shipped	(23)	(23)	(23)	(23)
Spoilage	(1)	(1)	(1)	(1)
Balance at December 31, 1981	19	16	8	8

Required Prepare a schedule for job number 487 of ending inventory costs for (a) raw materials by department, (b) work in process by department, and (c) cost of goods shipped. All spoilage costs are charged to cost of goods shipped.

[AICPA adapted]

15. *Equivalent Units: FIFO*
For each of the situations described below, determine the equivalent units completed using the FIFO method.

(a) Units transferred   40,000
      Beginning inventory   10,000 (50% complete)
      Ending inventory   6,000 (40% complete)

(b) Units started in production   60,000
      Beginning inventory   5,000 (70% complete)
      Ending inventory   7,500 (60% complete)

(c) Units started in production   50,000
      Units transferred out   60,000
      Ending inventory   10,000 (75% complete)
      Beginning inventory was 80% complete.

16. *Equivalent Units: Weighted Average*
Repeat Problem 15 using the weighted average method.

17. **Equivalent Units: FIFO**

For each of the situations described below, determine the equivalent units completed using the FIFO method.

(a) Beginning inventory   30,000 (70% complete)
     Ending inventory   20,000 (45% complete)
     Units started and completed   100,000

(b) Beginning inventory   20,000 (20% complete)
     Ending inventory   25,000 (10% complete)
     Units started in production   80,000

(c) Beginning inventory   30,000 (60% complete)
     Ending inventory   40,000 (40% complete)
     Units transferred   100,000

18. **Equivalent Units: Weighted Average**

Repeat Problem 17 using the weighted average method.

19. **Process Costing (Weighted Average Method)**

Ballinger Paper Products manufactures a high quality paper box. The box department conducts two separate operations: cutting and folding. The paper is first cut and trimmed to the dimensions of a box form by one machine group. The trimmings from this process have no scrap value. Box forms are then creased and folded—completed—by a second machine group. All work-in-process in the department is cut box forms that are ready for creasing and folding. These partly processed boxes are considered 50 percent complete as to conversion costs, that is, labor and overhead. The materials department maintains an inventory of paper in sufficient quantities to permit continuous processing, and transfers to the box department are made as needed. Immediately after folding, all good boxes are transferred to the finished goods department.

During June, 1981, the costs were

	Raw Materials	Conversion	Total
Work-in-process 6/1/81	$ 35,000	$ 20,000	$ 55,000
Started	280,000	226,000	506,000
Totals	$315,000	$246,000	$561,000

The opening inventory consisted of 800,000 units. During June, 5,500,000 units were started. The ending inventory consisted of 300,000 units.

(a) Using the weighted average method, calculate the equivalent units produced.
(b) Calculate the costs per equivalent unit for materials and conversion and the total cost per equivalent unit.

[AICPA adapted]

20. **Process Costing (FIFO Method)**

Using the data given for Ballinger Paper Products in Problem 19, calculate

(a) The equivalent units of production using the FIFO method.
(b) The materials cost, conversion cost, and total cost per equivalent unit for June.
(c) The total cost per unit of opening inventory completed during the month.

21. **Process Costing: Comprehensive**
Using the following information, prepare schedules indicating equivalent units, costs of units transferred, and ending work-in-process inventories relative to Processes A and B. (Units from Process A are transferred to Process B.) Use FIFO for Process A and the weighted average method for Process B. Allocate spoilage costs on the basis of the number of good units remaining.

	Process A	Process B
Beginning inventories	$ 4,500	$23,560 ($16,580 of which represents transferred-in costs)

Current Costs

Materials added continuously	$27,600	
Materials added at the end of process		$19,040
Labor and overhead	$36,800	$32,224

Production Data

Beginning inventories (units)	1,500 (50% complete)	2,500 (75% complete)
Units transferred	9,000	9,520
Units still in process	2,000 (40% complete)	1,900 (70% complete)
Units spoiled		
Normal	100[a]	60[b]
Abnormal	50	20

[a] Units are inspected at the end of Process A.
[b] Spoilage is detected when the units are 50 percent complete.

22. **Process Costing with Standard Costs**
The standard costs of processing Product A through Department 1 are as follows, with prices adjusted for freight and discounts. All materials are added at the beginning of the process.

BILL OF MATERIALS

No.	Description	Quantity per Unit	Price	Standard Cost per Unit
180	Processed oil	2 gallons	$.80	$1.60
190	Supplementary	1 gallon	.40	.40
				Total $2.00
Spoilage and waste allowance per unit				.15
Standard cost per unit				$2.15

DIRECT LABOR

Pay Grade	Actual Base
11	$3.00
12	3.20
13	3.60

$$\textit{Standard (average)} = \tfrac{1}{4}(\$3.00) + \tfrac{1}{2}(\$3.20) + \tfrac{1}{4}(\$3.60)$$
$$= \$.75 + \$1.60 + \$.90 = \$3.25 \text{ per hour}$$

The average standard labor is 2 hours per unit. Therefore, the standard direct labor cost is 2($3.25) = $6.50.

Standards for overhead are based on a flexible budget. A summary of this budget based on monthly allocations is reproduced below.

	18,000 hr	20,000 hr	22,000 hr	24,000 hr
Indirect materials and labor	$ 5,400	$ 6,000	$ 6,600	$ 7,200
Maintenance and miscellaneous variable overhead	9,200	10,000	10,800	11,600
Supervision	15,000	20,000	20,000	25,000
Depreciation	20,000	20,000	20,000	20,000
Miscellaneous fixed overhead	2,000	2,000	2,000	2,000
	$51,600	$58,000	$59,400	$65,800

Variable overhead rate	$.70/hour
Fixed overhead	
Normal volume	20,000 hours
Budgeted (based on 20,000 hr)	$44,000
Fixed overhead rate	$2.20/hour

The actual results for Department 1 are as follows:

Beginning inventory	0
Units placed in process	10,000
Ending inventory (50% complete)	2,000
Current costs	
Materials used (at standard)	$21,800
Labor	61,050
Overhead costs	
Indirect material and labor	5,735
Maintenance and miscellaneous variable overhead	9,500
Supervision	20,500
Depreciation	20,000
Miscellaneous fixed overhead	2,000

Actual hours worked: 18,500

Actual purchases: $25,400 (consisting of 24,000 gallons of processed oil and 12,000 gallons of supplementary)

Required (a) Calculate the equivalent units of work done under
   (1) Materials.
   (2) Conversion.
   (b) Calculate
   (1) Direct materials price variance.
   (2) Normal direct materials usage variance.
   (3) Abnormal direct materials usage variance.
   (c) Calculate
   (1) Direct labor rate variance.
   (2) Direct labor efficiency variance.
   (d) Show how (1) the variable overhead rate was calculated and (2) the fixed overhead budgeted amount was determined.
   (e) Determine all the variable and fixed overhead variances using the two-factor model.

23. *Allocation of Spoilage Costs*
   The data below summarize the operations of a processing department.

	Materials	Conversion
Current costs	$19,300	$210,650
Beginning inventory		
500 units	Complete	40% Complete
Costs	$5,000	$22,000
Units transferred 20,000 (total)	—	—
Ending inventory		
4,000 units	Complete	25% Complete
Spoilage [a]		
Normal: 200 units		
Abnormal: 100 units		

[a] Spoilage is detected when the units are 50 percent complete.

   (a) Calculate the equivalent units using weighted averages.
   (b) Determine the costs that should be allocated to
   (1) Normal and abnormal spoilage.
   (2) Units transferred (including spoilage costs).
   (3) Ending inventory (including spoilage costs, if appropriate).

24. *Process Costs and Spoilage*
   Poole, Inc., produces a chemical compound by a unique chemical process which Poole has divided into two departments, A and B, for accounting purposes. The process functions as follows:

   (1) The formula for the chemical compound requires one pound of Chemical X and one pound of Chemical Y. In the simplest sense, one pound of Chemical X is processed in Department A and transferred to Department B for further processing, where one pound of Chemical Y is added when the process is 50 percent complete. When the processing is complete in Department B, the finished chemical compound is transferred to finished goods. The process is continuous, operating twenty-four hours a day.

(2) Normal spoilage occurs in Department A. Five percent of Chemical X is lost in the first few seconds of processing.

(3) No spoilage occurs in Department B.

(4) In Department A conversion costs are incurred uniformly throughout the process, and they are allocated to good pounds produced because spoilage is normal.

(5) In Department B conversion costs are allocated equally to each equivalent pound of output.

(6) Poole's unit of measure for work-in-process and finished-goods inventories is pounds.

(7) The following data are available for the month of October 1981:

	Department A	Department B
Work in process, October 1	8,000 pounds	10,000 pounds
Stage of completion of beginning inventory (one batch per department)	$\frac{3}{4}$	$\frac{3}{10}$
Started or transferred in	50,000 pounds	?
Transferred out	46,500 good pounds	?
Work in process, October 31	?	?
Stage of completion of ending inventory (one batch per department)	$\frac{1}{3}$	$\frac{1}{5}$
Total equivalent pounds of material added in Department B	—	44,500 pounds

Required Prepare schedules computing equivalent unspoiled pounds of production (materials and conversion costs) for Department A and Department B for October 1981 using the FIFO method for inventory costing.

[AICPA adapted]

25. **Process Costing and Lower of Cost or Market**
You are engaged in an audit of the ABC Manufacturing Company's financial statements, and you are in the process of verifying the pricing of the company's inventory for work-in-process and finished goods. They are recorded on the company's books as follows:

Finished goods inventory, 110,000 units	$504,900
Work-in-process inventory, 90,000 units, 50% completed	$330,480

The company follows the practice of pricing the above inventories at the lower of cost or market using the FIFO method. You learn that materials are added to the production line at the start of the process, and that overhead is applied

EXHIBIT 12-7

	Units	Materials	Labor
Beginning inventory, January 1, 1982, 80% completed	100,000	$100,000	$160,000
Additional units started in 1982	500,000		
Material costs incurred		$550,000	
Labor costs incurred			$997,500
Units completed in 1982			
Good units	500,000		
Defective units	10,000		
Finished goods inventory at December 31, 1982, including 10,000 defective units	110,000		

to the product at the rate of 75 percent based on direct labor dollars. You also learn that the market value of the finished goods inventory and the work-in-process inventory is greater than the amounts shown above, with the exception of the defective units in the ending inventory of finished goods, the market value of which amounts to $1 per unit.

A review of the company's cost records shows the information given in Exhibit 12-7.

You also learn that the defective units occur at the end of the process, at the point of final inspection.

(a) Prepare schedules indicating effective or equivalent production; unit costs of production of materials, labor, and overhead; and pricing of inventories of finished goods, defective units, and work-in-process.
(b) Prepare the necessary journal entries, if any, to correctly state inventory valuation of finished goods and work-in-process. (Ignore income tax considerations.)

[AICPA adapted]

26. *Process Costs by Products*

The Adept Company is a manufacturer of two products known as "Prep" and "Pride." Incidental to the production of these two products, it produces a by-product known as "Wilton." The manufacturing process covers two departments, Grading and Saturating.

The manufacturing process begins in the Grading department when raw materials are started in process. Upon completion of processing in the Grading department, the by-product "Wilton" is produced, which accounts for 20 percent of the material output. This by-product needs no further processing and is transferred to finished goods.

The net realizable value of the by-product "Wilton" is accounted for as a reduction of the cost of materials in the Grading department. The current selling price of "Wilton" is $1.00 per pound and the estimated selling and delivery costs total $.10 per pound.

The remaining output is transferred to the Saturating department for the final phase of production. In the Saturating department, water is added at the beginning of the production process, which results in a 50 percent weight gain of the materials in production.

The following information is available for the month of November 1979:

	NOVEMBER 1		NOVEMBER 30
Inventories	Quantity (pounds)	Amount	Quantity (pounds)
Work in process			
Grading dept.	None	—	None
Saturating dept.	1,600	$17,600	2,000
Finished goods			
Prep	600	14,520	1,600
Pride	2,400	37,110	800
Wilton	None	—	None

The work-in-process inventory (labor and overhead) in the Saturating department is estimated to be 50 percent complete both at the beginning and end of November.

Costs of production for November are as follows:

Costs of Production	Materials Used	Labor and Overhead
Grading department	$265,680	$86,400
Saturating department	—	86,000

The material used in the Grading department weighed 36,000 pounds.
Adept uses the FIFO method of process costing.

Required Prepare a cost of production report for both the Grading and Saturating departments for the month of November. Show supporting computations in good form. The answer should include:
(1) Equivalent units of production (in pounds).
(2) Total manufacturing costs.
(3) Cost per equivalent unit (pounds).
(4) Dollar amount of ending work in process.
(5) Dollar amount of inventory cost transferred out.

[AICPA adapted]

27. *Process Costing with Spoilage*
The Dexter Production Company manufactures a single product. Its operations are a continuous process carried on in two departments—machining and finishing. In the production process, materials are added to the product in each department without increasing the number of units produced.

For the month of June the company records indicated the following production statistics for each department:

	Machining Department	Finishing Department
Units in process June 1	0	0
Units transferred from preceding department and put into production	0	60,000
Units started in production	80,000	—
Units completed and transferred out	60,000	50,000
Units in process, June 30[a]	20,000	8,000
Units spoiled in production	0	2,000
[a] Percent of completion of units in process June 30		
Materials	100%	100%
Labor	50%	70%
Overhead	25%	70%

The units spoiled in production had no scrap value and were 50 percent complete as to materials, labor, and overhead. The company's policy is to treat the cost of spoiled units in production as a separate element of cost in the department in which the spoilage occurs. Cost records showed the following charges for the month of June:

	Machining Department	Finishing Department
Materials	$240,000	$ 88,500
Labor	140,000	141,500
Overhead	65,000	25,700

For both the machining and finishing departments, calculate the equivalent units and the cost per unit for the month of June. Use the weighted average method.

[AICPA adapted]

13
Master Budgets

Up to this point we have viewed the budget process in a micro fashion. We answered such questions as: What is the department's overhead budget? What is the sales representative's budget? These budgets are considered micro because they describe the plan for a small unit within the organization. To direct the organization's activities properly, however, these budgets must be coordinated. Links must exist between the goals of the sales representatives and the production schedules of the department heads. Otherwise, chaos may result. Production may fall short of sales, leading to customer dissatisfaction, or it may exceed sales, resulting in excess inventory. Alternatively, the wrong goods may be produced, giving the firm both unhappy customers and surplus inventory.

A master budget reduces these potential problems by taking a macro view of the firm. Sales are related to production; required materials and machinery are coordinated with production plans. All aspects of production are integrated to permit management to forecast the firm's profitability and cash position. The master budget is an integrative tool that cuts across divisional boundaries in order to coordinate the firm's diverse activities.

Master budgets should be distinguished from two other types of budgets—operating and planning budgets. While master budgets provide plans for an entire system, operating budgets provide plans for the organization's subsystems; that is, operating budgets constitute the building blocks used to complete the master budget. Examples of operating budgets are manufacturing overhead budgets (such as that discussed in Chapter 6) and sales budgets for a division or territory. Since operating budgets differ in format, _all_ operating budgets need not be part of the master budget. Some are too micro (for example, a particular salesperson's quota for a one-month period); others may recast data already in the master budget.

A planning budget is similar in purpose to a master budget. It is a

493

projected course of action for one or more, *but not all,* subsystems of the organization. As such, its scope is more limited than the firm's master budget.

A firm may utilize planning budgets rather than a comprehensive master budget for a variety of reasons. The most common is that only a single aspect of the corporate resource allocation process is of concern to management at the time. For example, the firm may be concerned primarily with the adequacy of its cash position. If the cash budget indicates that all is well, it may be the sole statement produced for management's use. If it indicates a deficiency in the cash flows, then other components of the master budget process may have to be revised. In such a case, the generation of new forecasts and budgets continues until management finds an acceptable set of plans or budgets that together form a new master budget.

A specific planning budget may also be developed because its time horizon is different from that of the master budget. Thus, while the master budget typically provides a detailed plan for one year, many areas require estimates for longer time periods; for example, a five-year sales forecast or a three-year research and development plan may be required. Other plans may call for finer detail than the monthly data of the typical master budget. For example, a cash management problem may require weekly or daily data. We shall discuss planning budgets, particularly cash budgets, after completing our discussion of master budgets.

Elements of Successful Budgets

We have defined a budget as a formal, quantitative statement of anticipated resource flows. A budget thus reflects management's expectations concerning the organization's activities during a particular time period. A master budget is the vehicle for coordinating all of the individual budgets for an organization into an acceptable, firm-wide plan. The success of the master budget process depends on several essential elements:

(1) Forecasting the organization's activities.
(2) Coordinating these activities.
(3) Communicating the activities to all concerned.
(4) Acceptance of the plan by the participants.
(5) Providing a frame of reference for evaluation at the end of the period.

Continued success is usually enjoyed by firms that are regularly able to attain all of these goals. The master budget process, then, is the critical link between top management's plans and lower level managers' programs.

Forecasting

While it may be obvious that any plan requires some effort by management to predict the future, the complexity and expense of the master budget process requires management's best efforts to justify the costs. Many of the activities to be forecast are internal. These activities usually are easier to predict than external activities, particularly the nature of the economy and its impact on demand in a certain region or for a certain product. (For example, if there is a recession and the demand for furniture slumps, how will it affect a new line of Impey Recliners?) Although information on these external topics generally is abundant, the data may be conflicting and may not deal with exactly the question at hand. Fortunately, market researchers are skillful in dealing with these problems.

One of the benefits of a master budget is that it requires this forecasting behavior. A firm's managers must contemplate the future. The aim is to do it in a systematic fashion and end the process with a significantly better understanding of the firm's relationship to its environment. Since no master budget can be any better than its initial assumptions, the forecasts not only serve as starting points, but also are critical to the development of an accurate plan.

Coordinating

The coordinating aspect of budgets arises from the need to merge subsystem plans, since each subsystem's plans have implications for other units. Sales depends upon production to have the proper mix and quantities of goods. Production, in turn, makes its plans with the assumption that purchasing and personnel will supply the required material and human resources. And all functions require finance to maintain a critical level of solvency during the period. The budget serves to communicate these expectations and provide a means whereby subunits can adjust to one another. The result is a mutually acceptable and feasible plan.

This topic provides an important analogy with transfer pricing. In a sense, coordination with a master budget is achieved via communication and so-called "quantity" controls; the division's resources become specified in the budget. Conversely, coordination with a transfer price mechanism is achieved via communication and so-called "price" controls; the division's resources are self-selected subject to an internal pricing system.

Communicating

Although the master budget coordination function is important, it would be trivial if the plans were not communicated to the subunits. There not only must be an overall plan, that plan must be well known to the affected parties. No manager can respond to another's expectations for him unless the expectations are communicated to him. Moreover, the expectations must be communicated unambiguously and concisely, in an authoritative fashion. The budget process is intended to provide channels and incentives for honest communication and to give the parties involved a clearer picture of what is ultimately expected of them.

Acceptance

The acceptance of the budget is usually considered an integral part of the budget process and a necessary condition for its success. For the group to act in harmony, the members must not only know the plan, they must implement it. Acceptance can be achieved in any of a variety of ways.

Evaluating

Once a goal has been accepted, it forms a basis on which to assess the subsequent performance of the parties. A master budget, properly evolved, provides the managers with top management's best advice and its expectations for them. Managers should strive to fulfill these expectations. If we expect to achieve an intuitively reasonable solution, then the initial plan must be integrated into the evaluation process.

This view of the master budget, of course, merely summarizes our model in Chapter 5. We are interested in providing a mechanism to coordinate and motivate the various individuals' activities; this encompasses, it is important to remember, their motivation to work with the coordination mechanism.

Preparing the Master Budget

The development of the master budget consists of two types of activities—organizational processes and technical processes. The former refers to the manner in which people are organized and interact to achieve the best plan. The latter reflects the techniques used to produce a master budget from the data in the system. Each fulfills a needed function. It is tempting for accountants to emphasize the techniques that make the forecasts and integrate them into the organization's master budget. This is because computing a master budget is similar to recording past transactions, with the forecasts replacing real-world events.

However, the process an organization employs determines the quality of the data used. Certain people in an organization are better able to make the forecasts. Others are more critical for the acceptance and implementation of the plans. In total, the purpose of organizing the master budget process is to ensure selection of the best plan.

The Organization of the Process

Because of its importance, the master budget should be prepared in an organized manner. The details of the procedure vary with the organization of the firm. Factors such as the degree of centralization, geographic dispersion, and the nature of the product or products will affect the procedures adopted. However, the process can be discussed in general terms since the underlying procedure is much the same in all cases.

The Budget Committee

In most firms, the responsibility for formulating the budget rests with a budget committee. This group is responsible for the entire process leading to the master budget, although its decisions may be subject to a final review. The committee supervises the design of forms, sets deadlines, and reviews budget proposals. The procedures followed by this committee and other participants in the master budget process may be recorded in a budget manual.

The composition of the committee reflects one or more of several possible criteria. These are department or division of the firm, function, geographical region, and level of management. Each of these criteria has its own advantages and disadvantages. For example, a committee made up of divisional representatives (who are designated as such) will be capable of reflecting all aspects of a diverse organization's activities. Thus, a conglomerate may organize its budget committee so all the different companies are represented. However, such a committee may find it hard to function if its members take their charge as company representatives too seriously. Advocacy may replace analysis, and conflict may replace cooperation, which would work to the detriment of the firm and reduce the long-run benefit to the subunits. Regional or functional representation could have similar, though less extreme, dysfunctional effects.[1] In the final analysis, the effectiveness of the committee in performing its difficult task depends significantly upon the conditions existing on a daily basis in the organization. If intersubunit conflict is a way of life, then the budget process will be fraught with conflict. If cooperation usually prevails, it should carry over to the budget committee.

The Consultative Nature of the Process

The consultative model is an operational middle ground between the authoritarian and participative models of the standard-setting process. In this model, data about operations flow upward in the organization. Each level in the organization analyzes the data and prepares a report synthesizing its expectations for the coming period. Top management sets goals and integrates plans,

---

[1] See M. Schiff and A. Lewin, "The Impact of People on Budgets," *Accounting Rev.*, April 1970.

which are then communicated downward in the organization, with each superior using the budget set for him or her to establish standards for subordinates. In this manner, goals are transmitted downward through the organization, and budgets are set at each level.

The success of the consultative model depends upon the extent to which the downward flow of data includes not only management's plans, such as are manifested in budgets, but also an explanation relating the initial proposal of the subordinate to the final plan adopted by the organization. One of the ways this communication can be achieved is through repeated interaction between the superior and the subordinate during the process so that the subordinate is kept informed. Alternatively, the superior can explain the relationship at the end of the process. By providing the avenues for communication and consultation, the consultative model enhances the subordinate's view of his importance in the planning process. The rationale is that even if he cannot participate in the actual decision, he is gratified that others take cognizance of his expertise.

One risk inherent in the consultative model is that the subordinate's expectations may become the standards and he may be held to them rigidly because he set them for himself. This is in reality an authoritarian situation and not a true consultative situation. In an early study, Lowe and Shaw[2] found that, under such circumstances, sales managers learned to bias their sales forecasts downward. This may have occurred for either of two reasons. First, such a quasi-consultative situation is even more threatening than the pure authoritarian model because the subordinate sets his own standards. At the end of the period he finds he cannot reject the standards as being unreasonable, so he must rationalize the unfavorable differences away. Had management imposed the standards, the situation would have been less threatening. Second, some conflict is bound to be present as both superior and subordinate strive to achieve goals that are not completely congruent. There may be honest disagreements in the sense that both parties are trying to do their jobs as well as they can. In the Lowe and Shaw study, the sales managers strove to build in a cushion, or slack, to protect themselves, and the resulting forecast was less than they were capable of achieving. This kind of conflict is often accepted as part of the superior–subordinate "game."

The impact of the master budget process on the subunits has been subject to some study. Generally, the nature of the budget task precludes an authoritarian or downward flow approach. That is, there should be upward and horizontal flows of forecasts, plans, and other information. The amount of participation depends upon the system developed by the budget committee. The high degree of perceived participation possible in this process brings many of the potential benefits that are ascribed to it by its advocates.

---

[2] A. Lowe and R. Shaw, "An Analysis of Managerial Biasing: Evidence from a Company's Budgeting Process," *J. of Management Studies*, Oct. 1968.

However, the implicit need for cooperation among various levels raises two important issues. First, a more participative master budget process may be inconsistent with the organization's management philosophy. That is, it could lead to an increased desire for greater participation in other aspects of the organization's activities and thereby create conflict. Second, the budget process requires an expenditure of time and effort. Frictions can arise between levels and units as each strives to minimize its own work. Furthermore, each group may produce less than the requisite quality input to the process, necessitating extra effort by others, tighter controls by the committee, or inferior output from the budget process.

Put another way, what is optimal from the point of view of a subunit may not be optimal from the point of view of the firm as a whole. This arises because of interdependencies among subunits that, in the absence of hierarchical direction, the members of the subunits may not be motivated to recognize.

Statements of the Master Budget: A Simple Example

Although our first example of the master budget will be a simple one, it will serve to highlight the array of budgets coordinated via the master budget process. The second example will afford a more detailed discussion of the process.

Every summer Tony Hope has been awarded the franchise to run the refreshment stand at the Community Swim Club. The Club provides him with the small stand, but he must supply the various pieces of equipment, pay for utilities, and employ the personnel required. Mr. Hope has run the stand for several years as a profitable sideline. During this period he has acquired the necessary equipment. In addition, he has some supplies left over from last year, which are not shown on the balance sheet.

In early April, Mr. Hope is planning for the 1982 swimming season that will run from June 1 until August 31. Specifically, he wants to forecast two things:

(1) How profitable the stand will be in 1982.
(2) What the cash flows will be during this period.

To answer these questions, he must develop a projected income statement for the summer and a projected cash budget for the period from June through August. In addition, to obtain these data he must also develop estimates of sales, purchases, and operating costs. These estimates take the form of:

(1) A sales budget (in units and dollars).
(2) A purchase budget.
(3) An operating expense budget.

Mr. Hope's opening balance sheet for Hope's Community Swim Club Stand (H.C.S.C.S.) is shown in Exhibit 13-1. This sheet provides required information about the cash balance and equipment. Exhibit 13-2 begins the actual process of projecting the summer's statements. It reflects Mr. Hope's estimates of the summer's sales activity by month. Mr. Hope increased his estimates over last year for two reasons. First, last year was a rather cold summer. Second, the club has expanded its membership from 400 families to 450. He tempered his increase because he felt inflation would adversely affect his sales volume.

Exhibit 13-3 shows the projected dollar amount of sales at the expected 1982 prices. As indicated, hamburgers will sell for $1.50 and soda pop and snacks will sell for $.30. Since Mr. Hope's stand sells strictly for cash, the data in this exhibit will serve as both the sales figure in the projected income statement (Exhibit 13-7) and the monthly cash receipts in the cash budget (Exhibit 13-8).

Given the projected level of sales, Mr. Hope now must plan his purchases for the period. Because of a lack of storage space, concern over spoilage, and pilferage, Mr. Hope buys the snacks, hamburger patties, and buns two or three times each week. Thus the purchase budget (in units) is the same as the sales budget for these items (Exhibit 13-4). To obtain the syrup and CO_2 for the beverages, Mr. Hope anticipates making two large purchases during the summer: one in June, at the start of the season, and one in July, to carry him through the remainder of the summer. These purchases are included in the purchase budget in dollars (Exhibit 13-5.)

Mr Hope's suppliers bill him on a monthly basis. All of June's purchases are billed to him on or about July 1 and paid during that month. The same

EXHIBIT 13-1

Hope's Community Swim Club Stand
Balance Sheet
April 1, 1982

Assets		
Cash		$ 300
Prepaid insurance		150
Equipment		
Cost	$5,000	
Less: Accumulated depreciation	3,000	2,000
Total assets		$2,450
Proprietorship: T. Hope		$2,450

EXHIBIT 13-2

H.C.S.C.S.
Projected Sales in Units
June to August, 1982

	Hamburgers	Soda Pop	Snacks
June	1,350	3,750	4,000
July	1,600	5,000	3,350
August	1,550	4,750	3,900
Total	4,500	13,500	11,250

pattern is followed for July's and August's purchases. This means that each month's purchases appear one month later in the cash budget (see Exhibit 13-8).

Because Mr. Hope carries no inventory of perishables from one season to the next, purchases equal cost of sales on the summer's income statement.

Finally, Mr. Hope must estimate his operating costs. The overhead budget (Exhibit 13-6) summarizes these costs. The cost of wages, which Mr. Hope rounded off for each month, is based on an hourly rate of about $3.75 and a total of about 400 hours per month. Wages are a cash item in the overhead budget—that is, Mr. Hope uses and pays for them in the same cash budget period, the month. Utilities and supplies are credit items: They, like the hamburger patties and other purchases, are acquired in one month and paid for in the subsequent month. Finally, depreciation and insurance are noncash items during the period covered by the cash budget. Both result from the consumption of service potentials acquired and paid for prior to the start of the budget period. The insurance on the stand costs $150 per season and is paid once each year, in March. The depreciation expense is the allocation of the year's depreciation expense of $600 over the three months the stand is operating.

EXHIBIT 13-3

H.C.S.C.S.
Projected Sales
June to August, 1982

	Hamburgers[a]	Soda Pop[a]	Snacks[a]	Total
June	$2,025	$1,125	$1,200	$ 4,350
July	2,400	1,500	1,005	4,905
August	2,325	1,425	1,170	4,920
	$6,750	$4,050	$3,375	$14,175

[a] Selling prices: hamburgers, $1.50; soda pop, $.30; and snacks, $.30.

EXHIBIT 13-4_____

H.C.S.C.S.
Purchase Budget in Units
June to August, 1982

	Hamburger Patties	Buns	Snacks
June	1,350	1,350	4,000
July	1,600	1,600	3,350
August	1,550	1,550	3,900
	4,500	4,500	11,250

EXHIBIT 13-5_____

H.C.S.C.S.
Purchase Budget in Dollars
June to August, 1982

	Hamburger Patties[a]	Buns[a]	Snacks[a]	Syrup and CO_2	Total
June	$ 810	$135	$ 720	$1,000	$2,665
July	960	160	603	890	2,613
August	930	155	702	0	1,787
	$2,700	$450	$2,025	$1,890	$7,065

[a] Costs: patties, $.60; buns, $.10; and snacks, $.18.

EXHIBIT 13-6_____

H.C.S.C.S.
Overhead Budget
June to August, 1982

	June	July	August	Total
Cash item				
Wages	$1,500	$1,550	$1,550	$4,600
Credit items				
Supplies	60	80	70	210
Utilities	100	120	110	330
Noncash items				
Depreciation	200	200	200	600
Insurance	50	50	50	150
	$1,910	$2,000	$1,980	$5,890

_____EXHIBIT 13-7

H.C.S.C.S.
Projected Income Statement
June to August, 1982

Sales (from Exhibit 13-3)		$14,175
Less: Cost of sales (from Exhibit 13-5)		7,065
Gross margin		$ 7,110
Less: Overhead (from Exhibit 13-6)		
Labor	$4,600	
Supplies	210	
Utilities	330	
Depreciation	600	
Insurance	150	$ 5,890
Net profit (pre-tax)		$ 1,220

Exhibit 13-7 shows Hope's projected income statement for the summer from the stand. Because Hope's stand carries no inventory over from one year to the next, the cost of goods sold equals purchases and no separate calculation of the cost of sales is necessary. Typically, this is not the case and a separate calculation is required to project the cost of sales.

A single income statement is shown for the entire summer because this is all Hope required. If for some reason monthly income statements were required, they could be prepared.

The data from the cash budget summarize the amounts presented in the exhibits and the timing of payments explained earlier. Since all sales are cash, the cash inflow is reflected in the month the sale is made. Similarly,

_____EXHIBIT 13-8

H.C.S.C.S.
Cash Budget
June to September, 1982

	June	July	August	September
Opening balance	$ 300	$3,150	$3,680	$4,237
Add				
Receipts (from Exhibit 13-3)	4,350	4,905	4,920	0
Cash available	$4,650	$8,055	$8,600	$4,237
Less payment for:				
Raw materials (from Exhibit 13-5)	0	2,665	2,613	1,787
Wages (from Exhibit 13-6)	1,500	1,550	1,550	0
Supplies (from Exhibit 13-6)	0	60	80	70
Utilities (from Exhibit 13-6)	0	100	120	110
Cash disbursed	$1,500	$4,375	$4,363	$1,967
Ending balance	$3,150	$3,680	$4,237	$2,270

EXHIBIT 13-9————————————————————————————

H.C.S.C.S.
Balance Sheet
September 30, 1982

Assets		
Cash		$2,270
Equipment		
Cost	$5,000	
Less: Accumulated depreciation	$3,600	1,400
Total assets		$3,670
Proprietorship: T. Hope		
Opening balance		$2,450
Operating profit		1,220
Total proprietorship		$3,670

wages are paid on the final day of the month in which they are earned. Thus they are an outflow of that month. In contrast, the bills for most materials and supplies are paid one month after they are purchased. Thus June's purchases were paid for in July.

Two items, insurance and depreciation, did not involve a cash outlay during any of the months covered by the cash budget. Thus, while they are included in the income statement to match costs and revenues properly, they are irrelevant for the preparation of a cash budget. Note, however, that their consumption is reflected on the September 30, 1982, balance sheet (Exhibit 13-9). Accumulated depreciation has gone up by $600 and the prepaid insurance is no longer carried on the balance sheet.

The next example will deal with a more complex situation. However, the underlying concepts are not different from those just used in preparing budgets for the refreshment stand.

Statements of the Master Budget:————————— An Extended Example

Before enmeshing ourselves in detail, we should recognize that the individual firm chooses the sequence in which its budgets are presented, the titles of its budgets, and their organization. Other texts and budget manuals, while providing fundamentally the same budget data, may present the statements in a different order, use different labels, and combine two or more statements into a single budget. However, all budgets have the common goal of producing a detailed plan for the acquisition, storage, conversion, use, and sale of resources.

Mechanically, preparation of a master budget involves a set of technical procedures that generate the supporting schedules and aggregate them into a comprehensive statement of expected income and a new balance sheet for the end of the period. We have chosen one year as the time period to be described, although this too is a matter of individual firm choice. For convenience, we have used quarterly data, though monthly data would be more representative.

The starting point in preparing the master budget is the sales forecast for the period. Here we assume that expected sales is a variable exogenous to the firm and that the problem of estimating sales has been resolved through a combination of marketing and operating decisions. At this point the individual budgets begin to build on and relate to one another.

The sales forecast serves as the basis for developing a production budget for the period. Once the production budget is agreed upon, estimates can be made of the cash and noncash expenditures needed to produce the budgeted output. These estimates can be summarized into raw materials purchases, direct labor costs, and manufacturing overhead budgets. Total selling and production activities indicate the amounts of selling and administrative expenses that should be incurred. These individual budgets, along with schedules of collections and payables, may then be consolidated into the cash budget (given capital acquisitions anticipated), the projected income statement, and the projected balance sheet for the period. An illustration of how these different schedules may be integrated into a master budget follows.

Sales Budget.   Consider the sales budget illustrated in Exhibit 13-10. This is a simplified example of a sales budget for a firm producing only two types or classes of products. A firm's sales budget may be based on simple extrapolations of past sales or on sophisticated planning models. The choice of models probably depends in part on the complexity of the firm's operations.

The sales budget may, in addition, reflect the opinions of a variety of individuals. For example, some firms base sales data upon estimates provided by salespeople, the rationale being that they possess local information about sales potential. While this may be the case, there is evidence indicating that when sales personnel are allowed to set their own standards for future sales, they deliberately bias their estimates downward. Certainly, if this type of biasing behavior is present, it can weaken the value of the budgeting process. And in any event, the phenomenon underscores the importance of designing incentives to work with the firm's coordination mechanism.

The format selected for the sales budget statement depends on the structure of the organization's responsibility units, which are often called profit centers in this context. The sales forecast presents the estimates in a manner that permits each manager to determine his responsibility. For example, the sales data shown in Exhibit 13-10 are classified by responsibility units as well as by products and territories. Each budget should display the data in

EXHIBIT 13-10

J.D.D. Company
Sales Budget

	TERRITORY 1		TERRITORY 2		TERRITORY 3		TOTALS	
	Units	Dollars	Units	Dollars	Units	Dollars	Units	Dollars
Product J ($30 per unit)								
1st qtr.	7,000	$ 210,000	10,000	$ 300,000	9,000	$ 270,000	26,000	$ 780,000
2nd qtr.	8,000	240,000	11,000	330,000	9,000	270,000	28,000	840,000
3rd qtr.	11,000	330,000	14,000	420,000	9,000	270,000	34,000	1,020,000
4th qtr.	9,000	270,000	9,000	270,000	8,000	240,000	26,000	780,000
Totals	35,000	$1,050,000	44,000	$ 1,320,000	35,000	$ 1,050,000	114,000	$ 3,420,000
Product D ($40 per unit)								
1st qtr.	40,000	$1,600,000	75,000	$ 3,000,000	50,000	$ 2,000,000	165,000	$ 6,600,000
2nd qtr.	50,000	2,000,000	80,000	3,200,000	70,000	2,800,000	200,000	8,000,000
3rd qtr.	55,000	2,200,000	75,000	3,000,000	80,000	3,200,000	210,000	8,400,000
4th qtr.	50,000	2,000,000	60,000	2,400,000	75,000	3,000,000	185,000	7,400,000
Totals	195,000	$7,800,000	290,000	$11,600,000	275,000	$11,000,000	760,000	$30,400,000

such a way that each cell in the report matrix can be associated with a responsibility unit.

Production Budget. The sales budget becomes the basis for preparing the production budget (Exhibit 13-11). The objective of the production budget is to strike a balance between the output needed to meet this period's sales and the desired level of inventory at the end of the period so the firm will also be able to meet next period's sales. In the typical budget setting, these goods come from either the opening inventory or the current period's production. (Indeed, formal management science models may be used at this point.)

In the budget process, three of the four items in Exhibit 13-11 are usually known or set by firm policy. Opening and closing inventories are usually a function of expected sales, storage capacity, or (perhaps) storage life. Thus they can be treated as known. Similarly, the sales level was already projected in the sales budget. Thus the production budget calculates the level of production needed in the current period to meet these conditions.

Purchases Budget. The production budget indicates the number of units to be produced in each quarter, and it is therefore the basis for developing the amounts of materials, labor, and overhead necessary during the specified period. The materials purchases budget (Exhibit 13-12) summarizes the amounts of materials needed to meet the production goal set for each quarter.

—————————————————————————————————EXHIBIT 13-11

J.D.D. Company
Production Budget

Product J	Qtr. 1	Qtr. 2	Qtr. 3	Qtr. 4
Units to be sold[a]	26,000	28,000	34,000	26,000
Plus: Planned ending inventory	1,000	1,300	1,000	1,200
Units needed during the quarter	27,000	29,300	35,000	27,200
Less: Beginning inventory	700	1,000	1,300	1,000
Units to be produced	26,300	28,300	33,700	26,200
Total for the period: 114,500 units				
Product D				
Units to be sold[a]	165,000	200,000	210,000	185,000
Plus: Planned ending inventory	10,000	12,000	15,000	20,000
Units needed during the quarter	175,000	212,000	225,000	205,000
Less: Beginning inventory	5,000	10,000	12,000	15,000
Units to be produced	170,000	202,000	213,000	190,000
Total for the period: 775,000 units				

[a] Data from the sales budget (Exhibit 13-10).

EXHIBIT 13-12

J.D.D. Company
Materials Purchases Budget

	Qtr. 1	Qtr. 2	Qtr. 3	Qtr. 4
Plastic (⅝" sheet)				
Units to be used	100,000	300,000	200,000	50,000
Plus: Planned ending inventory	10,000	5,000	4,000	10,000
Units needed during the quarter	110,000	305,000	204,000	60,000
Less: Planned beginning inventory	15,000	10,000	5,000	4,000
Units to be purchased	95,000	295,000	199,000	56,000
Total: 645,000 units				
Steel (¼" sheet)				
Units to be used	100,000	100,000	175,000	150,000
Plus: Planned ending inventory	10,000	7,500	10,000	10,000
Units needed during the quarter	110,000	107,500	185,000	160,000
Less: Planned beginning inventory	10,000	10,000	7,500	10,000
Units to be purchased	100,000	97,500	177,500	150,000
Total: 525,000 units				
Wood (2" × 4" × 10")				
Units to be used	100,000	100,000	50,000	50,000
Plus: Planned ending inventory	10,000	10,000	8,000	20,000
Units needed during the quarter	110,000	110,000	58,000	70,000
Less: Planned beginning inventory	15,000	10,000	10,000	8,000
Units to be purchased	95,000	100,000	48,000	62,000
Total: 305,000 units				

These items are priced and a purchases budget prepared as shown in Exhibit 13-13.

Management may stockpile raw materials as well as finished goods. As a result, the desired ending inventory will fluctuate and the units purchased may differ from the amount required by expected production. Purchases may exceed the quantity used in production (what is called an inventory build up) or fall short of it (an inventory depletion). For example, the firm's policy in this area may encourage inventory fluctuations by setting the period's ending inventory at a fixed percentage of next period's sales. If this is the case, inventory will expand ahead of production and sales and decrease prior to the downturn in those areas. Other firms may have no definite policy, relying instead on the purchasing department to acquire materials as needed and at the best price. Because the master budget process requires planning of activities, it works against such a policy. In this example, the inventory level has been determined by management. However, they do not appear to follow any simple rule, such as making ending inventory a certain percentage of next period's projected sales.

—————————————————————————————— EXHIBIT 13-13

J.D.D. Company
Purchases Budget

	Qtr. 1	Qtr. 2	Qtr. 3	Qtr. 4
Cost of materials to be used	$2,000,000	$3,000,000	$3,000,000	$2,000,000
Plus: Planned ending inventory	200,000	150,000	160,000	250,000
Cost of materials needed	$2,200,000	$3,150,000	$3,160,000	$2,250,000
Less: Planned beginning inventory	250,000	200,000	150,000	160,000
Cost of materials to be purchased	$1,950,000	$2,950,000	$3,010,000	$2,090,000

Total purchases: $10,000,000[a]

[a] Purchases are on account. Payments are made within the discount period and in amounts sufficient to maintain a constant balance for Accounts Payable.

Direct Labor Budget.   Similarly, production of Products J and D in each quarter requires a certain number of direct labor hours. When these hours are costed at the standard labor rate, the direct labor budget can be calculated. An example of such a budget is given in Exhibit 13-14. Note that the hours required for a product in any period is the expected production (as shown by the production budget) times the expected direct labor hours per unit. For Product J this is 1 hour and for D it is ½ hour. The hourly rate is $15.

Manufacturing Overhead Budget.   The manufacturing overhead budget requires some additional comment. It is a summary budget of all overhead activities and therefore not disaggregated enough for detailed control purposes. As a summary of the various departmental budgets, it reflects all the cost assumptions and measurement problems present in overhead items. These different patterns of cost behavior are illustrated in the sample budget shown in Exhibit 13-15.

—————————————————————————————— EXHIBIT 13-14

J.D.D. Company
Direct Labor Budget

	Qtr. 1	Qtr. 2	Qtr. 3	Qtr. 4
Product J, hours[a]	26,300	28,300	33,700	26,200
Product D, hours[a]	85,000	101,000	106,500	95,000
Total hours	111,300	129,300	140,200	121,200
Total dollars	$1,669,500	$1,939,500	$2,103,000	$1,818,000

Total labor budget: $7,530,000

[a] Data from the production budget (Exhibit 13-11).

EXHIBIT 13-15

J.D.D. Company
Manufacturing Overhead Budget

	Qtr. 1	Qtr. 2	Qtr. 3	Qtr. 4	Totals
Heat	$ 50,000	$ 30,000	$ 10,000	$ 40,000	$ 130,000
Light	32,000	30,000	28,000	30,000	120,000
Power	58,950	62,350	63,990	60,940	246,230
Supplies	29,445	34,545	37,005	32,430	133,425
Maintenance	120,000	130,000	150,000	123,000	523,000
Rent	150,000	150,000	150,000	150,000	600,000
Depreciation	235,000	235,000	235,000	235,000	940,000
Indirect labor	39,260	46,060	49,340	43,240	177,900
Insurance	10,000	10,000	10,000	10,000	40,000
Totals	$724,655	$727,955	$733,335	$724,610	$2,910,555
Less: Depreciation	235,000	235,000	235,000	235,000	940,000
Cash payments	$489,655	$492,955	$498,335	$489,610	$1,970,555

Average overhead per unit of production is approximately $3.27; i.e., $2,910,555 ÷ 889,500 units.

The first two items in the budget, heat and light, vary primarily with environmental conditions rather than with the rate of production. Thus we have assumed that these costs can best be estimated by the exact relationship with the season. In contrast, power is semivariable with changes in volume. The variable rate is assumed to be $.10 per unit of production (fixed portion = $39,320). Supplies and indirect labor are considered to be strictly variable costs, with per unit rates of $.15 and $.20, respectively. Rent, depreciation, and insurance, which are usually fixed in the short run, are shown as fixed costs. The pattern for maintenance cost is usually the least clear. There typically is some change in maintenance cost in response to changes in the rate of production. For practical purposes, this cost equation usually cannot be developed from available data. Total maintenance cost is budgeted at a level roughly related to the amount of production planned for the quarter. While this assumption does not present a serious problem from the standpoint of budget preparation, the lack of any standard results in some difficulty in interpreting any deviations in performance from the budgeted amounts. For example, an over-budget expenditure when production is slack could reflect inefficiency, greater maintenance work because more time is available in which to perform it, or both.

The average overhead cost per unit of output (arithmetic mean over the year) is approximately $3.27. The average is based on the total number of units produced and, in the case of a multiproduct firm, assumes a given mix of products. The datum serves as an input for the cost of sales and for a projected statement of net income for the period. In a more detailed example,

_____ EXHIBIT 13-16

J.D.D. Company
Selling Expense Budget

	Qtr. 1	Qtr. 2	Qtr. 3	Qtr. 4	Total
Salaries	$ 250,000	$ 250,000	$ 250,000	$ 250,000	$1,000,000
Commissions[a]	208,000	249,000	265,000	230,000	952,000
Travel	160,000	170,000	170,000	160,000	660,000
Advertising	500,000	500,000	500,000	500,000	2,000,000
Telephone	10,000	10,000	10,000	10,000	40,000
Office rent	62,500	62,500	62,500	62,500	250,000
Shipping expenses[b]	38,200	45,600	48,800	42,200	174,800
Delivery expenses	40,000	50,000	60,000	50,000	200,000
Totals	$1,268,700	$1,337,100	$1,366,300	$1,304,700	$5,276,800

[a] Approximately 2.8 percent of sales.
[b] $.20 per unit sold (Exhibit 13-10).

_____

the overhead rates of each product would be used to determine the projected sales cost.

Since depreciation is a noncash expense, it is eliminated from the calculation of cash outflow in the manufacturing overhead budget.

Selling and Administrative Budgets.　　Exhibits 13-16 and 13-17 summarize the estimated costs of selling and administrative activities. We have sim-

_____ EXHIBIT 13-17

J.D.D. Company
General and Administrative Expense Budget

	Qtr. 1	Qtr. 2	Qtr. 3	Qtr. 4	Total
Officers' salaries	$ 450,000	$ 450,000	$ 450,000	$ 450,000	$1,800,000
Office salary	275,000	275,000	275,000	275,000	1,100,000
Auditor's fee	80,000	—	—	—	80,000
Corporate taxes	140,000	140,000	140,000	140,000	560,000
Supplies	20,000	20,000	20,000	20,000	80,000
Light and heat	30,000	5,000	5,000	20,000	60,000
Rent	95,000	95,000	95,000	95,000	380,000
Telephone	10,000	10,000	10,000	10,000	40,000
Donations	5,000	5,000	5,000	5,000	20,000
Depreciation	15,000	15,000	15,000	15,000	60,000
Totals	$1,120,000	$1,015,000	$1,015,000	$1,030,000	$4,180,000
Less: Depreciation	15,000	15,000	15,000	15,000	60,000
Cash payments	$1,105,000	$1,000,000	$1,000,000	$1,015,000	$4,120,000

EXHIBIT 13-18 _____

J.D.D. Company
Sales Revenue Budget
Net of Returns, Allowances, and Uncollectibles

	Qtr. 1	Qtr. 2	Qtr. 3	Qtr. 4	Totals
Gross sales[a]	$7,380,000	$8,840,000	$9,420,000	$8,180,000	$33,820,000
Returns and allowances (4%)	$ 295,200	$ 353,600	$ 376,800	$ 327,200	$ 1,352,800
Bad debts (2%)	147,600	176,800	188,400	163,600	676,400
Total deductions	$ 442,800	$ 530,400	$ 565,200	$ 490,800	$ 2,029,200
Net sales	$6,937,200	$8,309,600	$8,854,800	$7,689,200	$31,790,800

[a] Data from Exhibit 13-10.

_____

plified the administrative expense budget by assuming that most costs are essentially fixed. Selling expenses reflect two variable costs—commissions and shipping expenses. Commissions vary as a percentage of the dollar sales; shipping expenses vary with the number of units sold. Delivery expense is considered a step cost, with no cost equation specified.

Cash Receipts. Exhibits 13-18 and 13-19 illustrate the procedures for calculating cash receipts from sales. Exhibit 13-18 shows the calculations for determining the net dollar sales. An estimate of returns and allowances (4 percent of gross sales) and uncollectibles (2 percent of gross sales) is subtracted from gross sales to determine net sales. This amount is the revenue the firm expects to realize from total sales. However, adjustments for changes in receivable balances will be required to yield expected cash receipts from sales.

Net sales totals are then transferred to the accounts receivable schedules (Exhibit 13-19). Past collection experience indicates that the firm can expect to collect 88 percent of a quarter's net sales within the quarter in which the sales were made, another 10 percent in the following quarter, and the remaining 2 percent in the quarter after that.[3] The ending balance of accounts receivable will appear on the firm's quarterly balance sheet. Total collections will be transferred to the cash collections summary, Exhibit 13-20. This summary is self-explanatory. Other income consists of interest, dividends, and miscellaneous revenues; they are immaterial in amount. If the firm had cash sales, these would be entered directly in the summary of cash collections.

Cash Payments. Exhibit 13-21 summarizes the estimated cash payments. As indicated on the purchases budget (Exhibit 13-13), accounts payable are kept at a constant balance so that quarterly amounts of purchases are equiva-

_____

[3] These assumptions are merely illustrative and are not meant to represent any firm's actual experiences.

_____ EXHIBIT 13-19

J.D.D. Company
Estimated Collections on Accounts Receivable

	Qtr. 1	Qtr. 2	Qtr. 3	Qtr. 4
Net accounts receivable at the beginning of the quarter				
Previous quarter (12%)	$ 720,000[a]	$ 832,460	$ 997,150	$1,062,580
Second previous quarter (2%)	120,000[a]	120,000	138,740	166,190
Plus: Current sales, net	6,937,200	8,309,600	8,854,800	7,689,200
Total charges	$7,777,200	$9,262,060	$9,990,690	$8,917,970
Less: Collections				
Current quarter (88%)	$6,104,740	$7,312,450	$7,792,220	$6,766,500
Previous quarter (10%)	600,000[b]	693,720	830,960	885,480
Second previous quarter (2%)	120,000[b]	120,000	138,740	166,190
Total collections	$6,824,740	$8,126,170	$8,761,920	$7,818,170
Ending balance, accounts receivable[c]	$ 952,460	$1,135,890	$1,228,770	$1,099,800

[a] The balance sheet for January 1 (Exhibit 13-25) lists an accounts receivable balance of $840,000 = $720,000 + $120,000.

[b] $600,000 is 10% of the previous quarter's sales; the entire $120,000 of the second previous quarter will be collected in this quarter.

[c]
J.D.D. Company
Analysis of Accounts Receivable Balance

	Qtr. 1	Qtr. 2	Qtr. 3	Qtr. 4
Ending balance, accounts receivable				
From previous quarter	$ 120,000	$ 138,740	$ 166,190	$ 177,100
From current quarter				
10%	$ 693,720	$ 830,960	$ 885,480	$ 768,920
2%	138,740	166,190	177,100	153,780
Total, current quarter	$ 832,460	$ 997,150	$1,062,580	$ 922,700
Ending balance, accounts receivable	$ 952,460	$1,135,890	$1,228,770	$1,099,800

lent to the amount of cash paid to suppliers. We could have complicated the schedule by assuming the presence of a time lag as we did for cash collections. However, the technique would have been the same. Except for capital expansion, taxes, and interest, the items on the cash payments budget are taken from previous exhibits. (Exhibit numbers are given in parentheses.) Note the adjustments for depreciation in Exhibits 13-15 and 13-17. The tax payments are made in two installments and are for last year's liability. This year's taxes will be paid next year.[4]

_____
[4] We are ignoring, in the interest of simplicity, questions of estimated tax payments.

EXHIBIT 13-20 _____

J.D.D. Company
Summary of Cash Collections

	Qtr. 1	Qtr. 2	Qtr. 3	Qtr. 4	Totals
Collections of accounts receivable[a]	$6,824,740	$8,126,170	$8,761,920	$7,818,170	$31,531,000
Other income	50,000	60,000	30,000	30,000	170,000
Sale of assets[b]	200,000	—	—	100,000	300,000
Totals	$7,074,740	$8,186,170	$8,791,920	$7,948,170	$32,001,000

[a] Data from Exhibit 13-19.
[b] Cash received = Book value of assets sold. No gain or loss.

Interest payments are based on the loans outstanding at the end of each quarter. The opening equipment debt balance is $750,000 (Exhibit 13-25.) Interest is paid semiannually, on March 31 and September 30. From Exhibit 13-22, the capital budget, we note that additional long-term notes will be signed in the second and third quarters. Assuming no payments on principal, the loan balance stays at $750,000 for the first quarter, increases to $1,650,000 at the end of the second, and goes to $2,250,000 at the end of the third. At an interest rate of 6 percent, the firm would have an interest

EXHIBIT 13-21 _____

J.D.D. Company
Cash Payments Budget

	Qtr. 1	Qtr. 2	Qtr. 3	Qtr. 4	Totals
Materials (13-13)	$1,950,000	$2,950,000	$3,010,000	$2,090,000	$10,000,000
Labor (13-14)	1,669,500	1,939,500	2,103,000	1,818,000	7,530,000
Manufacturing burden (13-15)	489,655	492,955	498,335	489,610	1,970,555
Selling expense (13-16)	1,268,700	1,337,100	1,366,300	1,304,700	5,276,800
General and administrative expense (13-17)	1,105,000	1,000,000	1,000,000	1,015,000	4,120,000
Capital expansion (13-22)	280,000	120,000	70,000	120,000	590,000
Interest payments (13-25)	40,000	—	96,000	—	136,000
Income tax (13-25)	440,000	440,000	—	—	880,000
Dividends (assumed)	—	375,000	—	375,000	750,000
U.S. tax notes (assumed)	—	—	—	750,000	750,000
Total	$7,242,855	$8,654,555	$8,143,635	$7,962,310	$32,003,355

EXHIBIT 13-22

J.D.D. Company
Capital Budget

	Qtr. 1	Qtr. 2	Qtr. 3	Qtr. 4	Total
New machinery	$250,000	$1,000,000	$450,000	$100,000	$1,800,000
Capitalized mainte-nance	—	—	200,000	—	200,000
Miscellaneous capital additions	30,000	20,000	20,000	20,000	90,000
Capital budget	$280,000	$1,020,000	$670,000	$120,000	$2,090,000
Less: Notes on new machinery	—	900,000	600,000	—	1,500,000
Current cash expenditure	$280,000	$ 120,000	$ 70,000	$120,000	$ 590,000

expense of $30,000 for quarter 1, $30,000 for quarter 2, $66,000 for quarter 3, and $90,000 for quarter 4. The loans are obtained at the end of each of the respective quarters. Also from the January 1 balance sheet (Exhibit 13-25), we observe that interest payable was $10,000; therefore, interest paid will be $10,000 + $30,000 in the first quarter and $30,000 plus $66,000 or $96,000, in the third quarter. No interest would be paid in the second and fourth quarters. Interest expense will be noted on the budgeted income statement, which we will discuss later.

Capital Acquisitions.   Exhibit 13-22 illustrates purchases and major maintenance charges related to the fixed asset accounts. The cash outlays for the purchases are reduced by the amount of the notes on new machinery. We have indicated these debt instruments as reductions in cash outlays, but this is merely for convenience. The alternative would have been to show any financing as part of the cash collections schedule. However, except for accounts payable, this is the only outside financing contemplated during the next operating period. Therefore, we have indicated that the financing occurs in the quarters in which the fixed assets are acquired.

The summary of cash flows appears in Exhibit 13-23. This exhibit merely relates the cash receipts of Exhibit 13-20 to the cash payments in Exhibit 13-21.

Budgeted Net Income.   The budgeted income statements in Exhibit 13-24 are based on a simple average costing method for computing cost of goods by quarters. We took the total expected manufacturing costs—both fixed and variable—and divided this total by expected units to be produced (approximately 890,000). The resulting average cost per unit was then applied to

EXHIBIT 13-23 ——

J.D.D. Company
Summary Cash Budget

	Qtr. 1	Qtr. 2	Qtr. 3	Qtr. 4	Totals
Beginning balance[a]	$ 900,000	$ 731,885	$ 263,500	$ 911,785	$ 900,000
Budgeted receipts (13-20)	7,074,740	8,186,170	8,791,920	7,948,170	32,001,000
Budgeted disbursements (13-21)	(7,242,855)	(8,654,555)	(8,143,635)	(7,962,310)	(32,003,355)
Net change	(168,115)	(468,385)	648,285	(14,140)	(2,355)
Ending balance	$ 731,885	$ 263,500	$ 911,785	$ 897,645	$ 897,645

[a] See Exhibit 13-25; beginning balance of cash is $900,000.

the total number of units sold in order to approximate the cost of goods sold.

As a consequence of this technique, the difference between the total manufacturing charges during a quarter and the amount of charges assigned to cost of goods sold does not reflect the actual changes in the physical invento-

EXHIBIT 13-24 ——

J.D.D. Company
Budgeted Income Statement

	Qtr. 1	Qtr. 2	Qtr. 3	Qtr. 4	Totals
Sales (net) (13-18)	$6,937,200	$8,309,600	$8,854,800	$7,689,200	$31,790,800
Cost of sales (13-13, 14, 15)[a]	4,397,000	5,256,000	5,623,000	4,837,000	20,113,000
	$2,540,200	$3,053,600	$3,231,800	$2,852,200	$11,677,800
Selling expense (13-16)	$1,268,700	$1,337,100	$1,366,300	$1,304,700	$ 5,276,800
General and administrative expense (13-17)	1,120,000	1,015,000	1,015,000	1,030,000	4,180,000
Total operating expenses	$2,388,700	$2,352,100	$2,381,300	$2,334,700	$ 9,456,800
Net operating income	$ 151,500	$ 701,500	$ 850,500	$ 517,500	$ 2,221,000
Other income (13-20)	50,000	60,000	30,000	30,000	170,000
	$ 201,500	$ 761,500	$ 880,500	$ 547,500	$ 2,391,000
Interest expense	30,000	30,000	66,000	90,000	216,000
Pre-tax income	$ 171,500	$ 731,500	$ 814,500	$ 457,500	$ 2,175,000
Income tax[b]	68,600	292,600	325,800	183,000	870,000
Net profit	$ 102,900	$ 438,900	$ 488,700	$ 274,500	$ 1,305,000

[a] Based on an average cost of approximately $23.00 per unit.
[b] 40 percent of income.

ries of finished goods from quarter to quarter. For example, the cost of goods sold in quarter 1 totaled $4,397,000; total manufacturing charges for the quarter consisted of direct materials of $2,000,000 plus direct labor of $1,669,500 plus manufacturing overhead of $724,665, or a total of $4,394,155. This difference appears as a credit of $2,845 on the balance sheet (Exhibit 13-25), reflecting a decrease in inventories for quarter 1. However, total production in units exceeded sales, and an increase should have appeared.[5] In order to minimize the calculation problems involved in income determination by quarters, a simple average-costing method was used. An accurate measurement of the expected quarterly income of the firm and the appropriate balances for work-in-process and finished goods would be extremely difficult. Perhaps we would have obtained a more useful quarterly statement if we had carefully distinguished between the variable and fixed costs of producing and selling the different volumes, as under a direct costing method of reporting.[6] In any event, our simple method is sufficient to illustrate how the differences between production and sales costs are resolved by running the adjustments through inventories. The remaining components of the income statement do not require additional comment, since they are taken from exhibits discussed previously.

Budgeted Balance Sheet. Our final schedule, Exhibit 13-25, is a projected balance sheet by quarters. This schedule summarizes all the previous exhibits discussed and therefore incorporates all the assumptions necessary to prepare these preliminary statements—that is, the estimating procedures used to project total and quarterly sales, the amounts and proper combinations of inputs, the production rates necessary to meet the projected sales, the standards for producing the different kinds of products, the estimated amounts of overhead given the production schedule, and so on.

It is difficult, if not impossible, to estimate the degree of accuracy of the ending balance sheet, since we did not (and could not) specify the errors in the different estimates that support these balances. On the other hand, the figures are sufficient to serve top management's preliminary evaluation of the policies and plans tentatively adopted for the coming period. These policies and plans may be modified to the extent that management does not consider the final results satisfactory. For example, cash balances may be adjusted by borrowing or by issuing long-term instruments, or inventory balances may be adjusted by applying more detailed analyses to the amounts and timing of purchases and production. Perhaps the profit figures would be improved if management adopted new policies and plans. If management

---

[5] This result merely reflects the fact that the higher levels of production in the remaining quarters have reduced the average fixed overhead cost per unit. Similar kinds of adjustments would have been required if we had used standard costs of sales, since the uneven production levels would have produced volume variances in each quarter.

[6] This type of interim report is discussed by D. Green, Jr., in "Towards a Theory of Interim Reports," *J. of Accounting Research,* Spring 1964.

EXHIBIT 13-25

J.D.D. Company
Budgeted Balance Sheet

	Jan. 1	March 31	June 30	Sept. 30	Dec. 31
Assets					
Current					
Cash (13-23)	$ 900,000	$ 731,885	$ 263,500	$ 911,785	$ 897,645
U.S. tax notes (13-21)	40,000	40,000	40,000	40,000	790,000
Accounts receivable, net (13-19)	840,000	952,460	1,135,890	1,228,770	1,099,800
Inventories					
Materials (13-13)	250,000	200,000	150,000	160,000	250,000
Finished goods	285,000	285,000	285,000	285,000	285,000
Adjustment for inventory changes		(2,845)	408,610	621,945	327,555
Net current assets	$ 2,315,000	$ 2,206,500	$ 2,283,000	$ 3,247,500	$ 3,650,000
Plant and equipment (net)[a]	15,000,000	14,830,000	15,600,000	16,020,000	15,790,000
Total assets	$17,315,000	$17,036,500	$17,883,000	$19,267,500	$19,440,000
Equities					
Current liabilities					
Accounts payable	$ 350,000	$ 350,000	$ 350,000	$ 350,000	$ 350,000
Interest payable	10,000	—	30,000	—	90,000
Tax liability (13-24)	880,000	508,600	361,200	687,000	870,000
Total current liabilities	$ 1,240,000	$ 858,600	$ 741,200	$ 1,037,000	$ 1,310,000
Equipment debt	750,000	750,000	1,650,000	2,250,000	2,250,000
Total liabilities	$ 1,990,000	$ 1,608,600	$ 2,391,200	$ 3,287,000	$ 3,560,000
Capital Section					
Capital stock	$14,000,000	$14,000,000	$14,000,000	$14,000,000	$14,000,000
Retained earnings, beginning	1,325,000	1,325,000	1,427,900	1,419,800	1,980,500
Quarterly earnings (13-24)	—	102,900	438,900	488,700	274,500
Dividends (13-21)	—	—	(375,000)	—	(375,000)
Ending balance	$ 1,325,000	$ 1,427,900	$ 1,491,800	$ 1,980,500	$ 1,880,000
Total capital (ending balance plus capital stock)	15,325,000	15,427,900	15,491,800	15,980,500	15,880,000
Total liabilities	1,990,000	1,608,600	2,391,200	3,287,000	3,560,000
Total equities	$17,315,000	$17,036,500	$17,883,000	$19,267,500	$19,440,000

[a]

	Mar. 31	June 30	Sept. 30	Dec. 31
Opening balance	$15,000,000	$14,830,000	$15,600,000	$16,020,000
Acquisitions	280,000	1,020,000	670,000	120,000
Depreciation	(235,000)	(235,000)	(235,000)	(235,000)
	(15,000)	(15,000)	(15,000)	(15,000)
Dispositions	(200,000)			(100,000)
	$14,830,000	$15,600,000	$16,020,000	$15,790,000

is satisfied with the results of these preliminary estimates, the summary statements may be used as the initial benchmarks against which actual performances may be compared. If management is not satisfied, it has a basis for assessing the effects of changes in the various operating policies under its control.

Revision of Master Budgets

The usefulness of formal plans is now well established and has made such plans part of standard business practices. Variations in format or in data-collecting processes, or even the presence or absence of computers, does not detract from the central claim that successful firms allocate a significant amount of their resources to planning. But because of the costliness of a master budget and the amount of time elapsing between its completion and the period covered, changes do occur in the environment. Most of these are trivial and do not affect the firm's predetermined course of action. They may, however, alter the appropriateness of some of the data contained in the budget. When such changes occur, management is faced with two questions:

(1) Should the individual budgets be changed?
(2) Should the master budget be changed?

In practice the answer is usually yes in the first instance and very mixed in the second.

Individual department heads should be notified so that they can alter their activities as required. If a significant change in expected sales (up or down) occurs, the heads of purchasing and production must know this to avoid under- or overstocking. Failure to notify them would cause a breakdown of coordination.

The revision of the master budget is a more controversial topic. The work involved in initially formulating the budget is representative of what must occur if it is to be revised. The argument in favor of the revision is that it makes a better basis for control. By revising the budgets, all members of the firm are informed of the standard to which they will be held. Anything less than this raises a question of whether the subordinate will realize that the superior has changed the rules of the game.

Firms that do not make revisions base their position on two arguments. First, unless heavily automated the process is expensive and the benefits come not from a total revision but from ensuring that the right people receive the new information. Second, the evaluation process can consider these facts retrospectively once the change does occur. This approach is more or less a middle ground. While it argues for revision when changes do occur, it focuses on actual effects rather than projected changes. Supporters feel that this avoids making small changes in the plan that are of little consequence and keeps management from trying to outguess random fluctuations in their forecast.

Planning Budgets

At this point in our discussion, it will be worthwhile to examine planning budgets. At the outset, we indicated that planning budgets are used for periods different from those used for the comprehensive budget. For example, for its long-range or strategic planning,[7] management may wish to know expected sales figures for some period beyond that covered by the comprehensive budget, say for five years as opposed to one year. A sales forecast by product for the next five years will not be as detailed as the one-year forecast because of the estimation problems involved. However, it will show the expected level of sales in sufficient detail for management's purposes.

Perhaps the single most important planning budget requested by management for the day-to-day operation of the firm is a statement of projected cash receipts and disbursements, often called a cash budget. This statement is significant because most firms try to manage their cash position so as to minimize unnecessary borrowing and large unproductive balances. In the previous section, the components of a cash budget were contained in the summary Exhibit 13-23 and the related detailed Exhibits 13-20 and 13-21. However, these materials were embedded in the context of a larger problem. The illustration that follows focuses more clearly on the cash management problem.

Cash Budget Illustration[8]

The Standard Mercantile Corporation wishes to prepare a cash forecast by months for January, February, and March, 1982, to calculate the expected amount of cash on hand at the end of each month. Management is particularly concerned about its ability to repay a bank loan due on March 31, 1982. However, this is only one reason for calculating the ending cash balances. Should the summary of cash receipts and disbursements project an excess cash balance at any time, management will plan to invest it in short-term securities. Conversely, if a cash deficit should appear likely at any time, plans must be made to secure temporary financing. The facts of the problem are as follows.

The Standard Mercantile Corporation is a wholesaler and ends its fiscal

---

[7] G. Steiner, *Top Management Planning.* New York: Macmillan, 1969, or P. Lorange and R. Vancil, *Strategic Planning Systems.* Englewood Cliffs, N.J.: Prentice-Hall, 1977.

[8] Adapted from a C.P.A. Examination.

year on December 31. As the company's C.P.A., you have been requested in early January, 1982, to assist in the preparation of a cash forecast. The following information is available concerning the company's operations:

(1) Management believes that the 1981 sales pattern is a reasonable estimate of 1982 sales. Sales in 1981 were as follows:

January	$ 360,000
February	420,000
March	600,000
April	540,000
May	480,000
June	400,000
July	350,000
August	550,000
September	500,000
October	400,000
November	600,000
December	800,000
Total	$6,000,000

(2) The accounts receivable on December 31 total $380,000. Sales collections are generally made as follows:

During month of sale	60%
In first subsequent month	30%
In second subsequent month	9%
Uncollectible	1%

(3) The purchase cost of goods averages 60 percent of selling price. The cost of the inventory on hand on December 31 is $840,000, of which $30,000 is obsolete. Arrangements have been made to sell the obsolete inventory in January for $25,000 on a C.O.D. basis.

    The company wishes to maintain the end-of-month inventory at a level of three-months' sales as determined by the sales forecast for the next three months. All purchases are paid for on the tenth of the following month. Accounts payable for purchases on December 31 total $370,000.

(4) Recurring fixed expenses amount to $120,000 per month, including depreciation of $20,000. For accounting purposes, the company apportions the recurring fixed expenses to the various months in the same proportion as that month's estimated sales bears to the estimated total annual sales. Variable expenses amount to 10 percent of sales. Payments for expenses are made as follows:

	During Month Incurred	Following Month
Fixed expenses	100%	0
Variable expenses	70%	30%

(5) Annual property taxes amount to $50,000 and are paid in equal installments on December 31 and March 31. Property taxes are in addition to the expenses in item (4).

(6) It is anticipated that cash dividends of $20,000 will be paid each quarter on the fifteenth day of the third month of the quarter.

(7) During the winter, unusual advertising costs will be incurred, which will require cash payments of $10,000 in February and $15,000 in March. These advertising costs are in addition to the expenses in item (4).

(8) Equipment replacements are made at the rate of $3,000 per month.

(9) The company must pay $60,000 in March, 1982, to cover a portion of its obligation on its 1981 federal income tax.

(10) On December 31, 1981, the company had a bank loan with an unpaid balance of $280,000. The loan requires a principal payment of $20,000 on the last day of each month plus interest at 1½ percent per month on the unpaid balance on the first of the month. The entire balance is due on March 31, 1982.

(11) The cash balance on December 31, 1981, is $100,000.

Solution

While the problem could be attacked by beginning either with the cash receipts (essentially payments received on accounts receivable) or the cash disbursements (payments made for purchases of inventory and other goods and services), the cash receipts is the easier of the two in this problem. According to the data, January sales will amount to $360,000, February sales will amount to $420,000, and March sales will be $600,000. In addition, the accounts receivable balance on December 31, 1981, was $380,000 [item (2)]. The $380,000 consists of balances still due Standard Mercantile from November, 1981, sales totaling $60,000 (10 percent of $600,000), and December, 1981, sales still unpaid of $320,000 (40 percent of $800,000). These balances and the 1982 sales will be paid in a 60 percent, 30 percent, and 9 percent fashion, with 1 percent constituting bad debts [see item (2)]. The cash inflows from sales are summarized in Exhibit 13-26. Note, for example, that the January receipts on accounts receivable consisted of 60 percent of that month's sales ($360,000), 30 percent of the previous month's sales (December, $800,000), and 9 percent of the sales of the period two months previous (November, $600,000). Similar calculations resulted in the cash inflows from receivables shown for February and March. (You may wish to verify the calculations.) These receipts are included in the cash budget (Exhibit 13-28).

_____ EXHIBIT 13-26

Standard Mercantile Corporation
Schedule of Payments on Accounts Receivable
January–March, 1982

CASH RECEIVED IN

From Sales In	January	February	March
November	$ 54,000	—	—
December	240,000	$ 72,000	—
January	216,000	108,000	$ 32,400
February	—	252,000	126,000
March	—	—	360,000
	$510,000	$432,000	$518,400

The only other cash receipt item listed in the problem data is the sale of obsolete merchandise for $25,000 cash in January [item (3)]. This will be taken directly into the cash budget.

There are various items of cash disbursements. Several require no additional calculations and need only be included in the final cash budget. However, the payment of Standard Mercantile's accounts payable for merchandise requires that we first calculate the amount of the periodic purchases before arriving at the amount and timing of the payments on accounts payable. Item (3) stated that Standard Mercantile plans to maintain its end-of-month inventory at the level required to meet sales for the next three months. Thus, it must have available in January merchandise to cover January sales of $216,000 (60 percent of $360,000), plus $936,000 for sales in February, March, and April (60 percent of $1,560,000), less the beginning inventory of merchandise, $810,000. This requires purchases of $342,000. Similarly, at the end of February, management wishes to have on hand enough goods to meet the March, April, and May sales. Exhibit 13-27 shows these calculations. (Because the March purchases will not be paid until April, they were not calculated in this exhibit.)

The final statement employed by Standard Mercantile to assess its cash position from January through March is the cash budget, Exhibit 13-28. All of the cash receipt items were calculated in Exhibit 13-26, except for the proceeds from the sale of obsolete inventory.

The cash disbursements reflect a variety of transactions. The payments for inventory purchases are made in the month following the purchase. Thus, the January disbursement was to pay the accounts payable balance on December 31, 1981 [see item (3)], the February payment is for January's purchases, and the March payment is for February's purchases.

The operating expenses are of two types, fixed and variable. The fixed

EXHIBIT 13-27

Standard Mercantile Corporation
Purchases Schedule
January and February, 1982

	January	February
Sales forecast at retail (next three months)	$1,560,000	$1,620,000
Sales at cost (60% of retail)[a]	936,000	972,000
Plus: Cost of monthly sales[b]	216,000	252,000
Total requirement	$1,152,000	$1,224,000
Less: Beginning inventory	810,000[c]	936,000
Purchase requirements	$ 342,000	$ 288,000

[a] This is the desired ending inventory.
[b] 60 percent of the month's sales at retail.
[c] After allowing for the $30,000 of goods being sold as obsolete during January ($840,000 − $30,000 = $810,000).

expenses of $120,000 include $20,000 of depreciation expense, a noncash item [see item (4)]. Thus, the periodic cash outflow is only $100,000 per month. These expenses are paid in the month incurred. The variable operating expenses are given as 10 percent of sales. Since they are paid on a 70–30 percent basis, the cash outflow of any given month reflects partially that month's variable operating costs and partially those of the previous month. The calculation of the variable overhead cost payments is shown in the first footnote to the cash budget.

The other cash disbursements reflect the data given in the problem. The numbers in parentheses following items in the first column relate the outflow to the problem data.

In this case, the firm will not be able to pay off the note as required. In fact, the $289,300 cash deficit at the end of March suggests that Standard Mercantile's management should not only extend the loan but should also find a source of additional financing during February or March.

How management will meet these problems is not clear from the information supplied. However, a variety of possibilities exist besides an additional bank loan. For example, the company could maintain a smaller inventory. This would result in a cash saving, but it might also lead to lost sales because of stockouts. Similarly, management could attempt to delay payments of its liabilities, thereby again securing a temporary saving in cash outflow in the short run. However, this also could be detrimental in the long run. Finally, as part of the renegotiation of the loan, Standard Mercantile could arrange

EXHIBIT 13-28

Standard Mercantile Corporation
Cash Budget
January through March, 1982

	January	February	March
Opening cash balance (11)	$100,000	$ 88,600	$ 1,500
Cash receipts			
Regular sales	510,000	432,000	518,400
Sale of obsolete inventory (3)	25,000		
	$635,000	$520,600	$519,900
Cash disbursements			
Inventory purchases	$370,000	$342,000	$288,000
Fixed expenses	100,000	100,000	100,000
Variable expenses[a]	49,200	40,200	54,600
Property taxes (5)			25,000
Dividends (6)			20,000
Special advertising costs (7)		10,000	15,000
Equipment purchases (8)	3,000	3,000	3,000
Income tax (9)			60,000
Bank loan (10)			
Principal	20,000	20,000	240,000
Interest[b]	4,200	3,900	3,600
Total	$546,400	$519,100	$809,200
Ending cash balance (deficiency)	$ 88,600	$ 1,500	($289,300)

[a]

	January	February	March
1. Variable expenses	$ 36,000	$ 42,000	$ 60,000
2. Expense payments			
Paid in	January	February	March
Expense of			
December	$ 24,000		
January	25,200	$ 10,800	
February		29,400	$ 12,600
March			42,000
	$ 49,200	$ 40,200	$ 54,600

[b]

	January	February	March
Bank loan interest			
Balance	$280,000	$260,000	$240,000
Interest at 1½%	$ 4,200	$ 3,900	$ 3,600

to make no payments on principal in January and February. Whatever course the firm adopts, a new or modified version of Exhibit 13-28 will be needed. If several plans are considered, then many new cash budgets must be calculated. Some may extend beyond March if management is concerned about its ability to repay the loan at any time during 1982.

Other Approaches to Planning Budgets

The examples used in this chapter require a significant outlay of resources for any firm. Unfortunately, each is based on a particular set of assumptions and estimates. When those assumptions must be changed or when estimates prove inaccurate, the plans are suspect. However, a firm may find itself with precious little time to revise and update the current period's budget. The personnel required to do this are either concerned with day-to-day operations or already planning for next year. In either case, they are unavailable for use in revising this year's data.

A possible solution to this problem is found in the form of the assumptions made by planners. In the Standard Mercantile illustration, many of the periodic cash inflows and outflows can be reduced to formulas. For example, using the data given to describe collection of accounts receivable [item (2)], the cash receipts in month t are:

$$CR_t = .6S_t + .3S_{t-1} + .09S_{t-2}$$

where
$$CR_t = \text{cash receipts in month } t$$
$$S_t = \text{sales in month } t$$

Similar relations can be developed for other elements of the cash budget.

Once the set of equations is developed, Standard Mercantile can consider alternative estimates of the critical variables in the environment. What if the projected sales for January had been $400,000? Or if collection rates drop off, making Standard Mercantile wait longer for the cash from each month's sales? Questions like these and numerous others can be answered much more easily if Standard Mercantile has a model of its cash flow process.

Larger Models

The logical next step in the process is to take the model and put it on a computer. This eases the burden in calculating the effects of changes. Smaller models can even be programmed into pocket calculators; larger problems can be solved on mini computers. When the resulting statements are shown on visual displays, managers can "see" the effects of different policies and assumptions.

The use of computers allows additional tasks to be delegated to the budget model. To accomplish this, two approaches have recently been suggested. One uses mathematical programing models to plan and develop an optimal budget for the firm's operations. The other relies on simulation and is intended primarily to allow management to assess the effects of alternative strategies on current plans.[9]

---

[9] For a discussion of each, see A. Schreiber, ed., *Corporate Simulation Models.* Seattle: Graduate School of Business. University of Washington, 1970, and P. Grinyer and J. Wooler, *Corporate Models Today,* 2nd ed. London: Institute of Chartered Accountants in England and Wales, 1978.

Mathematical Programing Models.   Mathematical programing models seemingly provide the mechanism by which the budgetary process could be joined with the procedures used to select the optimal policies of the firm for a given operating period. Although the models discussed in the literature are not elaborate, they are sufficient to illustrate how mathematical programing can be used in financial planning.[10]

For example, the model of Ijiri *et al.* uses 19 equations and/or inequalities that must be satisfied in order for the financial accounts to reflect management's objectives. Some of the constraints represent physical limits on the transactions that can take place (for example, on the number of units that can be produced and the number of units that may be sold); others reflect management's objectives regarding the ending balances of some of the accounts (cash must be greater than or equal to x dollars); still others define the functional relationships necessary to budget items such as depreciation expense. As we would surmise, these equations reflect the same assumptions underlying the preparation of budgets in the exhibits throughout this chapter. A programing approach to budgeting will yield an optimal set of transactions, given management's objectives. These transactions are the basis for a projected income statement and balance sheet. Moreover, every programing solution also yields information on the effects of varying the constraints observed in the original solution. Such information may be used to evaluate the costs of imposing various restrictions on the transactions of the firm.

Simulation Models.   The use of computer-based simulation models to assist in the budget process is an extension of the power of the budgeting technique. The master budget provides the structure within which management can plan a coordinated set of activities. The computer provides the capacity to view a variety of alternatives and to include a large number of time periods. The use of computer models for this purpose is relatively recent, but the number of models actually in use is growing rapidly. Many believe that it is only a matter of time before what could be called the computer-augmented master budget process will be relatively common. However, the cost of such models may limit the number of firms that decide to implement them.

Recent developments in visual display techniques have given computer models an added boost. Not only can the computer develop, revise, and/or update a firm's plans quickly, it can display outputs in a manner easily assimilated by executives. It can plot trends and compare various alternative trends.

---

[10] See A. Charnes, W. Cooper, and Y. Ijiri, "Breakeven Budgeting and Programming to Goals," *J. of Accounting Research,* Spring 1963; Y. Ijiri, F. Levy, and R. Lyon, "A Linear Programming Model for Budgeting and Financial Planning," *J. of Accounting Research,* Autumn 1963; V. Jaaskelain, "A Goal Programming Model for Financial Planning," *Finnish J. of Economics,* 1971; and J. Callahan, "An Introduction to Financial Planning Through Goal Programming," *Cost and Management,* Jan.–Feb. 1973.

All this can be done in color on a single large screen or on personalized, smaller units. At present we have little insight into the impact of these "war rooms" on managerial decision making. It may be quite some time until we do. However, it is apparent that many firms are willing to spend large sums of money to make the output of their computers more accessible to managers. Planning would appear to be an aspect of managing that could benefit from these new managerial tools.

In the remaining sections of this chapter, simulation models are discussed in a very general manner. Students desiring a more detailed discussion should examine the references shown at the end of the chapter.

Characteristics of Budget Simulation Models.   Many considerations go into the final decision on the form of the budget simulation model. They are the same issues that are faced by anyone about to construct a simulation model. Although the choices made in some areas will restrict the options in others, these options are listed below as if each could be considered separately.

(1)   Whether to rent an already existing general purpose model from a consulting group or develop a specific model for the firm.

(2)   Whether to consider an integrated model of the firm as the initial goal or to construct a series of modules that can be run independently as they are completed.

(3)   Whether to aggregate by product lines, divisions, geographic considerations, or other factors.

(4)   Whether to include estimation routines for key variables or to input such variables from external sources.

(5)   Whether to follow probabilistic or deterministic analyses.

(6)   Whether to include interactive capabilities.

All of these considerations are important once management is committed to a simulation model. The initial decision of whether to acquire access to an existing model or to construct one's own is critical to many of the considerations that follow.[11] An examination of some general purpose programs indicates that unless the firm adapts the package, it will be acquiring a deterministic simulation that is concerned primarily with the traditional financial reports and ratios for the firm. However, such a general purpose program will offer some forecasting capabilities, will be interactive, and will permit the inclusion of data by profit centers if desired. Significantly, these models usually are financial models that require the user to produce most of the operating data in some other fashion. The model then integrates the cost data into the projected statements and the cash budget and calculates ratios for management.

----

[11] N. Statland and J. Worthington, "Software Packages: Are They for You?" *Todays Executive,* Winter 1979. The VisiCalc program for minicomputers provides an inexpensive package for the manager that can be run on a machine such as the Apple II.

In the J.D.D. Company example in this chapter, such a model would still require that all the operating budgets be produced outside the simulator.

General purpose models of this sort are useful to management in a manner analogous to break-even analysis. They can reduce a complex problem to a simple but still meaningful form for planning. By making some assumptions about cost behavior, cash flows, and revenues, management can use the program to project its income statement, balance sheet, and cash budget. By altering the assumptions, different conditions can be examined. The effectiveness of the technique depends upon the appropriateness of the simplified input data.

In contrast, a specialized model is vastly more detailed. By constructing its own model (or having others construct one), management can decide to produce as elegant a model as the cost would justify; it is not limited by the nature of an existing model. As usual, the choice depends upon the availability of the appropriate skills and management's assessment of the costs and benefits.

The decision of whether to produce an integrated model or a modular one is important for the firm designing its own system.

Firms do not usually begin with an integrated model. The reasons for this are obvious. It is cheaper and quicker to develop a module—say, for the marketing function or the production function—than it is to develop a firm-wide model. By pursuing a modular approach, the firm can focus on the most important facets of the operations first and have those modules on line earlier. Moreover, the designers can learn from each module, thereby lowering the total development cost. Since the time to develop and implement even a single module for an organization is substantial, the decision to employ a modular approach is probably sensible.

There is not the same degree of agreement on the level of aggregation as there is on the use of modules. Many firms adopt simulation models to aid the decisions of top management. This suggests that the aggregation should be at the level of divisions, products, and so forth. One rationalization for this concentration at the upper levels is that the organization's budget process at lower levels is already well developed and coordination is needed at the top. These firms perceive the budget simulation as a vehicle for reconciling and coordinating *inter*divisional effects rather than *intra*divisional effects.

In contrast, the users of a so-called "bottom-up approach" focus on the benefits of budget simulation to managers at lower levels. Simulation models at this level may possess greater validity in terms of the underlying relations, and they tend to be less complex than those for the firm as a whole. Moreover, the flexibility that simulation models provide may be more beneficial to lower level managers since they are the ones who must react to changes in the environment.

The choice between these two approaches is not an absolute one. It depends on which factors are most relevant in a given firm. Gershefski justified

Sun Oil's use of a "top-down approach" by suggesting that this was where the greatest need for improvement could be found.[12] Other firms have taken other courses of action.

Most models contain the capacity to estimate some parameter values as an integral part of the program. The extent to which the estimation techniques are present in a specialized model, and the extent to which they are used in a general model, depends upon the nature of the data available. Most simulations contain a marketing model and use regression analysis or exponential smoothing to forecast sales. Most financial reporting models use regression analysis for many categories of cost behavior. This is particularly true for the top-down models, where detailed operations data like those found in the master budget are not included. For example, the cost of goods sold is calculated as a function of sales. Other costs may be similarly analyzed using linear relations. However, managed or policy costs, such as advertising, are usually taken as a given, that is exogenous to the simulation.

Even when a program can estimate the parameter, the model usually permits management's estimates of sales and other variables to override the estimation technique. This capacity is an integral part of any human–machine interaction. Early planners recognized the need for a manager to interact with the model in order to secure its greatest benefits. By interacting with the simulator, the manager learns from it and is able to answer "what if" questions.

Finally, the models tend to be deterministic rather than probabilistic. Several reasons are possible. Paramount among these are cost, complexity, and user acceptance. The cost factor is obvious. The complexity is increased in a probabilistic model because the model builders must develop appropriate probability distributions for many variables. These distributions are often unknown, since the operating characteristics of firms are usually not stable over time. User acceptance is often a problem among lower level managers, who are reluctant to use probabilistic models. Since such acceptance is necessary, top managers may feel that it is more desirable to trade elegance and some potential insights for a higher rate of usage and interaction.

The Modules.   The number of modules to be included in the completed model depends in part on the manner in which the model builders break down the firm's operations. The typical breakdown is production, marketing, and finance. Other modules can be subsumed in these. Each module is as self-contained as possible, but a certain amount of interdependence must be recognized. This was illustrated in the static master budget example, where the sales data, an output of the marketing module, affected the production plan and the pro forma statements, parts of the production and financial modules.

---

[12] G. Gershefski, "Building a Corporate Financial Model," *Harvard Business Rev.,* July–Aug. 1969.

A typical marketing module is responsible for estimating sales in sufficient detail to permit the other modules to perform their tasks. Some marketing modules estimate price based upon historical and environmental data. Others require price to be entered from estimates from either the marketing department or the manager interacting with the simulation. Other data requirements depend upon the variables included in the functional relations contained in the model. Such data could include environmental conditions, changes in the number of outlets, prices of complements or substitutes, and the historical pattern of sales updated each time period to include the most recent results.

The production module is a model of the production process. In our static budget, it was the standard cost of the products. In the case of a firm with many products, the modeling is more complex. In addition to the technological relations it describes, a multiproduct production module requires that the marketing module (or marketing department, if no module exists) indicate the forecast sales volumes and timings of the sales. This permits the production module to determine if the desired goods can be ready as needed and provides the bases for the production budgets similar to those described earlier in the chapter—overhead budgets, purchase budgets, etc. The production module must also be updated to reflect any change in capacity due to capital expenditures or to planned sales or retirement of productive capacity. These data are usually part of the financial module.

Some production modules include a manpower dimension. Such a function is concerned with the staffing problem of skilled human resources. Just as a budget of the acquisition and retirement of equipment is necessary, it is important that personnel be available to operate the various machines. Thus, when such a question is important, management will request that it be included. Sometimes a separate manpower module is developed.

The financing module produces the pro forma statements based on data from sales and production modules as well as inputs from management (such as managed costs, financing, and capital inventments) and the data the module calculates internally (such as cost behavior and depreciation). A major output of this module is the cash budget and the pro forma income statement and balance sheet.

We have assumed that the capital budget is determined independently of this process and is included as an input to the financial module. Some model builders have separated the capital budget process and have included a capital budget module, which includes both the budget and the financing decision. While such a module may not usually be needed, a firm concerned with investigating various capital budgets and financing plans would find it useful. A separate module highlights the links between the capital budgeting decision and other decision units.

Cost Effectiveness of Simulations.   There is little question that simulation models offer their users clearcut benefits. The question is whether they are worth the cost of the time required to design, program, and properly implement them. Relatively simple models have required many "person-years" to develop. A complete system would clearly be an expenditure of major proportion, whereas the benefits derived from it, such as better management, are more difficult to quantify. Probably the most objectively measurable benefit is the cost savings of transferring the calculations to a computer. This is no small benefit when one recognizes the effort required for problems as simple as those contained in this chapter.

Another major benefit derived from the simulation model is the acceleration of control. The effects of projected trends can be ascertained and decisions reached quickly on a plan of action. When the manager is faced with a static budget formulated three to six months earlier, he may find himself without the capacity to evaluate alternatives. The simulation model gives him this added computational capacity. As usual, though, our cost–benefit philosophy is easier to talk about than implement.

FIGURE 13-1

Corporate model flow chart for a savings and loan.

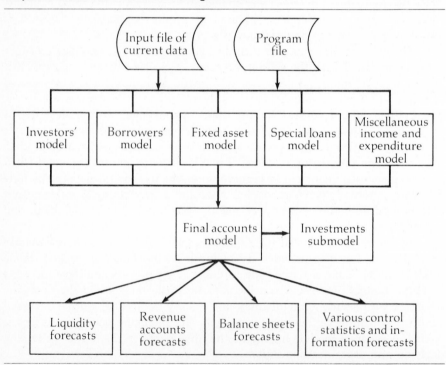

SOURCE: P. Grinyer and J. Wooller, *Corporate Models Today,* 2nd ed. London: Institute of Chartered Accountants in England and Wales, 1978, p. 115.

Some Examples of Corporate Models.   It would be cumbersome to repro-
duce a corporate model of any size in this text. However, benefits can be
derived from showing the structures of different models. Figure 13-1 shows
the flow chart of a savings and loan. It has been modifed slightly for presentation, but no substantive details have been omitted.

From the flow chart it is impossible to determine the detail present in
each of the submodels. However, the nature of a saving and loan's activities
suggests that the submodels should be less complex than those of a large,
multiproduct firm that produces and distributes consumer goods. The fixed

_____FIGURE 13-2

Corporate sales model.

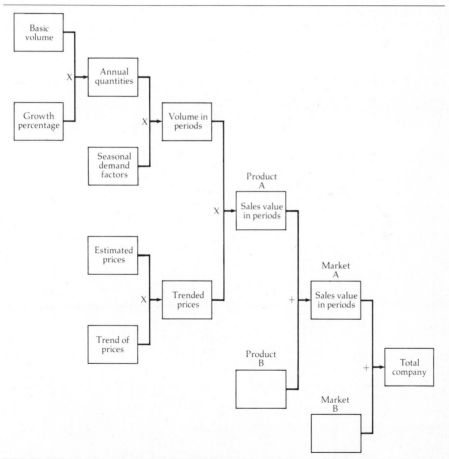

SOURCE: P. Grinyer and J. Wooller, *Corporate Models Today,* 2nd ed. London: Institute of Chartered
Accountants in England and Wales, 1978, p. 135.

FIGURE 13-3

Sales/production model.

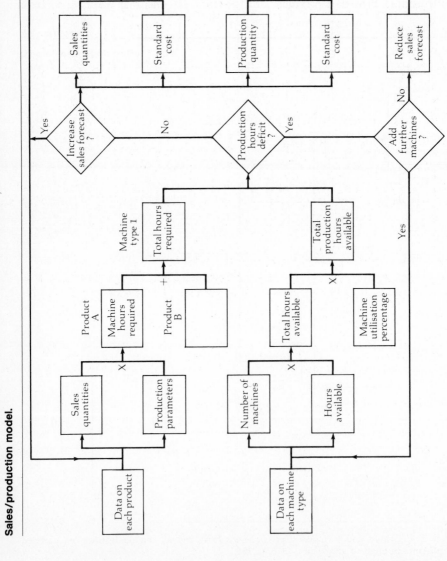

SOURCE: P. Grinyer and J. Wooller, *Corporate Models Today*, 2nd ed. London: Institute of Chartered Accountants in England and Wales, 1978, p. 136.

asset submodel is usually one of the simplest. It keeps the fixed asset records and calculates depreciation charges. As such, it is essentially a bookkeeping program. In contrast, the borrowers' submodel is usually one of the more complex. It calculates the cash flows, interest charges, various fees, and other factors related to the handling of the firm's clients. These data are utilized in developing the model's cash forecast and financial statements.

A more sophisticated borrowers' submodel would forecast the level of new loans based upon economic conditions, legal requirements, and other variables. In this model the level of new loans is taken as given externally. It is provided by management as part of the inputs to the program.

Figure 13-2 shows the details of the sales submodel used by a large plastics manufacturer. It permits management to vary several factors:

(1) The basic volume and price.
(2) Projected growth in volume and price.
(3) The nature of the seasonality.
(4) The firm's relative strength by product and by market.

The empty boxes labled "Product B" and "Market B" indicate the ability of the program to repeat the process for other products and other markets. When the submodel has completed the process, management can examine sales forecasts on a variety of dimensions—time, product, market, and so on. Importantly, management can generate the outcomes resulting from various sets of assumptions.

The submodel shown in Figure 13-2 is part of a larger model possessing the capacity to test sales estimates for their impact on the firm's productive capacity. Figure 13-3 shows how the model deals with this problem.

Summary

In this chapter, we have discussed and illustrated the budget process. Since the budget is both a tool that permits management to investigate the effects of alternatives and the plan against which performance is compared, it is part of the control process. It serves to communicate, coordinate, and anticipate the activities of the organization.

By its very nature, the master budget process is participative. As such, it requires substantial resource outlays by the firm. These outlays are justified if the budget leads to more efficient management. Even the computerized budget process requires the time of managers. However, in contrast to the noncomputerized static budget, the time is utilized in preparing better estimates and evaluating a greater array of alternatives. Ideally, the trade-off is not entirely computer time for human time, but also mechanical, structured tasks for ill-structured planning activities.

This chapter has presented a typical master budget, which reflects most of the features of the budget process. Names of the individual budgets, the sequence in which they are organized, and other details will vary from organization to organization, but the general process remains the same.

In many decision areas, management finds it useful to employ a planning budget for a single activity, usually covering a longer time period than is possible for a master budget. This was illustrated with a cash budget.

Finally, we discussed the characteristics and cost effectiveness of computerized simulation models.

Supplementary Readings

Articles

Callahan, J., "An Introduction to Financial Planning Through Goal Programming" *Cost and Management,* Jan.–Feb. 1973.

Greshefski, G., "Building a Corporate Financial Model," *Harvard Business Rev.,* July–Aug. 1969.

Gorman, T., "Corporate Financial Models for Planning and Control," *Price-Waterhouse Review,* Summer 1970.

Lowe, E. and R. Shaw, "An Example of Managerial Bias: Evidence from a Company's Budgeting Process," *J. of Management Studies,* 1968.

Schiff, M. and A. Lewin, "The Impact of People on Budgets," *Accounting Rev.,* April 1970.

Statland, N. and J. Worthington, "Software Packages: Are They for You?" *Todays Executive,* Winter 1979.

Surver, J. and F. Helmer, "Developing Budgetary Models for Greater Hospital Efficiency," *Management Accounting,* July 1979.

Books

Ijiri, Y., *Management Goals and Accounting for Control,* Chicago: Rand McNally, 1965.

Greshefski, G., *The Development and Application of a Corporate Financial Model.* Oxford, Ohio: Planning Executives Institute, 1968.

Grinyer, P. and J. Wooler, *Corporate Models Today: A Tool for Financial Management,* 2nd ed. London: Institute of Chartered Accountants in England and Wales, 1978.

Lorange, P. and R. Vancil, *Strategic Planning Systems.* Englewood Cliffs, NJ: Prentice-Hall, 1977.

Steiner, G., *Top Management Planning.* New York: MacMillan, 1969.

Welsch, G.A., *Budgeting: Profit Planning and Control.* Englewood Cliffs, NJ: Prentice-Hall, 1971.

Questions and Problems

1. Corporal Products has been told by its accounting firm, N.A. Associates, that its new N.A. Special Simulator program can be rented for a reasonable sum. This simulator does much of the work of preparing cash flow analyses and projected financial statements. To use the simulator, Corporal Products must be able to set its level of sales and sales prices and describe as a linear cost function its cost of goods sold and other operating costs. If Corporal Products rents the simulator, how would management use it? In what kind of planning situations would it help management?

2. In this chapter, the model has been one of relatively short-term plans (one year or less). How does this kind of planning compare to the longer term (sometimes called strategic) planning? What kind of decisions does management make when it does strategic planning? Finally, to what extent would you expect strategic planning to be participative?

3. A study of the budgeting process suggests that operating personnel react negatively to the budgetary process because the budget requires too many assumptions about the future. They feel it is of little use in controlling their operations and that the estimates are out of date before the budget is even implemented. Comment on the nature of the assumptions that underlie the budgetary process and discuss whether these assumptions justify the position indicated above.

4. Preparation of the master budget usually starts with estimated sales during the budgeted period. One method of obtaining estimates of sales is the so-called "grass-roots" method, which relies heavily on the estimates prepared by the salespeople in the field. Discuss the problem of bias in this method and indicate why it might arise.

5. **Modeling Cash Flow Relationships**

   Over the past several years, the Programme Corporation has encountered difficulties in estimating its cash flows. The result has been a rather strained relationship with its banker. Programme's controller would like to develop means by which he can forecast the firm's monthly operating cash flows. The following data were gathered to facilitate the development of such a forecast:

   (1) Sales have been and are expected to increase at .5 percent each month.

   (2) Thirty percent of each month's sales are for cash; the other 70 percent are on open account.

   (3) Of the credit sales, 80 percent are collected in the first month following the sale and the remaining 20 percent are collected in the second month. There are no bad debts.

   (4) Gross margin on sales averages 25 percent.

   (5) Programme purchases enough inventory each month to cover the following month's sales.

   (6) All inventory purchases are paid for in the month of purchase at a 2 percent cash discount.

   (7) Monthly expenses are: payroll, $15,000; rent, $400; depreciation, $120; and other cash expenses, 1 percent of that month's sales. There are no accruals.

(8) Ignore the effects of corporate income taxes, dividends, and equipment acquisitions.

Using this data, develop a mathematical model the controller can use for his calculations. Your model should be capable of calculating the monthly operating cash inflows and outflows for any specified month.

[ICMA adapted]

6. *Cash Budget*

The president of the J.N. Company has asked you to prepare a cash forecast for October, 1982. The company leases equipment to small business firms.

(1) You examine the contracts outstanding and determine that:
  (a) Rentals due in the current month are $100,000 (95 percent collection rate).
  (b) Rentals overdue one to three months are $35,000. Experience has shown that 80 percent of these overdue payments can be expected to be paid in October.
  (c) Accounts overdue four months or more come to $15,000. These accounts will yield approximately $8,000 in October; however, the extra expenses of collecting will reduce this figure to a net of $6,500.
(2) Most of the company's operating expenses consist of salaries paid to maintenance and service personnel. The J.N. Company schedules its service personnel very efficiently, with the result that service costs do not fluctuate much from month to month. Total service costs can be estimated by the equation $TSC = \$65,000 + \$0.20\Delta R$, where ΔR is the change in monthly rentals. Monthly rentals have increased by $15,000 for October.
(3) Other operating costs are fixed and consist of:

Supplies	$ 5,000
Rent	2,500
Administrative and sales salaries	22,000
Advertising	3,000
Commission on new rentals	5,500
	$38,000

(4) The company has a revolving loan balance with a limit of $25,000. The loan balance as of October 1 is $18,750. Interest per month is 1.5 percent of the beginning balance.
(5) New equipment purchases during October total $15,000, half of which will be financed by the seller.

Prepare a statement of cash receipts and disbursements for October, 1982.

7. *Cash Budget*

During the next quarter, the Zinger Company expects a total sales of 100,000 units at $10 per unit, distributed within the quarter as follows:

	January	February	March	Total
Credit	$200,000	$220,000	$230,000	$650,000
Cash	$100,000	$120,000	$130,000	$350,000

Each month, the company produces a sufficient number of units to meet the next month's sales (expected sales in April: credit, $210,000; cash, $115,000). Month-end raw materials inventory is maintained at 4,000 units. Purchases are made to meet the current month's production requirements. A safety stock of 6,000 finished units, in addition to the next month's sales requirements, is held in inventory.

Expected cost of goods sold

Raw materials	$1.25/unit
Direct labor	2.50/unit
Other variable costs—requiring	
cash payments	1.75/unit
Fixed costs (depreciation)	1.25/unit
	$6.75/unit

Other expenses

Variable selling and administrative expenses	$1.50/unit
Fixed selling and administrative expenses	$18,000/month[a]

[a] Assume that this amount is for salaries payable on the 15th of each month.

Payments to suppliers of all services are made in such a manner that the expected accounts payable balance at March 31 will be the same as at January 1 (ignore discounts).

Zinger collects 75 percent of the credit sales of a particular month within the month in which the sale was made. The other 25 percent is collected in the following month (ignore sales adjustments).

The company wishes to maintain a cash balance of $75,000, with deficiencies eliminated by borrowing the necessary amount on a short-term basis (at 10 percent interest). Borrowings are assumed to be made (on the basis of the budget) at the beginning of the month, with repayments on the 15th of the following month.

The balance sheet as of January 1 includes the following balances:

Cash	$ 75,000	Accounts payable	$55,000
Accounts receivable	42,000	Mortgage payable	
Raw materials	5,000	due in January	25,000
Finished goods	243,000	due in February	15,000
Work-in-process	—		
Fixed assets (net)	450,000		

Complete the following:

Total units to be produced in January _____
February _____
March _____
Total cash receipts in February _____
Total cash disbursements in February _____
Amount of credit sales in December _____
Amount of cash to be borrowed in January _____
February _____
March _____

8. **Budgets for Operating a Nonprofit Service Organization**
   DeMars College has asked your assistance in developing its budget for the 1982–83 academic year. You are supplied with the following data for the current year:

(1)

	Lower Division (Freshman–Sophomore)	Upper Division (Junior–Senior)
Average number of students per class	25	20
Average salary of faculty members	$25,000	$25,000
Average number of credit hours carried each year per student	33	30
Enrollment, including scholarship students	2,500	1,700
Average faculty teaching load in credit hours per year (10 classes of 3 credit hours)	30	30

For 1982–83, lower division enrollment is expected to increase by 10 percent, while the upper division's enrollment is expected to remain stable. Faculty salaries will be increased by a standard 5 percent, and additional merit increases to be awarded to individual faculty members will be $90,750 for the lower division and $85,000 for the upper division.

(2) The current budget is $210,000 for operation and maintenance of plant and equipment; this includes $90,000 for salaries and wages. Experience of the past three months suggests that the current budget is realistic, but that expected increases for 1982–83 are 5 percent in salaries and wages and $9,000 in other expenditures for operation and maintenance of plant and equipment.

(3) The college expects to award 25 tuition-free scholarships to lower division students and 15 to upper division students. Tuition is $50 per credit hour, and no other fees are charged.

Required (a) Prepare a schedule computing for 1982–83 by division: (1) the expected enrollment, (2) the total credit hours to be carried, and (3) the number of faculty members needed.

(b) Prepare a schedule computing the budget for faculty salaries, by division, for 1982–83.

(c) Prepare a schedule computing the tuition revenue budget, by division, for 1982–83.

[AICPA adapted]

9. *Purchase and Production Budgets*
  (1) The sales budget for the first five months of 1982 for a particular product line manufactured by F. Adams, Inc., is as follows:

January	8,000
February	7,500
March	7,000
April	6,750
May	7,200

Inventory of finished products at the end of each month is to be equal to the sales estimate for the next month. On January 1 there were 8,000 units on hand.

Each unit of product requires 3 pounds of Material X and 2 pounds of Material Y. Raw materials equal to one-half of the next month's requirements are to be on hand at the end of each month. This requirement was met on December 31, 1981.

Prepare a materials purchases budget for the first quarter of 1982. Summarize your answers as follows:

PRODUCTION REQUIREMENTS

	January	February	March
X	_____	_____	_____
Y	_____	_____	_____

  (2) The following amounts of X and Y are to be acquired from December, 1981, to March, 1982:

	December	January	February	March
X	22,500	22,000	21,000	21,500
Y	14,000	15,000	14,000	14,250

Each unit of X costs $5 (2 percent per 10 days; net 30 days) and each unit of Y costs $3 (2 percent per 10 days; net 30 days).

Orders for materials are placed on the 8th and 18th of each month. Each order is for one-half the current month's requirements. Lead time is five days. The company sends out its payments for materials nine days after receipt in order to take advantage of discounts.

Other operating expenses are approximately $8 per unit of product finished during the month plus fixed expenditures of $10,000 per month. They are paid in the month in which they are incurred.

Prepare a cash payment forecast for the quarter. Summarize your answers as follows:

CASH PAYMENTS

	January	February	March
Materials purchases	___	___	___
Expenses	___	___	___
Total	___	___	___

11. *Production—Purchase Budget*

The Windy Company produces two main products, L and N, which require the following types of subassemblies:

	Product L	Product N
A-3ZO	2 per unit	3 per unit
S-3ZL	5 per unit	—
S-3ZN	—	4 per unit

Subassemblies S-3ZL and S-3ZN are manufactured by Windy Company, while A-3ZO is purchased from local suppliers. Expected sales in units for the next five quarters for each product are as follows:

Product L

Quarter	1	2	3	4	5
Units	10,200	15,000	15,000	15,400	15,500

Product N

Quarter	1	2	3	4	5
Units	18,200	19,800	21,100	22,100	22,000

The O.R. Division has determined that production (and inventories) of the subproducts should be stabilized at the average of expected sales. Inventories carried over from last year are L, 3,000; N, 6,000; S-3ZL, 12,000; S-3ZN, 20,000; A-3ZO, 4,000

The cost of placing an order for A-3ZO is $30; the storage costs for this item are 1 percent per month; and the expected cost of each unit is $5. Inventories of L and N are to be about 30 percent of the next period's sales. Inventories of S-3ZL and S-3ZN should be about 25 percent of the next period's demand. Determine the production budget for the first three quarters (a) for L and N and (b) for S-3ZL and S-3ZN.

11. *Cash Flows*

The O'Hara News, a daily newspaper, services a community of 100,000. The paper has a circulation of 40,000, with 32,000 copies delivered to subscribers. The rate schedule for the paper is:

	Daily	Sunday
Single issue price	$0.15	$0.30
Weekly subscription	$1.00	
(includes daily and Sunday)		

The paper has experienced profitable operations, as can be seen from the income statement for the year ended December 30, 1981 (000s omitted):

Revenue		
Newspaper sales	$2,200	
Advertising sales	1,800	$4,000
Costs and expenses		
Personnel costs		
Commissions		
Carriers	$ 292	
Sales	73	
Advertising	48	
Salaries		
Administration	250	
Advertising	100	
Equipment operators	500	
Newsroom	400	
Employee benefits	195	$1,858
Newsprint		$ 834
Other supplies		417
Repairs		25
Depreciation		180
Property taxes		120
Building rental		80
Automobile leases		10
Other		90
Total costs and expenses		$3,614
Income before income taxes		$ 386
Income taxes		154
Net income		$ 232

The Sunday edition usually has twice as many pages as the daily editions. Analysis of direct edition variable costs for 1981 is shown in the schedule below:

	COST PER ISSUE	
	Daily	**Sunday**
Paper	$0.050	$0.100
Other supplies	0.025	0.050
Carrier and sales commissions	0.025	0.025
	$0.100	$0.175

Several changes in operations are scheduled for the next year, in addition to the need to recognize increasing costs:

(1) The building lease expired on December 30, 1981, and has been renewed with a change in the rental fee provisions from a straight fee to a fixed fee of $60,000 plus 1 percent of newspaper sales.

(2) The advertising department will eliminate the payment of a 4 percent advertising commission on contracts sold by its employees. An average of two-thirds of the advertising has been sold on a contract basis in the past. The salaries of the four who solicited advertising will be raised from $7,500 each to $14,000 each.

(3) Automobiles will no longer be leased. Employees whose jobs require automobiles will use their own and be reimbursed at $0.15 per mile. The leased cars were driven 80,000 miles in 1981, and it is estimated that the employees will drive some 84,000 miles next year on company business.

(4) Cost increases estimated for next year are:

Newsprint $0.01 per daily issue and $0.02 for the Sunday paper.

Salaries of equipment operators 8 percent.

Salaries of other employees 6 percent.

Employee benefits (from 15 percent of personnel costs, excluding carrier and sales commissions to 20 percent).

(5) Circulation increases of 5 percent in newstand and home delivery are anticipated.

(6) Advertising revenue is estimated at $1,890,000, with $1,260,000 from employee-solicited contracts.

Prepare a projected income statement for the O'Hara News for the 1982 fiscal year using a format that shows the total variable costs and total fixed costs for the newspaper (round calculations to the nearest thousand dollars).

[ICMA adapted]

12. **Projected Income Statement**

The management of O'Hara News is contemplating one additional proposal for the 1982 fiscal year: raising the rates for its newspaper to the following amounts:

	Daily	Sunday
Single issue price	$0.20	$0.40
Weekly subscription (includes daily and Sunday)	$1.25	

It is estimated that the newspaper's circulation would decline to 90 percent of the currently anticipated 1982 level for both newsstand and home delivery sales if this change is initiated. Using the data in the previous problem, calculate the effect on the projected 1982 income if this proposed rate change is implemented.

[ICMA adapted]

13. **Production and Sales Budgets for a Service-Oriented Agency**

The administrator of Wright Hospital has presented you with a number of service projections for the year ending June 30, 1983. Estimated room requirements for inpatients by type of service are:

Type of Patient	Total Patients Expected	AVERAGE NUMBER OF DAYS IN HOSPITAL		NUMBER OF PATIENTS SELECTING TYPES OF SERVICE			
					Semi-private		
		Regular	Medicare	Private	Private	Medicare	Ward
Medical	2,100	7	17	189	1,132	210	569
Surgical	2,400	10	15	324	1,620	240	216

Of the patients served by the hospital, 10 percent are expected to be Medicare patients, all of whom are expected to select semiprivate rooms. Daily rentals per patient are $250 for a private room, $200 for a semiprivate room, and $100 for a ward.

Operating room charges are based on "person-minutes" (the number of minutes the operating room is in use multiplied by the number of personnel assisting in the operation). The person-minute charges are $2.50 for inpatients and $5.00 for outpatients. Studies for the current year show that operations on inpatients are divided as follows:

Type of Operation	Number of Operations	Average Number of Minutes per Operation	Average Number of Personnel Required
A	800	30	4
B	700	45	5
C	300	90	6
D	200	120	8
	2,000		

The same proportion of inpatient operations is expected for the next fiscal year, and 180 outpatients are expected to use the operating room. Outpatient operations average 20 minutes and require the assistance of 3 persons. Assume that each surgical patient has one operation. (For example, an operation of Type A required 30 minutes and 4 people, or 120 person-minutes.)

Prepare schedules showing the computation of

(a) The number of patient-days (number of patients multiplied by average stay in hospital) expected, by type of patients and by type of room.
(b) The total number of person-minutes expected for operating room services for inpatients and outpatients. For inpatients, show the breakdown of total operating room use by person-minutes and by type of operation.
(c) Expected gross revenue from room rental.
(d) Expected gross revenue from operating room services.

[AICPA adapted]

14. *Flexible Budgets and Costs for Budgeted Income Statements*
A small Chicago firm has been operating on an actual cost basis. The company now wishes to adopt a flexible budgeting system. The system will be used primarily for control purposes but will also provide a pro forma income statement.

EXHIBIT 13-29————————————

	Jan.	Feb.	March	April	May	June
Output (in units)	12,500	12,600	14,500	14,750	16,000	14,000
Direct labor cost[a]	$43,760	$44,410	$50,775	$51,655	$56,025	$49,280
Direct materials	40,125	40,194	46,835	47,200	51,680	44,940
Overhead						
Indirect labor	18,000	18,080	19,745	19,947	21,120	19,340
Operating						
supplies	7,500	7,560	8,710	8,860	9,920	8,540
Power	7,500	7,520	7,900	7,950	8,200	7,800
Maintenance	12,000	12,010	13,000	13,050	14,100	13,000
Salaries	10,000	10,000	12,000	12,000	13,000	12,000
Depreciation	8,000	8,000	8,000	8,000	9,000	9,000
Tax and						
insurance	4,500	4,500	4,500	4,500	4,750	4,750
Miscellaneous	3,500	3,550	3,600	3,650	3,800	3,600

	July	Aug.	Sept.	Oct.	Nov.	Dec.
Expected production (in units)	13,500	14,000	14,800	15,500	16,000	14,000

[a] Each unit of output requires one hour of direct labor.

Data covering the past six months' activities are given in Exhibit 13-29.

(a) Using only the data supplied, prepare a flexible budget for July through December. State any assumptions you make concerning the data and the calculations.

(b) Indicate how these data may be used to prepare projected monthly income statements. What was the total cost per unit of output projected for July? For November?

15. *Budgeted Income and Cash Statements*

The Adams Company distributes brand-name products. All its sales are on account. In general, 70 percent of its monthly sales are collected in the month of the sale, 20 percent in the month following the sale, and 8 percent in the second month following the sale. The remaining 2 percent are uncollectible. Sales for the last two months were as follows: November, $17,500; and December, $20,000. An estimate of uncollectibles is provided at the end of each month. Uncollected accounts are written off in the third month after the sale.

Projected sales for the new quarter are as follows: January, $22,000; February, $23,500; and March, $24,000. Inventory is maintained at 75 percent of the expected sales for the next month. Purchases are made under the terms 2 percent per 10 days, net 30 days. The company always takes its discounts. Goods have been purchased at an average cost of 60 percent of gross sales. Assume that 80 percent of the purchases are paid in the month of purchase and the remaining 20 percent in the month following the purchase.

The cash account has a beginning balance of $7,500.

A note payable is due on July 1 of the coming year. The note is for $12,000 at 16 percent interest payable semiannually on January 1 and July 1. Taxes payable, due March 15, are $4,800.

Monthly fixed expenses are $2,500; other variable expenses are approximately 8 percent of sales. These expenses are paid in the month in which they are incurred.

(a) On the basis of the information supplied, prepare a cash budget for January and February.

(b) Prepare an income statement for January.

16. *Using Equations to Project Cash Flows*

In Problem 15, develop the equations needed to project cash receipts from sales and cash disbursements for accounts payable. Include in your model the equation needed to predict purchases.

If you have solved Problem 15, check your equation by using the data in Problem 15 and compare your two answers.

17. *Sales, Production, and Input Budgets*

The Scarborough Corporation manufactures and sells two products, Thingone and Thingtwo. In July, 1981, Scarborough's budget department gathered the following data in order to project sales and budget requirements for 1982.

1982 Projected Sales:

Product	Units	Price
Thingone	60,000	$ 70
Thingtwo	40,000	$100

1982 Inventories (in units):

Product	Expected Jan. 1, 1982	Desired Dec. 31, 1982
Thingone	20,000	25,000
Thingtwo	8,000	9,000

In order to produce one unit of Thingone and Thingtwo, the following raw materials are used:

		AMOUNT USED PER UNIT	
Raw Material	Unit	Thingone	Thingtwo
A	pounds	4	5
B	pounds	2	3
C	each		1

Projected data for 1982 with respect to raw materials are as follows:

Raw Material	Anticipated Purchase Price	Expected Inventories Jan. 1, 1982	Desired Inventories Dec. 31, 1982
A	$8	32,000 lbs.	36,000 lbs.
B	$5	29,000 lbs.	32,000 lbs.
C	$3	6,000 each	7,000 each

Projected direct labor requirements for 1982 and rates are as follows:

Product	Hours per Unit	Rate per Hour
Thingone	2	$6
Thingtwo	3	$8

Overhead is applied at the rate of $2 per direct labor hour.

Required Based upon the above projections and budget requirements for 1982 for Thingone and Thingtwo, prepare the following budgets for 1982:

(a) Sales budget (in dollars).
(b) Production budget (in units).
(c) Raw materials purchase budget (in quantities).
(d) Raw materials purchase budget (in dollars).
(e) Direct labor budget (in dollars).
(f) Budgeted finished goods inventory at December 31, 1982 (in dollars).

[AICPA adapted]

18. **Projected Income Statement and Cash Flow**
David Construction, Inc., builds heavy construction equipment for commercial and government purposes. Because of two new contracts and the anticipated purchase of new equipment, the management needs certain projections for the next two years. You have been requested to prepare these projections.

You have acquired the following information from the company's records and personnel:

(1) David Construction uses the completed contract method of accounting, whereby construction costs are capitalized until the contract is completed. Since all general and administrative expenses can be identified with a particular contract, they also are capitalized until the contract is completed.
(2) Two contracts will be started in 1982: Contracts A and B. These contracts are expected to be completed in December 1983 and December 1984, respectively. No other contracts will be started until these are completed. All other outstanding contracts were completed in 1981.

(3) Total estimated revenues for Contracts A and B are $2,000,000 and $1,500,000, respectively. The estimated cash collections per year are:

	1982	1983
Contract A	$ 800,000	$1,200,000
Contract B	300,000	450,000
	$1,100,000	$1,650,000

(4) Estimated construction costs to be incurred per contract, per year are:

	Contract A	Contract B
1982	$ 720,000	$ 250,000
1983	1,000,000	400,000
1984	—	650,000
	$1,720,000	$1,300,000

(5) Depreciation expense is included in these estimated construction costs. For 1982, 10 percent of the estimated construction costs represents depreciation expenses. For 1983 and 1984, 15 percent of the estimated construction costs represents depreciation expense. The cash portion of these estimated construction costs is paid as follows: 70 percent in the year incurred and 30 percent in the following year. On December 31, 1981, David owed creditors $612,400 in construction costs. They will be paid in 1982.

(6) Total general and administrative expenses (not included in construction costs) consist of a fixed portion of $7,000 each year for each contract, and a variable portion that is 1.5 percent of cash collected each year.

(7) David will acquire a new asset in 1983 for $700,000 and plans to pay for it that year.

(8) On December 31, 1981, David's cash balance is $72,000. When the cash balance falls below $70,000, David obtains short-term loans in multiples of $10,000. For purposes of this problem, ignore interest on short-term loans and ignore any repayments on these loans.

Prepare projected income statements and cash budgets for each of the calendar years 1982 and 1983.

[AICPA adapted]

19. **Projected Income Statement and Balance Sheet**

As chief budget officer for Day, Inc., you are given the responsibility for preparing the following final forecasted reports: the projected balance sheet and the income statement. Day, Inc., buys unfinished widgets and finishes them. You have been provided with the firm's balance sheet as of December 31, 1981, and the various budget schedules. Reproduced below are the balance sheet and the quarterly figures for the various budgets.

Prepare in good form the forecasted income statement for January–March 1982 and balance sheet for March 31, 1982.

Day, Inc.
Balance Sheet
December 31, 1981

Assets		Liabilities	
Current assets:		Current liabilities:	
Cash	$ 10,000	Accounts payable	$ 18,000
Accounts receivable	15,000	Accrued salaries payable	1,000
Inventory:[a]		Total current liabilities	$ 19,000
Raw materials	10,000		
Finished goods	20,000		
Prepaid rent	1,000		
Total current assets	$ 56,000	Stockholders' Equity	
Fixed assets:		Capital stock	$ 40,000
Equipment	$100,000	Retained earnings	70,000
Less: Accumulated depreciation	27,000	Total stockholders' equity	$110,000
Net equipment	$ 73,000	Total liabilities and	
Total assets	$129,000	stockholders' equity	$129,000

[a] All inventories are carried at their standard cost.

Forecasted Sales Budget
For Quarter Ending March 31, 1982

Product	Quantity	Selling Price	Gross Sales	Discounts and Allowances	Net Sales
Widget	10,000	$15	$150,000	$5,000	$145,000

Note: All sales are credit sales.

Production and Purchase Requirements Schedule
For Quarter Ending March 31, 1982

	Finished Widgets	Unfinished Widgets
Desired ending inventory	2,000 units	3,500 units
Period requirement	10,000 units	9,500 units
Total requirement	12,000 units	13,000 units
Less: Opening inventory	2,500 units	2,500 units
Unit requirement for quarter	9,500 units	10,500 units
Standard cost per unfinished widget		× $4
Dollar purchase requirement for raw materials		$42,000

Manufacturing Overhead
For Quarter Ending March 31, 1982

Actual Costs	Amount
Various wages, salaries, and fringe benefits	$ 9,000
Supplies	500
Utilities	500
Rent	6,000
Depreciation	3,000
Total	$19,000
Standard (9,500 direct labor hours at $2 per hour)	19,000
Over (under) applied overhead	$ 0

Selling and Administrative Expense Budgets
For Quarter Ending March 31, 1982

	Amount
Various selling expenses	$25,000
Administrative expenses	
Salaries	$13,000
Depreciation on office equipment	2,000
Total administrative expenses	$15,000

Standard Cost-Widget
For Quarter Ending March 31, 1982

Raw material: unfinished widget (1 unit at $4 per unit)	$4.00
Direct labor (1 hour at $2 per hour)	2.00
Manufacturing overhead (1 hour at $2 per hour)	2.00
Standard cost per unit	$8.00

Cash Budget
For Quarter Ending March 31, 1982

Opening balance	$ 10,000
Payment on accounts receivable	140,000
New 10 percent, 10-year debentures issued 3/31/82	20,000
Total available	$170,000
Disbursements	
Accounts payable-raw materials	$ 42,000
Direct labor	19,500
Overhead-manufacturing	15,000
Selling and administrative expenses	38,000
Prepaid rent	1,000
Equipment additions	25,000
Cash dividend	10,000
Total disbursements	$150,500
Closing balance	$ 19,500

Other Information: The income tax rate for 1982 is 40 percent. In 1981, Day, Inc., had prepaid its income taxes in full. In 1982, it plans to accrue its income taxes quarterly. Rent amounts to $6,000 per quarter and $1,000 is paid for in advance. Supplies and utilities expensed during the period are paid by the end of the quarter.

20. *Comprehensive Budgeting Problem*

Modern Products Corporation, a manufacturer of molded plastic containers, determined in October 1981 that it needed cash to continue operations. The corporation began negotiating for a one-month bank loan of $100,000 on November 1. In considering the loan, the bank requested a projected income statement and a cash budget for the month of November. The following information is available:

Sales were budgeted at 120,000 units per month in October, December, and January, and at 90,000 units in November.

The selling price is $2 per unit. Sales are billed on the 15th and the last day of each month. Terms are 6 percent per 10 days, net 30 days. Past experience indicates sales are made evenly throughout the month. Fifty percent of the customers pay the billed amount within the discount period. The remainder pay at the end of 30 days, except for bad debts, which average ½ percent of gross sales.

The inventory of finished goods on October 1 was 24,000 units. The finished goods inventory at the end of each month is to be maintained at 20 percent of sales anticipated for the following month. The production process is such that there is no work-in-process inventory.

The inventory of raw materials on October 1 was 22,800 pounds. At the end of each month the raw materials inventory is to be maintained at not less than 40 percent of production requirements for the following month. Materials are purchased locally. Minimum quantity is 25,000 pounds per shipment. Raw material purchases of each month are paid in the next month. Terms are net 30 days.

All salaries and wages are paid on the 15th and last day of each month for the period ending on the date of payment.

All manufacturing overhead and selling and administrative expenses are paid on the 10th of the month following the month in which the expenses are incurred. Selling expenses are 10 percent of gross sales. Administrative expenses, which include depreciation of $500 per month on office furniture and fixtures, total $33,000 per month.

The standard cost of a molded plastic container, based on normal production of 100,000 units per month, is as follows:

Materials, ½ pound	$ .50	
Labor	.40	
Variable overhead	.20	
Fixed overhead	.10	(total budgeted = $10,000)
Total	$1.20	

Fixed overhead includes depreciation on factory equipment of $4,000 per month. Over- or underabsorbed overhead (that is, differences between $10,000 and the amount assigned to production) is included in cost of sales. The cash balance on November 1 is expected to be $10,000.

Assuming the bank loan is granted, and ignoring income taxes:

(a) Prepare schedules computing inventory budgets by months for (1) finished goods production in units for October, November, and December (2) raw materials purchases in pounds for October and November.

(b) Prepare a projected income statement for the month of November.

(c) Prepare a cash forecast for the month of November showing the opening balance, receipts (itemized by dates of collection), disbursements, and balance at the end of the month.

[AICPA adapted]

21. *Projected Income Statement—A Linear Programing Approach*
Bi-Product Inc. produces two soap products, Clean and Powerful. The standard costs of processing Clean in Process C and Powerful in Process D are as follows:

	Clean Process C	Powerful Process D
Direct materials	$ .10 per pound	$ .12 per pound
Direct labor	3.40 per hour	3.45 per hour
Variable overhead (directly associated with each product)	.40 per labor hour	.47 per hour

Standard fixed costs are $.02 and $.025 per pound, respectively (these represent noncash expenditures). Each product requires approximately ¼ hour of labor time per 10 pounds of finished product. Clean is expected to sell for approximately $.31 per pound, while Powerful will probably sell for $.36 per pound.

These products pass through two common processes, A and B. In general, each product requires 0.5 pound of special mix per pound of finished product in Process A. Process A is limited to 1,000,000 pounds of total output per month in various combinations of Clean and Powerful. Both processes receive special treatment in Process B, which is capable of yielding either 1,200,000 pounds of Clean or 900,000 pounds of Powerful. Costs in Processes A and B are as follows:

		Process B	
	Process A	Clean	Powerful
Variable costs	$0.02 per pound of mix for each product	$0.025 per pound	$0.03 per pound
Fixed costs	$15,000	$18,000	

(a) Compute an optimal combination of Clean and Powerful that can serve as a basis for a budgeted income statement.

(b) Project an income statement by product. Allocate final costs of Processes A and B on the basis of the number of pounds of each product produced.

(c) Suppose the capacity of Process A could be expanded 10 percent at a cost of $15,000 (rental cost of equipment for one month). How would such an expansion affect the projected income figures?

(d) Discuss the possible uses of sensitivity analysis and linear programing in the budgetary process.

The Investment Decision

In our discussion of CVP analysis in Chapter 4, we assumed that a firm is committed to a fixed investment in various capacity resources, and, therefore, management's main problem was to determine optimal uses of these capacities. In this chapter we shall discuss some methods, and their accounting demands, for analyzing the effects of decisions to change the level of investment in capacities.

Many resources (assets) held by a firm are capable of providing productive services over a long time period. For example, a building may have a useful life of 40 years, and equipment may have 10 years. Even small units of machinery may be used for several years. The decision to invest in a long-lived asset exposes a firm to the risk that the net economic benefits from the asset may be less than anticipated, and this uncertainty about the realization of future net benefits tends to increase over time. Expected net benefits are usually expressed in terms of net cash inflows (for example, revenues less cash expenditures) and the delay in their receipt results in a form of opportunity cost. Let us review CVP analysis to see how this opportunity cost might enter the decision situation.

The Opportunity Cost of Invested Capital

In CVP analysis we tend to observe the decision rule to expand output (change output mix) if the expected incremental revenues from expanded outputs (different mixes) exceed the expected incremental costs, ignoring risk considerations. Incremental costs consist mostly of the out-of-pocket costs of producing and distributing output. For a single-product firm, the decision problem centers essentially on whether to use capacities at alternative levels. When we consider a multiproduct firm, however, an additional "cost" has to be taken into consideration—the opportunity costs of not being able to produce all possible outputs at any given level. If the increased output of one product, say Product A, requires a reduction in the output level of one or more alternative products, then the decision to expand the output of A must be charged with the loss in the net revenues of the alternative products. This loss is an opportunity cost of expanding the output of Product A.

This brings us to the point of whether there are other alternatives available to the firm and, therefore, other opportunity costs that we might include in the cost–volume–profit analysis. At least one alternative immediately comes to mind. At the beginning of any operating period, a firm has the option of halting production and selling its facilities. In ignoring this alternative, we assume that the net benefits from selling the facilities at the beginning of the period would be less than the total net benefits obtained from continuing an investment in the facilities during the operating period. A more thorough analysis would include a comparison between the alternatives of (1) selling the facilities at time t_0 and (2) producing an optimal output during one time period and selling the facilities at the end of that period, that is, at t_1.

Usually the omission of the alternative of selling the facilities is not a serious defect in cost–volume–profit analysis. For short operating periods it is unlikely that firms would observe a significantly different selling price for their facilities at the end of the period relative to the price at the beginning of the period. Also, the decline in the salvage value of usable fixed assets in the short run is often insignificant relative to the benefits received if the assets are used in productive processes. Therefore, the opportunity costs of holding an investment in productive facilities for short-run analyses can be considered negligible.

Consider now the effect of lengthening the time period during which a firm holds its facilities. Eventually, these facilities become inefficient and have to be scrapped. Thus, we would expect a significant decrease in their value between time t_0 and time t_n, where n is the number of periods the facilities can be operated efficiently. The firm's management must decide which alternative is worth more to the firm: (1) to operate the facilities for n periods, after which they will be scrapped or salvaged for $\$y$, or (2) to sell the facilities at t_0 for $\$x$, where x is greater than y. The nature of the problem can be illustrated by the following example.

Excess Present Value Criterion

A firm has facilities that can be sold at t_0 for $\$130,000$. Alternatively, these facilities may be used to produce a yearly output of 10,000 units that can be sold for $\$10$ each. The cost of producing and selling is $\$10,000$ per year plus $\$5$ a unit, or a total of $\$60,000$ for 10,000 units of output. Thus, the net annual cash inflows from operating the facilities are $\$100,000$ —

$60,000 = $40,000 per year.[1] The facilities may be sold for $15,000 at t_5 (the end of the fifth year).

For the moment we ignore the effect of income taxes. At first glance the optimal alternative seems apparent. If it holds the facilities, the firm can receive cash inflows of $40,000 each year for five years plus $15,000 at the end of that time (or total receipts of $215,000) compared with only $130,000 if the facilities are sold immediately. However, there are at least two other alternatives that we have not considered. If the firm sells its facilities for $130,000, it can invest the money in another project that may offer, with an equal degree of risk, a higher return than is promised by the operation of the facilities. As another alternative, the firm could distribute the $130,000 to its owners, who could use the money for consumption or for other investments available to them. Thus, the investment of $130,000 in the operation of the facilities costs the firm and its owners the net benefits obtainable from either of these alternative uses of the proceeds.

Note that since there are two or more possible uses of the firm's capital of $130,000, this capital becomes scarce relative to the demands that may be placed on it. Whenever an item becomes scarce it attains a value, and the use or consumption of this item results in an opportunity cost. Consequently, we must find some way to assign a cost of capital to the firm's use of $130,000 in the production of output for five operating periods.

Before we consider a method for doing this, however, let us determine what constitutes an investment in an economic asset. An investment in an economic asset is an investment in the right to receive the cash proceeds from the use of and ultimate sale or disposition of that asset. For example, an investment in a bond is an investment in the right to receive interest payments as specified and to receive the principal when the bond matures. An investment in a corporation's common stock is an investment in the right to receive dividends plus the proceeds when the stock is either sold by the investor in the market or redeemed by the corporation. Similarly, an investment in a producing asset is an investment in the right to the net receipts from the utilization of the asset plus the proceeds when the asset is ultimately sold or salvaged. Generally, net receipts are calculated as the cash received from the output of the asset minus all of the cash expenditures required to produce and distribute the output. In our example, the firm is investing $130,000 for the right to receive net cash inflows of $40,000 each year for five years plus $15,000 at the end of the fifth year.

Suppose that the firm has the alternative of investing the $130,000 for a period of one year in another asset of equal risk that will yield an annual rate of return r. If the firm followed this alternative, at the end of one year it would have the right to receive the original amount of $130,000 plus the

---

[1] Note that our prediction of the periodic cash flows assumes that the firm has solved its short-run allocation decision in each period.

interest on this amount, or $130,000 + r($130,000)$. If PV is the original amount invested, at the end of the first period the firm would have an asset worth $PV + rPV = PV(1 + r)$. Suppose the firm invested this entire amount during the second time period at the same rate.[2] The value of the asset at the end of the second year would be

$$PV(1 + r) + r[PV(1 + r)] = PV(1 + r)^2$$

In general, if the firm continues to reinvest its principal plus the interest, the asset will have a future value

$$FV = PV(1 + r)^n$$

where n is the number of time periods (years, in this case) for which the interest return is compounded.

If $FV = PV(1 + r)^n$, then

$$PV = FV(1 + r)^{-n} = FV \left[\frac{1}{(1 + r)^n} \right]$$

That is, if the firm will have an asset worth FV after n periods, then it would only be willing to pay PV *today* for the right to receive this future value. In terms of our example, the firm would not pay $40,000 today for the right to receive $40,000 cash one year from now; nor would it pay $40,000 to receive the second $40,000 two years from now. As long as the firm has an alternative use of its capital *today*, it will require some additional compensation to induce it to invest that capital and forgo its alternative use today. Thus, the firm will pay only $40,000[1/(1 + r)^1]$ for the first receipt and only $40,000[1/(1 + r)^2]$ for the second receipt, and so on.

The present value of the total set of cash receipts can be determined by summing up the present values of the individual cash receipts, or

$$PV_{asset} = \$40,000 \left[\frac{1}{(1 + r)} \right] + \$40,000 \left[\frac{1}{(1 + r)^2} \right] + \$40,000 \left[\frac{1}{(1 + r)^3} \right]$$

$$+ \$40,000 \left[\frac{1}{(1 + r)^4} \right] + \$40,000 \left[\frac{1}{(1 + r)^5} \right] + \$15,000 \left[\frac{1}{(1 + r)^5} \right]$$

Factoring out the $40,000 net cash operating inflows, gives us

---

[2] We are assuming that the future rate of return is equal for all time periods. This is convenient, since the mathematics of capital budgeting become tedious if we must allow for shifting rates of return. If interest rates vary for each period, as they do in practice, the value of the asset after one period would be $PV(1 + r_1)$, and at the end of the second period, $PV (1 + r_1)(1 + r_2)$, where r_1 and r_2 are the two rates. If the asset is invested for many time periods, the equation becomes unwieldy.

$$PV_{asset} = \$40,000 \left[\frac{1}{(1+r)} + \frac{1}{(1+r)^2} + \frac{1}{(1+r)^3} + \frac{1}{(1+r)^4} + \frac{1}{(1+r)^5} \right]$$

$$+ \$15,000 \left[\frac{1}{(1+r)^5} \right]$$

The elements in the large bracketed term are the present value factors of an annuity of $1 received for five periods at a rate r. The sum of the annuity factors, which may be expressed as the factor $[1 - (1+r)^{-n}]/r$, can be found in Table 14-4 in the appendix to this chapter. Students who are not familiar with compound interest calculations might be well advised to work through the appendix before continuing with this chapter.[3]

Let us suppose that the firm in our example considers that an investment in this asset should return at least 16 percent; that is, 16 percent is the compensation required to induce the firm to forgo using the $130,000 in an alternative investment. The present value of the series of $40,000 receipts at 16 percent is equal to[4]

$$PV_{\$40,000} = \$40,000(3.274) = \$130,960$$

The present value of the $15,000 salvage receipt is[5]

$$PV_{\$15,000} = \$15,000[1/(1.16)^5] = \$15,000(0.476) = \$7,140$$

Therefore, the present value of the right to all of the cash receipts, assuming a required rate of return of 16 percent, is equal to

$$PV_{asset} = \$130,960 + \$7,140 = \$138,100$$

If 16 percent does in fact measure the compensation required by the firm to devote capital to this asset, then the firm should be willing to make the investment, since it receives an asset worth $138,100 at a cost of only $130,000. The $8,100 excess is called the *excess present value* of the project; that is, it reflects the excess of the present value of the set of net cash receipts ($138,100) over the present value of the required outlay ($130,000). The *excess present value criterion for investment decisions* states: A firm or individual should

---

[3] The appendix includes a discussion of six tables of interest factors. Table 14-1 has factors for $(1 + r)^n$; Table 14-2 has factors for $[1/(1 + r)^n]$; Table 14-3 has factors for the future value of an annuity, which is rarely needed in capital budgeting; Table 14-4 has factors for the present value of an annuity, which are merely sums of the factors from Table 14-2 for the same values of r. Tables 14-5 and 14-6 contain factors for continuous discounting; these are described in the appendix. (Of course a hand calculator is more convenient. It also reduces rounding errors.)

[4] See Table 14-4, column headed 16 percent opposite $n = 5$. Note that 3.274 is the sum of the first five factors under 16 percent in Table 14-2.

[5] See Table 14-2, column headed 16 percent opposite $n = 5$.

invest in an asset if the present value of the net future cash receipts is at least equal to the asset's outlay cost, assuming that the "appropriate discount rate" is used to determine the present value of the future cash flows.

The logic of this argument depends on a perfectly functioning capital market. The *market price* of capital is assumed to be $(1 + r)^n$. Anyone can acquire a single dollar in exchange for a promise to return $(1 + r)^n$ at the end of n periods. Under such pristine conditions, our firm can *sell* its future outlays for $138,100. The discount rate, in other words, is a *market rate.* But because markets are not perfect, the use of a discounting approach raises the issue of what discount rate to use. Merely asking what the discount rate is signals that we do not have the type of market structure envisioned in an economics textbook.

Thus, in the world of business affairs, the "appropriate discount rate" is not obvious and will likely depend on several factors, such as the asset's risk class, expected future rates of inflation, consumption–investment trade-offs, and so on.[6] Movements in current investment interest rates reflect all of these factors jointly, and it is difficult—and usually not necessary—to break down an interest rate to reflect the individual contribution of each of these joint factors. For example, rather than adjusting future cash flows to reflect decreases in purchasing power—that is, to determine real cash flows—we can simply use the appropriate interest rates in the discounting process, which has a built-in adjustment for anticipated rates of inflation. A current yield of between 13 and 14 percent (before taxes) on corporate bonds is actually a geometric average of the interest rates over the future periods that the bond will be outstanding. For example, suppose a five-year bond will pay $1,000 per year for five years and its face value of $10,000 at the end of the fifth year. Interest rates are expected to be 10, 12, 14, 16, and 18 percent, respectively, for the next five years. If we used these rates to discount each cash receipt we would obtain a present value of approximately $8,765. This price would imply an average yield of about 13.5 percent over the five years.[7] Later in this chapter we discuss the problem of selecting the current discount rate appropriate for a particular risk class.

One more remark before continuing. In the 1980s, interest rates in the United States have skyrocketed. We have tried to use current rates in our

---

[6] A risk class is a set of assets whose returns are always scale multiples of one another (that is, perfectly correlated). If we have a nontrivial set of such assets, bought and sold in a perfect market, arbitrage would guarantee that prices differ only by the appropriate scale factor. If, in turn, we express the price as a discounting mechanism, each asset in the class would be discounted at the same rate, hence, the idea of applying a risk class specific discount rate to an asset's *expected* cash flows. The serious student should consult a basic finance text, such as J. Van Horne, *Financial Managemental Policy,* Englewood Cliffs, N.J.: Prentice-Hall, 1980, and then consult a theory text including those by Hirshleifer, Fama and Miller, or Haley and Schall, which are listed in the chapter's supplemental readings.

[7] Discount the $1,000 payments plus $10,000 received five years from now at a rate of 13.5 percent and the present value of these receipts will be approximately equal to $8,765.

illustrations and problems. If the rates in this chapter are considerably out of step with current rates, consider this a tour down memory lane. After all, it was not too long ago that a return of 7 percent on a government security was considered an attractive investment.

Internal Rate of Return Criterion

An alternative means of evaluating the degree of acceptability of investment alternatives is a variation of the present value criterion, at least in the typical decision problem of whether to invest in a project.[8] Under this criterion, an investment should be accepted if the time-adjusted rate of return of the project exceeds the required rate of return. The time-adjusted rate of return of a project is called its *internal rate of return.*

In our first example, we found that the present value of the inflows of the project was greater than its outlay, that is, $138,100 > $130,000. The present value of the inflows was determined using factors for a 16 percent rate of interest. If we refer to the two discounting tables used (Tables 14-2 and 14-4), we note that the factors for any year decrease as we move from lower to higher rates of interest. Suppose the required rate of return for this project were 20 percent. The discounted value of the project's net cash receipts would be

$$\$40,000(2.991) + \$15,000(.402) = \$125,670$$

which would be less than the outlay. Therefore, the firm should not invest in the project because the internal rate of return of the project would be less than the required rate of return.

The internal rate of return, r^*, earned on any project lasting n periods, can be calculated by solving the equation

$$\sum_{t=1}^{n} NR_t(1 + r^*)^{-t} - \text{Outlay} = 0$$

that is, by finding r^* such that the discounted value of the net cash receipts (NR_t) is exactly equal to the outlay cost, giving the project a zero excess present value. For the project in our example, the internal rate of return would be slightly higher than 19 percent, since

$$\sum_{t=1}^{5} NR_t(1.19)^{-t} - \$130,000 = \$267$$

---

[8] The two criteria can give different solutions if the problem is to select the best project from a set of mutually exclusive projects. Some of the circumstances leading to these conflicts in ranking are considered later.

If the net cash receipts are constant each year, r^* can be determined easily from Table 14-4. For example, suppose an outlay of \$1,200 will purchase the right to receive \$400 per year for five years. Setting up our equation,

$$\sum_{t=1}^{5} \$400(1 + r^*)^{-t} = \$1,200$$

Dividing both sides by \$400, we have

$$\sum_{t=1}^{5} (1 + r^*)^{-t} = 3.0$$

The left-hand side of the equation is the present value of \$1 received annually for 5 periods, which we can obtain from Table 14-4. If we run across the columns opposite $n = 5$, we find the factor 2.991 under the column for 20 percent. Because we would have to move to the left for a factor of 3.0, we know that the project will earn slightly less than 20 percent. Our decision, then, would be to invest in this project if the required rate of return for the project *is less* than 20 percent. (A hand calculator gives a more precise answer, indicating an internal rate of return of 19.86 percent.)

Note that this criterion gives the same decision for accepting or rejecting a single project as the excess present value criterion. If we insert a discount rate—that is, a cost of capital rate—less than 20 percent in the above equation—the discounted value of \$400 received for 5 years will exceed the outlay (have an excess present value) of \$1,200. For example, at 19 percent, the excess present value would be \$23.20. This is not to say that the internal rate of return and the excess present value criterion always result in the same investment decisions. As we show in Chapter 15, we can obtain two different rankings of the desirability of a set of projects when each criterion is applied to determine which project(s) should be chosen from a group of "mutually exclusive" projects (for example, we can select A or B but not both). Later we further discuss assumptions about the market for capital assets, which tend to support the use of the excess present value criterion rather than the internal rate of return. When we add the fact that the calculation of the internal rate of return can be tedious if yearly cash flows are not constant, and that we can obtain more than one solution if the yearly flows happen to flip-flop from positive to negative to positive, we might question the use of the internal rate of return criterion.

Nevertheless, many managements employ the internal rate of return as their investment criterion. If you must use the criterion, consider the possibility of obtaining different solutions with the excess present value criterion and interpreting the internal rate of return in light of that outcome. Remember, however, that the excess present value criterion is based on extremely restrictive market conditions. In fact, either approach is simplified and the choice between them is a situation-specific issue.

REVIEW PROBLEM 1
No Explicit Consideration of Tax Effects _____

Mr. X has $150,000 to invest in any one of three alternatives:

(1) Project A—Invest in a well-established business with the prospect of receiving $12,000 net after-tax cash receipts at the end of each year for five years, after which he could sell out for $150,000.

(2) Project B—Invest in a more risky operation that promises to return net after-tax cash receipts for five years according to the following schedule (including a "salvage value" at the end of five years as shown):

Year	0	1	2	3	4	5
Net operating cash inflows		$20,000	$20,000	$30,000	$30,000	$ 20,000
"Salvage value"						$100,000

(3) Project C—Invest in a radically new production process, which, if successful, promises large inflows at the end of years 3, 4, and 5, but no returns for years 1 and 2. The expected after-tax cash flows are as follows:

End of Year	0	1	2	3	4	5
Net operating cash inflows		$0	$0	$40,000	$40,000	$ 40,000
"Salvage value"						$175,000

Required (a) Suppose Mr. X discounted at 10 percent the after-tax cash inflows of each investment alternative. Using the factors from Tables 14-2 and 14-4 (where appropriate), determine which project would have the highest excess present value. Which would have the lowest? Do you think it is reasonable to use the same opportunity cost rate of interest to discount the flows of each project?

(b) Regardless of the answer to (a), Mr. X wonders how the projects would rank if he used three different discount rates, as follows:

> 8 percent for Project A
> 10 percent for Project B
> 16 percent for Project C

Compute the excess present value of each project using its appropriate rate and then indicate which project should be "purchased" by Mr. X.

(c) What is the internal rate of return for each project (relatively easy for A and C, but not for B).

(d) Suppose the operating cash inflows for Project A were

received evenly throughout each time period (for example, the $12,000 payments are received evenly from 0–1, 1–2, 2–3, 3–4, and 4–5) and the $150,000 "salvage value" for A were still received at the end of year 5. Mr. X wishes to determine the effect of using continuous discounting factors, shown in Tables 14-5 and 14-6, on the attractiveness of Project A. Calculate the excess present value of the cash flows for Project A using the factors under the 8 percent column in Table 14-6 for the $12,000 payments and the factor opposite .40 (equal to 5 × .08 = rt) from Table 14-5 for the $150,000 return of principal.

After-Tax Cash Flows

In general, the two discounting criteria in investment analysis that we have illustrated rely on the same data inputs. That is, regardless of the criterion used, we must work with estimates of the periodic net cash receipts for each project, and we must select the appropriate rate of discount for each project to determine if it earns a rate of return equal to or in excess of what it should.

Selection of the appropriate discount rate for each project, or each project risk class, will depend on our assumptions about the efficiency of the capital market and how firms and individual investors come together in this market. We defer until later a consideration of this problem. The estimates of net cash receipts constitute more of an accounting problem, but apart from repeating the discussion in Chapters 3 and 4, we cannot be any more specific about how to obtain the estimates. Obviously, the success of any investment project will depend ultimately on whether the cash receipts and cash disbursements occur as expected. The realization of these estimates will be affected both by economic factors outside the control of the decision maker and by how he or she reacts to these factors as they occur. Employing a discounting process in investment analysis helps the decision maker because estimates of net cash receipts that occur in later years have less impact on the final decision. For example, at a discount rate of 16 percent, cash receipts and disbursements occurring in year 5 will be weighted by the factor, .476 (Table 14-2, $n = 5$, $r = 16\%$). Those occurring in year 10 will be weighted by the factor, .227 (same table, $n = 10$, $r = 16\%$). Changing the latter cash estimates by as much as ±25 percent will affect their present values by only ±5.7 percent. These figures suggest that investments in the improvement of cash flow estimates should concentrate on those flows that occur in the near future (because they receive higher weights).

This brings us now to a different category of cash flow estimates—yearly or periodic income taxes. We cannot consider all aspects of the tax code that influence a project's net cash receipts. However, we should be aware of the more pervasive ones, such as investment credits against taxes payable, depreciation methods allowed, and taxes on gains and losses associated with asset sales. Taxes on net capital gains are generally set at lower rates than on income in general. On the other hand, assets depreciated at accelerated rates tend to lose this tax rate advantage. In fact, we often assume that gains and losses on the sale of a firm's operating assets are handled at regular income tax rates. Additional variations in the tax laws are introduced as we go along. (Tax laws frequently change, however, and we therefore attempt to introduce basic ideas without relying too explicitly on extant regulations.)

To illustrate some basic concepts in taxation, let us assume a manager of a manufacturing firm is faced with three mutually exclusive alternatives, which we shall call Plans A, B, and C.

Plan A—Keeping the Old Equipment. The firm currently owns equipment that produces 5,000 units per year that sell for $5 each. The total cash costs of production and distribution are represented by the linear cost model of

$$TC = \$10,000 + \$2x$$

That is, at an output of 5,000 units $TC = \$20,000$, and net receipts before taxes are $5,000 per year ($25,000 − $20,000).

The equipment can be sold today for $11,000. It has a remaining useful life of five years, after which it can be sold for $2,000. The equipment was originally purchased for $16,000 and has been depreciated for tax purposes to a book value of $12,000. Consequently, if the equipment were sold today, there would be a tax loss of $1,000, which would reduce the firm's taxes in the current period.

Recapping, we can view the retention of the old equipment as a decision to invest $11,000 plus the tax benefits of the loss on the sale (or the total cash forgone today) to buy the right to receive $5,000 net revenues *minus any taxes* each year for five years *plus* the salvage proceeds of $2,000 five years from now.

The net cash flows after taxes from operations in any period t can be calculated as

$$NCF_{at} = Revenues_t - Cash\ expenses_t - Taxes_t$$

where the subscript at indicates after taxes in period t. In general, taxes on operating flows are based on net income (that is, taxes = tax rate × net income). But for tax purposes net income is equal to revenues minus cash expenses allowed for deduction minus noncash expenses allowed for deduction. Letting TR equal the tax rate, we have

$$NCF_{at} = (Revenues - Cash\ expenses)_t$$
$$- TR(Revenues - Cash\ expenses - Noncash\ expenses)_t$$
$$= (1 - TR)(Revenues - Cash\ expenses)_t + TR(Noncash\ expenses)_t$$

EXHIBIT 14-1_____

Schedule of Plan A Cash Flows

	END OF YEAR					
	0	1	2	3	4	5
Effective outlay on investment						
Salvage proceeds given up	−$11,000					
Tax benefits of loss given up today = 0.48(−$1,000)	−480					
Net receipts						
From operations:						
(1 − TR)(Revenue − Cash expenses) + TR(Depreciation)		$3,560	$3,560	$3,560	$3,560	$3,560
From salvage						2,000
Totals	−$11,480	$3,560	$3,560	$3,560	$3,560	$5,560

The firm is assessed a marginal tax rate of 48 percent; that is, it has a sufficient number of profitable projects that the net income generated by Plan A equipment will be taxed at a rate of 48 percent. The only noncash deductions are for depreciation and for any losses on assets sold. Depreciation is calculated on a straight-line basis, using the book value of $12,000 and the salvage estimate of $2,000. In this case, depreciation is[9]

$$\frac{\$12,000 - \$2,000}{5} = \$2,000 \text{ per year}$$

Summarizing, the net after-tax cash operating inflows for Plan A are

$$(1 - .48)(\$5,000) + .48(\$2,000) = \$2,600 + \$960 = \$3,560 \text{ per year}$$

We can drop the time subscript since the flows are constant. All the relevant cash flows for this investment alternative can be displayed as in Exhibit 14-1.

Generally, discrete compounding formulas are used, as in Tables 14-1 to 14-4, if all cash flows occur at the end of a time period, without continuous compounding of interest. Continuous formulas could be used—Tables 14-5 and 14-6—but the bias in using discrete formulas is often negligible.

After-Tax Operating Cash Flows—Some General Considerations.   Our equation for after-tax flows can be generalized to handle all cash and noncash transactions that affect the calculation of taxable income. A cash transaction that affects the calculation of taxes may be calculated as $\pm(1 - $ TR)(Cash

---

[9] In general, straight-line depreciation is equal to $(1/n)$(Book value − Salvage), where n = number of years of remaining life. For a new asset, book value is merely cost.

transaction), the sign depending on whether the cash transaction is a receipt of revenue (positive) or an expense (negative). Similarly, a noncash transaction affecting taxes is calculated as ±TR(Noncash transaction), the sign depending on whether the noncash transaction reduces taxes (for example, from a deduction for depreciation or a loss on the sale of an asset) or increases taxes (for example, from a gain on exchange of other than "like-kind" assets). Because of the so-called depreciation recapture provisions, gains on the sale of operating assets rarely enjoy the preferential capital gains tax but are taxed at the ordinary income tax rate instead.

There are other kinds of tax effects that may be involved in an investment analysis; some of these are illustrated in subsequent examples and in various problems at the end of this chapter.

We now turn to Plans B and C, alternatives to keeping the present equipment.

Plan B—Purchase Standard New Equipment.   Under this plan, the firm can purchase a standardized set of equipment that will reduce operating costs relative to the old equipment. Specifically, with this equipment, output can be produced and distributed at variable costs of $1.25 per unit plus fixed cash expenditures of $12,000 per year, or $18,250 cash expenses each year to produce 5,000 units. Thus,

$$\text{Revenues} - \text{Cash expenses} = \$25,000 - \$18,250 = \$6,750$$

This equipment has a useful life of eight years, but we shall use five years as our cutoff date in order to compare this plan with Plan A. This requires an estimate of the salvage value of the equipment at two dates—at the end of five years when it can be sold, and at the end of eight years for tax depreciation calculations. The equipment will cost $18,000. For convenience, assume the tax guidelines indicate that the firm may use a zero salvage value after eight years. However, the firm can sell the equipment after five years for $5,000.

The tax guidelines also allow the firm to recognize accelerated depreciation on new equipment and machinery purchased after 1954. One accelerated depreciation method is called the *sum-of-the-years'-digits* method. In it, depreciation in any year, D_t, can be calculated as

$$D_t = \frac{n - (t - 1)}{n(n + 1)/2} (C - S)$$

where C is cost, S is salvage value, and n is defined as before.[10] Using our figures, depreciation for each of the first five years is

---

[10] The denominator is the sum of the arithmetic series of n terms $1 + 2 + 3 + \cdots + n$. Note that accelerated depreciation allows greater deductions in earlier years than straight-line depreciation, which results in higher tax savings in those earlier years.

$$D_1 = \frac{8-(1-1)}{8(9)/2}(\$18,000-0) = \left(\frac{8}{36}\right)(\$18,000) = \$4,000$$

$$D_2 = \frac{8-(2-1)}{36}(\$18,000-0) = \left(\frac{7}{36}\right)(\$18,000) = \$3,500$$

$$D_3 = \frac{8-(3-1)}{36}(\$18,000-0) = \left(\frac{6}{36}\right)(\$18,000) = \$3,000$$

$$D_4 = \frac{8-(4-1)}{36}(\$18,000-0) = \left(\frac{5}{36}\right)(\$18,000) = \$2,500$$

$$D_5 = \frac{8-(5-1)}{36}(\$18,000-0) = \left(\frac{4}{36}\right)(\$18,000) = \$2,000$$

Note that, after five years, this equipment would have a book value of

$$C - \sum_{t=1}^{5} D_t = \$18,000 - \$15,000 = \$3,000$$

If the firm sells the equipment then for \$5,000, it will have a taxable gain of \$5,000 − \$3,000 = \$2,000. The cash flow effect of this gain is − TR(\$2,000) = −.48(\$2,000) = −\$960.[11] The relevant cash flows for this alternative are shown in Exhibit 14-2.

You should also note, before proceeding, that our calculation of the tax effects is only suggestive of their general structure. The so-called Economic Recovery Tax Act of 1981, for example, actually abandons the concept of useful life and creates five classes of depreciable assets with prescribed depreciation lives and patterns. Some states, in turn, impose income tax regulations that vary with their federal counterparts. The important point to remember is that tax implications are not likely to be a simple function of cash flows in these types of problems. Rather, they reflect cash flows as well as taxable income computation regulations.

Plan C—Purchase Special-Purpose Equipment.   This equipment will reduce operating costs even more than Plan B equipment. Using the specially designed equipment, the 5,000 units of output can be produced and distributed at a cash outlay of \$.60 per unit plus \$13,500, or a total of \$16,500. Therefore, revenues minus cash expenses are \$25,000 − \$16,500 = \$8,500.

This equipment will cost \$21,600, and it too has a useful life of eight years. Again assume a zero salvage value after eight years for tax purposes, but a salvage value of \$2,500 if the equipment is sold at the end of five years. Sum-of-the-years'-digits depreciation is also used for this equipment; it is computed as follows:

---

[11] Note that if we always compute the tax effect of a sale as TR(Book Value$_t$ − Salvage$_t$), we will have the correct sign (+ for a loss and − for a gain).

_____ EXHIBIT 14-2

Schedule of Plan B Cash Flows

	YEAR					
	0	**1**	**2**	**3**	**4**	**5**
Outlay	−$18,000					
$(1 - TR)$(Revenue − Cash expenses)[a]		$3,510	$3,510	$3,510	$3,510	$3,510
TR(Depreciation) $= .48(D_t)$		1,920	1,680	1,440	1,200	960
$-TR$(Gain$_{t=5}$) $= -.48(\$2,000)$						−960
Salvage, at end of 5 years						5,000
	−$18,000	$5,430	$5,190	$4,950	$4,710	$8,510

[a] $.52(\$6,750)$

$$D_1 = \left(\frac{8}{36}\right)(\$21,600) = \$4,800$$

$$D_2 = \left(\frac{7}{36}\right)(\$21,600) = \$4,200$$

$$D_3 = \left(\frac{6}{36}\right)(\$21,600) = \$3,600$$

$$D_4 = \left(\frac{5}{36}\right)(\$21,600) = \$3,000$$

$$D_5 = \left(\frac{4}{36}\right)(\$21,600) = \$2,400$$

At the end of five years, the book value of the equipment will be $21,600 − $18,000 = $3,600. A comparison of the book value with the $2,500 received from the sale shows a tax loss of $1,100. The after-tax benefits of this loss are +.48 ($1,100) = +$528. The after-tax cash flows for this plan are given in Exhibit 14-3.

Ranking the Three Alternatives. We are now prepared to evaluate the three investment alternatives—Plan A versus Plan B versus Plan C. Remaining to be considered is the relevant cost-of-capital rate to apply in the discounting process. We shall assume that these three alternatives belong in the same risk class; that is, the same discount rate should be used in discounting the expected cash flows of each alternative. For illustrative purposes we assume that the firm's management believes a 10 percent discount rate is appropriate for discounting the after-tax cash flows for this type of investment project. The discounting calculations for each alternative are summarized in Exhibit 14-4.

EXHIBIT 14-3 _____

Schedule of Plan C Cash Flows

	YEAR					
	0	**1**	**2**	**3**	**4**	**5**
Outlay	−$21,600					
$(1 − TR)$(Revenue − Cash expenses)[a]		$4,420	$4,420	$4,420	$4,420	$4,420
TR(Depreciation) $= 0.48(D_t)$		2,304	2,016	1,728	1,440	1,152
$TR(Loss_{t=5}) = 0.48(\$1,100)$						528
Salvage at end of 5 years						2,500
	−$21,600	$6,724	$6,436	$6,148	$5,860	$8,600

[a] .52($8,500)

The excess present value criterion indicates that the firm should accept Plan C, because it offers the highest excess present value, $3,788 (versus $3,442 for Plan B and $3,255 for Plan A). This assumes that 10 percent measures the after-tax opportunity cost of providing capital for these projects as opposed to investing in other projects available to the firm (and its owners) that have the same degree of risk. If management has correctly assessed the opportunity cost of capital rate, then accepting Plan C should increase the present value of the owners' wealth by $3,788, all other things being equal.

Using Incremental Cash Flows. In the foregoing example we treated Plan A, the decision to retain the old equipment, as a separate capital budgeting decision. It is conceivable that all three plans could have resulted in negative excess present values, suggesting that the firm should discontinue the production of the 5,000 units of output and liquidate its present investment in equipment. The liquidation of the present equipment is often not an acceptable alternative; that is, production with present equipment is clearly profitable, so the typical analysis is concerned only with replacement. The replacement decision can be evaluated using only the incremental cash flows of investing in new equipment relative to operating the old equipment. In effect, the cash flows of Plan A become the base against which the cash flows of Plans B and C are assessed.

To illustrate, we show the incremental expected cash flows of Plan B over Plan A in Exhibit 14-5 [in all cases, we compute the difference (Cash flows)$_B$ − (Cash flows)$_A$].

Using this approach, we obtain an incremental excess present value for Plan B that is merely the excess present value of Plan B, calculated earlier, less the excess present value of Plan A, or $3,442 − $3,255 = $187 (from Exhibit 14-4). Obviously, if we were to calculate the incremental effects of

──**EXHIBIT 14-4**

Schedule of Excess Present Values of Each Alternative

	END OF YEAR					
	0	**1**	**2**	**3**	**4**	**5**
Plan A						
Net cash flows[a]	−$11,480	$3,560	$3,560	$3,560	$3,560	$5,560
Discount factors @ 10%	1.0	.909	.826	.751	.683	.621
Present values (PV)	−$11,480	$3,236	$2,941	$2,674	$2,431	$3,453
Excess present value:						
Σ PV of inflows	$14,735					
Less: Σ PV of outflows	11,480					
	$ 3,255					
Plan B						
Net cash flows[a]	−$18,000	$5,430	$5,190	$4,950	$4,710	$8,510
Discount factors @ 10%	1.0	.909	.826	.751	.683	.621
Present values (PV)	−$18,000	$4,936	$4,287	$3,717	$3,217	$5,285
Excess present value:						
Σ PV of inflows	$21,442					
Less: Σ PV of outflows	18,000					
	$ 3,442					
Plan C						
Net cash flows[a]	−$21,600	$6,724	$6,436	$6,148	$5,860	$8,600
Discount factors @ 10%	1.0	.909	.826	.751	.683	.621
Present values (PV)	−$21,600	$6,112	$5,316	$4,617	$4,002	$5,341
Excess present value:						
Σ PV of inflows	$25,388					
Less: Σ PV of outflows	21,600					
	$ 3,788					

[a] Net cash flows are from Exhibits 14-1, 14-2, and 14-3.

───

Plan C over Plan A, we should obtain the net difference in excess present values of $3,788 − $3,255 = $533.[12]

───────────────

[12] This can be demonstrated as follows:

(Excess present value)$_C$ − (Excess present value)$_A$

$$= \left[\sum_{t=1}^{5} \text{NR}_{C_{at}}(1.10)^{-t} - \text{Outlay}_C \right] - \left[\sum_{t=1}^{5} \text{NR}_{A_{at}}(1.10)^{-t} - \text{Outlay}_A \right]$$

$$= \left[\sum_{t=1}^{5} (1.10)^{-t}(\text{NR}_{C_{at}} - \text{NR}_{A_{at}}) - (\text{Outlay}_C - \text{Outlay}_A) \right]$$

which is the present value of the *incremental cash inflows* of Plan C less the *incremental outlay* of Plan C.

EXHIBIT 14-5————————————————————————————————————

Incremental Cash Flows

			YEAR (t)			
	0	**1**	**2**	**3**	**4**	**5**
Difference in outlay, Plan B—Plan A	−$6,520					
Difference in yearly cash inflows, Plan B—Plan A		$1,870	$1,630	$1,390	$1,150	$2,950
Discount factors @ 10%	1.0	.909	.826	.751	.683	.621
Present value of incremental flows	−$6,520	$1,700	$1,346	$1,044	$ 785	$1,832
Incremental inflows of Plan B	$6,707					
Incremental outlay of Plan B	6,520					
Incremental excess present value	$ 187					

In both cases the interpretation is as follows: The incremental outlays for Plans B and C ($6,520 and $10,120, respectively) will purchase incremental cash inflows over those generated by Plan A equipment. The present values of these incremental cash inflows exceed the incremental outlays, indicating that incremental investments in either set of new equipment will earn in excess of the appropriate cost-of-capital rate.

We illustrate the replacement problem by treating the cash flows of the present equipment as a separate decision. The number of calculations is the same, because we must measure the cash flows of all three sets of equipment regardless of how we display the analysis. Therefore, reporting the cash flows of the present equipment has a relatively low cost and may provide useful information in the event that a liquidation of the present equipment is a viable alternative.

Internal Rate of Return Versus Excess Present Value

We can now illustrate how the two discounting criteria can produce different rankings. Using the excess present value criterion, Plan C is preferred over Plan B, which is preferred over Plan A.

Let us now determine the internal rate of return of each project. This will require that we find r^* such that the following three equations hold:

$$\sum_{t=1}^{5} \text{NR}_{\text{A}at}(1 + r^*)^{-t} = \$11,480 \qquad [14\text{--}1]$$

$$\sum_{t=1}^{5} NR_{B_{at}}(1 + r^*)^{-t} = \$18,000 \qquad\qquad [14\text{--}2]$$

$$\sum_{t=1}^{5} NR_{C_{at}}(1 + r^*)^{-t} = \$21,600 \qquad\qquad [14\text{--}3]$$

For Plan A, $r^* \cong 20\%$; for Plan B, $r^* \cong 18\%$; and for Plan C, $r^* \cong 18\%$ (rounding off to the nearest whole percent in Table 14-2). Actually, the present values of the net cash inflows for the three plans at the interest rates indicated are \$11,452 (Plan A), \$17,489 (Plan B), and \$20,842 (Plan C). This means that each plan earns slightly less than the stated rates.[13]

Thus, according to the internal rate of return, Plan A is preferred over Plans B and C, which is different from the ranking obtained under the excess present value criterion. The internal rate of return actually reflects the return per dollar of investment, which implies that Plan A generates returns more efficiently than Plans B and C.[14] However, if the discount rate we use to find the present values of the inflows (10 percent) is a proper measure of the opportunity cost of providing funds to each of these investments, then it does not matter that Plan A returns more per dollar of investment. The firm's management can maximize the wealth of the owners by investing in projects that have the highest excess present value, always assuming the correct discount rates are applied. (See Chapter 15 for further discussion of this problem.)

In line with this, we might argue that Plan C probably constitutes a different class of investment. That is, special-purpose equipment generally has a thinner salvage market than general-purpose equipment. As a consequence, the salvage value of Plan C equipment would probably be low relative to the salvage values of the other two sets of equipment at any point in time from $t = 0$ to $t = 5$. The question, then, is whether the same discount rate should be applied to all three classes of equipment.

To illustrate the nature of the problem, suppose we used only a one-year horizon in the evaluation of the three plans. Offhand, we would expect the salvage value of Plan C equipment at the end of the first year to be a smaller percentage of its original outlay than the salvage values of Plans A and B equipment. Let us use the following hypothetical salvage values for

---

[13] That is, we would have to move to a lower interest column to solve the equation for each plan. In fact, the precise rates are 19.89, 16.81, and 16.48 percent.

[14] A variation of this criterion, designed to give the same result, requires that we divide the present values of the inflows of each investment by their respective outlays. The result is called the "present value index" and indicates the efficiency with which each project generates present values of inflows. For A, the index is \$14,735/\$11,480 = 1.28; for B, it is \$21,442/\$18,000 = 1.19; and for C, it is \$25,388/\$21,600 = 1.18. However, there is no conceptual basis for using this index, assuming capital markets are efficient and the proper discount rate is used to compute present values.

year 1 and, to simplify the analysis, we ignore losses on the sale of the assets: salvage for A = $9,500, salvage for B = $15,000, and salvage for C = $16,000 (a 25 percent decline in one year). The analysis would now indicate that Plan C no longer promises an excess present value. This is shown in Exhibit 14-6.

These are hypothetical figures, but they illustrate the kind of problem that may arise in practice when an attempt is made to compare alternatives

EXHIBIT 14-6

Analysis for One Year
for Plans A, B, and C

	End of Year 0	End of Year 1
Plan A		
Effective outlay	($11,480)	
Inflows		
Operating		$ 3,560
Salvage		9,500
Totals	($11,480)	$13,060
Present values (at 10%)		
Inflows	$11,871	
Outlay	(11,480)	
Excess present value	$ 391	
Plan B		
Outlay	($18,000)	
Inflows		
Operating		$ 5,430
Salvage		15,000
Totals	($18,000)	$20,430
Present values (at 10%)		
Inflows	$18,571	
Outlay	(18,000)	
Excess present value	$ 571	
Plan C		
Outlay	($21,600)	
Inflows		
Operating		$ 6,724
Salvage		16,000
Totals	($21,600)	$22,724
Present values (at 10%)		
Inflows	$20,656	
Outlay	(21,600)	
Excess present value (Negative)	($ 944)	

that may not be equivalent. Later on we discuss practical approaches to this situation, but for the moment we shall assume that if alternatives do belong to different risk classes, appropriate discount rates can be found for each.

Nondiscounting Approaches to Investment Analysis

Two other criteria are used to rank investment alternatives, but neither relies on discounted cash flows in the analysis. These are the *payback method* and the *accounting rate of return method.*

Payback

The payback method bases the choice of investment alternatives on the number of time periods required for projects to generate net cash receipts equal to their investment outlays. For example, as can be seen in Exhibit 14-4, Plan A will recover its outlay of $11,480 in about 3.2 years; however, Plans B and C require slightly longer to recover their investment outlays of $18,000 and $21,600, respectively. Thus, the payback criterion would rank Plan A over the other alternatives.[15]

There is a more fundamental relationship between the internal rate of return method and the payback method, although its theoretical significance is not clear. Suppose we have a project that will generate constant net cash receipts (NR) over n periods. The payback for this project would be simply the ratio, Outlay/NR. The internal rate of return for the project would be determined by solving the equation

$$\text{Outlay} = \sum_{t=1}^{n} NR_t (1 + r^*)^{-t}$$

But $NR_1 = NR_2 = \cdots = NR_n$, so the NR term can be factored out

$$\text{Outlay} = NR \sum_{t=1}^{n} (1 + r^*)^{-t}$$

Since the sum of the present value factors can be represented by the annuity formula (Table 14-4), this gives us

$$\text{Outlay} = NR \left[\frac{1 - \left(\frac{1}{1 + r^*}\right)^n}{r^*} \right]$$

---

[15] This happens to be consistent with the ranking of the internal rate of return criterion. However, this is coincidental.

Rearranging,

$$r^* = \frac{NR}{Outlay}\left[1 - \left(\frac{1}{1+r^*}\right)^n\right] = \frac{NR}{Outlay} - \frac{NR}{Outlay}\left(\frac{1}{1+r^*}\right)^n$$

Assuming $r^* > 0$, as n approaches infinity, the fraction $(1/1 + r^*)^n$ approaches zero; or

$$\lim_{n \to \infty} \frac{NR}{Outlay}\left(\frac{1}{1+r^*}\right)^n = 0$$

in which case, r^* is approximately equal to NR/Outlay, or to the reciprocal of the payback period. As n becomes large, the reciprocal of the payback period becomes a good estimate of a project's internal rate of return.[16] In general, the reciprocal of the payback period will overestimate the internal rate of return of a project by the amount

$$\frac{NR}{Outlay}\left(\frac{1}{1+r^*}\right)^n$$

(see the equations above).

A manager's reliance on the payback method for investment decisions suggests a conservative approach to investment analysis. We cannot be too critical of this attitude; in an uncertain world, it is intuitively appealing to rely more heavily on estimates associated with time periods less distant in the future. The payback method stresses the minimum number of time periods required to recoup the investment outlay and may motivate management to rely less on predictions of revenues and costs associated with time periods beyond the payback period.[17]

This particular feature of the payback method has also been a source of criticism of the method. By its nature, the payback method ignores the profitability of a project beyond the payback period. However, the method

---

[16] A more general and comprehensive treatment of this subject is given by M. Gordon, who first pointed out the relationship between the internal rate of return and the payback method. See M. Gordon, "The Payoff Period and the Rate of Profit," *J. of Business*, October 1955.

[17] The use of payback in this manner seems to have been a factor in the sequence of decisions made by the management of Convair during the development of the first jet airliners. Since it was difficult to estimate the total number of jets that would be sold, each new decision was conditioned by the likelihood of recouping investment outlays. See "How a Great Corporation Got Out of Control, Part I," *Fortune*, Jan. 1962, and Part II, Feb. 1962.

can be made more meaningful if we adjust for this factor. For every project, we can define the payback period as that period, PB, for which

$$\sum_{t=1}^{PB} NR_t = \text{Outlay}$$

where we sum up to the payback period, PB. Every project has a salvage value (sometimes negative) that can be estimated at various points in time. Therefore, the payback period can be defined as the shortest time span PB for which the following equality holds:

$$\sum_{t=1}^{PB} NR_t + \text{Salvage}_{PB} = \text{Cost outlay}$$

If we assume that the salvage value of a project at any point in time reflects (somewhat) the present value of the future cash flows generated by the project, then this modified method for computing the payback period should adjust for the profitability of a project beyond its payback period.

For example, consider the two projects for which data are given in Exhibit 14-7, only one of which can be accepted.

A decision based on the unadjusted payback method favors Project 1, and it is clear that the estimates of cash flows for the five time periods indicate that Project 2 has the highest excess present value. If the marketplace ranks the two projects in a similar manner, then it is reasonable to assume that their relative market values at the end of the first period, second period, third period, and so on, would reflect the more profitable flows of Project 2. Therefore, a comparison of the two projects on the assumption that they are salvaged after one year, two years, three years, and so on, should indicate the relative profitability of Project 2 over Project 1.

_____EXHIBIT 14-7

	Project 1	Project 2
Outlay at $t=0$	($1,000)	($5,000)
Inflows		
$t=1$	500	1,000
$t=2$	500	1,500
$t=3$	300	2,500
$t=4$	200	2,500
$t=5$	150	2,100
Excess present value @ 10%	$323	$2,038
Payback (as normally calculated)	2 periods	3 periods
Internal rate of return	24%	23%

Accounting Rate of Return

It is traditional in accounting to assume that the ratio of net annual income to beginning total investment is a measure of a firm's efficiency. If we ignore problems in measuring income and total investment, this is a reasonable assumption. A firm that earns the most income per dollar of investment is probably the most efficient firm in its risk class. It may also be reasonable to expect that firms that were efficient in the past will continue to be efficient in the future. This is the normal assumption underlying the use of the accounting rate of return as a basis for ranking firms as investment alternatives.

However, this criterion may not be valid for management's decisions about investment proposals. The accounting rate of return (ARR) does not take into account directly the differences between the timing of cash flows of different investment proposals. Moreover, if the periodic flows are not constant, it is necessary to average the flows in order to determine net annual income. Finally, there is some controversy over whether the calculation of the accounting rate of return should be based on the original outlay of each project or on the average investment in the project over its useful life (outlay divided by 2). Since the calculation of periodic income requires a deduction for depreciation, the investment in the project declines with this write-off.

We can illustrate some of these problems by again referring to the decision problem concerning Plans A, B, and C. The total after-tax income from each project is merely the sum of operating net cash receipts less (plus) the sum of noncash deductions (gains). The calculations are as follows:

	Total operating cash flows	−	Total depreciation	−	Losses (+ Gains)	=	Total income	Average income
Plan A	$17,800	−	$10,000		. . .	=	$ 7,800	$1,560
Plan B	$24,750	−	$15,000	+	$2,000	=	$11,750	$2,350
Plan C	$30,740	−	$18,000	−	$1,100	=	$11,640	$2,328

Using the original investment as the base, the respective accounting rates of return are[18]

$$ARR_A = \$1,560/\$12,000 = 13.00\%$$
$$ARR_B = \$2,350/\$18,000 = 13.06\%$$
$$ARR_C = \$2,328/\$21,600 = 10.78\%$$

---

[18] We use 12,000 as the base for Plan A because if the old equipment were retained the book value would not be adjusted downward to its current market price. This is consistent with the traditional historical cost principle of asset valuation in accounting.

Our rankings are now inverted relative to those obtained using the excess present value criterion. The inversion occurs primarily because the accounting rate of return weights all flows equally regardless of the time period in which they occur. Thus, the higher cash flows in the early years under Plans B and C are not given higher relative weights to counteract their higher investment outlays. This is ridiculous, because under most circumstances individuals would prefer to receive higher cash flows from an investment in earlier years than in later ones.[19]

REVIEW PROBLEM 2
Comparison of Investment Rules

Assume your firm is contemplating the replacement of some present equipment with equipment R. Information on the two alternatives available to the firm—that is, keep present equipment or acquire R—is shown below.

The marginal tax rate is 40 percent (to keep the arithmetic simple). Output sells for $10 per unit regardless of how it is produced. Depreciation information is based on the firm's tax rules.

Prepare an analysis of the cash flows associated with each alternative. Show your answers as indicated below.

(1) *Keep old equipment*

Present salvage value	$5,000
Present book value	$6,000
Cash operating costs:	
Variable	$6 per unit
Fixed	$10,000 per year
Remaining life	3 years
Salvage after 3 years	0
Present output	5,000 units per year
Depreciation method	straight line

Complete the following:

YEARS

Cash Flow Items	0	1	2	3
Cash foregone if asset is kept (including any tax adjustments)	_____			
After-tax operating inflows		_____	_____	_____
Tax effect of depreciation		_____	_____	_____
Net salvage (after tax)				_____

---

[19] If tax rates are expected to decline in the future, however, higher gross cash flows would be preferred in *later* years.

(2) *Equipment R*

Outlay price	$15,000
Useful life (IRS guidelines)	5 years
Salvage value (5 years)	$1,500
Salvage value (3 years)	$3,500
Cash operating costs:	
Variable	$4 per unit
Fixed	$15,000 per year
Expected output	5,000 units per year
Investment credit	appropriate for 5-year asset—taken in year 0[20]
Depreciation method	sum-of-the-years' digits (ignoring salvage up to 10% of cost)

Complete the following

YEARS

Cash Flow Items	0	1	2	3
Outlay	_____			
Investment credit	_____			
After-tax operating inflows		_____	_____	_____
Tax benefit of depreciation		_____	_____	_____
Salvage proceeds—gross				_____
Tax adjustment on salvage transaction				_____

(3) Suppose the total yearly cash flows for the two prospects in (a) and (b) were as follows:

YEAR

	0	1	2	3
(1) Keep	−$ 6,000	+$ 5,000	+$ 5,000	+$ 5,000
(2) Buy new	− 16,000	+ 10,000	+ 11,000	+ 12,000

(a) If the firm follows the excess present value rule and uses a 12 percent cost of capital rate for this project, should the firm:

(1) Keep the old asset irrespective of the attractiveness of the new asset? Show calculations given the following discount factors:

Year

	0	1	2	3
Factors	1.0	.90	.80	.70

Sum = 2.40

---

[20] The rates are 10 percent for an asset with $n \geq 7$; $\frac{2}{3}$(10 percent) for assets when n is 5 or 6; $\frac{1}{3}$(10 percent) if n is 3 or 4; and zero if $n < 3$. If the asset is sold prior to the year assumed to calculate the credit, re-calculate in that year and pay the government any excess to which you were not entitled at zero penalty interest.

(2)   Or sell the old and *buy* the new? Show calculations.
(b)   Set up the equations to calculate the internal rates of return for each investment alternative using the cash flow figures in (3) above. What decision would you recommend now?
(c)   Using the figures in (3) above, what is the payback period for each project?
(d)   Given your answers to (1) and (2), compute and compare the accounting rate of return for each project.

Investment Criteria and Accounting Measurements

We have now presented four rules for determining whether to invest in a long-lived asset: excess present value, internal rate of return, payback, and accounting rate of return. Note that all four criteria process essentially the same accounting measurements. In particular, the analysis of investment proposals rests on estimates of future revenues (if any), future cash expenses, and future taxes, and therefore on future noncash expenses. The particular criterion employed merely determines how these future flows will be analyzed. Since the way in which these flows are processed will have some effect on the decision maker's decision, we shall give some consideration here to theoretical underpinnings of the different criteria.

Unfortunately, the demands of practice exceed the capabilities of extant theory. From Chapter 4 we know that the economic theory of the firm is in a state of flux, and this fact affects long-run decision making as well. Under perfect market conditions and certainty, the excess present value criterion, with the discount rate interpreted as a market price of funds, has considerable appeal. Markets, of course, are not perfect. Uncertainty exists regardless of whether we formally acknowledge its presence, and insurance markets are limited. Thus, market value considerations do not provide an unassailable guide to action. In this sense, theory points toward discounting expected values at a rate consistent with the project's risk. Remember, however, that this approach entails an extrapolation of today's theory.[21]

It seems reasonable to prefer a discounting approach to investment analysis over a nondiscounting approach, provided we can determine the appropriate discount rate to use. We will begin by assuming that a firm's management is responsible for maximizing the present value of the owners' wealth. The

---

[21] A major issue here is analysis of possible tax effects, yet our theory rests almost entirely on a tax-free economic assumption. For detailed discussions, see J. Van Horne, *Financial Managemental Policy,* Englewood Cliffs, N.J.: Prentice-Hall, 1980; C. Haley and L. Schall, *The Theory of Financial Decisions,* New York: McGraw-Hill, 1979; E. Fama and M. Miller, *The Theory of Finance,* New York: Holt, Rinehart and Winston, 1972; E. Fama, "Risk-Adjusted Discount Rates and Capital Budgeting under Uncertainty," *J. of Financial Economics,* Aug. 1977; and H. DeAngelo, "Competition and Unanimity," *American Economic Rev.,* March 1981. Application of these considerations to income measurement is available in W. Beaver and J. Demski, "The Nature of Income Measurement," *Accounting Rev.,* Jan. 1977.

owners' wealth is partly a function of the expected net receipts that will be generated by the firm's productive assets. If the firm is a corporation whose ownership claims are traded in the securities market, the owners' wealth can be measured at any point in time by the aggregate market value of the securities outstanding (that is, price of each type of security multiplied by the number of each). Under these conditions, a firm's management should invest in an asset if the investment promises either to maintain or to increase the market value of the owners' securities. In perfect capital markets, this effect will be achieved if the discount rate used to calculate the present value of the asset's net cash inflows is commensurate with the asset's risk.

In an uncertain world, the riskiness of an individual asset is often represented by the "variance of the future return around its expected value."[22] That is, the future return of an asset is actually a random variable with some probability distribution. "The variance of a random variable is a commonly used measure of the dispersion of the probability distribution of that variable. As such, it can be used to indicate the degree of uncertainty with which expectations of the future are held."[23] However, if we wish to consider "riskiness," attention to individual assets may not be appropriate; instead we should consider the riskiness of a *portfolio* of assets.

Investment rules have recently been developed for the optimal management of portfolios of assets that are based on the overall expected return from all the assets in a portfolio and the variance of this overall return. The expected return of a portfolio is defined as the weighted sum of the expected returns of the individual assets. The variance of the portfolio's rate of return is the weighted sum of the variances of the rates of return of each asset in the portfolio plus the weighted sum of the covariances of these rates of return.[24] The weights are determined on the basis of the fractional amounts of the total portfolio investment represented by each asset.

Obviously, a firm can be viewed as a portfolio of productive assets, and the expected rate of return of this portfolio and its variance can be measured in the same manner (that is, in terms of individual variances and covariances). Therefore, an investment in a new asset can be evaluated in terms of how it is expected to affect the portfolio's rate of return and its variance.

A general rule for portfolio management is to minimize the variance for an expected rate of return from the portfolio or, equivalently, to maximize the expected rate of return for a given variance. This rule assumes that invest-

---

[22] R. Ball and P. Brown, "Portfolio Theory and Accounting," *J. of Accounting Research,* Autumn 1969, p. 301. Here we mean by variance the expected value of the squared deviations of the random variable around its mean.

[23] *Ibid.*

[24] The covariance between two random variables X_i, X_j is measured as

$$\text{Covar}(X_i X_j) = E[(X_i - E(X_i))(X_j - E(X_j))]$$

where E is the expectation operator.

ments are made by risk-averse investors who will accept more risk only if the expected compensation (rate of return) is increased accordingly. It would be a difficult rule to put into operation if all the inputs to the portfolio model had to be measured directly. Fortunately, it can be shown that under certain (restrictive) assumptions about the workings of the capital market, it is not necessary to measure the individual variances and covariances of the assets making up a portfolio.

The portfolio model has been extended to indicate that the expected rate of return on any one asset can be represented as a linear function of the expected rate of return for all assets traded in the economy.[25] For example, Sharpe has proposed that the expected one-period future rate of return on any asset i can be represented as:

$$E(R_i) = R_f + [E(\tilde{R}_m) - R_f] \frac{\text{Covar} (\tilde{R}_i, \tilde{R}_m)}{\text{Var} (\tilde{R}_m)}$$

where R_f can be interpreted as the available return to all investors on a risk-free asset, Var $(\tilde{R}_m)$ is the variance of the market rate of return $(\tilde{R}_m)$, and Covar $(\tilde{R}_i, \tilde{R}_m)$ is the covariance between the rate of return on asset i and the market rate of return.[26] (The terms with tildes, $\tilde{R}_i$ and $\tilde{R}_m$, denote random variables.) The fraction on the right is a measure of the risk of asset i relative to the risk of the market rate of return.

Even this would be difficult to measure in practice if Covar $(\tilde{R}_i, \tilde{R}_m)$ had to be estimated directly. However, if we can assume that market factors alone account for the riskiness of individual assets, then a simple regression model may be used to estimate the required rate of return for an asset. Letting I_m stand for an index of market performance, the rate of return of an asset can be estimated as

$$R_i = \alpha_i + \beta_i(I_m) + \epsilon_i$$

where ϵ_i is an error term satisfying the traditional assumptions of the regression model.[27] (This is the so-called "single-index" model.)

This is only a sketchy description of a complex theory of investment decisions under uncertainty. Moreover, we have ignored how (whether) differ-

---

[25] The extensions are the so-called capital-asset pricing models. See, for example, G. Foster, *Financial Statement Analysis,* Englewood Cliffs, N.J.: Pentice-Hall, 1979, Chapter 8 and the references therein.

[26] The assumptions underlying the Sharpe model are summarized in Ball and Brown, p. 306. As Fama indicates, equilibrium in the capital market would not be achieved unless the market return in this model represents the return from all the risky assets traded in the market. See E. Fama, "Risk, Return and Equilibrium: Some Clarifying Comments," *J. of Finance,* March 1968.

[27] In particular, the expected value of the error term is zero, it is assumed to have a constant variance around its mean over all observations, and the error terms are not correlated with the independent variable, I_m, or with each other.

ential tax rates on individuals and firms may affect equilibrium conditions in the capital market.[28] While this theory is constantly in a state of development, its implications for capital investment are straightforward.

The theory indicates that the required rate of return on any asset depends on the expected average rate of return on all assets traded in the economy. This is intuitively appealing, since in a competitive economy an investor can trade in numerous types of assets, and there is no reason to believe that the prices, and hence the rates of return, of these assets would be totally independent of one another. The theory also indicates that the required rate of return on any asset is the sum of the rate of return on what can be interpreted as a risk-free asset and the risk premium consisting of the difference between the average rate of return on all assets and the risk-free rate of return weighted by the fraction, Covar $(\tilde{R}_i, \tilde{R}_m)/\text{Var } (\tilde{R}_m)$. Note that the variance of the rate of return on any individual asset is not important as a measure of its riskiness. Rather, the appropriate measure of risk is the covariance between the asset's return and the rate on all assets traded in the economy. (Naturally, this same observation applies to the analysis of short-run risk and return trade-offs discussed in Chapter 4.)

This theory has been tested in the securities market, which has many of the characteristics of an efficient competitive market.[29] The same theory should also apply to productive assets, since the securities of a firm are nothing more than the claims on the earnings of these productive assets. However, measuring the required rate of return for a productive asset would require estimates of the covariances between the rates of return of productive assets and the market rate of return (under the same assumptions as the capital–asset pricing model referred to earlier; see footnote 25). The rate of return of any asset during period t is defined as the ratio

$$R_t = \frac{(\text{Net cash receipts})_t + (\text{Market price})_t - (\text{Market price})_{t-1}}{(\text{Market price})_{t-1}}$$

where the market price is the selling price of the asset at the two points in time. But a firm's productive assets are not traded extensively in the market, so their market prices are not directly available. One possibility is to use index numbers to determine the prices of used assets, but they are subject to various types of measurement errors.[30]

---

[28] See for example, R.H. Litzenberger and K. Ramaswany, "The Effects of Personal Taxes and Dividends on Capital Asset Prices: Theory and Empirical Evidence," *J. of Financial Economics,* June 1979.

[29] Efficient markets are defined in E. Fama, "Efficient Capital Markets: A Review of Theory and Empirical Work," *J. of Finance,* May 1970.

[30] One of the major problems in constructing index numbers is allowing for improved technology in new assets relative to used assets. It is difficult to assign values to improved technology and, therefore, to establish the value of a used asset at any point in time. A more sophisticated approach is treating the project's return as some "combination" of those available in the market. This then allows for an indirect pricing argument. See Haley and Schall, especially Chapter 17.

There is an alternative approach to this problem. Suppose there exists a firm which holds only one class of productive assets, where a "class" comprises a portfolio of assets whose performance differs from the portfolios of other firms holding that class by only a scale factor. Portfolios in the same class are subject to identical probability distributions of returns. The securities of this firm are traded in the market, and investors have the same expectations regarding the average expected earnings, $E(\overline{X})$, of the firm's class of productive assets. In equilibrium, the prices of such a firm's securities should adjust to reflect the market's assessment of the required rate of return on the firm's assets relative to the rates of return on all other assets in the economy. The required rate of return on this class of assets can be measured by[31]

$$\frac{E(\overline{X})}{\text{Market value of all securities}}$$

assuming the expected earnings extend into perpetuity.

It is reasonable to assume that over time the management of a firm that holds only one class of assets can estimate the required rate of return on its class of assets. Any other firm that anticipates an investment in the same class of assets can use the same required rate of return to evaluate the expected net cash flows. Thus, it is not uncommon for managers who deal in real estate to have an intuitive idea of the required rates of return of the classes of rental properties they hold, or for managers who invest in oil drilling to have an intuitive idea of the required rate of return from drilling, and so on.

In effect, we have taken a long route to arrive at a very simple operational rule for investment analysis. The accountant prepares estimates of the net cash flows that would occur in each period if the investment alternative were accepted. He or she would then use the discount rate that management feels is appropriate for the type of investment contemplated to discount these flows to their net excess present value. The required rate is assumed to be management's best estimate of the rate of return required to compensate the owners of the firm for the risk associated with an acceptance of the investment. The analysis completely ignores how the investment may be financed—whether by bonds, stocks, or internal cash generation.[32] The financial structure of the firm determines how security holders share in the risk of the firm's investment and how they receive their compensation for risk-

---

[31] This is a fundamental assumption followed by F. Modigliani and M.H. Miller in "The Cost of Capital, Corporation Finance and the Theory of Investment," *American Economic Rev.,* June 1958. The main objective of their article was to establish the independence between the required investment rate for an asset and its method of financing under appropriate market conditions.

[32] Again ignoring any potential effects of differential tax rates imposed on corporations and individuals and on different financial instruments. Further notice that the discount rate and cash flow estimates should also be price-level consistent. We would, presumably, discount price-level adjusted cash flows at a real rate, and unadjusted cash flows at a nominal rate.

taking. The required discount rate is determined by reference to the probability distributions of the cash flows generated by investments.

Admittedly, this is only a practical approach to the problem. However, at the very least it allows the individuals who bear the penalties for choosing the wrong discount rates—management—to determine what the investment rate should be.

Sensitivity Analysis in Capital Budgeting.   Sensitivity analysis may give management some insight into the relative risks of projects that appear at first to be in the same risk class. Several authors have proposed that the cash flow estimates used in an investment analysis be varied in order to assess the sensitivity of the investment decision to potential forecasting errors in the cash flows. As in any other kind of sensitivity analysis, estimates of revenues, cash expenses (including the effects of taxes), salvage values, and length of project lives could be systematically varied to determine the range and distribution of excess present values and internal rates of return should different events affecting cash flows occur in the future. The analysis would reveal which projects were more sensitive to particular forecasting errors. More important, it would also give some indication about the relative riskiness of different projects. This is the basic thrust of an approach originally proposed by Hertz.[33]

Basically, his approach requires a decision maker to specify the range in which different cash flow items (revenues, expenses, and so on) could be observed, with some minimal probability assessments for this range—for example, optimistic, most likely, and pessimistic values. Assuming that the different flows are independent, an analyst could randomly draw different combinations of possible cash flow outcomes from each project. These outcomes would yield different excess present values or rates of return. If enough outcomes were simulated, they could be summarized as frequency distributions that could be used as the basis for assessing the probabilities of the possible outcomes of each project.

To illustrate, Figure 14-1 shows the probability curves for two projects. The shape of the curve for alternative A suggests that this project promises a 5 percent rate of return with near certainty. In contrast, alternative B has a higher probability of returning a rate in excess of 5 percent—for example, there is a probability of .20 for a rate $\geq$ 10 percent—but it also has a higher probability of yielding a negative rate of return. That is, the probability of B returning a rate $\geq$ 0 is only 80 percent, whereas A promises a positive return with a probability of almost 1.0.

If the assumptions underlying the simulation are valid, then we would conclude that alternative B is a riskier project even though the expected rate

---

[33] See D. Hertz, "Risk Analysis in Capital Investment," *Harvard Business Rev.*, Jan.–Feb. 1964.

FIGURE 14-1

Probability graph for rates of return for alternative projects.

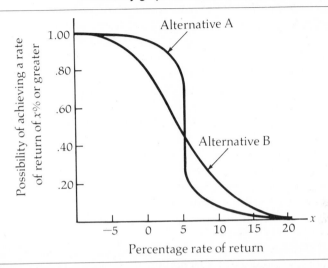

SOURCE: Reprinted by permission of the *Harvard Business Review.* Exhibit from "Investment Policies That Pay Off" by David B. Hertz (HBR, Jan.–Feb. 1964). Copyright © 1964 by the President and Fellows of Harvard College; all rights reserved.

of return for each is 5 percent.[34] Presumably, management could impose its preference for one project over another by varying the discount rate for the project with the greater risk. We should be careful in adopting this type of analysis. The required rates of return for projects in a competitive economy as sketched above are a function of the covariance of their returns with some market index. At best, the above approach represents an ad hoc way of determining the extent to which the cash flows of competing projects vary in the same manner in response to a common set of external events affecting the firm.

Theory Versus Practice

The conceptual superiority of the excess present value criterion in a setting of perfect markets under certainty has been accepted for some time. Yet not all firms adopt this method of analysis, and some even employ nondis-

---

[34] The main assumption that may be violated in practice is the one of independence. Revenues and expenses may be correlated, or changes in salvage values may encourage responses affecting the years of useful life. Thus, a more reasonable simulation may require drawing appropriate combinations of cash flow items based on their partial correlation coefficients. It is doubtful that these correlation coefficients are known.

counting criteria that are difficult to rationalize from a theoretical standpoint. However, we should be careful in evaluating these practices.[35]

First, many investment decisions by firms are somewhat automatic, since the alternatives available to them are limited. For example, firms are often faced with the decision to replace or not to replace a worn-out asset. The optimal decision may be intuitively obvious if the only alternative is to discontinue operations. In such cases, formal analyses of investment proposals are not required.

Second, a firm can use rule-of-thumb methods to screen projects that are obviously unacceptable. The payback criterion is easily implemented, and if the payback period of an investment almost coincides with its useful life, the chances are the project would not meet a required discounted rate of return.

Third, the different criteria often lead to the same rankings of investment alternatives, so firms would make similar decisions even if they employed different methods.[36] Fourth, the excess present value criterion is clearly superior only if the assumptions about the operations of capital markets and investors' expectations generally hold.

Finally, there has been speculation that managers may be influenced by accounting measurements of income—present and prospective—when evaluating a possible investment in capital assets. The income reported by a firm in its annual report is based on allocations of the acquisition costs of assets that are used in the income-generating process. Unfortunately, there still exist many problems concerning the allocation of costs of long-lived assets, both tangible and intangible. Accountants do not adjust all asset book values to their current prices, and in some cases (for example, research and development) an asset is not recorded at all. The result is that current accounting income may be adversely affected by certain investment transactions even though the investment promises an excess present value. The question is whether managers will forego or delay investments in order to avoid reporting lower income in their annual reports.

They may, but there are restrictions on their ability to forego profitable cash flows in favor of higher accounting incomes. After all, the owners of the firm may replace them with managers who may better act in the owners' interest(s). While we may question whether the competitive market for managerial talent works as efficiently as competitive markets for tangible goods, it is unlikely that none exists at all.[37] This, of course, returns us to the material of Chapter 5.

---

[35] One survey in the 1970s suggests a trend toward discounting methods. See T. Klammer, "Empirical Evidence of the Adoption of Sophisticated Capital Budgeting Techniques, *J. of Business*, July 1972.

[36] The relationship between the different methods is explored by M. Sarnat and H. Levy, "The Relationship of Rule of Thumb to the Internal Rate of Return: A Restatement and Generalization," *J. of Finance*, June 1969; also see their reference, 27.

[37] This issue is explored extensively by E. Fama, "Agency Problems and the Theory of the Firm," *J. of Political Economy*, April 1980.

Conclusion

Our main concern has been with the types of estimates that are essential to the implementation of various capital budgeting criteria. Fortunately, the four criteria discussed in this chapter all rely on the same types of accounting estimates: revenues from a project, the expenses incurred in generating the revenues, salvage values, and project lives. We discussed some of the conceptual issues concerning these different criteria because the specific criterion followed in a capital budgeting analysis has an influence on how the data should be displayed and the recommendations that will be made by an analyst. Various concerns about producing the essential estimates (along with value of information considerations) apply the ideas covered in Chapter 4.

In general, textbooks consistently recommend that investment decisions be made according to the excess present value rule. Certainly, the timing of cash flows and the risks associated with different investment projects should be factors in deciding whether to accept an investment alternative. The excess present value analysis handles these factors by using risk-adjusted interest rates in the discounting process. However, there are a number of implementation problems with this criterion, and we caution against a blind reliance on its superiority over other criteria for investment decisions.

In Chapter 15 we extend the discussion to consider conflicts between the two discounting criteria and investigate further the notion that the investment decision may be kept separate from the financing decision.

Appendix
Compound Interest: Notes and Tables

We have indicated that interest may be viewed as the cost of using capital. In terms of the management of corporate capital, the interest rate used in capital budgeting analysis represents the price that must be paid to compensate investors for the use of their funds to finance the operating assets of the firm.

The examples in the chapter illustrated the use of two kinds of interest formulas—the future value of an amount invested for n periods at a rate r, or $FV = PV(1 + r)^n$, and the present value of a sum to be received n periods from the present date, or $PV = FV(1 + r)^{-n}$. Two other general formulas are the future value of a series of n equal payments of $\$A$ and the present value of n equal payments of $\$A$. The latter two formulas facilitate the computations of future and present values of a long series of payments, providing these are all equal.

In addition to these discrete compounding formulas, capital budgeting analysis may also require the use of continuous discounting formulas in order to take into account the fact that the cash flows of a firm take place on a continuous basis.

This appendix illustrates the derivation and use of six compound interest formulas—four discrete and two continuous. Students who have studied compound interest in other courses may omit this appendix and proceed to the problems section.

Table 14-1. This table contains the values of $(1 + r)^n$ for different assumptions about r and n. Recall from the chapter that the future value of a lump sum PV invested for n periods at a rate r each period is equal to $PV(1 + r)^n$. For example, if $n = 2$ and $r = 4\%$, $PV(1.04)^2 = PV(1.0816)$, which is shown in Table 14-1 in the 4% column opposite $n = 2$.

Table 14-2. The present value of a lump sum to be received n interest periods from today can be calculated by reversing the process of finding future values. For example, if $PV(1 + r)^n = FV$, then

$$PV = \frac{FV}{(1 + r)^n} = FV(1 + r)^{-n}$$

Table 14-2 shows values for $(1 + r)^{-n}$ for different r and n. Since $(1.04)^2 = 1.0816$, it follows that

$$\frac{1}{(1.04)^2} = \frac{1}{1.0816} = 0.925$$

which appears in Table 14-2 in the second column $(r = 4\%)$ opposite $n = 2$.

Table 14-3: Future Value of an Annuity. Suppose n payments of amount A are to be invested at 4% (compounded). The first payment is invested in period 1, and the remaining $n - 1$ payments are spread out evenly over a time span of $n - 1$ periods. The sequence of payments and the number of periods during which each payment earns interest may be diagrammed as follows:

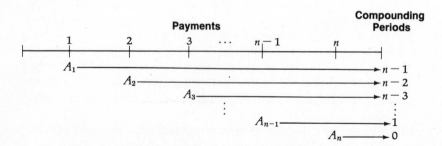

APPENDIX: COMPOUND INTEREST: NOTES AND TABLES

TABLE 14-1

Future Value of $1.00

$$FV = PV(1 + r)^n$$

n	2%	2½%	3%	4%	5%	6%	8%	10%
1	1.0200	1.0250	1.0300	1.0400	1.0500	1.0600	1.0800	1.1000
2	1.0404	1.0506	1.0609	1.0816	1.1025	1.1236	1.1664	1.2100
3	1.0612	1.0769	1.0927	1.1249	1.1576	1.1910	1.2597	1.3310
4	1.0824	1.1038	1.1255	1.1699	1.2155	1.2625	1.3605	1.4641
5	1.1041	1.1314	1.1593	1.2167	1.2763	1.3382	1.4693	1.6105
6	1.1262	1.1597	1.1941	1.2653	1.3401	1.4185	1.5869	1.7716
7	1.1487	1.1887	1.2299	1.3159	1.4071	1.5036	1.7138	1.9438
8	1.1717	1.2184	1.2668	1.3686	1.5775	1.5938	1.8509	2.1436
9	1.1951	1.2489	1.3048	1.4233	1.5513	1.6895	1.9990	2.3589
10	1.2190	1.2801	1.3439	1.4802	1.6289	1.7908	2.1589	2.5938
11	1.2434	1.3121	1.3842	1.5395	1.7103	1.8983	2.3316	2.8532
12	1.2682	1.3449	1.4258	1.6010	1.7959	2.0122	2.5182	3.1385
13	1.2936	1.3785	1.4685	1.6651	1.8856	2.1329	2.7196	3.4524
14	1.3195	1.4130	1.5126	1.7317	1.9799	2.2609	2.9372	3.7976
15	1.3459	1.4483	1.5580	1.8009	2.0709	2.3966	3.1722	4.1774
16	1.3728	1.4845	1.6047	1.8730	2.1829	2.5404	3.4259	4.5951
17	1.4002	1.5216	1.6528	1.9479	2.2920	2.6928	3.7000	5.0545
18	1.4282	1.5597	1.7024	2.0258	2.4066	2.8543	3.9960	5.5600
19	1.4568	1.5987	1.7535	2.1068	2.5270	3.0256	4.3157	6.1160
20	1.4859	1.6386	1.8061	2.1911	2.6533	3.2071	4.6610	6.7276
22	1.5460	1.7216	1.9161	2.3699	2.9253	3.6035	5.4365	8.1404
24	1.6084	1.8087	2.0328	2.5633	3.2251	4.0489	6.3412	9.8498
26	1.6734	1.9003	2.1566	2.7725	3.5557	4.5494	7.3964	11.9183
28	1.7410	1.9965	2.2879	2.9987	3.9201	5.1117	8.6271	14.4211
30	1.8114	2.0976	2.4273	3.2434	4.3219	5.7435	10.0627	17.4495
32	1.8845	2.2038	2.5751	3.5081	4.7649	6.4534	11.7371	21.1140
34	1.9607	2.3153	2.7319	3.7943	5.2533	7.2510	13.6901	25.5479
36	2.0399	2.4325	2.8983	4.1039	5.7918	8.1473	15.9682	30.9130
38	2.1223	2.5557	3.0748	4.4388	6.3855	9.1543	18.6253	37.4047
40	2.2080	2.6851	3.2620	4.8010	7.0400	10.2857	21.7245	45.2597
42	2.2972	2.8210	3.4607	5.1928	7.7616	11.5570	25.3395	54.7643
44	2.3901	2.9638	3.6715	5.6165	8.5572	12.9855	29.5560	66.2648
46	2.4866	3.1139	3.8950	6.0748	9.4343	14.5905	34.4741	80.1804
48	2.5871	3.2715	4.1323	6.5705	10.4013	16.3939	40.2106	97.0181
50	2.6916	3.4371	4.3839	7.1067	11.4674	18.4202	46.9016	117.3920
60	3.2810	4.3998	5.8916	10.5196	18.6792	32.9877	101.2571	304.4846

TABLE 14–2
Present value of $1.00

$$PV = FV(1 + r)^{-n}$$

n	2%	4%	6%	8%	10%	12%	14%	16%	18%	20%	22%	24%	26%	28%	30%	40%	50%
1	0.980	0.962	0.943	0.926	0.909	0.893	0.877	0.862	0.847	0.833	0.820	0.806	0.794	0.781	0.769	0.714	0.667
2	0.961	0.925	0.890	0.857	0.826	0.797	0.769	0.743	0.718	0.694	0.672	0.650	0.630	0.610	0.592	0.510	0.444
3	0.942	0.889	0.840	0.794	0.751	0.712	0.675	0.641	0.609	0.579	0.551	0.524	0.500	0.477	0.455	0.364	0.296
4	0.924	0.855	0.792	0.735	0.683	0.636	0.592	0.552	0.516	0.482	0.451	0.423	0.397	0.373	0.350	0.260	0.197
5	0.906	0.822	0.747	0.681	0.621	0.567	0.519	0.476	0.437	0.402	0.370	0.341	0.315	0.291	0.269	0.186	0.131
6	0.888	0.790	0.705	0.630	0.564	0.507	0.456	0.410	0.370	0.335	0.303	0.275	0.250	0.227	0.207	0.133	0.088
7	0.871	0.760	0.665	0.583	0.513	0.452	0.400	0.354	0.314	0.279	0.249	0.222	0.198	0.178	0.159	0.095	0.059
8	0.853	0.731	0.627	0.540	0.467	0.404	0.351	0.305	0.266	0.233	0.204	0.179	0.157	0.139	0.123	0.068	0.039
9	0.837	0.703	0.592	0.500	0.424	0.361	0.308	0.263	0.225	0.194	0.167	0.144	0.125	0.108	0.094	0.048	0.026
10	0.820	0.676	0.558	0.463	0.386	0.322	0.270	0.227	0.191	0.162	0.137	0.116	0.099	0.085	0.073	0.035	0.017
11	0.804	0.650	0.527	0.429	0.350	0.287	0.237	0.195	0.162	0.135	0.112	0.094	0.079	0.066	0.056	0.025	0.012
12	0.788	0.625	0.497	0.397	0.319	0.257	0.208	0.168	0.137	0.112	0.092	0.076	0.062	0.052	0.043	0.018	0.008
13	0.773	0.601	0.469	0.368	0.290	0.229	0.182	0.145	0.116	0.093	0.075	0.061	0.050	0.040	0.033	0.013	0.005
14	0.758	0.577	0.442	0.340	0.263	0.205	0.160	0.125	0.099	0.078	0.062	0.049	0.039	0.032	0.025	0.009	0.003
15	0.743	0.555	0.417	0.315	0.239	0.183	0.140	0.108	0.084	0.065	0.051	0.040	0.031	0.025	0.020	0.006	0.002
16	0.728	0.534	0.394	0.292	0.218	0.163	0.123	0.093	0.071	0.054	0.042	0.032	0.025	0.019	0.015	0.005	0.002
17	0.714	0.513	0.371	0.270	0.198	0.146	0.108	0.080	0.060	0.045	0.034	0.026	0.020	0.015	0.012	0.003	0.001
18	0.700	0.494	0.350	0.250	0.180	0.130	0.095	0.069	0.051	0.038	0.028	0.021	0.016	0.012	0.009	0.002	0.001
19	0.686	0.475	0.331	0.232	0.164	0.116	0.083	0.060	0.043	0.031	0.023	0.017	0.012	0.009	0.007	0.002	
20	0.673	0.456	0.312	0.215	0.149	0.104	0.073	0.051	0.037	0.026	0.019	0.014	0.010	0.007	0.005	0.001	

21	0.660	0.439	0.294	0.199	0.135	0.093	0.064	0.044	0.031	0.022	0.015	0.011	0.008	0.006	0.004	0.001
22	0.647	0.422	0.278	0.184	0.123	0.083	0.056	0.038	0.026	0.018	0.013	0.009	0.006	0.004	0.003	0.001
23	0.634	0.406	0.262	0.170	0.112	0.074	0.049	0.033	0.022	0.015	0.010	0.007	0.005	0.003	0.002	
24	0.622	0.390	0.247	0.158	0.102	0.066	0.043	0.028	0.019	0.013	0.008	0.006	0.004	0.003	0.002	
25	0.610	0.375	0.233	0.146	0.092	0.059	0.038	0.024	0.016	0.010	0.007	0.005	0.003	0.002	0.001	
26	0.598	0.361	0.220	0.135	0.084	0.053	0.033	0.021	0.014	0.009	0.006	0.004	0.002	0.002	0.001	
27	0.586	0.347	0.207	0.125	0.076	0.047	0.029	0.018	0.011	0.007	0.005	0.003	0.002	0.001	0.001	
28	0.574	0.333	0.196	0.116	0.069	0.042	0.026	0.016	0.010	0.006	0.004	0.002	0.002	0.001	0.001	
29	0.563	0.321	0.185	0.107	0.063	0.037	0.022	0.014	0.008	0.005	0.003	0.002	0.001	0.001	0.001	
30	0.552	0.308	0.174	0.099	0.057	0.033	0.020	0.012	0.007	0.004	0.003	0.002	0.001	0.001		
40	0.453	0.208	0.097	0.046	0.022	0.011	0.005	0.003	0.001	0.001						
50	0.372	0.141	0.054	0.021	0.009	0.003	0.001	0.001								

TABLE 14-3

Future value of annuity of $1.00 in arrears

$$FV_a = \frac{(1+r)^n - 1}{r}$$

n	2%	2½%	3%	4%	5%	6%	8%	10%
1	1.0000	1.0000	1.0000	1.0000	1.0000	1.0000	1.0000	1.0000
2	2.0200	2.0250	2.0300	2.0400	2.0500	2.0600	2.0800	2.1000
3	3.0604	3.0756	3.0909	3.1216	3.1525	3.1836	3.2464	3.3100
4	4.1216	4.1525	4.1836	4.2465	4.3101	4.3746	4.5061	4.6410
5	5.2040	5.2563	5.3091	5.4163	5.5256	5.6371	5.8666	6.1051
6	6.3081	6.3877	6.4684	6.6330	6.8019	6.9753	7.3359	7.7156
7	7.4343	7.5474	7.6625	7.8983	8.1420	8.3938	8.9228	9.4872
8	8.5830	8.7361	8.8923	9.2142	9.5491	9.8975	10.6366	11.4360
9	9.7546	9.9545	10.1591	10.5828	11.0266	11.4913	12.4876	13.5796
10	10.9497	11.2034	11.4639	12.0061	12.5779	13.1808	14.4866	15.9376
11	12.1687	12.4835	12.8078	13.4864	14.2068	14.9716	16.6455	18.5314
12	13.4121	13.7956	14.1920	15.0258	15.9171	16.8699	18.9771	21.3846
13	14.6803	15.1404	15.6178	16.6268	17.7130	18.8821	21.4953	24.5231
14	15.9739	16.5190	17.0863	18.2919	19.5986	21.0151	24.2149	27.9755
15	17.2934	17.9319	18.5989	20.0236	21.5786	23.2760	27.1521	31.7731
16	18.6393	19.3802	20.1569	21.8245	23.6575	25.6725	30.3243	35.9503
17	20.0121	20.8647	21.7616	23.6975	25.8404	28.2129	33.7502	40.5456
18	21.4123	22.3863	23.4144	25.6454	28.1324	30.9057	37.4502	45.6001
19	22.8406	23.9460	25.1169	27.6712	30.5390	33.7600	41.4463	51.1601
20	24.2974	25.5447	26.8704	29.7781	33.0660	36.7856	45.7620	57.2761
22	27.2990	28.8629	30.5368	34.2480	38.5052	43.3923	55.4568	71.4041
24	30.4219	32.3490	34.4265	39.0826	44.5020	50.8156	66.7648	88.4989
26	33.6709	36.0117	38.5530	44.3117	51.1135	59.1564	79.9544	109.1835
28	37.0512	39.8598	42.9309	49.9676	58.4026	68.5281	95.3388	134.2119
30	40.5681	43.9027	47.5754	56.0849	66.4388	79.0582	113.2832	164.4962
32	44.2270	48.1503	52.5028	62.7015	75.2988	90.8898	134.2135	201.1402
34	48.0338	52.6129	57.7302	69.8579	85.0670	104.1838	158.6267	245.4796
36	51.9944	57.3014	63.2759	77.5983	95.8363	119.1209	187.1021	299.1302
38	56.1149	62.2273	69.1594	85.9703	107.7095	135.9042	220.3159	364.0475
40	60.4020	67.4026	75.4013	95.0255	120.7998	154.7620	259.0565	442.5974
42	64.8622	72.8398	82.0232	104.8196	135.2318	175.9505	304.2435	537.6428
44	69.5027	78.5523	89.0484	115.4129	151.1430	199.7580	356.9496	652.6478
46	74.3306	84.5540	96.5015	126.8706	168.6852	226.5081	418.4261	791.8039
48	79.3535	90.8596	104.4084	139.2632	188.0254	256.5645	490.1322	960.1827
50	84.5794	97.4843	112.7969	152.6671	209.3480	290.3359	573.7702	1163.9209
60	114.0515	135.9916	163.0534	237.9907	353.5837	533.1282	1253.2133	3034.8470

Note that the first payment earns interest for $n - 1$ periods, whereas the last payment does not earn any interest.

The question we are interested in is: What is the value of this sequence of payments at the end of period n, that is, at the date of the last payment?

This value may be obtained by summing the values of these payments as of this date. The first payment will build to a future value of $A_1(1 + r)^{n-1}$, the second to a future value of $A_2(1 + r)^{n-2}$, the third to a future value of $A_3(1 + r)^{n-3}$, etc., with the nth payment equal to $A_n(1 + r)^0$, or $A_n(1) = A_n$. If we let FV_a represent the future value of this series of payments, we may write it as

$$FV_a = A_n(1 + r)^0 + A_{n-1}(1 + r)^1 + A_{n-2}(1 + r)^2 + \cdots + A_3(1 + r)^{n-3}$$
$$+ A_2(1 + r)^{n-2} + A_1(1 + r)^{n-1} \quad [1]$$

Since $A_1 = A_2 = A_3 = \cdots = A_n = A$,

$$FV_a = A[(1 + r)^0 + (1 + r)^1 + (1 + r)^2 + \cdots + (1 + r)^{n-3}$$
$$+ (1 + r)^{n-2} + (1 + r)^{n-1}] \quad [2]$$

If we now multiply both sides of this equation by $(1 + r)$, we have

$$FV_a(1 + r) = A[(1 + r)^1 + (1 + r)^2 + (1 + r)^3 + \cdots + (1 + r)^{n-2}$$
$$+ (1 + r)^{n-1} + (1 + r)^n] \quad [3]$$

Subtracting [2] from [3] and canceling out the appropriate terms, we obtain

$$FV_a + rFV_a - FV_a = A[(1 + r)^n - (1 + r)^0]$$

and

$$FV_a = A\left(\frac{(1 + r)^n - (1 + r)^0}{r}\right) = A\left(\frac{(1 + r)^n - 1}{r}\right) \quad [4]$$

This is the formula for determining the future value of a series of equal payments, or the future value of an annuity, where A occurs at the end of the period.

Table 14-4: Present Value of an Annuity.   The sequence of cash flows in this situation is similar to the one associated with Table 14-3, except that we are now interested in the present value of a series of equal payments of amount A. Assume that the first payment is made one time period from now, the second two periods from now, and so on, with the nth payment made n periods from now. The sequence of payments and the periods of discount appear as shown on page 598.

TABLE 14-4

Present Value of an Annuity of $1.00 in Arrears

$$PV_a = \frac{1 - (1 + r)^{-n}}{r}$$

n	2%	4%	6%	8%	10%	12%	14%	16%	18%	20%	22%	24%	25%	26%	28%	30%	40%	50%
1	0.980	0.962	0.943	0.926	0.909	0.893	0.877	0.862	0.847	0.833	0.820	0.806	0.800	0.794	0.781	0.769	0.714	0.667
2	1.942	1.886	1.833	1.783	1.736	1.690	1.647	1.605	1.566	1.528	1.492	1.457	1.440	1.424	1.392	1.361	1.224	1.111
3	2.884	2.775	2.673	2.577	2.487	2.402	2.322	2.246	2.174	2.106	2.042	1.981	1.952	1.923	1.868	1.816	1.589	1.407
4	3.808	3.630	3.465	3.312	3.170	3.037	2.914	2.798	2.690	2.589	2.494	2.404	2.362	2.320	2.241	2.166	1.849	1.605
5	4.713	4.452	4.212	3.993	3.791	3.605	3.433	3.274	3.127	2.991	2.864	2.745	2.689	2.635	2.532	2.436	2.035	1.737
6	5.601	5.242	4.917	4.623	4.355	4.111	3.889	3.685	3.498	3.326	3.167	3.020	2.951	2.885	2.759	2.643	2.168	1.824
7	6.472	6.002	5.582	5.206	4.868	4.564	4.288	4.039	3.812	3.605	3.416	3.242	3.161	3.083	2.937	2.802	2.263	1.883
8	7.325	6.733	6.210	5.747	5.335	4.968	4.639	4.344	4.078	3.837	3.619	3.421	3.329	3.241	3.076	2.925	2.331	1.922
9	8.162	7.435	6.802	6.247	5.759	5.328	4.946	4.607	4.303	4.031	3.786	3.566	3.463	3.366	3.184	3.019	2.379	1.948
10	8.983	8.111	7.360	6.710	6.145	5.650	5.216	4.833	4.494	4.192	3.923	3.682	3.571	3.465	3.269	3.092	2.414	1.965
11	9.787	8.760	7.887	7.139	6.495	5.988	5.453	5.029	4.656	4.327	4.035	3.776	3.656	3.544	3.335	3.147	2.438	1.977
12	10.575	9.385	8.384	7.536	6.814	6.194	5.660	5.197	4.793	4.439	4.127	3.851	3.725	3.606	3.387	3.190	2.456	1.985
13	11.343	9.986	8.853	7.904	7.103	6.424	5.842	5.342	4.910	4.533	4.203	3.912	3.780	3.656	3.427	3.223	2.468	1.990
14	12.106	10.563	9.295	8.244	7.367	6.628	6.002	5.468	5.008	4.611	4.265	3.962	3.824	3.695	3.459	3.249	2.477	1.993
15	12.849	11.118	9.712	8.559	7.606	6.811	6.142	5.575	5.092	4.675	4.315	4.001	3.859	3.726	3.483	3.268	2.484	1.995
16	13.578	11.652	10.106	8.851	7.824	6.974	6.265	5.669	5.162	4.730	4.357	4.033	3.887	3.751	3.503	3.283	2.489	1.997
17	14.292	12.166	10.477	9.122	8.022	7.120	6.373	5.749	5.222	4.775	4.391	4.059	3.910	3.771	3.518	3.295	2.492	1.998
18	14.992	12.659	10.828	9.372	8.201	7.250	6.467	5.818	5.273	4.812	4.419	4.080	3.928	3.786	3.529	3.304	2.494	1.999
19	15.678	13.134	11.158	9.604	8.365	7.366	6.550	5.877	5.316	4.844	4.442	4.097	3.942	3.799	3.539	3.311	2.496	1.999
20	16.351	13.590	11.470	9.818	8.514	7.469	6.623	5.929	5.353	4.870	4.460	4.110	3.954	3.808	3.546	3.316	2.497	1.999

21	17.011	14.029	11.764	10.017	8.649	7.562	6.687	5.973	5.384	4.891	4.476	4.121	3.963	3.816	3.551	3.320	2.498	2.000
22	17.658	14.451	12.042	10.201	8.772	7.645	6.743	6.011	5.410	4.909	4.488	4.130	3.970	3.822	3.556	3.323	2.498	2.000
23	18.292	14.857	12.303	10.371	8.883	7.718	6.792	6.044	5.432	4.925	4.499	4.137	3.976	3.827	3.559	3.325	2.499	2.000
24	18.914	15.247	12.550	10.529	8.985	7.784	6.835	6.073	5.451	4.937	4.507	4.143	3.981	3.831	3.562	3.327	2.499	2.000
25	19.523	15.622	12.783	10.675	9.077	7.843	6.873	6.097	5.467	4.948	4.514	4.147	3.985	3.834	3.564	3.329	2.499	2.000
26	20.121	15.983	13.003	10.810	9.161	7.896	6.906	6.118	5.480	4.956	4.520	4.151	3.988	3.837	3.566	3.330	2.500	2.000
27	20.707	16.330	13.211	10.935	9.237	7.943	6.935	6.136	5.492	4.964	4.524	4.154	3.990	3.839	3.567	3.331	2.500	2.000
28	21.281	16.663	13.406	11.051	9.307	7.984	6.961	6.152	5.502	4.970	4.528	4.157	3.992	3.840	3.568	3.331	2.500	2.000
29	21.844	16.984	13.591	11.158	9.370	8.022	6.983	6.166	5.510	4.975	4.531	4.159	3.994	3.841	3.569	3.332	2.500	2.000
30	22.396	17.292	13.765	11.258	9.427	8.055	7.003	6.177	5.517	4.979	4.534	4.160	3.995	3.842	3.569	3.332	2.500	2.000
40	27.355	19.793	15.046	11.925	9.779	8.244	7.105	6.234	5.548	4.997	4.544	4.166	3.999	3.846	3.571	3.333	2.500	2.000
50	31.424	21.482	15.762	12.234	9.915	8.304	7.133	6.246	5.554	4.999	4.545	4.167	4.000	3.846	3.571	3.333	2.500	2.000

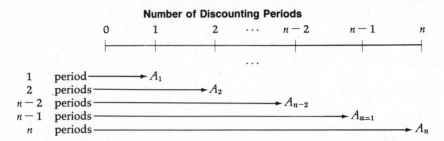

If we let PV_a represent the present value of this series of payments, we can write it as

$$PV_a = A\left[\frac{1}{(1+r)} + \frac{1}{(1+r)^2} + \cdot\cdot\cdot + \frac{1}{(1+r)^{n-2}} + \frac{1}{(1+r)^{n-1}} + \frac{1}{(1+r)^n}\right] \quad [5]$$

since $A_1 = A_2 = \cdot\cdot\cdot = A_n = A$, and we assume an interest rate of r. Multiplying both sides of [5] by $(1 + r)$, we have

$$(1+r)PV_a = A\left[1 + \frac{1}{(1+r)} + \frac{1}{(1+r)^2} + \cdot\cdot\cdot + \frac{1}{(1+r)^{n-3}} \right.$$

$$\left. + \frac{1}{(1+r)^{n-2}} + \frac{1}{(1+r)^{n-1}}\right] \quad [6]$$

Subtracting [5] from [6], we have

$$PV_a + rPV_a - PV_a = A\left[1 - \frac{1}{(1+r)^n}\right]$$

and

$$PV_a = A\left[\frac{1 - 1/(1+r)^n}{r}\right] = A\left[\frac{1 - (1+r)^{-n}}{r}\right]$$

Tables 14-5 and 14-6: Continuous Discounting.   The compound interest formulas illustrated above deal with cash flows that occur at discrete points of time and that are to be compounded at these times. In most capital budgeting analyses the assumption is that cash flows take place at the end of each year (or the beginning of each year) and that interest is compounded annually. In real life, of course, cash flows in and out of a firm on a continuous basis. Hence, continuous discounting formulas, which take into account the effects of cash flow turnovers and the receipts of cash on a continuous basis, are more accurate.

Table 14-5 shows the continuous discounting factors for adjusting an amount received or paid in a lump sum at the end of t periods from now at a rate of r. The formula is $PV = FV (e^{-rt})$, where $e = 2.718$ (approximately),

TABLE 14-5

Continuous Discount Factor

$PV = FV(e^{-rt})$

rt	e^{-rt}	rt	e^{-rt}	rt	e^{-rt}
.00	1.000	.30	.741	2.30	.100
.01	.990	.35	.705	2.40	.091
.02	.980	.40	.670	2.50	.082
.03	.970	.45	.638	2.60	.074
.04	.961	.50	.607	2.70	.067
.05	.951	.55	.577	2.80	.061
.06	.942	.60	.549	2.90	.055
.07	.932	.65	.522	3.00	.050
.08	.923	.70	.497	3.10	.045
.09	.914	.75	.472	3.20	.041
.10	.905	.80	.449	3.40	.033
.11	.896	.85	.427	3.60	.027
.12	.887	.90	.407	3.80	.022
.13	.878	.95	.387	4.00	.018
.14	.869	1.00	.368	4.20	.015
.15	.861	1.05	.350	4.40	.012
.16	.852	1.10	.333	4.60	.010
.17	.844	1.15	.317	4.80	.008
.18	.835	1.20	.301	5.00	.007
.19	.827	1.25	.287	5.50	.004
.20	.819	1.30	.273	6.00	.002
.21	.811	1.40	.247		
.22	.803	1.50	.223		
.23	.795	1.60	.202		
.24	.787	1.70	.183		
.25	.779	1.80	.165		
.26	.771	1.90	.150		
.27	.763	2.00	.135		
.28	.756	2.10	.122		
.29	.748	2.20	.111		

Taken from H. Bierman, Jr., L.E. Fouraker, and R.K. Jaedicke, *Quantitative Analysis for Business Decisions.* Homewood, Ill.: Irwin, 1961, p. 335.

r = interest rate per year, and t = time in years. These discounting factors assume that interest is compounded continuously during the time period rather than monthly, quarterly, or semiannually. Notice that for 10% and $t = 1$, the factor is .905, which is less than the discrete discount factor of .909 in Table 14-2 for $r = 10\%$.

TABLE 14-6————————————————————————————————

Factors for Discounting Cash Flows Spread Evenly Throughout
the Time Period $t-1$ to t

$$PV = FV\left[\frac{e^r - 1}{re^{rt}}\right]$$

Period ($t-1$ to t)	4%	5%	6%	8%	10%	12%	15%	18%	20%	25%
0–1	.9901	.9754	.9706	.9610	.9516	.9423	.9286	.9152	.9063	.8848
1–2	.9418	.9278	.9141	.8872	.8611	.8358	.7993	.7644	.7421	.6891
2–3	.9049	.8826	.8608	.8189	.7791	.7413	.6879	.6385	.6075	.5366
3–4	.8694	.8395	.8107	.7560	.7050	.6574	.5921	.5333	.4974	.4179
4–5	.8353	.7986	.7635	.6979	.6379	.5831	.5096	.4455	.4072	.3255
5–6	.8026	.7596	.7191	.6442	.5772	.5172	.4386	.3721	.3334	.2535
6–7	.7711	.7226	.6772	.5947	.5223	.4587	.3775	.3108	.2730	.1974
7–8	.7409	.6874	.6377	.5490	.4726	.4068	.3250	.2596	.2235	.1538
8–9	.7118	.6538	.6006	.5068	.4276	.3608	.2797	.2168	.1830	.1197
9–10	.6839	.6220	.5656	.4678	.3869	.3200	.2407	.1811	.1498	.0933
10–11	.6571	.5916	.5327	.4318	.3501	.2838	.2072	.1513	.1227	.0726
11–12	.6313	.5628	.5017	.3986	.3168	.2517	.1783	.1264	.1004	.0566
12–13	.6066	.5353	.5724	.3680	.2866	.2233	.1535	.1055	.0822	.0441
13–14	.5828	.5092	.4449	.3397	.2594	.1980	.1321	.0882	.0673	.0343
14–15	.5599	.4844	.4190	.3136	.2347	.1756	.1137	.0736	.0551	.0267
15–16	.5380	.4608	.3946	.2895	.2123	.1558	.0979	.0615	.0451	.0208
16–17	.5169	.4383	.3716	.2672	.1921	.1382	.0842	.0514	.0370	.0162
17–18	.4966	.4169	.3500	.2467	.1739	.1225	.0725	.0429	.0303	.0126
18–19	.4772	.3966	.3296	.2277	.1573	.1087	.0624	.0358	.0248	.0098
19–20	.4584	.3772	.3104	.2102	.1423	.0964	.0537	.0299	.0203	.0077

Table 14-6 gives the adjustment factors for discounting on a continuous basis an amount received or paid continuously during time period t. This formula would be appropriate for discounting yearly sales receipts or yearly production costs that are spread out evenly during the year. The formula is

$$PV = FV\left[\frac{e^r - 1}{re^{rt}}\right]$$

Supplementary Readings—————————————————————————

Articles

Ball, R., and P. Brown, "Portfolio Theory and Accounting," *J. of Accounting Research*, Autumn 1969.

Davidson, S., and D. Drake, "Selecting the Best Depreciation Policy," *J. of Business*,

Oct. 1961; a later version is "The 'Best' Tax Depreciation Method—1964," July 1964.

Fama, E., "Efficient Capital Markets: A Review of Theory and Empirical Work," *J. of Finance,* May 1970.

Fama, E., "Risk-Adjusted Discount Rates and Capital Budgeting Under Uncertainty," *J. of Financial Economics,* Aug. 1971.

Fama, E., "Risk, Return, and Equilibrium: Some Clarifying Comments," *J. of Finance,* March 1968.

Gordon, M., "The Payoff Period and the Rate of Profit," *J. of Business,* Oct. 1955.

Lintner, J., "The Valuation of Risk Assets and the Selection of Risky Investments in Stock Portfolios and Capital Budgets," *Review of Economics and Statistics,* Feb. 1965.

Manès, R., "A New Dimension to Break-Even Analysis," *J. of Accounting Research,* Spring 1966.

Modigliani, F., and M.H. Miller, "The Cost of Capital, Corporate Finance, and the Theory of Investment," *American Economic Rev.,* June 1958.

Sharpe, W., "Capital Asset Prices: A Theory of Market Equilibrium Under Conditions of Risk," *J. of Finance,* Sept. 1964.

Books

Bierman, H., Jr. and S. Smidt, *The Capital Budgeting Decision.* New York: Macmillan, 1980.

Fama, E. and Miller, M., *The Theory of Finance.* New York: Holt, Rinehart and Winston, 1972.

Foster, G., *Financial Statement Analysis.* Englewood Cliffs, N.J.: Prentice-Hall, 1979, Sec. III.

Haley, C. and L. Schall, *The Theory of Financial Decisions.* New York: McGraw-Hill, 1978.

Hirshleifer, J., *Investment, Interest and Capital.* Englewood Cliffs, N.J.: Prentice-Hall, 1970.

Sharpe, W., *Investments,* 2nd ed. Englewood Cliffs, N.J.: Prentice-Hall, 1981.

Van Horne, J.C., *Fundamentals of Financial Management.* Englewood Cliffs, N.J.: Prentice-Hall, 1980.

Questions and Problems

1. The cost of capital for a firm is a measure of an opportunity cost. Discuss.
2. What criteria might be used to select depreciation methods for tax purposes?[38] (As one source for your answer, see S. Davidson and D. Drake, "Selecting

---

[38] The three main methods of depreciation allowed for tax purposes are the straightline method, the sum-of-the-years'-digits method, and the double-declining balance method. The equation for the latter is $D_t = (2/n)$ (Asset balance)$_{t-1}$. For $t = 1$, $D_1 = (2/n)$ (Cost); for $t = 2$, $D_2 = (2/n)$ (Cost $- D_1$); for $t = 3$, $D_3 = (2/n)$ (Cost $- D_1 - D_2$), and so on. At any time, the remaining asset balance can be written off on a straight-line basis over the remaining years of life. Notice that the double-declining balance method ignores salvage values, but the switchover would have to include a salvage estimate, if appropriate. Currently, salvage may be ignored in any depreciation method up to 10 percent of the asset's cost; but the final year of depreciation, D_n, should not exceed (Book value$_n$ − Salvage value$_n$).

the Best Depreciation Policy," *J. of Business,* Oct. 1961; a related article appears in the *J. of Business,* July 1964.

3. Define for an investment project (in words or symbols):

   (a) the payback.
   (b) the internal rate of return (often called the project rate of return).
   (c) the excess present value.

4. Some recent studies of the capital budgeting process in industry have found that the less sophisticated models, such as payback, are much more prevalent in practice than models such as internal rate of return and excess present value. How do you explain this?

5. Comment on the following statement: "The assumptions of the capital budgeting models are convenient for purposes of analysis but are not realistic. Thus, there are valid reasons for rejecting them in practice."

   (a) What are the assumptions?
   (b) Do you agree with the conclusion above?

6. One of the problems in applying any model of rational behavior to individuals is the need to know the individual's utility function. Because it is felt that these utility functions are nonlinear over the relevant range, we cannot assume that all dollars are equally valuable to the recipient; for example, a gift of $5,000 immediately is to most people more than 5,000 times as valuable as the gift of one dollar. Similarly, a loss of 90 percent of a person's total wealth has a penalty greater than nine times the penalty of a loss of 10 percent of his wealth (for example, bankruptcy may result). With respect to the management of corporate capital:

   (a) Do you feel nonlinearities exist? Why?
   (b) If you were to try to develop a utility function to apply to a firm's decisions, what difficulties would you expect to encounter?

7. What is the significance of the payback calculation? What are its limitations?
8. Evaluate critically the accountant's rate-of-return method.
9. Several years ago an aircraft company was considering the production of a passenger jet that would have a considerable advantage in speed, comfort, and size over present passenger jets. The company had no previous experience in building passenger jets, and the management had to decide whether to engage in the research and development of the jet or concentrate on military contracts.

   It was very difficult to estimate the total costs of developing, testing, and building the new jet. However, the company was able to obtain contracts for the sale of the aircraft that were believed sufficient to cover the total costs of research, development, and meeting the contracts. The contracts were conditional on the performance of the new jet; specifically, it had to be the fastest jet in the air on the date of the first delivery.

   The management used a payback analysis covering three years to justify the firm's entry into the passenger-jet business.

Discuss management's problem in terms of the payback analysis. Consider this problem in relation to the fundamental criticism of payback analysis—the analysis does not consider the profitability of the project beyond the payback date. What are the potential profits beyond the payback date? (P.S. They lost their gamble!)

10. Capital expenditure analysis involves, essentially, the calculation of cash flows relating to two or more investment proposals. Suppose a firm is contemplating whether to modernize its present facilities or to invest in a new and more efficient set of facilities. How would you treat each of the following items in your cash flow analysis of Project A (modernize) and Project B (replace)? Include also what tables of discount factors you would use. Assume that each project will have a useful life of five years. Summarize your answers as follows:

Effect of Item on Cash Flow in Years Indicated

	0	1	2	3	4	5
Project A Description of item						
Project B Description of item						

(a) The costs of modernization are expected to total $150,000 spread out over two years as follows: first year, $100,000; second year, $50,000; both amounts are disbursed evenly during the year.

(b) At the end of the five-year time span, the remodeled facilities will be removed at a cost of $15,000 less $10,000 for salvage.[39]

(c) The company will use the straight-line method of depreciation with the salvage estimate given in (b), above. (Assume the facilities are put into operation as expenditures are completed at the end of each year; use a tax rate of $t, 0 < t < 1.0$.)

(d) The remodeled facilities will be used to produce one of the company's new products. The costs are estimated as follows:

Direct material and direct labor	$2.00 per unit
Variable overhead	$.30 per unit
Fixed expenditures	$25,000.00 per year

During the past few years the company has processed an average of 50,000 units of this product annually. During the next five years an average volume of 60,000 units is expected. The yearly volume will take the following distribution:

---

[39] The net is tax deductible.

Year	1	2	3	4	5
Volume	52,000	55,000	60,000	63,000	70,000

These output estimates also apply if new facilities are purchased.

(e) If the new facilities are purchased, the old equipment will be removed, with part of it being scrapped and the remaining part traded in on the new facilities. The part traded in has a book value of $25,000; however, the company has been given a cash allowance by the dealer of only $15,000 on the new facilities.[40]

(f) The new facilities will reduce the materials and labor costs by approximately 20 percent and variable overhead by 40 percent. These savings are due in part to a $5,000 addition to fixed expenditures. The new facilities have an invoice price of $190,000.

(g) The new facilities will be depreciated over five years using the sum-of-the-years'-digits method. The estimate of salvage value for tax depreciation is $20,000. However, the company expects to sell the facilities for only $15,000.

(h) The new facilities will eliminate plant storage space that has been used for miscellaneous items. Although this space is not of direct use to the firm, management believes its opportunity cost is $5,000 per year (net of taxes).

11. *Capital Expenditure Analysis and Net Income Determination*
An automobile company expanded its facilities in the early 1960s in anticipation of an expanded market for its products. The expansion consisted of constructing new assembly plants in several key locations. The operating statements for the years 1966, 1967, and 1968 appeared as follows:

	1966	**1967**	**1968**
Units sold	840,000	820,000	750,000
Financial data (thousands of dollars):			
Sales	$2,080	$2,050	$1,875
Variable costs	1,550	1,538	1,387
Fixed costs			
Factory	220	225	230
Selling and administrative	210	215	220
Total costs	$1,980	$1,978	$1,837
Net income	$ 100	$ 72	$ 38

The 1969 management team forecasted expected sales for the next six years (1969–1974) and realized that at least one of the old assembly plants could be shut down and the contents and building salvaged at a value of perhaps $15,000,000. However, the assembly plant did produce cash savings in satisfying the Midwest market for automobiles. Estimated savings averaged about $15 per unit assembled. The number of units that would be affected each year

---

[40] For tax purposes, book value of old facilities is added to cash paid to determine the depreciation base of the new asset. See also part (f).

was estimated as follows (use an 8 percent cost-of-capital rate if appropriate to the problem):

Year	1969	1970	1971	1972	1973	1974
Units	275,000	300,000	315,000	325,000	330,000	340,000

If the plant is salvaged, the company will report an accounting loss on the transaction of approximately $50 million. This plant accounts for $12.5 million of the fixed factory costs reported in 1968; $11.5 million of this amount is depreciation on the plant assets. A new management took control of the company in 1969 and immediately ordered this facility closed down as well as any others that were not needed to process expected units of output. Discuss the action taken by the new management. Which action do you think the old management would have taken? Use figures to support your answers, both before and after taxes.

12. *Sensitivity of Investment Decisions to Tax Laws*
In late 1966, Congress suspended the investment credit and considered suspending the accelerated depreciation provisions regarding qualified assets.[41] Assume that in 1966 a firm contemplated the purchase of a qualifying asset to be put into operation late in 1967. The asset could be purchased in 1966 but it would remain idle for the intervening period 1966–67. The asset was expected to yield savings in operating costs of $1.10 per unit and was expected to have a useful life of five years with an expected salvage rate of approximately 10 percent. These estimates are consistent with the IRS guidelines for similar assets. (The tax code permits the taxpayer to ignore salvage value in computing depreciation of up to 10 percent of the assets' cost. This provision was not expected to be canceled in 1966.)

The number of units expected to be produced in each of the years of operation was as follows:

Year	1967–68	1968–69	1969–70	1970–71	1971–72
Units	52,000	55,000	60,000	60,000	55,000

Production is evenly spaced throughout the year. However, discounting the savings at the end of each operating year is not expected to distort the decision process. The company believes that a 12 percent cost of capital rate (applied after taxes have been considered) is appropriate for this asset. The asset had an outlay cost of $150,000 in 1966 and an expected cost of $162,000 (approximately) in 1967.

---

[41] The tax credit in force in 1966 allowed a deduction from the tax liability of the firm equal to 7 percent of the gross price of a new asset if the service life of the asset was eight years or more; $\frac{2}{3}$ of 7 percent if the service life was greater than six but less than eight years; and $\frac{1}{3}$ of 7 percent if the service life was greater than four but less than six years. If the asset was sold prior to the time contemplated, the credit was recomputed and the firm was liable (at no interest penalty) for any part of the credit to which it was not entitled. For example, if a credit of 7 percent (Cost) were taken initially, but then the asset were sold at the end of the sixth year, the firm would owe .07 (Cost) − ($\frac{2}{3}$) (.07) Cost = ($\frac{1}{3}$) (.07) Cost to the government. The investment tax credit in effect in 1981 was similar to the above, except the appropriate years were 7, 5, and 3 (instead of 8, 6, and 4), and the credit was 10 percent of the outlay.

(a) Set up an analysis that could have been used to guide management in deciding whether to purchase the asset in late 1966, prior to the suspension date, or in late 1967. Use a tax rate of 50 percent. The discount factors for each year, $r = 12\%$, are as follows:

Year	1	2	3	4	5	6
Factor	0.89	0.80	0.71	0.64	0.57	0.51

Use the sum-of-the-years' digits for calculating accelerated depreciation.

(b) Compare the after-tax value of depreciation calculated by the double-declining balance method with that calculated by the sum-of-the-years'-digits method. Assume that a switch to straight line is made in years 4 and 5 in order to write down the undepreciated balance existing at the end of year 3.

13. **Cash Flow and Short EPV Problems (Ignoring Taxes)**

Sum Company is considering replacing one of its machines with a new model, which would substantially reduce labor costs. The old machine has a net book value of $100,000 and a resale value of $10,000. The labor costs under the old machine are six men at $16,000 per year. The new machine requires only one operator, who would receive $20,000 per year.

The company is concerned about its guaranteed annual wage agreement, which requires it to pay any discharged worker his or her full salary for one calendar year. Four of the six operators will be discharged if the new machine is acquired. They will receive their full salaries for one year even though they will render no services to the company. The two other operators will be transferred to new jobs that can be filled by hiring less skilled labor. The less skilled workers will receive $15,000 annually. However, the old workers will continue to receive their old salaries.

The machines' operating costs and capacities are identical in all other respects. While the new machine has a physical life of 15 years, both machines have an economic life of only five years. No scrap value is expected at that time. The new machine will cost $200,000.

(a) Using the form illustrated in Problem 10, indicate the relevant cash flows.
(b) Assuming a cost of capital of 10 percent, indicate whether the new machine should be acquired. (Ignore income taxes.)
(c) The department manager suggests that the economic life might well be only four years. How does this affect the decision?
(d) Without calculation, would an overestimation of the firm's cost of capital alter this decision? Why?
(e) The firm is concerned that its cost of capital might in fact be 16 percent. Does this alter the analysis?
(f) The manufacturer has indicated that the price may be increased to $220,000. How would this alter your analysis?

14. *Comparison of Methods (Ignoring Taxes)*

One of the department heads feels that acquiring a new type of lathe would result in substantial savings to his department. He has submitted the following data about the new lathe and the old one.

	New Lathe	Old Lathe
Capacity	1,000 units per day	1,000 units per day
Labor	2 operators	3 operators
	at $12,000 per year	at $12,000 per year
Maintenance	$1,000 per year	$1,400 per year
Waste, scrap, etc.	$200 per year	$600 per year
Length of life	6 years	4 years

The old machine can be sold for $10,000 today. The new machine will cost $70,000 installed. For purposes of analysis, a four-year life and scrap values of zero and $20,000, respectively, should be used. Using an incremental approach to the data, calculate:

(a) The payback period.
(b) The internal rate of return.
(c) The excess present value index assuming a cost of capital of 10 percent.
(d) The accountant's rate of return. (Book value of the old machine today is $5,000.)

15. *Length of Time Used for Analysis of Alternatives*

In Problem 14, management policy precluded any estimates of cost savings beyond four years. Management justified this policy because of the difficulty in forecasting the future.

(a) What decision(s) would be open to management at year 4 if it did not replace the old machine today?
(b) Suppose the new machine could be sold for $2,000 at the end of year 6. A new machine like the old one can be purchased for $30,000, but it only has a four year life. Which machine(s) should the department head acquire?

16. *Effect of Timing of Cash Flows (Ignoring Taxes)*

The Grand Company has developed a new product for which they anticipate a growing demand. During the first year that the product will be on the market, sales are expected to be 20,000 units. Each year thereafter for eight years the company expects demand to increase by 10,000 units per year, reaching a peak of 100,000 units in the ninth year. After the ninth year, it expects sales to stabilize at the 100,000 figure. Ignore any consideration of excess capacity.

The company must choose between two alternative production arrangements:

(a) Buy a large, heavy-duty machine with a capacity of 100,000 units per year and an estimated service life of 10 years. This machine would cost $60,000 and would have no scrap value at the end of its service life.

(b) Buy today a smaller, lighter machine with a capacity of 60,000 units per year and an estimated service life of five years. Five years from today the company estimates that they could buy two more machines to replace the one that will be worn out. The smaller machines will cost $50,000 each when purchased now and five years from now. There will be no scrap value at the end of the service life.

Local real estate taxes and insurance for each year are expected to run 5 percent of the original cost of the equipment in use. Maintenance cost is expected to be $1,000 per year on the large machine and $700 per year on each of the smaller machines. Labor and material cost per unit is expected to be the same under either arrangement.

Calculate the present value of the costs of each machine using a discount rate of 10 percent; using a discount rate of 16 percent. What other factors might affect your decision regarding which size machine to acquire?

17. *Image Building (Ignoring Taxes)*

In anticipation of his job after graduation, a student to whom we shall assign the alias of Gossett wishes to trade in his 1970 Pinto on a BMW. Being a typical staid potential BMW owner, he wishes to rationalize this decision on economic grounds. He feels that by disposing of his Pinto he saves himself a major overhaul immediately and a new pair of studded tires and four regular ones. The studded tires will cost him about $270 and the regular ones $200. A major overhaul will cost $2,200. In addition, he feels that the BMW will enhance his image on the job. This will mean faster promotions and more pay, probably about $3,500 a year. A summary of the other relevant (and perhaps irrelevant) data is presented below (ignore taxes):

Cost of BMW: $30,000 plus his old car
Life: five years
Scrap value: $25,000
Scrap value of Pinto after five years: 0
Annual operating costs for a typical year

	BMW	Pinto
Gasoline and oil	$3,100	$2,050
Insurance	1,500	1,100
Maintenance and other repairs	400	1,100
Total	$5,000	$4,250

Ignoring any effects after five years, calculate

(a) The payback period.
(b) The internal rate of return.

18. *Incremental Replacement Analysis with Taxes*

Jones Warehousing has placed a noncancelable order with Kit-Cat Tractor Company for a new diesel warehouse forklift designed to meet Jones's specifications. However, as a representative for Eel Electric Carts, you would like to sell them your new battery-powered forklift. They are interested, but the recent order makes any changeover seem impossible at this time.

Since you are interested in making the sale, use the data shown in Exhibit 14-8 to ascertain if your electric forklift would be a better investment even if the new diesel forklift must be junked.

EXHIBIT 14-8

	Cost for Electric Forklift	Cost for Diesel Forklift
Life: eight years in each case		
Purchase price	$15,000	$14,500[a]
Annual operating cost	300	1,000
Driver cost	18,000	18,000
Repairs	50	250
Insurance	50	150
Scrap value at the end of useful life	300	300
Value of diesel tractor sold today as "used"		$ 1,000
Depreciation method: sum-of-the-years' digits[b]		
Tax rate: 50%		

[a] Book value
[b] Ignore scrap value in computing tax depreciation, except in last year.

(a) Set up the incremental cash flows if the electric forklift is acquired.

(b) What is the approximate payback period for the incremental investments?

19. *Payback Reciprocal (Ignoring Taxes)*

Jones Warehousing is considering a conveyor belt system for its freight transfer section. Such a system would increase efficiency and reduce operating costs. However, it would increase the firm's capital investment. The platform manager's best estimate of the effects of the new system are as follows:

(1) The work force could be cut from ten men to six. The other workers would be shifted to other jobs that the firm is now trying to fill. The typical warehouse worker now receives $18,000 per year.

(2) The conveyor is powered by electricity, and the electric company estimates the quarterly electric bill after the conveyor is installed at $1,000. Currently, the electric bill for the firm is $250 per quarter.

(3) Insurance on the equipment is $100 per year.

(4) Breakage is reduced by the conveyor; it could be reduced by as much as $15,000 per year. However this is still small relative to Jones's total breakage.

Therefore, the result will be only a nominal, approximately $100, reduction in the cost of insurance against breakage and theft.

(5) The equipment costs $120,000. The installation will be performed by Jones's repair crew during their usual working hours. It is estimated that it will take five workers ten working days at $32 per worker per day.

(6) During the period when installation is taking place, the loading dock area will be congested and ten dock workers will work overtime. The total overtime bill for the workers during this period is estimated at $2,000.

(7) Normal maintenance on the equipment should be about $38,000 per year, which includes minor repairs and parts.

(8) With proper repair, the system could last for about 25 years. However, Jones does not expect to use this building for more than 10 years.

(9) Once the conveyor system is installed it has no scrap value. The cost of removal offsets any revenue it might realize.

Calculate

(a) The cash inflows and outflows in the form suggested in Problem 10.
(b) The payback period and payback reciprocal.
(c) The actual internal (or project) rate of return.

20. *Example of the Usefulness of Payback (Ignoring Taxes)*
XYZ Table Tennis Ball Company has always found the filling of cartons to be costly because it must be done either by hand—as is now the case—or with expensive machinery. Management determined that the volume has never been sufficient to justify the cost of the machine. Recently an employee designed a system that partially automates the process. Management is enthusiastic about it because it utilizes some of their present equipment.

The new method retains some of the workers who now do the task manually. They will place the empty boxes in larger containers open and up. These boxes pass under a new set of pneumatic "guns" that fill the container. The packages of balls are then closed by hand.

The new system will reduce the labor force by about 25 percent. Management expects to save a proportional percentage of the department's labor costs, which last year were $30,000. The unit itself will cost about $15,000 to build and test prior to operation. It is expected that other operating costs relating to the new process will be about $5,000 per year.

Based on the above data,

(a) Calculate the payback period and payback reciprocal.
(b) Assume the useful life of the new process will be twice the payback life. Should management invest in it?

21. *Different Capacity Machines (Including Taxes)*
Dy-Nal Fall Makers, a manufacturer of wigs, is considering two machines manufactured by the same firm. The smaller machine is capable of producing efficiently

20,000 to 60,000 wigs per year according to the manufacturer's specifications. The larger unit can produce from 30,000 to 70,000 wigs efficiently per year. Outside of these ranges the machines tend to function very poorly and the manufacturer does not recommend their use. Outlay costs are $63,000 for the larger machine and $52,500 for the smaller one. If appropriate, assume that taxes are 40 percent and that Dy-Nal uses a cost-of-capital rate of 10 percent.

According to the sales representative for their manufacturer, the smaller machine costs about $40,000 per year plus $4 per wig made. The larger machine costs $65,000 plus $3.50 per wig. Useful life is five years (no salvage value).

(a) Analyze the data so that once you are given Dy-Nal's average rate of production you can tell them which machine to buy.
(b) If the larger machine's variable costs were reduced to only $3 per wig, how would this affect your analysis?

22. **Project Sensitivity: Changes in Sales and Selling Price[42] (Ignoring Taxes)**
Assume that a firm is contemplating an expansion of its facilities. It expects to sell an additional 1,000,000 units per year, although the actual output will probably range from 800,000 to 1,250,000 units per year. The following investments are required:

Land	$ 25,000
Buildings	250,000
Equipment	450,000
Working capital	275,000
	$1,000,000

The sales price of the units will be set initially at $1 per unit. The variable costs of production are set at $.25 per unit. Fixed cost outlays will be $450,000. The project will have a useful life of 10 years. No salvage value is expected for the equipment; the building and land will probably have a market value of $100,000 after 10 years.

Assuming the company has a cutoff rate of 12 percent, calculate the excess present value for the project under the following conditions:

(a) Sales prices of $.90, $1.00, and $1.10; output at 1,000,000 units.
(b) Outputs of 900,000 per year, 1,000,000 per year, 1,100,000 per year, and 1,250,000 per year, given a sales price of $1.00 per unit.
(c) The combination: sales price of $.90 and output of 1,250,000; sales price of $1.10 and output of 900,000 per year.

Discuss the use of this type of analysis as a basis for assessing the riskiness of the project.

---

[42] This problem is based on material in an unpublished paper by Morlin J. Vincent, University of Chicago, 1966.

23. *Cash Flow Analysis (Including Taxes)*

A firm is contemplating the replacement of its present equipment with Machine A. Information for the two alternatives available to the firm, that is, keep the present machine or buy Machine A, is given in Exhibit 14-9.

The tax rate is 40 percent. Output sells for $7 per unit regardless of the method of production. Depreciation methods are for tax purposes. Gains and losses on sales of assets are treated as adjustments to taxable income.

EXHIBIT 14-9————————————————————————————

Keep Present Machine

Present salvage value	$6,200
Book value	$7,000
Operating costs	
Variable	$3 per unit
Fixed outlays	$10,000 per year
Remaining life	4 years
Salvage value at end of four years	$600
Present output	10,000 units per year
Depreciation method	straight-line (using $600 salvage estimate)

Machine A

Outlay cost	$16,000
Useful life	6 years (IRS guideline)
Salvage value at end of six years	$460
Salvage value at end of four years	$2,840
Operating costs	
Variable	$2.40 per unit
Fixed	$12,000 per year
Expected output	10,000 units

Investment credit applies (claim will be taken one year hence)[a]
Depreciation method—sum-of-the-years'-digits

---

[a] For information on the investment credit, see footnotes 20 and 41, this chapter.

(a) Prepare an analysis of cash flows relative to each alternative (assume a four-year analysis).

(b) What is the approximate number of periods required to recover the incremental investment in Machine A over the alternative of keeping the present equipment?

(c) Using your cash flow figures, evaluate the replacement proposal using the excess present value criterion (cost of capital is 12 percent).

24. *Evaluating an Investment Request (Taxes Included)*

Assume a department of your firm has some assets with a book value of $50,000, which are used to produce a single product with operating costs as follows:

Direct materials	$2.50 per unit
Direct labor	$4.50 per unit
Overhead	
Variable	$1.50 per unit
Fixed (exclusive of noncash expenses)	$15,000 per year if output is between 15,000 and 20,000 units

Output for the next five years, the remaining life of the old assets, is expected to average 22,000 units per year. In this range, fixed overhead expenses (exclusive of noncash expenses) will increase from $15,000 to $18,000.

The facilities are depreciated on a straight-line basis for tax purposes with an estimated salvage at the end of five years of $10,000. The net salvage (proceeds less removal costs) is $5,000. If the facilities are sold today, they will yield net proceeds of $35,000.

The manager of the department has requested approval of a proposal to replace the old assets with new assets costing $130,000. The new assets have an expected life of eight years (the tax guidelines) with a salvage estimate of 15 percent of original cost. The manager's proposal indicates that an investment in the new assets should yield a rate of return in excess of the firm's cost of capital of 10 percent (using after-tax flows based on sum-of-the-years'-digits depreciation). The manager's analysis, which is based on the following supplementary information, is reproduced in Exhibit 14-10.

Outlay	$130,000
Operating costs with new assets:	
Direct materials and labor	$5.80 per unit
Overhead	
Variable	$1.20 per unit
Fixed (cash expenditures only)	$21,000 per year for output range of 20,000–25,000 units
Salvage estimate at the end of 8 years	$19,500
Salvage estimate at the end of 5 years	$30,000

The marginal tax rate is 52 percent.

(a) You are asked to verify the figures indicated in Exhibit 14-10 by superscript letters a through f. Show your calculations, and state whether the department manager's analysis is correct.

(b) Using the cash flow figures in Exhibit 14-10, set up the equation for determining the internal rate of return on this project.

(c) How long will it take the firm to recover its cash outlay (that is, what is the payback of the project)?

(d) Using the figures from Exhibit 14-10, what is the average accounting rate of return on the project?

EXHIBIT 14-10

End of Year	0	1	2	3	4	5
Outlay	($130,000)					
Less: Opportunity cost of holding old assets	42,200[a]					
Net incremental outlay	($ 87,800)					
Investment credit (10%)		$13,000[b]				
Savings in operating costs (after taxes)		14,400[c]	$14,400	$14,400	$14,400	$14,400
Savings from additional depreciation		9,331[d1]	7,685[d2]	6,038	2,746	1,100
Incremental salvage value after 5 years						25,000[e]
Less: Incremental tax paid on difference between salvage proceeds and book value						−4,240[f]
Net cash flows	($ 87,800)	$36,731	$22,085	$20,438	$17,146	$36,260
Present value of cash flows (at 10%)	($87,800)	$33,392	18,242	15,349	11,710	22,517
Present value of inflows	$ 97,660					
Less: Outlay	87,800					
Excess present value	$ 9,860					

NOTE: Superscripts a through f identify data referred to in part (a) of Problem 24.

---

*25. **Short-Run Production Schedules and Capacity Expansion**

Refer to the data for Springfield Manufacturing Company in Problem 25 Chapter 4 (page 000). The initial problem dealt with determining an allocation of the firm's production and sales resources among three products for the year 1980. Another issue is the level of these resources themselves. Suppose that (1) the basic cost and demand structures and parameters will exist for the next five years and (2) the firm's cost of capital is 15 percent.

(a) What is the maximum amount Springfield should be willing to pay for machinery that would increase the capacity of department 1 by 20,000 hours? Assume that the machinery has a five-year life and will have zero salvage value in five years.

(b) What is the maximum amount Springfield should be willing to pay for machinery that would increase the capacity of department 2 by 20,000 hours? Again assume a five-year life and zero salvage value.

(c) What is the maximum amount Springfield should be willing to pay for *both* the machinery in (a) and the machinery in (b)?

(d) How would relaxation of assumption (1) affect your answers in (a), (b), and (c)?

15
Additional Considerations in Capital Investment Analysis: Discontinuities, Leasing, and Differential Tax Benefits

$\mathbf{I}$n Chapter 14 we observed that different rankings in the desirability of investment projects may arise when two discounting criteria—excess present value and internal rate of return—are applied to the same set of projects. There are two general conditions under which this conflict may be encountered: when the projects require different outlays or when they have different useful lives. Each is an example of a type of discontinuity problem. In the first case we either accept each project at 100 percent of its outlay or reject it completely. In the second, the lack of perfect markets for "used" assets often makes it more profitable to hold and use an asset for its normal useful life rather than to sell it at an earlier stage. As a result, it is difficult to compare an asset with a useful life of three years with a similar asset whose useful life is five years. We discuss these discontinuity problems in the first section of this chapter.

Leasing is another aspect of investment analysis which may affect the ranking of projects, depending on the terms of the lease. In general, entering into a financial lease (one with debt contract features) can be viewed as a decision to engage in a special type of financing—a decision that is normally kept separate from the investment decision. However, the various income tax rules governing leases and asset purchases may require that we analyze the investment decision and the financing decision together. A major portion of this chapter deals with the somewhat complex analysis of the lease-or-buy decision.

In the final section of this chapter we discuss how differential tax rates that apply to ordinary income and to net capital gains affect special types of investment analyses. The preferential rate on capital gains—approximately

615

30 percent—makes it worthwhile to convert ordinary income determinants into capital gain determinants. For example, at one time a large car rental firm used accelerated depreciation for the first two years of life of its cars, received tax benefits of 48 percent of each year's depreciation deduction, and then recognized a capital gain on sale of the cars that was taxed at about 25 percent. The "rules" have changed for this type of transaction, resulting in the so-called depreciation recapture provisions. Essentially, the gain on the sale of operating assets, which can be treated as a capital gain, is reduced by the excess of accelerated over straight-line depreciation. The amount not treated as a capital gain is included in ordinary income. We will illustrate how these differential tax rates can encourage certain types of asset transactions.

Two final notes before proceeding: We observed in Chapter 14 that borrowing rates in the United States are varying rapidly, so the rates we use in the various illustrations and problems may not be current. The appropriate analyses, however, do not change with fluctuating interest rates.

Second, it is important to remember that we currently lack adequate theory in capital investment analyses. The excess present value criterion is well grounded in a world of certainty and complete, perfect markets. But the topics in this chapter—discontinuities, taxes, and leases—simply do not exist in a perfect market setting. Thus, lacking the guidance of a completed theory, we essentially confine ourselves to one in which a risk class with known capital cost (or market requirement) is operative.

Conditions Leading to Conflicts in Investment Rankings

Differences in Outlays

The excess present value criterion yields a relatively straightforward rule for investment decisions: Invest in a project if the present value of net cash inflows is greater than the outlay cost of the project. As indicated in Chapter 14, a positive excess present value indicates that a project earns a rate of return in excess of the firm's cost of capital, which is also consistent with the internal rate-of-return criterion. Hence, there should be no conflict between the two discounting criteria when the decision is limited to the "go–no-go" type of investment decision.

However, different rankings of the desirability of projects can arise when the decision involves the selection of the best single project or group of projects from a set of mutually exclusive investment alternatives. The firm in the example in Chapter 14 had to decide which plan was the "best" from the set of three alternatives: Plans A, B, and C. As it turned out, Plan C offered the highest excess present value of the three plans, but Plan A had the highest internal rate of return. The conflict arises between the two criteria whenever the mutually exclusive projects require different outlays, as they did in that example.

In general, the internal rate of return measures the efficiency of the capital invested in a project; that is, it reflects the discounted return per dollar of investment. Therefore, a project requiring a small outlay may promise a very high rate of return and yet produce a lower excess present value than another project requiring a considerably higher outlay.

To illustrate, consider the following two proposals:

	Project 1	Project 2
Outlay ($t=0$)	−$1,000	−$ 600
Inflow ($t=1$)	$1,750	$1,200
Excess present value @ 20%	$ 458*	$ 400
Internal rate of return	75%	100%*

The preferred alternative under each of the two criteria is indicated by an asterisk. How can this conflict be resolved?

We might argue that, since Project 1 requires a higher initial outlay, it constitutes a different risk from Project 2. If so, 20 percent should not be used to discount the cash flows of both projects. For example, if we used a 30 percent discount rate for Project 1, its excess present value would only be $346, which would rank it below Project 2 under both criteria.

However, projects are not necessarily more risky merely because they require higher outlays. Projects belong in the same risk class if their cash flows are perfectly positively correlated; that is, their cash flows are drawn from the same probability distribution. If Projects 1 and 2 belong to the same risk class, investors' decisions should not be affected by differences in outlays.

Assuming they are in the same risk class, we can resolve the issue as follows: Project 1 may be viewed as a single project that will earn a rate of return of 75 percent on an investment of $1,000. This alternative can be compared with the combined decision of investing $600 in Project 2, which will earn 100 percent, *and* $400 in some unknown alternative that belongs to the same risk class. In the absence of information to the contrary, we would assume that the $400 will be invested in projects in the same risk class that will tend to earn the cost-of-capital rate of 20 percent.

Hence, it is now obvious why Project 1 would be preferred. It will yield a terminal wealth of $1,750 at the end of one year, whereas Project 2, plus the $400 incremental outlay in some other project earning 20 percent, will yield a terminal wealth of only $1,200 + $400 (1.20) = $1,680. This combined decision results in an average rate of return of only 68 percent [$\frac{6}{10}$(100 percent)+ $\frac{4}{10}$(20 percent)], which is less than the 75 percent return from Project 1—assuming throughout that we are considering projects from the same risk class.

An interesting question is what rate of return would be required on the incremental investment of $400 to make the firm indifferent between Project 1 and the combined decision. This can be determined by solving the simple equation $400 = \$550[1/(1 + r^*)]$, where r^* represents the indifference rate. For this situation, $r^* = 37.5\%$.[1] Thus, if the firm could invest the $400 in another project that would earn a rate of return in excess of 37.5 percent, then it should select Project 2 and this other project over Project 1.[2]

Unequal Lives

A similar conflict can arise when mutually exclusive projects with unequal lives are compared under the two criteria. This conflict can also be resolved by examining the reinvestment assumption for the project with the shorter life.

We illustrate this problem by another simple example. Assume we wish to compare the two projects in the same risk class for which data are given in Exhibit 15-1. (The asterisk indicates the higher ranking.) If the $880 received from Project B were invested at 10 percent for four years (from year 1 to year 5), it would build to a future value of $1,288, which is less than the terminal wealth of $1,613 for Project A. Hence, the firm would be better off investing $300 at 40 percent for five years than investing $300 at 193 percent for one year and $880 at 10 percent for four years.[3]

---

[1] Actually, the rate of return as advanced by Irving Fisher was not designed to be used as a ranking device between two projects. Fisher's rate of return is a marginal rate of return, which reflects the rate r^* that makes the investor indifferent between two mutually exclusive projects. See A. Alchian, "The Rate of Interest, Fisher's Rate of Return over Costs, and Keynes' 'Internal Rate of Return,'" in *Management of Corporate Capital*, E. Solomon (ed.), New York: Free Press, 1959.

[2] Terminal wealth at 37.5 percent would be $1,200 + $400(1.375) = $1,750, which is the same as the terminal wealth of Project 1.

[3] Again, the rate of return that would be required on the $880 for four years to make the firm indifferent between the two projects can be determined by solving the equation

$$\$880(1 + r^*)^4 = \$1,613$$

To simplify matters, we convert the equation to the form

$$(1 + r^*)^{-4} = \frac{\$880}{\$1,613} = 0.546$$

and use Table 14-2, which gives us $r^* = 16\%$.

_____EXHIBIT 15-1

	Project A	Project B
Outlay	−$ 300	−$300
Inflows		
Year 1	0	880
2	0	0
3	0	0
4	0	0
5	1,613	0
Present value of inflows @ 10%	$1,002	$800
Less outlay	300	300
Excess present value	$ 702*	$500
Internal rate of return	40%	193%*

Budget Constraints: Combining Aspects of Both Conditions

Our discussion of the use of the excess present value criterion implies that the marketplace is willing to supply unlimited funds to the firm, provided these funds can and will be invested in projects that have positive excess present values at appropriate costs of capital.[4] We hesitate, therefore, to consider some of the problems caused by a firm's decision to impose constraints on the amount of capital it will invest in any one time period. In practice, however, there is often a need for a firm to limit the amount of funds for investment, especially in the short run. For example, there are administrative costs associated with issuing securities, and firms try to predict their capital requirements in advance in order to consolidate them into a single security issue. Similarly, divisions of firms tend to develop independently their own requirements for capital, and when these are brought together at the corporate level, central management may be faced with an allocation problem. In effect, the imposition of a budget restriction creates the problem of choosing the best set of projects from a population of mutually exclusive investment alternatives. That is, the budget may not be sufficient to allow the acceptance of all projects, so at the margin the acceptance of one project precludes the acceptance of others. The result is another situation in which conflicts can arise among the various investment criteria.

Nevertheless, the excess present value criterion can still be used as the basis for determining the optimal allocation of a firm's budget. However,

_____

[4] The "will be" qualifier here is important. Motivation issues concern a potential lender. The proposed project may be displaced by one that is more risky, thereby lowering the lender's repayment odds. See R. Holthausen, "Evidence on the Effect of Bond Covenants and Management Compensation Contracts on the Choice of Accounting Techniques: The Case of Depreciation Switch-Back" and R. Leftwich, "Evidence of the Impact of Mandatory Changes in Accounting Principles on Corporate Loan Agreements," both in _J. of Accounting and Economics,_ March 1981.

EXHIBIT 15-2

	Project 1	Project 2	Project 3	Project 4
Outlay ($t = 0$)	−$250	−$400	−$100	−$150
Inflows				
$t = 1$	0	134	40	0
$t = 2$	0	134	40	0
$t = 3$	0	134	40	0
$t = 4$	0	134	40	0
$t = 5$	525	134	40	340
Present value of inflows @ 12%	$298	$483	$144	$193
Excess present value (EPV)	48	83	44	43
Internal rate of return (IRR)	16%	20%	29%	18%
Present value index (PVI)	1.192	1.207	1.440	1.287

the analysis is not as straightforward as we would like, primarily because of the problem of discontinuities. The nature of the problem is best illustrated with another simple example.

A firm's management wishes to allocate $750 of capital funds over the set of four projects listed in Exhibit 15-2. In addition to the excess present value and internal rate of return, the firm's accountant has provided a calculation of the present value index, which indicates the present value per dollar of investment generated by each project. This provides another basis for allocating a capital budget, although its theoretical underpinnings are controversial.[5]

Using the three methods, the project rankings would be as follows:

Excess Present Value	Internal Rate of Return	Present Value Index
2	3	3
1	2	4
3	4	2
4	1	1

The budget limit of $750 would be allocated to Projects 2, 1, and 3 (EPV); to Projects 3, 2, and 4 (IRR); or to Projects 3, 4, and 2 (PVI). Note that the first allocation consumes the entire budget, but the second and third allocations use only $650 of the budget allowance. However, the $100 left over from the latter two allocations is not sufficient to permit the acceptance of Project 1. This is an example of the effect of a discontinuity on the allocation decision (that is, a project must be accepted or rejected in total).

The first allocation yields a total of $175 in excess present value, but the second and third yield only $170 in total excess present value. Therefore, the maximum excess present value results from the first allocation. Keep in

[5] As H. Weingartner has demonstrated, the present value index criterion effectively imposes a budget constraint by imputing a cost of acquiring funds. See his article "The Excess Present Value Index—A Theoretical Basis and Critique," *J. of Accounting Research*, Autumn 1963.

mind, however, that the application of this criterion assumes that the $100 left over from the other two allocations would be invested in projects that would earn income at the cost-of-capital rate. An investment at the cost-of-capital rate yields an excess present value of zero.

In this case, the excess present value criterion gave us the optimal allocation without any additional analysis.

Suppose now that only $650 is available for capital investments. An application of the excess present value criterion would allocate this budget to Projects 2 and 1, consuming the $650 and yielding a total excess present value of $131. However, the same amount could be distributed over Projects 2, 3, and 4, which also consumes the entire budget but yields $170 of total excess present value. This is another example of the effect of discontinuities.

The possibility of discontinuities prevents us from formulating a general rule as to which method of ranking leads to the optimal allocation of a capital budget. Often, the acceptance of a project requires an immediate expenditure of the entire outlay, and this may not represent the best allocation of the budget. If a large number of projects must be considered, the analysis may have to rely on integer programing methods to obtain, say, an excess present value maximizing allocation.[6]

REVIEW PROBLEM 1
Present Value Versus Internal Rate of Return _____

(A) We have indicated that there are two basic situations wherein the excess present value method and the internal rate of revenue method may yield different decisions:

(1) Difference in length of project life. Consider two mutually exclusive projects, X and Y, which have the following cash flows:

	X	Y
Outlay	($1,000)	($1,000)
Inflows		
Years 1–6 inclusive	$271 per year	
Years 1–3 inclusive		$460 per year

(a) Determine the excess present value of each project using a 10 percent cost-of-capital rate.

(b) Determine (approximately) the internal rate of return for each product.

(c) Assuming the rankings differ in (a) and (b), which project would you recommend to management and why?

(2) Difference in outlays. Consider again two projects that are mutually exclusive and have the following cash flows:

_____

[6] For example, see H. Weingartner, *Mathematical Programming and the Analysis of Capital Budgeting Problems*. Englewood Cliffs, N.J.: Prentice-Hall, 1962.

	X	Y
Outlay	($2,000)	($5,000)
Inflows, years 1 and 2	$1,340 per year	$3,270 per year

Repeat (a), (b), and (c) of part (1) for these two projects, using a cost-of-capital rate of 12 percent in (a).

(B) Generally the conflict in ranking two projects by the internal rate of return and the excess present value methods can be resolved by considering explicitly the reinvestment rates expected for the difference in life spans or the difference in initial outlays, or both. We can do this by finding the interest rate that sets the excess present values of both projects equal.

(1) Refer to the data of part (A). Calculate the interest rates that would make both projects equally profitable under the assumptions given in (A-1 and A-2) above.

(2) How would you interpret these interest rates?

Leasing: A Special Form of Financing

A firm may have the option of either buying or renting a long-lived asset. If it buys the asset, the firm bears all the ownership risks, including the economic risk that the asset may not prove to be as profitable as originally envisioned. Leasing or renting an asset may remove or reduce the economic risk in return for a financial risk. Often, a lease contract requires payments over the entire lease period regardless of whether the firm continues to use the asset. This type of contract is called a noncancelable, or financial, lease to distinguish it from a lease agreement that is renewable at the option of either party at the end of each time period—for example, monthly or yearly.[7]

The financial lease causes some problems in capital budgeting analysis, because entering into an agreement to make a specified series of payments on the lease is substantially equivalent to borrowing money from a lending institution. Hence, a firm that signs a noncancelable lease has effectively combined two decisions into one: the decision to acquire the asset and the decision to finance the asset through debt. This assumes that a noncancelable lease places the same financial demands on the firm as that of a bond or long-term note. Whether this is true depends on the exact nature of the lease contract; but, in general, a noncancelable lease has many of the same requirements as a serial bond or note.

Let us assume that a financial lease is a form of debt and examine the problem.

---

[7] A cancelable lease is called an operating lease. An operating lease does not create a problem in a capital budgeting framework, because payments on this type of lease are treated like any other kind of operating expense.

The Leasing Decision Ignoring Taxes

If the firm is not subject to income taxes, the analysis of the leasing decision is relatively straightforward. Suppose the firm can buy an asset for $1,500 that has an estimated life of five years and a zero salvage value. The same asset is available under a five-year financial lease that requires yearly payments of $450. However, these payments include a charge of $33.90 per year for maintenance and other services that the firm would incur if it purchased the asset. Thus, the net payments under the lease for the use of the asset are only $416.10 per year.

Management goes through a normal capital budgeting analysis and determines that the acquisition of the asset promises an excess present value, using its cost-of-capital rate of 14 percent. The firm has a line of credit available from a bank that charges an interest rate of 10 percent on borrowed funds.

In the absence of tax considerations, management's decision is fairly obvious. The firm can acquire the machine by paying cash, borrowing from the bank, or signing the lease commitment. Whether the firm should pay cash or borrow is a question we defer for the moment. However, we can consider which of the two forms of borrowing is more attractive.

If the firm borrows from the bank, it will have to pay 10 percent interest, which can be translated into yearly payments of about $395.70, or $20.40 per year less than if it leased the asset. That is, the present value of an annuity of $395.70 at 10 percent is $1,500, which is the amount the firm would have to borrow. The set of lease payments implies that the lessor is charging 12 percent interest, since the present value of an annuity of $416.10 per year for five years at 12 percent is $1,500.[8] Assuming the lease is equivalent to borrowing, then the firm is better off paying $395.70 per year instead of $416.10. In general (ignoring taxes), a firm (or individual) would want to pay less interest than more.

Leasing with Current Income Tax Laws

We may have to qualify the previous statement slightly when we consider the effect of income tax laws. When a firm buys an asset and borrows the purchase price, it is allowed to deduct each year the depreciation on the asset and the interest paid on the debt. However, if the firm leases an asset, the entire lease payment is deductible during the year in which it is paid. Thus, an evaluation of the lease-or-buy decision must now include an assessment of the amounts and patterns of deductions available under each alterna-

---

[8] That is, $416.10(3.605) = $1,500$, where 3.605 is the present value factor from Table 14-4 for five years at 12 percent. Further note that if perfect markets were present, we would not expect to see *any* leasing under these conditions; the market price is simply not competitive.

EXHIBIT 15-3

		BUY AND BORROW	
Year	Lease Payments	Depreciation	Interest (10%)[a]
1	$ 395.70	$ 500	$150.00
2	395.70	400	125.40
3	395.70	300	98.40
4	395.70	200	68.67
5	395.70	100	35.97
Total deductions	$1,978.50	$1,500	$478.44

[a] The interest is computed on the beginning-of-the-year balance. Thus, $150 is 10 percent of $1,500. At the beginning of year 2, the balance is $1,500 − ($395.70 − $150) = $1,254.30. At year 3, it is $1,254.30 − ($395.70 − $125.40) = $984, and so on. A rounding error of 6 cents accumulates by year 5.

tive. We shall consider the problem in two stages. (Investment credit provisions are also likely to be present.)

When Lease and Borrowing Rates Are Equal. Suppose the firm can lease the asset or borrow the purchase price at the same effective interest rate. For example, assume the net lease payments and the debt payments are both equal to $395.70 per year. If the asset is purchased, the firm will deduct depreciation under the sum-of-the-years'-digits method.[9] The yearly tax deductions under each plan—that is, lease versus buy and borrow—are shown in Exhibit 15-3.

Note that when the lease and the borrowing plans require the same cash payments, the total deductions under the two plans are the same—in this case, 5($395.70) = $1,500 depreciation + $478.50 interest (except for the small rounding error). However, the timing of the deductions is not the same; the lease deductions are constant each year, but the depreciation and interest deductions are accelerated. In the first year, the buy-and-borrow arrangement results in a total deduction of $620, whereas the lease deduction is only $395.70. It is not until after the third year that the lease deductions exceed the deductions for depreciation and interest. But since early deductions are generally preferred over late deductions, these figures suggest that the buy-and-borrow plan is a better alternative for the firm.

Let us look at the problem in a slightly different way. Both forms of

---

[9] Recall that sum-of-the-years'-digits depreciation in year t, D_t, is computed as

$$D_t = \frac{n - (t-1)}{n(n+1)/2} (C - S)$$

where n is the number of years, C is cost, and S is salvage.

debt require the same cash payments and the same amounts of interest. They differ only in the amount of noninterest deductions. If the firm buys the asset, its noninterest deductions consist of each year's depreciation. If the firm leases the asset, its noninterest deductions are simply the lease payments less the interest:

Year	Lease Payment	—	Interest	=	Noninterest Deduction
1	$395.70		150.00		$ 245.70
2	395.70		125.40		270.30
3	395.70		98.40		297.30
4	395.70		68.67		327.03
5	395.70		35.97		359.73
					$1,500.06

Recall that the depreciation deductions are included in the capital investment analysis since they have a favorable effect on cash flows of a project equal to TR(Depreciation)$_t$. If we view the noninterest deductions of leases as equivalent to the depreciation deductions, we see that leasing reduces the tax benefits of noninterest deductions in the first three years by the difference TR(Depreciation − Noninterest lease deduction).

This single example should not be interpreted to mean that leasing will generally be inferior to a borrowing arrangement. For one thing, the lessor can require accelerated payments, which provide large deductions in the early years of the lease contract. For example, suppose a lease contract for a $1,500 asset required payments distributed as follows (where the discount factor is for $r = 8\%$):

Year	Payment	Discount Factor	Discounted Value
1	$ 650	.926	$ 601.90
2	550	.857	471.35
3	450	.794	357.30
4	50	.735	36.75
5	50	.681	34.05
Totals	$1,750		$1,501.35

If the firm "borrowed" this amount from the lessor, its implicit interest costs would be as follows:

Year 1	$120.10
Year 2	77.70
Year 3	39.95
Year 4	7.15
Year 5	3.70

Using these figures we note that the noninterest deductions of the lease will exceed the depreciation deductions in the first three years. Specifically:

Year	Lease Payment	− Interest	= Noninterest Deduction	Depreciation
1	$650	$120.10	529.90	$500
2	550	77.70	472.30	400
3	450	39.95	410.05	300
4	50	7.15	42.85	200
5	50	3.70	46.30	100

The question now is, how much is this difference worth to the firm? Recall that cash flows for the investment decision are discounted by the appropriate cost of capital for the project. Therefore, the value of the noninterest deductions over the depreciation deductions can be calculated as

$$\sum_t \text{TR (Lease noninterest deduction} - \text{Depreciation deduction)}_t \, (1 + \rho)^{-t}$$

where ρ is the appropriate cost of capital for the project. Assuming $\rho =$ 10% and a tax rate of 45 percent, the value of the above stream is as given in Exhibit 15-4.

This example illustrates how the tax laws may require a combined investment–financing decision. Suppose that an investment analysis of a project results in a negative excess present value. Normally, the analysis would stop there. However, if the project can be leased, the noninterest deductions may exceed the depreciation deductions to such an extent that the leased project will have an excess present value.

The sum of the discounted values illustrated in Exhibit 15-4 is called the *operating* advantage of the lease. It summarizes the discounted after-tax benefits of the excess of noninterest lease deductions over depreciation deductions. Its significance at this point is that it may alter the investment decision of a project that other criteria indicate to be unprofitable.

However, a problem arises when a lessor accelerates lease payments to provide larger deductions to the lessee in the earlier years of the contract. The U.S. Internal Revenue Service may interpret an accelerated lease contract

EXHIBIT 15-4

Year	TR(Lease − Depreciation)[a]	Discount Factor	Discounted Value
1	$13.46	.909	$12.24
2	32.54	.826	26.87
3	49.52	.751	37.19
4	−70.72	.683	−48.30
5	−24.17	.621	−15.01
Total			$12.99

[a] The deductions should sum to 0, but we have rounding errors equal to $.63.

as a sale by the lessor and a purchase by the lessee, thus requiring the lessee to record interest and depreciation rather than the lease payments on his or her tax return.

REVIEW PROBLEM 2

Assume a firm has the option of leasing an asset for five years or buying it outright. The lease payments are $5,000 per year. Based on the lessor's implicit interest rate of 16 percent, the purchase price is $16,370. The firm's borrowing rate for this asset is also 16 percent, its cost-of-capital rate is 20 percent, and its marginal tax rate is 45 percent. There is no salvage value for tax or other purposes.

(a) Suppose the firm's management decided to compare after-tax cash outlays of leasing to after-tax cash outlays to purchase using cash. Which option would it take, given an objective of minimizing the present value of total after-tax outlays? Use straight-line depreciation for five years.

(b) You are disturbed because a comparison of leasing with buying clearly biases decisions in favor of leasing. Why? You suggest instead that the comparison be based on leasing versus buy-and-borrow.

Show the after-tax cash outlays for leasing and for buy-and-borrow. In presenting your figures, split the lease payments into interest and noninterest deductions in order to highlight the critical differences in cash flows. Use sum-of-the-years'-digits depreciation for the buy-borrow option.

(c) On the basis of your analysis in (b), which option would you recommend to management? If it is different from their choice in (a), explain your different preference ranking.

When Interest Rates Differ. The lease-or-buy analysis becomes more complex when the firm can borrow at one interest rate but the lessor charges a different borrowing rate. Usually we assume that the lessor charges a higher interest rate than the firm would have to pay if it borrowed. In some cases, the lessor may provide credit to a lessee when the latter's bank refuses the loan. For example, the bank may feel that the lessee has an excess amount of debt outstanding. Institutional constraints may prevent the bank from extending credit when the borrower cannot provide sufficient security. The lessor is not subject to the same constraints and may be willing to provide credit under a lease at a higher rate of interest than the lessee would normally pay on a bank loan.[10]

Another argument for higher interest rates is less convincing than the

---

[10] In a sense, this assumption implies that the bank refuses to loan the funds even though the borrower would be willing to pay higher rates of interest. This may be reasonable since there are laws that prevent a lender from charging an explicit rate of interest higher than some stated percentage.

previous one. We generally assume that a lessor wishes to earn the cost of capital on a lease contract. Since a lessor's cost-of-capital rate may be higher than a financial institution's lending rate, the lease will have higher interest rates. This argument is difficult to justify, however. A lessor is normally required to quote a selling price on the asset he or she is willing to lease. This selling price becomes the basis for determining the amount of interest the lessee would pay if he or she leased the asset. It is reasonable to assume that the lessor would set the selling price to include some amount of profit over the cost of acquiring the asset. Thus, the spread between the total amount of the lease payments and the lessor's cost of acquiring the asset is composed of two forms of compensation: a profit on the asset (based on a quoted selling price) and the interest payments (total payments less selling price). How the lessor divides compensation between the two factors will depend on the specific circumstances.

Arguments may support the assumption that the lease contract will carry a *lower* interest rate than that available from a lending institution. A lessor often provides maintenance services whose cost is included in the lease payments. If the lessee buys the asset he or she must either provide maintenance services or purchase them. In evaluating the lease contract, the lessee would subtract an estimate of the cost of maintenance services from the lease payments to arrive at the net payments. The lessee's estimate of the cost of maintenance services may even be higher if he or she provides the services than if the lessor has built the services into the lease payments. That is, the lessor may enjoy economies of scale since he or she maintains and services a larger set of assets than the lessee. Thus, the net lease payments may result in a lower implicit interest charge than the lessee could obtain elsewhere.

Consider another possibility. When the lessee evaluates the buying decision, he or she must estimate the eventual salvage value of the asset. When the lessor sets lease payments a similar salvage estimate must be made, and this will have some bearing on the lease payments charged. The lessee is not in the asset-selling business and may have less knowledge about the available markets for used assets. The lessor is probably closer to the used asset market and will be in a better position to know the future demand for leased assets when the contracts expire. This could result in the lessor setting a higher salvage value for the asset than the estimate set by the lessee. The lessee must treat the estimate of the asset's salvage value as an additional payment on the lease.[11] But if the lessee's estimate is lower than the lessor's,

---

[11] That is, when a firm or individual leases an asset with no purchase option at the end of the lease, any salvage value of the asset at the end of the period is forgone and must be viewed as an additional payment to the lessor. This complicates the calculation somewhat, so in our examples we have assumed a zero salvage value for the asset. In the problem section and in later examples, positive salvage values are assumed.

the total net payments on the lease may reflect a lower interest rate than the lessee could obtain from a lending institution.

In other words, we should not automatically assume that leasing will carry higher interest rates than borrowing. There are conditions that could result in interest rates that are higher or lower in the leasing arrangement than those available through conventional financing (borrowing). Our concern now is how differences in interest rates affect the analysis of the lease-or-buy decision.

Financial and Operating Analyses of Leasing.   In the following example we shall assume a lease contract carries an implicit interest rate that is different from the rate the firm would pay on funds borrowed from a lending institution. This creates some ambiguity as to how to compare the lease and the buy-and-borrow alternatives. We might discount the respective cash flow streams at the firm's cost of capital or we might employ an internal rate of return analysis. Remember, however, that the lease combines investment and financing considerations. An alternative approach recognizes this fact and proceeds in two stages wherein we compute a financial effect and an operating effect.[12] We will use 10 percent and 8 percent for the lease rate and the borrowing rate, respectively. The nature of the analysis, however, would not change if we used different (higher) rates for each.

A firm can acquire the services of an asset for five years by signing a noncancelable lease contract that requires yearly payments of $1,000. The asset can also be purchased at a price of $3,791, which implies a 10 percent rate of interest on the lease.[13] The firm's management believes that funds can be borrowed at a marginal rate of 8 percent. If the asset is purchased, it can be depreciated according to the sum-of-the-years'-digits method. (Further note the assumption that if the asset is purchased the firm's capital structure calls for a conventional loan contract.)

We now separate the relative advantage or disadvantage of leasing compared with borrowing into a financial advantage or disadvantage, which considers the effect of paying a lower or higher interest rate on the lease, and an operating advantage or disadvantage, which considers the effect of the different noninterest deductions available from leasing and from buying.

To compute the former, we merely discount the lease payments at the firm's current borrowing rate and determine if their present value is less than (advantage) or greater than (disadvantage) the purchase price, which would be the amount of the debt if funds were borrowed. In our example, the

---

[12] The analysis to follow was first proposed by R. Vancil. See his article "Lease or Borrow—New Method of Analysis," *Harvard Business Rev.*, Sept.–Oct. 1961.

[13] That is, since $1,000x = $3,791$, $x = 3.791$, which is the annuity factor for $r = 10\%$ and $n = 5$ (Table 14-4).

$1,000 payments discounted at 8 percent have a present value of $3,993, which is $202 greater than the purchase price. This means that the firm is incurring a debt of $202 more than it would through borrowing, which is equivalent to saying that the firm could save interest payments that have a present value of $202 if it borrowed the funds instead of leasing the asset. Because these extra interest payments are tax deductible, we assume that the lease contract could reduce the value of the firm's stock by $(1 - TR)$ ($202). Using a tax rate of 48 percent, the financial disadvantage of the lease is .52($202) = $105.04. This calculation summarizes the effect of paying $1,000 per year under the lease contract as opposed to paying about $950 per year if the purchase price of $3,791 were borrowed at 8 percent.[14]

Recall that the operating advantage or disadvantage of the lease is computed from the differences between the noninterest deductions under each plan. For the buy-and-borrow decision, the noninterest deductions consist of the depreciation allowed in each year. (For simplicity, we ignore investment tax credit provisions of the tax code.) The noninterest deduction on the lease consists of the payments less the interest charges each year. There has been some controversy concerning the proper rate to use in computing the interest charges. For example, we could use either the borrowing rate[15] or the implicit interest rate charged by the lessor to determine the interest charges of the lease. If the firm borrows the purchase price, it will pay $949.41 per year for five years, or a total of $4,747.05. The total amount of interest will be ($4,747.05 − $3,791.00) = $956.05.

If the firm leases the asset it will pay total interest of ($5,000 − $3,791) = $1,209, or an incremental amount of $252.95. This difference in interest deductions, spread over five years (that is, $1,000.00 − $949.41 per year) has a present value of $202—see footnote 14, this chapter.

In effect, the calculation of the financial disadvantage, adjusted for taxes, is merely designed to reflect the *incremental* effect of paying a different (here, higher) rate of interest on the lease than the rate available through a standard loan. Once this incremental effect is removed, both plans will be on an equal footing as far as interest deductions are concerned. This means we should now remove total interest of $1,209 (equal to $252.95 + $956.05) from the lease payments in order to calculate the noninterest portion of the payments, which are then compared to the noninterest deductions through buying. The only way to accomplish this is to use the implicit rate of interest charged by the lessor—approximately 10 percent—to determine the interest portion of the lease payments. The relevant calculations are shown in Exhibit 15-5.

---

[14] That is, $3.993x = $3,791$, where 3.993 is the annuity factor for $r = 8\%$ and $n = 5$. Solving, $x = 949.41. Note that ($1,000 − $949.41) (3.993) = $202.

[15] For example, Bower *et al.* use the borrowing rate to break out the noninterest deduction, but this creates a subsequent problem in amortizing the loan balance of $3,791. See R. Bower, F. Herringer, and J. Williamson, "Lease Evaluation," *Accounting Rev.*, April 1966.

————————————————————————————————————EXHIBIT 15-5

Year	Depreciation[a]	Lease Balance, End of Year	Interest @ 10%	Lease Deduction[b]
0		$3,791.00		
1	$1,263.67	3,170.10	$379.10	$620.90
2	1,010.94	2,487.11	317.01	682.99
3	758.20	1,735.82	248.71	751.29
4	505.47	909.40	173.58	826.42
5	252.73	0	90.94	909.06

[a] $\frac{5}{15}($3,791)$, $\frac{4}{15}($3,791)$, $\frac{3}{15}($3,791)$, and so on.
[b] Lease payment less interest. Some error due to rounding.

We now compare the two streams of noninterest deductions by taking the difference, Lease − Depreciation, and assuming a 48 percent tax rate:

Year	Lease	Depreciation	Difference	Difference × Tax Rate
1	$620.90 −	$1,263.67 =	−$642.77	−$308.53
2	682.99 −	1,010.94 =	− 327.95	− 157.42
3	751.29 −	758.20 =	− 6.91	− 3.32
4	826.42 −	505.47 =	+ 320.95	+ 154.06
5	909.06 −	252.73 =	+ 656.33	+ 315.04

Suppose the firm has a cost-of-capital rate of 12 percent. If we use that rate to discount the differences in tax benefits of the two flows, the operating disadvantage of the lease (a negative figure) would be as follows:

Lease operating advantage
$= -$308.53(.893) - $157.42(.797) - $3.32(.712) + $154.06(.636)$
$+$315.04(.567)$
$= -$275.52 - $125.46 - $2.36 + $97.98 + 178.63
$= -$126.73$

The total disadvantage of the lease is the sum of the two components:

Total disadvantage $= $105.04 + 126.73
$= 231.77

Note that we use the cost-of-capital rate for the project to discount the after-tax differences between the lease noninterest deductions and the buy-and-borrow noninterest deductions. The assumption here is that since the after-tax benefits of depreciation are presumably discounted by the cost-of-capital rate in investment analysis, this rate should be used to assess the incremental effect of any noninterest deductions under the lease contract (in this case, the incremental effect is negative).[16]

The justification for using the borrowing rate to discount the incremental effect of paying more interest under the lease (or less, as the case may be) comes from accepted theories in finance. Under rather strict assumptions, it can be shown that the value of the firm will increase (decrease) if the firm can "refund" its debt with lower (higher) interest costs by an amount equal to the discounted value of the differences between the present interest costs and the new interest costs over the future time interval of the debt. The discount rate used in the calculation is the interest rate on the new debt, which can be viewed as the opportunity cost rate at which the firm could borrow. Of course, these "strict assumptions" are easier to invoke than to observe, and alternative evaluation procedures reflect this fact.

Alternative Approaches to the Leasing Decision

The lease-or-buy analysis just described consists essentially in splitting the total tax deductions under leasing—the total of the lease payments themselves—between interest deductions and noninterest deductions. Doing this assumes we accept the notion that one stream of deductions, the interest portion, should be discounted at the borrowing rate whereas the other stream, the noninterest portion, should be discounted at the cost-of-capital rate. In effect this implies that one stream of deductions is less risky than the other. Of course, both components of the lease payments are equally risky. We know of no lease contracts stipulating that if the firm no longer wishes to use the leased asset, it need only pay the interest portion of the lease payment. The same holds true should the firm decide to buy the asset and borrow an amount equal to the purchase price; that is, it must make the payments regardless of whether it continues to use the asset.

Traditionally, it has been assumed that since depreciation is part of the operating expenses used to determine operating income, it represents a more risky stream of deductions compared with interest payments. However, this view is somewhat naive. As long as a firm has sufficient revenues to cover its expenses, the total depreciation deduction is just as certain as the interest deduction. The only uncertainty is the pattern of the deduction, which depends on the depreciation method used, the estimate of the asset's service life, and the salvage value of the asset at the time it is actually salvaged. Indeed, if the firm decides to abandon the asset before its normal life expires, the difference between the unamortized portion of the asset cost and its salvage value at the time it is abandoned is deducted immediately. In that event, the firm may receive deductions even earlier than it had originally anticipated.

---

[16] This too is subject to controversy. See J. Van Horne, *Financial Management and Policy*. Prentice-Hall, 1980.

Controversy over the points raised in the previous paragraph has led some to reject the two-stage, two-interest rate approach to the analysis of the leasing decision. In doing so, some have also changed the nature of the comparison, and instead of comparing leasing with buy-and-borrow, they compare the cash flows under leasing with the cash flows under the assumption that the firm buys the asset and pays cash. If a noncancelable lease is equivalent to borrowing—and that is the assumption underlying the SEC's *Accounting Series Release No. 147* and the FASB's *Opinion No. 13*—it is inappropriate to compare a decision to buy and finance with debt with a decision to buy and pay cash. Rather, the comparison should be to a decision to buy and finance with an alternative source of debt.

Once we accept the notion to compare leasing to buy-and-borrow, the issue of applying two different rates to the different deductions or using a single discounting rate for all deductions for each alternative may be a trivial one. We might guess that once the deductions are arranged under each alternative, the optimal decision of whether to lease or buy-and-borrow is often unaffected by the use of a single discounting rate or the use of two different rates as in our example. We assume that if only one discount rate is used, that rate is also used to discount the total tax deductions under both alternatives. The critical aspect in the analysis is that once we accept the fact that the lease payment represents interest and noninterest deductions for tax purposes, we must then compare these deductions to the interest and noninterest deductions under the buy-and-borrow alternative (the latter is mostly depreciation).

Other Complications: Salvage Values, Gains/Losses on Sale, and Maintenance

When a firm buys an asset, it receives the right to any cash salvage value of that asset when it is abandoned. This right does not usually extend to the firm under a leasing contract, and any salvage value foregone under the lease contract must be treated as an additional *implicit* cash payment to the lessor—a payment that is not tax deductible. To illustrate, suppose a firm has the option of entering into a leasing contract that requires cash payments of $1,000 per year for five years or of buying the asset for $3,715 cash. If the asset is purchased, the total depreciation will be limited to $3,215, because the tax (and expected) salvage value is $500. The firm's borrowing rate is 10 percent. If we merely discount the explicit payments of $1,000 per year for five years at 10 percent we obtain a present value of $3,791—only $76 more than the purchase price. This fact suggests that the lessor is charging an implicit rate approximately equal to the firm's borrowing rate. The firm could go to another creditor, however, and sign a 10 percent loan agreement to pay $x per year for five years plus a lump-sum payment of $500 at the end of five years to acquire the $3,715 asset. As we would guess, the equal payments under this borrowing contract would be less than $1,000, indicating the lease's financial disadvantage. Specifically, the firm's payments under its borrowing alternative would be only $898.18, since $898.18(3.791) + $500(.621) = $3,715 (approximately), where the numbers in the parentheses are the 10 percent discount factors for a five-year annuity and a lump-sum payment at the end of five years, respectively. The $101.82 difference between the two annual payment streams represents a 2 percent premium charged by the lessor (use the appropriate factors for 12 percent to discount the $1,000 payments and the $500 implicit payment). If we use the two-stage approach described above, the financial disadvantage of the lease is equal to $(1 - TR)$ $101.82(3.791)$.

Now suppose that the tax guidelines require the firm to use a salvage value of $1,000 at the end of year 5, even though the firm expects to receive only the original $500. Should the firm buy the asset, it will depreciate $2,715 over five years and then receive an additional deduction of $500 at the end of year 5 because the book value at that time will be $1,000. If we ignored this loss, we would understate the total noninterest deductions under the buy-and-borrow contract because the total depreciation recognized would only be $2,715. The simplest way to handle this loss is simply to add the $500 to the depreciation recognized in year 5 before comparing the noninterest deductions under the two alternatives. Obviously, if there were a gain on the final sale of the asset, we would subtract the gain from the last year's depreciation.

One final complication in comparing leasing with buy-and-borrow (or to buy, for that matter) occurs when the operating expenses under the two alternatives are not the same. This often arises when the lease contract includes provisions for maintenance and repairs that the lessee would have to provide or purchase if he or she bought the asset. The practical approach to this problem is merely to deduct the estimated value of these and other ancillary services from the lease payments, thus obtaining net payments for the acquisition of the asset. We would then compare net lease payments with borrowing payments, with implicit interest charges based on these net payments rather than on their gross amounts. Recall that this is how we handled such a payment in our first illustration in this section on leasing.

REVIEW PROBLEM 3
Capital Budgeting and Leasing

(A) Suppose the following data regarding a capital asset are available to you.

	YEAR			
	0	1	2	3
Outlay	$36,000			
Revenues		$40,000	$40,000	$40,000

YEAR

	0	1	2	3
Variable and fixed cash expenses—includes $1,000 for maintenance		16,000	16,000	16,000
Salvage value (ignore in computing depreciation for taxes*)				2,000
Investment credit applies in Year 1 (10%, 6⅔%, and 3⅓% for 7, 5, and 3 years, respectively)				
Tax rate = 40% each year				
Depreciation method—sum of the year's digits				

Interest rate factors:	**Year**	**12%**	**14%**	**18%**
	1	.89	.88	.85
	2	.80	.77	.72
	3	.70	.67	.61

Cost of capital for this asset is 18%.

Using the format below, show the after-tax flows if the asset is purchased for cash.

YEAR

		0	1	2	3
(1)	Investment outlay				
(2)	Investment credit				
(3)	After-tax flows from (Revenues − Cash Expenses)				
(4)	After-tax benefits from depreciation, assuming full year for year 3				
(5)*	After-tax salvage proceeds (recall you ignored $S = \$2,000$ in computing depreciation)				

(B) Suppose your firm could borrow the outlay price of $36,000 from the bank, paying interest at a rate of 12 percent. The firm wishes to set up the payments such that it pays $x per year for three years plus $2,000 at the end of year 3.

(1) Using the discount factors for 12 percent, calculate the yearly payments (round off). (This can be set up as a simple annuity problem.)

(2) Suppose the payments were $14,500; hypothetical interest and principal payments would be as follows:

Year	Interest	Principal
1	$4,400	$10,100
2	3,200	11,300
3	1,900	12,600
Salvage		2,000
	Total	$36,000

Suppose this option were substituted in the cash-flow analysis in (A) instead of the outlay. Show how the cash-flow figures would be modified. Label each type of flow and include tax effects.

	AMOUNTS FOR YEAR			
Type of Cash Flows	0	1	2	3
(1)				
(2)				
(3)				
(4)				
(5)				
(6)				

(C) The firm may also lease the asset making three yearly payments of $16,500. This figure includes a charge of $1,000 for maintenance services that were included as a cash expense in part (A). If we chose this option, how would the cash-flow figures be modified? Show again as follows:

	AMOUNTS FOR YEARS			
Type of Cash Flows	0	1	2	3
(1)				
(2)				
(3)				
(4)				
(5)				
(6)				

(D) We can now compare and contrast various approaches to leasing versus buy-and-borrow.
  (1) One option is to discount the cash flows from parts (A), (B), and (C) using the firm's cost-of-capital rate of 18 percent, and then choose the option with the highest excess present value. What is the main criticism of this approach?
  (2) Another approach (proposed by R. Johnson and W. Lewellen,

Problem 14 this chapter) is to discount some of the differential flows by the cost-of-capital rate (for example, after-tax flows from depreciation and net salvage proceeds) and use the debt rate to discount the lease payments. This assumes that we are only interested in comparing the *incremental* effects of Plan (A) (buy) versus Plan (C) (lease). Justify the use of two different rates. What other flows might be discounted by the debt rate?

(3) A third option, described in this chapter, is to compare differential effects of Plan _____ to Plan _____ *(fill-in)*. This is done in two stages (also using two different discount rates).

    (a) The financial disadvantage (advantage) of the lease is designed to measure the differential effects of interest. Using the appropriate cash-flow figures, write the equation for this computation and identify each variable. (Note, we have adjusted for the salvage value by computing "equivalent" borrowing payments of $14,500—see (B-1) and (B-2) above.)

    (b) The second computation compares the effect of differential noninterest tax deductions on the lease. Determine the "operating" advantage or disadvantage of the lease, assuming the lease has an implicit interest rate of 14 percent (there will be a round-off error of approximately $10).

Differential Tax Benefits

We shall begin this section by commenting on a feature of the investment tax credit rules that had an impact on the leasing of large assets (rolling stock of railroads, aircraft, tankers, and so on). The tax credit laws generally prevented some firms from taking advantage of all the tax credits they might have earned during a single year. To illustrate, let us assume that the tax credit on a jetliner is approximately $5 million. Assume also that the maximum tax credit originally allowed during a single year is approximately 50 percent of the firm's tax liability. Thus, the firm acquiring the jet must earn about $10 million in order to take its maximum credit in the year in which it purchased the aircraft, assuming an average tax rate of 50 percent. If the average tax rate were 45 percent the firm's before-tax income must be approximately $11.1 million to qualify for the $5 million credit. Suppose an airline purchases six aircraft during a single year. Its before-tax income must be between $60 and $66 million to take advantage of its maximum credits. Several of the large U.S. airlines have never earned that amount in one year.

Tax credit laws contained carryback and carryforward provisions for any credits not taken during a current year. However, during periods of rapid growth—for example, switching from propeller to jet fleets—these carryback and carryover provisions did not provide much relief for firms making large capital investments; that is, the credits would have expired before the firms could accumulate sufficient income to exhaust them. This apparently led to an increase in the leasing of aircraft from banks during the 1960s and the first half of the 1970s. Banks were in the opposite position vis-à-vis airlines— banks did not have to make large capital investments for their own businesses, but they had sufficient before-tax income to absorb large investment credits. The result was a unique sharing of the tax credits between the lessor firms and the lessee firms.

This situation tended to change in the late 1970s. Inflation, increases in air travel around the world, and other factors led to increases in the salvage values of certain airliners that had been depreciated by the airlines. These increased salvage values were not incorporated into the IRS guidelines, so airlines could receive tax benefits on the depreciation of aircraft at the normal tax rates—say, 45–50 percent—and then recognize a tax gain on the sale of the aircraft—some of which could be taxed at the capital gain tax rate of less than 30 percent—to the extent they could avoid depreciation recapture rules. Since airlines have not been in a period of increased capital expenditures in recent years, they have begun to move from leasing back to purchasing aircraft.

There is nothing (morally) wrong with taking advantage of differential tax rates if that is the way the Code is written. But the scenario above does indicate how differential tax inputs can dramatically affect an industry, given certain economic events. Today a similar phenomenon seems to be affecting the housing market: More and more rental units are being converted to purchased units. This conversion not only provides the former renter (now owner) with current deductions for interest and taxes (formerly accruing to landlords), but also promises a beneficial tax rate on any capital gain, assuming inflation continues to raise the replacement cost of housing. Indeed, the homeowner who reaches age 55 may exclude up to $150,000 of a gain on the sale of a personal residence. (This is a once-in-a-lifetime election.) We can begin to understand the large increase in housing demand as a result of double-digit inflation. We might also note here that inflation rates move individuals into higher tax brackets, so current deductions for interest and taxes also become more attractive. These deductions would be equally attractive to landlords who could pass some of their benefits through to the renter in the form of reduced rent payments. Finally, the consumption of housing services from ownership completely escapes the income tax laws.

Again, the main point is that the differential benefits of taxation alter individuals' and firms' investment behavior. Another illustration concerns the purchase and sale of a professional athletic team. During the 1960s the Code allowed the purchaser of a sports team to allocate much of the acquisition cost of a franchise and the players (often a lump-sum purchase price) to the cost of acquiring the players rather than to the franchise. This benefited the purchaser because the acquisition costs of players (assets) could be depreciated according to normal tax guidelines—for example, for five years or more. In contrast, the cost of acquiring the franchise could not be depreciated, because it was assumed that the franchise did not deteriorate. Of course, any difference between the original acquisition price of the franchise and the price received on its eventual sale would be treated as a capital gain (or loss).

Now consider the following scenario. A group of investors in relatively high marginal tax brackets obtain a franchise and players for X, a lump-sum investment. They operate the franchise for about five years, after which the total acquisition cost allocated to the players has been depreciated at the normal rates. The players still have a playing value, since the IRS guidelines do not determine their total useful playing years. Assume then that the franchise plus these players could now be sold for Y. A potential purchaser, perhaps a new syndicate, observes that about 90 percent of the Y acquisition cost could be assigned to the players, which could then be depreciated again at the regular rates—in effect, a second round of depreciation for many of the players. In turn, the former owners would recognize a capital gain on the sale of the franchise equal to the current value of the players less their reduced book value. The depreciation recapture rules might require that this gain be taxed at normal rates, but the sale might go through because of the potential depreciation benefits to the new owners. Indeed, the owners could easily make up figures in this situation to motivate the sale of the franchise merely to take advantage of the differential benefits of taxation, which is what we do in the next Review Problem.

This type of situation was restricted when the IRS won a court case against an Atlanta sports team. In that case, the IRS succeeded in assigning much of the purchase price of the team (a franchise and players) to the franchise, which could not be depreciated. Hence, the conversion of depreciation to capital gain to depreciation is now more difficult, and changes in ownership of sports teams depend on other economic factors.

These are but a few examples of how differential tax benefits influence individuals and firms to move into and out of contracts that may seem out of character.[17] Witness the popular types of investments by professionals and entertainment stars, like oil drilling, farms, and real estate. Inflation and high marginal tax rates will motivate individuals to invest in firms as a means of seeking out these tax relief measures. As noted in Chapter 14, the differential tax rates in the current tax code may lead to a more complicated analysis of equilibrium values of firms.

REVIEW PROBLEM 4

A sports team investor owns a franchise and players with a book value of $2.25 million. The players have been fully depreciated but their playing value produces after-tax operating cash inflows (that is, revenues less

---

[17] Another dimension of investment surfaces if we assume uncertainty. A risk-neutral individual who faces a progressive tax structure will act as if he were risk averse toward pretax income! See J. Fellingham and M. Wolfson, "The Effects of Alternative Income Tax Structures on Risk Taking in Capital Markets," *National Tax Journal,* Dec. 1978.

cash expense) of $1.75 million per year for five years. The franchise could then be sold for $2.25 million.

The investor has found a potential buyer for the franchise and players who is willing to pay $10 million for this asset provided the acquisition cost of the players leads to suitable tax benefits. Both parties agree on the $1.75 million estimate of after-tax operating cash inflows. The seller suggests a split of $7.75 million for the players and $2.25 million for the franchise (the current book value). The players would be depreciated on an accelerated (sum-of-the-years' digits) basis, $n = 5$, $S = 0$. The buyer also assumes the franchise could be sold for $2.25 million after five years.

Show that the above information indicates that it is not in the best interests of the current owner to continue to hold this asset but that at the same time it is a profitable investment for the new buyer. Although it may not be an accurate assumption, assume the current owner will be taxed at 30 percent on the capital gain.[18] Also assume 14 percent discount factors and a normal tax rate of 50 percent.

Conclusion

In this chapter we have discussed some of the controversial issues in investment analysis. For the most part, these issues arise simply because theory has not developed to a point where agreement can be reached on the optimal investment strategies under conditions of market imperfections and uncertainty.

Nevertheless, managers must make investment decisions, and the discussion of the arguments for and against various investment strategies may provide a basis for decision making that goes beyond mere intuition. There seems to be strong agreement that some form of discounting model is appropriate for investment decisions even under conditions of uncertainty. Unfortunately, the actual measurement of the appropriate discount rate to use in the model is difficult to obtain in practice.

There also seems to be agreement that a financial lease should be considered a special form of debt and as such should be evaluated against alternative forms of financing available to a firm. But here again, theory does not provide an unequivocal approach to analyzing whether to lease or buy an asset. The rule is generally to separate financial from investment decisions. However, a lease payment represents a joint payment for the services of an asset as well as a charge for financing (interest).

Again, we must emphasize that the entire leasing analysis assumes that a noncancelable lease is in fact another form of borrowing. Of course, not all leasing contracts are equivalent to borrowing. In fact, the accounting profession is somewhat reluctant to treat all leases as debt and effectively allows

---

[18] In practice, some of this gain would be taxed at ordinary rates because of the recapture rules. We ignore these rules here.

some contracts to escape a recording on a firm's balance sheet.[19] There are also some qualitative factors involved in a leasing arrangement that tend to reduce our confidence in the debt assumption.[20] A leasing contract permits a firm to transfer some of the uncertainties of asset ownership to the lessor. For example, the lease contract is fixed regardless of the costs of maintenance of the particular asset during the years in which it is used. Similarly, fixed lease payments in effect guarantee a certain salvage value of the asset as far as the lessee is concerned, because the lessor estimates a salvage value and fixes the payments accordingly. Any penalties for errors in the salvage estimate must usually be borne by the lessor.[21]

Finally, a lease contract may permit the lessee to obtain tax benefits that he or she could otherwise not claim. To illustrate, consider the investment credit of the 1960s that permitted a firm to deduct from its tax bill 7 percent of the cost of an asset if the asset had a tax life of eight years or more.[22] However, the total amount of investment credits that would be allowed in any taxable year was limited to $25,000 plus 50 percent of the tax liability over $25,000. Any unused tax credits had carryback and carryover provisions. However, firms discovered a way to obtain the benefits immediately. In general, financial lending institutions had a great potential for absorbing investment credits since they were profitable and therefore had high tax liabilities but did not require large amounts of operating assets. Hence, agreements were made whereby the financial institutions purchased the operating assets of a prospective lessee, thus capturing the investment credit, and then passed on some of the benefits to the lessee at the end of the leasing period under

---

[19] The criteria for determining when a lease is debt are described in FASB *Statement No. 13* (Amended and Interpreted thru May 1980), *Accounting for Leases.* Stamford, Conn.: Financial Accounting Standards Board, 1980.

[20] Other features of leasing are discussed in R. Vancil, *Leasing of Industrial Equipment.* New York: McGraw-Hill, 1963 and W. Ferrara *et al., Lease Purchase Decision.* New York: National Association of Accountants, 1980.

[21] This is not always the case; the leasing contract may require additional payments by the lessee if the salvage proceeds of the leased asset fall below a certain amount.

[22] Two-thirds of 7 percent could be deducted if the asset life for tax purposes was less then eight but at least six years, and ⅓ of 7 percent could be deducted for assets with a tax life of four to six years. Recent class life system (CLS) and asset depreciation range (ADR) provisions from the Revenue Act of 1971 further alter deduction comparisons. The tax credit rate in effect in 1979 was 10 percent rather then 7 percent, and the relevant lives were three years (receive ⅓ of 10 percent), five years (receive ⅔ of 10 percent), and seven years (receive 10 percent). In turn, the Economic Recovery Tax Act of 1981 further changed the provision. The central new feature is an abandonment of useful life, with a few classes of assets with prescribed lives and depreciation patterns. The investment tax credit is 6 percent in the 3 year class and 10 percent in the 5, 10, and 15 year classes. Lease provisions that allow the credit have been considerably relaxed. And the depreciation schedules become mixtures of declining balance and sum-of-the-years' digits. Old rules apply to assets placed in service prior to the Act. Finally, the upper limit on the annual investment credit allowed is being relaxed, and by 1982, it will be up to 90 percent of the tax liability in excess of $25,000 (formerly, it was 50 percent of the excess).

a purchase–option arrangement. (Indeed, the ability to do this has been considerably increased by provisions in the 1981 Tax Act.)

Many of these investment credit provisions are in current tax laws, but the specific provisions should be checked by reference to appropriate texts. This admonition is especially important because the tax laws are being subjected to a major restructuring at the time of this writing. Tax provisions change constantly, and an additional dimension to investment analysis concerns speculation on the timing and content of such changes.

Our final word here is a reminder of the shortage of theory. Leasing is perplexing because of market imperfections. Discounting is emphasized in the text because it is clearly used in practice. But to what extent the illustrated discounting approach represents theoretical perfection or the simplicity in preparation theme of the *nouvelle cuisine* remains unclear.

Supplementary Readings

Articles

Alchian, A., "The Rate of Interest, Fisher's Rate of Return over Costs, and Keynes' 'Internal Rate of Return,' " *American Economic Rev.,* Dec. 1955.

Bower, R., F. Herringer, and J. Williamson, "Lease Evaluation," *Accounting Rev.,* April 1966.

Hirshleifer, J., "Risk, the Discount Rate, and Investment Decisions," *American Economic Rev.,* May 1961.

Miller, M. and C. Upton, "Leasing, Buying, and the Cost of Capital Services," *J. of Finance,* June 1976.

Myers, S. *et al.,* "Valuation of Financial Lease Contracts," *J. of Finance,* July 1976.

Vancil, R., "Lease or Borrow—New Method of Analysis," *Harvard Business Rev.,* Sept.–Oct. 1961.

Weingartner, H., "The Excess Present Value Index—A Theoretical Basis and Critique," *J. of Accounting Research,* Autumn 1963.

Books

Bierman, H., Jr., and S. Smidt, *The Capital Budgeting Decision,* 5th ed. New York: Macmillan, 1980.

Ferrara, W., J. Thies, and M. Dirsmith, *The Lease Purchase Decision.* New York: National Association of Accountants, 1980.

Hawkins, D., and M. Wehle, *Accounting for Leases.* New York: Research Foundation of Financial Executives Institute, 1973.

Van Horne, J., *Financial Management and Policy.* Englewood Cliffs, N.J.: Prentice-Hall, 1980.

Weingartner, H., *Mathematical Programming and the Analysis of Capital Budgeting Decisions.* Englewood Cliffs, N.J.: Prentice-Hall, 1962.

Questions and Problems

1. It has been said that the internal rate of return and the excess present value methods give the same results for "accept or reject" decisions. Explain why.
2. Much of the theory underlying capital investment criteria assumes the existence of perfect capital markets. In a perfect capital market a firm does not have to impose a budget on the amount of funds devoted to capital expenditures. Indicate situations wherein the imposition of capital budgets seems, at least administratively, to be a reasonable policy to follow.
3. A manager makes the following statement: "Whenever we want to avoid a review of our investment proposals or to circumvent a budget limit set by top management, we merely enter into a leasing agreement that permits us to acquire the asset with rental payments obtained from our operating budget." Discuss this procedure.
4. A manager raises the following issue: The cost of capital for a firm measures the rate of interest that the marketplace demands as compensation for an investment in a firm of a given risk class. Therefore, it is the marketplace's, and not the manager's, assessment of the risk of individual projects that is important. Comment on this issue, including the implications of this statement on the use of subjective probabilities in capital budgeting analyses.
5. In the analysis of a lease-or-buy decision, is it always feasible for the decision to invest to be kept separate from the decision to finance?

6. **Multiple Rates**

   (1) Assume that a firm is considering the following investment proposal:

	Year 1	Year 2	Year 3
Outlay ($160)			
Cash flows at end of year	$500	($500)*	$160

   * Indicates a negative cash flow.

   (a) Calculate the excess present value for the project, assuming a cost-of-capital rate of 10 percent.
   (b) Repeat (a) using rates of 20 percent and 40 percent.
   (c) Comment on your results. What is the internal rate of return for the project?

   (2) Suppose that the project outlay and cash flows were as follows:

	Year 1	Year 2	Year 3
Outlay ($125)			
Cash flows at end of year	$500	($550)	$160

   Calculate the excess present value for this project using rates of 10 percent and 40 percent. Discuss your results.

7. **Capital Budgets and the Discontinuity Problem**
   The central management of Synchro Systems, Inc., has received requests for capital funds from its various divisions. The quarterly budget for capital expendi-

EXHIBIT 15-6_____

Division A

Proposal 1: Replace machinery

Outlay	($130,000)
Present value of inflows	153,000
Present value index	1.17

Proposal 2: Expand warehouse

Outlay	($50,000)
Present value of inflows	65,000
Present value index	1.30

Division B

Proposal 1: Expand new territory

Outlay	($100,000)
Present value of inflows	120,000
Present value index	1.20

Proposal 2: Remodel sales division

Outlay	($40,000)
Present value of inflows	50,000
Present value index	1.25

Proposal 3: Expand productive facilities

Outlay	($170,000)
Present value of inflows	200,000
Present value index	1.17

Division C

Proposal 1: Develop product characteristics

Outlay	($100,000)
Present value of inflows	125,000
Present value index	1.25

Proposal 2: Acquire new office machinery

Outlay	($75,000)
Present value of inflows	105,000
Present value index	1.40

Proposal 3: Expand distributive facilities

Outlay	($80,000)
Present value of inflows	105,000
Present value index	1.31

tures has been estimated at $500,000, and central management prefers to stay within this estimate. The various proposals are summarized in Exhibit 15-6 (all flows are after tax).

(a) Using excess present values, determine how central management should allocate its $500,000.
(b) Repeat part (a) using the present value index.
(c) What other factors should be considered in allocating the funds to the different divisions?
(d) What kind of analysis would you follow if the division managers asked central management to borrow from the budgets for the next few quarters?

8. **The Purchasing and Financing Decision**

The following problem illustrates the types of alternatives that may be evaluated relative to a capital budgeting decision.

The Baker Casting Company is considering the purchase of a new machine that will result in operating savings of $1,000 per year for six years. The following options are available:

(1) Purchase the machine at a cost of $4,000. Estimated salvage value at the end of six years is $300. Freight costs are $150, to be paid by shipper.

(2) Purchase the machine on a conditional sales contract. The payments are $975 per year.

(3) Lease the machine for six years at a yearly rental of $1,025 per year. The lease has a noncancelable clause for three years. The lessor promises to provide the company with new features on the machine, as they become available, at no extra cost. These features would have favorable effects on operating expenses as the machine ages, but these effects cannot be quantified at the time of purchase.

(4) Lease the machine for six years on a yearly contract basis. The rental would be set at $1,100 per year.

Discuss each of these alternatives, indicating how you would compare them in terms of present (discounted) values.

9. **The Leasing Question**

The G Company sells computer services to its clients. On January 1, 1982, the company decided to buy a new computer. Information pertaining to the new computer is given in Exhibit 15-7.

If the company purchases the computer, it will pay cash. The G Company follows an investment rule that uses an 18 percent rate of return as a cutoff point. The company may borrow at a rate of 14 percent. The rental contract is noncancelable and runs for three years.

_____EXHIBIT 15-7

Purchase price	$275,000		
Maintenance, taxes, and insurance	25,000 per year		
Rental price (includes maintenance, taxes, and insurance)	90,000 per year + 10% of billings		
Useful life—3 years			
Salvage value	120,000		
Depreciation method—sum-of-the-years'-digits (tax and book)			
Tax rate—48%			
Estimated billings	**Year 1**	**Year 2**	**Year 3**
	$230,000	$250,000	$240,000
Operating expenses	75,000 per year		
Startup costs	20,000		
Purchase option	125,000 at end of year 3		

(a) Prepare an analysis of these two alternatives and indicate which alternative should be followed.

(b) How would you evaluate these alternatives if the lease were cancelable?

[AICPA adapted]

10. ***Comprehensive Problem in Leasing and Capital Budgeting***

On January 1, 1982, executives of Dingman Manufacturing Co. are considering the following alternatives:

(1) They will completely overhaul six machines at a combined cost of $75,000. The machines will then have a remaining useful life of eight years. The costs of operating these machines are estimated according to the standard cost per unit of output as

Direct materials	$1.25
Direct labor	2.50
Variable overhead	1.25

for an expected output of 25,000 units per year. In the past, the actual costs have averaged $.10 per unit above standard.

The present salvage value of the machines is $2,000 (book value is $2,500). The expected salvage value at the end of year 8 is negligible and therefore can be ignored.

(2) They will purchase new machines from either Gaynes, Inc., or the Rich Company. These new machines have a capacity rated at 150 percent of the machines in (1). In addition, their operation is expected to offer economies derived from the following:

	Gaynes	Rich
Direct materials	$1.20	$1.15
Direct labor	2.40	2.40
Variable overhead	1.20	1.20

Expected annual output is the same as in (1); that is, 25,000 units per year.

If new machines are purchased, Dingman may pay cash or finance payments as follows:

	Gaynes	Rich
Cash price per machine	$19,355	$22,500
Financing		
Down payment per machine	3,750	6,250
Annual payments for eight years, per machine, before taxes	3,592	3,740

(3) They will lease machines from Gaynes or Rich, either without a purchase option (Plan A) or with one (Plan B).

	Gaynes	**Rich**
Plan A (noncancelable lease)		
Lease payments per machine		
Years 1 through 4	$4,746	$5,304*
Years 5 through 8	$4,746	$5,304*
Plan B		
Lease payments per machine		
Years 1 through 4	$4,746	$5,304*
Purchase option	Original cost	Original cost
at the end of year 4	minus a credit	minus a credit
	of $6,575	of $8,000

* The Rich plan includes a savings of $125 per machine per year in maintenance costs.

Assume a tax rate of 50 percent, a borrowing rate of 16 percent, and a cost-of-capital rate of 20 percent. Use straight-line depreciation for (1) (that is, the overhaul) and sum-of-the-years'-digits for the machines purchased from either Gaynes or Rich. The new machines permit the 10 percent investment credit (assume the tax provisions apply).

(a) Set up the cash inflows and outflows for alternatives (1) and (2). Indicate the discounting formulas with the appropriate rates.
(b) Assuming Dingman decides to purchase the new machines, evaluate the alternatives in (2) and in Plan A of (3) for the Rich Company and Gaynes, Inc. Be specific in your calculations. Then evaluate the alternatives in Plan B against those in Plan A for both companies.

11. **Refunding**[23]
Assume that a company has a $40,000,000 bond issue outstanding. Interest on the old bonds is paid at a rate of 15 percent. The remaining life of the bonds is 15 years. Unamortized premium on the bonds is $700,000; unamortized issue costs are $75,000.

The redemption price on the old bonds is 105 percent, with a 60-day call notice. Other redemption costs are $20,000. New issue costs are estimated at $225,000. Interest rates are expected to fall to about 12 percent.

Determine whether the company should refund the old issue on the assumption that the interest rate will fall 3 percentage points. Use a tax rate of 50 percent. *Hint:* Treat as a problem similar to that of analyzing the financial effect of a lease.

12. **Tax Incentives**
The investment credit in the 1970s allowed a credit against a firm's tax liability up to 10 percent of investments made in qualified assets. However, the credit

---

[23] This problem was adapted from E.A. Spiller, Jr., "Time-Adjusted Breakeven Rate for Refunding," *Financial Executive*, July 1963.

was limited to $25,000 plus 50 percent of the tax liability over that amount, assuming that the tax liability of the firm exceeds $25,000 (otherwise, the credit is limited to the amount of the tax liability). Any unused credits could be carried back three years and carried forward five years. However, the amounts that could be applied to prior or future years were also limited to the maximum stated above.

Suppose you were the president of a large airline and had to purchase an average of 20 new aircraft each year for the next five years at an average cost of $30 million each. The amount of the credit available on these investments would average close to $60 million a year. Assume the tax liability for the past four years has averaged only $50 million per year. Hence the company's allowable credit would be only about $25 million each year.

In order to obtain additional credits, you wonder whether you should lease the aircraft or acquire firms whose income could absorb your unused credits.

Discuss the impact of this or other tax laws on the decision to lease, to buy, or to acquire other firms.

13. *Eichenfield's Folly—"A Pitch for Leasing"* [24]
S. Eichenfield, an officer of a leasing company, prepared the tables presented in Exhibit 15-8 to indicate why it would be profitable to a firm to lease a particular piece of equipment.

The equipment costs $56,000. It has a ten-year life for tax depreciation, with a salvage estimate of $1,000 (which can be ignored if desired). The decision horizon for this asset is five years (the term of the lease contract). The firm is in the 48 percent tax bracket.

Point out any defects in this analysis. Suppose the asset has a positive salvage value after five years (for example, $8,000). How would this affect the rankings? Is double-declining balance the best depreciation method for tax purposes? Prepare a proper analysis of this lease.

EXHIBIT 15-8————————————————————————————————

(1) Five-Year Lease

Year	Rental ($1,190 Per Month)	Tax Saving 48%	Net Cash Cost	Cumulative Net Cash Cost
1	$14,280	$6,854	$7,426	$ 7,426
2	14,280	6,854	7,426	14,852
3	14,280	6,854	7,426	22,278
4	14,280	6,854	7,426	29,704
5	14,280	6,854	7,426	37,130
	$71,400			

---

[24] Adapted from a problem originally developed by D. Green.

——————————————— EXHIBIT 15-8 Continued

(2) Five-Year Bank Loan, $56,000
6% Interest, Double-Declining Balance Depreciation
10-Year Life

Year	Payments ($1,083 Per Month)	Depreciation 20% of Book Balance	Interest 6%	Tax Saving 48%	Net Cash Cost	Cumulative Net Cash Cost
1	$12,996	$11,200	$3,091	$6,860	$ 6,136	$ 6,136
2	12,996	8,960	2,480	5,491	7,505	13,641
3	12,996	7,168	1,831	4,320	8,676	22,317
4	12,996	5,734	1,142	3,300	9,696	32,013
5	12,996	4,587	410	2,399	10,597	42,610
	$64,980	$37,649				

(3) Cash Purchase; $56,000

Year		Depreciation (10 Years)	Tax Savings 48%	Cumulative Net Cash Cost
0	$56,000			
1		$11,200	$5,376	$50,624
2		8,960	4,301	46,323
3		7,168	3,441	42,882
4		5,734	2,752	40,130
5		4,587	2,202	37,928
	$56,000	$37,649		

14. **Lease Versus Buy Versus Borrow**

The authors of an article on leasing[25] propose that the alternatives to be considered consist of Lease versus Buy. This is in contrast to the method we have followed in this chapter, which approached the problem in two stages: (a) determine whether to buy the asset, then (b) determine whether to borrow or lease. Of course, these two stages are related and, in fact, there is disagreement as to whether they can be treated as separate analyses.

In their article, Johnson and Lewellen compare the net present value of the buy decision with the net present value of the lease decision. In equation form, net present value of the buy decision is

$$NPV_B = \sum_{t=1}^{n} \frac{(Rev_t - CE_t)(1 - TR) + TR\,(Depr_t)}{(1+\rho)^t} + \frac{S - TR(S - BV)}{(1+\rho)^n} - Cost$$

where Rev_t = Revenues received in period t

CE_t = Cash expenses in period t

———
[25] R. Johnson and W. Lewellen, "Analysis of the Lease-or-Buy Decision," *J. of Finance*, Sept. 1972.

$S = $ Salvage

$BV = $ Book value

$\rho = $ Cost-of-capital rate

$r = $ Interest rate on debt

$Depr_t = $ Depreciation in period t

That is, NPV_B equals the sum of the discounted values of the after-tax operating flows plus the present value of the net salvage proceeds (that is, salvage less taxes on a gain or plus tax savings on a loss) minus the cost of the asset.

The net present value of the lease is defined as follows, where L_t is the net lease payment in year t:

$$NPV_L = \sum_{t=1}^{n} \frac{(REV_t - CE'_t)(1 - TR)}{(1 + \rho)^t} - \sum_{t=1}^{n} \frac{L_t(1 - TR)}{(1 + r)^t}$$

where CE'_t represents the operating expenses if the asset is leased. Note that the lease payments are discounted at the borrowing rate (net of taxes).

The rule would be to accept the alternative—NPV_B or NPV_L—with the highest value; that is, buy if $NPV_B - NPV_L > 0$; otherwise lease.

Assume we are dealing with a three-year asset that will generate revenues of $15,000 per year, incurring variable and fixed cash expenditures of $10,800 per year. Included in the latter is an estimate for repairs and maintenance of $1,000 that will be eliminated if the asset is leased. The cost of the asset is $9,000, with a zero expected salvage value.

The firm uses a cost of capital for this asset of 12 percent; its marginal borrowing rate is 8 percent. Its tax rate is 45 percent.

The leasing company will provide the asset at a cost of $4,500 per year, which includes a charge for maintenance and repairs.

The company would use the sum-of-the-years'-digits method of depreciation. The tax credit can be ignored for this problem. Some interest rate factors appear below

Period	6%	8%	10%	12%	14%	16%
1	.94	.93	.91	.89	.88	.86
2	.89	.86	.83	.80	.77	.74
3	.84	.79	.75	.71	.67	.64

(a) Using the format below, determine the net after-tax inflows for each year. Also indicate the appropriate discount factors for each year on the assumption that the firm uses the excess present value method to determine whether to acquire an asset.

Year	0	1	2	3
(1) Investment				
(2) (Revenue—Cash expense)				
(3) After-tax value of item (2)				
(4) Depreciation expense in each period				

Year	0	1	2	3
(5) Tax savings from depreciation				
(6) Net cash flows [(1) and (3) + (5)]				
(7) Discount factors				

(b) Using the two-stage approach to leasing, determine whether the firm should buy (borrow) or lease. (Use net lease payments for your calculations.)

(1) What is the financial advantage (disadvantage) of a lease? Explain.

(2) Assuming an interest rate of 8 percent for the lease and depreciation costs of $4,000, $3,000, and $2,000, calculate the noninterest deductions under each alternative. Show calculations as follows:

NONINTEREST DEDUCTIONS

Year	Lease	Buy	Net (Lease Minus Buy)
1			
2			
3			

(3) According to this approach, should we lease or buy-and-borrow? Explain.

(c) Using the "new" method, we would determine whether to buy or lease on the basis of the following equation (salvage is zero, no gain or loss at retirement):

$$(NPV_B - NPV_L) = \sum_{t=1}^{n} \left[\frac{TR\ (Depr_t)}{(1 + \rho)^t} + \frac{(1 - TR)L_t}{(1 + r)^t} \right] - Cost$$

Would we come up with the same decision? Explain.

15. *Probabilistic Estimates*

Famous Sluggers, Inc., manufactures a line of novelties featuring the autographs of various baseball stars. They sign a star player to a multiple-year contract that guarantees him a minimum pay and a fixed percent of their gross revenues from his products. Since they can market only a limited number of players' novelties, they try to sign only established stars. However, they will sign a rookie who seems likely to achieve stardom.

At present, they are considering a rookie named "Ep" Mikstein. All reports indicate that within a year or two he will be a superstar of the same magnitude as Jackson, Mays, Clemente, and Robinson. Because the decision involves so much uncertainty, management has brought all its available data to you. After reviewing the data below (taken from the Mikstein file), you are expected to aid management in its decision to offer him a five-year contract.

Regarding: Berkeley "Ep" Mikstein   *Date:* December 25, 1981
Age: 23 years   *Bats:* Left
Team: Walla-Walla Salmons
Prospects: While this is "Ep's" first year in the major leagues with the Salmons, he cannot miss. As we have indicated in our five-year projection, he may be a year or two away from the kind of performance that achieves large sales volume. However, by 1984 he will be well known and one of our best sellers *if our estimates are correct.*

Five-Year Projection

1982		1983		1984	
Rating	*Probability*	*Rating*	*Probability*	*Rating*	*Probability*
0.88	0.30	0.85	0.20	0.94	0.15
0.86	0.40	0.87	0.60	0.92	0.70
0.84	0.30	0.90	0.20	0.89	0.15

1985		1986	
Rating	*Probability*	*Rating*	*Probability*
0.91	0.20	0.92	0.10
0.93	0.60	0.94	0.80
0.95	0.20	0.96	0.10

The ratings assigned to his potential performance are the result of Famous Sluggers' elaborate prediction model to evaluate performers. It weights the effects of batting average, home runs, rbi's, and other variables and then relates them to an estimate of sales volume. The sales volume associated with each rating is shown in Exhibit 15-9. Each unit sells for $20 net.

For calculations of this type, Famous Sluggers has found that a fixed cost of $600,000 annually and variable costs of 70 percent per sales dollar are quite satisfactory. This will project all the incremental costs associated with signing Mikstein except his fee and initial advertising of $1.5 million. They expect to offer Mikstein a guarantee of $25,000 per year plus a 10 percent commission on the contribution margin ($6).

The contract must be renegotiated after five years without any option to Famous Sluggers or Mikstein. Thus, there is no residual value to it. The first

EXHIBIT 15-9

Rating	Volume (in Units)	Rating	Volume (in Units)
0.84	50,000	0.90	275,000
0.85	100,000	0.91	312,500
0.86	150,000	0.92	375,000
0.87	187,500	0.93	450,000
0.88	200,000	0.94	500,000
0.89	250,000	0.95	587,500
		0.96	625,000

five years are the only years to be considered in your analysis. Famous Sluggers signs only select ballplayers to contracts. They never offer a player a contract unless the expected return is at least 20 percent, the firm's minimum acceptable rate of return.

Analyze the cash flows involved to ascertain if Famous Sluggers ought to sign Mikstein at this time. How would the contract look through Mikstein's eyes?

16. **Some Tax Considerations of Gifts**

The J.E. Company makes a computer game that has required substantial investments in plant assets, engineering talents, and set-up costs. Labor and material costs, however, are relatively low, given the game's selling price of $10 each. The standard production cost per game is $1 for variable (out-of-pocket) costs and $5 for fixed overhead (allocated on the assumption that 100,000 units are produced each period—hence, fixed overhead is $500,000 in total). Selling and administrative out-of-pocket costs for 100,000 units sold total $150,000. The estimated cost function for selling and administrative costs (S & A) is $TC_{S\&A} = \$50,000 + \$1$ (sales in units).

Assume that sales seem to be lagging in the current period and that only 80,000 units will be sold. The standard net income for 80,000 units is as follows:

Sales	$800,000
Cost of Goods Sold at Standard	480,000 (equal to $6 × 80,000 units)
Gross Margin at Standard	$320,000
Selling and Administrative at Standard	130,000
	$190,000
Tax at 40%	76,000
Net After-tax income	$114,000

The firm anticipates a normal sales level of 100,000 units in future years and production in the current operating period will be cut to 80,000 units in order to keep inventory levels relatively in line with sales. This will reduce the period's net income before taxes by $5 × 20,000 units = $100,000, which will show up as a volume variance given the firm will not produce 100,000 units. (Normally, this is treated as an adjustment to standard cost of goods sold.)

A nationwide organization for disadvantaged youths has appealed to the management of the J.E. Company, asking them to contribute 20,000 units to their youth rehabilitation projects. The 20,000 units would be deducted from the firm's income for tax purposes at the standard production rate of $6 per unit.

(a) Show the effect of adopting this proposal on this year's income statement. Assume the company will produce 100,000 units instead of 80,000, thus eliminating the anticipated volume variance of $100,000. Compare the after-tax income under this proposal with the amount reported if J.E. produced and sold only 80,000 units and recognized the $100,000 volume variance in the current period.

(b) Compute the after-tax cash flows that would accrue to the firm under each alternative. Assume all fixed costs are noncash allocations of previous investments (unrealistic, but since the total costs will be the same under each alternative, it does not matter).

(c) Your answer to (b) should have resulted in a preference for producing and selling 80,000 units. Suppose now that J.E. had actually produced 100,000 units before realizing it would not be able to sell more than 80,000 in this period. The 20,000 units must be held in inventory incurring *extra* storage costs of $.50 per unit (out-of-pocket) before being sold next period. To adjust inventories, J.E. would produce only 80,000 units next period, so the company would obtain the tax benefit of the $100,000 volume variance on next year's tax bill. What is the preferred alternative now? It might be easier to do this using an incremental format. Assume a discount rate of 12 percent for the volume variance deduction.

(d) In some cases, a deduction for a donated capital asset may be claimed at the current value (selling price) of the asset. Moreover, no recognition of a capital gain on the transfer is required. At one time, the firms' donations of units from inventory enjoyed the same tax benefit. Assume J.E. could deduct the donation at an average price of $10 per unit. What is the net advantage of the donation now? [Assume the facts in (b) above.]

16
Inventory Models

In this final chapter we provide another example of the interplay between decision making and accounting by examining a firm's inventory decisions. We noted in Chapters 14 and 15 that determining the firm's optimal portfolio of assets is a complex matter. Here we continue exploring the accounting dimensions of this class of problems, confining ourselves to assets that are acquired, held, consumed, and so on.

Before proceeding, however, it is important to place the chapter topic and our treatment of it in perspective. One thing to notice at the outset is the pervasive nature of inventories: Examples include raw materials, work-in-process, and finished goods in a typical manufacturing setting; stock in warehouses, in transit, in "back rooms," and on shelves in merchandising; water in reservoirs; cash; oil in the ground; and so on. Moreover, varying amounts of complexity can be and have been modeled here. For example, one or more assets might be involved, one or more storage facilities might be involved, demand might be known or unknown as well as systematically vary from period to period. The cost structure might reflect "quantity discounts," tax considerations, or the product's perishability (as in blood banks or cash accounts during inflationary conditions). The inventory policy itself might be based on periodic observation—such as a monthly observation—or perpetual observation, which might be provided by computer-based merchandising systems. Shortages might be lost, might lead to expediting cost, or might affect future demand.

A complete survey of the inventory problem is obviously too complex for one chapter. Indeed, entire textbooks have been devoted to discussions about appropriate models for various operating conditions. Fortunately, the general nature of the accounting issues that arise with the use of formal inventory models can be discussed within the context of a simple model. Hence, we shall confine our discussion to the economic order quantity model and the accounting issues associated with its use. After developing the basic

655

model, we shall consider the accounting issues related to predicting the model's parameters, supplying data to implement inventory management systems, and evaluating alternative inventory management systems.

Because our purpose here is to explore accounting issues and not to survey inventory theory, the inventory model is extremely simple. The simple economic order quantity model coupled with a safety stock and some type of demand forecasting mechanism is the most common form of formal inventory management. Indeed, it is readily available in standard software packages.

A Simple Inventory Model

Inventory models are designed to achieve a balance between the costs of acquiring and holding inventory and the (opportunity) costs of not holding inventory. There are three general motives for holding inventories: the transactions motive, the precautionary motive, and the speculative motive.[1]

The transactions motive, which is the need to hold inventory to meet production and sales requirements, is present whenever production cannot (feasibly or economically) respond instantaneously to demand. Moreover, the transactions motive is the *only* motive operative if (1) the firm is able to predict with perfect certainty the demand for its outputs and inputs, and (2) it knows with certainty that the prices of inputs will remain constant for some reasonable length of time.

In the absence of the first condition the precautionary motive would influence the firm's decision. The firm might hold additional amounts of inventories against the possibility that it had underestimated the demand for its outputs or inputs, or both. That is, the firm would hold precautionary amounts of inventory because the costs of potential shortages (which we call *stockouts*) are greater than the costs of holding the additional inventory. Similarly, if the firm expected future input prices to change, it might hold more or less inventory in order to speculate on the expected increase or decrease in future prices. However, the firm could not stop all purchases in any period even if it anticipated a decline in future prices, because that would be inconsistent with the transactions motive for stocking inventories. In general, the firm would continue to cut back inventories only as long as the costs of stockouts did not become prohibitive.

Costs Relevant to Inventory Policies

Suppose a firm decides that D units of some inventoriable item must be acquired during some future period of length T, and no such items are currently in stock. The two aspects of inventory policy to be determined are (1) the

---

[1] M. Starr and D. Miller, *Inventory Control: Theory and Practice.* Englewood Cliffs, N.J.: Prentice-Hall, 1962, p. 17 (attributed to K. Arrow's classification).

number of units to acquire at any given time and (2) the time to place specific orders. We shall concentrate on the first (the order quantity) issue throughout most of this section.

Clearly, the firm could acquire all D units now and merely draw them out of inventory when they are needed. Alternatively, the firm might order the units so that they arrive just as they are needed, with no inventory stock whatever. Neither approach is likely to be optimal because of the various costs involved. Three types of costs influence optimal inventory policies: the costs of acquiring inventories, the costs of holding inventories, and the costs of holding insufficient inventories (stockout costs).

To explore the relationship among these types of costs, let us suppose that the firm decides to order q units at a time, with each successive order timed to arrive just as the inventory is depleted. Under such a policy no stockouts will occur, and any consideration of stockout costs is therefore irrelevant. Assuming constant usage of the total amount D over time T, we obtain the replenishment–usage pattern depicted in Figure 16-1, in which t_s denotes the time between receipt of the orders.

As an illustration, let us assume a time period of length $T = 30$ days, total demand of $D = 30$ units, and an order quantity of $q = 5$ units (with $t_s = 5$ days). The total number of orders will be 30/5 = 6 per month. Since the rate of decrease in inventory is constant, the inventory level will drop from 5 to 4 after one day, from 4 to 3 after two days, and so on until the end of the fifth day when it reaches zero units. The inventory pattern can be described as in Exhibit 16-1.

Because no stockout costs are incurred with this system, the total monthly inventory costs will be equal to the sum of the monthly acquisition and storage costs. If the firm purchases its inventory, the acquisition costs will consist of the purchase costs and the costs of placing and receiving an

FIGURE 16-1

Inventory levels assuming a constant rate of demand and immediate replacement of q.

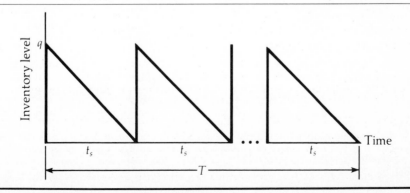

EXHIBIT 16-1

End of Time Period	Level of Inventory
0	5
1	4
2	3
3	2
4	1
5	0

Number of time periods: 6   Total $\overline{15}$

Average inventory on hand: $\frac{15}{6} = 2.5$

order of inventory.[2] Purchase costs would consist of such items as the purchase price and delivery cost. The costs of placing and receiving an order would include:

1. The costs of reviewing and determining the amounts to acquire and of clerically processing the order.
2. The costs incurred in inspecting the order and placing it in storage.
3. The costs of processing the purchase payments.

The costs of placing and receiving an order are not easy to measure. Many of them are common costs to other functions. That is, the personnel who receive and process orders and payments usually have a number of duties, and therefore they provide joint services. In such cases, it is difficult to determine the incremental costs of processing a particular purchasing order. A plot of these costs against the number of orders, for example, would more than likely reveal a spurious relationship (or a step-cost function). An accurate analysis of clerical costs would probably require multiple regression techniques to take into account the effects of other activities.[3]

In any event, some acquisition costs may depend on the total number of units ordered, D, and others may depend on how many separate orders are placed.[4] Still other costs may be fixed. To model these costs, we adopt a simple, tractable cost function and represent total acquisition cost by $G + PD + C_p(D/q)$. G represents acquisition costs that are totally independent of the number of units ordered or the number of separate orders placed. C_p denotes the constant cost of placing an order and D/q is, of course, the total

---

[2] If a firm produced its own inventory, we would have to substitute manufacturing costs and setup costs for purchase and acquisition costs. Moreover, without instantaneous production the graph of the situation would be different from that shown in Figure 16-1. The production situation is illustrated in Problem 17 at the end of the chapter.

[3] See Chapter 3 for a discussion of the problems involved in using multivariate analysis for cost estimation.

[4] There is, of course, a simplification inherent in this approach. Varying q varies the time at which the purchase price payments will be made, and hence cash flow timing considerations are present. We generally suppress these, however, because suppression provides a fairly simple model.

number of orders placed. P, in turn, represents the constant cost of acquiring one unit, aside from the ordering and fixed costs. Observe that the minimum total acquisition cost would be $G + PD + C_p$, when $q = D$.

Consider now the inventory holding costs. Some of the more common types of holding costs are:

1. The cost of money tied up in inventory (the interest or opportunity cost of having money invested in inventory).
2. The costs of storage (rental or opportunity cost of providing space for inventories).
3. The costs of obsolescence and deterioration of inventory (including breakage and theft).
4. The costs of insurance and taxes (usually based on the value of inventory held by the firm).

To introduce these costs explicitly, we again use a simple, tractable cost function. The most common assumption is that total inventory costs are a constant amount plus an amount that varies with the average level of inventory on hand. With the no-stockout pattern depicted in Figure 16-1, the average inventory is simply $q/2$. Hence, we represent the total inventory holding cost by $H + C_s q/2$, where C_s denotes the holding cost (over time of length T) per unit of average inventory and H denotes the inventory related costs that are totally independent of the order quantity chosen.

Carrying or holding costs can usually be quantified as a certain amount per dollar of inventory investment, since many of these costs vary as a function of the investment in inventory. Often, as in the case of taxes, insurance, storage costs, and the opportunity costs of invested capital, they can be estimated with a reasonable degree of accuracy. Deterioration and obsolescence may be more difficult to estimate, but these costs are usually not critical to the inventory decision. Quite clearly though, H, like $G + PD$, is not a determinant of the optimal policy.

The Economic Order Quantity Model

With these cost functions, we can now determine the optimal order quantity. We continue to assume that stockouts are not permitted. A firm that adopts a no-stockout policy is implicitly placing a high cost on stockouts. This may be a reasonable policy, because good service may be the primary consideration in achieving sales.

We further assume that the following relevant cost function and demand parameters are known with certainty:

$D =$ total demand during time period T
$C_p =$ incremental acquisition cost per order
$C_s =$ incremental holding cost per unit of average inventory

The total inventory costs over T will equal the sum of the acquisition and holding costs. If we delete the components of these costs that are independent of the order quantity q, the total inventory costs will be[5]

$$TC = \frac{C_s q}{2} + \frac{C_p D}{q} \qquad [16\text{--}1]$$

We can determine a minimum for this total cost function by differentiating [16–1] with respect to q and setting the derivative equal to zero.[6] The result is

$$q^* = \sqrt{\frac{2C_p D}{C_s}} \qquad [16\text{--}2]$$

Therefore, from [16–1], the minimum total inventory cost is:

$$TC^* = \frac{\sqrt{2C_p D/C_s}\ C_s}{2} + \frac{C_p D}{\sqrt{2C_p D/C_s}} \qquad [16\text{--}1a]$$

$$= \sqrt{2C_p D C_s}$$

Given q^*, from [16–2], we can also determine the optimal number of orders, N^*:

$$N^* = \frac{D}{q^*}$$

$$= \frac{D}{\sqrt{2C_p D/C_s}} \qquad [16\text{--}3]$$

$$= \sqrt{\frac{D C_s}{2C_p}}$$

---

[5] Technically, we assume an infinite horizon with exactly D units of demand each period and the period cost structure given in [1]. We then select q, to minimize the period cost in [1].

[6] $\dfrac{d\,TC}{dq} = \dfrac{C_s}{2} - \dfrac{C_p D}{q^2} = 0$, or $\dfrac{C_s}{2} = \dfrac{C_p D}{q^2}$. Hence, $q^2 = \dfrac{C_p D}{C_s/2} = \dfrac{2C_p D}{C_s}$,

and the optimal quantity q^* is

$$q^* = \sqrt{2C_p D/C_s}$$

We can test for a minimum by establishing whether the second derivative is positive for all values of q^*:

$$\frac{d}{dq}\left(\frac{d\,TC}{dq}\right) = -\left(\frac{-2q C_p D}{q^4}\right) = \frac{2q C_p D}{q^4} = \frac{2C_p D}{q^3}$$

Since all the variables take on positive values only, this is a sufficient condition.

This is the so-called economic order quantity, or EOQ, model. It is generally regarded as the first successful use of management science modeling techniques.

As an example, assume that a firm has a demand D for 3,600 units a year, that its purchase costs are \$22.23 per order, and that its storage costs are \$1 per unit per year. We then have

$$q^* = \sqrt{\frac{2C_pD}{C_s}} = \sqrt{\frac{2(22.23)(3,600)}{1}} = 400 \text{ units}$$

$$N^* = \frac{3,600}{q^*} = \frac{3,600}{400} = 9$$

and, from [16–1a].

$$TC^* = \sqrt{2C_pDC_s} = \sqrt{2(22.23)(3,600)(1)} = \$400$$

The Question of Stockouts

An alternative to the EOQ model would be to introduce explicitly the cost of stockouts and let the model itself properly balance acquisition, storage, and stockout costs. This is typically accomplished by approximating the stockout cost (which reflects possible lost orders, tarnished reputation, and additional processing) as a linear function of the average stockout. We develop this procedure at length in the appendix to this chapter.

We might therefore conclude that a policy of allowing no stockouts implicitly assumes that the stockout cost (per unit of average stockout) is large (technically, unbounded). A better interpretation is that, for a simplified model, management perceives that the solution with no stockouts allowed is superior to that with stockouts allowed.

In particular, allowing no stockouts is difficult to rationalize if the model is perfectly specified. Demand or replenishment uncertainty, however, would likely increase management's interest in carrying *more* average inventory than the amount determined in a simple application of the EOQ analysis.

Lead Time and Safety Stocks

The effect of demand or replenishment uncertainty can, perhaps, be shown by focusing on the optimal time to issue replenishment orders. If replenishment is instantaneous, we would reorder whenever the actual inventory dropped to zero in the above model. If there is a constant lead time—the time between placing and receiving an order—we would merely adjust the reorder time to compensate for the usage that would occur during the lead time. That is, we would set the reorder time so that the order arrives precisely as the inventory level falls to zero. Indeed, under conditions of certainty we would not even have to monitor the system to implement the policy. We would know, at the start of the period, exactly when to schedule the arrival of each order.

Of course certainty is more a convenient modeling assumption than a description of reality. Because it is likely that both the demand and the lead time will be uncertain, the firm can never be sure that no stockouts will occur. A possible solution here is to supplement the system with a base or safety stock designed to guard against stockouts due to excessive demand during the lead time. The firm then monitors the inventory level and issues a reorder of an appropriate size whenever the predetermined minimum level is reached. Clearly, this introduces another decision variable and further complicates the analysis. As with stockouts, this added feature provides no new insights into the accounting issues we now discuss, so we shall not pursue it.

Accounting Issues

The accounting issues that arise with the adoption of formal inventory models fall into the three broad categories of parameter prediction, implementation, and evaluation. The simple EOQ model, for example, requires a prediction of the incremental cost of processing an order, and the firm's accounting system typically provides the basis for making such a prediction. Similarly, these models require supporting inventory records that signal reorders and help to evaluate the individuals responsible for having inventory available when needed. Finally, the firm's accounting system provides a basis for evaluating alternative inventory management policies.

Parameter Prediction

Perhaps the most obvious accounting issue is the necessity of predicting the model's parameters—for example, the demand, order cost, and holding cost parameters in the simple EOQ model. Resolution of these issues, of course, follows the basic ideas expressed in Chapters 1 and 3. That is, we concern ourselves with the degree to which accurate measurements of these parameters can be obtained at reasonable cost and the extent to which accurate measurements are useful. Clearly, the degree of accuracy that is worthwhile depends on the inventory model's sensitivity to errors in parameter measurement.

To develop this theme, suppose a firm must design an inventory policy to guide the acquisition of some type of raw material input. The firm requires 3,600 units of this material per year, and management has decided to use the EOQ model to guide its inventory policy. Only the acquisition cost and holding cost parameters, C_p and C_s, are in question.

Assume that the purchase price of the material is \$1.50 per unit, and average delivery costs add another $1 per unit. Time records indicate that an employee can process an average of 20 units per hour into inventory— unpacking, checking, and storing. Inventory can also be withdrawn at an average rate of 20 units per hour.

It takes the inventory personnel approximately one hour to process a purchase order. Other order related costs, such as processing payment for the order and other paper work, average $2.23 per order.

The total cost of maintaining the firm's storage facility amounts to about $50,000 per year in depreciation, insurance, fixed personnel costs, and so on. In addition, checking the items in inventory requires about .015 labor hour per unit of average inventory.

The firm generally requires a 20 percent (pretax) return on investments in inventories. Labor cost averages $10 per hour, and recent regression analysis of the firm's overhead indicates that overhead increases at an average rate of $10 per hour of labor.

The EOQ model requires predicted values for D, C_s, and C_p for equation [16–2]. D is, of course, 3,600 units per year. The cost of processing an order is $2.23 per order plus one hour of labor. Labor, in turn, costs $10 per hour, and associated overhead adds another $10 per labor hour. Hence, our estimate of C_p is $20 + $2.23 = $22.23 per order.

The prediction of holding cost is more complicated. An obvious cost is the checking at .015 labor hour per unit of average inventory or using the cost of $20 per labor hour, $.30 per average unit of inventory. Difficulty arises in accounting for the opportunity cost of the funds invested in the inventory. By acquiring the material before it is actually used, the firm incurs purchase, delivery, and receiving costs earlier than necessary. These costs total $1.50 per unit purchase price, $1 per unit delivery cost, and $1 per unit receiving cost, or $3.50 per unit. At the 20 percent capital rate, the implicit investment costs are $.70 per unit of average inventory. Observe that the inventory withdrawal costs are not included here; they occur only at the time of use and are thus not incurred earlier than necessary. Also, as in the acquisition cost analysis, we are concerned with only those holding costs that are actually affected by the order quantity. Therefore, our prediction is $C_s = $.30 + $.70 = $1 per unit of average inventory.

Recall that these were the values assumed in our original example. When we insert them into equations [16–1] and [16–2], we obtain $q^* = 400$ and $TC^* = 400, as before:

$$q^* = \sqrt{\frac{2C_p D}{C_s}} = \sqrt{\frac{2(22.23)(3,600)}{1}} = 400 \text{ units per order}$$

and

$$TC^* = \sqrt{2C_p D C_s} = \sqrt{2(22.23)(3,600)(1)} = \$400 \text{ per year}$$

We can rely on accounting records to provide a basis for predicting the model's cost parameters. However, the requisite analysis may be far more complex than we can hope to communicate in a textbook illustration. For example, we need to predict how total acquisition and holding costs vary as the order quantity is varied. Merely observing, as in the illustration, that inventory receiving and/or checking take, on average, z units of labor does not imply that the total labor hours will actually vary in this proportion as we vary the amount ordered or stored. Similar comments apply to the overhead prediction. Determining which labor costs will, in fact, vary with the inventory policy is difficult in almost any setting. Whether it is reasonable (or useful) to assume complete variability as in the example is a question that we cannot analyze here.

However, absolute accuracy is not essential in measuring these parameters. To illustrate, suppose the storage cost per unit is actually $C_s' = \$1.50$. Using $q^* = 400$ determined with the incorrect parameter, we would incur actual incremental holding and acquisition costs of

$$\frac{C_s' q}{2} + \frac{C_p D}{q} = \frac{\$1.5(400)}{2} + \frac{\$22.23(3,600)}{400} = \$500 \text{ per year}$$

The optimal order quantity is, however,

$$q^{*\prime} = \sqrt{\frac{2(22.23)(3,600)}{1.5}} = 327 \text{ units per order}$$

and the minimum cost is

$$\sqrt{2(22.23)(3,600)(1.5)} = \$490 \text{ per year}$$

That is, a 50 percent error in predicting the holding cost per unit results in an additional cost of $\$500 - \$490 = \$10$ per year, which is hardly disastrous. Indeed, the additional cost is only 2 percent above the minimum policy cost. This type of insensitivity to cost prediction errors is characteristic of the EOQ model.

Similarly, suppose the actual storage cost per unit is $C_s' = \$.50$. Using $q^* = 400$ would now result in incremental holding and acquisition costs of

$$\frac{\$.50(400)}{2} + \frac{\$22.23(3,600)}{400} = \$300 \text{ per year}$$

But the minimum cost would be

$$\sqrt{2(22.23)(3,600)(.5)} = \$283 \text{ per year}$$

with an optimal order quantity of

$$\sqrt{\frac{2(22.23)(3,600)}{.5}} = 566 \text{ units per order}$$

The additional cost in this case would therefore be $300 - $283 = $17 per year.

Now, we link this observation directly with the conceptual discussion in Chapter 1. Suppose the actual storage cost parameter will be $.50, $1.00, or $1.50, with respective probabilities of .25, .50, and .25. Without additional information, suppose management will use $q^* = 400$ (determined by using the *expected value* of C_s in the EOQ model). The expected annual cost of such a policy is

$$.25(\$300) + .50(\$400) + .25(\$500) = \$400 \text{ per year}$$

But if the C_s parameter is correctly ascertained before the reorder policy is determined, the expected cost will be:

$$.25(\$283) + .50(\$400) + .25(\$490) = \$393.25 \text{ per year}$$

Thus, the expected value of perfect storage cost information is

$$\$400 - \$393.25 = \$6.75 \text{ per annum}$$

Further note that this is merely the expected value of the above calculated additional cost figures:

$$.25(\$300 - \$283) + .50(\$400 - \$400) + .25(\$500 - \$490) = \$6.75$$

These various data and calculations are summarized in Exhibit 16-2.

_____**EXHIBIT 16-2**

Expected Value of Perfect C_s Information
($D = 3,600$, $C_p = \$22.23$)

	EVENT		
	$C_s = \$.50$	$C_s = \$1.00$	$C_s = \$1.50$
Optimal policy with perfect information: $q^* =$	566	400	327
Total cost of optimal policy	$283	$400	$490
Total cost of $q^* = 400$ policy	$300	$400	$500
Probability	.25	.50	.25

To further illustrate the simple inventory model's sensitivity to cost prediction errors and the value of perfect information calculation, let us suppose the C_p parameter is in question. Let $D = 3,600$ units per year, $C_s = \$1.00$ and $C_p = \$13.23$, $\$22.23$, or $\$31.23$, with respective probabilities of $\frac{1}{3}$, $\frac{1}{3}$, and $\frac{1}{3}$. The expected value of C_p is therefore $\$22.23$ per order. Without additional information, the $q^* = 400$ policy will be implemented. The student should confirm that the expected value of perfect C_p information is $\$5.67$ per annum in this case.[7]

Of course, in a more complex story the cost parameters would vary simultaneously. Suppose overhead actually increases at a rate of $\$5$ per labor hour, instead of the $\$10$ per hour originally predicted. Actual labor and overhead cost, then, will be $\$15$ per labor hour. As a result, the correct C_p value is $\$17.23$, and the correct C_s value is $\$.875$.[8] Using the originally determined $q^* = 400$ units, actual incremental holding and acquisition costs will be

$$\frac{C_s' q}{2} + \frac{C_p' D}{q} = \frac{\$.875(400)}{2} + \frac{\$17.23(3,600)}{400} = \$330 \text{ per year}$$

and the minimum incremental cost will be

$$\sqrt{2C_p' D C_s'} = \sqrt{2(17.23)(3,600)(.875)} = \$329 \text{ per year}$$

with an optimal order quantity of

$$q^{*'} = \sqrt{\frac{2(17.23)(3,600)}{.875}} = 377 \text{ units per order}$$

In this case, the cost of the overhead prediction error is merely $\$330 - \$329 = \$1$ per year.[9] Continuing the calculations to obtain an expected value of information calculation should be obvious.[10]

---

[7] The minimum annual cost when $C_p = \$13.23$ is $\$309$; when $C_p = \$31.23$, it is $\$474$.

[8] The incremental order cost is one labor hour plus $\$2.23$ in miscellaneous costs; at $\$10 + \$5 = \$15$ per hour, this amounts to $\$17.23$ per order. Checking costs are $.015(\$15) = \$.225$ per average unit. Funds committed amount to $\$1.50$ price $+ \$1$ delivery $+ \$15/20$ receiving, or $\$3.25$. Hence, at 20 percent, the opportunity cost is $\$.650$; $C_s' = \$.225 + \$.650 = \$.875$ per average unit of inventory.

[9] See J. Demski and G. Feltham, "Forecast Evaluation." *Accounting Rev.*, July 1972, for an extensive discussion of the analysis of forecast errors and the selection of an optimal forecast.

[10] For completeness, suppose the overhead increases at a rate of $\$5$, $\$10$, or $\$15$ per labor hour, with each event being equally likely. (Under the $\$15$ event we have $C_p = \$27.23$ and $C_s = \$1.125$.) Without additional information, the $\$10$ rate will be assumed and the $q^* = 400$ policy implemented. Actual expected costs total $\frac{1}{3}$ $(330 + 400 + 470)$, and under perfect overhead information the minimum expected costs total $\frac{1}{3}$ $(329 + 400 + 470)$ where we have rounded to the nearest dollar. Quite clearly, the value of perfect overhead information is therefore $\$.33$ per annum.

Implementation Issues

Implementing formal inventory models raises even more issues than those that arise in predicting a model's parameters. For example, a certain amount of recordkeeping is necessary to implement any periodic reorder system. To appreciate this, recall that the policies we have discussed assume the inventory level is being monitored. Once the level falls to a specified point, a reorder is issued. This monitoring might be accomplished either with a computer-based perpetual inventory mechanism or with a simple "two-bin" procedure in which the reorder is executed when the first bin is emptied. (Indeed, models that formally recognize uncertain demand are based on perpetual or periodic monitoring policies.)

Certain recordkeeping procedures are also essential to the maintenance of the policy as well. We would not establish an inventory policy and never expect to update it for changing circumstances. Therefore, some attention must be devoted to acquiring sufficient information to update demand, cost, and policy specifications.

Clearly, the costs of implementing inventory policies may discourage management from carefully controlling the firm's inventories. (Remember, no implementation cost is recognized in our simple EOQ model or in its more sophisticated descendants.) A firm's diversity of operations may require holding in excess of 50,000 separate items of inventory. Fortunately, in most situations a small number of items tend to account for a large proportion of the total value of inventory held by the firm. For example, one particular firm reported that 10 percent of all inventory items accounted for approximately 77 percent of the value of its inventory; similarly, another 20 percent of the inventory accounted for an additional 17+ percent of the value, so that 30 percent of the total number of items in inventory represented approximately 95 percent of the inventory's total value.[11] This is a rather common phenomenon that has led to the use of the so-called ABC system of classifying inventory items. Using the figures above, class A items would consist of the 10 percent of items that accounted for 77 percent of the inventory value; class B, the 20 percent that accounted for 17+ percent of the value; and class C, the remaining 70 percent of the inventory items (5 percent of the value). Class A items would receive the greatest amount of attention in the control system, with formal models to determine the decision rules to be followed for many of the items in this class. Class C items would be left to more informal methods of control. The ABC system of classification has permitted the use of inventory models in otherwise impractical situations. (Of course, such a scheme presumes value is a good indicator of the benefits associated with careful control.)

---

[11] "Techniques in Inventory Management," *N.A.A. Research Report No. 40.* New York: National Association of Accountants, 1964.

Another set of implementation issues concerns the motivation of person-nel to follow appropriate stocking policies. While the cost structure assumed in, say, the simple EOQ model is quite straightforward, management often evaluates inventory personnel against an alternative cost structure. This type of evaluation may motivate these persons to make dysfunctional decisions. For example, a purchasing agent is often evaluated in terms of the prices he or she pays for items relative to a standard price. The deviation from this standard is evaluated without reference to any effect on storage costs.

To illustrate how these issues originate, let us return to our example and suppose that the individual responsible for acquiring the basic material has the option of purchasing the entire required 3,600 units at a price of $1.30 per unit. The alternative, of course, is to purchase the 3,600 units during the year at $1.50 per unit. If the purchasing agent is evaluated solely in terms of the purchase price he incurs, his performance will show a net savings to the firm of ($1.50 − $1.30)(3,600) = $720 for the year, assuming he accepts this special supply offer. However, the incremental cost incurred in accepting the offer will be $22.23, the incremental acquisition cost for the single order, plus holding costs of ($3,600/2)($.96) = $1,728. The net cost to the firm will be −$720 + $22 + $1,728 = $1,030. (Note that we adjusted the holding cost here to reflect the lower purchase price and therefore the lower investment per unit of inventory.) If we compare this inventory cost with the optimal cost of $400 per year (based on $q^* = 400$), we see that the firm has incurred $630 more than optimal cost. Myopic focus on the purchase price alone may not motivate the inventory manager to make decisions in the firm's best interests.

Indeed, it is difficult to analyze price speculation opportunities within this context. To illustrate, suppose that the same inventory manager has the option of purchasing only 600 units at a distressed price. An analysis of this alternative must incorporate the effect it will have on future orders and inventory levels. For example, if he relies on $q^* = 400$ for all other orders except this special 600 unit order, he will end the year with nine orders and 200 units in ending inventory. Conversely, if the offer is rejected, he will also end the year with nine orders, but with precisely zero ending inven-tory units. The key to the analysis of the offer lies in how the ending inventory is to be treated or in whether the $q^* = 400$ policy will be implemented for the remaining 3,000 units should the offer be accepted.

Total System Evaluation

A final accounting issue that arises in the use of formal inventory models is the analysis of alternative inventory management systems. This entails far more than merely worrying about order quantities. Costs relating to safety stocks, stockouts, and recordkeeping must also be included in the analysis. Moreover, basic management policies—such as how closely each class of inventoriable items will be controlled (for example, through the ABC system) and coordinated—are also subject to scrutiny in this type of analysis. For example, to analyze a hierarchical arrangement in which, say, end-product demand creates subassembly demands, and subassembly demands create raw material demands, we might treat the levels as independent and apply the analysis at each level. Using independently determined order quantities or lot sizes, however, may lead to unbalanced inventory combinations. Moreover, the derived demand in the lower levels is apt to be quite "lumpy," as when 1,000 units of a final product are placed in production and all requisite subassemblies are required at nearly the same instant. As a result, we become highly suspicious of an inventory management approach based on the usual inventory modeling assumptions. A somewhat popular approach in such settings, material requirements planning, or MRP,[12] recognizes the interdependence of each inventory level and permits the use of alternative acquisition policies at each level. Total system evaluation is aimed at helping management decide whether more sophisticated control mechanisms—such as extensions of the EOQ model in conjunction with an MRP system—are cost effective.[13]

This type of analysis is far more complex than we have shown in our illustrations. But the basic method of analysis still holds: Alternative policies are evaluated by focusing on the consequences of each.[14]

Conclusion

As a final exercise in examining the interplay between accounting and decision making, we have discussed the most elementary formal inventory models that depend on balancing various inventory costs. Using *any* such model creates a demand for parameter estimation. This is (or should be) a continuing theme that derives its conceptual orientation from the cost and value of information calculations originally presented in Chapter 1. Use of *any* such model also creates a demand for various implementation supports. We have to know the inventory level (continuously or periodically), and we want data that are useful in updating the system as its environment changes as well as in

---

[12] See, for example, R. Chase and N. Aquilano, *Production and Operations Management.* Homewood, Ill.: Irwin, 1977.

[13] See E. Gardner and D. Dannenbring, "Using Optimal Policy Surfaces to Analyze Aggregate Inventory Tradeoffs," *Management Science,* August 1979.

[14] A.H. Packer, for example, reports a case analysis of a firm's inventory management system. Using the simple EOQ model with appropriate safety stocks and exponential smoothing to predict demand requirements, he was able to maintain the current level of inventory service at a substantial reduction in inventory costs. Focusing on 24,000 different inventory items, he estimated the net savings to be about $165,000 per year. See "Simulation and Adaptive Forecasting as Applied to Inventory Control," *Operations Research,* July–August, 1967. A similar study using a more sophisticated model is reported in D. Gross *et al.,* "Bridging the Gap Between Mathematical Inventory Theory and the Construction of a Workable Model—A Case Study," *International Journal of Production Research,* 1972.

evaluating managers charged with implementing the system. And lest we feel such issues are mundane to the point of irrelevance, firms have historically found it useful to implement only the simplest inventory models.

Finally, use of *any* such model represents management's choice of a model in which analysis costs and benefits are somehow balanced. Review of this decision creates a demand for total system evaluation, and this places demands on the accounting system. It is important to recognize that a number of specific inventory costs are usually not recorded in the financial accounts of the firm. One example is the opportunity cost of holding or not holding sufficient inventories. Those inventory costs that are in the accounts often are not recorded in a manner consistent with their incorporation in an inventory model. For example, the clerical costs of processing orders or payments are recorded in the general category of office salaries and wages, and the costs of receiving and inspecting inventory shipments may be buried in some other overhead category, such as storage. The costs of taxes and insurance may be the only major inventory cost items that can be taken from the accounts with a minimum of effort.

Whether accounting records should be more sensitive to inventory policy evaluation demands is a situation specific issue. It is, however, a design question that must, implicitly or explicitly, be addressed in resolution of the firm's information problem.

REVIEW PROBLEM

A firm must acquire 15,000 units of raw material X each quarter. Cost analysis reveals the following approximate *quarterly* inventory cost:

$$\text{Cost} = \$3,000 + \$145(\text{Number of orders})$$
$$+ \$.22(\text{Value of average inventory on hand})$$

Raw material X costs $200 per unit.

Required (a) Determine the economic order quantity.
  (b) List and comment on the important assumptions in your determination in part (a) above.
  (c) Suppose the order cost will be $100 or $190 with equal probability. Determine how much the firm should pay to learn the actual value before implementing an EOQ policy. (Assume your policy in (a) above will, in the absence of additional information, be implemented.)

Appendix
The Effect of Stockouts

The simple economic order quantity, or EOQ, model can be modified to reflect a more general case in which stockouts are permitted. If a firm permits stockouts, then it effectively delays reorder beyond the point at which total inventory is depleted. Of course, these orders must be made up when new inventory items are received; these are called "back-orders." Suppose that q units are still ordered, but a portion of the order is used to fill back-orders. This results in only s units being stored in inventory; that is, $q - s$ is the quantity of back-orders. Obviously, then, the firm can reduce its storage cost by allowing back-orders.

Unfortunately, back-orders result in a different type of cost. At the very least, the firm will incur additional processing and shipping costs, because back-orders will have to be filled as soon as possible. In addition, back-orders may create customer dissatisfaction, which can eventually result in lost sales.

By their nature, stockout costs are difficult to estimate. For example, the costs of filling back-orders may not be constant for each order. Some of the "extra" costs of processing back-orders will vary with the rate of activity of the firm.

The costs of lost sales are even more difficult to estimate. An estimate should probably consider the number of orders that are permanently lost to the firm because some orders were not filled on time. Indeed, if a firm thought it would permanently lose orders because of back-orders, it would probably not permit them. As a result, back-order costs are generally estimated to be the additional costs of processing and shipping.

The effects of stockouts on our inventory system are shown in Figure 16-2. Upon receipt of q units, the stockouts are immediately satisfied and a net of s units is placed in inventory. Two variables now determine an optimal inventory policy: the order quantity q and the stockout amount $q - s$.

Observe in Figure 16-2 that the firm will now have an average inventory of $s/2$ units during the time segment t_1. Similarly, during the time segment t_2, the firm will have an average inventory shortage, or stockout, of $(q - s)/2$ units. Also, the average inventory over the horizon t_s will be $(s/2)(t_1/t_s)$. Algebraic reduction shows this average inventory to be $s^2/2q$ units. Similarly, the average stockout over the entire period will be $(q - s)^2/2q$ units.[15] Now

---

[15] Note in Figure 16-2 that ABC and AFE are similar triangles. Hence, $t_1/t_s = s/q$, and

$$\frac{s}{2}\left(\frac{t_1}{t_s}\right) = \frac{s}{2}\left(\frac{s}{q}\right) = \frac{s^2}{2q}$$

Similarly,

$$\frac{q-s}{2}\left(\frac{t_2}{t_s}\right) = \frac{q-s}{2}\left(\frac{t_s - t_1}{t_s}\right) = \frac{q-s}{2}\left(1 - \frac{t_1}{t_s}\right)$$

$$= \frac{q-s}{2}\left(1 - \frac{s}{q}\right) = \frac{(q-s)^2}{2q}$$

FIGURE 16-2

Relationship of order quantity q to stock levels s and stockouts $q - s$.

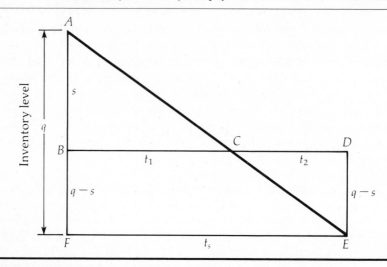

make the tractable assumption that the total stockout costs are C_0 per unit of average stockout. The total cost related to inventory policy, consisting of holding, stockout, and acquisition components, is then given by

$$TC = \frac{s^2 C_s}{2q} + \frac{(q-s)^2 C_0}{2q} + \frac{C_p D}{q} \qquad [16\text{-}4]$$

If we differentiate [16-4] with respect to q and s, we can solve for the optimal q and s, which we label q^{**} and s^*

$$q^{**} = \sqrt{\frac{2 C_p D}{C_s}} \cdot \sqrt{\frac{C_s + C_0}{C_0}} \qquad [16\text{-}5]$$

$$s^* = \sqrt{\frac{2 C_p D}{C_s}} \cdot \sqrt{\frac{C_0}{C_s + C_0}} \qquad [16\text{-}6]$$

Similarly, the total cost equation, given s^* and q^{**}, becomes

$$TC^* = \sqrt{2 C_p D C_s} \cdot \sqrt{\frac{C_0}{C_s + C_0}} \qquad [16\text{-}7]$$

Note that as C_0 increases without bound, the second expression in [16-5] approaches the value of 1 and the result is the original EOQ formula, equation [16-2]. Therefore, the original EOQ formula may be viewed as a special case of [16-5] wherein stockout costs C_0 are assumed to be infinite.

An example from Chapter 16 may be used to illustrate how the EOQ is modified for stockout costs. In that example the firm's demand for inventory is 3,600 units per year, its purchase costs are $22.23 per order, and its storage costs are $1 per unit per year. The calculated EOQ for this firm is 400 units. Assume now that the firm estimates its stockout costs at $5.50 per unit of average stockout. According to equation [16–5],

$$q^{**} = \sqrt{\frac{2C_p D}{C_s}} \cdot \sqrt{\frac{C_s + C_0}{C_0}}$$

$$= 400\sqrt{1.18} = 400(1.09)$$

$$= 436$$

Therefore, $N^* = 3,600/436 = 8.3$ orders (approximately). Similarly, from equation [16–6],

$$s^* = \sqrt{\frac{2C_p D}{C_s}} \cdot \sqrt{\frac{C_0}{C_s + C_0}}$$

$$= 400(0.92)$$

$$= 368$$

This results in the following inventory decision rules: Order 436 units, and permit back-orders of 68 units per period. The total policy-related cost, from equation [16–7], will be equal to

$$TC^* = \sqrt{2C_p DC_s} \cdot \sqrt{\frac{C_0}{C_s + C_0}}$$

$$= \$400(0.92)$$

$$= \$368$$

We can verify this figure as follows. On the basis of slightly less than 8.3 orders, the purchasing cost will be approximately $184. If we assume a constant rate of usage of 10 units per day, the firm will be out of stock approximately 6.8 days per cycle, or a total of 56.2 days for the year. Total stockout costs, therefore, will be approximately $29 (56.2 days is 1.87 months; the stockout rate is 0.458 per unit per month, and the average amount of stockouts is 34 units). Similarly, the firm will hold an average of 184 units for approximately 304 days (360 − 56), which is slightly over 10 months. At a monthly cost of storage of $.083 per unit, the storage costs are approximately $155. Thus, $184 + $29 + $155 = $368.

Supplementary Readings

Articles

Bunch, R.,"The Effect of Payment Terms on Economic Order Quantity Determination,"
Management Accounting (formerly *N.A.A. Bull.*), Jan. 1967.

Cohen, M. and R. Halperin, "Optimal Inventory Order Policy for a Firm Using the
LIFO Inventory Costing Method," *J. of Accounting Research,* Autumn 1980.

Demski, J. and G. Feltham, "Forecast Evaluation," *Accounting Rev.,* July 1972.

Packer, A., "Simulation and Adaptive Forecasting as Applied to Inventory Control,"
Operations Research, July–August 1967.

Shegda, M. and H. Weinberg, "Costs for Inventory Control and Production Planning,"
N.A.A. Bull., July 1964.

Books

Buffa, E. and J. Miller, *Production-Inventory Systems: Planning and Control.* Homewood, Ill.:
Irwin, 1979.

Chase, R. and N. Aquilano, *Production and Operations Management,* 3rd ed. Homewood,
Ill.: Irwin, 1981.

Eppen, G. and F. Gould, *Quantitative Concepts for Management: Decision Making without Algorithms.* Englewood Cliffs, N.J.: Prentice-Hall, 1979.

Fetter, R.B. and W.C. Dalleck, *Decision Models for Inventory Management.* Homewood, Ill.:
Irwin, 1961. Chapter II has an excellent discussion on input data.

Hadley, G. and T.M. Whitin, *Analysis of Inventory Systems.* Englewood Cliffs, N.J.: Prentice-Hall, 1963.

Itami, H., *Adaptive Behavior: Management Control and Information Analysis.* Sarasota, Fla.:
American Accounting Association, 1977.

Johnson, L.A. and D.C. Montgomery, *Operations Records in Production Planning, Scheduling
and Inventory Control.* New York: Wiley, 1974.

Naddor, E., *Inventory Systems.* New York: Wiley, 1966.

Orlicky, J., *Material Requirements Planning.* New York: McGraw-Hill, 1975.

Starr, M.K. and D. Miller, *Inventory Control: Theory and Practice.* Englewood Cliffs, N.J.:
Prentice-Hall, 1962.

"Techniques in Inventory Management," *N.A.A. Research Report No. 40.* New York:
National Association of Accountants, 1964.

Questions and Problems

1. The following statement has been made about inventory models: "Where such techniques were found in use, company accounting personnel had rarely participated in the application even though the methods rest upon cost data."[16] Discuss this situation and indicate the extent to which inventory costs are, or should be, collected in the financial accounts.

2. The two relevant cost parameters considered in the EOQ model are purchase order costs C_p and storage or holding costs C_s. Indicate whether the following costs are likely to be variable, semivariable, fixed, or semifixed. What estimating methods could be applied in determining their relationship to inventory policies?

> *Purchase order costs*
>> Purchase order forms
>> Receiving forms
>> Clerical processing of order
>> Inspection of shipments
>> Clerical processing of payments
>> Transportation costs
>
> *Storage costs*
>> Insurance
>> Taxes
>> Breakage
>> Warehouse rental
>> Warehouse light, heat, and security guard
>> Interest on investment

3. Define *lead time* and *safety stock,* and indicate how the two concepts are related.

4. **Economic Order Quantity**
Given the following data, compute the reorder quantity, the number of orders, and the total cost of the resulting inventory policies. Suppose that the lead time is 18 calendar days and that the company works approximately 260 days per year. What is the approximate reorder level?

$$D = 2{,}400 \text{ units per year}$$

$$C_p = \$12$$

$$C_s = 12\% \text{ per year}$$

$$P = \$10 \text{ per unit}$$

5. **Lot Size and Demand**

   (a) Using equation [16–2] and the following data, determine the amount by which demand would have to increase before the lot size q^* would double.

---

[16] "Techniques in Inventory Management," p. 3.

$$D = 3,600 \text{ units per year}$$

$$C_p = \$22.23 \text{ per order}$$

$$C_s = \$1 \text{ per year}$$

(b) The inventory turnover ratio,

$$\frac{\text{Cost of goods sold}}{\text{Average inventory on hand}}$$

is used to determine the efficiency of a firm's inventory policies. Discuss the use of this ratio in light of your answer to part (a).

6. **Fluctuating Rates of Demand**
The inventory models discussed in this chapter are based on an assumption of constant demand in each subperiod t_s. Suppose demand did fluctuate from one subperiod to the next. Explain why these simple inventory models would no longer be appropriate to this type of inventory problem.

7. **Economic Order Quantity**
A firm's total annual inventory costs are approximated by:

$\$2,400 + \$395(\text{Demand}) + \$50(\text{Number of orders}) + \$8(\text{Average inventory}).$

Demand is expected to be 5,000 units during the coming year. Determine the optimal order quantity.

8. **EOQ and Value of Order Cost Information**
Consider the basic data in Problem 7 above. Without additional information, the policy determined above will be implemented. Assume, however, that the C_p parameter will be $25, $50, or $75 with equal probability. $D = 5,000$ units and $C_s = \$8$ per average unit, what is the expected value of perfect C_p information?

9. **EOQ and Value of Storage Cost Information**
Consider the basic data in Problem 7 above. Without additional information, the policy determined above will be implemented. Now assume the storage cost parameter C_s will be either $6 or $10 with equal probability. Assuming $D = 5,000$ units and $C_p = \$50$ per order, what is the expected value of perfect C_s information?

10. **EOQ and Value of C_p and C_s Information**
Consider the basic data in Problems 7, 8, and 9 above. Without additional information, the policy determined in Problem 7 will be implemented. Assume the order cost parameter C_p will be $25, $50, or $75 (with equal probability) and that the storage cost parameter C_s will be $6 or $10 (with equal probability). Also assume the two parameters are independent (implying the joint probability

that $C_p = 25$ and $C_s = 6$ is $\frac{1}{6}$, and so on). What is the expected value of perfect C_p *and* C_s information?

11. ***Relevant Inventory Costs***[17]
The Supersap Corporation distributes widgets to the upper delta region of the Sunswop River. The demand for widgets is constant and Supersap is able to predict the annual demand with considerable accuracy. The predicted demand for the next couple of years is 200,000 widgets per year.

Supersap purchases its widgets from a supplier in Calton at a price of $20 per widget. In order to transport the purchases from Calton to the upper delta region, Supersap must charter a ship. The charter service usually charges $1,000 per trip plus $2 per widget (this includes the cost of loading the ship). The ship has a capacity of 10,000 widgets. Placing each order, including arranging for the boat, requires about five hours of employee time. It takes a week for an order to arrive at the Supersap warehouse.

When a boat arrives at the Supersap warehouse, the widgets can be un-loaded at a rate of 25 per hour per employee. The unloading equipment used by each employee is rented from a local supplier at a rate of $5 per hour. Supervisory time for each shipload is about four hours.

Supersap leases a large warehouse for storing the widgets; it has a capacity of 15,000 widgets. The employees working in the warehouse have several tasks:

(1) Placing the widgets into storage, after they are unloaded, can be done at the rate of about 40 per hour.
(2) Checking and cleaning the widgets in inventory requires about one-half hour per widget per year.
(3) Removing a widget from inventory and preparing it for shipment to a customer requires about one-eighth hour.
(4) Security guards and general maintenance require about 10,000 hours per year.

The average cost per hour of labor is approximately $10 (including fringe benefits). Supersap has developed the following prediction equation for its general overhead (excluding shipping materials, fringe benefits, and equipment rental).

Predicted overhead for the year = $1,000,000 + ($8)(Total labor hours)

The materials used to ship one widget to a customer cost $1 and the delivery costs average about $2 per widget.

The company requires a before-tax rate of return of 20 percent on its investment.

(a) Supersap has decided to base its ordering policy on an EOQ model. What amount should they order each time, and what should they use as the reorder point?

---

[17] Prepared by G. Feltham, University of British Columbia.

(b) If the true overhead prediction equation is

$$\$800,000 + (\$12)(\text{Total labor hours})$$

what is the opportunity cost of the prediction error?

12. **EOQ and Value of Overhead Information**
Return to the Supersap Corporation in Problem 11. The policy determined in part (a) will be implemented without additional information. The variable overhead, however, will be $4 per labor hour with probability $\frac{1}{4}$, $8 per labor hour with probability $\frac{1}{2}$, and $12 per labor hour with probability $\frac{1}{4}$. What is the expected value of learning the "true" variable overhead rate before the inventory policy is implemented?

13. **Opportunity Cost Measurement**
Mr. Swish, an aggressive entrepreneur, is working on some make-or-buy decisions and related inventory system. For one such product (and you may assume, for purposes of argument, that all such situations are independent), he decides to use the classic economic order quantity model with no stockouts to determine an optimal order size. He initially predicts that annual demand will be 2,000 units, that each unit will cost $45, that the incremental cost of processing each order (and receiving the ordered goods) will be $67, and that the incremental cost of storage will be $6 per unit per year.

(a) What is the optimal order quantity?
(b) What is the incremental cost of following the policy in (a), above?
(c) Suppose that Swish is incorrect in his $67 incremental cost per order prediction but is precisely correct in all other predictions. State the equation to predict the maximum amount Swish should pay to discover the true incremental cost per order if (1) this true cost is $33 per order and (2) in the absence of any knowledge to the contrary, Swish will implement the solution in (a) and will not alter it for one full year.
(d) What happens to your answer in (c) if we admit that Swish has also made errors in predicting demand, price, and the cost of storage?
(e) Suppose Swish implements the solution in (a) for two years. Further suppose that all his initial predictions were (and are) correct, except that the actual incremental cost of storage is $20 per average unit. If it costs Swish $4 to alter his inventory policy, state the equation to determine the opportunity cost of not changing his inventory policy at the beginning of the second year. Note: You may assume that the inventory cycle precisely repeats every year; otherwise, you would have to adjust for nonintegral values.
(f) Suppose that the true cost of a stockout to Swish is $18 per unit per year; further suppose that all other predictions are as given in (a). State the equation to determine the opportunity cost to Swish of using the economic order quantity model without stockouts if, indeed, stockouts are possible at the $18 figure. Assume that Swish will implement the incorrect model's solution [that is, (a)] for one year.

(g) What happens to your answer in (f) if each parameter prediction (demand, cost of storage, cost of purchasing, and cost of stockout) is incorrect?

14. **Stockout Costs**
   (a) Assume the same data as in Problem 4 but with the addition of stockout costs of $6 per unit per year. Calculate q^{**} and s^* and explain the significance of $(q^{**} - s^*)$.
   (b) Using the data above, calculate the effect on q^{**}, s^*, and TC of a possible error of $+ 10$ percent in (1) C_p; (2) C_s; and (3) C_0.
      Which of these possible errors has the most effect on the optimal policies of the firm? Suppose the estimate of C_p is based on the "visual curve" technique described in Chapter 3. A special cost study has been proposed whose purpose is to obtain accurate measures, within $.005, of the costs of placing orders and storing inventory on hand. The proposal contains a request for $100 to undertake the study. Evaluate this proposal.

*15. Suppose C_p is the out-of-pocket cash flow associated with processing a purchase order and P is the out-of-pocket cash flow per unit purchased. Thus, if 10 units are purchased, the net cash outflow at the time of purchase is $10P + C_p$. No other cash flows are involved at the time of purchase.
   Further suppose that D units are required per year and that p is the firm's (annual) cost of capital. What is the present value of relying on an order quantity of q? How does this compare with the cost function used in the EOQ model?

*16. **Speculation and Inventory Policies**
   M. Gordon has stated that the efficiency of the purchasing agent cannot be assessed unless we provide some means of crediting (debiting) him or her for the savings (losses) effected through the proper timing of purchases. (See his "Toward a Theory of Responsibility Accounting Systems," N.A.A. Bull., Dec. 1963, pp. 8–9). His illustration indicates that the differences between the expected or standard price of the purchased product and the actual prices cannot be used to determine the success or failure of a purchasing agent's attempt to speculate.
   It costs Smith & Sons, Inc., $15 to place an order; they require a total of 4,200 units during the year (the firm works 280 days a year), and storage costs are approximately 12½ percent per year per unit. The expected price per unit is $10.

   (a) What is the optimal order size? (Round off to whole units.)
   (b) Suppose the purchasing agent anticipates a price increase of 5 percent. The company can store 480 units in excess of its order size at a storage cost of 2 percent per month per unit. Should the additional units be purchased?
   (c) The agent decided to speculate, and the price of the units actually rose from $10 to $10.30 per unit. What is the net gain or loss we can assign to this decision?
   (d) Prices are expected to increase by 5 percent. What additional storage costs per unit can the agent afford to pay and still show a gain from speculation?

*17. **EOQ and Production Lots**

A firm can produce its own units at a rate of M per day. Setup costs per production run are C_u (corresponding to C_p). The demand rate is d units per day, with a total demand of D units. The length of the run is equal to Q/M, that is, the amount produced each run divided by the production rate. Maximum inventory (assuming a zero beginning inventory each run) is equal to $(M - d)$ times the length of the run, or $(M - d)Q/M$, and average inventory is $(M - d)Q/2M$. Using C_s to represent storage costs during time period T, the total cost of this type of inventory is

$$TC = \frac{D}{Q} C_u + (M - d)\frac{Q}{2M} C_s$$

and

$$\frac{dTC}{dQ} = -\frac{DC_u}{Q^2} + \frac{M-d}{2M} C_s = 0$$

with

$$Q^* = \sqrt{\frac{2DC_u M}{C_s (M - d)}}$$

In graphical terms, this inventory policy behaves as shown in Figure 16-3. Solve for Q^*, assuming that

$$D = 750 \text{ units per year}$$

$$C_u = \$25 \text{ per run}$$

$$C_s = \$2.50 \text{ per unit per time period } T$$

$$M = 20 \text{ units per day}$$

$$d = 10 \text{ units per day}$$

What kinds of costs might be included in the \$25 estimate of C_u?

FIGURE 16-3

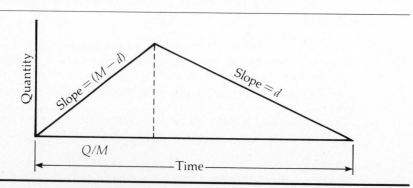

Solutions to Review Problems

1. (a) Expected net gain if the manager implements the new technique:

$$.60(\$30,000) + .40(-\$40,000) = \$2,000$$

Expected net gain if he does not implement the technique:

$$.60(\$0) \quad + .40(\$0) \quad\quad = \$0$$

(b) If the manager knows the high savings event will occur, he will implement and capture the $30,000 gain. If he knows the low savings event will occur, he will retain the status quo and avoid the $40,000 loss. Hence, we have:

Expected value of gain under perfect information

$$.60(\$30,000) + .40(\$0) = \$18,000$$

Less expected value of gain under no information

$$= \$\ 2,000$$

Expected value of perfect information

$$= \$16,000$$

This quantity, $16,000, bounds the manager's ability to improve his decision. Without any improvement, he has an expected gain of $2,000. With perfect information (information such that he knows exactly what will happen before he acts), he would have an expected gain of $18,000.

CHAPTER 2 _____

1. (a) Cost of direct materials:

Beginning inventory	$10,000
Add: Purchases	50,000
Available for use	60,000
Less: Ending inventory	12,000
Raw material used in production	$48,000

   (b) Cost of goods manufactured:

Beginning inventory of work-in-process		$ 30,000
Add: Production costs		
Raw material (a above)	$48,000	
Direct labor costs	50,000	
Overhead allocated to production	45,000	
		143,000
Total costs: Work-in process		173,000
Less: Ending Inventory of work-in-process		23,000
Costs to finished goods (Costs of goods manufactured)		$150,000

   (c) Cost of goods sold:

Beginning inventory—Finished Goods	$ 20,000
Add: Costs of goods manufactured (b above)	150,000
Finished goods available for sale	170,000
Less: Ending inventory — finished goods	70,000
Costs of goods sold	$140,000

   (d) Overhead rate per labor hour:

$$\frac{\$45,000}{10,000 \text{ hr}} = \$4.50 \text{ per labor hour}$$

2. (a) Semivariable. Some electricity is needed for light and, perhaps, heat; and a variable portion is likely to be related to operating machinery.
   (b) Fixed. (Ignoring the possibility of a profit-sharing bonus).
   (c) Fixed. Some question may be raised about the level of advertising being related to current production. However, the important

aspect is that once committed, this cost is unchanging in response to volume changes. That is, if sales rise 15 percent above the forecast, is advertising raised? For some firms the cost may be semifixed if volume is markedly different from the projected levels.

(d) Fixed. An exception would be the units of production basis of depreciation. Another would be in a period of exceptionally heavy usage, which could shorten the useful life.

(e) Fixed.

(f) Probably semivariable, but depends on company policy. Airlines service equipment after a given number of flying hours. Cars may be serviced after either a mileage or time limit expires. Different conditions lead to different answers.

(g) Semivariable; if a company retains skilled workers during slack periods as a matter of policy.

(h) Variable

(i) Semifixed.

(j) Semivariable over its entire range. However, we would consider it fixed or variable if we are confined to one portion of it.

(k) Probably variable. Overtime premiums would be variable with output, corresponding to regular wage rates for direct labor. However, overtime might be incurred at irregular times producing somewhat of a discontinuous function. For example, the cost function for output during normal hours might be $TC = a + bx_1$ where $x \leq x_1 =$ the output at which point overtime is incurred. Following that point, the variable rate would increase to $(b + OT)$. Hence the cost function over the entire output would be $TC = a + b(x) + OTP\ (x - x_1)$ assuming $x > x_1$. Graphically, the function might appear as follows:

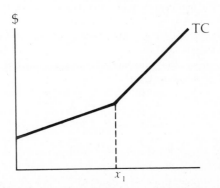

Of course, the firm might plan on a regular amount of overtime for each worker so that effectively the total wage per unit is $[b + k(OTP)]$ for all units of output where k = "planned" overtime hours as a fraction of straight time hours.

(l) Fixed; property taxes and insurance will be based upon the amounts of inventory, machines, and equipment held at the time of the audit. Assuming these levels are relatively fixed, the corresponding charges for taxes and maintenance would be fixed also.

3. (1) b.

(2) f.

(3) i. Note that the slope of the variable portion is .01 per dollar of sales and would go through the origin.

(4) j. Choice (f) ignores the minimum.

(5) g. Note that the cost of 1,000 widgets ($1,000) exceeds the cost of 1001 ($800.80).

(6) a.

(7) b.

(8) b. Note that when the work force is paid for an hour, this is not necessarily *working* the hour. The insurance cost is based on the latter and they vary directly with production. If it were based on the number of hours for which they are paid, graph (a) applies for a work force of constant size.

(9) b.

(10) e.

4. (a) The types of decisions under control of the unit head consist largely of the allocations of individuals possessing different levels of skills, i, to tasks, j. Presumably there is an optional allocation of each individual *skill* level to each *task required*, subject to the availability of individuals who have these skills. The budget for labor cost would be based on some *average* labor cost per task, given past observations. If better (worse) than average allocations are made currently, the total labor costs incurred should be lower (higher) than the product: average labor cost per task times number of tasks performed.

The average may be affected over time, however, by the mix of skills made available to the unit head. This may be a partial responsibility of the head or a responsibility of the personnel department. Such an average is a useful benchmark only to the extent that the mix of tasks to be performed does not change much over time.

(b) Using the optimal skills of labor for each task should result in less waste in materials and supplies. Hence, the unit head would be responsible for the amount of these costs as well.

In many situations, it may also be possible for unit heads to trade off price and quality of one type of material against the price–quality combination of other types of material. Presumably higher prices are associated with higher grades of material, and a unit head would have to determine what combination best fits the technology. This suggests that evaluations of the performance of unit heads should focus on total costs incurred relative to the budget.

(c) Supplies, clean-up labor, utility costs (to some extent); maintenance; overtime costs. In general, these costs would be controllable.

(d) Depreciation based on the passage of time; rent or leasing costs; taxes and insurance, supervising labor, and other costs related to capacity levels of fixed resources. Since these resources appear to be "assigned" to the unit head by higher levels of management, they would not be controllable.

5. (1) a.   (6) b.
   (2) d.   (7) c.
   (3) e.   (8) h.
   (4) f.   (9) i.
   (5) i.   (10) g.

(11) g. While the company has said he must entertain these customers, they did not specify how lavishly.

(12) g.

(13) g. He controls the salesmen who in turn make this decision.

(Note: All of this analysis assumes this is the *only* way to use the excess capacity.)

CHAPTER 3

1. (a) $a = \sum\limits_{i=1}^{n}$ Fixed costs $= \$9,000 + \$10,000 + \$12,000 = \$31,000$

$$b = \sum\limits_{i=1}^{n} \frac{\text{variable costs at } x = 20,000}{x = 20,000}$$

$$= \frac{\$40,000 + \$60,000 + \$20,000 + \$26,000}{20,000}$$

$$= \frac{\$146,000}{20,000} = \$7.30$$

$\hat{T}C_{AC.} = \$31,000 + \$7.30x$

(b) $b = \dfrac{\$177,000 - \$106,000}{20,000 - 10,000} = \dfrac{TC_{x=H} - TC_{x=L}}{x_H - x_L} = \dfrac{\$71,000}{1,000} = \$7.10$

$a = TC_{x=H} - \$7.10(x_H) = TC_{x=L} - \$7.10(x_L)$
$= \$177,000 - \$7.10(20,000) = \$106,000 - \$7.10(10,000)$
$= \$ 35,000$

$\hat{T}C_{HL} = \$35,000 + \$7.10x$

(c) If an item is strictly variable, the intercept is zero so that TC/x is a constant over all output observations. Checking each item classified as variable, we note that for materials, labor, indirect supplies, this condition holds (that is, $\$40,000/20,000 = \$20,000/10,000$; $\$60,000/20,000 = \$30,000/10,000$ and $\$20,000/20,000 = \$10,000/10,000$ for the three cost items respectively). This is not true, however, for indirect labor, which has lower average costs for higher levels of output. Specifically, the average for indirect labor at 20,000 is $\$26,000/20,000 = \$1.30$; but at 10,000, the average is $\$18,000/10,000 = \$1.80$. Also, utilities were classified as strictly fixed, which is obviously not consistent with the data. Using the high low-method for each results in the following estimate:

Indirect labor:

$$b = \frac{\$26,000 - \$18,000}{20,000 - 10,000} = \$.80$$

$$a = \underline{\underline{10,000}}$$

Utilities:

$$b = \frac{\$9,000 - \$6,000}{20,000 - 10,000} = \$.30$$

$$a = \underline{\underline{3,000}}$$

To reconcile, under the account classification method we assigned a variable cost of $1.30 to indirect labor—$.50 excess—and zero to utilities—$.30 deficiency—which nets out to a $.20 reduction to get to $7.10 under the high-low method. For fixed costs we understated the fixed cost component of indirect labor by $10,000 and overstated it for utilities by $6,000; a net shortage of $4,000.

2. (a) This is a subjective approach to the problem and visual curve-fitting is unlikely to resolve the issue. However, if later supported by supplementary analysis based on regression results, the graphical approach can provide us with clues as to which activity basis is likely to provide the best estimate of costs.

On the basis of the graphs below, it appears that DLH (direct labor hours) is the best activity basis for this department.

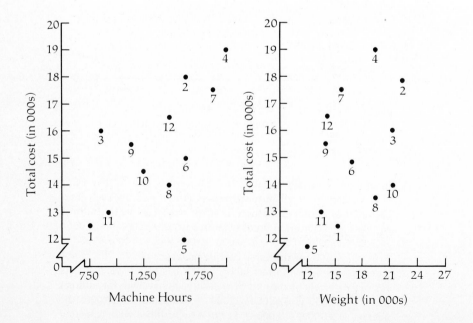

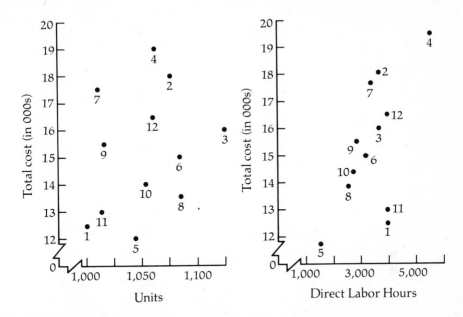

(b) (1) High-low method:

	Cost	**Volume**
High	$19,200	5,350 DLH
Low	11,800	1,600 DLH
Difference	$ 7,400	3,750 DLH

Variable cost: $7,400 ÷ 3,750 DLH = $1.973 per DLH
Fixed cost:* $11,800 − $1.973(1600) = $8643.20
Fixed cost:* $19,200 − $1.973(5350) = $8644.45

* Discrepancy due to rounding error. Actual variable cost is $1.97 ⅓ per unit.

(2) The "normal" equations are:

$$\Sigma y = na + b\Sigma x$$
$$\Sigma xy = a\Sigma x + b\Sigma x^2$$

$$182,900 = 12a + 41,130b$$
$$641,476,000 = 41,130a + 151,658,500b$$
$$626,889,750 = 41,130a + 140,973,075b$$
$$14,586,250 = 0 + 10,685,425b$$
$$b = 1.3651 \doteq 1.365$$
$$a = 10,563.129 \doteq 10,563$$

The prediction equation is

$$\widehat{OVHD} = 10,563 + 1.365DLH$$

(c) (1) The "normal" equations are:

$$\Sigma y = na + b\Sigma x \qquad 182{,}900 = 12a + 17{,}050b$$
$$\Sigma xy = a\Sigma x + b\Sigma x^2 \qquad 265{,}994{,}000 = 17{,}050a + 26{,}255{,}350b$$
$$259{,}870{,}417 = 17{,}050a + 24{,}225{,}208b$$
$$6{,}123{,}583 = 0 + 2{,}030{,}142b$$
$$b = 3.01633 \doteq 3.016$$
$$a = 10{,}955.960c \doteq 10{,}956$$

The prediction equation is:

$$\widehat{\text{OVHD}} = 10{,}956 + 3.016 \ (\text{machine hours})$$

(2) OVHD

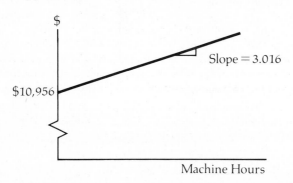

(d) *Additional considerations.* Since each manager finds a different activity
base to be advantageous, it is possible that all the alternatives
may have some explanatory power; that is, "there may be some
truth to each." The effect of the proposed solution on each manager's incentives must be carefully considered.

Presumably each manager's products make use of different
proportions of the sealing department's inputs, or there would
be no controversy. One possible compromise would be to include
all the proposed independent variables in a multitude regression
framework. However, if the independent variables are highly
colinear, the estimated cost coefficient for some inputs might
be subject to a wide margin of error, distorting incentives beyond
those presented by the best simple regression cost estimate. On
the other hand, if variables are omitted that are important and
uncorrelated with those included, the overall estimate of marginal
cost will be subject to more error than necessary.

3. (a) Profit expected at 18,000 units = ($12 − $9.00) 18,000 − $39,000
= π or, $54,000 − $39,000 = $15,000 profit

(b) Profit expected at 20,000 units = ($12 − $8.50) 20,000 − $52,150
= π or $70,000 − $52,150 = $17,850 profit

(c) If management would have known that only 18,000 units would
have been sold, the fixed selling and administrative costs would
have been kept at $14,000. Profit would have been $13,000 as
in (a) above. Actual profit = 18,000 ($12 − $7.50) − $52,150 −

$1,000 storage costs (presumably, the extra 2,000 units will be sold in the next period), or $9,850. Opportunity Loss = $13,000 − $9,850 = $3,150

(d) The measure is an upper bound on the improvement in decisions if perfect information were available. Of course, perfect information can rarely be obtained, but instead we receive information that only allows us to revise our probabilities of a particular state occurring (see Chapter 1). This is not to say the measure is not a useful one to obtain. Suppose the value of perfect information about particular outcomes is trivial (decisions are relatively insensitive to estimation errors). Then a decision maker is justified in not investing significant amounts of resources to improve his estimates before making his decisions. Alternatively, suppose the value of perfect information is quite high. Then a decision maker would want to consider investing in information production even if the outcome will be in the form of imperfect information. The difficulty is what to do when the value of perfect information falls within these two extremes. Whether any particular item of imperfect information should be acquired is a cost/benefit decision.

4. (a) Regression ignoring the timing of the observations: Let Total Cost = y, volume (units) = x.

y	x	$y \cdot x$	x^2
11.0	1.0	11.00	1.00
14.5	1.5	21.75	2.25
16.5	2.0	33.00	4.00
18.0	2.5	45.00	6.25
17.0	2.0	34.00	4.00
15.5	1.5	23.25	2.25
92.5	10.5	168.00	19.75

$\Sigma y = na + b\Sigma x$ or $92.5 = 6a + b\,(10.5)$

$\Sigma xy = a\Sigma x + b\Sigma x^2$ $168.0 = a(10.5) + b(19.75)$

$$a = 15.41667 - b(1.75)$$
$$19.75\ b = 168 - 10.5(15.41667 - 1.75b)$$
$$= 168 - 161.87504 + 18.375b$$
$$1.375b = 6.125$$
$$b = 4.4545$$
$$a = 7.6213$$

x	Actual Y	Predicted Y	Error (Act-Predicted)	(Error)²
1.0	11.0	12.0758	−1.0758	1.15735
1.5	14.5	14.3030	+ .1970	.03881
2.0	16.5	16.5303	− .0303	.00918
2.5	18.0	18.7576	− .7576	.57396
2.0	17.0	16.5303	+ .4697	.22062
1.5	15.5	14.3030	+1.1970	1.43281
			$\Sigma = 0$	$\Sigma = 3.43273$

(b) Regression including dummy variable. Let $y = $ Total cost, $x_1 = $ volume (units), and $x_2 = $ dummy.

y	x_1	x_2	$y \cdot x_1$	$y \cdot x_2$	x_1^2	x_2^2	$x_1 \cdot x_2$
11.0	1.0	0	11.00	0	1.00	0	0
14.5	1.5	0	21.75	0	2.25	0	0
16.5	2.0	0	33.00	0	4.00	0	0
18.0	2.5	0	45.00	0	6.25	0	0
17.0	2.0	1	34.00	17.0	4.00	1	1.5
15.5	1.5	1	23.25	15.5	2.75	1	1.0
92.5	10.5	2.0	168.00	32.5	19.75	2.0	2.5

$$92.5 = 6a + b_1 (10.5) + b_2 (2.0)$$
$$168.0 = a(10.5) + b_1(19.75) + b_2 (2.5)$$
$$32.5 = a(2.0) + b_1 (2.5) + b_2(2.0)$$

Solving

$$a = 7.20$$
$$b_1 = 4.45 \text{ (rounded off)}$$
$$b_2 = 1.25 \text{ (rounded off)}$$

x_1	x_2	*Actual*	*Predicted*	*Error*	*(Error)^2*
1.0	0	11.0	11.65	$-.65$	.423
1.5	0	14.5	13.88	.62	.384
2.0	0	16.5	16.10	.40	.160
2.5	0	18.0	18.33	$-.33$	.109
1.5	1.0	17.0	17.35	$-.35$	.125
1.0	1.0	15.5	15.13	.32	.102
					1.301

Note the reduction in the sum of the squared error (from 3.433 to 1.301) from the introduction of the dummy variable. Effectively, the dummy variable raises the intercept from 7.20 to 8.45 (7.20 + 1.25) whenever production drops below its previous level. That is, if production is decreasing, the estimate is:

$$E(TC) = 7.20 + 4.45 \ x_1 + 1.25 \ (1.0)$$
$$= 8.45 + 4.45 \ x_1$$

In contrast, our first regression line merely "splits" the observations. Its intercept of 7.62 falls between the intercepts of the prediction lines in (b) above, and the slopes in parts (a) and (b) are the same.

(c) In actual practice it is unlikely that the sequence of observations would be so ordered. Instead we are more likely to find a random pattern of plus and minus changes in production levels. It is unlikely that cost stickiness, if present, would be spotted in these situations. Also, even if there were sequences of plus and minus changes in output around a general upward trend, it is unlikely

that an examination of the observations would reveal cost stickiness. The cost observations would tend to produce a ratchet-
type of cost function where costs would decrease at a lower
rate when production was decreasing, then remain at a fairly
constant level as output increases to the original level, then increase at the normal rate as original levels of output are surpassed.
This is illustrated as follows

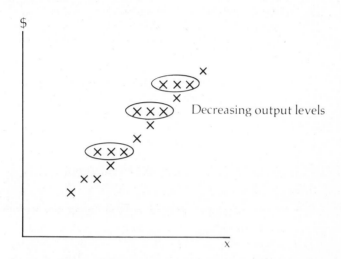

If we did not suspect cost stickiness, we might view different cost observations for the same output levels as merely due
to random causes. In short, our priors about the existence or
nonexistence of cost stickiness will determine the extent to which
we are likely to be able to detect its effects on cost estimation.

With more observations, ill-behaved regression residuals
(high autocorrelations, excessive number of "runs" of residuals
with the same sign) might be suggestive of cost stickiness if
there are sequences of plus and minus changes in output.

5. (Based on natural logs.)

(a) $\log(580) = \log a - l(\log 50)$ or

$$6.36303 = \log a - l(3.91202)$$

Similarly

$$\log(398) = \log a - l(\log 150)$$
$$5.98645 = \log a - l(5.01604)$$

Solving for l:

$$6.36303 - \log a + 3.91202(l) = 5.98645 - \log a + 5.01064(l)$$
$$.37658 = 1.09862(l)$$
$$.34278 = l$$

Solving for a:

$$6.36303 = \log a - l(3.91202) \text{ or}$$
$$6.36303 + .34278(3.91202) = \log a$$
$$7.70399 = \log a$$
$$2217 = a$$

(b) $\log (y_{200}) = \log 2217 - l(\log 200)$
$\log (y_{200}) = 7.70399 - .34278 (5.2983)$
$\quad\quad = 7.70399 - 1.81615$
$\log (y_{200}) = 5.88784$
$\quad\quad y = 361 \text{ (approx)}$

Total hours $200(361) = 72,200$
$\quad\quad x = 200$
Total hours $150(398) = \underline{59,700}$
$\quad\quad x = 150$
Incremental hours   12,500

(c) Incremental costs $= 12,500(\$10/\text{hr}) = \$125,000$

CHAPTER 4

1. (a) Line BB' represents 0 (zero) profit or loss.
    (b) The horixontal axis AE represents *output levels* usually in units, and the vertical axis AF represents *profit* (above point B) *or loss* (below point B).
    (c) Point C represents the *break-even point*.
    (d) The distance DE' divided by distance AE' *is the contribution margin* (usually expressed per unit of output).

2. (a) Contribution margin per unit is $\$10 - \$5.90 = \$4.10$. Total fixed costs is $\$61,500$. Break-even in units is $\$61,500/\$4.10 = 15,000$ units or 15,000 $\times \$10 = \$150,000$ in sales dollars. The latter is also equal to $\$61,500 \div (10 - 5.90)/\$10 = \$61,500/\$.41$.
    (b) Profit will be $\$4.10(20,000 - 15,000) = \$20,500$, that is, contribution margin $\times$ units sold in excess of break-even. The calculation can be checked as follows: Total sales at 20,000 units minus Total costs at 20,000 units $= \$200,000$ minus $\$67,500 + \$5.90 (20,000) = \$200,000 - \$179,500 = \$20,500$.
    (c) New selling price: $= \$10 - \$.50 = \$9.50$.
         New volume $= 1.15(20,000) = 23,000$ units.
         New variable cost per unit, $\$5.10$ up to 21,000, $\$5.20$ beyond 21,000.
         New fixed costs $= \$61,500 + \$7,500 = \$69,000$.
         New profit $= \$9.50(23,000) - \$69,000 - \$5.9(21,000) - \$6.00(2,000)$
         $= \$218,500 - [\$69,000 + \$123,900 + \$12,000] = \$218,500 - \$204,900$
         $= \$13,600$.
         Proof:
         Increase in contribution margin from extra sales $= 1,000 (\$9.50 - \$5.90) + 2,000 (\$9.5 - \$6.0) = 1,000 (\$3.60) + 2,000 (\$3.50) = + \$10,600$.

Decrease in contribution margin on original 20,000 = 20,000 ($.50) = −10,000.

Net change = +600 in contribution margin.

Less extra fixed costs of $7,500 = −$6,900 net loss (20,500 − 6,900) = $13,600.

(d) Sales = 1.2(20,000) = 24,000. Net sales = $9.9(24,000) less $20,000 allowance = $217,660. Total costs (using above figures) = $61,500 + $5.9(21,000) + $6.0(3,000) = $61,500 + $123,900 + $18,000 = $203,400. $217,600 − $203,400 = $14,200

(e) We know the solution will be an output greater than 21,000 units; let this be x.

$20,500 = $3.6(21,000) + $3.5(x) − $69,000

$13,900 = $3.5(x)

$$x = 3,972 \text{ units}$$

Solution: 21,000 + 3,972 = 24,972 units.

(f) Again, let x represent the excess over 21,000 units.

$20,500 = $4.0(21,000) + $3.9(x) − $61,500 − $20,000

$20,500 = $3.9(x) + $2,500

$$x = 4,615 \text{ units}$$

Solution: 21,000 + 4,615 = 25,615 units which is not feasible.

3. (a) (1) Reducing fixed costs by $20 million reduced the break-even point by 100,000 units. This is equivalent to saying the firm could increase profit by $20 million by going from 250,000 to 350,000 units. Hence $\Delta\pi/\Delta x$ = $20,000,000/100,000 = $200 per unit.

   (2) Previous break-even point was 350,000. At $200 CM per unit, this provides a total contribution margin of $70 million. Since total CM = total fixed costs at break-even, fixed costs were $70 million and are now $50 million.

   (3) 300,000 × $200 = $60 million total CM. With old FC of $70 million, the loss would have been $10 million = $200 (50,000 units below break-even).

   (4) 400,000 × $200 or $80 million less $50 million fixed costs = 30 million profit.

(b) Selling price constant over entire range of output.
Variable costs constant over entire range of output.
Mix of output constant over entire range of output.

4. (a) Incremental costs = $5,000 materials + $600 labor + $720 overhead = $6,320.

(b) Same as above plus $8 × 40 = $320 or $6,640.

(c) $6,320 + $4,000 lost contribution margin = $10,320.

(d) At $10, total incremental costs would be $5,600 for direct material and labor + $400 for overhead = $6,000. Incremental profit would be $10,000 − $6,000 = $4,000. At $18, incremental profit would be $10,000 − $6,320 or $3,680. At $26, total incremental costs would be $5,600 + $1,040 = $6,640. Incremental profit would be $10,000 − 6,640 = $3,360. The optimal choice in each case is to accept the offer. Knowing the actual costs does not change this decision. Hence information on actual costs is not worth anything.

(e) Because it fails to consider other possible uses of the overhead information.

5. (a) Presumably, we could process 2,000 units of Product A with 6,000 hours of capacity. If sold now, 2,000 × $5 of total revenues could be obtained. If processed further, 2,000 × $8 = $16,000 total revenues could be obtained. Thus, the firm could acquire $6,000 incremental revenues while incurring $3,000 + $1(2,000) = $5,000 incremental costs from processing: OPTIMAL DECISION = Process further.

(b) $2,000(p-5) = \$3,000 + \$1(2,000)$
     $2,000p = \$15,000$
     $p = \$7.50$

(c) $(\$8 - \$5)x = \$3,000 + \$1(x)$
     $(\$3 - \$1)x = \$3,000$
     $x = 1,500$

At $x = 1,500$, the firm receives $3(1,500) = $4,500 incremental revenue and incurs $3,000 + $1,500 incremental costs.

6. (a) Produce, if the incremental costs of producing are less than the incremental costs of buying—assuming no capacity constraints.

Part	#11	#12	#13	#14
Cost of Buying (per unit)	$2.00	$5	$14	$4.25
Cost of Producing	$1.75	$3.50	$ 9.50	$4.50
Savings (Loss)	$ .25	$1.50	$ 4.50	$(.25)

Produce #11, #12, #13; buy #14.

(b) With a single capacity constraint, maximize the savings per hour of scarce capacity.

	#11	#12	#13
Savings per unit	$.25	$1.50	$4.50
Capacity required per unit	½ hr	1 hr	4 hr
Savings per hour	$.50	$1.50	$1.125

Best Use of Capacity—assign to #12 until its requirements are fulfilled; then #13 and #11 in that order.
Capacity available = 150,000 hours.
#12 Requirement = 80,000 × 1 = 80,000 hours.
#13 Requirement = 15,000 × 4 = 60,000 hours.
#11 receives 10,000 hours. Produce 20,000 units and buy 80,000 units of #11.

(c) Left to the student.

7. (a)
	x_1	x_2
Contribution Margins	$19.00	$22.00
Using A Estimates	−6.00	−7.00
	$13.00	$15.00

SOLUTION (See graph below)

$$x_1 = 300$$
$$x_2 = 100$$
$$\text{Total CM} = 300(\$13) + 100(\$15) = \underline{\$5,400}$$

(Note: TCM at $x_1 = 400$ is $5,200; TCM at $x_2 = 250$ is $3,750)

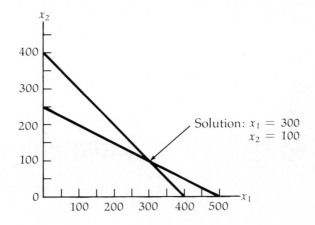

(b) If the B estimates are used, contribution margins become ($19 − $4) = $15 for x_1 and ($22 − $8) = $14 for x_2.

   (1) At $x_1 = 300$ and $x_2 = 100$, TCM′ = 300($15) + 100($14) = $5,900.
      At $x_1 = 400$, $x_2 = 0$, TCM′ = 400($15) + 0($14) = $6,000.
   (2) Actual TCM would be TCM$_{act}$ = 400($13) + 0($15) = $5,200.
      At optimal, TCM$_{opt}$ = 300($13) + 100($15) = $5,400. Cost equals $200 less TCM.

(c) 1/2 ($200) = $100.

CHAPTER 6 ─────────────────────────────────

1. Utilizing the cost relations in Exhibit 6-4, we substitute 75,000 for x and calculate total costs.

Account	Actual	Budget		Difference
Labor	$62,000		($.80)(75,000) = $60,000	$2,000
Electricity	6,500	$1,000 +	($.08)(75,000) = 7,000	(500)
Equipment rental	2,100	$2,000	2,000	100
Maintenance supplies	1,255	$ 250 +	($0.05)(75,000) = 1,375	(120)
Total	$71,855		$70,375	$1,480

2. *Materials.* Since the bolt contains 900 usable flags, the cost per 100 is 100/900 of the cost of the bolt, or $6. Added to this is $1, the cost of 100 poles.

Labor. The labor consists of two steps, cutting and assembling. The cutters do 180 flags in an hour, so 100/180 of an hour is required to do 100. The assemblers are able to do 200 flags in an hour, so a lot of 100 will require 100/200 of an hour.

Overhead. Initially the depreciation and rent can be classified as fixed because they are the same for both budgets. All others require the high-low approach to approximate the variable cost.

Utilities: $(\$3,920 - \$3,500) \div (960 - 750) = \$420 \div 210 = \underline{\underline{\$2 \text{ per}}}$ m.h.

Fixed Cost $= \$3,500 - \$2(750) = \$3,500 - \$1,500 = \underline{\underline{\$2,000}}$

Supplies: $(\$960 - \$750) \div (960 - 750) = \$210 \div 210 = \underline{\underline{\$1 \text{ per m.h.}}}$

Fixed Cost $= \$750 - \$1(750) = \$750 - \$750 = \underline{\underline{O}}$

Fringe benefits: $(\$1,920 - \$1,500) \div (960 - 750) = \$420 \div 201 = \underline{\underline{\$2}}$ per m.h.

Fixed Cost $= \$1,500 - \$2(750) = \$1,500 - \$1,500 = \underline{\underline{O}}$

The fixed cost per lot required us to find the portion of the total fixed costs allocated to each lot. This is 1/900 of the fixed cost, since normal volume is 900 machine hours. Therefore the fixed cost *per machine hour* is $5,400 ÷ 900, or $6. Since it takes one-half hour to do 100 flags, the cost per lot of 100 is $3. The individual accounts included in the fixed costs are calculated in the same fashion. Each item is 1/1,800 of its respective cost. These results are summarized in the following table.

Marston Manufacturing
Standard Cost Sheet: 100 Flags
1982

Raw materials	Cost per 100
Cloth (⅑ of a bolt @ $54 per bolt)	$ 6.00
Poles (100 poles @ $1 per 100)	1.00
Total materials	$ 7.00

Labor	
Cutting (⅝ hour @ $3.60 per hour)	$ 2.00
Assembly (½ hour @ $3.60 per hour)	1.80
Total labor	$ 3.80

Overhead	
Variable	
Utilities (½ hour @ $2 per hour)	$ 1.00
Supplies (½ hour @ $1 per hour)	.50
Fringe benefits (½ hour @ $2 per hour)	1.00
Total variable overhead cost	$ 2.50

Fixed

Utilities	$2,000	$ 1.11
Depreciation	1,000	.56
Rent	2,400	1.33
Total fixed cost per 100 @ 900 m.h.	$5,400	$ 3.00
Total standard cost per 100		$16.30

3. A bolt of cloth is now expected to yield only 890 flags (1,000 − 100 − 10 = 890). The cost per flag is then $54 ÷ 890 = $.0607, amounting to $6.07 per hundred. The poles now yield only 97 per bundle of 100. This is a cost of $1.00 ÷ 97 = $.0103 per pole. Thus the standard cost per hundred good flags for poles is $1.03. This yields a materials standard of $6.07 plus $1.03, or $7.10, instead of $7.00 per 100.

CHAPTER 7

1. The following diagrams show the answers to parts (a) and (b). The calculations under each diagram show the answer to (c).

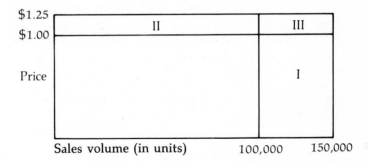

I	(Quantity variance):	50,000 units × $1	= $50,000F
II	(Price variance):	$.25 × 100,000 units =	25,000F
III	(Joint variance):	$.25 × 50,000 units =	12,500F
	Total variance		$87,500F

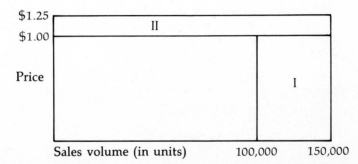

I (Quantity variance): 50,000 units × $1 = $50,000F

II (Price variance): $.25 × 150,000 units = 37,500F

Total variance $87,500F

2. (a) Raw materials

Actual cost	$587,000
Actual quantity at standard price (200,000 lb @ $3)	600,000
Price variance	$ 13,000F
Actual quantity used at standard price (163,000 lb @ $3)	$489,000
Standard quantity used at standard price (3 × 55,000 × $3)	495,000
Quantity variance	$ 6,000F
Total raw materials variance = $13,000F + $6,000F =	$ 19,000F

Labor variances

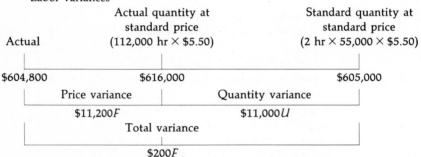

	Actual quantity at standard price (112,000 hr × $5.50)	Standard quantity at standard price (2 hr × 55,000 × $5.50)
Actual		
$604,800	$616,000	$605,000
	Price variance	Quantity variance
	$11,200F	$11,000U
	Total variance	
	$200F	

(b) Materials variances

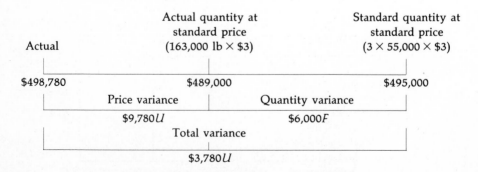

	Actual quantity at standard price (163,000 lb × $3)	Standard quantity at standard price (3 × 55,000 × $3)
Actual		
$498,780	$489,000	$495,000
	Price variance	Quantity variance
	$9,780U	$6,000F
	Total variance	
	$3,780U	

3.

	Actual	Actual quantity at standard price $464,000 + \$2$ DLH	Standard quantity at standard price $464,000 + \$4x$
Fixed	$465,500	Fixed $464,000	Fixed $464,000
Variable	229,600	Variable 224,000	Variable 220,000
	$695,100	$688,000	$684,000

Price variance		Quantity variance	
Fixed	$1,500$U$	Fixed	—
Variable	5,600U	Variable	$4,000$U$
	7,100U		$4,000$U$

Total variance	
Fixed	$ 1,500U
Variable	9,600U
	$11,100$U$

4.   Standard Cost

Raw material[a] 3 pounds @ $3 per pound		$ 9.00
Direct labor[a] 2 hours @ $5.50 per hour		11.00
Overhead		
Variable[b]: $2 per direct labor hour	$4	
Fixed[c]: $4 per direct labor hour	8	12.00
Total standard cost		$32.00

[a] Given in Review Problem 2.

[b] Given in Review Problem 3.

[c] Budgeted fixed costs are given in Review Problem 3 as $464,000. Fixed cost per direct labor hour is $464,000 ÷ 116,000 direct labor hours or $4.

Volume Variance

Normal volume	58,000 units
Actual volume	55,000
Shortfall in Production	3,000 units
Fixed overhead per unit	× $8
Volume variance	$24,000 U

5.   See diagram.

$F =$ Fixed cost
$N =$ Normal volume
$A =$ Actual volume worked
$S =$ Standard volume of work produced

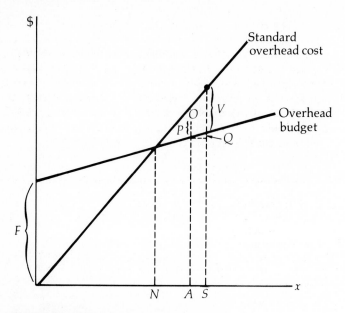

O = Actual cost
P = Price (or spending) variance
Q = Quantity (or efficiency) variance
V = Volume variance

		Actual	Budget	Difference
6. (a)	Sales	$275,000	$180,000	$ 95,000
	Less: Cost of sales	212,500	105,000	107,500
	Gross profit	$ 62,500	$ 75,000	$(12,500)
	Less: Administrative expense	$ 20,000	$ 18,000	2,000
	Marketing expense	30,000	25,000	5,000
	Net pretax profit	$ 12,500	$ 32,000	$(19,500)

(b) Sales variances:

Price effect [($11–12) × 25,000 units]	$ 25,000U
Quantity effect [10,000 units × $12]	120,000F
	$ 95,000F

(c) Cost of sales variance

Price effect [($8.50 − 7.00) × 25,000]	$ 37,500U
Quantity effect (10,000 × $7)	70,000U
	$107,500$U$

(d) In this problem we know the price reduction was done deliberately in an attempt to attract new business. As the result, we
can attribute the price effect on the budgeted volume to the
price reduction. Thus the net increase in revenues was $95,000.

The critical question is which of the cost effects relate to the expanded volume. Without question the quantity effect of $70,000 did. However, it is unlikely that the expanded volume caused the $1.50 rise in the cost per unit. Thus the price effect on the planned volume is not a result of the decision. The critical question is whether the decision to go ahead was made with knowledge of the price rise or not. If it was, then the relevant costs would be $85,000 ($70,000 + $15,000) and the effect of the price cut was to raise the gross margin by $10,000.

CHAPTER 9

1. (a)

Cash inflow from X (10 units @ $8)		$ 80
Cash inflow from Y (30 units @ $4)		120
Total cash inflow		$200
Less Department 1 costs		
Cost of A	$100	
Cash outflow for processing X and Y	50	$150
Contribution per unit of A		$ 50

Decision: Process A

(b)

Cash inflow from U (5 units @ $25)		$125
Cash inflow from T (3 units @ $0)		0
Total cash inflow		$125
Less:		
Opportunity value of X (10 units @ $8)	$ 80	
Cash outflow from Department 2	60	$140
Excess of cash outflows over cash inflows		($ 15)

Decision: Sell X for $P_x = 8 rather than process X further

(c)

Cash inflow from Q (45 units @ $10)		$450
Less:		
Opportunity value of X (10 units @ $8)	$ 80	
Opportunity value of S (20 units @ $1)	20	
Cash outflow from Department 3	120	
Cash outflow from Department 4	90	$310
Contribution		$140

Decision: Manufacture Q

(d)

Cash inflow from Q (45 units at $10 per unit)		$450
Less:		
Cash outflow from purchase of X		
(10 units @ $15)	$150	
Cash outflow from purchase of S		
(20 units @ $5)	100	
Cash outflow from Department 3	120	
Cash outflow from Department 4	90	$460
Excess of cash outflows over cash inflows		($ 10)

Decision: Reject

2.
Cash inflow from sale of Z	100($5000) = $500,000	
Less cash outflow from production		
Direct labor	100($ 900)	90,000
Variable overhead	100($1350)	135,000
Direct material	100($ 850)	85,000
Fixed		50,000
Net inflow		$140,000
Less: Opportunity value of Y	100($1500)	150,000
Net loss		$ (10,000)

3. (a)
Incremental revenue: 10 ($2,000) =		$20,000
Incremental cost		
Direct labor: 10 ($500) =	$5,000	
Direct material: 10 ($800) =	8,000	
Maintenance: 10 ($50)(.01)(500) =	2,500	
Variable overhead: 10 (1.50 − 0.50) 500 =	5,000	20,500
		$ (500)

(b) The above analysis coincides with that based on the standard variable cost datum. The allocation allows us to forego explicit recognition of maintenance effects. Of course, if fixed maintenance cost was also included in the variable overhead, we would be overstating the incremental cost.

CHAPTER 11

1. Part A

The statement that the firm uses a FIFO cost flow assumption for determining its cost of goods sold is not relevant in this case since actual costs equalled standard costs (no variances were observed). This must also be true for the unit cost of the beginning inventory.

(a) The direct costing standard cost would be

$$
\begin{array}{l}
\$\ 6.00\ \text{DM} \\
4.00\ \text{DL} \\
\underline{2.00\ \text{VOH}} \\
\$12.00\ \text{per unit manufactured}
\end{array}
$$

(b) The amount of selling expense can be used to determine the number of units sold: $150,000 − Fixed costs of $70,000 = $80,000 Variable selling costs. At $2.00 per unit (table footnote b), 40,000 units were sold.

Sales		$1,000,000
Less: Variable costs		
of manufacturing (40,000 × 12)	480,000	
Manufacturing margin	520,000	
Less: Variable selling costs	80,000	
Contribution margin		$440,000

Less: Fixed costs		
Manufacturing	108,000	
Selling	70,000	
Administrative	200,000	378,000
Profit before taxes		$ 62,000

(c) Finished goods inventory would be carried at $12.00 per unit—variable manufacturing cost per unit only—or a total of $24,000. Under absorption, finished goods inventory would be $15.00 × 2,000 = $30,000.

(d) Fixed cost in beginning finished goods inventory was 6,000 × $3.00 = $18,000. Fixed cost in ending finished goods inventory is 2,000 × $3.00 = $6,000. The change in Fixed costs in inventory was $6,000 − $18,000 = −$12,000. Absorption income − Direct income = $50,000 − 62,000 = −$12,000. (Note: The firm manufactured 36,000 units and sold 40,000—that is, $108,000/$3.00 = 36,000 units for normal volume. No volume variance means production = normal volume).

1. Part B

(a)

Sales (36,000 × $25)		$900,000
Standard cost of goods sold—		
absorption (36,000 × $15)		$540,000
Standard gross margin		$360,000
Variances		
Direct materials	+$10,000$U$	
Direct labor	+ 4,000U	
Variable overhead	+ 2,000U	
Fixed overhead	− 12,000F	
Net		$ 4,000U
Actual gross margin		$356,000

(b)

Variances charged—direct costing		
Direct materials	+$10,000$U$	
Direct labor	+ 4,000U	
Variable overhead	+ 2,000U	
Fixed overhead (spending only—see below)	0	
Net	16,000U	

Total fixed overhead variance		−$ 12,000F
Less: Volume variance		
Fixed overhead budgeted	$108,000	
Fixed overhead at standard (40,000 × $3.00)	120,000	
Volume variance		− $12,000
Spending variance is zero.		

(c) To compute the difference in net income between absorption and direct costing, we first calculate the manufacturing margin under direct: $900,000 - 36,000 ($12) - $108,000 fixed manufacturing = $900,000 - $540,000 = $360,000; less variable variances of $16,000 net [(b) above] = $344,000. Absorption income - Direct income = $356,000 - $344,000 = $12,000 = change in units in inventory × F.O.H. rate per unit = +4,000 ($3) = $12,000.

(d) Average unit costs in the prior period was $15.00 per unit (recall, there were no variances). Ending inventory was 2,000 @ $15.00 = $30,000. Average unit cost this period was as follows:

Direct materials
  40,000 × $6.00 + $10,000 = $250,000 actual
Direct labor
  40,000 × $4 + $4,000   = 164,000 actual
Variable overhead
  40,000 × $2 + $2,000   =   82,000
Fixed overhead   = 108,000
                               _____
Total $604,000

$$\frac{\$604,000}{40,000} = \$15.10$$

Ending inventory: 2,000 beginning inventory + 40,000 produced - 36,000 sold = 6,000 units. Ending inventory = 6,000 ($15.10) = $90,600 for absorption. For direct, 6,000 (496,000 ÷ 40,000) = 6,000 × $12.4 = $74,400.

2. (a)

	P_1	P_2
Variable costs		
S_1	$10,000	
S_2		$20,000
Fixed costs		
S_1	$ 8,000	
S_2		$10,000
	$18,000	$30,000
Average cost per hr		
of service received	$18	$16.67
	(=$18,000/1,000)	($30,000/1,800)

(b)

	S_1	S_2	P_1	P_2
(1) Variable				
Costs	$10,000	$20,000		
S_1 allocation	(10,000)	5,000	$5,000	
S_2 allocation		(25,000)		25,000
Total			5,000	25,000
Fixed				
Costs	$ 8,000	$10,000		
S_1 Allocation	(8,000)	4,000	4,000	
S_2 Allocation		(14,000)		14,000
Totals			$9,000	$39,000
Average cost				
per hr			$9.00	$21.67

(c)   Variable costs

$$S_1 = \$10,000 + \tfrac{1}{10} (\$20,000 + \tfrac{5}{10} S_1)$$
$$= \$10,000 + \$2,000 + \tfrac{1}{20} (S_1)$$
$$\tfrac{19}{20} S_1 = \$12,000$$
$$S_1 = \$12,632$$
$$S_2 = \$20,000 + \tfrac{5}{10} (12,632)$$
$$S_2 = \$26,316$$

Allocations: To $P_1 = \tfrac{1}{2}$ ($12,632) = $ 6,316
To $P_2 = .90$ ($26,316) = $\underline{\quad 23,684}$
Total $\qquad\qquad$ $30,000

Fixed costs

$$S_1 = \$8,000 + \tfrac{1}{10} (\$10,000 + \tfrac{5}{10} S_1)$$
$$= \$9,000 + \tfrac{1}{20} (S_1)$$
$$\tfrac{19}{20} S_1 = \$9,000$$
$$S_1 = \$9,474$$
$$S_2 = \$10,000 + \tfrac{5}{10} (\$9,474)$$
$$= \$14,737$$

Allocations: To $P_1 = \tfrac{1}{2}$($9,474) = $4,737
To $P_2 = .90$($14,737) = $13,263
Total Cost Allocations

	P_1	P_2	Total
To	$6,316	$23,684	$30,000
	4,737	13,263	18,000
	$11,053	$36,947	$48,000
Average cost per hr	$11.05	$20.53	

(d)   When the services of any one department are supplied in an uneven manner to the producing departments, as in the above. Note that P_2 uses 90 percent of S_2's services which in turn uses 50 percent of S_1's services. Hence, using our equations from (c) above, P_1 and P_2 account for the following amounts of services concerned.
For P_1

$$S_1 = 2,000 \text{ hr} + \tfrac{1}{10} (2,000 \text{ hr} + \tfrac{5}{10} S_1)$$
$$= 2,200 \text{ hr} + \tfrac{1}{20} S_1$$
$$\tfrac{19}{20} S_1 = 2,200 \text{ hr}$$
$$S_1 = 2,316 \text{ hr}$$
$$.5(2,316) = 1,158 \text{ hr}$$

For P_2

$$S_2 = 2,000 \text{ hr} + .5(2,316 \text{ hr})$$
$$= 3,158 \text{ hr}$$
$$.9(3,158) = 2,842 \text{ hr}$$

3. (a) (1) Net realizable value of output after further processing

Product	A	B	Total
Sales revenues	$100,000	40,000	$140,000
Separable	15,000	15,000	30,000
Costs			
Net realizable value	$ 85,000	$25,000	$110,000
Ratios	85/110	25/110	
Allocation percentage	77.3%	22.7%	

Total costs to allocate $80,000 + .75($1,000) = $80,750
Allocation to A = $62,420   Cost/unit = $6.242
Allocation to B = $18,330   Cost/unit = $3.666
           $80,750

(2) Net realizable value of output — at split-off price for A

Product	A	B	Total
Net realizable value	$60,000	$25,000	$85,000
Ratios	60/85	25/85	
Percentages	70.6%	29.4%	

Allocation
.706 ($80,750) $57,010   Cost/unit = $5.701
.294 ($80,750) $23,740   Cost/unit = $4.748

(3) Unit cost basis

$80,750/15,000 = $5.3833
Costs to A   = $53,833
Costs to B   = $26,917

(b) One half output sold after processing

	A	B	Total
Revenues	$50,000	$20,000	$70,000
Separable costs			
(1.50; 3.00)	7,500	7,500	15,000
	$42,500	$12,500	$55,000
Joint costs			
(6.242; 3.666)	31,210	9,165	40,375
Gross Margin	$11,290	$ 3,335	$14,625

B_p units would be recorded at a *credit* value of $.75 per unit. Net profit at disposal would be 0. An alternative would be to ignore any inventory of B_p and record the $.75 charge as an addition to cost of goods sold as B_p was sold. Note also that if the $.75 credit per unit of B_p in inventory were shown as an inventory adjustment account the cost valuation of A and B would net out to a total of $80,000—e.g., at split-off, A is recorded at $62,420 and B is recorded as $18,330. This sums to $80,750, less a credit for B_p of $750 = $80,000.

(c)

	A	B	Total
Total revenues	$100,000	$40,000	$140,000
Separable costs	15,000	15,000	30,000
	$ 85,000	$25,000	$110,000
Joint costs			
(A) (1)	$ 62,420	$18,330	$ 80,750
(A) (2)	57,010	23,740	80,750
(A) (3)	53,833	26,917	80,750
Gross Margin in all cases			$ 29,250

CHAPTER 12

1. (a) The overhead rate for 1982 is found by dividing 1982's expected overhead costs ($33,600) by the expected direct labor hours (8,400).

$$\$33,600 \div 8,400 \text{ DLH} = \underline{\$4/\text{DLH}}$$

(b)

Cadillac

Materials: January	$1,000	
February	100	$1,100
Labor: January (50 DLH @ $15/DLH)	750	
February (220 DLH @ $15/DLH)	3,300	4,050
Overhead (270 DLH @ $4/DLH)		1,080
		$6,230

VW

Materials	$ 500
Labor (160 DLH @ $15/DLH)	2,400
Overhead (160 DLH @ $4/DLH)	640
	$3,540

(c) The only job uncompleted at the end of February is the Omni. Costs on that are:

Materials	$1,200
Labor (310 DLH @ $15/hr.)	4,650
Overhead (310 DLH @ $4/hr.)	1,240
	$7,090

(d)

Overhead, applied (690 hr. @ $4/hr.)	$2,760
Actual [given in part (4)]	2,600
Over applied overhead (a credit)	$ 160

(e) As presented, the monthly figure has no meaning at all, since Carl's estimated costs and volume are for the entire year. The firm is hoping to be accurate over that length of time, not for each month. If it had a budget for February's overhead costs and the hours to be worked, then those comparisons would be of interest.

2. (a) Under the weighted average method all costs are treated as if they were incurred in the current period (April) and all finished goods are treated as if they were started and completed in this period. The equivalent units calculations are as follows:

Materials

Rods finished	42,200
Ending inventory (600 × 100%)	600
Equivalent units	42,800

Data for Conversion Costs

Rods finished	42,200
Ending inventory (600 × ⅓)	200
	42,400

The cost per unit is therefore:

COSTS

	April	Opening Inventory	Total	Equivalent Units	Unit Cost
Materials	$125,700	$2,340	$128,040	42,800	$2.992
Labor	83,600	1,155	84,755	42,400	1.999
Overhead	66,880	1,050	67,930	42,400	1.602
	$276,180	$4,545	$280,725		$6.593

(b) The allocation of the $280,725 between finished goods and ending work-in-process under the weighted average approach is:

Finished goods:		
(42,200 @ $6.593)		$278,225
Work-in-process:		
Materials (600 @ $2.992)	$1,795	
Labor (200 @ $1.999)	400	
Overhead (200 @ $1.602)	320	2,515
		$280,740[a]

[a] Difference between $280,725 total cost and this figure is due to a rounding error.

CHAPTER 14

1. (a) Present values of each alternative
   (1) Present value of $12,000 per year for 5 years (Table 14–4) is $45,492. Present value of $150,000 received after 5 years

(Table 14–2) is $93,150. Total present value is $138,642.
Net present value is $138,642 − 150,000 = −$11,358.
(2) Present value of operating flows

	YEAR				
	1	2	3	4	5
Flows	$ 20,000	$20,000	$30,000	$30,000	$ 30,000
Salvage					$100,000
	$ 20,000	$20,000	$30,000	$30,000	$130,000
P.V. factors	.909	.826	.751	.683	.621 (Table 14–2)
Present values	$ 18,180	$16,520	$22,530	$20,490	$ 80,730

Total $158,450
Net   −150,000
          +$ 8,450

(3) Present value of 3rd projects' flows
Operating $40,000 (2.487)(.826) = $82,170
Present value of "salvage" = $175,000 (.621) = $108,675
Total present value = $190,845
Net present value = $190,845 − 150,000 = $40,845

(b) (1) Using 8 percent for Project A
$ 12,000(3.993) = $ 47,915
$150,000 (.681)   102,150
            $150,065
Net present value = $150,065 − $150,000 = $65

(2) Present value of each year's flows—using 10 percent—would
be the same as above—that is, a net present value of $8,450.

(3) Using 16 percent for Project C = $40,000 (2.246)(.743) +
$175,000(.476) = 66,751 + 83,300 = $150,051.
Net present value = ($150,051 − $150,000) = $51

(c) Given the net present values of (1) and (3) are only $65 and
$51 respectively, we could assume each has an internal rate of
return approximately equal to the discount rates used to compute
their net present values—i.e., 8+ percent and 16+ percent respectively.

For Project B, the positive net present value of $8,450 indi-
cates an internal rate of return in excess of 10 percent. Try 12
percent:

	YEAR				
	1	2	3	4	5
Present value	$17,860	$15,940	$21,360	$19,080	$73,710

Total is $147,950, indicating the internal rate is less than 12 percent but probably more than 11 percent. Calculators could be used to determine a more definitive answer, but for what purpose? A rate between 11 and 12 percent is a good enough answer.

(d) Present value of $12,000 per year, 5 years, flows spread evenly throughout each year = $12,000 (.9610 + .8872 + .8189 + .7560 + .6979) = $12,000 (4.121) = $49,452. Present value of $150,000, received at the end of year 5, discounted continuously is $150,000 (.670) = $100,500 or a total of 149,952. Note the lower factor for the 150,000 receipt at year 5. In Table 14–2, r = 8%, n = 5 gives a factor of .681. In contrast, the annuity factor from Table 14–6 (i.e., 4.121) exceeds that from Table 14–4 (= 3.993).

2. (1) Keep old equipment

	YEAR			
	0	**1**	**2**	**3**
Cash foregone if asset is kept				
Present salvage	$5,000			
Tax benefits				
.4(6000 − 5000)	400			
	−$5,400			
(I-TR) Operating flows				
= .6($50,000 − $30,000 − $10,000)		+$6,000	+$6,000	+$6,000
TR(Depreciation) = .4($6000/3)		+$ 800	+$ 800	+$ 800
Net salvage, year 3				0
Net cash flows	−$5,400	+$6,800	+$6,800	+$6,800

If the asset is kept, the firm gives up $5,400 at t = 0 to "buy" future cash receipts of $6,800 per year for 3 years.

(2)

	YEAR			
	0	**1**	**2**	**3**
Net asset outlay	−$15,000			
Investment credit	+$ 1,000			−$ 500[a]
(1-TR) Operating flow				
= .6($50,000 − 20,000 − 15,000)		+$ 9,000	+$ 9,000	+$ 9,000
TR (Depreciation) assume 5 years,				
0 salvage		+$ 2,000	+$ 1,600	+$ 1,200
salvage, n = 3				+$ 3,500
TR (Book-salvage), year				
3 = .4(3,000 − 3,500)				−$ 200
Net cash flows	−$14,000	+$11,000	+$10,600	+$13,000

[a] Payment of investment credit to bring it in line with a 3 year asset.

(3) (a)

(1) Net present value—Holding old asset
Present value of
inflows = $5,000 (2.40)   = $12,000
Present value of cash foregone   − 6,000
Excess present value $ 6,000

(2) Present value of inflows—New
= $10,000(.90) + 11,000(.80) + 12,000(.70)
= $9,000 + 8,800 + 8,400
= $26,200
Outlay   − 16,000
Excess present value $10,200

Since $10,200 > $6,000, sell the old and buy the new. Equivalently, if the firm sells the old asset, it receives $6,000, but gives up $5,000 per year for 3 years. Netting these against the new asset, we have an incremental outlay of $10,000 [−16,000 − (−6,000)] which brings in incremental inflows of ($10,000 − 5,000 in year 1, ($11,000 − 5,000) in year 2 and ($12,000 − 5,000) in year 3.

Net excess present value, (New − Old)
−$10,000 + $5,000(.90) + $6,000(.80) + $7,000(.70)
= −$10,000 + $4,500 + $4,800 + $4,900
= +$4,200

This is the difference in the excess present values of the projects (i.e., $10,200 vs. $6,000).

(b) Solve for $r_i{}^*$ such that

(1) $$\$6,000 \equiv \$5,000\left(\frac{1}{1+r_1{}^*}\right) + \$5,000\left(\frac{1}{1+r_1{}^*}\right)^2 + \$5,000\left(\frac{1}{1+r_1{}^*}\right)^3$$

(2) $$\$16,000 \equiv \$10,000\left(\frac{1}{1+r_2{}^*}\right) + 11,000\left(\frac{1}{1+r_2{}^*}\right)^2 + \$12,000\left(\frac{1}{1+r_2{}^*}\right)^3$$

The internal rate of return for project (1) is about 65 percent. For (2) it is approximately 45 percent. Hence, (1) now looks more attractive than (2). See Review Problem 1 Chapter 15 for additional examples for switches.

(c) The payback for project (1) is 1.2 years; for project (2) it is approximately 1.55 years

(d) The accounting rate of return is average income/investment. For (1) the income each year is $6,000 - 2,000 depreciation or $4,000. $4,000/5,400 = .741. For (2) income is ($15,000 - 5,000) + ($15,000 - 4,000) + ($15,000 - 3,000) = $10,000 + $11,000 + $12,000 = $33,000. Add the gain of $500 and average income is 33,500/3 = $11,167. $11,167/14,000 = .798.

CHAPTER 15

1. (A) (1) (a) For Project X, the present value of a six-year annuity of $271 at 10 percent is 4.355($271) = $1,180. Hence, the excess present value of Project X is $1,180 - $1,000 = $180. The present value of project Y is: (2.487) $460 - $1,000 = $1,144 - $1,000 = $144. On the basis of the excess present value rule, Project X is to be preferred over Y.

(b) However, the internal rates of return for the projects suggest a different ranking.

PROJECT

	X*	Y**
Internal rate of return	16%	18%

$$* \text{ For X, present value factor } = \frac{\$1,000}{\$271} = 3.69.$$

$$**\text{For Y, present value factor} = \frac{\$1,000}{\$460} = 2.174$$

(c) Project X should be recommended on the basis of the excess present value criterion. The problem cannot be resolved unless we have some information about the firm's opportunities in years 4 through 6. In the absence of any additional information we must assume that proceeds from each project will be reinvested by the firm in other projects earning 10 percent. Therefore, the preference for Project X can be justified by comparing the future wealth of the firm as of year 6, given an investment in each project.

Investing in Project X will create a future value of net receipts of $271(7.7156) = $2,091. Project Y will create a future value of $460(3.310)(1.33) = $2,027 (this is the future value of a three-year annuity which is reinvested for 3 more years). The difference of $64 is equal to the difference in the excess present values of the projects—i.e., $180 - $144 = $36—invested for 6 years at 10 percent.

(2) (a)

	Project X	Project Y
Outlay	($2,000)	($5,000)
Present value of inflows*	$2,265	$5,526
Excess present value	$ 265	$ 526

* At 12 percent.

(b)

	Project X	Project Y
Outlay	($2,000)	($5,000)
Receipts each year	$1,340	$3,270
Present value factor (outlay/receipts)	1.492	1.529
Internal rate of return	22%	20%

(c) Here again the problem is to determine what the firm can do with the extra $3,000 left over if Project X is accepted. The present value criterion implies that 12 percent measures the opportunity cost of funds, so we must assume the $3,000 of extra funds will be invested at 12 percent. Therefore, the comparison above should be adjusted as follows:

X: Invest $2,000 to return $1,340 a year for 2 years plus $3,000 at 12 percent;

Y: Invest $5,000 to return $3,270 a year for 2 years. Project X will build to a future value of $1,340 (2.12) + $3,000(1.2544) = $2,841 + $3,763 = $6,604. Project Y will build to a future value of $3,270(2.12) = $6,932. Hence, Project Y should be recommended.

(B) (1) (a) For the problem in (1) we would be indifferent when the future values of each project are equal. For the first 3 years assume the proceeds of each project are invested at 10 percent. At the end of year 3, Project X will have a future value of $271(3.31) = $897. Project Y will have a future value of $460(3.3) = $1,524. For the next three years we would be indifferent between projects X and Y if, at an interest rate of r:

$$(1 + r)^3 \$897 + \$271 \left[\frac{(1 + r)^3 - 1}{r} \right] = \$1,524(1 + r)^3,$$

$$\$271 \left[\frac{(1 + r)^3 - 1}{r} \right] = 1,524(1 + r)^3 - \$897(1 + r)^3$$

$$= (1 + r)^3(\$1,524 - 897) = (1 + r)^3 \$627$$

$$\left[\frac{(1 + r)^3 - 1}{r} \right] = (1 + r)^3 \frac{\$627}{\$271}$$

$$\left[\frac{(1+r)^3-1}{r(1+r)^3}\right] = \$2.21$$

$$\left[\frac{1-\dfrac{1}{(1+r)^3}}{r}\right] = \$2.21.$$

That is, the present value of a 3 year annuity of $1 is $2.21. This implies an interest rate of approximately 17 percent. An alternative is to compute the indifference rate for the entire 6 year period. This gives an indifference rate of about 14 percent, i.e., solve for r as follows:

$$\$271\left[\frac{(1+r)^3-1}{r}\right](1+r)^3 + \$271\left[\frac{(1+r)^3-1}{r}\right]$$
$$= \left[\frac{(1+r)^3-1}{r}\right](1+r)^3\$460$$

(b) We would be indifferent between the two projects when the following equality holds

$$\$1,340\left[\frac{(1+r)^2-1}{r}\right] + \$3,000(1+r)^2$$
$$= \$3,270\left[\frac{(1+r)^2-1}{r}\right]$$

$$\$3,000(1+r)^2 = (\$3,270 - 1,340)\left[\frac{(1+r)^2-1}{r}\right]$$

$$\frac{\$3,000}{\$1,930}(1+r)^2 = \left[\frac{(1+r)^2-1}{r}\right]$$

$$\$1.55 = \left[\frac{1-\dfrac{1}{(1+r)^2}}{r}\right]$$

This implies an interest rate of approximately 19 percent. (See Table 14–4 for the present value of an annuity of 2 years.)

(2) These indifference rates may be viewed as reinvestment rates which will make the future value of both projects equal. These rates have been called "Fisher's" indifference rates (see A. Alchian, cited in the additional readings).

2. (a) Cash outlays for each alternative
   (1) Purchase for cash

YEAR

	0	1	2	3	4	5
Outlay	−$16,370					
TR(Depreciation) = .45($16,370/5)		$1,473.30	$1,473.30	$1,473.30	$1,473.30	$1,473.30
Totals	−$16,370	+$1,473.30	+$1,473.30	+$1,473.30	+$1,473.30	+$1,473.30

Present values
at 20% $= -\$16,370 + \$1,473.30(2.991) = -\$16,370 + \$4,407$

$= -\$11,963$

(2) Lease

YEAR

	0	1	2	3	4	5
Payments		−$5,000	−$5,000	−$5,000	−$5,000	−$5,000
Tax benefits = .45(5,000)		2,250	2,250	2,250	2,250	2,250
After tax flows = (1-TR)(−5,000)		−$2,750	−$2,750	−$2,750	−$2,750	−$2,750

Present values
at 20% $=$ −$2,750 (2.991)

$=$ −$8,225.25

Since the lessor's payments are based on a 16 percent discount rate, discounting the after-tax flows at 20 percent will make the leasing alternative more attractive.

(b) The bias is due to the difference in the cost of capital rate vs. the lessor's rate (See above).

(1) Buy/Borrow

YEAR

	1	2	3	4	5
Payments (Same as lease)	−$5,000	−$5,000	−$5,000	−$5,000	−$5,000
TR(Depreciation)	.45(5,457) = +$2,456	.45(4,365) = $1,964	.45(3,274) = $1,473	.45(2,183) = 982	.45(1,091) = $491
TR (Interest)*	+1,179	+1,007	+808	+578	+311
Net after tax payments	−$1,365	−$2,029	−$2,719	−$3,440	−$4,198

(2) Lease

YEAR

	1	2	3	4	5
Payments	−$5,000	−$5,000	−$5,000	−$5,000	−$5,000
TR (Interest) same as above	+ 1,179	+ 1,007	+ 808	+ 578	+ 311
TR (Non-interest deduction)	+ 1,071	+ 1,243	+1,442	+ 1,672	+ 1,939
Net after-tax = $(1 - TR)(.5000)$	−$2,750	−$2,750	−$2,750	−$2,750	−$2,750

*	Interest	Payment on Principal	New Balance
1	$2,619	$2,381	$13,989
2	2,238	2,762	11,227
3	1,796	3,204	8,023
4	1,285	3,715	4,308
5	692	4,308	
(To Balance)		Non-Interest Deductions = $16,370	

(3) Obviously Buy/Borrow has a lower present value of net after tax payments, no matter which discount rate is used. Note both options result in a total after tax outlay of $13,750. But the accelerated depreciation deductions delay the payments till later.

3. (A) Purchase for cash

YEAR

	0	1	2	3
(1) Outlay	−$36,000			
(2) Investment credit	+ 1,200			
(3) $(1 - TR)$ (Revenues − Cash expenses)		+$8,400	+$8,400	+$8,400
(4) TR (Depreciation) = .4 ($18,000; $12,000; $6,000)		7,200	4,800	2,400
(5) Salvage				+ 2,000
TR (Book value − Salvage) = .4 (0 − $2,000)				− 800
Net cash flows	−$34,800	+$15,600	+$13,200	+$12,000

(B) (1) $36,000 = X(2.39) + $2,000(.70)$
     $14,477 = X$
     (2.39 is the annuity factor for 12%, $n = 3$)

(2)

	YEAR			
	0	**1**	**2**	**3**
(1) Payments		−$14,500	−$14,500	−$16,500*
(2) Investment credit	+$1,200			
(3) $(1 - TR)(R - CE)$		+ 8,400	+ 8,400	+ 8,400
(4) TR (Depreciation)		+ 7,200	+ 4,800	+ 2,400
(5) Net salvage				+ 1,200
(6) TR (Interest)		+ 1,760	+ 1,280	+ 760
Net cash flows	+1,200	+$ 2,860	−$ 20	−$ 3,740

* Recall 2,000 Payment at Year 3

> Notice that by assuming the first payment is not until the end of year 1, the firm has no net cash investment if it borrows. An alternative is to assume the first payment is due immediately.

(C)

	YEAR			
	0	**1**	**2**	**3**
(1) Lease payments		−$16,500	−$16,500	−$16,500
(2) Investment credit	+$1,200			
(3) $(1 - TR)(R - CE)$		+ 9,000	+ 9,000	+ 9,000
(4) TR (Lease payments)		+ 6,600	+ 6,600	+ 6,600
(5) No salvage				
(6) —				
Net Cash Flows	+$1,200	−$ 900	−$ 900	−$ 900

* Adjusted for savings in maintenance. Note, the same result is obtained if we use .6 ($14,000) as before and reduce the payments to $15,500. That is, +$8,400 + TR (15,500) = $14,600; when netted against the payment of $15,500, we have a net −$900.

(D) (1) Using the rate of 18 percent penalizes the cash purchase option which requires the asset to earn 18 percent. Indeed, the net cash flows in (A) when discounted at 18 percent do not sum to a positive number (The project has a *negative* excess present value of $30,084 − 34,800 = −$4,716).

In contrast, by assuming the payments are delayed one year, the net cash flows for the loan option have a net present value of +$1,335. If the payments are moved forward to years 0, 1, 2, the net cash flows would then appear as follows:

YEAR

	0	1	2	3
	−$13,300	+$2,860	−$2,020	+$12,760
Discount factors	1.0	.85	.72	.61
Present values	−$13,300	+$2,431	−$1,454	+$ 7,784

which sums to a negative − $4,539.

Note that the lease option also appears more attractive than buying since the net present value of the flows +$1,200, −$900, −$900, −$900 is only −$762 (vs. − $4,716 above).

(2) Some cash flows are assumed to occur with certainty—e.g., interest and payments on principal. Other flows such as the tax benefits of depreciation and salvage are more uncertain depending on the firm's marginal tax rate. If the firm does not earn a profit the tax rate is zero. But the loan payments must still be made.

But this is an extreme. If the firm continues to earn a profit, the depreciation deductions will generate cash inflows (savings from taxes). And if the asset is scrapped for less than the assumed salvage value, the firm will report a loss, receiving tax benefits of TR (Book − Salvage). Similarly, if the asset is scrapped before the useful life, say t, the firm receives S_t + TR (Book$_t$ − S_t). Hence, the cash flows under the "buy" option are relatively certain if the firm continues to earn a proft. Any flows considered relatively certain could be discounted at a lower rate. For example, if the firm borrows, the payments are just as certain as the lease payments.

(3) Plan B to Plan C

(a) $($15,500 - 14,500) (1 - TR) \left(\dfrac{1}{1.12}\right)$

$+ ($15,500 - 14,500) (1 - TR) \left(\dfrac{1}{1.12}\right)^2$

$+ ($15,500 - 16,500) (1 - TR) \left(\dfrac{1}{1.12}\right)^3$

$= $1,000 (1 - TR) \left[\left(\dfrac{1}{1.12}\right) + \left(\dfrac{1}{1.12}\right)^2\right]$

$-100 (1 - TR)\left(\dfrac{1}{1.12}\right)^3$

We simply discount the after tax differences in the two payment streams by the debt rate. Any difference must represent more or less interest under one option versus the other.

(b)

End of Year	Lease Balance	14.0% Interest	Payment on Principal
0	$36,000		
1	25,540	$5,040	$10,460
2	13,616	3,576	11,924
3	22	1,906	13,594

	Non-Interest	Deductions	
			(L – B/B)
Year	Lease	Buy/Borrow	Differences
1	$10,460	$18,000	−$7,540
2	11,924	12,000	− 76
3	13,594	4,000 (Net of gain)	+ 9,594

$$\text{TR (Differences)} \left(\frac{1}{1.18}\right)^t = .4(-\$7,540 \left(\frac{1}{1.18}\right)$$

$$+ .4(-\$76)\left(\frac{1}{1.18}\right)^2 + .4(\$9,594)\left(\frac{1}{1.18}\right)^3$$

$$= -\$2,556 + (-\$22) + \$2,336$$
$$= -\$242, \text{ which represents a lease disadvantage}$$

4. (A) Present value of net cash flows—Present owner (in millions)

	YEAR					
	0	**1**	**2**	**3**	**4**	**5**
Current selling price foregone	−$10.0					
Less taxes of .3 ($2.25 − 10) =	2.325					
	−$7.675					
After tax operating flows		$1.75	1.75	1.75	1.75	1.75
Tax benefits from depreciation		0	0	0	0	0
Net salvage, year 5						$2.25

Net present value $= -\$7.675 + \$1.75(3.433) + \$2.25(.519)$
$= -\$7.675 + \$6.007 + \$1.167$
$= -\$.501$

Decision: Sell

(B) Present value of net cash flows—New owner (in millions)

	YEAR				
	0	**1**	**2**	**3**	**4**	**5**
Cash outlay	−$10.0				
After-tax operating flows		$1.75	1.75	1.75	1.75	1.75
TR (Depreciation)		1.29	1.03	.775	.517	.258
Salvage						2.25
		$3.04	$2.78	$2.525	$2.267	$4.258

$$\text{Net present value} = -\$10.0 + 2.67 + 2.14 + 1.70 + 1.34 + 2.21$$
$$= -\$10.0 + \$10.06$$
$$= +\$.06$$

Decision: Buy

CHAPTER 16 _____

(a) We have $C_p = 145$, $D = 15,000$, and $C_s = .22(200) = 44$. Hence the optimal order quantity is

$$q^* = \sqrt{\frac{2DC_p}{C_s}}$$

$$= \sqrt{\frac{2 \cdot 15,000 \cdot 145}{44}}$$

$$= \sqrt{98,863.64} \doteq 314 \text{ units per order}$$

(b) The important assumptions are that demand is known and uniform, that the cost structure is known (as specified), and that no stockouts are allowed.

(c) Suppose $C_p = 100$. The optimal policy is

$$q^* = \sqrt{\frac{2 \cdot 15,000 \cdot 100}{44}} = 261$$

with a quarterly cost of

$$\$3,000 + 100(15,000/261) + 44(261/2) = \$14,489$$
$$= \$3,000 + \sqrt{2 \cdot 15,000 \cdot 100 \cdot 44}.$$

The $q = 314$ policy, however, provides a quarterly cost of

$$\$3,000 + 100(15,000/314) + 44(314/2) = \$14,685$$

Now suppose $C_p = 190$. The optimal policy is

$$q^* = \sqrt{\frac{2 \cdot 15{,}000 \cdot 190}{44}} \doteq 360$$

with a quarterly cost of

$$\$3{,}000 + 190(15{,}000/360) + 44(360/2) = \$18{,}837$$

The $q = 314$ policy, however, provides a quarterly cost of

$$\$3{,}000 + 190(15{,}000/314) + 44(314/2) = \$18{,}984$$

Hence, with perfect C_p information we have an expected cost of

$$\tfrac{1}{2}[\$14{,}489 + 18{,}837] = \$16{,}663$$

while without we have

$$\tfrac{1}{2}[\$14{,}685 + 18{,}984] = \$16{,}835$$

which implies an information value of $172.

Of course, the problem is more delicate than we imply. The $172 figure is a quarterly datum. Will the firm learn the actual C_p at the end of the quarter? If so, then the various policies are "out of phase" and $172 can be interpreted as only an estimate of the return to information. (What is the inventory position at the end of the first quarter under each of the policies?)

Index

A 2
B 3
C 4
D 5
E 6
F 7
G 8
H 9
I 0
J 1